Creation, Life and Beauty,

undone by death and wrongdoing,

regained by God's surprising victory,

AS TOLD IN
THE BOOKS OF **THE**
HOLY BIBLE
NEW INTERNATIONAL VERSION®

Biblica Transforming lives through God's Word

Call us today or visit us online to receive a free catalog featuring hundreds of
biblical resources priced for ministry.

Website: Biblica.com
E-mail: CustomerCare@Biblica.com

Phone: 800-524-1588
Mail: 1820 Jet Stream Drive
Colorado Springs, CO 80921-3696

Biblica provides God's Word to people through Bible
translation & publishing, and Bible engagement in
Africa, Asia Pacific, Europe, Latin America, Middle
East, North America, and South Asia. Through its
worldwide reach, Biblica engages people with God's
Word so that their lives are transformed through a
relationship with Jesus Christ.

Eng. NT NIV 220140/220145/220147/220148/220149
220151/220155/220156/220157/220158/220210/220211
36500/3000/3000/10000/14000/8500/7800/33000/8000/15600/7200/17500

01/15
Printed in the U.S.A

THE STORY OF GOD AND THE WORLD,
INVITING YOU TO

TAKE UP YOUR ROLE IN THE
DRAMA
OF THE BIBLE

"... this is how God fulfilled what he had foretold through all the prophets, saying that his Messiah would suffer. Repent, then, and turn to God, so that your sins may be wiped out, that times of refreshing may come from the Lord, and that he may send the Messiah, who has been appointed for you—even Jesus. Heaven must receive him until the time comes for God to restore everything, as he promised long ago through his holy prophets."

The book of Acts

THE DRAMA
OF THE BIBLE
IN SIX ACTS

The Bible is a collection of letters, poems, stories, visions, prophetic oracles, wisdom and other kinds of writing. The first step to good Bible reading and understanding is to engage these collected works as the different kinds of writing that they are, and to read them as whole books. We encourage you to read big, to not merely take in little fragments of the Bible. The introductions at the start of each book will help you to do this.

But it is also important not to view the Bible as a gathering of unrelated writings. Overall, the Bible is a narrative. These books come together to tell God's true story and his plan to set the world right again. This story of the Bible falls naturally into six key major acts, which are briefly summarized below.

> "I had always felt life first as a story: and if there is a story, there is a story-teller."
>
> G.K. Chesterton

But even more precisely, we can say the story of the Bible is a drama. The key to a drama is that it has to be acted out, performed, lived. It can't remain as only words on a page. A drama is an activated story. The Bible was written so we could enter into its story. It is meant to be lived.

All of us, without exception, live our lives as a drama. We are on stage every single day. What will we say? What will we do? According to which story will we live? If we are not answering these questions with the biblical script, we will follow another. We can't avoid living by someone's stage instructions, even if merely our own.

This is why another key to engaging the Bible well is to recognize that its story has not ended. God's saving action continues. We are all invited to take up our own roles in this ongoing story of redemption and new creation. So, welcome to the drama of the Bible. Welcome to the story of how God intends to renew your life, and the life of the world. God himself is calling you to engage with his word.

Act 1: GOD'S INTENTION

 The drama begins (in the first pages of the book of Genesis) with God already on the stage creating a world. He makes a man and a woman, Adam and Eve, and places them in the Garden of Eden to work it and take care of it. The earth is created to be their home. God's intention is for humanity to be in close, trusting relationship with him and in harmony with the rest of creation that surrounds them.

In a startling passage, the Bible tells us that human beings are God's image-bearers, created to share in the task of bringing God's wise and beneficial rule to the rest of the world. Male and female together, we are significant, decision-making, world-shaping beings. This is our vocation, our purpose as defined in the biblical story.

An equally remarkable part of Act 1 is the description of God as coming into the garden to be with the first human beings. Not only is the earth the God-intended place for humanity, God himself comes to make the beautiful new creation his home as well.

God then gives his own assessment of the whole creation: *God saw all that he had made, and it was very good.* Act 1 reveals God's original desire for the world. It shows us that life itself is a gift from the Creator. It tells us what we were made for and provides the setting for all the action that follows.

Act 2: EXILE

 Tension and conflict are introduced to the story when Adam and Eve decide to go their own way and seek their own wisdom. They listen to the deceptive voice of God's enemy, Satan, and doubt God's trustworthiness. They decide to live apart from the word that God himself has given them. They decide to be a law to themselves.

The disobedience of Adam and Eve—the introduction of sin into our world—is presented in the Bible as having devastating consequences. Humans were created for healthy, life-giving relationship: with God, with each other, and with the rest of creation. But now humanity must live with the fracturing of all these relations and with the resulting shame, brokenness, pain, loneliness—and death.

Heaven and earth—God's realm and our realm—were intended to be united. God's desire from the beginning was clearly to live with us in the world he made. But now God is hidden. Now it is possible to be in our world and not know him, not experience his presence, not follow his ways, not live in gratitude.

As a result of this rebellion, the first exile in the story takes place. The humans are driven away from God's presence. Their offspring throughout history will seek to find their way back to the source of life. They will devise any number of philosophies and religions, trying to make sense of a fallen, yet haunting world. But death now stalks them, and they will find that they cannot escape it. Having attempted to live apart from God and his good word, humans will find they have neither God nor life.

New questions arise in the drama: Can the curse on creation be overcome and the relationship between God and humanity restored? Can heaven and earth be reunited? Or did God's enemy effectively end the plan and subvert the story?

Act 3: CALLING ISRAEL TO A MISSION

 We see the direction of God's redemptive plan when he calls Abraham, promising to make him into a great nation. God narrows his focus and concentrates on one group of people. But the ultimate goal remains the same: to bless all the peoples on earth and remove the curse from creation.

When Abraham's descendants are enslaved in Egypt, a central pattern in the story is set: God hears their cries for help and comes to set them free. God makes a covenant with this new nation of Israel at Mt. Sinai. Israel is called by God to be a light to the nations, showing the world what it means to follow God's ways for living. If they will do this, he will bless them in their new land and will come to live with them.

However, God also warns them that if they are

not faithful to the covenant, he will send them away, just as he did with Adam and Eve. In spite of God's repeated warnings through his prophets, Israel seems determined to break the covenant. So God abandons the holy temple—the sign of his presence with his people—and it is smashed by pagan invaders. Israel's capital city Jerusalem is sacked and burned.

Abraham's descendants, chosen to reverse the failure of Adam, have now apparently also failed. The problem this poses in the biblical story is profound. Israel, sent as the divine answer to Adam's fall, cannot escape Adam's sin. God, however, remains committed to his people and his plan, so he sows the seed of a different outcome. He promises to send a new king, a descendant of Israel's great King David, who will lead the nation back to its destiny. The very prophets who warned Israel of the dire consequences of its wrongdoing also pledge that the good news of God's victory will be heard in Israel once again.

Act 3 ends tragically, with God apparently absent and the pagan nations ruling over Israel. But the hope of a promise remains. There is one true God. He has chosen Israel. He will return to his people to live with them again. He will bring justice, peace and healing to Israel, and then to the world. He will do this in a final and climactic way. God will send his anointed one—the Messiah. He has given his word on this.

Act 4: THE SURPRISING VICTORY OF JESUS

"He is the god made manifest . . . the universal savior of human life." These words referring to Caesar Augustus (found in a Roman inscription from 4 BC in Ephesus) proclaim the gospel of the Roman Empire. This version of the good news announces that Caesar is the lord who brings peace and prosperity to the world.

Into this empire a son of David is born, and he announces the gospel of God's kingdom. Jesus of Nazareth brings the good news of the coming of God's reign. He begins to show what God's new creation looks like. He announces the end of Israel's exile and the forgiveness of sins. He heals the sick and raises the dead. He overcomes the dark spiritual powers. He welcomes sinners and those considered unclean. Jesus renews the nation, rebuilding the twelve tribes of Israel around himself in a symbolic way.

But the established religious leaders are threatened by Jesus and his kingdom, so they have him brought before the Roman governor. During the very week that the Jews were remembering and celebrating Passover—God's ancient rescue of his people from slavery in Egypt—the Romans nail Jesus to a cross and kill him as a false king.

But the Bible claims that this defeat is actually

God's greatest victory. How? Jesus willingly gives up his life as a sacrifice on behalf of the nation, on behalf of the world. Jesus takes onto himself the full force of evil and empties it of its power. In this surprising way, Jesus fights and wins Israel's ultimate battle. The real enemy was never Rome, but the spiritual powers that lie behind Rome and every other kingdom whose weapon is death. Through his blood Jesus pays the price and reconciles everything in heaven and on earth to God.

God then publicly declares this victory by reversing Jesus' death sentence and raising him back to life. The resurrection of Israel's king shows that the great enemies of God's creation—sin and death—really have been defeated. The resurrection is the great sign that the new creation has begun.

Jesus is the fulfillment of Israel's story and a new start for the entire human race. Death came through the first man, Adam. The resurrection of the dead comes through the new man, Jesus. God's original intention is being reclaimed.

Act 5: THE RENEWED PEOPLE OF GOD

 If the key victory has already been secured, why is there an Act 5? The answer is that God wants the victory of Jesus to spread to all the nations of the world. The risen Jesus says to his disciples, *"Peace be with you! As the Father has sent me, I am sending you."* So this new act in the drama tells the story of how the earliest followers of Jesus began to spread the good news of God's reign.

According to the New Testament, all those who belong to Israel's Messiah are children of Abraham, heirs of both the ancient promises and the ancient mission. The task of bringing blessing to the peoples of the world has been given again to Abraham's family. Their mission is to live out the liberating message of the good news of God's kingdom.

God is gathering people from all around the world and forming them into assemblies of Jesus-followers— his church. Together they are God's new temple, the place where his Spirit lives. They are the community of those who have pledged their allegiance to Jesus as the true Lord of the world. They have crossed from death into new life, through the power of God's Spirit. They demonstrate God's love across the usual boundaries of race, class, tribe and nation.

Forgiveness of sins and reconciliation with God can now be announced to all. Following in the steps of Jesus, his followers proclaim this gospel in both word and deed. The power of this new, God-given life breaking into the world is meant to be shown by the real-world actions of the Christian community. But the message also has a warning. When the Messiah returns, he will come as the rightful judge of the world.

The Bible is the story of the central struggle weaving its way through the history of the world. And now the story arrives at our own time, enveloping us in its drama.

So the challenge of a decision confronts us. What will we do? How will we fit into this story? What role will we play? God is inviting us to be a part of his mission of re-creation—of bringing restoration, justice and forgiveness. We are to join in the task of making things new, to be a living sign of what is to come when the drama is complete.

Act 6: GOD COMES HOME

 God's future has come into our world through the work of Jesus the Messiah. But for now, the present evil age also continues. Brokenness, wrongdoing, sickness and even death remain. We live in the time of the overlap of the ages, the time of in-between. The final Act is coming, but it has not yet arrived.

We live in the time of invitation, when the call of the gospel goes out to every creature. Of course, many still live as though God doesn't exist. They do not acknowledge the rule of the Messiah. But the day is coming when Jesus will return to earth and the reign of God will become an uncontested reality throughout the world.

God's presence will be fully and openly with us once again, as it was at the beginning of the drama. God's plan of redemption will reach its goal. The creation will experience its own Exodus, finding freedom from its bondage to decay. Pain and tears, regret and shame, suffering and death will be no more.

When the day of resurrection arrives God's people will find that their hope has been realized. The dynamic force of an indestructible life will course through their bodies. Empowered by the Spirit, and unhindered by sin and death, we will pursue our original vocation as a renewed humanity. We will be culture makers, under God but over the world. Having been remade in the image of Christ, we will share in bringing his wise, caring rule to the earth.

At the center of it all will be God himself. He will return and make his home with us, this time in a new heavens and a new earth. We, along with the rest of creation, will worship him perfectly and fulfill our true calling. God will be all in all, and the whole world will be full of his glory.

WHAT NOW?

The preceding overview of the drama of the Bible is meant to give you a framework so you can begin to read the books that make up the story. The summary we've provided is merely an invitation for you to engage the sacred books themselves.

Many people today follow the practice of reading only small, fragmentary snippets of the Bible—verses—and often in isolation from the books of which they are a part. This does not lead to good Bible understanding. We encourage you instead to take in whole books, the way their authors wrote them. This is really the only way to gain deep insight to the Scriptures.

Go deep and read big.

The more you immerse yourself in the script of this drama, the better you will be able to find your own place in the story. The following page, called *Living the Script*, will help you with practical next steps for taking up your role in the Bible's drama of renewal.

LIVING
THE SCRIPT

From the beginning God made it clear that he intends for us to be significant players in his drama. No doubt, it is first and foremost God's story. But we can't passively sit back and just watch what happens. At every stage he invites humans to participate with him.

Here are three key steps to finding your place in the drama:

1. IMMERSE YOURSELF IN THE BIBLE

If we are unfamiliar with the text of the drama itself, there's no chance of living our parts well. Only when we read both deeply and widely in the Bible, marinating in it and letting it soak into our lives, will we be prepared to effectively take up our roles. The more we read the Bible, the better readers we will become. Rather than skimming the surface, we will become skilled at interpreting and practicing what we read.

2. COMMIT TO FOLLOW JESUS

We've all taken part in the brokenness and wrongdoing that came into the story in Act 2. The victory of Jesus in Act 4 now offers us the opportunity to have our lives turned around. Our sins can be forgiven. We can become part of God's story of new creation.

Turn away from your wrongdoing. God has acted through the death and resurrection of the Messiah to deal decisively with evil—in your life and in the life of the world. His death was a sacrifice, and his resurrection a new beginning. Acknowledge that Jesus is the rightful ruler of the world, and commit to follow him and join with God's people.

3. LIVE YOUR PART

Followers of Jesus are gospel players in local communities living out the biblical drama together. But we do not have an exact script for our lines and actions in the drama today. Our history has not yet been written. And we can't just repeat lines from earlier acts in the drama. So what do we do?

We read the Bible to understand what God has already done, especially through Jesus the Messiah, and to know how we carry this story forward. *The Bible helps us answer the key question about everything we say and do: Is this an appropriate and fitting way to live out the story of Jesus today?* This is how we put the Scriptures into action. Life's choices can be messy, but God has given us his word and promised us his Spirit to guide us on the way. You are God's artwork, created to do good works. May your life be a gift of beauty back to him.

For more help in understanding the Bible
and finding your place in its story, go to

Biblica.com/LivingTheScript

ACT 1

God's Intention: Creation

ACT 3

Calling Israel to a Mission: Abraham ca. 2100 BC

Exile: The Fall into Sin

ACT 2

ACT 4

Jesus Dies ca. AD 30; 3 Days Later He Rises from the Dead

The Surprising Victory of Jesus

WORLD EVENTS

Pyramids built, 2500's BC
Hinduism gains influence in India, 1100's BC
Buddhism founded in India, 500's BC
Alexander the Great begins rule, 336 BC
China begins construction on The Great Wall, 214 BC
Rise of the Roman Empire, 27 BC

THE DRAMA OF THE BIBLE:
A Visual Chronology

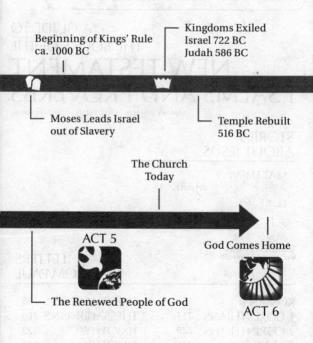

Beginning of Kings' Rule
ca. 1000 BC

Kingdoms Exiled
Israel 722 BC
Judah 586 BC

Moses Leads Israel
out of Slavery

Temple Rebuilt
516 BC

The Church
Today

ACT 5

God Comes Home

The Renewed People of God

ACT 6

A GUIDE TO
THE BOOKS OF THE
NEW TESTAMENT, PSALMS AND PROVERBS

(pause and pray before you read the Scriptures)

STORIES ABOUT JESUS

LETTERS FROM PAUL

Israel's continuing story and its climax in
THE LIFE, DEATH
AND RESURRECTION OF
JESUS THE MESSIAH,
the announcement of
GOD'S VICTORY OVER HUMANITY'S
ENEMIES SIN AND DEATH,
and the invitation for
ALL PEOPLES TO BE
RECONCILED TO GOD
and to share in his
RESTORATION OF ALL THINGS,

PRESENTED
IN THE BOOKS OF THE
NEW TESTAMENT

THE WORLD OF JESUS
Israel in the First Century

THE GOSPEL GOES OUT
TO THE FIRST CENTURY WORLD

ITALY

Rome

MACEDONIA

Philippi

Thessalonica

Corinth

ACHAIA

MALTA

GALATIA

ASIA

Ephesus · Colossae

PATMOS

CRETE

CYPRUS

Antioch

Damascus

Caesarea

ISRAEL

Jerusalem

JUDEA

EGYPT

MEDITERRANEAN SEA

3

MATTHEW

Matthew's purpose is to show that God has kept his ancient promises to Israel through the life, death and resurrection of Jesus the Messiah. The long-expected reign of heaven is now coming to earth, bringing the Jewish story to its climax. Matthew begins by highlighting that Jesus was the son of David, Israel's most famous king, and the son of Abraham, Israel's founding patriarch. Jesus is the true Israelite and God's promised Messiah.

The Messiah is shown as reliving the story of Israel—going down into the Jordan River, facing temptation in the wilderness, gathering twelve disciples as twelve new tribes, ascending a mountain to deliver a new Torah, etc. The author highlights the idea of Jesus as a new Moses by collecting his teachings into five long speeches. These are marked off by some variation of the phrase *When Jesus had finished saying these things*. Just as the Torah had five books, Matthew presents five major sections.

The book concludes by telling how Jesus brought about the great new act of redemption for his people. As in the story of Israel's Exodus, a Passover meal is celebrated and then deliverance comes. Jesus gives his life for the sake of the world and is then raised from the dead. At the beginning of the book, Jesus is given the name *Immanuel*, meaning "God with us." At the end, Jesus sends his followers into the world with the promise that *surely I am with you always*.

---

1 This is the genealogy[a] of Jesus the Messiah[b] the son of David, the son of Abraham:

2 Abraham was the father of Isaac,
Isaac the father of Jacob,
Jacob the father of Judah and his brothers,
3 Judah the father of Perez and Zerah, whose mother was Tamar,
Perez the father of Hezron,
Hezron the father of Ram,
4 Ram the father of Amminadab,
Amminadab the father of Nahshon,
Nahshon the father of Salmon,
5 Salmon the father of Boaz, whose mother was Rahab,
Boaz the father of Obed, whose mother was Ruth,
Obed the father of Jesse,
6 and Jesse the father of King David.

David was the father of Solomon, whose mother had been Uriah's wife,
7 Solomon the father of Rehoboam,
Rehoboam the father of Abijah,
Abijah the father of Asa,
8 Asa the father of Jehoshaphat,
Jehoshaphat the father of Jehoram,

---

a 1 Or *is an account of the origin*   b 1 Or *Jesus Christ. Messiah* (Hebrew) and *Christ* (Greek) both mean *Anointed One*; also in verse 18.

Jehoram the father of Uzzi-
ah,
⁹Uzziah the father of Jotham,
Jotham the father of Ahaz,
Ahaz the father of Hezekiah,
¹⁰Hezekiah the father of Manasseh,
Manasseh the father of
Amon,
Amon the father of Josiah,
¹¹and Josiah the father of Jeconiah*a* and his brothers at
the time of the exile to Babylon.

¹²After the exile to Babylon:
Jeconiah was the father of
Shealtiel,
Shealtiel the father of Zerubbabel,
¹³Zerubbabel the father of Abihud,
Abihud the father of Eliakim,
Eliakim the father of Azor,
¹⁴Azor the father of Zadok,
Zadok the father of Akim,
Akim the father of Elihud,
¹⁵Elihud the father of Eleazar,
Eleazar the father of Matthan,
Matthan the father of Jacob,
¹⁶and Jacob the father of Joseph, the husband of Mary,
and Mary was the mother
of Jesus who is called the
Messiah.

¹⁷Thus there were fourteen generations in all from Abraham to
David, fourteen from David to the
exile to Babylon, and fourteen from
the exile to the Messiah.

¹⁸This is how the birth of Jesus
the Messiah came about*b*: His
mother Mary was pledged to be
married to Joseph, but before they
came together, she was found to be
pregnant through the Holy Spirit.
¹⁹Because Joseph her husband was
faithful to the law, and yet*c* did not
want to expose her to public disgrace, he had in mind to divorce
her quietly.

²⁰But after he had considered
this, an angel of the Lord appeared
to him in a dream and said, "Joseph
son of David, do not be afraid to take
Mary home as your wife, because
what is conceived in her is from the
Holy Spirit. ²¹She will give birth to
a son, and you are to give him the
name Jesus,*d* because he will save
his people from their sins."

²²All this took place to fulfill
what the Lord had said through the
prophet: ²³"The virgin will conceive
and give birth to a son, and they will
call him Immanuel"*e* (which means
"God with us").

²⁴When Joseph woke up, he did
what the angel of the Lord had
commanded him and took Mary
home as his wife. ²⁵But he did not
consummate their marriage until
she gave birth to a son. And he gave
him the name Jesus.

2 After Jesus was born in Bethlehem in Judea, during the time
of King Herod, Magi*f* from the east
came to Jerusalem ²and asked,
"Where is the one who has been
born king of the Jews? We saw his
star when it rose and have come to
worship him."

³When King Herod heard this he
was disturbed, and all Jerusalem
with him. ⁴When he had called together all the people's chief priests
and teachers of the law, he asked
them where the Messiah was to be

---

a 11 That is, Jehoiachin; also in verse 12   *b 18* Or *The origin of Jesus the Messiah was like this*
c 19 Or *was a righteous man and*   *d 21* *Jesus* is the Greek form of *Joshua*, which means *the LORD*
saves.   *e 23* Isaiah 7:14   *f 1* Traditionally *wise men*

born. [5]"In Bethlehem in Judea," they replied, "for this is what the prophet has written:

[6] " 'But you, Bethlehem, in the
    land of Judah,
  are by no means least among
    the rulers of Judah;
  for out of you will come a ruler
    who will shepherd my people
      Israel.'[a]"

[7]Then Herod called the Magi secretly and found out from them the exact time the star had appeared. [8]He sent them to Bethlehem and said, "Go and search carefully for the child. As soon as you find him, report to me, so that I too may go and worship him."

[9]After they had heard the king, they went on their way, and the star they had seen when it rose went ahead of them until it stopped over the place where the child was. [10]When they saw the star, they were overjoyed. [11]On coming to the house, they saw the child with his mother Mary, and they bowed down and worshiped him. Then they opened their treasures and presented him with gifts of gold, frankincense and myrrh. [12]And having been warned in a dream not to go back to Herod, they returned to their country by another route.

[13]When they had gone, an angel of the Lord appeared to Joseph in a dream. "Get up," he said, "take the child and his mother and escape to Egypt. Stay there until I tell you, for Herod is going to search for the child to kill him."

[14]So he got up, took the child and his mother during the night and left for Egypt, [15]where he stayed until the death of Herod. And so was fulfilled what the Lord had said

through the prophet: "Out of Egypt I called my son."[b]

[16]When Herod realized that he had been outwitted by the Magi, he was furious, and he gave orders to kill all the boys in Bethlehem and its vicinity who were two years old and under, in accordance with the time he had learned from the Magi. [17]Then what was said through the prophet Jeremiah was fulfilled:

[18]"A voice is heard in Ramah,
    weeping and great mourning,
  Rachel weeping for her children
    and refusing to be comforted,
    because they are no more."[c]

[19]After Herod died, an angel of the Lord appeared in a dream to Joseph in Egypt [20]and said, "Get up, take the child and his mother and go to the land of Israel, for those who were trying to take the child's life are dead."

[21]So he got up, took the child and his mother and went to the land of Israel. [22]But when he heard that Archelaus was reigning in Judea in place of his father Herod, he was afraid to go there. Having been warned in a dream, he withdrew to the district of Galilee, [23]and he went and lived in a town called Nazareth. So was fulfilled what was said through the prophets, that he would be called a Nazarene.

3 In those days John the Baptist came, preaching in the wilderness of Judea [2]and saying, "Repent, for the kingdom of heaven has come near." [3]This is he who was spoken of through the prophet Isaiah:

"A voice of one calling in the
    wilderness,
  'Prepare the way for the Lord,
    make straight paths for him.' "[d]

---

[a] 6 Micah 5:2,4   [b] 15 Hosea 11:1   [c] 18 Jer. 31:15   [d] 3 Isaiah 40:3

⁴John's clothes were made of camel's hair, and he had a leather belt around his waist. His food was locusts and wild honey. ⁵People went out to him from Jerusalem and all Judea and the whole region of the Jordan. ⁶Confessing their sins, they were baptized by him in the Jordan River.

⁷But when he saw many of the Pharisees and Sadducees coming to where he was baptizing, he said to them: "You brood of vipers! Who warned you to flee from the coming wrath? ⁸Produce fruit in keeping with repentance. ⁹And do not think you can say to yourselves, 'We have Abraham as our father.' I tell you that out of these stones God can raise up children for Abraham. ¹⁰The ax is already at the root of the trees, and every tree that does not produce good fruit will be cut down and thrown into the fire.

¹¹"I baptize you with*a* water for repentance. But after me comes one who is more powerful than I, whose sandals I am not worthy to carry. He will baptize you with*a* the Holy Spirit and fire. ¹²His winnowing fork is in his hand, and he will clear his threshing floor, gathering his wheat into the barn and burning up the chaff with unquenchable fire."

¹³Then Jesus came from Galilee to the Jordan to be baptized by John. ¹⁴But John tried to deter him, saying, "I need to be baptized by you, and do you come to me?"

¹⁵Jesus replied, "Let it be so now; it is proper for us to do this to fulfill all righteousness." Then John consented.

¹⁶As soon as Jesus was baptized, he went up out of the water. At that moment heaven was opened, and he saw the Spirit of God descending like a dove and alighting on him. ¹⁷And a voice from heaven said, "This is my Son, whom I love; with him I am well pleased."

4 Then Jesus was led by the Spirit into the wilderness to be tempted*b* by the devil. ²After fasting forty days and forty nights, he was hungry. ³The tempter came to him and said, "If you are the Son of God, tell these stones to become bread."

⁴Jesus answered, "It is written: 'Man shall not live on bread alone, but on every word that comes from the mouth of God.'*c*"

⁵Then the devil took him to the holy city and had him stand on the highest point of the temple. ⁶"If you are the Son of God," he said, "throw yourself down. For it is written:

" 'He will command his angels
        concerning you,
    and they will lift you up in
        their hands,
    so that you will not strike your
        foot against a stone.'*d*"

⁷Jesus answered him, "It is also written: 'Do not put the Lord your God to the test.'*e*"

⁸Again, the devil took him to a very high mountain and showed him all the kingdoms of the world and their splendor. ⁹"All this I will give you," he said, "if you will bow down and worship me."

¹⁰Jesus said to him, "Away from me, Satan! For it is written: 'Worship the Lord your God, and serve him only.'*f*"

¹¹Then the devil left him, and angels came and attended him.

¹²When Jesus heard that John had been put in prison, he withdrew to Galilee. ¹³Leaving Nazareth, he

---

a 11 Or in   *b 1* The Greek for *tempted* can also mean *tested.*   *c 4* Deut. 8:3
d 6 Psalm 91:11,12   *e 7* Deut. 6:16   *f 10* Deut. 6:13

went and lived in Capernaum, which was by the lake in the area of Zebulun and Naphtali— ¹⁴to fulfill what was said through the prophet Isaiah:

¹⁵ "Land of Zebulun and land of
        Naphtali,
    the Way of the Sea, beyond the
        Jordan,
    Galilee of the Gentiles—
¹⁶ the people living in darkness
    have seen a great light;
    on those living in the land of the
        shadow of death
    a light has dawned."ᵃ

¹⁷From that time on Jesus began to preach, "Repent, for the kingdom of heaven has come near."

¹⁸As Jesus was walking beside the Sea of Galilee, he saw two brothers, Simon called Peter and his brother Andrew. They were casting a net into the lake, for they were fishermen. ¹⁹"Come, follow me," Jesus said, "and I will send you out to fish for people." ²⁰At once they left their nets and followed him.

²¹Going on from there, he saw two other brothers, James son of Zebedee and his brother John. They were in a boat with their father Zebedee, preparing their nets. Jesus called them, ²²and immediately they left the boat and their father and followed him.

²³Jesus went throughout Galilee, teaching in their synagogues, proclaiming the good news of the kingdom, and healing every disease and sickness among the people. ²⁴News about him spread all over Syria, and people brought to him all who were ill with various diseases, those suffering severe pain, the demon-possessed, those having seizures, and the paralyzed; and he healed them.

²⁵Large crowds from Galilee, the Decapolis,ᵇ Jerusalem, Judea and the region across the Jordan followed him.

5 Now when Jesus saw the crowds, he went up on a mountainside and sat down. His disciples came to him, ²and he began to teach them. He said:

³ "Blessed are the poor in spirit,
    for theirs is the kingdom of
        heaven.
⁴ Blessed are those who mourn,
    for they will be comforted.
⁵ Blessed are the meek,
    for they will inherit the earth.
⁶ Blessed are those who
        hunger and thirst for
        righteousness,
    for they will be filled.
⁷ Blessed are the merciful,
    for they will be shown mercy.
⁸ Blessed are the pure in heart,
    for they will see God.
⁹ Blessed are the peacemakers,
    for they will be called children
        of God.
¹⁰ Blessed are those who
        persecuted because of
        righteousness,
    for theirs is the kingdom of
        heaven.

¹¹ "Blessed are you when people insult you, persecute you and falsely say all kinds of evil against you because of me. ¹²Rejoice and be glad, because great is your reward in heaven, for in the same way they persecuted the prophets who were before you.

¹³ "You are the salt of the earth. But if the salt loses its saltiness, how can it be made salty again? It is no longer good for anything, except to be thrown out and trampled underfoot.

ᵃ 16 Isaiah 9:1,2   ᵇ 25 That is, the Ten Cities

14 "You are the light of the world. A town built on a hill cannot be hidden. 15 Neither do people light a lamp and put it under a bowl. Instead they put it on its stand, and it gives light to everyone in the house. 16 In the same way, let your light shine before others, that they may see your good deeds and glorify your Father in heaven.

17 "Do not think that I have come to abolish the Law or the Prophets; I have not come to abolish them but to fulfill them. 18 For truly I tell you, until heaven and earth disappear, not the smallest letter, not the least stroke of a pen, will by any means disappear from the Law until everything is accomplished. 19 Therefore anyone who sets aside one of the least of these commands and teaches others accordingly will be called least in the kingdom of heaven, but whoever practices and teaches these commands will be called great in the kingdom of heaven. 20 For I tell you that unless your righteousness surpasses that of the Pharisees and the teachers of the law, you will certainly not enter the kingdom of heaven.

21 "You have heard that it was said to the people long ago, 'You shall not murder,*a* and anyone who murders will be subject to judgment.' 22 But I tell you that anyone who is angry with a brother or sister*b,c* will be subject to judgment. Again, anyone who says to a brother or sister, 'Raca,'*d* is answerable to the court. And anyone who says, 'You fool!' will be in danger of the fire of hell.

23 "Therefore, if you are offering your gift at the altar and there remember that your brother or sister has something against you, 24 leave your gift there in front of the altar. First go and be reconciled to them; then come and offer your gift.

25 "Settle matters quickly with your adversary who is taking you to court. Do it while you are still together on the way, or your adversary may hand you over to the judge, and the judge may hand you over to the officer, and you may be thrown into prison. 26 Truly I tell you, you will not get out until you have paid the last penny.

27 "You have heard that it was said, 'You shall not commit adultery.'*e* 28 But I tell you that anyone who looks at a woman lustfully has already committed adultery with her in his heart. 29 If your right eye causes you to stumble, gouge it out and throw it away. It is better for you to lose one part of your body than for your whole body to be thrown into hell. 30 And if your right hand causes you to stumble, cut it off and throw it away. It is better for you to lose one part of your body than for your whole body to go into hell.

31 "It has been said, 'Anyone who divorces his wife must give her a certificate of divorce.'*f* 32 But I tell you that anyone who divorces his wife, except for sexual immorality, makes her the victim of adultery, and anyone who marries a divorced woman commits adultery.

33 "Again, you have heard that it was said to the people long ago, 'Do not break your oath, but fulfill to the Lord the vows you have made.' 34 But I tell you, do not swear an oath at all: either by heaven, for it is God's throne; 35 or by the earth, for it is his footstool; or by Jerusalem, for it is the city of the Great King. 36 And

---

a 21 Exodus 20:13   *b* 22 The Greek word for *brother or sister* (*adelphos*) refers here to a fellow disciple, whether man or woman; also in verse 23.   *c* 22 Some manuscripts *brother or sister without cause*   *d* 22 An Aramaic term of contempt   *e* 27 Exodus 20:14   *f* 31 Deut. 24:1

do not swear by your head, for you cannot make even one hair white or black. ³⁷All you need to say is simply 'Yes' or 'No'; anything beyond this comes from the evil one.ᵃ

³⁸"You have heard that it was said, 'Eye for eye, and tooth for tooth.'ᵇ ³⁹But I tell you, do not resist an evil person. If anyone slaps you on the right cheek, turn to them the other cheek also. ⁴⁰And if anyone wants to sue you and take your shirt, hand over your coat as well. ⁴¹If anyone forces you to go one mile, go with them two miles. ⁴²Give to the one who asks you, and do not turn away from the one who wants to borrow from you.

⁴³"You have heard that it was said, 'Love your neighborᶜ and hate your enemy.' ⁴⁴But I tell you, love your enemies and pray for those who persecute you, ⁴⁵that you may be children of your Father in heaven. He causes his sun to rise on the evil and the good, and sends rain on the righteous and the unrighteous. ⁴⁶If you love those who love you, what reward will you get? Are not even the tax collectors doing that? ⁴⁷And if you greet only your own people, what are you doing more than others? Do not even pagans do that? ⁴⁸Be perfect, therefore, as your heavenly Father is perfect.

6 "Be careful not to practice your righteousness in front of others to be seen by them. If you do, you will have no reward from your Father in heaven.

²"So when you give to the needy, do not announce it with trumpets, as the hypocrites do in the synagogues and on the streets, to be honored by others. Truly I tell you, they

have received their reward in full. ³But when you give to the needy, do not let your left hand know what your right hand is doing, ⁴so that your giving may be in secret. Then your Father, who sees what is done in secret, will reward you.

⁵"And when you pray, do not be like the hypocrites, for they love to pray standing in the synagogues and on the street corners to be seen by others. Truly I tell you, they have received their reward in full. ⁶But when you pray, go into your room, close the door and pray to your Father, who is unseen. Then your Father, who sees what is done in secret, will reward you. ⁷And when you pray, do not keep on babbling like pagans, for they think they will be heard because of their many words. ⁸Do not be like them, for your Father knows what you need before you ask him.

⁹"This, then, is how you should pray:

" 'Our Father in heaven,
    hallowed be your name,
¹⁰your kingdom come,
    your will be done,
        on earth as it is in heaven.
¹¹Give us today our daily bread.
¹²And forgive us our debts,
    as we also have forgiven our
        debtors.
¹³And lead us not into temptation,ᵈ
    but deliver us from the evil
        one.ᵉ'

¹⁴For if you forgive other people when they sin against you, your heavenly Father will also forgive you. ¹⁵But if you do not forgive others their sins, your Father will not forgive your sins.

ᵃ 37 Or *from evil*   ᵇ 38 Exodus 21:24; Lev. 24:20; Deut. 19:21   ᶜ 43 Lev. 19:18
ᵈ 13 The Greek for *temptation* can also mean *testing*.   ᵉ 13 Or *from evil*; some late manuscripts one, / *for yours is the kingdom and the power and the glory forever. Amen.*

16"When you fast, do not look somber as the hypocrites do, for they disfigure their faces to show others they are fasting. Truly I tell you, they have received their reward in full. 17But when you fast, put oil on your head and wash your face, 18so that it will not be obvious to others that you are fasting, but only to your Father, who is unseen; and your Father, who sees what is done in secret, will reward you.

19"Do not store up for yourselves treasures on earth, where moths and vermin destroy, and where thieves break in and steal. 20But store up for yourselves treasures in heaven, where moths and vermin do not destroy, and where thieves do not break in and steal. 21For where your treasure is, there your heart will be also.

22"The eye is the lamp of the body. If your eyes are healthy,a your whole body will be full of light. 23But if your eyes are unhealthy,b your whole body will be full of darkness. If then the light within you is darkness, how great is that darkness!

24"No one can serve two masters. Either you will hate the one and love the other, or you will be devoted to the one and despise the other. You cannot serve both God and money.

25"Therefore I tell you, do not worry about your life, what you will eat or drink; or about your body, what you will wear. Is not life more than food, and the body more than clothes? 26Look at the birds of the air; they do not sow or reap or store away in barns, and yet your heavenly Father feeds them. Are you not much more valuable than they? 27Can any one of you by worrying add a single hour to your lifec?

28"And why do you worry about clothes? See how the flowers of the field grow. They do not labor or spin. 29Yet I tell you that not even Solomon in all his splendor was dressed like one of these. 30If that is how God clothes the grass of the field, which is here today and tomorrow is thrown into the fire, will he not much more clothe you — you of little faith? 31So do not worry, saying, 'What shall we eat?' or 'What shall we drink?' or 'What shall we wear?' 32For the pagans run after all these things, and your heavenly Father knows that you need them. 33But seek first his kingdom and his righteousness, and all these things will be given to you as well. 34Therefore do not worry about tomorrow, for tomorrow will worry about itself. Each day has enough trouble of its own.

7 "Do not judge, or you too will be judged. 2For in the same way you judge others, you will be judged, and with the measure you use, it will be measured to you.

3"Why do you look at the speck of sawdust in your brother's eye and pay no attention to the plank in your own eye? 4How can you say to your brother, 'Let me take the speck out of your eye,' when all the time there is a plank in your own eye? 5You hypocrite, first take the plank out of your own eye, and then you will see clearly to remove the speck from your brother's eye.

6"Do not give dogs what is sacred; do not throw your pearls to pigs. If you do, they may trample them under their feet, and turn and tear you to pieces.

7"Ask and it will be given to you; seek and you will find; knock and

---

a 22 The Greek for *healthy* here implies *generous.* b 23 The Greek for *unhealthy* here implies stingy.   c 27 Or *single cubit to your height*

the door will be opened to you. [8]For everyone who asks receives; the one who seeks finds; and to the one who knocks, the door will be opened.

[9]"Which of you, if your son asks for bread, will give him a stone? [10]Or if he asks for a fish, will give him a snake? [11]If you, then, though you are evil, know how to give good gifts to your children, how much more will your Father in heaven give good gifts to those who ask him! [12]So in everything, do to others what you would have them do to you, for this sums up the Law and the Prophets.

[13]"Enter through the narrow gate. For wide is the gate and broad is the road that leads to destruction, and many enter through it. [14]But small is the gate and narrow the road that leads to life, and only a few find it.

[15]"Watch out for false prophets. They come to you in sheep's clothing, but inwardly they are ferocious wolves. [16]By their fruit you will recognize them. Do people pick grapes from thornbushes, or figs from thistles? [17]Likewise, every good tree bears good fruit, but a bad tree bears bad fruit. [18]A good tree cannot bear bad fruit, and a bad tree cannot bear good fruit. [19]Every tree that does not bear good fruit is cut down and thrown into the fire. [20]Thus, by their fruit you will recognize them.

[21]"Not everyone who says to me, 'Lord, Lord,' will enter the kingdom of heaven, but only the one who does the will of my Father who is in heaven. [22]Many will say to me on that day, 'Lord, Lord, did we not prophesy in your name and in your name drive out demons and in your name perform many miracles?'

[23]Then I will tell them plainly, 'I never knew you. Away from me, you evildoers!'

[24]"Therefore everyone who hears these words of mine and puts them into practice is like a wise man who built his house on the rock. [25]The rain came down, the streams rose, and the winds blew and beat against that house; yet it did not fall, because it had its foundation on the rock. [26]But everyone who hears these words of mine and does not put them into practice is like a foolish man who built his house on sand. [27]The rain came down, the streams rose, and the winds blew and beat against that house, and it fell with a great crash."

[28]When Jesus had finished saying these things, the crowds were amazed at his teaching, [29]because he taught as one who had authority, and not as their teachers of the law.

8 When Jesus came down from the mountainside, large crowds followed him. [2]A man with leprosy[a] came and knelt before him and said, "Lord, if you are willing, you can make me clean."

[3]Jesus reached out his hand and touched the man. "I am willing," he said. "Be clean!" Immediately he was cleansed of his leprosy. [4]Then Jesus said to him, "See that you don't tell anyone. But go, show yourself to the priest and offer the gift Moses commanded, as a testimony to them."

[5]When Jesus had entered Capernaum, a centurion came to him, asking for help. [6]"Lord," he said, "my servant lies at home paralyzed, suffering terribly."

[a] 2 The Greek word traditionally translated *leprosy* was used for various diseases affecting the skin.

7 Jesus said to him, "Shall I come and heal him?"

8 The centurion replied, "Lord, I do not deserve to have you come under my roof. But just say the word, and my servant will be healed. 9 For I myself am a man under authority, with soldiers under me. I tell this one, 'Go,' and he goes; and that one, 'Come,' and he comes. I say to my servant, 'Do this,' and he does it."

10 When Jesus heard this, he was amazed and said to those following him, "Truly I tell you, I have not found anyone in Israel with such great faith. 11 I say to you that many will come from the east and the west, and will take their places at the feast with Abraham, Isaac and Jacob in the kingdom of heaven. 12 But the subjects of the kingdom will be thrown outside, into the darkness, where there will be weeping and gnashing of teeth."

13 Then Jesus said to the centurion, "Go! Let it be done just as you believed it would." And his servant was healed at that moment.

14 When Jesus came into Peter's house, he saw Peter's mother-in-law lying in bed with a fever. 15 He touched her hand and the fever left her, and she got up and began to wait on him.

16 When evening came, many who were demon-possessed were brought to him, and he drove out the spirits with a word and healed all the sick. 17 This was to fulfill what was spoken through the prophet Isaiah:

"He took up our infirmities
    and bore our diseases." [a]

18 When Jesus saw the crowd around him, he gave orders to cross to the other side of the lake. 19 Then a teacher of the law came to him and said, "Teacher, I will follow you wherever you go."

20 Jesus replied, "Foxes have dens and birds have nests, but the Son of Man has no place to lay his head."

21 Another disciple said to him, "Lord, first let me go and bury my father."

22 But Jesus told him, "Follow me, and let the dead bury their own dead."

23 Then he got into the boat and his disciples followed him. 24 Suddenly a furious storm came up on the lake, so that the waves swept over the boat. But Jesus was sleeping. 25 The disciples went and woke him, saying, "Lord, save us! We're going to drown!"

26 He replied, "You of little faith, why are you so afraid?" Then he got up and rebuked the winds and the waves, and it was completely calm.

27 The men were amazed and asked, "What kind of man is this? Even the winds and the waves obey him!"

28 When he arrived at the other side in the region of the Gadarenes, [b] two demon-possessed men coming from the tombs met him. They were so violent that no one could pass that way. 29 "What do you want with us, Son of God?" they shouted. "Have you come here to torture us before the appointed time?"

30 Some distance from them a large herd of pigs was feeding. 31 The demons begged Jesus, "If you drive us out, send us into the herd of pigs."

32 He said to them, "Go!" So they came out and went into the pigs, and the whole herd rushed down

---

a 17 Isaiah 53:4 (see Septuagint)   b 28 Some manuscripts *Gergesenes*; other manuscripts *Gerasenes*

the steep bank into the lake and died in the water. ³³Those tending the pigs ran off, went into the town and reported all this, including what had happened to the demon-possessed men. ³⁴Then the whole town went out to meet Jesus. And when they saw him, they pleaded with him to leave their region.

9 Jesus stepped into a boat, crossed over and came to his own town. ²Some men brought to him a paralyzed man, lying on a mat. When Jesus saw their faith, he said to the man, "Take heart, son; your sins are forgiven."

³At this, some of the teachers of the law said to themselves, "This fellow is blaspheming!"

⁴Knowing their thoughts, Jesus said, "Why do you entertain evil thoughts in your hearts? ⁵Which is easier: to say, 'Your sins are forgiven,' or to say, 'Get up and walk'? ⁶But I want you to know that the Son of Man has authority on earth to forgive sins." So he said to the paralyzed man, "Get up, take your mat and go home." ⁷Then the man got up and went home. ⁸When the crowd saw this, they were filled with awe; and they praised God, who had given such authority to man.

⁹As Jesus went on from there, he saw a man named Matthew sitting at the tax collector's booth. "Follow me," he told him, and Matthew got up and followed him.

¹⁰While Jesus was having dinner at Matthew's house, many tax collectors and sinners came and ate with him and his disciples. ¹¹When the Pharisees saw this, they asked his disciples, "Why does your teacher eat with tax collectors and sinners?"

¹²On hearing this, Jesus said, "It is not the healthy who need a doctor, but the sick. ¹³But go and learn what this means: 'I desire mercy, not sacrifice.'^a For I have not come to call the righteous, but sinners."

¹⁴Then John's disciples came and asked him, "How is it that we and the Pharisees fast often, but your disciples do not fast?"

¹⁵Jesus answered, "How can the guests of the bridegroom mourn while he is with them? The time will come when the bridegroom will be taken from them; then they will fast.

¹⁶"No one sews a patch of unshrunk cloth on an old garment, for the patch will pull away from the garment, making the tear worse. ¹⁷Neither do people pour new wine into old wineskins. If they do, the skins will burst; the wine will run out and the wineskins will be ruined. No, they pour new wine into new wineskins, and both are preserved."

¹⁸While he was saying this, a synagogue leader came and knelt before him and said, "My daughter has just died. But come and put your hand on her, and she will live." ¹⁹Jesus got up and went with him, and so did his disciples.

²⁰Just then a woman who had been subject to bleeding for twelve years came up behind him and touched the edge of his cloak. ²¹She said to herself, "If I only touch his cloak, I will be healed."

²²Jesus turned and saw her. "Take heart, daughter," he said, "your faith has healed you." And the woman was healed at that moment.

²³When Jesus entered the synagogue leader's house and saw the noisy crowd and people playing pipes, ²⁴he said, "Go away. The girl

^a 13 Hosea 6:6

is not dead but asleep." But they laughed at him. 25 After the crowd had been put outside, he went in and took the girl by the hand, and she got up. 26 News of this spread through all that region.

27 As Jesus went on from there, two blind men followed him, calling out, "Have mercy on us, Son of David!"

28 When he had gone indoors, the blind men came to him, and he asked them, "Do you believe that I am able to do this?"

"Yes, Lord," they replied.

29 Then he touched their eyes and said, "According to your faith let it be done to you"; 30 and their sight was restored. Jesus warned them sternly, "See that no one knows about this." 31 But they went out and spread the news about him all over that region.

32 While they were going out, a man who was demon-possessed and could not talk was brought to Jesus. 33 And when the demon was driven out, the man who had been mute spoke. The crowd was amazed and said, "Nothing like this has ever been seen in Israel."

34 But the Pharisees said, "It is by the prince of demons that he drives out demons."

35 Jesus went through all the towns and villages, teaching in their synagogues, proclaiming the good news of the kingdom and healing every disease and sickness. 36 When he saw the crowds, he had compassion on them, because they were harassed and helpless, like sheep without a shepherd. 37 Then he said to his disciples, "The harvest is plentiful but the workers are few. 38 Ask the Lord of the harvest, therefore, to send out workers into his harvest field."

10 Jesus called his twelve disciples to him and gave them authority to drive out impure spirits and to heal every disease and sickness.

2 These are the names of the twelve apostles: first, Simon (who is called Peter) and his brother Andrew; James son of Zebedee, and his brother John; 3 Philip and Bartholomew; Thomas and Matthew the tax collector; James son of Alphaeus, and Thaddaeus; 4 Simon the Zealot and Judas Iscariot, who betrayed him.

5 These twelve Jesus sent out with the following instructions: "Do not go among the Gentiles or enter any town of the Samaritans. 6 Go rather to the lost sheep of Israel. 7 As you go, proclaim this message: 'The kingdom of heaven has come near.' 8 Heal the sick, raise the dead, cleanse those who have leprosy,^{a} drive out demons. Freely you have received; freely give.

9 "Do not get any gold or silver or copper to take with you in your belts— 10 no bag for the journey or extra shirt or sandals or a staff, for the worker is worth his keep. 11 Whatever town or village you enter, search there for some worthy person and stay at their house until you leave. 12 As you enter the home, give it your greeting. 13 If the home is deserving, let your peace rest on it; if it is not, let your peace return to you. 14 If anyone will not welcome you or listen to your words, leave that home or town and shake the dust off your feet. 15 Truly I tell you, it will be more bearable for Sodom and Gomorrah on the day of judgment than for that town.

---

^{a} 8 The Greek word traditionally translated *leprosy* was used for various diseases affecting the skin.

16 "I am sending you out like sheep among wolves. Therefore be as shrewd as snakes and as innocent as doves. 17 Be on your guard; you will be handed over to the local councils and be flogged in the synagogues. 18 On my account you will be brought before governors and kings as witnesses to them and to the Gentiles. 19 But when they arrest you, do not worry about what to say or how to say it. At that time you will be given what to say, 20 for it will not be you speaking, but the Spirit of your Father speaking through you.

21 "Brother will betray brother to death, and a father his child; children will rebel against their parents and have them put to death. 22 You will be hated by everyone because of me, but the one who stands firm to the end will be saved. 23 When you are persecuted in one place, flee to another. Truly I tell you, you will not finish going through the towns of Israel before the Son of Man comes.

24 "The student is not above the teacher, nor a servant above his master. 25 It is enough for students to be like their teachers, and servants like their masters. If the head of the house has been called Beelzebul, how much more the members of his household!

26 "So do not be afraid of them, for there is nothing concealed that will not be disclosed, or hidden that will not be made known. 27 What I tell you in the dark, speak in the daylight; what is whispered in your ear, proclaim from the roofs. 28 Do not be afraid of those who kill the body but cannot kill the soul. Rather, be afraid of the One who can destroy both soul and body in hell. 29 Are not two sparrows sold for a penny? Yet not one of them will fall to the ground outside your Father's care.[a] 30 And even the very hairs of your head are all numbered. 31 So don't be afraid; you are worth more than many sparrows.

32 "Whoever acknowledges me before others, I will also acknowledge before my Father in heaven. 33 But whoever disowns me before others, I will disown before my Father in heaven.

34 "Do not suppose that I have come to bring peace to the earth. I did not come to bring peace, but a sword. 35 For I have come to turn

" 'a man against his father,
      a daughter against her mother,
   a daughter-in-law against her
         mother-in-law—
36   a man's enemies will be the
         members of his own
         household.'[b]

37 "Anyone who loves their father or mother more than me is not worthy of me; anyone who loves their son or daughter more than me is not worthy of me. 38 Whoever does not take up their cross and follow me is not worthy of me. 39 Whoever finds their life will lose it, and whoever loses their life for my sake will find it.

40 "Anyone who welcomes you welcomes me, and anyone who welcomes me welcomes the one who sent me. 41 Whoever welcomes a prophet as a prophet will receive a prophet's reward, and whoever welcomes a righteous person as a righteous person will receive a righteous person's reward. 42 And if anyone gives even a cup of cold water to one of these little ones who is my disciple, truly I tell you, that person will certainly not lose their reward."

a 29 Or will; or knowledge   b 36 Micah 7:6

11 After Jesus had finished instructing his twelve disciples, he went on from there to teach and preach in the towns of Galilee.[a]

2When John, who was in prison, heard about the deeds of the Messiah, he sent his disciples 3to ask him, "Are you the one who is to come, or should we expect someone else?"

4Jesus replied, "Go back and report to John what you hear and see: 5The blind receive sight, the lame walk, those who have leprosy[b] are cleansed, the deaf hear, the dead are raised, and the good news is proclaimed to the poor. 6Blessed is anyone who does not stumble on account of me."

7As John's disciples were leaving, Jesus began to speak to the crowd about John: "What did you go out into the wilderness to see? A reed swayed by the wind? 8If not, what did you go out to see? A man dressed in fine clothes? No, those who wear fine clothes are in kings' palaces. 9Then what did you go out to see? A prophet? Yes, I tell you, and more than a prophet. 10This is the one about whom it is written:

" 'I will send my messenger
   ahead of you,
who will prepare your way
   before you.'[c]

11Truly I tell you, among those born of women there has not risen anyone greater than John the Baptist; yet whoever is least in the kingdom of heaven is greater than he. 12From the days of John the Baptist until now, the kingdom of heaven has been subjected to violence,[d] and violent people have been raiding it. 13For all the Prophets and the

Law prophesied until John. 14And if you are willing to accept it, he is the Elijah who was to come. 15Whoever has ears, let them hear.

16"To what can I compare this generation? They are like children sitting in the marketplaces and calling out to others:

17 " 'We played the pipe for you,
      and you did not dance;
   we sang a dirge,
      and you did not mourn.'

18For John came neither eating nor drinking, and they say, 'He has a demon.' 19The Son of Man came eating and drinking, and they say, 'Here is a glutton and a drunkard, a friend of tax collectors and sinners.' But wisdom is proved right by her deeds."

20Then Jesus began to denounce the towns in which most of his miracles had been performed, because they did not repent. 21"Woe to you, Chorazin! Woe to you, Bethsaida! For if the miracles that were performed in you had been performed in Tyre and Sidon, they would have repented long ago in sackcloth and ashes. 22But I tell you, it will be more bearable for Tyre and Sidon on the day of judgment than for you. 23And you, Capernaum, will you be lifted to the heavens? No, you will go down to Hades.[e] For if the miracles that were performed in you had been performed in Sodom, it would have remained to this day. 24But I tell you that it will be more bearable for Sodom on the day of judgment than for you."

25At that time Jesus said, "I praise you, Father, Lord of heaven and earth, because you have hidden

---

a 1 Greek *in their towns*   b 5 The Greek word traditionally translated *leprosy* was used for various diseases affecting the skin.   c 10 Mal. 3:1   d 12 Or *been forcefully advancing*
e 23 That is, the realm of the dead

these things from the wise and learned, and revealed them to little children. 26 Yes, Father, for this is what you were pleased to do.

27 "All things have been committed to me by my Father. No one knows the Son except the Father, and no one knows the Father except the Son and those to whom the Son chooses to reveal him.

28 "Come to me, all you who are weary and burdened, and I will give you rest. 29 Take my yoke upon you and learn from me, for I am gentle and humble in heart, and you will find rest for your souls. 30 For my yoke is easy and my burden is light."

12 At that time Jesus went through the grainfields on the Sabbath. His disciples were hungry and began to pick some heads of grain and eat them. 2 When the Pharisees saw this, they said to him, "Look! Your disciples are doing what is unlawful on the Sabbath."

3 He answered, "Haven't you read what David did when he and his companions were hungry? 4 He entered the house of God, and he and his companions ate the consecrated bread — which was not lawful for them to do, but only for the priests. 5 Or haven't you read in the Law that the priests on Sabbath duty in the temple desecrate the Sabbath and yet are innocent? 6 I tell you that something greater than the temple is here. 7 If you had known what these words mean, 'I desire mercy, not sacrifice,'[a] you would not have condemned the innocent. 8 For the Son of Man is Lord of the Sabbath."

9 Going on from that place, he went into their synagogue, 10 and a man with a shriveled hand was there. Looking for a reason to bring charges against Jesus, they asked him, "Is it lawful to heal on the Sabbath?"

11 He said to them, "If any of you has a sheep and it falls into a pit on the Sabbath, will you not take hold of it and lift it out? 12 How much more valuable is a person than a sheep! Therefore it is lawful to do good on the Sabbath."

13 Then he said to the man, "Stretch out your hand." So he stretched it out and it was completely restored, just as sound as the other. 14 But the Pharisees went out and plotted how they might kill Jesus.

15 Aware of this, Jesus withdrew from that place. A large crowd followed him, and he healed all who were ill. 16 He warned them not to tell others about him. 17 This was to fulfill what was spoken through the prophet Isaiah:

18 "Here is my servant whom I have
         chosen,
     the one I love, in whom I
         delight;
     I will put my Spirit on him,
         and he will proclaim justice to
             the nations.
19 He will not quarrel or cry out;
     no one will hear his voice in
         the streets.
20 A bruised reed he will not break,
     and a smoldering wick he will
         not snuff out,
     till he has brought justice
         through to victory.
21   In his name the nations will
         put their hope."[b]

22 Then they brought him a demon-possessed man who was blind and mute, and Jesus healed him, so that he could both talk and see. 23 All the people were astonished and said, "Could this be the Son of David?"

---

[a] 7 Hosea 6:6   [b] 21 Isaiah 42:1-4

24But when the Pharisees heard this, they said, "It is only by Beelzebul, the prince of demons, that this fellow drives out demons."

25Jesus knew their thoughts and said to them, "Every kingdom divided against itself will be ruined, and every city or household divided against itself will not stand. 26If Satan drives out Satan, he is divided against himself. How then can his kingdom stand? 27And if I drive out demons by Beelzebul, by whom do your people drive them out? So then, they will be your judges. 28But if it is by the Spirit of God that I drive out demons, then the kingdom of God has come upon you.

29"Or again, how can anyone enter a strong man's house and carry off his possessions unless he first ties up the strong man? Then he can plunder his house.

30"Whoever is not with me is against me, and whoever does not gather with me scatters. 31And so I tell you, every kind of sin and slander can be forgiven, but blasphemy against the Spirit will not be forgiven. 32Anyone who speaks a word against the Son of Man will be forgiven, but anyone who speaks against the Holy Spirit will not be forgiven, either in this age or in the age to come.

33"Make a tree good and its fruit will be good, or make a tree bad and its fruit will be bad, for a tree is recognized by its fruit. 34You brood of vipers, how can you who are evil say anything good? For the mouth speaks what the heart is full of. 35A good man brings good things out of the good stored up in him, and an evil man brings evil things out of the evil stored up in him. 36But I tell you that everyone will have to give account on the day of judgment for every empty word they have spoken. 37For by your words you will be acquitted, and by your words you will be condemned."

38Then some of the Pharisees and teachers of the law said to him, "Teacher, we want to see a sign from you."

39He answered, "A wicked and adulterous generation asks for a sign! But none will be given it except the sign of the prophet Jonah. 40For as Jonah was three days and three nights in the belly of a huge fish, so the Son of Man will be three days and three nights in the heart of the earth. 41The men of Nineveh will stand up at the judgment with this generation and condemn it; for they repented at the preaching of Jonah, and now something greater than Jonah is here. 42The Queen of the South will rise at the judgment with this generation and condemn it; for she came from the ends of the earth to listen to Solomon's wisdom, and now something greater than Solomon is here.

43"When an impure spirit comes out of a person, it goes through arid places seeking rest and does not find it. 44Then it says, 'I will return to the house I left.' When it arrives, it finds the house unoccupied, swept clean and put in order. 45Then it goes and takes with it seven other spirits more wicked than itself, and they go in and live there. And the final condition of that person is worse than the first. That is how it will be with this wicked generation."

46While Jesus was still talking to the crowd, his mother and brothers stood outside, wanting to speak to him. 47Someone told him, "Your mother and brothers are standing outside, wanting to speak to you."

⁴⁸He replied to him, "Who is my mother, and who are my brothers?" ⁴⁹Pointing to his disciples, he said, "Here are my mother and my brothers. ⁵⁰For whoever does the will of my Father in heaven is my brother and sister and mother."

13 That same day Jesus went out of the house and sat by the lake. ²Such large crowds gathered around him that he got into a boat and sat in it, while all the people stood on the shore. ³Then he told them many things in parables, saying: "A farmer went out to sow his seed. ⁴As he was scattering the seed, some fell along the path, and the birds came and ate it up. ⁵Some fell on rocky places, where it did not have much soil. It sprang up quickly, because the soil was shallow. ⁶But when the sun came up, the plants were scorched, and they withered because they had no root. ⁷Other seed fell among thorns, which grew up and choked the plants. ⁸Still other seed fell on good soil, where it produced a crop—a hundred, sixty or thirty times what was sown. ⁹Whoever has ears, let them hear."

¹⁰The disciples came to him and asked, "Why do you speak to the people in parables?"

¹¹He replied, "Because the knowledge of the secrets of the kingdom of heaven has been given to you, but not to them. ¹²Whoever has will be given more, and they will have an abundance. Whoever does not have, even what they have will be taken from them. ¹³This is why I speak to them in parables:

"Though seeing, they do not see;
    though hearing, they do not
        hear or understand.

¹⁴In them is fulfilled the prophecy of Isaiah:

" 'You will be ever hearing but
        never understanding;
    you will be ever seeing but
        never perceiving.
¹⁵For this people's heart has
        become calloused;
    they hardly hear with their
        ears,
    and they have closed their
        eyes.
Otherwise they might see with
        their eyes,
    hear with their ears,
    understand with their hearts
and turn, and I would heal
        them.' ᵃ

¹⁶But blessed are your eyes because they see, and your ears because they hear. ¹⁷For truly I tell you, many prophets and righteous people longed to see what you see but did not see it, and to hear what you hear but did not hear it.

¹⁸"Listen then to what the parable of the sower means: ¹⁹When anyone hears the message about the kingdom and does not understand it, the evil one comes and snatches away what was sown in their heart. This is the seed sown along the path. ²⁰The seed falling on rocky ground refers to someone who hears the word and at once receives it with joy. ²¹But since they have no root, they last only a short time. When trouble or persecution comes because of the word, they quickly fall away. ²²The seed falling among the thorns refers to someone who hears the word, but the worries of this life and the deceitfulness of wealth choke the word, making it unfruitful. ²³But the seed falling on good soil refers to someone who hears

ᵃ 15 Isaiah 6:9,10 (see Septuagint)

the word and understands it. This is the one who produces a crop, yielding a hundred, sixty or thirty times what was sown."

24 Jesus told them another parable: "The kingdom of heaven is like a man who sowed good seed in his field. 25 But while everyone was sleeping, his enemy came and sowed weeds among the wheat, and went away. 26 When the wheat sprouted and formed heads, then the weeds also appeared.

27 "The owner's servants came to him and said, 'Sir, didn't you sow good seed in your field? Where then did the weeds come from?'

28 "'An enemy did this,' he replied.

"The servants asked him, 'Do you want us to go and pull them up?'

29 "'No,' he answered, 'because while you are pulling the weeds, you may uproot the wheat with them. 30 Let both grow together until the harvest. At that time I will tell the harvesters: First collect the weeds and tie them in bundles to be burned; then gather the wheat and bring it into my barn.'"

31 He told them another parable: "The kingdom of heaven is like a mustard seed, which a man took and planted in his field. 32 Though it is the smallest of all seeds, yet when it grows, it is the largest of garden plants and becomes a tree, so that the birds come and perch in its branches."

33 He told them still another parable: "The kingdom of heaven is like yeast that a woman took and mixed into about sixty pounds[a] of flour until it worked all through the dough."

34 Jesus spoke all these things to the crowd in parables; he did not say anything to them without using a parable. 35 So was fulfilled what was spoken through the prophet:

> "I will open my mouth in parables,
> I will utter things hidden since the creation of the world."[b]

36 Then he left the crowd and went into the house. His disciples came to him and said, "Explain to us the parable of the weeds in the field."

37 He answered, "The one who sowed the good seed is the Son of Man. 38 The field is the world, and the good seed stands for the people of the kingdom. The weeds are the people of the evil one, 39 and the enemy who sows them is the devil. The harvest is the end of the age, and the harvesters are angels.

40 "As the weeds are pulled up and burned in the fire, so it will be at the end of the age. 41 The Son of Man will send out his angels, and they will weed out of his kingdom everything that causes sin and all who do evil. 42 They will throw them into the blazing furnace, where there will be weeping and gnashing of teeth. 43 Then the righteous will shine like the sun in the kingdom of their Father. Whoever has ears, let them hear.

44 "The kingdom of heaven is like treasure hidden in a field. When a man found it, he hid it again, and then in his joy went and sold all he had and bought that field.

45 "Again, the kingdom of heaven is like a merchant looking for fine pearls. 46 When he found one of great value, he went away and sold everything he had and bought it.

47 "Once again, the kingdom of heaven is like a net that was let down into the lake and caught all

---

[a] 33 Or about 27 kilograms   [b] 35 Psalm 78:2

kinds of fish. 48When it was full, the fishermen pulled it up on the shore. Then they sat down and collected the good fish in baskets, but threw the bad away. 49This is how it will be at the end of the age. The angels will come and separate the wicked from the righteous 50and throw them into the blazing furnace, where there will be weeping and gnashing of teeth.

51"Have you understood all these things?" Jesus asked.

"Yes," they replied.

52He said to them, "Therefore every teacher of the law who has become a disciple in the kingdom of heaven is like the owner of a house who brings out of his storeroom new treasures as well as old."

53When Jesus had finished these parables, he moved on from there. 54Coming to his hometown, he began teaching the people in their synagogue, and they were amazed. "Where did this man get this wisdom and these miraculous powers?" they asked. 55"Isn't this the carpenter's son? Isn't his mother's name Mary, and aren't his brothers James, Joseph, Simon and Judas? 56Aren't all his sisters with us? Where then did this man get all these things?" 57And they took offense at him.

But Jesus said to them, "A prophet is not without honor except in his own town and in his own home."

58And he did not do many miracles there because of their lack of faith.

14 At that time Herod the tetrarch heard the reports about Jesus, 2and he said to his attendants, "This is John the Baptist; he has risen from the dead! That is why miraculous powers are at work in him."

3Now Herod had arrested John and bound him and put him in prison because of Herodias, his brother Philip's wife, 4for John had been saying to him: "It is not lawful for you to have her." 5Herod wanted to kill John, but he was afraid of the people, because they considered John a prophet.

6On Herod's birthday the daughter of Herodias danced for the guests and pleased Herod so much 7that he promised with an oath to give her whatever she asked. 8Prompted by her mother, she said, "Give me here on a platter the head of John the Baptist." 9The king was distressed, but because of his oaths and his dinner guests, he ordered that her request be granted 10and had John beheaded in the prison. 11His head was brought in on a platter and given to the girl, who carried it to her mother. 12John's disciples came and took his body and buried it. Then they went and told Jesus.

13When Jesus heard what had happened, he withdrew by boat privately to a solitary place. Hearing of this, the crowds followed him on foot from the towns. 14When Jesus landed and saw a large crowd, he had compassion on them and healed their sick.

15As evening approached, the disciples came to him and said, "This is a remote place, and it's already getting late. Send the crowds away, so they can go to the villages and buy themselves some food."

16Jesus replied, "They do not need to go away. You give them something to eat."

17"We have here only five loaves of bread and two fish," they answered.

18"Bring them here to me," he

said. 19And he directed the people to sit down on the grass. Taking the five loaves and the two fish and looking up to heaven, he gave thanks and broke the loaves. Then he gave them to the disciples, and the disciples gave them to the people. 20They all ate and were satisfied, and the disciples picked up twelve basketfuls of broken pieces that were left over. 21The number of those who ate was about five thousand men, besides women and children.

22Immediately Jesus made the disciples get into the boat and go on ahead of him to the other side, while he dismissed the crowd. 23After he had dismissed them, he went up on a mountainside by himself to pray. Later that night, he was there alone, 24and the boat was already a considerable distance from land, buffeted by the waves because the wind was against it.

25Shortly before dawn Jesus went out to them, walking on the lake. 26When the disciples saw him walking on the lake, they were terrified. "It's a ghost," they said, and cried out in fear.

27But Jesus immediately said to them: "Take courage! It is I. Don't be afraid."

28"Lord, if it's you," Peter replied, "tell me to come to you on the water."

29"Come," he said.

Then Peter got down out of the boat, walked on the water and came toward Jesus. 30But when he saw the wind, he was afraid and, beginning to sink, cried out, "Lord, save me!"

31Immediately Jesus reached out his hand and caught him. "You of little faith," he said, "why did you doubt?"

32And when they climbed into the boat, the wind died down. 33Then those who were in the boat worshiped him, saying, "Truly you are the Son of God."

34When they had crossed over, they landed at Gennesaret. 35And when the men of that place recognized Jesus, they sent word to all the surrounding country. People brought all their sick to him 36and begged him to let the sick just touch the edge of his cloak, and all who touched it were healed.

15 Then some Pharisees and teachers of the law came to Jesus from Jerusalem and asked, 2"Why do your disciples break the tradition of the elders? They don't wash their hands before they eat!"

3Jesus replied, "And why do you break the command of God for the sake of your tradition? 4For God said, 'Honor your father and mother'*a* and 'Anyone who curses their father or mother is to be put to death.'*b* 5But you say that if anyone declares that what might have been used to help their father or mother is 'devoted to God,' 6they are not to 'honor their father or mother' with it. Thus you nullify the word of God for the sake of your tradition. 7You hypocrites! Isaiah was right when he prophesied about you:

8 " 'These people honor me with
        their lips,
    but their hearts are far from
        me.
9 They worship me in vain;
    their teachings are merely
        human rules.'*c*

10Jesus called the crowd to him and said, "Listen and understand. 11What goes into someone's mouth does not defile them, but what

a 4 Exodus 20:12; Deut. 5:16   *b* 4 Exodus 21:17; Lev. 20:9   *c* 9 Isaiah 29:13

comes out of their mouth, that is what defiles them."

[12] Then the disciples came to him and asked, "Do you know that the Pharisees were offended when they heard this?"

[13] He replied, "Every plant that my heavenly Father has not planted will be pulled up by the roots. [14] Leave them; they are blind guides.[a] If the blind lead the blind, both will fall into a pit."

[15] Peter said, "Explain the parable to us."

[16] "Are you still so dull?" Jesus asked them. [17] "Don't you see that whatever enters the mouth goes into the stomach and then out of the body? [18] But the things that come out of a person's mouth come from the heart, and these defile them. [19] For out of the heart come evil thoughts—murder, adultery, sexual immorality, theft, false testimony, slander. [20] These are what defile a person; but eating with unwashed hands does not defile them."

[21] Leaving that place, Jesus withdrew to the region of Tyre and Sidon. [22] A Canaanite woman from that vicinity came to him, crying out, "Lord, Son of David, have mercy on me! My daughter is demon-possessed and suffering terribly."

[23] Jesus did not answer a word. So his disciples came to him and urged him, "Send her away, for she keeps crying out after us."

[24] He answered, "I was sent only to the lost sheep of Israel."

[25] The woman came and knelt before him. "Lord, help me!" she said.

[26] He replied, "It is not right to take the children's bread and toss it to the dogs."

[27] "Yes it is, Lord," she said. "Even the dogs eat the crumbs that fall from their master's table."

[28] Then Jesus said to her, "Woman, you have great faith! Your request is granted." And her daughter was healed at that moment.

[29] Jesus left there and went along the Sea of Galilee. Then he went up on a mountainside and sat down. [30] Great crowds came to him, bringing the lame, the blind, the crippled, the mute and many others, and laid them at his feet; and he healed them. [31] The people were amazed when they saw the mute speaking, the crippled made well, the lame walking and the blind seeing. And they praised the God of Israel.

[32] Jesus called his disciples to him and said, "I have compassion for these people; they have already been with me three days and have nothing to eat. I do not want to send them away hungry, or they may collapse on the way."

[33] His disciples answered, "Where could we get enough bread in this remote place to feed such a crowd?"

[34] "How many loaves do you have?" Jesus asked.

"Seven," they replied, "and a few small fish."

[35] He told the crowd to sit down on the ground. [36] Then he took the seven loaves and the fish, and when he had given thanks, he broke them and gave them to the disciples, and they in turn to the people. [37] They all ate and were satisfied. Afterward the disciples picked up seven basketfuls of broken pieces that were left over. [38] The number of those who ate was four thousand men, besides women and children. [39] After Jesus had sent the crowd away,

---

[a] 14 Some manuscripts blind guides of the blind

he got into the boat and went to the vicinity of Magadan.

16 The Pharisees and Sadducees came to Jesus and tested him by asking him to show them a sign from heaven.

2 He replied, "When evening comes, you say, 'It will be fair weather, for the sky is red,' 3 and in the morning, 'Today it will be stormy, for the sky is red and overcast.' You know how to interpret the appearance of the sky, but you cannot interpret the signs of the times.*a* 4 A wicked and adulterous generation looks for a sign, but none will be given it except the sign of Jonah." Jesus then left them and went away.

5 When they went across the lake, the disciples forgot to take bread. 6 "Be careful," Jesus said to them. "Be on your guard against the yeast of the Pharisees and Sadducees."

7 They discussed this among themselves and said, "It is because we didn't bring any bread."

8 Aware of their discussion, Jesus asked, "You of little faith, why are you talking among yourselves about having no bread? 9 Do you still not understand? Don't you remember the five loaves for the five thousand, and how many basketfuls you gathered? 10 Or the seven loaves for the four thousand, and how many basketfuls you gathered? 11 How is it you don't understand that I was not talking to you about bread? But be on your guard against the yeast of the Pharisees and Sadducees."

12 Then they understood that he was not telling them to guard against the yeast used in bread, but against the teaching of the Pharisees and Sadducees.

13 When Jesus came to the region of Caesarea Philippi, he asked his disciples, "Who do people say the Son of Man is?"

14 They replied, "Some say John the Baptist; others say Elijah; and still others, Jeremiah or one of the prophets."

15 "But what about you?" he asked. "Who do you say I am?"

16 Simon Peter answered, "You are the Messiah, the Son of the living God."

17 Jesus replied, "Blessed are you, Simon son of Jonah, for this was not revealed to you by flesh and blood, but by my Father in heaven. 18 And I tell you that you are Peter,*b* and on this rock I will build my church, and the gates of Hades*c* will not overcome it. 19 I will give you the keys of the kingdom of heaven; whatever you bind on earth will be*d* bound in heaven, and whatever you loose on earth will be*d* loosed in heaven." 20 Then he ordered his disciples not to tell anyone that he was the Messiah.

21 From that time on Jesus began to explain to his disciples that he must go to Jerusalem and suffer many things at the hands of the elders, the chief priests and the teachers of the law, and that he must be killed and on the third day be raised to life.

22 Peter took him aside and began to rebuke him. "Never, Lord!" he said. "This shall never happen to you!"

23 Jesus turned and said to Peter, "Get behind me, Satan! You are a stumbling block to me; you do not have in mind the concerns of God, but merely human concerns."

24 Then Jesus said to his disciples, "Whoever wants to be my

a 2,3 Some early manuscripts do not have *When evening comes . . . of the times.*   *b 18* The Greek word for *Peter* means *rock.*   *c 18* That is, the realm of the dead   *d 19* Or *will have been*

disciple must deny themselves and take up their cross and follow me. [25] For whoever wants to save their life[a] will lose it, but whoever loses their life for me will find it. [26] What good will it be for someone to gain the whole world, yet forfeit their soul? Or what can anyone give in exchange for their soul? [27] For the Son of Man is going to come in his Father's glory with his angels, and then he will reward each person according to what they have done.

[28] "Truly I tell you, some who are standing here will not taste death before they see the Son of Man coming in his kingdom."

17 After six days Jesus took with him Peter, James and John the brother of James, and led them up a high mountain by themselves. [2] There he was transfigured before them. His face shone like the sun, and his clothes became as white as the light. [3] Just then there appeared before them Moses and Elijah, talking with Jesus.

[4] Peter said to Jesus, "Lord, it is good for us to be here. If you wish, I will put up three shelters — one for you, one for Moses and one for Elijah."

[5] While he was still speaking, a bright cloud covered them, and a voice from the cloud said, "This is my Son, whom I love; with him I am well pleased. Listen to him!"

[6] When the disciples heard this, they fell facedown to the ground, terrified. [7] But Jesus came and touched them. "Get up," he said. "Don't be afraid." [8] When they looked up, they saw no one except Jesus.

[9] As they were coming down the mountain, Jesus instructed them,

"Don't tell anyone what you have seen, until the Son of Man has been raised from the dead."

[10] The disciples asked him, "Why then do the teachers of the law say that Elijah must come first?"

[11] Jesus replied, "To be sure, Elijah comes and will restore all things. [12] But I tell you, Elijah has already come, and they did not recognize him, but have done to him everything they wished. In the same way the Son of Man is going to suffer at their hands." [13] Then the disciples understood that he was talking to them about John the Baptist.

[14] When they came to the crowd, a man approached Jesus and knelt before him. [15] "Lord, have mercy on my son," he said. "He has seizures and is suffering greatly. He often falls into the fire or into the water. [16] I brought him to your disciples, but they could not heal him."

[17] "You unbelieving and perverse generation," Jesus replied, "how long shall I stay with you? How long shall I put up with you? Bring the boy here to me." [18] Jesus rebuked the demon, and it came out of the boy, and he was healed at that moment.

[19] Then the disciples came to Jesus in private and asked, "Why couldn't we drive it out?"

[20] He replied, "Because you have so little faith. Truly I tell you, if you have faith as small as a mustard seed, you can say to this mountain, 'Move from here to there,' and it will move. Nothing will be impossible for you." [21][b]

[22] When they came together in Galilee, he said to them, "The Son of Man is going to be delivered into the hands of men. [23] They will kill

---

[a] 25 The Greek word means either *life* or *soul*; also in verse 26.　　[b] 21 Some manuscripts include here words similar to Mark 9:29.

him, and on the third day he will be raised to life." And the disciples were filled with grief.

²⁴After Jesus and his disciples arrived in Capernaum, the collectors of the two-drachma temple tax came to Peter and asked, "Doesn't your teacher pay the temple tax?"

²⁵"Yes, he does," he replied.

When Peter came into the house, Jesus was the first to speak. "What do you think, Simon?" he asked. "From whom do the kings of the earth collect duty and taxes—from their own children or from others?"

²⁶"From others," Peter answered.

"Then the children are exempt," Jesus said to him. ²⁷"But so that we may not cause offense, go to the lake and throw out your line. Take the first fish you catch; open its mouth and you will find a four-drachma coin. Take it and give it to them for my tax and yours."

18 At that time the disciples came to Jesus and asked, "Who, then, is the greatest in the kingdom of heaven?"

²He called a little child to him, and placed the child among them. ³And he said: "Truly I tell you, unless you change and become like little children, you will never enter the kingdom of heaven. ⁴Therefore, whoever takes the lowly position of this child is the greatest in the kingdom of heaven. ⁵And whoever welcomes one such child in my name welcomes me.

⁶"If anyone causes one of these little ones—those who believe in me—to stumble, it would be better for them to have a large millstone hung around their neck and to be drowned in the depths of the sea.

⁷Woe to the world because of the things that cause people to stumble! Such things must come, but woe to the person through whom they come! ⁸If your hand or your foot causes you to stumble, cut it off and throw it away. It is better for you to enter life maimed or crippled than to have two hands or two feet and be thrown into eternal fire. ⁹And if your eye causes you to stumble, gouge it out and throw it away. It is better for you to enter life with one eye than to have two eyes and be thrown into the fire of hell.

¹⁰"See that you do not despise one of these little ones. For I tell you that their angels in heaven always see the face of my Father in heaven. [11]ᵃ

¹²"What do you think? If a man owns a hundred sheep, and one of them wanders away, will he not leave the ninety-nine on the hills and go to look for the one that wandered off? ¹³And if he finds it, truly I tell you, he is happier about that one sheep than about the ninety-nine that did not wander off. ¹⁴In the same way your Father in heaven is not willing that any of these little ones should perish.

¹⁵"If your brother or sisterᵇ sins,ᶜ go and point out their fault, just between the two of you. If they listen to you, you have won them over. ¹⁶But if they will not listen, take one or two others along, so that 'every matter may be established by the testimony of two or three witnesses.'ᵈ ¹⁷If they still refuse to listen, tell it to the church; and if they refuse to listen even to the church, treat them as you would a pagan or a tax collector.

ᵃ 11 Some manuscripts include here the words of Luke 19:10.   ᵇ 15 The Greek word for *brother or sister* (*adelphos*) refers here to a fellow disciple, whether man or woman; also in verses 21 and 35.   ᶜ 15 Some manuscripts *sins against you*   ᵈ 16 Deut. 19:15

18"Truly I tell you, whatever you bind on earth will be*a* bound in heaven, and whatever you loose on earth will be*a* loosed in heaven.

19"Again, truly I tell you that if two of you on earth agree about anything they ask for, it will be done for them by my Father in heaven. 20For where two or three gather in my name, there am I with them."

21Then Peter came to Jesus and asked, "Lord, how many times shall I forgive my brother or sister who sins against me? Up to seven times?"

22Jesus answered, "I tell you, not seven times, but seventy-seven times.*b*

23"Therefore, the kingdom of heaven is like a king who wanted to settle accounts with his servants. 24As he began the settlement, a man who owed him ten thousand bags of gold*c* was brought to him. 25Since he was not able to pay, the master ordered that he and his wife and his children and all that he had be sold to repay the debt.

26"At this the servant fell on his knees before him. 'Be patient with me,' he begged, 'and I will pay back everything.' 27The servant's master took pity on him, canceled the debt and let him go.

28"But when that servant went out, he found one of his fellow servants who owed him a hundred silver coins.*d* He grabbed him and began to choke him. 'Pay back what you owe me!' he demanded.

29"His fellow servant fell to his knees and begged him, 'Be patient with me, and I will pay it back.'

30"But he refused. Instead, he went off and had the man thrown into prison until he could pay the debt. 31When the other servants saw what had happened, they were outraged and went and told their master everything that had happened.

32"Then the master called the servant in. 'You wicked servant,' he said, 'I canceled all that debt of yours because you begged me to. 33Shouldn't you have had mercy on your fellow servant just as I had on you?' 34In anger his master handed him over to the jailers to be tortured, until he should pay back all he owed.

35"This is how my heavenly Father will treat each of you unless you forgive your brother or sister from your heart."

19 When Jesus had finished saying these things, he left Galilee and went into the region of Judea to the other side of the Jordan. 2Large crowds followed him, and he healed them there.

3Some Pharisees came to him to test him. They asked, "Is it lawful for a man to divorce his wife for any and every reason?"

4"Haven't you read," he replied, "that at the beginning the Creator 'made them male and female,'*e* 5and said, 'For this reason a man will leave his father and mother and be united to his wife, and the two will become one flesh'?*f* 6So they are no longer two, but one flesh. Therefore what God has joined together, let no one separate."

7"Why then," they asked, "did Moses command that a man give his wife a certificate of divorce and send her away?"

---

a 18 Or *will have been* *b* 22 Or *seventy times seven*
was worth about 20 years of a day laborer's wages.
was the usual daily wage of a day laborer (see 20:2). *c* 24 Greek *ten thousand talents*; a talent
  d 28 Greek *a hundred denarii*; a denarius
  e 4 Gen. 1:27 *f* 5 Gen. 2:24

8 Jesus replied, "Moses permitted you to divorce your wives because your hearts were hard. But it was not this way from the beginning. 9 I tell you that anyone who divorces his wife, except for sexual immorality, and marries another woman commits adultery."

10 The disciples said to him, "If this is the situation between a husband and wife, it is better not to marry."

11 Jesus replied, "Not everyone can accept this word, but only those to whom it has been given. 12 For there are eunuchs who were born that way, and there are eunuchs who have been made eunuchs by others — and there are those who choose to live like eunuchs for the sake of the kingdom of heaven. The one who can accept this should accept it."

13 Then people brought little children to Jesus for him to place his hands on them and pray for them. But the disciples rebuked them.

14 Jesus said, "Let the little children come to me, and do not hinder them, for the kingdom of heaven belongs to such as these." 15 When he had placed his hands on them, he went on from there.

16 Just then a man came up to Jesus and asked, "Teacher, what good thing must I do to get eternal life?"

17 "Why do you ask me about what is good?" Jesus replied. "There is only One who is good. If you want to enter life, keep the commandments."

18 "Which ones?" he inquired.

Jesus replied, " 'You shall not murder, you shall not commit adultery, you shall not steal, you shall not give false testimony, 19 honor your father and mother,'[a] and 'love your neighbor as yourself.'[b]

20 "All these I have kept," the young man said. "What do I still lack?"

21 Jesus answered, "If you want to be perfect, go, sell your possessions and give to the poor, and you will have treasure in heaven. Then come, follow me."

22 When the young man heard this, he went away sad, because he had great wealth.

23 Then Jesus said to his disciples, "Truly I tell you, it is hard for someone who is rich to enter the kingdom of heaven. 24 Again I tell you, it is easier for a camel to go through the eye of a needle than for someone who is rich to enter the kingdom of God."

25 When the disciples heard this, they were greatly astonished and asked, "Who then can be saved?"

26 Jesus looked at them and said, "With man this is impossible, but with God all things are possible."

27 Peter answered him, "We have left everything to follow you! What then will there be for us?"

28 Jesus said to them, "Truly I tell you, at the renewal of all things, when the Son of Man sits on his glorious throne, you who have followed me will also sit on twelve thrones, judging the twelve tribes of Israel. 29 And everyone who has left houses or brothers or sisters or father or mother or wife[c] or children or fields for my sake will receive a hundred times as much and will inherit eternal life. 30 But many who are first will be last, and many who are last will be first.

20 "For the kingdom of heaven is like a landowner who went out

---

a 19 Exodus 20:12-16; Deut. 5:16-20   b 19 Lev. 19:18   c 29 Some manuscripts do not have or wife.

early in the morning to hire workers for his vineyard. ²He agreed to pay them a denarius*a* for the day and sent them into his vineyard.

³"About nine in the morning he went out and saw others standing in the marketplace doing nothing. ⁴He told them, 'You also go and work in my vineyard, and I will pay you whatever is right.' ⁵So they went.

"He went out again about noon and about three in the afternoon and did the same thing. ⁶About five in the afternoon he went out and found still others standing around. He asked them, 'Why have you been standing here all day long doing nothing?'

⁷" 'Because no one has hired us,' they answered.

"He said to them, 'You also go and work in my vineyard.'

⁸"When evening came, the owner of the vineyard said to his foreman, 'Call the workers and pay them their wages, beginning with the last ones hired and going on to the first.'

⁹"The workers who were hired about five in the afternoon came and each received a denarius. ¹⁰So when those came who were hired first, they expected to receive more. But each one of them also received a denarius. ¹¹When they received it, they began to grumble against the landowner. ¹²'These who were hired last worked only one hour,' they said, 'and you have made them equal to us who have borne the burden of the work and the heat of the day.'

¹³"But he answered one of them, 'I am not being unfair to you, friend. Didn't you agree to work for a denarius? ¹⁴Take your pay and go. I want to give the one who was hired last the same as I gave you. ¹⁵Don't I

have the right to do what I want with my own money? Or are you envious because I am generous?'

¹⁶"So the last will be first, and the first will be last."

¹⁷Now Jesus was going up to Jerusalem. On the way, he took the Twelve aside and said to them, ¹⁸"We are going up to Jerusalem, and the Son of Man will be delivered over to the chief priests and the teachers of the law. They will condemn him to death ¹⁹and will hand him over to the Gentiles to be mocked and flogged and crucified. On the third day he will be raised to life!"

²⁰Then the mother of Zebedee's sons came to Jesus with her sons and, kneeling down, asked a favor of him.

²¹"What is it you want?" he asked.

She said, "Grant that one of these two sons of mine may sit at your right and the other at your left in your kingdom."

²²"You don't know what you are asking," Jesus said to them. "Can you drink the cup I am going to drink?"

"We can," they answered.

²³Jesus said to them, "You will indeed drink from my cup, but to sit at my right or left is not for me to grant. These places belong to those for whom they have been prepared by my Father."

²⁴When the ten heard about this, they were indignant with the two brothers. ²⁵Jesus called them together and said, "You know that the rulers of the Gentiles lord it over them, and their high officials exercise authority over them. ²⁶Not so with you. Instead, whoever wants to become great among you must be your

---

a 2 A denarius was the usual daily wage of a day laborer.

servant, 27and whoever wants to be first must be your slave— 28just as the Son of Man did not come to be served, but to serve, and to give his life as a ransom for many."

29As Jesus and his disciples were leaving Jericho, a large crowd followed him. 30Two blind men were sitting by the roadside, and when they heard that Jesus was going by, they shouted, "Lord, Son of David, have mercy on us!"

31The crowd rebuked them and told them to be quiet, but they shouted all the louder, "Lord, Son of David, have mercy on us!"

32Jesus stopped and called them. "What do you want me to do for you?" he asked.

33"Lord," they answered, "we want our sight."

34Jesus had compassion on them and touched their eyes. Immediately they received their sight and followed him.

21 As they approached Jerusalem and came to Bethphage on the Mount of Olives, Jesus sent two disciples, 2saying to them, "Go to the village ahead of you, and at once you will find a donkey tied there, with her colt by her. Untie them and bring them to me. 3If anyone says anything to you, say that the Lord needs them, and he will send them right away."

4This took place to fulfill what was spoken through the prophet:

5 "Say to Daughter Zion,
    'See, your king comes to you,
  gentle and riding on a donkey,
    and on a colt, the foal of a
      donkey.' "a

6The disciples went and did as Jesus had instructed them. 7They brought the donkey and the colt and placed their cloaks on them for Jesus to sit on. 8A very large crowd spread their cloaks on the road, while others cut branches from the trees and spread them on the road. 9The crowds that went ahead of him and those that followed shouted,

"Hosannab to the Son of David!"

"Blessed is he who comes in the name of the Lord!"c

"Hosannab in the highest heaven!"

10When Jesus entered Jerusalem, the whole city was stirred and asked, "Who is this?"

11The crowds answered, "This is Jesus, the prophet from Nazareth in Galilee."

12Jesus entered the temple courts and drove out all who were buying and selling there. He overturned the tables of the money changers and the benches of those selling doves. 13"It is written," he said to them, " 'My house will be called a house of prayer,'d but you are making it 'a den of robbers.'e"

14The blind and the lame came to him at the temple, and he healed them. 15But when the chief priests and the teachers of the law saw the wonderful things he did and the children shouting in the temple courts, "Hosanna to the Son of David," they were indignant.

16"Do you hear what these children are saying?" they asked him.

"Yes," replied Jesus, "have you never read,

" 'From the lips of children and infants

a 5 Zech. 9:9   b 9 A Hebrew expression meaning "Save!" which became an exclamation of praise; also in verse 15   c 9 Psalm 118:25,26   d 13 Isaiah 56:7   e 13 Jer. 7:11

you, Lord, have called forth
your praise'[a]?"

[17] And he left them and went out
of the city to Bethany, where he
spent the night.

[18] Early in the morning, as Jesus
was on his way back to the city, he
was hungry. [19] Seeing a fig tree by
the road, he went up to it but found
nothing on it except leaves. Then
he said to it, "May you never bear
fruit again!" Immediately the tree
withered.

[20] When the disciples saw this,
they were amazed. "How did the
fig tree wither so quickly?" they
asked.

[21] Jesus replied, "Truly I tell you, if
you have faith and do not doubt, not
only can you do what was done to
the fig tree, but also you can say to
this mountain, 'Go, throw yourself
into the sea,' and it will be done. [22] If
you believe, you will receive whatever you ask for in prayer."

[23] Jesus entered the temple courts,
and, while he was teaching, the
chief priests and the elders of the
people came to him. "By what authority are you doing these things?"
they asked. "And who gave you this
authority?"

[24] Jesus replied, "I will also ask
you one question. If you answer
me, I will tell you by what authority I am doing these things. [25] John's
baptism—where did it come from?
Was it from heaven, or of human
origin?"

They discussed it among themselves and said, "If we say, 'From
heaven,' he will ask, 'Then why
didn't you believe him?' [26] But if
we say, 'Of human origin'—we are
afraid of the people, for they all hold
that John was a prophet."

[27] So they answered Jesus, "We
don't know."

Then he said, "Neither will I tell
you by what authority I am doing
these things.

[28] "What do you think? There was
a man who had two sons. He went to
the first and said, 'Son, go and work
today in the vineyard.'

[29] "'I will not,' he answered, but
later he changed his mind and
went.

[30] "Then the father went to the
other son and said the same thing.
He answered, 'I will, sir,' but he did
not go.

[31] "Which of the two did what his
father wanted?"

"The first," they answered.

Jesus said to them, "Truly I tell
you, the tax collectors and the prostitutes are entering the kingdom of
God ahead of you. [32] For John came
to you to show you the way of righteousness, and you did not believe
him, but the tax collectors and the
prostitutes did. And even after you
saw this, you did not repent and believe him.

[33] "Listen to another parable:
There was a landowner who planted a vineyard. He put a wall around
it, dug a winepress in it and built
a watchtower. Then he rented the
vineyard to some farmers and
moved to another place. [34] When
the harvest time approached, he
sent his servants to the tenants to
collect his fruit.

[35] "The tenants seized his servants; they beat one, killed another,
and stoned a third. [36] Then he sent
other servants to them, more than
the first time, and the tenants treated them the same way. [37] Last of all,
he sent his son to them. 'They will
respect my son,' he said.

---

[a] 16 Psalm 8:2 (see Septuagint)

38 "But when the tenants saw the son, they said to each other, 'This is the heir. Come, let's kill him and take his inheritance.' 39 So they took him and threw him out of the vineyard and killed him.

40 "Therefore, when the owner of the vineyard comes, what will he do to those tenants?"

41 "He will bring those wretches to a wretched end," they replied, "and he will rent the vineyard to other tenants, who will give him his share of the crop at harvest time."

42 Jesus said to them, "Have you never read in the Scriptures:

" 'The stone the builders rejected
        has become the cornerstone;
    the Lord has done this,
        and it is marvelous in our
            eyes'a?

43 "Therefore I tell you that the kingdom of God will be taken away from you and given to a people who will produce its fruit. 44 Anyone who falls on this stone will be broken to pieces; anyone on whom it falls will be crushed."b

45 When the chief priests and the Pharisees heard Jesus' parables, they knew he was talking about them. 46 They looked for a way to arrest him, but they were afraid of the crowd because the people held that he was a prophet.

22 Jesus spoke to them again in parables, saying: 2 "The kingdom of heaven is like a king who prepared a wedding banquet for his son. 3 He sent his servants to those who had been invited to the banquet to tell them to come, but they refused to come.

4 "Then he sent some more servants and said, 'Tell those who have been invited that I have prepared my dinner: My oxen and fattened cattle have been butchered, and everything is ready. Come to the wedding banquet.'

5 "But they paid no attention and went off—one to his field, another to his business. 6 The rest seized his servants, mistreated them and killed them. 7 The king was enraged. He sent his army and destroyed those murderers and burned their city.

8 "Then he said to his servants, 'The wedding banquet is ready, but those I invited did not deserve to come. 9 So go to the street corners and invite to the banquet anyone you find.' 10 So the servants went out into the streets and gathered all the people they could find, the bad as well as the good, and the wedding hall was filled with guests.

11 "But when the king came in to see the guests, he noticed a man there who was not wearing wedding clothes. 12 He asked, 'How did you get in here without wedding clothes, friend?' The man was speechless.

13 "Then the king told the attendants, 'Tie him hand and foot, and throw him outside, into the darkness, where there will be weeping and gnashing of teeth.'

14 "For many are invited, but few are chosen."

15 Then the Pharisees went out and laid plans to trap him in his words. 16 They sent their disciples to him along with the Herodians. "Teacher," they said, "we know that you are a man of integrity and that you teach the way of God in accordance with the truth. You aren't swayed by others, because you pay no attention to who they are. 17 Tell us then, what is your opinion? Is

---

a 42 Psalm 118:22,23   b 44 Some manuscripts do not have verse 44.

it right to pay the imperial tax[a] to Caesar or not?"

18 But Jesus, knowing their evil intent, said, "You hypocrites, why are you trying to trap me? 19 Show me the coin used for paying the tax." They brought him a denarius, 20 and he asked them, "Whose image is this? And whose inscription?"

21 "Caesar's," they replied.

Then he said to them, "So give back to Caesar what is Caesar's, and to God what is God's."

22 When they heard this, they were amazed. So they left him and went away.

23 That same day the Sadducees, who say there is no resurrection, came to him with a question. 24 "Teacher," they said, "Moses told us that if a man dies without having children, his brother must marry the widow and raise up offspring for him. 25 Now there were seven brothers among us. The first one married and died, and since he had no children, he left his wife to his brother. 26 The same thing happened to the second and third brother, right on down to the seventh. 27 Finally, the woman died. 28 Now then, at the resurrection, whose wife will she be of the seven, since all of them were married to her?"

29 Jesus replied, "You are in error because you do not know the Scriptures or the power of God. 30 At the resurrection people will neither marry nor be given in marriage; they will be like the angels in heaven. 31 But about the resurrection of the dead—have you not read what God said to you, 32 'I am the God of Abraham, and the God of Isaac, and the God of Jacob'[b]? He is not the God of the dead but of the living."

33 When the crowds heard this, they were astonished at his teaching.

34 Hearing that Jesus had silenced the Sadducees, the Pharisees got together. 35 One of them, an expert in the law, tested him with this question: 36 "Teacher, which is the greatest commandment in the Law?"

37 Jesus replied: "'Love the Lord your God with all your heart and with all your soul and with all your mind.'[c] 38 This is the first and greatest commandment. 39 And the second is like it: 'Love your neighbor as yourself.'[d] 40 All the Law and the Prophets hang on these two commandments."

41 While the Pharisees were gathered together, Jesus asked them, 42 "What do you think about the Messiah? Whose son is he?"

"The son of David," they replied.

43 He said to them, "How is it then that David, speaking by the Spirit, calls him 'Lord'? For he says,

44 "'The Lord said to my Lord:
    "Sit at my right hand
until I put your enemies
    under your feet."'[e]

45 If then David calls him 'Lord,' how can he be his son?" 46 No one could say a word in reply, and from that day on no one dared to ask him any more questions.

23 Then Jesus said to the crowds and to his disciples: 2 "The teachers of the law and the Pharisees sit in Moses' seat. 3 So you must be careful to do everything they tell you. But do not do what they do, for they do not practice what they preach. 4 They tie up heavy, cumbersome loads and put them on other people's shoulders, but they

---

a 17 A special tax levied on subject peoples, not on Roman citizens   b 32 Exodus 3:6
c 37 Deut. 6:5   d 39 Lev. 19:18   e 44 Psalm 110:1

themselves are not willing to lift a finger to move them.

⁵"Everything they do is done for people to see: They make their phylacteries*a* wide and the tassels on their garments long; ⁶they love the place of honor at banquets and the most important seats in the synagogues; ⁷they love to be greeted with respect in the marketplaces and to be called 'Rabbi' by others.

⁸"But you are not to be called 'Rabbi,' for you have one Teacher, and you are all brothers. ⁹And do not call anyone on earth 'father,' for you have one Father, and he is in heaven. ¹⁰Nor are you to be called instructors, for you have one Instructor, the Messiah. ¹¹The greatest among you will be your servant. ¹²For those who exalt themselves will be humbled, and those who humble themselves will be exalted.

¹³"Woe to you, teachers of the law and Pharisees, you hypocrites! You shut the door of the kingdom of heaven in people's faces. You yourselves do not enter, nor will you let those enter who are trying to. [14]*b*

¹⁵"Woe to you, teachers of the law and Pharisees, you hypocrites! You travel over land and sea to win a single convert, and when you have succeeded, you make them twice as much a child of hell as you are.

¹⁶"Woe to you, blind guides! You say, 'If anyone swears by the temple, it means nothing; but anyone who swears by the gold of the temple is bound by that oath.' ¹⁷You blind fools! Which is greater: the gold, or the temple that makes the gold sacred? ¹⁸You also say, 'If anyone swears by the altar, it means nothing; but anyone who swears by the gift on the altar is bound by

that oath.' ¹⁹You blind men! Which is greater: the gift, or the altar that makes the gift sacred? ²⁰Therefore, anyone who swears by the altar swears by it and by everything on it. ²¹And anyone who swears by the temple swears by it and by the one who dwells in it. ²²And anyone who swears by heaven swears by God's throne and by the one who sits on it.

²³"Woe to you, teachers of the law and Pharisees, you hypocrites! You give a tenth of your spices—mint, dill and cumin. But you have neglected the more important matters of the law—justice, mercy and faithfulness. You should have practiced the latter, without neglecting the former. ²⁴You blind guides! You strain out a gnat but swallow a camel.

²⁵"Woe to you, teachers of the law and Pharisees, you hypocrites! You clean the outside of the cup and dish, but inside they are full of greed and self-indulgence. ²⁶Blind Pharisee! First clean the inside of the cup and dish, and then the outside also will be clean.

²⁷"Woe to you, teachers of the law and Pharisees, you hypocrites! You are like whitewashed tombs, which look beautiful on the outside but on the inside are full of the bones of the dead and everything unclean. ²⁸In the same way, on the outside you appear to people as righteous but on the inside you are full of hypocrisy and wickedness.

²⁹"Woe to you, teachers of the law and Pharisees, you hypocrites! You build tombs for the prophets and decorate the graves of the righteous. ³⁰And you say, 'If we had lived in the days of our ancestors,

---

a 5 That is, boxes containing Scripture verses, worn on forehead and arm   *b 14* Some manuscripts include here words similar to Mark 12:40 and Luke 20:47.

we would not have taken part with them in shedding the blood of the prophets.' ³¹So you testify against yourselves that you are the descendants of those who murdered the prophets. ³²Go ahead, then, and complete what your ancestors started!

³³"You snakes! You brood of vipers! How will you escape being condemned to hell? ³⁴Therefore I am sending you prophets and sages and teachers. Some of them you will kill and crucify; others you will flog in your synagogues and pursue from town to town. ³⁵And so upon you will come all the righteous blood that has been shed on earth, from the blood of righteous Abel to the blood of Zechariah son of Berekiah, whom you murdered between the temple and the altar. ³⁶Truly I tell you, all this will come on this generation.

³⁷"Jerusalem, Jerusalem, you who kill the prophets and stone those sent to you, how often I have longed to gather your children together, as a hen gathers her chicks under her wings, and you were not willing. ³⁸Look, your house is left to you desolate. ³⁹For I tell you, you will not see me again until you say, 'Blessed is he who comes in the name of the Lord.'ᵃ'

24 Jesus left the temple and was walking away when his disciples came up to him to call his attention to its buildings. ²"Do you see all these things?" he asked. "Truly I tell you, not one stone here will be left on another; every one will be thrown down."

³As Jesus was sitting on the Mount of Olives, the disciples came to him privately. "Tell us," they said, "when will this happen, and what will be the sign of your coming and of the end of the age?"

⁴Jesus answered: "Watch out that no one deceives you. ⁵For many will come in my name, claiming, 'I am the Messiah,' and will deceive many. ⁶You will hear of wars and rumors of wars, but see to it that you are not alarmed. Such things must happen, but the end is still to come. ⁷Nation will rise against nation, and kingdom against kingdom. There will be famines and earthquakes in various places. ⁸All these are the beginning of birth pains.

⁹"Then you will be handed over to be persecuted and put to death, and you will be hated by all nations because of me. ¹⁰At that time many will turn away from the faith and will betray and hate each other, ¹¹and many false prophets will appear and deceive many people. ¹²Because of the increase of wickedness, the love of most will grow cold, ¹³but the one who stands firm to the end will be saved. ¹⁴And this gospel of the kingdom will be preached in the whole world as a testimony to all nations, and then the end will come.

¹⁵"So when you see standing in the holy place 'the abomination that causes desolation,'ᵇ spoken of through the prophet Daniel—let the reader understand—¹⁶then let those who are in Judea flee to the mountains. ¹⁷Let no one on the housetop go down to take anything out of the house. ¹⁸Let no one in the field go back to get their cloak. ¹⁹How dreadful it will be in those days for pregnant women and nursing mothers! ²⁰Pray that your flight will not take place in winter or on the Sabbath. ²¹For then there will be great distress, unequaled from

ᵃ 39 Psalm 118:26   ᵇ 15 Daniel 9:27; 11:31; 12:11

the beginning of the world until now—and never to be equaled again. [22]"If those days had not been cut short, no one would survive, but for the sake of the elect those days will be shortened. [23]At that time if anyone says to you, 'Look, here is the Messiah!' or, 'There he is!' do not believe it. [24]For false messiahs and false prophets will appear and perform great signs and wonders to deceive, if possible, even the elect. [25]See, I have told you ahead of time.

[26]"So if anyone tells you, 'There he is, out in the wilderness,' do not go out; or, 'Here he is, in the inner rooms,' do not believe it. [27]For as lightning that comes from the east is visible even in the west, so will be the coming of the Son of Man. [28]Wherever there is a carcass, there the vultures will gather.

[29]"Immediately after the distress of those days

" 'the sun will be darkened,
    and the moon will not give its
        light;
the stars will fall from the sky,
    and the heavenly bodies will
        be shaken.'[a]

[30]"Then will appear the sign of the Son of Man in heaven. And then all the peoples of the earth[b] will mourn when they see the Son of Man coming on the clouds of heaven, with power and great glory.[c] [31]And he will send his angels with a loud trumpet call, and they will gather his elect from the four winds, from one end of the heavens to the other.

[32]"Now learn this lesson from the fig tree: As soon as its twigs get tender and its leaves come out, you know that summer is near. [33]Even so, when you see all these things, you know that it[d] is near, right at the door. [34]Truly I tell you, this generation will certainly not pass away until all these things have happened. [35]Heaven and earth will pass away, but my words will never pass away.

[36]"But about that day or hour no one knows, not even the angels in heaven, nor the Son,[e] but only the Father. [37]As it was in the days of Noah, so it will be at the coming of the Son of Man. [38]For in the days before the flood, people were eating and drinking, marrying and giving in marriage, up to the day Noah entered the ark; [39]and they knew nothing about what would happen until the flood came and took them all away. That is how it will be at the coming of the Son of Man. [40]Two men will be in the field; one will be taken and the other left. [41]Two women will be grinding with a hand mill; one will be taken and the other left.

[42]"Therefore keep watch, because you do not know on what day your Lord will come. [43]But understand this: If the owner of the house had known at what time of night the thief was coming, he would have kept watch and would not have let his house be broken into. [44]So you also must be ready, because the Son of Man will come at an hour when you do not expect him.

[45]"Who then is the faithful and wise servant, whom the master has put in charge of the servants in his household to give them their food at the proper time? [46]It will be good for that servant whose master finds him doing so when he returns.

---

[a] 29 Isaiah 13:10; 34:4   [b] 30 Or the tribes of the land   [c] 30 See Daniel 7:13-14.   [d] 33 Or he
[e] 36 Some manuscripts do not have nor the Son.

47 Truly I tell you, he will put him in charge of all his possessions. 48 But suppose that servant is wicked and says to himself, 'My master is staying away a long time,' 49 and he then begins to beat his fellow servants and to eat and drink with drunkards. 50 The master of that servant will come on a day when he does not expect him and at an hour he is not aware of. 51 He will cut him to pieces and assign him a place with the hypocrites, where there will be weeping and gnashing of teeth.

25 "At that time the kingdom of heaven will be like ten virgins who took their lamps and went out to meet the bridegroom. 2 Five of them were foolish and five were wise. 3 The foolish ones took their lamps but did not take any oil with them. 4 The wise ones, however, took oil in jars along with their lamps. 5 The bridegroom was a long time in coming, and they all became drowsy and fell asleep.

6 "At midnight the cry rang out: 'Here's the bridegroom! Come out to meet him!'

7 "Then all the virgins woke up and trimmed their lamps. 8 The foolish ones said to the wise, 'Give us some of your oil; our lamps are going out.'

9 " 'No,' they replied, 'there may not be enough for both us and you. Instead, go to those who sell oil and buy some for yourselves.'

10 "But while they were on their way to buy the oil, the bridegroom arrived. The virgins who were ready went in with him to the wedding banquet. And the door was shut.

11 "Later the others also came. 'Lord, Lord,' they said, 'open the door for us!'

12 "But he replied, 'Truly I tell you, I don't know you.'

13 "Therefore keep watch, because you do not know the day or the hour.

14 "Again, it will be like a man going on a journey, who called his servants and entrusted his wealth to them. 15 To one he gave five bags of gold, to another two bags, and to another one bag,[a] each according to his ability. Then he went on his journey. 16 The man who had received five bags of gold went at once and put his money to work and gained five bags more. 17 So also, the one with two bags of gold gained two more. 18 But the man who had received one bag went off, dug a hole in the ground and hid his master's money.

19 "After a long time the master of those servants returned and settled accounts with them. 20 The man who had received five bags of gold brought the other five. 'Master,' he said, 'you entrusted me with five bags of gold. See, I have gained five more.'

21 "His master replied, 'Well done, good and faithful servant! You have been faithful with a few things; I will put you in charge of many things. Come and share your master's happiness!'

22 "The man with two bags of gold also came. 'Master,' he said, 'you entrusted me with two bags of gold; see, I have gained two more.'

23 "His master replied, 'Well done, good and faithful servant! You have been faithful with a few things; I will put you in charge of many things. Come and share your master's happiness!'

24 "Then the man who had re-

---

[a] 15 Greek *five talents . . . two talents . . . one talent*; also throughout this parable; a talent was worth about 20 years of a day laborer's wage.

ceived one bag of gold came. 'Master,' he said, 'I knew that you are a hard man, harvesting where you have not sown and gathering where you have not scattered seed. 25So I was afraid and went out and hid your gold in the ground. See, here is what belongs to you.'

26"His master replied, 'You wicked, lazy servant! So you knew that I harvest where I have not sown and gather where I have not scattered seed? 27Well then, you should have put my money on deposit with the bankers, so that when I returned I would have received it back with interest.

28" 'So take the bag of gold from him and give it to the one who has ten bags. 29For whoever has will be given more, and they will have an abundance. Whoever does not have, even what they have will be taken from them. 30And throw that worthless servant outside, into the darkness, where there will be weeping and gnashing of teeth.'

31"When the Son of Man comes in his glory, and all the angels with him, he will sit on his glorious throne. 32All the nations will be gathered before him, and he will separate the people one from another as a shepherd separates the sheep from the goats. 33He will put the sheep on his right and the goats on his left.

34"Then the King will say to those on his right, 'Come, you who are blessed by my Father; take your inheritance, the kingdom prepared for you since the creation of the world. 35For I was hungry and you gave me something to eat, I was thirsty and you gave me something to drink, I was a stranger and you invited me in, 36I needed clothes and you clothed me, I was sick and

you looked after me, I was in prison and you came to visit me.'

37"Then the righteous will answer him, 'Lord, when did we see you hungry and feed you, or thirsty and give you something to drink? 38When did we see you a stranger and invite you in, or needing clothes and clothe you? 39When did we see you sick or in prison and go to visit you?'

40"The King will reply, 'Truly I tell you, whatever you did for one of the least of these brothers and sisters of mine, you did for me.'

41"Then he will say to those on his left, 'Depart from me, you who are cursed, into the eternal fire prepared for the devil and his angels. 42For I was hungry and you gave me nothing to eat, I was thirsty and you gave me nothing to drink, 43I was a stranger and you did not invite me in, I needed clothes and you did not clothe me, I was sick and in prison and you did not look after me.'

44"They also will answer, 'Lord, when did we see you hungry or thirsty or a stranger or needing clothes or sick or in prison, and did not help you?'

45"He will reply, 'Truly I tell you, whatever you did not do for one of the least of these, you did not do for me.'

46"Then they will go away to eternal punishment, but the righteous to eternal life."

26 When Jesus had finished saying all these things, he said to his disciples, 2"As you know, the Passover is two days away—and the Son of Man will be handed over to be crucified."

3Then the chief priests and the elders of the people assembled in the palace of the high priest, whose name was Caiaphas, ⁴and they schemed to arrest Jesus secretly and kill him. ⁵"But not during the festival," they said, "or there may be a riot among the people."

⁶While Jesus was in Bethany in the home of Simon the Leper, ⁷a woman came to him with an alabaster jar of very expensive perfume, which she poured on his head as he was reclining at the table.

⁸When the disciples saw this, they were indignant. "Why this waste?" they asked. ⁹"This perfume could have been sold at a high price and the money given to the poor."

¹⁰Aware of this, Jesus said to them, "Why are you bothering this woman? She has done a beautiful thing to me. ¹¹The poor you will always have with you,ᵃ but you will not always have me. ¹²When she poured this perfume on my body, she did it to prepare me for burial. ¹³Truly I tell you, wherever this gospel is preached throughout the world, what she has done will also be told, in memory of her."

¹⁴Then one of the Twelve—the one called Judas Iscariot—went to the chief priests ¹⁵and asked, "What are you willing to give me if I deliver him over to you?" So they counted out for him thirty pieces of silver. ¹⁶From then on Judas watched for an opportunity to hand him over.

¹⁷On the first day of the Festival of Unleavened Bread, the disciples came to Jesus and asked, "Where do you want us to make preparations for you to eat the Passover?"

¹⁸He replied, "Go into the city to a certain man and tell him, 'The Teacher says: My appointed time is near. I am going to celebrate the Passover with my disciples at your house.'" ¹⁹So the disciples did as

Jesus had directed them and prepared the Passover.

²⁰When evening came, Jesus was reclining at the table with the Twelve. ²¹And while they were eating, he said, "Truly I tell you, one of you will betray me."

²²They were very sad and began to say to him one after the other, "Surely you don't mean me, Lord?"

²³Jesus replied, "The one who has dipped his hand into the bowl with me will betray me. ²⁴The Son of Man will go just as it is written about him. But woe to that man who betrays the Son of Man! It would be better for him if he had not been born."

²⁵Then Judas, the one who would betray him, said, "Surely you don't mean me, Rabbi?"

Jesus answered, "You have said so."

²⁶While they were eating, Jesus took bread, and when he had given thanks, he broke it and gave it to his disciples, saying, "Take and eat; this is my body."

²⁷Then he took a cup, and when he had given thanks, he gave it to them, saying, "Drink from it, all of you. ²⁸This is my blood of theᵇ covenant, which is poured out for many for the forgiveness of sins. ²⁹I tell you, I will not drink from this fruit of the vine from now on until that day when I drink it new with you in my Father's kingdom."

³⁰When they had sung a hymn, they went out to the Mount of Olives.

³¹Then Jesus told them, "This very night you will all fall away on account of me, for it is written:

" 'I will strike the shepherd,
        and the sheep of the flock will
                be scattered.'ᶜ

ᵃ 11 See Deut. 15:11.   ᵇ 28 Some manuscripts the new   ᶜ 31 Zech. 13:7

³²But after I have risen, I will go ahead of you into Galilee."

³³Peter replied, "Even if all fall away on account of you, I never will."

³⁴"Truly I tell you," Jesus answered, "this very night, before the rooster crows, you will disown me three times."

³⁵But Peter declared, "Even if I have to die with you, I will never disown you." And all the other disciples said the same.

³⁶Then Jesus went with his disciples to a place called Gethsemane, and he said to them, "Sit here while I go over there and pray." ³⁷He took Peter and the two sons of Zebedee along with him, and he began to be sorrowful and troubled. ³⁸Then he said to them, "My soul is overwhelmed with sorrow to the point of death. Stay here and keep watch with me."

³⁹Going a little farther, he fell with his face to the ground and prayed, "My Father, if it is possible, may this cup be taken from me. Yet not as I will, but as you will."

⁴⁰Then he returned to his disciples and found them sleeping. "Couldn't you men keep watch with me for one hour?" he asked Peter. ⁴¹"Watch and pray so that you will not fall into temptation. The spirit is willing, but the flesh is weak."

⁴²He went away a second time and prayed, "My Father, if it is not possible for this cup to be taken away unless I drink it, may your will be done."

⁴³When he came back, he again found them sleeping, because their eyes were heavy. ⁴⁴So he left them and went away once more and prayed the third time, saying the same thing.

⁴⁵Then he returned to the disciples and said to them, "Are you still sleeping and resting? Look, the hour has come, and the Son of Man is delivered into the hands of sinners. ⁴⁶Rise! Let us go! Here comes my betrayer!"

⁴⁷While he was still speaking, Judas, one of the Twelve, arrived. With him was a large crowd armed with swords and clubs, sent from the chief priests and the elders of the people. ⁴⁸Now the betrayer had arranged a signal with them: "The one I kiss is the man; arrest him." ⁴⁹Going at once to Jesus, Judas said, "Greetings, Rabbi!" and kissed him.

⁵⁰Jesus replied, "Do what you came for, friend."ᵃ

Then the men stepped forward, seized Jesus and arrested him. ⁵¹With that, one of Jesus' companions reached for his sword, drew it out and struck the servant of the high priest, cutting off his ear.

⁵²"Put your sword back in its place," Jesus said to him, "for all who draw the sword will die by the sword. ⁵³Do you think I cannot call on my Father, and he will at once put at my disposal more than twelve legions of angels? ⁵⁴But how then would the Scriptures be fulfilled that say it must happen in this way?"

⁵⁵In that hour Jesus said to the crowd, "Am I leading a rebellion, that you have come out with swords and clubs to capture me? Every day I sat in the temple courts teaching, and you did not arrest me. ⁵⁶But this has all taken place that the writings of the prophets might be fulfilled." Then all the disciples deserted him and fled.

⁵⁷Those who had arrested Jesus

ᵃ 50 Or "Why have you come, friend?"

took him to Caiaphas the high priest, where the teachers of the law and the elders had assembled. 58 But Peter followed him at a distance, right up to the courtyard of the high priest. He entered and sat down with the guards to see the outcome.

59 The chief priests and the whole Sanhedrin were looking for false evidence against Jesus so that they could put him to death. 60 But they did not find any, though many false witnesses came forward.

Finally two came forward 61 and declared, "This fellow said, 'I am able to destroy the temple of God and rebuild it in three days.'"

62 Then the high priest stood up and said to Jesus, "Are you not going to answer? What is this testimony that these men are bringing against you?" 63 But Jesus remained silent.

The high priest said to him, "I charge you under oath by the living God: Tell us if you are the Messiah, the Son of God."

64 "You have said so," Jesus replied. "But I say to all of you: From now on you will see the Son of Man sitting at the right hand of the Mighty One and coming on the clouds of heaven."[a]

65 Then the high priest tore his clothes and said, "He has spoken blasphemy! Why do we need any more witnesses? Look, now you have heard the blasphemy. 66 What do you think?"

"He is worthy of death," they answered.

67 Then they spit in his face and struck him with their fists. Others slapped him 68 and said, "Prophesy to us, Messiah. Who hit you?"

69 Now Peter was sitting out in the courtyard, and a servant girl came to him. "You also were with Jesus of Galilee," she said.

70 But he denied it before them all. "I don't know what you're talking about," he said.

71 Then he went out to the gateway, where another servant girl saw him and said to the people there, "This fellow was with Jesus of Nazareth."

72 He denied it again, with an oath: "I don't know the man!"

73 After a little while, those standing there went up to Peter and said, "Surely you are one of them; your accent gives you away."

74 Then he began to call down curses, and he swore to them, "I don't know the man!"

Immediately a rooster crowed. 75 Then Peter remembered the word Jesus had spoken: "Before the rooster crows, you will disown me three times." And he went outside and wept bitterly.

27 Early in the morning, all the chief priests and the elders of the people made their plans how to have Jesus executed. 2 So they bound him, led him away and handed him over to Pilate the governor.

3 When Judas, who had betrayed him, saw that Jesus was condemned, he was seized with remorse and returned the thirty pieces of silver to the chief priests and the elders. 4 "I have sinned," he said, "for I have betrayed innocent blood."

"What is that to us?" they replied. "That's your responsibility."

5 So Judas threw the money into the temple and left. Then he went away and hanged himself.

6 The chief priests picked up the coins and said, "It is against the law to put this into the treasury, since it is blood money." 7 So they de-

―――――――――――――――
[a] 64 See Psalm 110:1; Daniel 7:13.

cided to use the money to buy the potter's field as a burial place for foreigners. [8]That is why it has been called the Field of Blood to this day. [9]Then what was spoken by Jeremiah the prophet was fulfilled: "They took the thirty pieces of silver, the price set on him by the people of Israel, [10]and they used them to buy the potter's field, as the Lord commanded me."[a]

[11]Meanwhile Jesus stood before the governor, and the governor asked him, "Are you the king of the Jews?"

"You have said so," Jesus replied.

[12]When he was accused by the chief priests and the elders, he gave no answer. [13]Then Pilate asked him, "Don't you hear the testimony they are bringing against you?" [14]But Jesus made no reply, not even to a single charge—to the great amazement of the governor.

[15]Now it was the governor's custom at the festival to release a prisoner chosen by the crowd. [16]At that time they had a well-known prisoner whose name was Jesus[b] Barabbas. [17]So when the crowd had gathered, Pilate asked them, "Which one do you want me to release to you: Jesus Barabbas, or Jesus who is called the Messiah?" [18]For he knew it was out of self-interest that they had handed Jesus over to him.

[19]While Pilate was sitting on the judge's seat, his wife sent him this message: "Don't have anything to do with that innocent man, for I have suffered a great deal today in a dream because of him."

[20]But the chief priests and the elders persuaded the crowd to ask for Barabbas and to have Jesus executed.

[21]"Which of the two do you want me to release to you?" asked the governor.

"Barabbas," they answered.

[22]"What shall I do, then, with Jesus who is called the Messiah?" Pilate asked.

They all answered, "Crucify him!"

[23]"Why? What crime has he committed?" asked Pilate.

But they shouted all the louder, "Crucify him!"

[24]When Pilate saw that he was getting nowhere, but that instead an uproar was starting, he took water and washed his hands in front of the crowd. "I am innocent of this man's blood," he said. "It is your responsibility!"

[25]All the people answered, "His blood is on us and on our children!"

[26]Then he released Barabbas to them. But he had Jesus flogged, and handed him over to be crucified.

[27]Then the governor's soldiers took Jesus into the Praetorium and gathered the whole company of soldiers around him. [28]They stripped him and put a scarlet robe on him, [29]and then twisted together a crown of thorns and set it on his head. They put a staff in his right hand. Then they knelt in front of him and mocked him. "Hail, king of the Jews!" they said. [30]They spit on him, and took the staff and struck him on the head again and again. [31]After they had mocked him, they took off the robe and put his own clothes on him. Then they led him away to crucify him.

[32]As they were going out, they met a man from Cyrene, named Simon, and they forced him to carry

---

[a] 10 See Zech. 11:12,13; Jer. 19:1-13; 32:6-9. [b] 16 Many manuscripts do not have Jesus; also in verse 17.

the cross. 33They came to a place called Golgotha (which means "the place of the skull"). 34There they offered Jesus wine to drink, mixed with gall; but after tasting it, he refused to drink it. 35When they had crucified him, they divided up his clothes by casting lots. 36And sitting down, they kept watch over him there. 37Above his head they placed the written charge against him: THIS IS JESUS, THE KING OF THE JEWS.

38Two rebels were crucified with him, one on his right and one on his left. 39Those who passed by hurled insults at him, shaking their heads 40and saying, "You who are going to destroy the temple and build it in three days, save yourself! Come down from the cross, if you are the Son of God!" 41In the same way the chief priests, the teachers of the law and the elders mocked him. 42"He saved others," they said, "but he can't save himself! He's the king of Israel! Let him come down now from the cross, and we will believe in him. 43He trusts in God. Let God rescue him now if he wants him, for he said, 'I am the Son of God.'" 44In the same way the rebels who were crucified with him also heaped insults on him.

45From noon until three in the afternoon darkness came over all the land. 46About three in the afternoon Jesus cried out in a loud voice, *"Eli, Eli,a lema sabachthani?"* (which means "My God, my God, why have you forsaken me?").b

47When some of those standing there heard this, they said, "He's calling Elijah."

48Immediately one of them ran and got a sponge. He filled it with wine vinegar, put it on a staff, and offered it to Jesus to drink. 49The rest said, "Now leave him alone. Let's see if Elijah comes to save him."

50And when Jesus had cried out again in a loud voice, he gave up his spirit.

51At that moment the curtain of the temple was torn in two from top to bottom. The earth shook, the rocks split 52and the tombs broke open. The bodies of many holy people who had died were raised to life. 53They came out of the tombs after Jesus' resurrection andc went into the holy city and appeared to many people.

54When the centurion and those with him who were guarding Jesus saw the earthquake and all that had happened, they were terrified, and exclaimed, "Surely he was the Son of God!"

55Many women were there, watching from a distance. They had followed Jesus from Galilee to care for his needs. 56Among them were Mary Magdalene, Mary the mother of James and Joseph,d and the mother of Zebedee's sons.

57As evening approached, there came a rich man from Arimathea, named Joseph, who had himself become a disciple of Jesus. 58Going to Pilate, he asked for Jesus' body, and Pilate ordered that it be given to him. 59Joseph took the body, wrapped it in a clean linen cloth, 60and placed it in his own new tomb that he had cut out of the rock. He rolled a big stone in front of the entrance to the tomb and went away. 61Mary Magdalene and the other Mary were sitting there opposite the tomb.

a 46 Some manuscripts *Eloi, Eloi*   *b 46* Psalm 22:1   *c 53* Or *tombs, and after Jesus' resurrection they*   *d 56* Greek *Joses,* a variant of *Joseph*

62The next day, the one after Preparation Day, the chief priests and the Pharisees went to Pilate. 63"Sir," they said, "we remember that while he was still alive that deceiver said, 'After three days I will rise again.' 64So give the order for the tomb to be made secure until the third day. Otherwise, his disciples may come and steal the body and tell the people that he has been raised from the dead. This last deception will be worse than the first."

65"Take a guard," Pilate answered. "Go, make the tomb as secure as you know how." 66So they went and made the tomb secure by putting a seal on the stone and posting the guard.

28 After the Sabbath, at dawn on the first day of the week, Mary Magdalene and the other Mary went to look at the tomb.

2There was a violent earthquake, for an angel of the Lord came down from heaven and, going to the tomb, rolled back the stone and sat on it. 3His appearance was like lightning, and his clothes were white as snow. 4The guards were so afraid of him that they shook and became like dead men.

5The angel said to the women, "Do not be afraid, for I know that you are looking for Jesus, who was crucified. 6He is not here; he has risen, just as he said. Come and see the place where he lay. 7Then go quickly and tell his disciples: 'He has risen from the dead and is going ahead of you into Galilee. There you will see him.' Now I have told you."

8So the women hurried away from the tomb, afraid yet filled with joy, and ran to tell his disciples. 9Suddenly Jesus met them. "Greetings," he said. They came to him, clasped his feet and worshiped him. 10Then Jesus said to them, "Do not be afraid. Go and tell my brothers to go to Galilee; there they will see me."

11While the women were on their way, some of the guards went into the city and reported to the chief priests everything that had happened. 12When the chief priests had met with the elders and devised a plan, they gave the soldiers a large sum of money, 13telling them, "You are to say, 'His disciples came during the night and stole him away while we were asleep.' 14If this report gets to the governor, we will satisfy him and keep you out of trouble." 15So the soldiers took the money and did as they were instructed. And this story has been widely circulated among the Jews to this very day.

16Then the eleven disciples went to Galilee, to the mountain where Jesus had told them to go. 17When they saw him, they worshiped him; but some doubted. 18Then Jesus came to them and said, "All authority in heaven and on earth has been given to me. 19Therefore go and make disciples of all nations, baptizing them in the name of the Father and of the Son and of the Holy Spirit, 20and teaching them to obey everything I have commanded you. And surely I am with you always, to the very end of the age."

MARK

Mark appears to be written for an audience in Rome. A Roman centurion's declaration near the end of the book—*Surely this man was the Son of God!*—models the witness to Jesus this gospel calls for.

The opening half of this fast-moving drama keys on the question: *Who do you say I am?* An episode at the end of the first half shows Jesus healing a blind man in two stages, so that he slowly comes to see. In the same way the disciples have only gradually come to recognize who Jesus is. Then in a key moment in the story, between its two halves, Peter confesses that Jesus is the Messiah.

Now the conflict moves out into the open. Jesus has come to introduce a radical new way of life that will undercut existing power relationships. The second half of the drama depicts this in three acts:

: First, Jesus and his disciples travel to Jerusalem.
: Next, Jesus teaches in the temple and clashes with the established leadership.
: In the final act, that leadership executes its plan and has Jesus arrested and crucified, seemingly overturning all he has done. But then God overturns their deed and raises Jesus to life. So Mark's readers are called to be faithful to Jesus, even in suffering, because this is how God continues to overturn the existing order and establish the way of life that Jesus taught.

---

1 The beginning of the good news about Jesus the Messiah,[a] the Son of God,[b] 2 as it is written in Isaiah the prophet:

"I will send my messenger ahead of you,
who will prepare your way"[c] —

3 "a voice of one calling in the wilderness,
'Prepare the way for the Lord,
make straight paths for him.'"[d]

4 And so John the Baptist appeared in the wilderness, preaching a baptism of repentance for the forgiveness of sins. 5 The whole Judean countryside and all the people of Jerusalem went out to him. Confessing their sins, they were baptized by him in the Jordan River. 6 John wore clothing made of camel's hair, with a leather belt around his waist, and he ate locusts and wild honey. 7 And this was his message: "After me comes the one more powerful than I, the straps of whose sandals I am not worthy to stoop down and untie. 8 I baptize you with[e] water, but he will baptize you with[e] the Holy Spirit."

9 At that time Jesus came from Nazareth in Galilee and was baptized by John in the Jordan. 10 Just as Jesus was coming up out of the water, he saw heaven being torn open and the Spirit descending on him like a dove. 11 And a voice came from heaven: "You are my Son, whom I love; with you I am well pleased."

---

[a] 1 Or *Jesus Christ. Messiah* (Hebrew) and *Christ* (Greek) both mean *Anointed One.*   [b] 1 Some manuscripts do not have *the Son of God.*   [c] 2 Mal. 3:1   [d] 3 Isaiah 40:3   [e] 8 Or *in*

¹²At once the Spirit sent him out into the wilderness, ¹³and he was in the wilderness forty days, being tempted[a] by Satan. He was with the wild animals, and angels attended him.

¹⁴After John was put in prison, Jesus went into Galilee, proclaiming the good news of God. ¹⁵"The time has come," he said. "The kingdom of God has come near. Repent and believe the good news!"

¹⁶As Jesus walked beside the Sea of Galilee, he saw Simon and his brother Andrew casting a net into the lake, for they were fishermen. ¹⁷"Come, follow me," Jesus said, "and I will send you out to fish for people." ¹⁸At once they left their nets and followed him.

¹⁹When he had gone a little farther, he saw James son of Zebedee and his brother John in a boat, preparing their nets. ²⁰Without delay he called them, and they left their father Zebedee in the boat with the hired men and followed him.

²¹They went to Capernaum, and when the Sabbath came, Jesus went into the synagogue and began to teach. ²²The people were amazed at his teaching, because he taught them as one who had authority, not as the teachers of the law. ²³Just then a man in their synagogue who was possessed by an impure spirit cried out, ²⁴"What do you want with us, Jesus of Nazareth? Have you come to destroy us? I know who you are—the Holy One of God!"

²⁵"Be quiet!" said Jesus sternly. "Come out of him!" ²⁶The impure spirit shook the man violently and came out of him with a shriek.

²⁷The people were all so amazed that they asked each other, "What is this? A new teaching—and with authority! He even gives orders to impure spirits and they obey him." ²⁸News about him spread quickly over the whole region of Galilee.

²⁹As soon as they left the synagogue, they went with James and John to the home of Simon and Andrew. ³⁰Simon's mother-in-law was in bed with a fever, and they immediately told Jesus about her. ³¹So he went to her, took her hand and helped her up. The fever left her and she began to wait on them.

³²That evening after sunset the people brought to Jesus all the sick and demon-possessed. ³³The whole town gathered at the door, ³⁴and Jesus healed many who had various diseases. He also drove out many demons, but he would not let the demons speak because they knew who he was.

³⁵Very early in the morning, while it was still dark, Jesus got up, left the house and went off to a solitary place, where he prayed. ³⁶Simon and his companions went to look for him, ³⁷and when they found him, they exclaimed: "Everyone is looking for you!"

³⁸Jesus replied, "Let us go somewhere else—to the nearby villages—so I can preach there also. That is why I have come." ³⁹So he traveled throughout Galilee, preaching in their synagogues and driving out demons.

⁴⁰A man with leprosy[b] came to him and begged him on his knees, "If you are willing, you can make me clean."

⁴¹Jesus was indignant.[c] He

---

[a] 13 The Greek for *tempted* can also mean *tested.* [b] 40 The Greek word traditionally translated *leprosy* was used for various diseases affecting the skin. [c] 41 Many manuscripts *Jesus was filled with compassion*

reached out his hand and touched the man. "I am willing," he said. "Be clean!" ⁴²Immediately the leprosy left him and he was cleansed.

⁴³Jesus sent him away at once with a strong warning: ⁴⁴"See that you don't tell this to anyone. But go, show yourself to the priest and offer the sacrifices that Moses commanded for your cleansing, as a testimony to them." ⁴⁵Instead he went out and began to talk freely, spreading the news. As a result, Jesus could no longer enter a town openly but stayed outside in lonely places. Yet the people still came to him from everywhere.

2 A few days later, when Jesus again entered Capernaum, the people heard that he had come home. ²They gathered in such large numbers that there was no room left, not even outside the door, and he preached the word to them. ³Some men came, bringing to him a paralyzed man, carried by four of them. ⁴Since they could not get him to Jesus because of the crowd, they made an opening in the roof above Jesus by digging through it and then lowered the mat the man was lying on. ⁵When Jesus saw their faith, he said to the paralyzed man, "Son, your sins are forgiven."

⁶Now some teachers of the law were sitting there, thinking to themselves, ⁷"Why does this fellow talk like that? He's blaspheming! Who can forgive sins but God alone?"

⁸Immediately Jesus knew in his spirit that this was what they were thinking in their hearts, and he said to them, "Why are you thinking these things? ⁹Which is easier: to say to this paralyzed man, 'Your sins are forgiven,' or to say, 'Get up, take your mat and walk'? ¹⁰But

I want you to know that the Son of Man has authority on earth to forgive sins." So he said to the man, ¹¹"I tell you, get up, take your mat and go home." ¹²He got up, took his mat and walked out in full view of them all. This amazed everyone and they praised God, saying, "We have never seen anything like this!"

¹³Once again Jesus went out beside the lake. A large crowd came to him, and he began to teach them. ¹⁴As he walked along, he saw Levi son of Alphaeus sitting at the tax collector's booth. "Follow me," Jesus told him, and Levi got up and followed him.

¹⁵While Jesus was having dinner at Levi's house, many tax collectors and sinners were eating with him and his disciples, for there were many who followed him. ¹⁶When the teachers of the law who were Pharisees saw him eating with the sinners and tax collectors, they asked his disciples: "Why does he eat with tax collectors and sinners?"

¹⁷On hearing this, Jesus said to them, "It is not the healthy who need a doctor, but the sick. I have not come to call the righteous, but sinners."

¹⁸Now John's disciples and the Pharisees were fasting. Some people came and asked Jesus, "How is it that John's disciples and the disciples of the Pharisees are fasting, but yours are not?"

¹⁹Jesus answered, "How can the guests of the bridegroom fast while he is with them? They cannot, so long as they have him with them. ²⁰But the time will come when the bridegroom will be taken from them, and on that day they will fast. ²¹"No one sews a patch of unshrunk cloth on an old garment.

Otherwise, the new piece will pull away from the old, making the tear worse. 22And no one pours new wine into old wineskins. Otherwise, the wine will burst the skins, and both the wine and the wineskins will be ruined. No, they pour new wine into new wineskins."

23One Sabbath Jesus was going through the grainfields, and as his disciples walked along, they began to pick some heads of grain. 24The Pharisees said to him, "Look, why are they doing what is unlawful on the Sabbath?"

25He answered, "Have you never read what David did when he and his companions were hungry and in need? 26In the days of Abiathar the high priest, he entered the house of God and ate the consecrated bread, which is lawful only for priests to eat. And he also gave some to his companions."

27Then he said to them, "The Sabbath was made for man, not man for the Sabbath. 28So the Son of Man is Lord even of the Sabbath."

3 Another time Jesus went into the synagogue, and a man with a shriveled hand was there. 2Some of them were looking for a reason to accuse Jesus, so they watched him closely to see if he would heal him on the Sabbath. 3Jesus said to the man with the shriveled hand, "Stand up in front of everyone."

4Then Jesus asked them, "Which is lawful on the Sabbath: to do good or to do evil, to save life or to kill?" But they remained silent.

5He looked around at them in anger and, deeply distressed at their stubborn hearts, said to the man, "Stretch out your hand." He stretched it out, and his hand was completely restored. 6Then the Pharisees went out and began to plot with the Herodians how they might kill Jesus.

7Jesus withdrew with his disciples to the lake, and a large crowd from Galilee followed. 8When they heard about all he was doing, many people came to him from Judea, Jerusalem, Idumea, and the regions across the Jordan and around Tyre and Sidon. 9Because of the crowd he told his disciples to have a small boat ready for him, to keep the people from crowding him. 10For he had healed many, so that those with diseases were pushing forward to touch him. 11Whenever the impure spirits saw him, they fell down before him and cried out, "You are the Son of God." 12But he gave them strict orders not to tell others about him.

13Jesus went up on a mountainside and called to him those he wanted, and they came to him. 14He appointed twelve*a* that they might be with him and that he might send them out to preach 15and to have authority to drive out demons. 16These are the twelve he appointed: Simon (to whom he gave the name Peter), 17James son of Zebedee and his brother John (to them he gave the name Boanerges, which means "sons of thunder"), 18Andrew, Philip, Bartholomew, Matthew, Thomas, James son of Alphaeus, Thaddaeus, Simon the Zealot 19and Judas Iscariot, who betrayed him.

20Then Jesus entered a house, and again a crowd gathered, so that he and his disciples were not even able to eat. 21When his family*b* heard about this, they went to take charge of him, for they said, "He is out of his mind."

a 14 Some manuscripts twelve—designating them apostles—   b 21 Or his associates

²²And the teachers of the law who came down from Jerusalem said, "He is possessed by Beelzebul! By the prince of demons he is driving out demons."

²³So Jesus called them over to him and began to speak to them in parables: "How can Satan drive out Satan? ²⁴If a kingdom is divided against itself, that kingdom cannot stand. ²⁵If a house is divided against itself, that house cannot stand. ²⁶And if Satan opposes himself and is divided, he cannot stand; his end has come. ²⁷In fact, no one can enter a strong man's house without first tying him up. Then he can plunder the strong man's house. ²⁸Truly I tell you, people can be forgiven all their sins and every slander they utter, ²⁹but whoever blasphemes against the Holy Spirit will never be forgiven; they are guilty of an eternal sin."

³⁰He said this because they were saying, "He has an impure spirit."

³¹Then Jesus' mother and brothers arrived. Standing outside, they sent someone in to call him. ³²A crowd was sitting around him, and they told him, "Your mother and brothers are outside looking for you."

³³"Who are my mother and my brothers?" he asked.

³⁴Then he looked at those seated in a circle around him and said, "Here are my mother and my brothers! ³⁵Whoever does God's will is my brother and sister and mother."

4 Again Jesus began to teach by the lake. The crowd that gathered around him was so large that he got into a boat and sat in it out on the lake, while all the people were along the shore at the water's edge. ²He taught them many things by parables, and in his teaching said: ³"Listen! A farmer went out to sow his seed. ⁴As he was scattering the seed, some fell along the path, and the birds came and ate it up. ⁵Some fell on rocky places, where it did not have much soil. It sprang up quickly, because the soil was shallow. ⁶But when the sun came up, the plants were scorched, and they withered because they had no root. ⁷Other seed fell among thorns, which grew up and choked the plants, so that they did not bear grain. ⁸Still other seed fell on good soil. It came up, grew and produced a crop, some multiplying thirty, some sixty, some a hundred times."

⁹Then Jesus said, "Whoever has ears to hear, let them hear."

¹⁰When he was alone, the Twelve and the others around him asked him about the parables. ¹¹He told them, "The secret of the kingdom of God has been given to you. But to those on the outside everything is said in parables ¹²so that,

" 'they may be ever seeing but
        never perceiving,
    and ever hearing but never
        understanding;
    otherwise they might turn and
        be forgiven!' ᵃ

¹³Then Jesus said to them, "Don't you understand this parable? How then will you understand any parable? ¹⁴The farmer sows the word. ¹⁵Some people are like seed along the path, where the word is sown. As soon as they hear it, Satan comes and takes away the word that was sown in them. ¹⁶Others, like seed sown on rocky places, hear the word and at once receive it with joy. ¹⁷But since they have no root, they last only a short time. When

ᵃ 12 Isaiah 6:9,10

trouble or persecution comes because of the word, they quickly fall away. [18]Still others, like seed sown among thorns, hear the word; [19]but the worries of this life, the deceitfulness of wealth and the desires for other things come in and choke the word, making it unfruitful. [20]Others, like seed sown on good soil, hear the word, accept it, and produce a crop—some thirty, some sixty, some a hundred times what was sown."

[21]He said to them, "Do you bring in a lamp to put it under a bowl or a bed? Instead, don't you put it on its stand? [22]For whatever is hidden is meant to be disclosed, and whatever is concealed is meant to be brought out into the open. [23]If anyone has ears to hear, let them hear."

[24]"Consider carefully what you hear," he continued. "With the measure you use, it will be measured to you—and even more. [25]Whoever has will be given more; whoever does not have, even what they have will be taken from them."

[26]He also said, "This is what the kingdom of God is like. A man scatters seed on the ground. [27]Night and day, whether he sleeps or gets up, the seed sprouts and grows, though he does not know how. [28]All by itself the soil produces grain—first the stalk, then the head, then the full kernel in the head. [29]As soon as the grain is ripe, he puts the sickle to it, because the harvest has come."

[30]Again he said, "What shall we say the kingdom of God is like, or what parable shall we use to describe it? [31]It is like a mustard seed, which is the smallest of all seeds on earth. [32]Yet when planted, it grows and becomes the largest of all garden plants, with such big branches that the birds can perch in its shade."

[33]With many similar parables Jesus spoke the word to them, as much as they could understand. [34]He did not say anything to them without using a parable. But when he was alone with his own disciples, he explained everything.

[35]That day when evening came, he said to his disciples, "Let us go over to the other side." [36]Leaving the crowd behind, they took him along, just as he was, in the boat. There were also other boats with him. [37]A furious squall came up, and the waves broke over the boat, so that it was nearly swamped. [38]Jesus was in the stern, sleeping on a cushion. The disciples woke him and said to him, "Teacher, don't you care if we drown?"

[39]He got up, rebuked the wind and said to the waves, "Quiet! Be still!" Then the wind died down and it was completely calm.

[40]He said to his disciples, "Why are you so afraid? Do you still have no faith?"

[41]They were terrified and asked each other, "Who is this? Even the wind and the waves obey him!"

5 They went across the lake to the region of the Gerasenes.[a] [2]When Jesus got out of the boat, a man with an impure spirit came from the tombs to meet him. [3]This man lived in the tombs, and no one could bind him anymore, not even with a chain. [4]For he had often been chained hand and foot, but he tore the chains apart and broke the irons on his feet. No one was strong enough to subdue him. [5]Night and day among the tombs and in the hills he would cry out and cut himself with stones.

---

[a] 1 Some manuscripts *Gadarenes*; other manuscripts *Gergesenes*

⁶When he saw Jesus from a distance, he ran and fell on his knees in front of him. ⁷He shouted at the top of his voice, "What do you want with me, Jesus, Son of the Most High God? In God's name don't torture me!" ⁸For Jesus had said to him, "Come out of this man, you impure spirit!"

⁹Then Jesus asked him, "What is your name?"

"My name is Legion," he replied, "for we are many." ¹⁰And he begged Jesus again and again not to send them out of the area.

¹¹A large herd of pigs was feeding on the nearby hillside. ¹²The demons begged Jesus, "Send us among the pigs; allow us to go into them." ¹³He gave them permission, and the impure spirits came out and went into the pigs. The herd, about two thousand in number, rushed down the steep bank into the lake and were drowned.

¹⁴Those tending the pigs ran off and reported this in the town and countryside, and the people went out to see what had happened. ¹⁵When they came to Jesus, they saw the man who had been possessed by the legion of demons, sitting there, dressed and in his right mind; and they were afraid. ¹⁶Those who had seen it told the people what had happened to the demon-possessed man—and told about the pigs as well. ¹⁷Then the people began to plead with Jesus to leave their region.

¹⁸As Jesus was getting into the boat, the man who had been demon-possessed begged to go with him. ¹⁹Jesus did not let him, but said, "Go home to your own people and tell them how much the Lord has done for you, and how he has

had mercy on you." ²⁰So the man went away and began to tell in the Decapolis[a] how much Jesus had done for him. And all the people were amazed.

²¹When Jesus had again crossed over by boat to the other side of the lake, a large crowd gathered around him while he was by the lake. ²²Then one of the synagogue leaders, named Jairus, came, and when he saw Jesus, he fell at his feet. ²³He pleaded earnestly with him, "My little daughter is dying. Please come and put your hands on her so that she will be healed and live." ²⁴So Jesus went with him.

A large crowd followed and pressed around him. ²⁵And a woman was there who had been subject to bleeding for twelve years. ²⁶She had suffered a great deal under the care of many doctors and had spent all she had, yet instead of getting better she grew worse. ²⁷When she heard about Jesus, she came up behind him in the crowd and touched his cloak, ²⁸because she thought, "If I just touch his clothes, I will be healed." ²⁹Immediately her bleeding stopped and she felt in her body that she was freed from her suffering.

³⁰At once Jesus realized that power had gone out from him. He turned around in the crowd and asked, "Who touched my clothes?"

³¹"You see the people crowding against you," his disciples answered, "and yet you can ask, 'Who touched me?'"

³²But Jesus kept looking around to see who had done it. ³³Then the woman, knowing what had happened to her, came and fell at his feet and, trembling with fear, told him the whole truth. ³⁴He said

---

[a] 20 That is, the Ten Cities

to her, "Daughter, your faith has healed you. Go in peace and be freed from your suffering."

35 While Jesus was still speaking, some people came from the house of Jairus, the synagogue leader. "Your daughter is dead," they said. "Why bother the teacher anymore?"

36 Overhearing[a] what they said, Jesus told him, "Don't be afraid; just believe."

37 He did not let anyone follow him except Peter, James and John the brother of James. 38 When they came to the home of the synagogue leader, Jesus saw a commotion, with people crying and wailing loudly. 39 He went in and said to them, "Why all this commotion and wailing? The child is not dead but asleep." 40 But they laughed at him.

After he put them all out, he took the child's father and mother and the disciples who were with him, and went in where the child was. 41 He took her by the hand and said to her, *"Talitha koum!"* (which means "Little girl, I say to you, get up!"). 42 Immediately the girl stood up and began to walk around (she was twelve years old). At this they were completely astonished. 43 He gave strict orders not to let anyone know about this, and told them to give her something to eat.

6 Jesus left there and went to his hometown, accompanied by his disciples. 2 When the Sabbath came, he began to teach in the synagogue, and many who heard him were amazed.

"Where did this man get these things?" they asked. "What's this wisdom that has been given him? What are these remarkable miracles he is performing? 3 Isn't this the carpenter? Isn't this Mary's son and the brother of James, Joseph,[b] Judas and Simon? Aren't his sisters here with us?" And they took offense at him.

4 Jesus said to them, "A prophet is not without honor except in his own town, among his relatives and in his own home." 5 He could not do any miracles there, except lay his hands on a few sick people and heal them. 6 He was amazed at their lack of faith.

Then Jesus went around teaching from village to village. 7 Calling the Twelve to him, he began to send them out two by two and gave them authority over impure spirits.

8 These were his instructions: "Take nothing for the journey except a staff—no bread, no bag, no money in your belts. 9 Wear sandals but not an extra shirt. 10 Whenever you enter a house, stay there until you leave that town. 11 And if any place will not welcome you or listen to you, leave that place and shake the dust off your feet as a testimony against them."

12 They went out and preached that people should repent. 13 They drove out many demons and anointed many sick people with oil and healed them.

14 King Herod heard about this, for Jesus' name had become well known. Some were saying,[c] "John the Baptist has been raised from the dead, and that is why miraculous powers are at work in him."

15 Others said, "He is Elijah."

And still others claimed, "He is a prophet, like one of the prophets of long ago."

16 But when Herod heard this, he

---

said, "John, whom I beheaded, has been raised from the dead!"

17 For Herod himself had given orders to have John arrested, and he had him bound and put in prison. He did this because of Herodias, his brother Philip's wife, whom he had married. 18 For John had been saying to Herod, "It is not lawful for you to have your brother's wife." 19 So Herodias nursed a grudge against John and wanted to kill him. But she was not able to, 20 because Herod feared John and protected him, knowing him to be a righteous and holy man. When Herod heard John, he was greatly puzzled[a]; yet he liked to listen to him.

21 Finally the opportune time came. On his birthday Herod gave a banquet for his high officials and military commanders and the leading men of Galilee. 22 When the daughter of[b] Herodias came in and danced, she pleased Herod and his dinner guests.

The king said to the girl, "Ask me for anything you want, and I'll give it to you." 23 And he promised her with an oath, "Whatever you ask I will give you, up to half my kingdom."

24 She went out and said to her mother, "What shall I ask for?"

"The head of John the Baptist," she answered.

25 At once the girl hurried in to the king with the request: "I want you to give me right now the head of John the Baptist on a platter."

26 The king was greatly distressed, but because of his oaths and his dinner guests, he did not want to refuse her. 27 So he immediately sent an executioner with orders to bring John's head. The man went,

beheaded John in the prison, 28 and brought back his head on a platter. He presented it to the girl, and she gave it to her mother. 29 On hearing of this, John's disciples came and took his body and laid it in a tomb.

30 The apostles gathered around Jesus and reported to him all they had done and taught. 31 Then, because so many people were coming and going that they did not even have a chance to eat, he said to them, "Come with me by yourselves to a quiet place and get some rest."

32 So they went away by themselves in a boat to a solitary place. 33 But many who saw them leaving recognized them and ran on foot from all the towns and got there ahead of them. 34 When Jesus landed and saw a large crowd, he had compassion on them, because they were like sheep without a shepherd. So he began teaching them many things.

35 By this time it was late in the day, so his disciples came to him. "This is a remote place," they said, "and it's already very late. 36 Send the people away so that they can go to the surrounding countryside and villages and buy themselves something to eat."

37 But he answered, "You give them something to eat."

They said to him, "That would take more than half a year's wages[c]! Are we to go and spend that much on bread and give it to them to eat?"

38 "How many loaves do you have?" he asked. "Go and see."

When they found out, they said, "Five—and two fish."

39 Then Jesus directed them to have all the people sit down in groups on the green grass. 40 So they

---

[a] 20 Some early manuscripts *he did many things*   [b] 22 Some early manuscripts *When his daughter*   [c] 37 Greek *take two hundred denarii*

sat down in groups of hundreds and fifties. ⁴¹Taking the five loaves and the two fish and looking up to heaven, he gave thanks and broke the loaves. Then he gave them to his disciples to distribute to the people. He also divided the two fish among them all. ⁴²They all ate and were satisfied, ⁴³and the disciples picked up twelve basketfuls of broken pieces of bread and fish. ⁴⁴The number of the men who had eaten was five thousand.

⁴⁵Immediately Jesus made his disciples get into the boat and go on ahead of him to Bethsaida, while he dismissed the crowd. ⁴⁶After leaving them, he went up on a mountainside to pray.

⁴⁷Later that night, the boat was in the middle of the lake, and he was alone on land. ⁴⁸He saw the disciples straining at the oars, because the wind was against them. Shortly before dawn he went out to them, walking on the lake. He was about to pass by them, ⁴⁹but when they saw him walking on the lake, they thought he was a ghost. They cried out, ⁵⁰because they all saw him and were terrified.

Immediately he spoke to them and said, "Take courage! It is I. Don't be afraid." ⁵¹Then he climbed into the boat with them, and the wind died down. They were completely amazed, ⁵²for they had not understood about the loaves; their hearts were hardened.

⁵³When they had crossed over, they landed at Gennesaret and anchored there. ⁵⁴As soon as they got out of the boat, people recognized Jesus. ⁵⁵They ran throughout that whole region and carried the sick on mats to wherever they heard he was.

⁵⁶And wherever he went — into villages, towns or countryside — they placed the sick in the marketplaces. They begged him to let them touch even the edge of his cloak, and all who touched it were healed.

7 The Pharisees and some of the teachers of the law who had come from Jerusalem gathered around Jesus ²and saw some of his disciples eating food with hands that were defiled, that is, unwashed. ³(The Pharisees and all the Jews do not eat unless they give their hands a ceremonial washing, holding to the tradition of the elders. ⁴When they come from the marketplace they do not eat unless they wash. And they observe many other traditions, such as the washing of cups, pitchers and kettles.*ᵃ*)

⁵So the Pharisees and teachers of the law asked Jesus, "Why don't your disciples live according to the tradition of the elders instead of eating their food with defiled hands?"

⁶He replied, "Isaiah was right when he prophesied about you hypocrites; as it is written:

" 'These people honor me with
    their lips,
but their hearts are far from
    me.
⁷They worship me in vain;
    their teachings are merely
      human rules.'ᵇ

⁸You have let go of the commands of God and are holding on to human traditions."

⁹And he continued, "You have a fine way of setting aside the commands of God in order to observeᶜ your own traditions! ¹⁰For Moses said, 'Honor your father and mother,'ᵈ and, 'Anyone who curses their

---

ᵃ 4 Some early manuscripts pitchers, kettles and dining couches   ᵇ 6,7 Isaiah 29:13   ᶜ 9 Some manuscripts set up   ᵈ 10 Exodus 20:12; Deut. 5:16

father or mother is to be put to death.'[a] 11But you say that if anyone declares that what might have been used to help their father or mother is Corban (that is, devoted to God)— 12then you no longer let them do anything for their father or mother. 13Thus you nullify the word of God by your tradition that you have handed down. And you do many things like that."

14Again Jesus called the crowd to him and said, "Listen to me, everyone, and understand this. 15Nothing outside a person can defile them by going into them. Rather, it is what comes out of a person that defiles them." [16][b]

17After he had left the crowd and entered the house, his disciples asked him about this parable. 18"Are you so dull?" he asked. "Don't you see that nothing that enters a person from the outside can defile them? 19For it doesn't go into their heart but into their stomach, and then out of the body." (In saying this, Jesus declared all foods clean.)

20He went on: "What comes out of a person is what defiles them. 21For it is from within, out of a person's heart, that evil thoughts come— sexual immorality, theft, murder, 22adultery, greed, malice, deceit, lewdness, envy, slander, arrogance and folly. 23All these evils come from inside and defile a person."

24Jesus left that place and went to the vicinity of Tyre.[c] He entered a house and did not want anyone to know it; yet he could not keep his presence secret. 25In fact, as soon as she heard about him, a woman whose little daughter was possessed by an impure spirit came

and fell at his feet. 26The woman was a Greek, born in Syrian Phoenicia. She begged Jesus to drive the demon out of her daughter.

27"First let the children eat all they want," he told her, "for it is not right to take the children's bread and toss it to the dogs."

28"Lord," she replied, "even the dogs under the table eat the children's crumbs."

29Then he told her, "For such a reply, you may go; the demon has left your daughter."

30She went home and found her child lying on the bed, and the demon gone.

31Then Jesus left the vicinity of Tyre and went through Sidon, down to the Sea of Galilee and into the region of the Decapolis.[d] 32There some people brought to him a man who was deaf and could hardly talk, and they begged Jesus to place his hand on him.

33After he took him aside, away from the crowd, Jesus put his fingers into the man's ears. Then he spit and touched the man's tongue. 34He looked up to heaven and with a deep sigh said to him, *"Ephphatha!"* (which means "Be opened!"). 35At this, the man's ears were opened, his tongue was loosened and he began to speak plainly.

36Jesus commanded them not to tell anyone. But the more he did so, the more they kept talking about it. 37People were overwhelmed with amazement. "He has done everything well," they said. "He even makes the deaf hear and the mute speak."

8 During those days another large crowd gathered. Since they had nothing to eat, Jesus called his

---

[a] 10 Exodus 21:17; Lev. 20:9   [b] 16 Some manuscripts include here the words of 4:23.
[c] 24 Many early manuscripts *Tyre and Sidon*   [d] 31 That is, the Ten Cities

disciples to him and said, ²"I have compassion for these people; they have already been with me three days and have nothing to eat. ³If I send them home hungry, they will collapse on the way, because some of them have come a long distance."

⁴His disciples answered, "But where in this remote place can anyone get enough bread to feed them?"

⁵"How many loaves do you have?" Jesus asked.

"Seven," they replied.

⁶He told the crowd to sit down on the ground. When he had taken the seven loaves and given thanks, he broke them and gave them to his disciples to distribute to the people, and they did so. ⁷They had a few small fish as well; he gave thanks for them also and told the disciples to distribute them. ⁸The people ate and were satisfied. Afterward the disciples picked up seven basketfuls of broken pieces that were left over. ⁹About four thousand were present. After he had sent them away, ¹⁰he got into the boat with his disciples and went to the region of Dalmanutha.

¹¹The Pharisees came and began to question Jesus. To test him, they asked him for a sign from heaven. ¹²He sighed deeply and said, "Why does this generation ask for a sign? Truly I tell you, no sign will be given to it." ¹³Then he left them, got back into the boat and crossed to the other side.

¹⁴The disciples had forgotten to bring bread, except for one loaf they had with them in the boat. ¹⁵"Be careful," Jesus warned them. "Watch out for the yeast of the Pharisees and that of Herod."

¹⁶They discussed this with one another and said, "It is because we have no bread."

¹⁷Aware of their discussion, Jesus asked them: "Why are you talking about having no bread? Do you still not see or understand? Are your hearts hardened? ¹⁸Do you have eyes but fail to see, and ears but fail to hear? And don't you remember? ¹⁹When I broke the five loaves for the five thousand, how many basketfuls of pieces did you pick up?"

"Twelve," they replied.

²⁰"And when I broke the seven loaves for the four thousand, how many basketfuls of pieces did you pick up?"

They answered, "Seven."

²¹He said to them, "Do you still not understand?"

²²They came to Bethsaida, and some people brought a blind man and begged Jesus to touch him. ²³He took the blind man by the hand and led him outside the village. When he had spit on the man's eyes and put his hands on him, Jesus asked, "Do you see anything?"

²⁴He looked up and said, "I see people; they look like trees walking around."

²⁵Once more Jesus put his hands on the man's eyes. Then his eyes were opened, his sight was restored, and he saw everything clearly. ²⁶Jesus sent him home, saying, "Don't even go into*ª* the village."

²⁷Jesus and his disciples went on to the villages around Caesarea Philippi. On the way he asked them, "Who do people say I am?"

²⁸They replied, "Some say John the Baptist; others say Elijah; and still others, one of the prophets."

²⁹"But what about you?" he asked. "Who do you say I am?"

ª 26 Some manuscripts *go and tell anyone in*

Peter answered, "You are the Messiah."

30 Jesus warned them not to tell anyone about him.

31 He then began to teach them that the Son of Man must suffer many things and be rejected by the elders, the chief priests and the teachers of the law, and that he must be killed and after three days rise again. 32 He spoke plainly about this, and Peter took him aside and began to rebuke him.

33 But when Jesus turned and looked at his disciples, he rebuked Peter. "Get behind me, Satan!" he said. "You do not have in mind the concerns of God, but merely human concerns."

34 Then he called the crowd to him along with his disciples and said: "Whoever wants to be my disciple must deny themselves and take up their cross and follow me. 35 For whoever wants to save their life*a* will lose it, but whoever loses their life for me and for the gospel will save it. 36 What good is it for someone to gain the whole world, yet forfeit their soul? 37 Or what can anyone give in exchange for their soul? 38 If anyone is ashamed of me and my words in this adulterous and sinful generation, the Son of Man will be ashamed of them when he comes in his Father's glory with the holy angels.

9 And he said to them, "Truly I tell you, some who are standing here will not taste death before they see that the kingdom of God has come with power."

2 After six days Jesus took Peter, James and John with him and led them up a high mountain, where they were all alone. There he was transfigured before them. 3 His clothes became dazzling white, whiter than anyone in the world could bleach them. 4 And there appeared before them Elijah and Moses, who were talking with Jesus.

5 Peter said to Jesus, "Rabbi, it is good for us to be here. Let us put up three shelters—one for you, one for Moses and one for Elijah." 6 (He did not know what to say, they were so frightened.)

7 Then a cloud appeared and covered them, and a voice came from the cloud: "This is my Son, whom I love. Listen to him!"

8 Suddenly, when they looked around, they no longer saw anyone with them except Jesus.

9 As they were coming down the mountain, Jesus gave them orders not to tell anyone what they had seen until the Son of Man had risen from the dead. 10 They kept the matter to themselves, discussing what "rising from the dead" meant.

11 And they asked him, "Why do the teachers of the law say that Elijah must come first?"

12 Jesus replied, "To be sure, Elijah does come first, and restores all things. Why then is it written that the Son of Man must suffer much and be rejected? 13 But I tell you, Elijah has come, and they have done to him everything they wished, just as it is written about him."

14 When they came to the other disciples, they saw a large crowd around them and the teachers of the law arguing with them. 15 As soon as all the people saw Jesus, they were overwhelmed with wonder and ran to greet him.

16 "What are you arguing with them about?" he asked.

17 A man in the crowd answered,

---

a 35 The Greek word means either *life* or *soul*; also in verses 36 and 37.

"Teacher, I brought you my son, who is possessed by a spirit that has robbed him of speech. 18Whenever it seizes him, it throws him to the ground. He foams at the mouth, gnashes his teeth and becomes rigid. I asked your disciples to drive out the spirit, but they could not."

19"You unbelieving generation," Jesus replied, "how long shall I stay with you? How long shall I put up with you? Bring the boy to me."

20So they brought him. When the spirit saw Jesus, it immediately threw the boy into a convulsion. He fell to the ground and rolled around, foaming at the mouth.

21Jesus asked the boy's father, "How long has he been like this?"

"From childhood," he answered. 22"It has often thrown him into fire or water to kill him. But if you can do anything, take pity on us and help us."

23"'If you can'?" said Jesus. "Everything is possible for one who believes."

24Immediately the boy's father exclaimed, "I do believe; help me overcome my unbelief!"

25When Jesus saw that a crowd was running to the scene, he rebuked the impure spirit. "You deaf and mute spirit," he said, "I command you, come out of him and never enter him again."

26The spirit shrieked, convulsed him violently and came out. The boy looked so much like a corpse that many said, "He's dead." 27But Jesus took him by the hand and lifted him to his feet, and he stood up.

28After Jesus had gone indoors, his disciples asked him privately, "Why couldn't we drive it out?"

29He replied, "This kind can come out only by prayer.a"

30They left that place and passed through Galilee. Jesus did not want anyone to know where they were, 31because he was teaching his disciples. He said to them, "The Son of Man is going to be delivered into the hands of men. They will kill him, and after three days he will rise." 32But they did not understand what he meant and were afraid to ask him about it.

33They came to Capernaum. When he was in the house, he asked them, "What were you arguing about on the road?" 34But they kept quiet because on the way they had argued about who was the greatest.

35Sitting down, Jesus called the Twelve and said, "Anyone who wants to be first must be the very last, and the servant of all."

36He took a little child whom he placed among them. Taking the child in his arms, he said to them, 37"Whoever welcomes one of these little children in my name welcomes me; and whoever welcomes me does not welcome me but the one who sent me."

38"Teacher," said John, "we saw someone driving out demons in your name and we told him to stop, because he was not one of us."

39"Do not stop him," Jesus said. "For no one who does a miracle in my name can in the next moment say anything bad about me, 40for whoever is not against us is for us. 41Truly I tell you, anyone who gives you a cup of water in my name because you belong to the Messiah will certainly not lose their reward.

42"If anyone causes one of these little ones—those who believe in me—to stumble, it would be better for them if a large millstone were hung around their neck and

a 29 Some manuscripts *prayer and fasting*

they were thrown into the sea. 43If your hand causes you to stumble, cut it off. It is better for you to enter life maimed than with two hands to go into hell, where the fire never goes out. [44]a 45And if your foot causes you to stumble, cut it off. It is better for you to enter life crippled than to have two feet and be thrown into hell. [46]a 47And if your eye causes you to stumble, pluck it out. It is better for you to enter the kingdom of God with one eye than to have two eyes and be thrown into hell, 48where

" 'the worms that eat them do not
    die,
and the fire is not quenched.'b

49Everyone will be salted with fire. 50"Salt is good, but if it loses its saltiness, how can you make it salty again? Have salt among yourselves, and be at peace with each other."

10 Jesus then left that place and went into the region of Judea and across the Jordan. Again crowds of people came to him, and as was his custom, he taught them.

2Some Pharisees came and tested him by asking, "Is it lawful for a man to divorce his wife?"

3"What did Moses command you?" he replied.

4They said, "Moses permitted a man to write a certificate of divorce and send her away."

5"It was because your hearts were hard that Moses wrote you this law," Jesus replied. 6"But at the beginning of creation God 'made them male and female.'c 7'For this reason a man will leave his father and mother and be united to his wife,d 8and the two will become

one flesh.'e So they are no longer two, but one flesh. 9Therefore what God has joined together, let no one separate."

10When they were in the house again, the disciples asked Jesus about this. 11He answered, "Anyone who divorces his wife and marries another woman commits adultery against her. 12And if she divorces her husband and marries another man, she commits adultery."

13People were bringing little children to Jesus for him to place his hands on them, but the disciples rebuked them. 14When Jesus saw this, he was indignant. He said to them, "Let the little children come to me, and do not hinder them, for the kingdom of God belongs to such as these. 15Truly I tell you, anyone who will not receive the kingdom of God like a little child will never enter it." 16And he took the children in his arms, placed his hands on them and blessed them.

17As Jesus started on his way, a man ran up to him and fell on his knees before him. "Good teacher," he asked, "what must I do to inherit eternal life?"

18"Why do you call me good?" Jesus answered. "No one is good— except God alone. 19You know the commandments: 'You shall not murder, you shall not commit adultery, you shall not steal, you shall not give false testimony, you shall not defraud, honor your father and mother.'f"

20"Teacher," he declared, "all these I have kept since I was a boy."

21Jesus looked at him and loved him. "One thing you lack," he said. "Go, sell everything you have and

---

a 44,46 Some manuscripts include here the words of verse 48.   b 48 Isaiah 66:24   c 6 Gen. 1:27   d 7 Some early manuscripts do not have and be united to his wife.   e 8 Gen. 2:24   f 19 Exodus 20:12-16; Deut. 5:16-20

give to the poor, and you will have treasure in heaven. Then come, follow me."

22 At this the man's face fell. He went away sad, because he had great wealth.

23 Jesus looked around and said to his disciples, "How hard it is for the rich to enter the kingdom of God!"

24 The disciples were amazed at his words. But Jesus said again, "Children, how hard it is[a] to enter the kingdom of God! 25 It is easier for a camel to go through the eye of a needle than for someone who is rich to enter the kingdom of God."

26 The disciples were even more amazed, and said to each other, "Who then can be saved?"

27 Jesus looked at them and said, "With man this is impossible, but not with God; all things are possible with God."

28 Then Peter spoke up, "We have left everything to follow you!"

29 "Truly I tell you," Jesus replied, "no one who has left home or brothers or sisters or mother or father or children or fields for me and the gospel 30 will fail to receive a hundred times as much in this present age: homes, brothers, sisters, mothers, children and fields—along with persecutions—and in the age to come eternal life. 31 But many who are first will be last, and the last first."

32 They were on their way up to Jerusalem, with Jesus leading the way, and the disciples were astonished, while those who followed were afraid. Again he took the Twelve aside and told them what was going to happen to him. 33 "We are going up to Jerusalem," he said, "and the Son of Man will be delivered over to the chief priests and the teachers of the law. They will condemn him to death and will hand him over to the Gentiles, 34 who will mock him and spit on him, flog him and kill him. Three days later he will rise."

35 Then James and John, the sons of Zebedee, came to him. "Teacher," they said, "we want you to do for us whatever we ask."

36 "What do you want me to do for you?" he asked.

37 They replied, "Let one of us sit at your right and the other at your left in your glory."

38 "You don't know what you are asking," Jesus said. "Can you drink the cup I drink or be baptized with the baptism I am baptized with?"

39 "We can," they answered.

Jesus said to them, "You will drink the cup I drink and be baptized with the baptism I am baptized with, 40 but to sit at my right or left is not for me to grant. These places belong to those for whom they have been prepared."

41 When the ten heard about this, they became indignant with James and John. 42 Jesus called them together and said, "You know that those who are regarded as rulers of the Gentiles lord it over them, and their high officials exercise authority over them. 43 Not so with you. Instead, whoever wants to become great among you must be your servant, 44 and whoever wants to be first must be slave of all. 45 For even the Son of Man did not come to be served, but to serve, and to give his life as a ransom for many."

46 Then they came to Jericho. As Jesus and his disciples, together with a large crowd, were leaving the city, a blind man, Bartimaeus (which means "son of Timaeus"), was sitting by the roadside begging.

_____
a 24 Some manuscripts *is for those who trust in riches*

⁴⁷When he heard that it was Jesus of Nazareth, he began to shout, "Jesus, Son of David, have mercy on me!"

⁴⁸Many rebuked him and told him to be quiet, but he shouted all the more, "Son of David, have mercy on me!"

⁴⁹Jesus stopped and said, "Call him."

So they called to the blind man, "Cheer up! On your feet! He's calling you." ⁵⁰Throwing his cloak aside, he jumped to his feet and came to Jesus.

⁵¹"What do you want me to do for you?" Jesus asked him.

The blind man said, "Rabbi, I want to see."

⁵²"Go," said Jesus, "your faith has healed you." Immediately he received his sight and followed Jesus along the road.

11 As they approached Jerusalem and came to Bethphage and Bethany at the Mount of Olives, Jesus sent two of his disciples, ²saying to them, "Go to the village ahead of you, and just as you enter it, you will find a colt tied there, which no one has ever ridden. Untie it and bring it here. ³If anyone asks you, 'Why are you doing this?' say, 'The Lord needs it and will send it back here shortly.' "

⁴They went and found a colt outside in the street, tied at a doorway. As they untied it, ⁵some people standing there asked, "What are you doing, untying that colt?" ⁶They answered as Jesus had told them to, and the people let them go. ⁷When they brought the colt to Jesus and threw their cloaks over it, he sat on it. ⁸Many people spread their cloaks on the road, while others spread branches they had cut in the fields. ⁹Those who went ahead and those who followed shouted,

"Hosanna!ᵃ"

"Blessed is he who comes in the name of the Lord!"ᵇ

¹⁰"Blessed is the coming kingdom of our father David!"

"Hosanna in the highest heaven!"

¹¹Jesus entered Jerusalem and went into the temple courts. He looked around at everything, but since it was already late, he went out to Bethany with the Twelve.

¹²The next day as they were leaving Bethany, Jesus was hungry. ¹³Seeing in the distance a fig tree in leaf, he went to find out if it had any fruit. When he reached it, he found nothing but leaves, because it was not the season for figs. ¹⁴Then he said to the tree, "May no one ever eat fruit from you again." And his disciples heard him say it.

¹⁵On reaching Jerusalem, Jesus entered the temple courts and began driving out those who were buying and selling there. He overturned the tables of the money changers and the benches of those selling doves, ¹⁶and would not allow anyone to carry merchandise through the temple courts. ¹⁷And as he taught them, he said, "Is it not written: 'My house will be called a house of prayer for all nations'ᶜ? But you have made it 'a den of robbers.'ᵈ"

¹⁸The chief priests and the teachers of the law heard this and began looking for a way to kill him, for they feared him, because the whole crowd was amazed at his teaching.

ᵃ 9 A Hebrew expression meaning "Save!" which became an exclamation of praise; also in verse 10   ᵇ 9 Psalm 118:25,26   ᶜ 17 Isaiah 56:7   ᵈ 17 Jer. 7:11

19When evening came, Jesus and his disciplesa went out of the city.

20In the morning, as they went along, they saw the fig tree withered from the roots. 21Peter remembered and said to Jesus, "Rabbi, look! The fig tree you cursed has withered!"

22"Have faith in God," Jesus answered. 23"Trulyb I tell you, if anyone says to this mountain, 'Go, throw yourself into the sea,' and does not doubt in their heart but believes that what they say will happen, it will be done for them. 24Therefore I tell you, whatever you ask for in prayer, believe that you have received it, and it will be yours. 25And when you stand praying, if you hold anything against anyone, forgive them, so that your Father in heaven may forgive you your sins." [26]c

27They arrived again in Jerusalem, and while Jesus was walking in the temple courts, the chief priests, the teachers of the law and the elders came to him. 28"By what authority are you doing these things?" they asked. "And who gave you authority to do this?"

29Jesus replied, "I will ask you one question. Answer me, and I will tell you by what authority I am doing these things. 30John's baptism—was it from heaven, or of human origin? Tell me!"

31They discussed it among themselves and said, "If we say, 'From heaven,' he will ask, 'Then why didn't you believe him?' 32But if we say, 'Of human origin' . . ." (They feared the people, for everyone held that John really was a prophet.)

33So they answered Jesus, "We don't know."

Jesus said, "Neither will I tell you by what authority I am doing these things."

12 Jesus then began to speak to them in parables: "A man planted a vineyard. He put a wall around it, dug a pit for the winepress and built a watchtower. Then he rented the vineyard to some farmers and moved to another place. 2At harvest time he sent a servant to the tenants to collect from them some of the fruit of the vineyard. 3But they seized him, beat him and sent him away empty-handed. 4Then he sent another servant to them; they struck this man on the head and treated him shamefully. 5He sent still another, and that one they killed. He sent many others; some of them they beat, others they killed.

6"He had one left to send, a son, whom he loved. He sent him last of all, saying, 'They will respect my son.'

7"But the tenants said to one another, 'This is the heir. Come, let's kill him, and the inheritance will be ours.' 8So they took him and killed him, and threw him out of the vineyard.

9"What then will the owner of the vineyard do? He will come and kill those tenants and give the vineyard to others. 10Haven't you read this passage of Scripture:

"'The stone the builders rejected
    has become the cornerstone;
11 the Lord has done this,
    and it is marvelous in our
      eyes'd?"

12Then the chief priests, the teachers of the law and the elders looked for a way to arrest him be-

---

a 19 Some early manuscripts came, Jesus in God," Jesus answered. 23"truly   b 22,23 Some early manuscripts "If you have faith   c 26 Some manuscripts include here words similar to Matt. 6:15.   d 11 Psalm 118:22,23

cause they knew he had spoken the parable against them. But they were afraid of the crowd; so they left him and went away.

13Later they sent some of the Pharisees and Herodians to Jesus to catch him in his words. 14They came to him and said, "Teacher, we know that you are a man of integrity. You aren't swayed by others, because you pay no attention to who they are; but you teach the way of God in accordance with the truth. Is it right to pay the imperial tax[a] to Caesar or not? 15Should we pay or shouldn't we?"

But Jesus knew their hypocrisy. "Why are you trying to trap me?" he asked. "Bring me a denarius and let me look at it." 16They brought the coin, and he asked them, "Whose image is this? And whose inscription?"

"Caesar's," they replied.

17Then Jesus said to them, "Give back to Caesar what is Caesar's and to God what is God's."

And they were amazed at him.

18Then the Sadducees, who say there is no resurrection, came to him with a question. 19"Teacher," they said, "Moses wrote for us that if a man's brother dies and leaves a wife but no children, the man must marry the widow and raise up offspring for his brother. 20Now there were seven brothers. The first one married and died without leaving any children. 21The second one married the widow, but he also died, leaving no child. It was the same with the third. 22In fact, none of the seven left any children. Last of all, the woman died too. 23At the resurrection[b] whose wife will she be, since the seven were married to her?"

24Jesus replied, "Are you not in error because you do not know the Scriptures or the power of God? 25When the dead rise, they will neither marry nor be given in marriage; they will be like the angels in heaven. 26Now about the dead rising—have you not read in the Book of Moses, in the account of the burning bush, how God said to him, 'I am the God of Abraham, the God of Isaac, and the God of Jacob'[c]? 27He is not the God of the dead, but of the living. You are badly mistaken!"

28One of the teachers of the law came and heard them debating. Noticing that Jesus had given them a good answer, he asked him, "Of all the commandments, which is the most important?"

29"The most important one," answered Jesus, "is this: 'Hear, O Israel: The Lord our God, the Lord is one.[d] 30Love the Lord your God with all your heart and with all your soul and with all your mind and with all your strength.'[e] 31The second is this: 'Love your neighbor as yourself.'[f] There is no commandment greater than these."

32"Well said, teacher," the man replied. "You are right in saying that God is one and there is no other but him. 33To love him with all your heart, with all your understanding and with all your strength, and to love your neighbor as yourself is more important than all burnt offerings and sacrifices."

34When Jesus saw that he had answered wisely, he said to him, "You are not far from the kingdom

---

of God." And from then on no one dared ask him any more questions.

35 While Jesus was teaching in the temple courts, he asked, "Why do the teachers of the law say that the Messiah is the son of David? 36 David himself, speaking by the Holy Spirit, declared:

" 'The Lord said to my Lord:
    "Sit at my right hand
until I put your enemies
    under your feet." ' [a]

37 David himself calls him 'Lord.' How then can he be his son?"

The large crowd listened to him with delight.

38 As he taught, Jesus said, "Watch out for the teachers of the law. They like to walk around in flowing robes and be greeted with respect in the marketplaces, 39 and have the most important seats in the synagogues and the places of honor at banquets. 40 They devour widows' houses and for a show make lengthy prayers. These men will be punished most severely."

41 Jesus sat down opposite the place where the offerings were put and watched the crowd putting their money into the temple treasury. Many rich people threw in large amounts. 42 But a poor widow came and put in two very small copper coins, worth only a few cents.

43 Calling his disciples to him, Jesus said, "Truly I tell you, this poor widow has put more into the treasury than all the others. 44 They all gave out of their wealth; but she, out of her poverty, put in everything — all she had to live on."

13 As Jesus was leaving the temple, one of his disciples said to him, "Look, Teacher! What massive stones! What magnificent buildings!"

2 "Do you see all these great buildings?" replied Jesus. "Not one stone here will be left on another; every one will be thrown down."

3 As Jesus was sitting on the Mount of Olives opposite the temple, Peter, James, John and Andrew asked him privately, 4 "Tell us, when will these things happen? And what will be the sign that they are all about to be fulfilled?"

5 Jesus said to them: "Watch out that no one deceives you. 6 Many will come in my name, claiming, 'I am he,' and will deceive many. 7 When you hear of wars and rumors of wars, do not be alarmed. Such things must happen, but the end is still to come. 8 Nation will rise against nation, and kingdom against kingdom. There will be earthquakes in various places, and famines. These are the beginning of birth pains.

9 "You must be on your guard. You will be handed over to the local councils and flogged in the synagogues. On account of me you will stand before governors and kings as witnesses to them. 10 And the gospel must first be preached to all nations. 11 Whenever you are arrested and brought to trial, do not worry beforehand about what to say. Just say whatever is given you at the time, for it is not you speaking, but the Holy Spirit.

12 "Brother will betray brother to death, and a father his child. Children will rebel against their parents and have them put to death. 13 Everyone will hate you because of me, but the one who stands firm to the end will be saved.

14 "When you see 'the abomina-

a 36 Psalm 110:1

tion that causes desolation'[a] standing where it[b] does not belong—let the reader understand—then let those who are in Judea flee to the mountains. [15]Let no one on the housetop go down or enter the house to take anything out. [16]Let no one in the field go back to get their cloak. [17]How dreadful it will be in those days for pregnant women and nursing mothers! [18]Pray that this will not take place in winter, [19]because those will be days of distress unequaled from the beginning, when God created the world, until now—and never to be equaled again.

[20]"If the Lord had not cut short those days, no one would survive. But for the sake of the elect, whom he has chosen, he has shortened them. [21]At that time if anyone says to you, 'Look, here is the Messiah!' or, 'Look, there he is!' do not believe it. [22]For false messiahs and false prophets will appear and perform signs and wonders to deceive, if possible, even the elect. [23]So be on your guard; I have told you everything ahead of time.

[24]"But in those days, following that distress,

"'the sun will be darkened,
    and the moon will not give its
        light;
[25]the stars will fall from the sky,
    and the heavenly bodies will
        be shaken.'[c]

[26]"At that time people will see the Son of Man coming in clouds with great power and glory. [27]And he will send his angels and gather his elect from the four winds, from the ends of the earth to the ends of the heavens.

[28]"Now learn this lesson from the fig tree: As soon as its twigs get tender and its leaves come out, you know that summer is near. [29]Even so, when you see these things happening, you know that it[b] is near, right at the door. [30]Truly I tell you, this generation will certainly not pass away until all these things have happened. [31]Heaven and earth will pass away, but my words will never pass away.

[32]"But about that day or hour no one knows, not even the angels in heaven, nor the Son, but only the Father. [33]Be on guard! Be alert[d]! You do not know when that time will come. [34]It's like a man going away: He leaves his house and puts his servants in charge, each with their assigned task, and tells the one at the door to keep watch.

[35]"Therefore keep watch because you do not know when the owner of the house will come back—whether in the evening, or at midnight, or when the rooster crows, or at dawn. [36]If he comes suddenly, do not let him find you sleeping. [37]What I say to you, I say to everyone: 'Watch!'"

14 Now the Passover and the Festival of Unleavened Bread were only two days away, and the chief priests and the teachers of the law were scheming to arrest Jesus secretly and kill him. [2]"But not during the festival," they said, "or the people may riot."

[3]While he was in Bethany, reclining at the table in the home of Simon the Leper, a woman came with an alabaster jar of very expensive perfume, made of pure nard. She broke the jar and poured the perfume on his head.

---

[a] 14 Daniel 9:27; 11:31; 12:11   [b] 14,29 Or he   [c] 25 Isaiah 13:10; 34:4   [d] 33 Some manuscripts alert and pray

⁴Some of those present were saying indignantly to one another, "Why this waste of perfume? ⁵It could have been sold for more than a year's wages[a] and the money given to the poor." And they rebuked her harshly.

⁶"Leave her alone," said Jesus. "Why are you bothering her? She has done a beautiful thing to me. ⁷The poor you will always have with you,[b] and you can help them any time you want. But you will not always have me. ⁸She did what she could. She poured perfume on my body beforehand to prepare for my burial. ⁹Truly I tell you, wherever the gospel is preached throughout the world, what she has done will also be told, in memory of her."

¹⁰Then Judas Iscariot, one of the Twelve, went to the chief priests to betray Jesus to them. ¹¹They were delighted to hear this and promised to give him money. So he watched for an opportunity to hand him over.

¹²On the first day of the Festival of Unleavened Bread, when it was customary to sacrifice the Passover lamb, Jesus' disciples asked him, "Where do you want us to go and make preparations for you to eat the Passover?"

¹³So he sent two of his disciples, telling them, "Go into the city, and a man carrying a jar of water will meet you. Follow him. ¹⁴Say to the owner of the house he enters, 'The Teacher asks: Where is my guest room, where I may eat the Passover with my disciples?' ¹⁵He will show you a large room upstairs, furnished and ready. Make preparations for us there."

¹⁶The disciples left, went into the city and found things just as Jesus had told them. So they prepared the Passover.

¹⁷When evening came, Jesus arrived with the Twelve. ¹⁸While they were reclining at the table eating, he said, "Truly I tell you, one of you will betray me — one who is eating with me."

¹⁹They were saddened, and one by one they said to him, "Surely you don't mean me?"

²⁰"It is one of the Twelve," he replied, "one who dips bread into the bowl with me. ²¹The Son of Man will go just as it is written about him. But woe to that man who betrays the Son of Man! It would be better for him if he had not been born."

²²While they were eating, Jesus took bread, and when he had given thanks, he broke it and gave it to his disciples, saying, "Take it; this is my body."

²³Then he took a cup, and when he had given thanks, he gave it to them, and they all drank from it.

²⁴"This is my blood of the[c] covenant, which is poured out for many," he said to them. ²⁵"Truly I tell you, I will not drink again from the fruit of the vine until that day when I drink it new in the kingdom of God."

²⁶When they had sung a hymn, they went out to the Mount of Olives.

²⁷"You will all fall away," Jesus told them, "for it is written:

"'I will strike the shepherd,
    and the sheep will be
        scattered.'[d]

²⁸But after I have risen, I will go ahead of you into Galilee."

²⁹Peter declared, "Even if all fall away, I will not."

---

[a] 5 Greek *than three hundred denarii*   [b] 7 See Deut. 15:11.   [c] 24 Some manuscripts *the new*   [d] 27 Zech. 13:7

³⁰"Truly I tell you," Jesus answered, "today—yes, tonight—before the rooster crows twice[a] you yourself will disown me three times."

³¹But Peter insisted emphatically, "Even if I have to die with you, I will never disown you." And all the others said the same.

³²They went to a place called Gethsemane, and Jesus said to his disciples, "Sit here while I pray." ³³He took Peter, James and John along with him, and he began to be deeply distressed and troubled. ³⁴"My soul is overwhelmed with sorrow to the point of death," he said to them. "Stay here and keep watch."

³⁵Going a little farther, he fell to the ground and prayed that if possible the hour might pass from him. ³⁶"Abba,[b] Father," he said, "everything is possible for you. Take this cup from me. Yet not what I will, but what you will."

³⁷Then he returned to his disciples and found them sleeping. "Simon," he said to Peter, "are you asleep? Couldn't you keep watch for one hour? ³⁸Watch and pray so that you will not fall into temptation. The spirit is willing, but the flesh is weak."

³⁹Once more he went away and prayed the same thing. ⁴⁰When he came back, he again found them sleeping, because their eyes were heavy. They did not know what to say to him.

⁴¹Returning the third time, he said to them, "Are you still sleeping and resting? Enough! The hour has come. Look, the Son of Man is delivered into the hands of sinners. ⁴²Rise! Let us go! Here comes my betrayer!"

⁴³Just as he was speaking, Judas, one of the Twelve, appeared.

With him was a crowd armed with swords and clubs, sent from the chief priests, the teachers of the law, and the elders.

⁴⁴Now the betrayer had arranged a signal with them: "The one I kiss is the man; arrest him and lead him away under guard." ⁴⁵Going at once to Jesus, Judas said, "Rabbi!" and kissed him. ⁴⁶The men seized Jesus and arrested him. ⁴⁷Then one of those standing near drew his sword and struck the servant of the high priest, cutting off his ear.

⁴⁸"Am I leading a rebellion," said Jesus, "that you have come out with swords and clubs to capture me? ⁴⁹Every day I was with you, teaching in the temple courts, and you did not arrest me. But the Scriptures must be fulfilled." ⁵⁰Then everyone deserted him and fled.

⁵¹A young man, wearing nothing but a linen garment, was following Jesus. When they seized him, ⁵²he fled naked, leaving his garment behind.

⁵³They took Jesus to the high priest, and all the chief priests, the elders and the teachers of the law came together. ⁵⁴Peter followed him at a distance, right into the courtyard of the high priest. There he sat with the guards and warmed himself at the fire.

⁵⁵The chief priests and the whole Sanhedrin were looking for evidence against Jesus so that they could put him to death, but they did not find any. ⁵⁶Many testified falsely against him, but their statements did not agree.

⁵⁷Then some stood up and gave this false testimony against him: ⁵⁸"We heard him say, 'I will destroy this temple made with human hands and in three days will build another,

---

[a] 30 Some early manuscripts do not have *twice*.   [b] 36 Aramaic for *father*

not made with hands.' " 59Yet even then their testimony did not agree.

60Then the high priest stood up before them and asked Jesus, "Are you not going to answer? What is this testimony that these men are bringing against you?" 61But Jesus remained silent and gave no answer.

Again the high priest asked him, "Are you the Messiah, the Son of the Blessed One?"

62"I am," said Jesus. "And you will see the Son of Man sitting at the right hand of the Mighty One and coming on the clouds of heaven."

63The high priest tore his clothes. "Why do we need any more witnesses?" he asked. 64"You have heard the blasphemy. What do you think?"

They all condemned him as worthy of death. 65Then some began to spit at him; they blindfolded him, struck him with their fists, and said, "Prophesy!" And the guards took him and beat him.

66While Peter was below in the courtyard, one of the servant girls of the high priest came by. 67When she saw Peter warming himself, she looked closely at him.

"You also were with that Nazarene, Jesus," she said.

68But he denied it. "I don't know or understand what you're talking about," he said, and went out into the entryway.a

69When the servant girl saw him there, she said again to those standing around, "This fellow is one of them." 70Again he denied it.

After a little while, those standing near said to Peter, "Surely you are one of them, for you are a Galilean."

71He began to call down curses, and he swore to them, "I don't know this man you're talking about."

72Immediately the rooster crowed the second time.b Then Peter remembered the word Jesus had spoken to him: "Before the rooster crows twicec you will disown me three times." And he broke down and wept.

15 Very early in the morning, the chief priests, with the elders, the teachers of the law and the whole Sanhedrin, made their plans. So they bound Jesus, led him away and handed him over to Pilate.

2"Are you the king of the Jews?" asked Pilate.

"You have said so," Jesus replied.

3The chief priests accused him of many things. 4So again Pilate asked him, "Aren't you going to answer? See how many things they are accusing you of."

5But Jesus still made no reply, and Pilate was amazed.

6Now it was the custom at the festival to release a prisoner whom the people requested. 7A man called Barabbas was in prison with the insurrectionists who had committed murder in the uprising. 8The crowd came up and asked Pilate to do for them what he usually did.

9"Do you want me to release to you the king of the Jews?" asked Pilate, 10knowing it was out of self-interest that the chief priests had handed Jesus over to him. 11But the chief priests stirred up the crowd to have Pilate release Barabbas instead.

12"What shall I do, then, with the one you call the king of the Jews?" Pilate asked them.

13"Crucify him!" they shouted.

14"Why? What crime has he committed?" asked Pilate.

But they shouted all the louder, "Crucify him!"

---

a 68 Some early manuscripts *entryway and the rooster crowed*   b 72 Some early manuscripts do not have *the second time.*   c 72 Some early manuscripts do not have *twice.*

¹⁵Wanting to satisfy the crowd, Pilate released Barabbas to them. He had Jesus flogged, and handed him over to be crucified.

¹⁶The soldiers led Jesus away into the palace (that is, the Praetorium) and called together the whole company of soldiers. ¹⁷They put a purple robe on him, then twisted together a crown of thorns and set it on him. ¹⁸And they began to call out to him, "Hail, king of the Jews!" ¹⁹Again and again they struck him on the head with a staff and spit on him. Falling on their knees, they paid homage to him. ²⁰And when they had mocked him, they took off the purple robe and put his own clothes on him. Then they led him out to crucify him.

²¹A certain man from Cyrene, Simon, the father of Alexander and Rufus, was passing by on his way in from the country, and they forced him to carry the cross. ²²They brought Jesus to the place called Golgotha (which means "the place of the skull"). ²³Then they offered him wine mixed with myrrh, but he did not take it. ²⁴And they crucified him. Dividing up his clothes, they cast lots to see what each would get.

²⁵It was nine in the morning when they crucified him. ²⁶The written notice of the charge against him read: THE KING OF THE JEWS.

²⁷They crucified two rebels with him, one on his right and one on his left. [28] ᵃ ²⁹Those who passed by hurled insults at him, shaking their heads and saying, "So! You who are going to destroy the temple and build it in three days, ³⁰come down from the cross and save yourself!" ³¹In the same way the chief priests and the teachers of the law mocked him among themselves. "He saved others," they said, "but he can't save himself! ³²Let this Messiah, this king of Israel, come down now from the cross, that we may see and believe." Those crucified with him also heaped insults on him.

³³At noon, darkness came over the whole land until three in the afternoon. ³⁴And at three in the afternoon Jesus cried out in a loud voice, *"Eloi, Eloi, lema sabachthani?"* (which means "My God, my God, why have you forsaken me?").ᵇ

³⁵When some of those standing near heard this, they said, "Listen, he's calling Elijah."

³⁶Someone ran, filled a sponge with wine vinegar, put it on a staff, and offered it to Jesus to drink. "Now leave him alone. Let's see if Elijah comes to take him down," he said.

³⁷With a loud cry, Jesus breathed his last.

³⁸The curtain of the temple was torn in two from top to bottom. ³⁹And when the centurion, who stood there in front of Jesus, saw how he died,ᶜ he said, "Surely this man was the Son of God!"

⁴⁰Some women were watching from a distance. Among them were Mary Magdalene, Mary the mother of James the younger and of Joseph,ᵈ and Salome. ⁴¹In Galilee these women had followed him and cared for his needs. Many other women who had come up with him to Jerusalem were also there.

⁴²It was Preparation Day (that is, the day before the Sabbath). So as evening approached, ⁴³Joseph of Arimathea, a prominent member of the Council, who was himself waiting

---

ᵃ 28 Some manuscripts include here words similar to Luke 22:37.   ᵇ 34 Psalm 22:1
ᶜ 39 Some manuscripts *saw that he died with such a cry*   ᵈ 40 Greek *Joses*, a variant of *Joseph*; also in verse 47

for the kingdom of God, went boldly to Pilate and asked for Jesus' body. 44Pilate was surprised to hear that he was already dead. Summoning the centurion, he asked him if Jesus had already died. 45When he learned from the centurion that it was so, he gave the body to Joseph. 46So Joseph bought some linen cloth, took down the body, wrapped it in the linen, and placed it in a tomb cut out of rock. Then he rolled a stone against the entrance of the tomb. 47Mary Magdalene and Mary the mother of Joseph saw where he was laid.

16 When the Sabbath was over, Mary Magdalene, Mary the mother of James, and Salome bought spices so that they might go to anoint Jesus' body. 2Very early on the first day of the week, just after sunrise, they were on their way to the tomb 3and they asked each other, "Who will roll the stone away from the entrance of the tomb?"

4But when they looked up, they saw that the stone, which was very large, had been rolled away. 5As they entered the tomb, they saw a young man dressed in a white robe sitting on the right side, and they were alarmed.

6"Don't be alarmed," he said. "You are looking for Jesus the Nazarene, who was crucified. He has risen! He is not here. See the place where they laid him. 7But go, tell his disciples and Peter, 'He is going ahead of you into Galilee. There you will see him, just as he told you.'"

8Trembling and bewildered, the women went out and fled from the tomb. They said nothing to anyone, because they were afraid.a

[The earliest manuscripts and some other ancient witnesses do not have verses 9–20.]

9When Jesus rose early on the first day of the week, he appeared first to Mary Magdalene, out of whom he had driven seven demons. 10She went and told those who had been with him and who were mourning and weeping. 11When they heard that Jesus was alive and that she had seen him, they did not believe it.

12Afterward Jesus appeared in a different form to two of them while they were walking in the country. 13These returned and reported it to the rest; but they did not believe them either.

14Later Jesus appeared to the Eleven as they were eating; he rebuked them for their lack of faith and their stubborn refusal to believe those who had seen him after he had risen.

15He said to them, "Go into all the world and preach the gospel to all creation. 16Whoever believes and is baptized will be saved, but whoever does not believe will be condemned. 17And these signs will accompany those who believe: In my name they will drive out demons; they will speak in new tongues; 18they will pick up snakes with their hands; and when they drink deadly poison, it will not hurt them at all; they will place their hands on sick people, and they will get well."

19After the Lord Jesus had spoken to them, he was taken up into heaven and he sat at the right hand of God. 20Then the disciples went out and preached everywhere, and the Lord worked with them and confirmed his word by the signs that accompanied it.

a 8 Some manuscripts have the following ending between verses 8 and 9, and one manuscript has it after verse 8 (omitting verses 9-20): Then they quickly reported all these instructions to those around Peter. After this, Jesus himself also sent out through them from east to west the sacred and imperishable proclamation of eternal salvation. Amen.

LUKE

The books of Luke and Acts are two volumes of a single work (see p. 148 for a more detailed introduction to Acts). Together they tell the story of how God first invited the people of Israel, and then all nations, to follow Jesus. In the first volume, the movement is toward Jerusalem, the center of Jewish national life. In the second, the movement is from Jerusalem to other nations, closing with Paul proclaiming the kingdom of God in Rome, the capital of the empire.

Luke addresses his history to *most excellent Theophilus*, most likely a Roman official. His volumes are stocked with details from sources Luke had available: letters, speeches, songs, travel accounts, trial transcripts and biographical anecdotes. Luke's purpose is to show the fulfillment of God's plan to bring his light to the world through Israel. The earliest Jesus-followers take up this calling by announcing Jesus' victory over sin and death to all the nations.

The first volume, Luke's telling of the story of Jesus, has three main sections:

: First, Jesus ministers in Galilee, the northern area of the land of Israel.
: Next, he takes a long journey to Jerusalem, during which he welcomes people into the way of God's reign and challenges Israel's current understanding of the kingdom.
: Third, Luke tells how Jesus gives his life in Jerusalem and then rises from the dead to be revealed as Israel's King and the world's true Lord.

---

1 Many have undertaken to draw up an account of the things that have been fulfilled[a] among us, ²just as they were handed down to us by those who from the first were eyewitnesses and servants of the word. ³With this in mind, since I myself have carefully investigated everything from the beginning, I too decided to write an orderly account for you, most excellent Theophilus, ⁴so that you may know the certainty of the things you have been taught.

⁵In the time of Herod king of Judea there was a priest named Zechariah, who belonged to the priestly division of Abijah; his wife Elizabeth was also a descendant of Aaron. ⁶Both of them were righteous in the sight of God, observing all the Lord's commands and decrees blamelessly. ⁷But they were childless because Elizabeth was not able to conceive, and they were both very old.

⁸Once when Zechariah's division was on duty and he was serving as priest before God, ⁹he was chosen by lot, according to the custom of the priesthood, to go into the temple of the Lord and burn incense. ¹⁰And when the time for the burning of incense came, all the assembled worshipers were praying outside.

¹¹Then an angel of the Lord ap-

---

a 1 Or *been surely believed*

peared to him, standing at the right side of the altar of incense. 12When Zechariah saw him, he was startled and was gripped with fear. 13But the angel said to him: "Do not be afraid, Zechariah; your prayer has been heard. Your wife Elizabeth will bear you a son, and you are to call him John. 14He will be a joy and delight to you, and many will rejoice because of his birth, 15for he will be great in the sight of the Lord. He is never to take wine or other fermented drink, and he will be filled with the Holy Spirit even before he is born. 16He will bring back many of the people of Israel to the Lord their God. 17And he will go on before the Lord, in the spirit and power of Elijah, to turn the hearts of the parents to their children and the disobedient to the wisdom of the righteous — to make ready a people prepared for the Lord."

18Zechariah asked the angel, "How can I be sure of this? I am an old man and my wife is well along in years."

19The angel said to him, "I am Gabriel. I stand in the presence of God, and I have been sent to speak to you and to tell you this good news. 20And now you will be silent and not able to speak until the day this happens, because you did not believe my words, which will come true at their appointed time."

21Meanwhile, the people were waiting for Zechariah and wondering why he stayed so long in the temple. 22When he came out, he could not speak to them. They realized he had seen a vision in the temple, for he kept making signs to them but remained unable to speak.

23When his time of service was completed, he returned home. 24After this his wife Elizabeth became pregnant and for five months remained in seclusion. 25"The Lord has done this for me," she said. "In these days he has shown his favor and taken away my disgrace among the people."

26In the sixth month of Elizabeth's pregnancy, God sent the angel Gabriel to Nazareth, a town in Galilee, 27to a virgin pledged to be married to a man named Joseph, a descendant of David. The virgin's name was Mary. 28The angel went to her and said, "Greetings, you who are highly favored! The Lord is with you."

29Mary was greatly troubled at his words and wondered what kind of greeting this might be. 30But the angel said to her, "Do not be afraid, Mary; you have found favor with God. 31You will conceive and give birth to a son, and you are to call him Jesus. 32He will be great and will be called the Son of the Most High. The Lord God will give him the throne of his father David, 33and he will reign over Jacob's descendants forever; his kingdom will never end."

34"How will this be," Mary asked the angel, "since I am a virgin?"

35The angel answered, "The Holy Spirit will come on you, and the power of the Most High will overshadow you. So the holy one to be born will be calleda the Son of God. 36Even Elizabeth your relative is going to have a child in her old age, and she who was said to be unable to conceive is in her sixth month. 37For no word from God will ever fail."

38"I am the Lord's servant," Mary

---

a 35 Or So the child to be born will be called holy,

answered. "May your word to me be fulfilled." Then the angel left her.

39 At that time Mary got ready and hurried to a town in the hill country of Judea, 40 where she entered Zechariah's home and greeted Elizabeth. 41 When Elizabeth heard Mary's greeting, the baby leaped in her womb, and Elizabeth was filled with the Holy Spirit. 42 In a loud voice she exclaimed: "Blessed are you among women, and blessed is the child you will bear! 43 But why am I so favored, that the mother of my Lord should come to me? 44 As soon as the sound of your greeting reached my ears, the baby in my womb leaped for joy. 45 Blessed is she who has believed that the Lord would fulfill his promises to her!"

46 And Mary said:

"My soul glorifies the Lord
47   and my spirit rejoices in God
          my Savior,
48 for he has been mindful
      of the humble state of his
          servant.
    From now on all generations will
          call me blessed,
49   for the Mighty One has done
          great things for me—
      holy is his name.
50 His mercy extends to those who
          fear him,
    from generation to generation.
51 He has performed mighty deeds
          with his arm;
    he has scattered those who
          are proud in their inmost
          thoughts.
52 He has brought down rulers
          from their thrones
    but has lifted up the humble.
53 He has filled the hungry with
          good things
    but has sent the rich away
          empty.
54 He has helped his servant Israel,

remembering to be merciful
55 to Abraham and his descendants
          forever,
    just as he promised our
          ancestors."

56 Mary stayed with Elizabeth for about three months and then returned home.

57 When it was time for Elizabeth to have her baby, she gave birth to a son. 58 Her neighbors and relatives heard that the Lord had shown her great mercy, and they shared her joy.

59 On the eighth day they came to circumcise the child, and they were going to name him after his father Zechariah, 60 but his mother spoke up and said, "No! He is to be called John."

61 They said to her, "There is no one among your relatives who has that name."

62 Then they made signs to his father, to find out what he would like to name the child. 63 He asked for a writing tablet, and to everyone's astonishment he wrote, "His name is John." 64 Immediately his mouth was opened and his tongue set free, and he began to speak, praising God. 65 All the neighbors were filled with awe, and throughout the hill country of Judea people were talking about all these things. 66 Everyone who heard this wondered about it, asking, "What then is this child going to be?" For the Lord's hand was with him.

67 His father Zechariah was filled with the Holy Spirit and prophesied:

68 "Praise be to the Lord, the God
          of Israel,
    because he has come to his
          people and redeemed
          them.

69 He has raised up a horn[a] of
  salvation for us
    in the house of his servant
      David
70 (as he said through his holy
    prophets of long ago),
71 salvation from our enemies
    and from the hand of all who
      hate us—
72 to show mercy to our ancestors
    and to remember his holy
      covenant,
73   the oath he swore to our father
      Abraham:
74 to rescue us from the hand of our
    enemies,
  and to enable us to serve him
    without fear
75   in holiness and righteousness
    before him all our days.

76 And you, my child, will be called
  a prophet of the Most High;
  for you will go on before the
    Lord to prepare the way
      for him,
77 to give his people the knowledge
    of salvation
  through the forgiveness of
    their sins,
78 because of the tender mercy of
    our God,
  by which the rising sun will
    come to us from heaven
79 to shine on those living in
    darkness
  and in the shadow of death,
  to guide our feet into the path of
    peace."

80 And the child grew and became
strong in spirit[b]; and he lived in the
wilderness until he appeared publicly to Israel.

2 In those days Caesar Augustus
  issued a decree that a census

should be taken of the entire Roman world. 2(This was the first
census that took place while[c] Qui-
rinius was governor of Syria.) 3And
everyone went to their own town to
register.

4So Joseph also went up from
the town of Nazareth in Galilee to
Judea, to Bethlehem the town of
David, because he belonged to the
house and line of David. 5He went
there to register with Mary, who
was pledged to be married to him
and was expecting a child. 6While
they were there, the time came for
the baby to be born, 7and she gave
birth to her firstborn, a son. She
wrapped him in cloths and placed
him in a manger, because there was
no guest room available for them.

8And there were shepherds living out in the fields nearby, keeping
watch over their flocks at night. 9An
angel of the Lord appeared to them,
and the glory of the Lord shone
around them, and they were terrified. 10But the angel said to them,
"Do not be afraid. I bring you good
news that will cause great joy for
all the people. 11Today in the town
of David a Savior has been born to
you; he is the Messiah, the Lord.
12This will be a sign to you: You will
find a baby wrapped in cloths and
lying in a manger."

13Suddenly a great company of
the heavenly host appeared with
the angel, praising God and saying,

14 "Glory to God in the highest
    heaven,
  and on earth peace to those on
    whom his favor rests."

15When the angels had left them
and gone into heaven, the shep-

---

[a] 69 Horn here symbolizes a strong king.   [b] 80 Or in the Spirit   [c] 2 Or This census took place
before

herds said to one another, "Let's go to Bethlehem and see this thing that has happened, which the Lord has told us about."

¹⁶So they hurried off and found Mary and Joseph, and the baby, who was lying in the manger. ¹⁷When they had seen him, they spread the word concerning what had been told them about this child, ¹⁸and all who heard it were amazed at what the shepherds said to them. ¹⁹But Mary treasured up all these things and pondered them in her heart. ²⁰The shepherds returned, glorifying and praising God for all the things they had heard and seen, which were just as they had been told.

²¹On the eighth day, when it was time to circumcise the child, he was named Jesus, the name the angel had given him before he was conceived.

²²When the time came for the purification rites required by the Law of Moses, Joseph and Mary took him to Jerusalem to present him to the Lord ²³(as it is written in the Law of the Lord, "Every firstborn male is to be consecrated to the Lord"ᵃ), ²⁴and to offer a sacrifice in keeping with what is said in the Law of the Lord: "a pair of doves or two young pigeons."ᵇ

²⁵Now there was a man in Jerusalem called Simeon, who was righteous and devout. He was waiting for the consolation of Israel, and the Holy Spirit was on him. ²⁶It had been revealed to him by the Holy Spirit that he would not die before he had seen the Lord's Messiah. ²⁷Moved by the Spirit, he went into the temple courts. When the parents brought in the child Jesus to do

for him what the custom of the Law required, ²⁸Simeon took him in his arms and praised God, saying:

²⁹ "Sovereign Lord, as you have promised,
   you may now dismissᶜ your servant in peace.
³⁰For my eyes have seen your salvation,
³¹   which you have prepared in the sight of all nations:
³²a light for revelation to the Gentiles,
   and the glory of your people Israel."

³³The child's father and mother marveled at what was said about him. ³⁴Then Simeon blessed them and said to Mary, his mother: "This child is destined to cause the falling and rising of many in Israel, and to be a sign that will be spoken against, ³⁵so that the thoughts of many hearts will be revealed. And a sword will pierce your own soul too."

³⁶There was also a prophet, Anna, the daughter of Penuel, of the tribe of Asher. She was very old; she had lived with her husband seven years after her marriage, ³⁷and then was a widow until she was eighty-four.ᵈ She never left the temple but worshiped night and day, fasting and praying. ³⁸Coming up to them at that very moment, she gave thanks to God and spoke about the child to all who were looking forward to the redemption of Jerusalem.

³⁹When Joseph and Mary had done everything required by the Law of the Lord, they returned to Galilee to their own town of Nazareth. ⁴⁰And the child grew and became strong; he was filled with

ᵃ 23 Exodus 13:2,12   ᵇ 24 Lev. 12:8   ᶜ 29 Or promised, / now dismiss   ᵈ 37 Or then had been a widow for eighty-four years.

wisdom, and the grace of God was on him.

⁴¹Every year Jesus' parents went to Jerusalem for the Festival of the Passover. ⁴²When he was twelve years old, they went up to the festival, according to the custom. ⁴³After the festival was over, while his parents were returning home, the boy Jesus stayed behind in Jerusalem, but they were unaware of it. ⁴⁴Thinking he was in their company, they traveled on for a day. Then they began looking for him among their relatives and friends. ⁴⁵When they did not find him, they went back to Jerusalem to look for him. ⁴⁶After three days they found him in the temple courts, sitting among the teachers, listening to them and asking them questions. ⁴⁷Everyone who heard him was amazed at his understanding and his answers. ⁴⁸When his parents saw him, they were astonished. His mother said to him, "Son, why have you treated us like this? Your father and I have been anxiously searching for you."

⁴⁹"Why were you searching for me?" he asked. "Didn't you know I had to be in my Father's house?"ᵃ ⁵⁰But they did not understand what he was saying to them.

⁵¹Then he went down to Nazareth with them and was obedient to them. But his mother treasured all these things in her heart. ⁵²And Jesus grew in wisdom and stature, and in favor with God and man.

3 In the fifteenth year of the reign of Tiberius Caesar — when Pontius Pilate was governor of Judea, Herod tetrarch of Galilee, his brother Philip tetrarch of Iturea and Traconitis, and Lysanias tetrarch of Abilene — ²during the high-priesthood of Annas and Caiaphas,

the word of God came to John son of Zechariah in the wilderness. ³He went into all the country around the Jordan, preaching a baptism of repentance for the forgiveness of sins. ⁴As it is written in the book of the words of Isaiah the prophet:

"A voice of one calling in the
        wilderness,
'Prepare the way for the Lord,
    make straight paths for him.
⁵ Every valley shall be filled in,
    every mountain and hill made
        low.
The crooked roads shall become
        straight,
    the rough ways smooth.
⁶ And all people will see God's
    salvation.' "ᵇ

⁷John said to the crowds coming out to be baptized by him, "You brood of vipers! Who warned you to flee from the coming wrath? ⁸Produce fruit in keeping with repentance. And do not begin to say to yourselves, 'We have Abraham as our father.' For I tell you that out of these stones God can raise up children for Abraham. ⁹The ax is already at the root of the trees, and every tree that does not produce good fruit will be cut down and thrown into the fire."

¹⁰"What should we do then?" the crowd asked.

¹¹John answered, "Anyone who has two shirts should share with the one who has none, and anyone who has food should do the same."

¹²Even tax collectors came to be baptized. "Teacher," they asked, "what should we do?"

¹³"Don't collect any more than you are required to," he told them.

¹⁴Then some soldiers asked him, "And what should we do?"

ᵃ 49 Or be about my Father's business   ᵇ 6 Isaiah 40:3-5

He replied, "Don't extort money and don't accuse people falsely—be content with your pay."

15 The people were waiting expectantly and were all wondering in their hearts if John might possibly be the Messiah. 16 John answered them all, "I baptize you with[a] water. But one who is more powerful than I will come, the straps of whose sandals I am not worthy to untie. He will baptize you with[a] the Holy Spirit and fire. 17 His winnowing fork is in his hand to clear his threshing floor and to gather the wheat into his barn, but he will burn up the chaff with unquenchable fire." 18 And with many other words John exhorted the people and proclaimed the good news to them.

19 But when John rebuked Herod the tetrarch because of his marriage to Herodias, his brother's wife, and all the other evil things he had done, 20 Herod added this to them all: He locked John up in prison.

21 When all the people were being baptized, Jesus was baptized too. And as he was praying, heaven was opened 22 and the Holy Spirit descended on him in bodily form like a dove. And a voice came from heaven: "You are my Son, whom I love; with you I am well pleased."

23 Now Jesus himself was about thirty years old when he began his ministry. He was the son, so it was thought, of Joseph,

the son of Heli, 24 the son of Matthat,
the son of Levi, the son of Melki,
the son of Jannai, the son of Joseph,
25 the son of Mattathias, the son of Amos,
the son of Nahum, the son of Esli,
the son of Naggai, 26 the son of Maath,
the son of Mattathias, the son of Semein,
the son of Josek, the son of Joda,
27 the son of Joanan, the son of Rhesa,
the son of Zerubbabel, the son of Shealtiel,
the son of Neri, 28 the son of Melki,
the son of Addi, the son of Cosam,
the son of Elmadam, the son of Er,
29 the son of Joshua, the son of Eliezer,
the son of Jorim, the son of Matthat,
the son of Levi, 30 the son of Simeon,
the son of Judah, the son of Joseph,
the son of Jonam, the son of Eliakim,
31 the son of Melea, the son of Menna,
the son of Mattatha, the son of Nathan,
the son of David, 32 the son of Jesse,
the son of Obed, the son of Boaz,
the son of Salmon,[b] the son of Nahshon,
33 the son of Amminadab, the son of Ram,[c]
the son of Hezron, the son of Perez,

---

a 16 Or *in*   *b 32* Some early manuscripts *Sala*   *c 33* Some manuscripts *Amminadab, the son of Admin, the son of Arni*; other manuscripts vary widely.

the son of Judah, 34the son of Jacob,
the son of Isaac, the son of Abraham,
the son of Terah, the son of Nahor,
35the son of Serug, the son of Reu,
the son of Peleg, the son of Eber,
the son of Shelah, 36the son of Cainan,
the son of Arphaxad, the son of Shem,
the son of Noah, the son of Lamech,
37the son of Methuselah, the son of Enoch,
the son of Jared, the son of Mahalalel,
the son of Kenan, 38the son of Enosh,
the son of Seth, the son of Adam,
the son of God.

4 Jesus, full of the Holy Spirit, left the Jordan and was led by the Spirit into the wilderness, 2where for forty days he was tempted*a* by the devil. He ate nothing during those days, and at the end of them he was hungry.

3The devil said to him, "If you are the Son of God, tell this stone to become bread."

4Jesus answered, "It is written: 'Man shall not live on bread alone.'*b*"

5The devil led him up to a high place and showed him in an instant all the kingdoms of the world. 6And he said to him, "I will give you all their authority and splendor; it has been given to me, and I can give it to anyone I want

to. 7If you worship me, it will all be yours."

8Jesus answered, "It is written: 'Worship the Lord your God and serve him only.'*c*"

9The devil led him to Jerusalem and had him stand on the highest point of the temple. "If you are the Son of God," he said, "throw yourself down from here. 10For it is written:

"'He will command his angels
　concerning you
　　to guard you carefully;
11they will lift you up in their
　hands,
　　so that you will not strike your
　　　foot against a stone.'*d*"

12Jesus answered, "It is said: 'Do not put the Lord your God to the test.'*e*"

13When the devil had finished all this tempting, he left him until an opportune time.

14Jesus returned to Galilee in the power of the Spirit, and news about him spread through the whole countryside. 15He was teaching in their synagogues, and everyone praised him.

16He went to Nazareth, where he had been brought up, and on the Sabbath day he went into the synagogue, as was his custom. He stood up to read, 17and the scroll of the prophet Isaiah was handed to him. Unrolling it, he found the place where it is written:

18"The Spirit of the Lord is on me,
　because he has anointed me
　　to proclaim good news to the
　　　poor.

---

a 2 The Greek for *tempted* can also mean *tested.*　　*b 4* Deut. 8:3　　*c 8* Deut. 6:13
d 11 Psalm 91:11,12　　*e 12* Deut. 6:16

He has sent me to proclaim
freedom for the prisoners
and recovery of sight for the
blind,
to set the oppressed free,
19 to proclaim the year of the
Lord's favor."*a*

20 Then he rolled up the scroll, gave it back to the attendant and sat down. The eyes of everyone in the synagogue were fastened on him. 21 He began by saying to them, "Today this scripture is fulfilled in your hearing."

22 All spoke well of him and were amazed at the gracious words that came from his lips. "Isn't this Joseph's son?" they asked.

23 Jesus said to them, "Surely you will quote this proverb to me: 'Physician, heal yourself!' And you will tell me, 'Do here in your hometown what we have heard that you did in Capernaum.'"

24 "Truly I tell you," he continued, "no prophet is accepted in his hometown. 25 I assure you that there were many widows in Israel in Elijah's time, when the sky was shut for three and a half years and there was a severe famine throughout the land. 26 Yet Elijah was not sent to any of them, but to a widow in Zarephath in the region of Sidon. 27 And there were many in Israel with leprosy*b* in the time of Elisha the prophet, yet not one of them was cleansed—only Naaman the Syrian."

28 All the people in the synagogue were furious when they heard this. 29 They got up, drove him out of the town, and took him to the brow of the hill on which the town was built, in order to throw him off the cliff. 30 But he walked right through the crowd and went on his way.

31 Then he went down to Capernaum, a town in Galilee, and on the Sabbath he taught the people. 32 They were amazed at his teaching, because his words had authority.

33 In the synagogue there was a man possessed by a demon, an impure spirit. He cried out at the top of his voice, 34 "Go away! What do you want with us, Jesus of Nazareth? Have you come to destroy us? I know who you are—the Holy One of God!"

35 "Be quiet!" Jesus said sternly. "Come out of him!" Then the demon threw the man down before them all and came out without injuring him.

36 All the people were amazed and said to each other, "What words these are! With authority and power he gives orders to impure spirits and they come out!" 37 And the news about him spread throughout the surrounding area.

38 Jesus left the synagogue and went to the home of Simon. Now Simon's mother-in-law was suffering from a high fever, and they asked Jesus to help her. 39 So he bent over her and rebuked the fever, and it left her. She got up at once and began to wait on them.

40 At sunset, the people brought to Jesus all who had various kinds of sickness, and laying his hands on each one, he healed them. 41 Moreover, demons came out of many people, shouting, "You are the Son of God!" But he rebuked them and would not allow them to speak, because they knew he was the Messiah.

---

a 19 Isaiah 61:1,2 (see Septuagint); Isaiah 58:6   *b* 27 The Greek word traditionally translated *leprosy* was used for various diseases affecting the skin.

⁴²At daybreak, Jesus went out to a solitary place. The people were looking for him and when they came to where he was, they tried to keep him from leaving them. ⁴³But he said, "I must proclaim the good news of the kingdom of God to the other towns also, because that is why I was sent." ⁴⁴And he kept on preaching in the synagogues of Judea.

5 One day as Jesus was standing by the Lake of Gennesaret,ᵃ the people were crowding around him and listening to the word of God. ²He saw at the water's edge two boats, left there by the fishermen, who were washing their nets. ³He got into one of the boats, the one belonging to Simon, and asked him to put out a little from shore. Then he sat down and taught the people from the boat.

⁴When he had finished speaking, he said to Simon, "Put out into deep water, and let down the nets for a catch."

⁵Simon answered, "Master, we've worked hard all night and haven't caught anything. But because you say so, I will let down the nets."

⁶When they had done so, they caught such a large number of fish that their nets began to break. ⁷So they signaled their partners in the other boat to come and help them, and they came and filled both boats so full that they began to sink.

⁸When Simon Peter saw this, he fell at Jesus' knees and said, "Go away from me, Lord; I am a sinful man!" ⁹For he and all his companions were astonished at the catch of fish they had taken, ¹⁰and so were James and John, the sons of Zebedee, Simon's partners.

Then Jesus said to Simon, "Don't be afraid; from now on you will fish for people." ¹¹So they pulled their boats up on shore, left everything and followed him.

¹²While Jesus was in one of the towns, a man came along who was covered with leprosy.ᵇ When he saw Jesus, he fell with his face to the ground and begged him, "Lord, if you are willing, you can make me clean."

¹³Jesus reached out his hand and touched the man. "I am willing," he said. "Be clean!" And immediately the leprosy left him.

¹⁴Then Jesus ordered him, "Don't tell anyone, but go, show yourself to the priest and offer the sacrifices that Moses commanded for your cleansing, as a testimony to them."

¹⁵Yet the news about him spread all the more, so that crowds of people came to hear him and to be healed of their sicknesses. ¹⁶But Jesus often withdrew to lonely places and prayed.

¹⁷One day Jesus was teaching, and Pharisees and teachers of the law were sitting there. They had come from every village of Galilee and from Judea and Jerusalem. And the power of the Lord was with Jesus to heal the sick. ¹⁸Some men came carrying a paralyzed man on a mat and tried to take him into the house to lay him before Jesus. ¹⁹When they could not find a way to do this because of the crowd, they went up on the roof and lowered him on his mat through the tiles into the middle of the crowd, right in front of Jesus.

²⁰When Jesus saw their faith, he said, "Friend, your sins are forgiven."

ᵃ 1 That is, the Sea of Galilee   ᵇ 12 The Greek word traditionally translated *leprosy* was used for various diseases affecting the skin.

²¹The Pharisees and the teachers of the law began thinking to themselves, "Who is this fellow who speaks blasphemy? Who can forgive sins but God alone?"

²²Jesus knew what they were thinking and asked, "Why are you thinking these things in your hearts? ²³Which is easier: to say, 'Your sins are forgiven,' or to say, 'Get up and walk'? ²⁴But I want you to know that the Son of Man has authority on earth to forgive sins." So he said to the paralyzed man, "I tell you, get up, take your mat and go home." ²⁵Immediately he stood up in front of them, took what he had been lying on and went home praising God. ²⁶Everyone was amazed and gave praise to God. They were filled with awe and said, "We have seen remarkable things today."

²⁷After this, Jesus went out and saw a tax collector by the name of Levi sitting at his tax booth. "Follow me," Jesus said to him, ²⁸and Levi got up, left everything and followed him.

²⁹Then Levi held a great banquet for Jesus at his house, and a large crowd of tax collectors and others were eating with them. ³⁰But the Pharisees and the teachers of the law who belonged to their sect complained to his disciples, "Why do you eat and drink with tax collectors and sinners?"

³¹Jesus answered them, "It is not the healthy who need a doctor, but the sick. ³²I have not come to call the righteous, but sinners to repentance."

³³They said to him, "John's disciples often fast and pray, and so do the disciples of the Pharisees, but yours go on eating and drinking."

³⁴Jesus answered, "Can you make the friends of the bridegroom fast while he is with them? ³⁵But the time will come when the bridegroom will be taken from them; in those days they will fast."

³⁶He told them this parable: "No one tears a piece out of a new garment to patch an old one. Otherwise, they will have torn the new garment, and the patch from the new will not match the old. ³⁷And no one pours new wine into old wineskins. Otherwise, the new wine will burst the skins; the wine will run out and the wineskins will be ruined. ³⁸No, new wine must be poured into new wineskins. ³⁹And no one after drinking old wine wants the new, for they say, 'The old is better.'"

6 One Sabbath Jesus was going through the grainfields, and his disciples began to pick some heads of grain, rub them in their hands and eat the kernels. ²Some of the Pharisees asked, "Why are you doing what is unlawful on the Sabbath?"

³Jesus answered them, "Have you never read what David did when he and his companions were hungry? ⁴He entered the house of God, and taking the consecrated bread, he ate what is lawful only for priests to eat. And he also gave some to his companions." ⁵Then Jesus said to them, "The Son of Man is Lord of the Sabbath."

⁶On another Sabbath he went into the synagogue and was teaching, and a man was there whose right hand was shriveled. ⁷The Pharisees and the teachers of the law were looking for a reason to accuse Jesus, so they watched him closely to see if he would heal on the Sabbath. ⁸But Jesus knew what they were thinking and said to the man with the shriveled hand, "Get

up and stand in front of everyone."
So he got up and stood there.

⁹Then Jesus said to them, "I ask you, which is lawful on the Sabbath: to do good or to do evil, to save life or to destroy it?"

¹⁰He looked around at them all, and then said to the man, "Stretch out your hand." He did so, and his hand was completely restored. ¹¹But the Pharisees and the teachers of the law were furious and began to discuss with one another what they might do to Jesus.

¹²One of those days Jesus went out to a mountainside to pray, and spent the night praying to God. ¹³When morning came, he called his disciples to him and chose twelve of them, whom he also designated apostles: ¹⁴Simon (whom he named Peter), his brother Andrew, James, John, Philip, Bartholomew, ¹⁵Matthew, Thomas, James son of Alphaeus, Simon who was called the Zealot, ¹⁶Judas son of James, and Judas Iscariot, who became a traitor.

¹⁷He went down with them and stood on a level place. A large crowd of his disciples was there and a great number of people from all over Judea, from Jerusalem, and from the coastal region around Tyre and Sidon, ¹⁸who had come to hear him and to be healed of their diseases. Those troubled by impure spirits were cured, ¹⁹and the people all tried to touch him, because power was coming from him and healing them all.

²⁰Looking at his disciples, he said:

"Blessed are you who are poor,
    for yours is the kingdom of
        God.
²¹Blessed are you who hunger
    now,

for you will be satisfied.
Blessed are you who weep now,
    for you will laugh.
²²Blessed are you when people
    hate you,
    when they exclude you and
        insult you
    and reject your name as evil,
        because of the Son of Man.

²³"Rejoice in that day and leap for joy, because great is your reward in heaven. For that is how their ancestors treated the prophets.

²⁴"But woe to you who are rich,
    for you have already received
        your comfort.
²⁵Woe to you who are well fed now,
    for you will go hungry.
Woe to you who laugh now,
    for you will mourn and weep.
²⁶Woe to you when everyone
        speaks well of you,
    for that is how their ancestors
        treated the false prophets.

²⁷"But to you who are listening I say: Love your enemies, do good to those who hate you, ²⁸bless those who curse you, pray for those who mistreat you. ²⁹If someone slaps you on one cheek, turn to them the other also. If someone takes your coat, do not withhold your shirt from them. ³⁰Give to everyone who asks you, and if anyone takes what belongs to you, do not demand it back. ³¹Do to others as you would have them do to you.

³²"If you love those who love you, what credit is that to you? Even sinners love those who love them. ³³And if you do good to those who are good to you, what credit is that to you? Even sinners do that. ³⁴And if you lend to those from whom you expect repayment, what credit is that to you? Even sinners lend to sinners, expecting to be repaid in

full. 35But love your enemies, do good to them, and lend to them without expecting to get anything back. Then your reward will be great, and you will be children of the Most High, because he is kind to the ungrateful and wicked. 36Be merciful, just as your Father is merciful.

37"Do not judge, and you will not be judged. Do not condemn, and you will not be condemned. Forgive, and you will be forgiven. 38Give, and it will be given to you. A good measure, pressed down, shaken together and running over, will be poured into your lap. For with the measure you use, it will be measured to you."

39He also told them this parable: "Can the blind lead the blind? Will they not both fall into a pit? 40The student is not above the teacher, but everyone who is fully trained will be like their teacher.

41"Why do you look at the speck of sawdust in your brother's eye and pay no attention to the plank in your own eye? 42How can you say to your brother, 'Brother, let me take the speck out of your eye,' when you yourself fail to see the plank in your own eye? You hypocrite, first take the plank out of your eye, and then you will see clearly to remove the speck from your brother's eye.

43"No good tree bears bad fruit, nor does a bad tree bear good fruit. 44Each tree is recognized by its own fruit. People do not pick figs from thornbushes, or grapes from briers. 45A good man brings good things out of the good stored up in his heart, and an evil man brings evil things out of the evil stored up in his heart. For the mouth speaks what the heart is full of.

46"Why do you call me, 'Lord,

Lord,' and do not do what I say? 47As for everyone who comes to me and hears my words and puts them into practice, I will show you what they are like. 48They are like a man building a house, who dug down deep and laid the foundation on rock. When a flood came, the torrent struck that house but could not shake it, because it was well built. 49But the one who hears my words and does not put them into practice is like a man who built a house on the ground without a foundation. The moment the torrent struck that house, it collapsed and its destruction was complete."

7 When Jesus had finished saying all this to the people who were listening, he entered Capernaum. 2There a centurion's servant, whom his master valued highly, was sick and about to die. 3The centurion heard of Jesus and sent some elders of the Jews to him, asking him to come and heal his servant. 4When they came to Jesus, they pleaded earnestly with him, "This man deserves to have you do this, 5because he loves our nation and has built our synagogue." 6So Jesus went with them.

He was not far from the house when the centurion sent friends to say to him: "Lord, don't trouble yourself, for I do not deserve to have you come under my roof. 7That is why I did not even consider myself worthy to come to you. But say the word, and my servant will be healed. 8For I myself am a man under authority, with soldiers under me. I tell this one, 'Go,' and he goes; and that one, 'Come,' and he comes. I say to my servant, 'Do this,' and he does it."

9When Jesus heard this, he was amazed at him, and turning to the crowd following him, he said, "I tell you, I have not found such great faith even in Israel." ¹⁰Then the men who had been sent returned to the house and found the servant well.

¹¹Soon afterward, Jesus went to a town called Nain, and his disciples and a large crowd went along with him. ¹²As he approached the town gate, a dead person was being carried out—the only son of his mother, and she was a widow. And a large crowd from the town was with her. ¹³When the Lord saw her, his heart went out to her and he said, "Don't cry."

¹⁴Then he went up and touched the bier they were carrying him on, and the bearers stood still. He said, "Young man, I say to you, get up!" ¹⁵The dead man sat up and began to talk, and Jesus gave him back to his mother.

¹⁶They were all filled with awe and praised God. "A great prophet has appeared among us," they said. "God has come to help his people." ¹⁷This news about Jesus spread throughout Judea and the surrounding country.

¹⁸John's disciples told him about all these things. Calling two of them, ¹⁹he sent them to the Lord to ask, "Are you the one who is to come, or should we expect someone else?"

²⁰When the men came to Jesus, they said, "John the Baptist sent us to you to ask, 'Are you the one who is to come, or should we expect someone else?'"

²¹At that very time Jesus cured many who had diseases, sicknesses and evil spirits, and gave sight to many who were blind. ²²So he replied to the messengers, "Go back and report to John what you have seen and heard: The blind receive sight, the lame walk, those who have leprosy[a] are cleansed, the deaf hear, the dead are raised, and the good news is proclaimed to the poor. ²³Blessed is anyone who does not stumble on account of me."

²⁴After John's messengers left, Jesus began to speak to the crowd about John: "What did you go out into the wilderness to see? A reed swayed by the wind? ²⁵If not, what did you go out to see? A man dressed in fine clothes? No, those who wear expensive clothes and indulge in luxury are in palaces. ²⁶But what did you go out to see? A prophet? Yes, I tell you, and more than a prophet. ²⁷This is the one about whom it is written:

" 'I will send my messenger
        ahead of you,
    who will prepare your way
        before you.'[b]

²⁸I tell you, among those born of women there is no one greater than John; yet the one who is least in the kingdom of God is greater than he."

²⁹(All the people, even the tax collectors, when they heard Jesus' words, acknowledged that God's way was right, because they had been baptized by John. ³⁰But the Pharisees and the experts in the law rejected God's purpose for themselves, because they had not been baptized by John.)

³¹Jesus went on to say, "To what, then, can I compare the people of this generation? What are they like? ³²They are like children sitting in

---

a 22 The Greek word traditionally translated *leprosy* was used for various diseases affecting the skin. b 27 Mal. 3:1

the marketplace and calling out to each other:

"'We played the pipe for you,
     and you did not dance;
we sang a dirge,
     and you did not cry.'

33 For John the Baptist came neither eating bread nor drinking wine, and you say, 'He has a demon.' 34 The Son of Man came eating and drinking, and you say, 'Here is a glutton and a drunkard, a friend of tax collectors and sinners.' 35 But wisdom is proved right by all her children."

36 When one of the Pharisees invited Jesus to have dinner with him, he went to the Pharisee's house and reclined at the table. 37 A woman in that town who lived a sinful life learned that Jesus was eating at the Pharisee's house, so she came there with an alabaster jar of perfume. 38 As she stood behind him at his feet weeping, she began to wet his feet with her tears. Then she wiped them with her hair, kissed them and poured perfume on them.

39 When the Pharisee who had invited him saw this, he said to himself, "If this man were a prophet, he would know who is touching him and what kind of woman she is—that she is a sinner."

40 Jesus answered him, "Simon, I have something to tell you."

"Tell me, teacher," he said.

41 "Two people owed money to a certain moneylender. One owed him five hundred denarii,[a] and the other fifty. 42 Neither of them had the money to pay him back, so he forgave the debts of both. Now which of them will love him more?"

43 Simon replied, "I suppose the one who had the bigger debt forgiven."

"You have judged correctly," Jesus said.

44 Then he turned toward the woman and said to Simon, "Do you see this woman? I came into your house. You did not give me any water for my feet, but she wet my feet with her tears and wiped them with her hair. 45 You did not give me a kiss, but this woman, from the time I entered, has not stopped kissing my feet. 46 You did not put oil on my head, but she has poured perfume on my feet. 47 Therefore, I tell you, her many sins have been forgiven—as her great love has shown. But whoever has been forgiven little loves little."

48 Then Jesus said to her, "Your sins are forgiven."

49 The other guests began to say among themselves, "Who is this who even forgives sins?"

50 Jesus said to the woman, "Your faith has saved you; go in peace."

8 After this, Jesus traveled about from one town and village to another, proclaiming the good news of the kingdom of God. The Twelve were with him, 2 and also some women who had been cured of evil spirits and diseases: Mary (called Magdalene) from whom seven demons had come out; 3 Joanna the wife of Chuza, the manager of Herod's household; Susanna; and many others. These women were helping to support them out of their own means.

4 While a large crowd was gathering and people were coming to Jesus from town after town, he told this parable: 5 "A farmer went out to sow his seed. As he was scattering the seed, some fell along the path; it

_____
a 41 A denarius was the usual daily wage of a day laborer (see Matt. 20:2).

was trampled on, and the birds ate it up. ⁶Some fell on rocky ground, and when it came up, the plants withered because they had no moisture. ⁷Other seed fell among thorns, which grew up with it and choked the plants. ⁸Still other seed fell on good soil. It came up and yielded a crop, a hundred times more than was sown."

When he said this, he called out, "Whoever has ears to hear, let them hear."

⁹His disciples asked him what this parable meant. ¹⁰He said, "The knowledge of the secrets of the kingdom of God has been given to you, but to others I speak in parables, so that,

" 'though seeing, they may not
    see;
    though hearing, they may not
    understand.'ᵃ

¹¹"This is the meaning of the parable: The seed is the word of God. ¹²Those along the path are the ones who hear, and then the devil comes and takes away the word from their hearts, so that they may not believe and be saved. ¹³Those on the rocky ground are the ones who receive the word with joy when they hear it, but they have no root. They believe for a while, but in the time of testing they fall away. ¹⁴The seed that fell among thorns stands for those who hear, but as they go on their way they are choked by life's worries, riches and pleasures, and they do not mature. ¹⁵But the seed on good soil stands for those with a noble and good heart, who hear the word, retain it, and by persevering produce a crop.

¹⁶"No one lights a lamp and hides it in a clay jar or puts it under a bed. Instead, they put it on a stand, so that those who come in can see the light. ¹⁷For there is nothing hidden that will not be disclosed, and nothing concealed that will not be known or brought out into the open. ¹⁸Therefore consider carefully how you listen. Whoever has will be given more; whoever does not have, even what they think they have will be taken from them."

¹⁹Now Jesus' mother and brothers came to see him, but they were not able to get near him because of the crowd. ²⁰Someone told him, "Your mother and brothers are standing outside, wanting to see you."

²¹He replied, "My mother and brothers are those who hear God's word and put it into practice."

²²One day Jesus said to his disciples, "Let us go over to the other side of the lake." So they got into a boat and set out. ²³As they sailed, he fell asleep. A squall came down on the lake, so that the boat was being swamped, and they were in great danger.

²⁴The disciples went and woke him, saying, "Master, Master, we're going to drown!"

He got up and rebuked the wind and the raging waters; the storm subsided, and all was calm. ²⁵"Where is your faith?" he asked his disciples.

In fear and amazement they asked one another, "Who is this? He commands even the winds and the water, and they obey him."

²⁶They sailed to the region of the Gerasenes,ᵇ which is across the lake from Galilee. ²⁷When Jesus stepped ashore, he was met by a demon-possessed man from the

town. For a long time this man had not worn clothes or lived in a house, but had lived in the tombs. 28When he saw Jesus, he cried out and fell at his feet, shouting at the top of his voice, "What do you want with me, Jesus, Son of the Most High God? I beg you, don't torture me!" 29For Jesus had commanded the impure spirit to come out of the man. Many times it had seized him, and though he was chained hand and foot and kept under guard, he had broken his chains and had been driven by the demon into solitary places.

30Jesus asked him, "What is your name?"

"Legion," he replied, because many demons had gone into him. 31And they begged Jesus repeatedly not to order them to go into the Abyss.

32A large herd of pigs was feeding there on the hillside. The demons begged Jesus to let them go into the pigs, and he gave them permission. 33When the demons came out of the man, they went into the pigs, and the herd rushed down the steep bank into the lake and was drowned.

34When those tending the pigs saw what had happened, they ran off and reported this in the town and countryside, 35and the people went out to see what had happened. When they came to Jesus, they found the man from whom the demons had gone out, sitting at Jesus' feet, dressed and in his right mind; and they were afraid. 36Those who had seen it told the people how the demon-possessed man had been cured. 37Then all the people of the region of the Gerasenes asked Jesus to leave them, because they were overcome with fear. So he got into the boat and left.

38The man from whom the demons had gone out begged to go with him, but Jesus sent him away, saying, 39"Return home and tell how much God has done for you." So the man went away and told all over town how much Jesus had done for him.

40Now when Jesus returned, a crowd welcomed him, for they were all expecting him. 41Then a man named Jairus, a synagogue leader, came and fell at Jesus' feet, pleading with him to come to his house 42because his only daughter, a girl of about twelve, was dying.

As Jesus was on his way, the crowds almost crushed him. 43And a woman was there who had been subject to bleeding for twelve years,a but no one could heal her. 44She came up behind him and touched the edge of his cloak, and immediately her bleeding stopped.

45"Who touched me?" Jesus asked.

When they all denied it, Peter said, "Master, the people are crowding and pressing against you."

46But Jesus said, "Someone touched me; I know that power has gone out from me."

47Then the woman, seeing that she could not go unnoticed, came trembling and fell at his feet. In the presence of all the people, she told why she had touched him and how she had been instantly healed. 48Then he said to her, "Daughter, your faith has healed you. Go in peace."

49While Jesus was still speaking, someone came from the house of Jairus, the synagogue leader. "Your

a 43 Many manuscripts years, and she had spent all she had on doctors

daughter is dead," he said. "Don't bother the teacher anymore."

⁵⁰Hearing this, Jesus said to Jairus, "Don't be afraid; just believe, and she will be healed."

⁵¹When he arrived at the house of Jairus, he did not let anyone go in with him except Peter, John and James, and the child's father and mother. ⁵²Meanwhile, all the people were wailing and mourning for her. "Stop wailing," Jesus said. "She is not dead but asleep."

⁵³They laughed at him, knowing that she was dead. ⁵⁴But he took her by the hand and said, "My child, get up!" ⁵⁵Her spirit returned, and at once she stood up. Then Jesus told them to give her something to eat. ⁵⁶Her parents were astonished, but he ordered them not to tell anyone what had happened.

9 When Jesus had called the Twelve together, he gave them power and authority to drive out all demons and to cure diseases, ²and he sent them out to proclaim the kingdom of God and to heal the sick. ³He told them: "Take nothing for the journey—no staff, no bag, no bread, no money, no extra shirt. ⁴Whatever house you enter, stay there until you leave that town. ⁵If people do not welcome you, leave their town and shake the dust off your feet as a testimony against them." ⁶So they set out and went from village to village, proclaiming the good news and healing people everywhere.

⁷Now Herod the tetrarch heard about all that was going on. And he was perplexed because some were saying that John had been raised from the dead, ⁸others that Elijah had appeared, and still others that one of the prophets of long ago had come back to life. ⁹But Herod said,

"I beheaded John. Who, then, is this I hear such things about?" And he tried to see him.

¹⁰When the apostles returned, they reported to Jesus what they had done. Then he took them with him and they withdrew by themselves to a town called Bethsaida, ¹¹but the crowds learned about it and followed him. He welcomed them and spoke to them about the kingdom of God, and healed those who needed healing.

¹²Late in the afternoon the Twelve came to him and said, "Send the crowd away so they can go to the surrounding villages and countryside and find food and lodging, because we are in a remote place here."

¹³He replied, "You give them something to eat."

They answered, "We have only five loaves of bread and two fish—unless we go and buy food for all this crowd." ¹⁴(About five thousand men were there.)

But he said to his disciples, "Have them sit down in groups of about fifty each." ¹⁵The disciples did so, and everyone sat down. ¹⁶Taking the five loaves and the two fish and looking up to heaven, he gave thanks and broke them. Then he gave them to the disciples to distribute to the people. ¹⁷They all ate and were satisfied, and the disciples picked up twelve basketfuls of broken pieces that were left over.

¹⁸Once when Jesus was praying in private and his disciples were with him, he asked them, "Who do the crowds say I am?"

¹⁹They replied, "Some say John the Baptist; others say Elijah; and still others, that one of the prophets of long ago has come back to life."

20"But what about you?" he asked. "Who do you say I am?"

Peter answered, "God's Messiah."

21Jesus strictly warned them not to tell this to anyone. 22And he said, "The Son of Man must suffer many things and be rejected by the elders, the chief priests and the teachers of the law, and he must be killed and on the third day be raised to life."

23Then he said to them all: "Whoever wants to be my disciple must deny themselves and take up their cross daily and follow me. 24For whoever wants to save their life will lose it, but whoever loses their life for me will save it. 25What good is it for someone to gain the whole world, and yet lose or forfeit their very self? 26Whoever is ashamed of me and my words, the Son of Man will be ashamed of them when he comes in his glory and in the glory of the Father and of the holy angels.

27"Truly I tell you, some who are standing here will not taste death before they see the kingdom of God."

28About eight days after Jesus said this, he took Peter, John and James with him and went up onto a mountain to pray. 29As he was praying, the appearance of his face changed, and his clothes became as bright as a flash of lightning. 30Two men, Moses and Elijah, appeared in glorious splendor, talking with Jesus. 31They spoke about his departure,*a* which he was about to bring to fulfillment at Jerusalem. 32Peter and his companions were very sleepy, but when they became fully awake, they saw his glory and the two men standing with him. 33As the men were leaving Jesus,

Peter said to him, "Master, it is good for us to be here. Let us put up three shelters—one for you, one for Moses and one for Elijah." (He did not know what he was saying.)

34While he was speaking, a cloud appeared and covered them, and they were afraid as they entered the cloud. 35A voice came from the cloud, saying, "This is my Son, whom I have chosen; listen to him." 36When the voice had spoken, they found that Jesus was alone. The disciples kept this to themselves and did not tell anyone at that time what they had seen.

37The next day, when they came down from the mountain, a large crowd met him. 38A man in the crowd called out, "Teacher, I beg you to look at my son, for he is my only child. 39A spirit seizes him and he suddenly screams; it throws him into convulsions so that he foams at the mouth. It scarcely ever leaves him and is destroying him. 40I begged your disciples to drive it out, but they could not."

41"You unbelieving and perverse generation," Jesus replied, "how long shall I stay with you and put up with you? Bring your son here."

42Even while the boy was coming, the demon threw him to the ground in a convulsion. But Jesus rebuked the impure spirit, healed the boy and gave him back to his father. 43And they were all amazed at the greatness of God.

While everyone was marveling at all that Jesus did, he said to his disciples, 44"Listen carefully to what I am about to tell you: The Son of Man is going to be delivered into the hands of men." 45But they did not understand what this meant. It was hidden from them, so that

a 31 Greek *exodus*

they did not grasp it, and they were afraid to ask him about it.

46 An argument started among the disciples as to which of them would be the greatest. 47 Jesus, knowing their thoughts, took a little child and had him stand beside him. 48 Then he said to them, "Whoever welcomes this little child in my name welcomes me; and whoever welcomes me welcomes the one who sent me. For it is the one who is least among you all who is the greatest."

49 "Master," said John, "we saw someone driving out demons in your name and we tried to stop him, because he is not one of us."

50 "Do not stop him," Jesus said, "for whoever is not against you is for you."

51 As the time approached for him to be taken up to heaven, Jesus resolutely set out for Jerusalem. 52 And he sent messengers on ahead, who went into a Samaritan village to get things ready for him; 53 but the people there did not welcome him, because he was heading for Jerusalem. 54 When the disciples James and John saw this, they asked, "Lord, do you want us to call fire down from heaven to destroy them[a]?" 55 But Jesus turned and rebuked them. 56 Then he and his disciples went to another village.

57 As they were walking along the road, a man said to him, "I will follow you wherever you go."

58 Jesus replied, "Foxes have dens and birds have nests, but the Son of Man has no place to lay his head."

59 He said to another man, "Follow me."

But he replied, "Lord, first let me go and bury my father."

60 Jesus said to him, "Let the dead bury their own dead, but you go and proclaim the kingdom of God."

61 Still another said, "I will follow you, Lord; but first let me go back and say goodbye to my family."

62 Jesus replied, "No one who puts a hand to the plow and looks back is fit for service in the kingdom of God."

10 After this the Lord appointed seventy-two[b] others and sent them two by two ahead of him to every town and place where he was about to go. 2 He told them, "The harvest is plentiful, but the workers are few. Ask the Lord of the harvest, therefore, to send out workers into his harvest field. 3 Go! I am sending you out like lambs among wolves. 4 Do not take a purse or bag or sandals; and do not greet anyone on the road.

5 "When you enter a house, first say, 'Peace to this house.' 6 If someone who promotes peace is there, your peace will rest on them; if not, it will return to you. 7 Stay there, eating and drinking whatever they give you, for the worker deserves his wages. Do not move around from house to house.

8 "When you enter a town and are welcomed, eat what is offered to you. 9 Heal the sick who are there and tell them, 'The kingdom of God has come near to you.' 10 But when you enter a town and are not welcomed, go into its streets and say, 11 'Even the dust of your town we wipe from our feet as a warning to you. Yet be sure of this: The kingdom of God has come near.' 12 I tell you, it will be more bearable on that day for Sodom than for that town.

13 "Woe to you, Chorazin! Woe to

---

[a] 54 Some manuscripts *them, just as Elijah did*   [b] 1 Some manuscripts *seventy*; also in verse 17

you, Bethsaida! For if the miracles that were performed in you had been performed in Tyre and Sidon, they would have repented long ago, sitting in sackcloth and ashes. ¹⁴But it will be more bearable for Tyre and Sidon at the judgment than for you. ¹⁵And you, Capernaum, will you be lifted to the heavens? No, you will go down to Hades.ᵃ

¹⁶"Whoever listens to you listens to me; whoever rejects you rejects me; but whoever rejects me rejects him who sent me."

¹⁷The seventy-two returned with joy and said, "Lord, even the demons submit to us in your name."

¹⁸He replied, "I saw Satan fall like lightning from heaven. ¹⁹I have given you authority to trample on snakes and scorpions and to overcome all the power of the enemy; nothing will harm you. ²⁰However, do not rejoice that the spirits submit to you, but rejoice that your names are written in heaven."

²¹At that time Jesus, full of joy through the Holy Spirit, said, "I praise you, Father, Lord of heaven and earth, because you have hidden these things from the wise and learned, and revealed them to little children. Yes, Father, for this is what you were pleased to do.

²²"All things have been committed to me by my Father. No one knows who the Son is except the Father, and no one knows who the Father is except the Son and those to whom the Son chooses to reveal him."

²³Then he turned to his disciples and said privately, "Blessed are the eyes that see what you see. ²⁴For I tell you that many prophets and kings wanted to see what you see

but did not see it, and to hear what you hear but did not hear it."

²⁵On one occasion an expert in the law stood up to test Jesus. "Teacher," he asked, "what must I do to inherit eternal life?"

²⁶"What is written in the Law?" he replied. "How do you read it?"

²⁷He answered, " 'Love the Lord your God with all your heart and with all your soul and with all your strength and with all your mind'ᵇ; and, 'Love your neighbor as yourself.'ᶜ"

²⁸"You have answered correctly," Jesus replied. "Do this and you will live."

²⁹But he wanted to justify himself, so he asked Jesus, "And who is my neighbor?"

³⁰In reply Jesus said: "A man was going down from Jerusalem to Jericho, when he was attacked by robbers. They stripped him of his clothes, beat him and went away, leaving him half dead. ³¹A priest happened to be going down the same road, and when he saw the man, he passed by on the other side. ³²So too, a Levite, when he came to the place and saw him, passed by on the other side. ³³But a Samaritan, as he traveled, came where the man was; and when he saw him, he took pity on him. ³⁴He went to him and bandaged his wounds, pouring on oil and wine. Then he put the man on his own donkey, brought him to an inn and took care of him. ³⁵The next day he took out two denariiᵈ and gave them to the innkeeper. 'Look after him,' he said, 'and when I return, I will reimburse you for any extra expense you may have.'

³⁶"Which of these three do you

ᵃ 15 That is, the realm of the dead   ᵇ 27 Deut. 6:5   ᶜ 27 Lev. 19:18   ᵈ 35 A denarius was the usual daily wage of a day laborer (see Matt. 20:2).

think was a neighbor to the man who fell into the hands of robbers?"

37The expert in the law replied, "The one who had mercy on him."

Jesus told him, "Go and do likewise."

38As Jesus and his disciples were on their way, he came to a village where a woman named Martha opened her home to him. 39She had a sister called Mary, who sat at the Lord's feet listening to what he said. 40But Martha was distracted by all the preparations that had to be made. She came to him and asked, "Lord, don't you care that my sister has left me to do the work by myself? Tell her to help me!"

41"Martha, Martha," the Lord answered, "you are worried and upset about many things, 42but few things are needed—or indeed only one.a Mary has chosen what is better, and it will not be taken away from her."

11 One day Jesus was praying in a certain place. When he finished, one of his disciples said to him, "Lord, teach us to pray, just as John taught his disciples."

2He said to them, "When you pray, say:

" 'Father,b
hallowed be your name,
your kingdom come.c
3 Give us each day our daily
bread.
4 Forgive us our sins,
for we also forgive everyone
who sins against us.d
And lead us not into
temptation.e' "

5Then Jesus said to them, "Suppose you have a friend, and you go to him at midnight and say, 'Friend, lend me three loaves of bread; 6a friend of mine on a journey has come to me, and I have no food to offer him.' 7And suppose the one inside answers, 'Don't bother me. The door is already locked, and my children and I are in bed. I can't get up and give you anything.' 8I tell you, even though he will not get up and give you the bread because of friendship, yet because of your shameless audacityf he will surely get up and give you as much as you need.

9"So I say to you: Ask and it will be given to you; seek and you will find; knock and the door will be opened to you. 10For everyone who asks receives; the one who seeks finds; and to the one who knocks, the door will be opened.

11"Which of you fathers, if your son asks forg a fish, will give him a snake instead? 12Or if he asks for an egg, will give him a scorpion? 13If you then, though you are evil, know how to give good gifts to your children, how much more will your Father in heaven give the Holy Spirit to those who ask him!"

14Jesus was driving out a demon that was mute. When the demon left, the man who had been mute spoke, and the crowd was amazed. 15But some of them said, "By Beelzebul, the prince of demons, he is driving out demons." 16Others tested him by asking for a sign from heaven.

17Jesus knew their thoughts and

---

a 42 Some manuscripts but only one thing is needed   b 2 Some manuscripts Our Father
in heaven   c 2 Some manuscripts come. May your will be done on earth as it is in heaven.
d 4 Greek everyone who is indebted to us   e 4 Some manuscripts temptation, but deliver us from
the evil one   f 8 Or yet to preserve his good name   g 11 Some manuscripts for bread, will give
him a stone? Or if he asks for

said to them: "Any kingdom divided against itself will be ruined, and a house divided against itself will fall. 18 If Satan is divided against himself, how can his kingdom stand? I say this because you claim that I drive out demons by Beelzebul. 19 Now if I drive out demons by Beelzebul, by whom do your followers drive them out? So then, they will be your judges. 20 But if I drive out demons by the finger of God, then the kingdom of God has come upon you.

21 "When a strong man, fully armed, guards his own house, his possessions are safe. 22 But when someone stronger attacks and overpowers him, he takes away the armor in which the man trusted and divides up his plunder.

23 "Whoever is not with me is against me, and whoever does not gather with me scatters.

24 "When an impure spirit comes out of a person, it goes through arid places seeking rest and does not find it. Then it says, 'I will return to the house I left.' 25 When it arrives, it finds the house swept clean and put in order. 26 Then it goes and takes seven other spirits more wicked than itself, and they go in and live there. And the final condition of that person is worse than the first."

27 As Jesus was saying these things, a woman in the crowd called out, "Blessed is the mother who gave you birth and nursed you."

28 He replied, "Blessed rather are those who hear the word of God and obey it."

29 As the crowds increased, Jesus said, "This is a wicked generation. It asks for a sign, but none will be given it except the sign of Jonah. 30 For as Jonah was a sign to the Ninevites, so also will the Son of Man be to this generation. 31 The Queen of the South will rise at the judgment with the people of this generation and condemn them, for she came from the ends of the earth to listen to Solomon's wisdom; and now something greater than Solomon is here. 32 The men of Nineveh will stand up at the judgment with this generation and condemn it, for they repented at the preaching of Jonah; and now something greater than Jonah is here.

33 "No one lights a lamp and puts it in a place where it will be hidden, or under a bowl. Instead they put it on its stand, so that those who come in may see the light. 34 Your eye is the lamp of your body. When your eyes are healthy,[a] your whole body also is full of light. But when they are unhealthy,[b] your body also is full of darkness. 35 See to it, then, that the light within you is not darkness. 36 Therefore, if your whole body is full of light, and no part of it dark, it will be just as full of light as when a lamp shines its light on you."

37 When Jesus had finished speaking, a Pharisee invited him to eat with him; so he went in and reclined at the table. 38 But the Pharisee was surprised when he noticed that Jesus did not first wash before the meal.

39 Then the Lord said to him, "Now then, you Pharisees clean the outside of the cup and dish, but inside you are full of greed and wickedness. 40 You foolish people! Did

a 34 The Greek for *healthy* here implies *generous.* b 34 The Greek for *unhealthy* here implies *stingy.*

not the one who made the outside make the inside also? 41 But now as for what is inside you—be generous to the poor, and everything will be clean for you.

42 "Woe to you Pharisees, because you give God a tenth of your mint, rue and all other kinds of garden herbs, but you neglect justice and the love of God. You should have practiced the latter without leaving the former undone.

43 "Woe to you Pharisees, because you love the most important seats in the synagogues and respectful greetings in the marketplaces.

44 "Woe to you, because you are like unmarked graves, which people walk over without knowing it."

45 One of the experts in the law answered him, "Teacher, when you say these things, you insult us also."

46 Jesus replied, "And you experts in the law, woe to you, because you load people down with burdens they can hardly carry, and you yourselves will not lift one finger to help them.

47 "Woe to you, because you build tombs for the prophets, and it was your ancestors who killed them. 48 So you testify that you approve of what your ancestors did; they killed the prophets, and you build their tombs. 49 Because of this, God in his wisdom said, 'I will send them prophets and apostles, some of whom they will kill and others they will persecute.' 50 Therefore this generation will be held responsible for the blood of all the prophets that has been shed since the beginning of the world, 51 from the blood of Abel to the blood of Zechariah, who was killed between the altar and the sanctuary. Yes, I tell you,

this generation will be held responsible for it all.

52 "Woe to you experts in the law, because you have taken away the key to knowledge. You yourselves have not entered, and you have hindered those who were entering."

53 When Jesus went outside, the Pharisees and the teachers of the law began to oppose him fiercely and to besiege him with questions, 54 waiting to catch him in something he might say.

12 Meanwhile, when a crowd of many thousands had gathered, so that they were trampling on one another, Jesus began to speak first to his disciples, saying: "Be[a] on your guard against the yeast of the Pharisees, which is hypocrisy. 2 There is nothing concealed that will not be disclosed, or hidden that will not be made known. 3 What you have said in the dark will be heard in the daylight, and what you have whispered in the ear in the inner rooms will be proclaimed from the roofs.

4 "I tell you, my friends, do not be afraid of those who kill the body and after that can do no more. 5 But I will show you whom you should fear: Fear him who, after your body has been killed, has authority to throw you into hell. Yes, I tell you, fear him. 6 Are not five sparrows sold for two pennies? Yet not one of them is forgotten by God. 7 Indeed, the very hairs of your head are all numbered. Don't be afraid; you are worth more than many sparrows.

8 "I tell you, whoever publicly acknowledges me before others, the Son of Man will also acknowledge before the angels of God. 9 But whoever disowns me before others will be disowned before the angels of

---

a 1 Or speak to his disciples, saying: "First of all, be

God. ¹⁰And everyone who speaks a word against the Son of Man will be forgiven, but anyone who blasphemes against the Holy Spirit will not be forgiven.

¹¹"When you are brought before synagogues, rulers and authorities, do not worry about how you will defend yourselves or what you will say, ¹²for the Holy Spirit will teach you at that time what you should say."

¹³Someone in the crowd said to him, "Teacher, tell my brother to divide the inheritance with me."

¹⁴Jesus replied, "Man, who appointed me a judge or an arbiter between you?" ¹⁵Then he said to them, "Watch out! Be on your guard against all kinds of greed; life does not consist in an abundance of possessions."

¹⁶And he told them this parable: "The ground of a certain rich man yielded an abundant harvest. ¹⁷He thought to himself, 'What shall I do? I have no place to store my crops.'

¹⁸"Then he said, 'This is what I'll do. I will tear down my barns and build bigger ones, and there I will store my surplus grain. ¹⁹And I'll say to myself, "You have plenty of grain laid up for many years. Take life easy; eat, drink and be merry."'

²⁰"But God said to him, 'You fool! This very night your life will be demanded from you. Then who will get what you have prepared for yourself?'

²¹"This is how it will be with whoever stores up things for themselves but is not rich toward God."

²²Then Jesus said to his disciples: "Therefore I tell you, do not worry about your life, what you will eat; or about your body, what you will

wear. ²³For life is more than food, and the body more than clothes. ²⁴Consider the ravens: They do not sow or reap, they have no storeroom or barn; yet God feeds them. And how much more valuable you are than birds! ²⁵Who of you by worrying can add a single hour to your life[a]? ²⁶Since you cannot do this very little thing, why do you worry about the rest?

²⁷"Consider the wild flowers grow. They do not labor or spin. Yet I tell you, not even Solomon in all his splendor was dressed like one of these. ²⁸If that is how God clothes the grass of the field, which is here today, and tomorrow is thrown into the fire, how much more will he clothe you—you of little faith! ²⁹And do not set your heart on what you will eat or drink; do not worry about it. ³⁰For the pagan world runs after all such things, and your Father knows that you need them. ³¹But seek his kingdom, and these things will be given to you as well.

³²"Do not be afraid, little flock, for your Father has been pleased to give you the kingdom. ³³Sell your possessions and give to the poor. Provide purses for yourselves that will not wear out, a treasure in heaven that will never fail, where no thief comes near and no moth destroys. ³⁴For where your treasure is, there your heart will be also.

³⁵"Be dressed ready for service and keep your lamps burning, ³⁶like servants waiting for their master to return from a wedding banquet, so that when he comes and knocks they can immediately open the door for him. ³⁷It will be good for those servants whose master finds them watching when he comes. Truly I tell you, he will dress

_____
ᵃ 25 Or single cubit to your height

himself to serve, will have them recline at the table and will come and wait on them. 38It will be good for those servants whose master finds them ready, even if he comes in the middle of the night or toward daybreak. 39But understand this: If the owner of the house had known at what hour the thief was coming, he would not have let his house be broken into. 40You also must be ready, because the Son of Man will come at an hour when you do not expect him."

41Peter asked, "Lord, are you telling this parable to us, or to everyone?"

42The Lord answered, "Who then is the faithful and wise manager, whom the master puts in charge of his servants to give them their food allowance at the proper time? 43It will be good for that servant whom the master finds doing so when he returns. 44Truly I tell you, he will put him in charge of all his possessions. 45But suppose the servant says to himself, 'My master is taking a long time in coming,' and he then begins to beat the other servants, both men and women, and to eat and drink and get drunk. 46The master of that servant will come on a day when he does not expect him and at an hour he is not aware of. He will cut him to pieces and assign him a place with the unbelievers.

47"The servant who knows the master's will and does not get ready or does not do what the master wants will be beaten with many blows. 48But the one who does not know and does things deserving punishment will be beaten with few blows. From everyone who has been given much, much will be demanded; and from the one who has been entrusted with much, much more will be asked.

49"I have come to bring fire on the earth, and how I wish it were already kindled! 50But I have a baptism to undergo, and what constraint I am under until it is completed! 51Do you think I came to bring peace on earth? No, I tell you, but division. 52From now on there will be five in one family divided against each other, three against two and two against three. 53They will be divided, father against son and son against father, mother against daughter and daughter against mother, mother-in-law against daughter-in-law and daughter-in-law against mother-in-law."

54He said to the crowd: "When you see a cloud rising in the west, immediately you say, 'It's going to rain,' and it does. 55And when the south wind blows, you say, 'It's going to be hot,' and it is. 56Hypocrites! You know how to interpret the appearance of the earth and the sky. How is it that you don't know how to interpret this present time?

57"Why don't you judge for yourselves what is right? 58As you are going with your adversary to the magistrate, try hard to be reconciled on the way, or your adversary may drag you off to the judge, and the judge turn you over to the officer, and the officer throw you into prison. 59I tell you, you will not get out until you have paid the last penny."

13 Now there were some present at that time who told Jesus about the Galileans whose blood Pilate had mixed with their sacrifices. 2Jesus answered, "Do you think that these Galileans were worse sinners than all the other

Galileans because they suffered this way? [3]I tell you, no! But unless you repent, you too will all perish. [4]Or those eighteen who died when the tower in Siloam fell on them—do you think they were more guilty than all the others living in Jerusalem? [5]I tell you, no! But unless you repent, you too will all perish.

[6]Then he told this parable: "A man had a fig tree growing in his vineyard, and he went to look for fruit on it but did not find any. [7]So he said to the man who took care of the vineyard, 'For three years now I've been coming to look for fruit on this fig tree and haven't found any. Cut it down! Why should it use up the soil?'

[8]"'Sir,' the man replied, 'leave it alone for one more year, and I'll dig around it and fertilize it. [9]If it bears fruit next year, fine! If not, then cut it down.'"

[10]On a Sabbath Jesus was teaching in one of the synagogues, [11]and a woman was there who had been crippled by a spirit for eighteen years. She was bent over and could not straighten up at all. [12]When Jesus saw her, he called her forward and said to her, "Woman, you are set free from your infirmity." [13]Then he put his hands on her, and immediately she straightened up and praised God.

[14]Indignant because Jesus had healed on the Sabbath, the synagogue leader said to the people, "There are six days for work. So come and be healed on those days, not on the Sabbath."

[15]The Lord answered him, "You hypocrites! Doesn't each of you on the Sabbath untie your ox or donkey from the stall and lead it out to give it water? [16]Then should not this woman, a daughter of Abraham, whom Satan has kept bound for eighteen long years, be set free on the Sabbath day from what bound her?"

[17]When he said this, all his opponents were humiliated, but the people were delighted with all the wonderful things he was doing.

[18]Then Jesus asked, "What is the kingdom of God like? What shall I compare it to? [19]It is like a mustard seed, which a man took and planted in his garden. It grew and became a tree, and the birds perched in its branches."

[20]Again he asked, "What shall I compare the kingdom of God to? [21]It is like yeast that a woman took and mixed into about sixty pounds[a] of flour until it worked all through the dough."

[22]Then Jesus went through the towns and villages, teaching as he made his way to Jerusalem. [23]Someone asked him, "Lord, are only a few people going to be saved?"

He said to them, [24]"Make every effort to enter through the narrow door, because many, I tell you, will try to enter and will not be able to. [25]Once the owner of the house gets up and closes the door, you will stand outside knocking and pleading, 'Sir, open the door for us.'

"But he will answer, 'I don't know you or where you come from.'

[26]"Then you will say, 'We ate and drank with you, and you taught in our streets.'

[27]"But he will reply, 'I don't know you or where you come from. Away from me, all you evildoers!'

[28]"There will be weeping there, and gnashing of teeth, when you see Abraham, Isaac and Jacob and all the prophets in the kingdom of

---

[a] 21 Or about 27 kilograms

God, but you yourselves thrown out. ²⁹People will come from east and west and north and south, and will take their places at the feast in the kingdom of God. ³⁰Indeed there are those who are last who will be first, and first who will be last."

³¹At that time some Pharisees came to Jesus and said to him, "Leave this place and go somewhere else. Herod wants to kill you."

³²He replied, "Go tell that fox, 'I will keep on driving out demons and healing people today and tomorrow, and on the third day I will reach my goal.' ³³In any case, I must press on today and tomorrow and the next day—for surely no prophet can die outside Jerusalem!

³⁴"Jerusalem, Jerusalem, you who kill the prophets and stone those sent to you, how often I have longed to gather your children together, as a hen gathers her chicks under her wings, and you were not willing. ³⁵Look, your house is left to you desolate. I tell you, you will not see me again until you say, 'Blessed is he who comes in the name of the Lord.'ᵃ"

14 One Sabbath, when Jesus went to eat in the house of a prominent Pharisee, he was being carefully watched. ²There in front of him was a man suffering from abnormal swelling of his body. ³Jesus asked the Pharisees and experts in the law, "Is it lawful to heal on the Sabbath or not?" ⁴But they remained silent. So taking hold of the man, he healed him and sent him on his way.

⁵Then he asked them, "If one of you has a childᵇ or an ox that falls into a well on the Sabbath day, will you not immediately pull it out?" ⁶And they had nothing to say.

⁷When he noticed how the guests picked the places of honor at the table, he told them this parable: ⁸"When someone invites you to a wedding feast, do not take the place of honor, for a person more distinguished than you may have been invited. ⁹If so, the host who invited both of you will come and say to you, 'Give this person your seat.' Then, humiliated, you will have to take the least important place. ¹⁰But when you are invited, take the lowest place, so that when your host comes, he will say to you, 'Friend, move up to a better place.' Then you will be honored in the presence of all the other guests. ¹¹For all those who exalt themselves will be humbled, and those who humble themselves will be exalted."

¹²Then Jesus said to his host, "When you give a luncheon or dinner, do not invite your friends, your brothers or sisters, your relatives, or your rich neighbors; if you do, they may invite you back and so you will be repaid. ¹³But when you give a banquet, invite the poor, the crippled, the lame, the blind, ¹⁴and you will be blessed. Although they cannot repay you, you will be repaid at the resurrection of the righteous."

¹⁵When one of those at the table with him heard this, he said to Jesus, "Blessed is the one who will eat at the feast in the kingdom of God."

¹⁶Jesus replied: "A certain man was preparing a great banquet and invited many guests. ¹⁷At the time of the banquet he sent his servant to tell those who had been invited, 'Come, for everything is now ready.'

¹⁸"But they all alike began to make excuses. The first said, 'I have

---

ᵃ 35 Psalm 118:26   ᵇ 5 Some manuscripts donkey

just bought a field, and I must go and see it. Please excuse me.'

¹⁹ "Another said, 'I have just bought five yoke of oxen, and I'm on my way to try them out. Please excuse me.'

²⁰ "Still another said, 'I just got married, so I can't come.'

²¹ "The servant came back and reported this to his master. Then the owner of the house became angry and ordered his servant, 'Go out quickly into the streets and alleys of the town and bring in the poor, the crippled, the blind and the lame.'

²² " 'Sir,' the servant said, 'what you ordered has been done, but there is still room.'

²³ "Then the master told his servant, 'Go out to the roads and country lanes and compel them to come in, so that my house will be full. ²⁴ I tell you, not one of those who were invited will get a taste of my banquet.' "

²⁵ Large crowds were traveling with Jesus, and turning to them he said: ²⁶ "If anyone comes to me and does not hate father and mother, wife and children, brothers and sisters — yes, even their own life — such a person cannot be my disciple. ²⁷ And whoever does not carry their cross and follow me cannot be my disciple.

²⁸ "Suppose one of you wants to build a tower. Won't you first sit down and estimate the cost to see if you have enough money to complete it? ²⁹ For if you lay the foundation and are not able to finish it, everyone who sees it will ridicule you, ³⁰ saying, 'This person began to build and wasn't able to finish.'

³¹ "Or suppose a king is about to go to war against another king.

Won't he first sit down and consider whether he is able with ten thousand men to oppose the one coming against him with twenty thousand? ³² If he is not able, he will send a delegation while the other is still a long way off and will ask for terms of peace. ³³ In the same way, those of you who do not give up everything you have cannot be my disciples.

³⁴ "Salt is good, but if it loses its saltiness, how can it be made salty again? ³⁵ It is fit neither for the soil nor for the manure pile; it is thrown out.

"Whoever has ears to hear, let them hear."

15 Now the tax collectors and sinners were all gathering around to hear Jesus. ² But the Pharisees and the teachers of the law muttered, "This man welcomes sinners and eats with them."

³ Then Jesus told them this parable: ⁴ "Suppose one of you has a hundred sheep and loses one of them. Doesn't he leave the ninety-nine in the open country and go after the lost sheep until he finds it? ⁵ And when he finds it, he joyfully puts it on his shoulders ⁶ and goes home. Then he calls his friends and neighbors together and says, 'Rejoice with me; I have found my lost sheep.' ⁷ I tell you that in the same way there will be more rejoicing in heaven over one sinner who repents than over ninety-nine righteous persons who do not need to repent.

⁸ "Or suppose a woman has ten silver coins[a] and loses one. Doesn't she light a lamp, sweep the house and search carefully until she finds it? ⁹ And when she finds it, she calls her friends and neighbors together

---

ᵃ 8 Greek *ten drachmas*, each worth about a day's wages

and says, 'Rejoice with me; I have found my lost coin.' ¹⁰In the same way, I tell you, there is rejoicing in the presence of the angels of God over one sinner who repents."

¹¹Jesus continued: "There was a man who had two sons. ¹²The younger one said to his father, 'Father, give me my share of the estate.' So he divided his property between them.

¹³"Not long after that, the younger son got together all he had, set off for a distant country and there squandered his wealth in wild living. ¹⁴After he had spent everything, there was a severe famine in that whole country, and he began to be in need. ¹⁵So he went and hired himself out to a citizen of that country, who sent him to his fields to feed pigs. ¹⁶He longed to fill his stomach with the pods that the pigs were eating, but no one gave him anything.

¹⁷"When he came to his senses, he said, 'How many of my father's hired servants have food to spare, and here I am starving to death! ¹⁸I will set out and go back to my father and say to him: Father, I have sinned against heaven and against you. ¹⁹I am no longer worthy to be called your son; make me like one of your hired servants.' ²⁰So he got up and went to his father.

"But while he was still a long way off, his father saw him and was filled with compassion for him; he ran to his son, threw his arms around him and kissed him.

²¹"The son said to him, 'Father, I have sinned against heaven and against you. I am no longer worthy to be called your son.'

²²"But the father said to his servants, 'Quick! Bring the best robe and put it on him. Put a ring on his finger and sandals on his feet. ²³Bring the fattened calf and kill it. Let's have a feast and celebrate. ²⁴For this son of mine was dead and is alive again; he was lost and is found.' So they began to celebrate.

²⁵"Meanwhile, the older son was in the field. When he came near the house, he heard music and dancing. ²⁶So he called one of the servants and asked him what was going on. ²⁷'Your brother has come,' he replied, 'and your father has killed the fattened calf because he has him back safe and sound.'

²⁸"The older brother became angry and refused to go in. So his father went out and pleaded with him. ²⁹But he answered his father, 'Look! All these years I've been slaving for you and never disobeyed your orders. Yet you never gave me even a young goat so I could celebrate with my friends. ³⁰But when this son of yours who has squandered your property with prostitutes comes home, you kill the fattened calf for him!'

³¹"'My son,' the father said, 'you are always with me, and everything I have is yours. ³²But we had to celebrate and be glad, because this brother of yours was dead and is alive again; he was lost and is found.'"

16 Jesus told his disciples: "There was a rich man whose manager was accused of wasting his possessions. ²So he called him in and asked him, 'What is this I hear about you? Give an account of your management, because you cannot be manager any longer.'

³"The manager said to himself, 'What shall I do now? My master is taking away my job. I'm not strong enough to dig, and I'm ashamed to beg— ⁴I know what I'll do so that,

when I lose my job here, people will welcome me into their houses.'

⁵ "So he called in each one of his master's debtors. He asked the first, 'How much do you owe my master?'

⁶ " 'Nine hundred gallonsᵃ of olive oil,' he replied.

"The manager told him, 'Take your bill, sit down quickly, and make it four hundred and fifty.'

⁷ "Then he asked the second, 'And how much do you owe?'

" 'A thousand bushelsᵇ of wheat,' he replied.

"He told him, 'Take your bill and make it eight hundred.'

⁸ "The master commended the dishonest manager because he had acted shrewdly. For the people of this world are more shrewd in dealing with their own kind than are the people of the light. ⁹ I tell you, use worldly wealth to gain friends for yourselves, so that when it is gone, you will be welcomed into eternal dwellings.

¹⁰ "Whoever can be trusted with very little can also be trusted with much, and whoever is dishonest with very little will also be dishonest with much. ¹¹ So if you have not been trustworthy in handling worldly wealth, who will trust you with true riches? ¹² And if you have not been trustworthy with someone else's property, who will give you property of your own?

¹³ "No one can serve two masters. Either you will hate the one and love the other, or you will be devoted to the one and despise the other. You cannot serve both God and money."

¹⁴ The Pharisees, who loved money, heard all this and were sneering at Jesus. ¹⁵ He said to them, "You are the ones who justify yourselves in the eyes of others, but God knows your hearts. What people value highly is detestable in God's sight.

¹⁶ "The Law and the Prophets were proclaimed until John. Since that time, the good news of the kingdom of God is being preached, and everyone is forcing their way into it. ¹⁷ It is easier for heaven and earth to disappear than for the least stroke of a pen to drop out of the Law.

¹⁸ "Anyone who divorces his wife and marries another woman commits adultery, and the man who marries a divorced woman commits adultery.

¹⁹ "There was a rich man who was dressed in purple and fine linen and lived in luxury every day. ²⁰ At his gate was laid a beggar named Lazarus, covered with sores ²¹ and longing to eat what fell from the rich man's table. Even the dogs came and licked his sores.

²² "The time came when the beggar died and the angels carried him to Abraham's side. The rich man also died and was buried. ²³ In Hades, where he was in torment, he looked up and saw Abraham far away, with Lazarus by his side. ²⁴ So he called to him, 'Father Abraham, have pity on me and send Lazarus to dip the tip of his finger in water and cool my tongue, because I am in agony in this fire.'

²⁵ "But Abraham replied, 'Son, remember that in your lifetime you received your good things, while Lazarus received bad things, but now he is comforted here and you are in agony. ²⁶ And besides all this, between us and you a great chasm has been set in place, so that those who want to go from here to you

---

ᵃ 6 Or about 3,000 liters   ᵇ 7 Or about 30 tons

cannot, nor can anyone cross over from there to us.'

27"He answered, 'Then I beg you, father, send Lazarus to my family, 28for I have five brothers. Let him warn them, so that they will not also come to this place of torment.'

29"Abraham replied, 'They have Moses and the Prophets; let them listen to them.'

30" 'No, father Abraham,' he said, 'but if someone from the dead goes to them, they will repent.'

31"He said to him, 'If they do not listen to Moses and the Prophets, they will not be convinced even if someone rises from the dead.' "

17 Jesus said to his disciples: "Things that cause people to stumble are bound to come, but woe to anyone through whom they come. 2It would be better for them to be thrown into the sea with a millstone tied around their neck than to cause one of these little ones to stumble. 3So watch yourselves.

"If your brother or sister[a] sins against you, rebuke them; and if they repent, forgive them. 4Even if they sin against you seven times in a day and seven times come back to you saying 'I repent,' you must forgive them."

5The apostles said to the Lord, "Increase our faith!"

6He replied, "If you have faith as small as a mustard seed, you can say to this mulberry tree, 'Be uprooted and planted in the sea,' and it will obey you.

7"Suppose one of you has a servant plowing or looking after the sheep. Will he say to the servant when he comes in from the field,

'Come along now and sit down to eat'? 8Won't he rather say, 'Prepare my supper, get yourself ready and wait on me while I eat and drink; after that you may eat and drink'? 9Will he thank the servant because he did what he was told to do? 10So you also, when you have done everything you were told to do, should say, 'We are unworthy servants; we have only done our duty.' "

11Now on his way to Jerusalem, Jesus traveled along the border between Samaria and Galilee. 12As he was going into a village, ten men who had leprosy[b] met him. They stood at a distance 13and called out in a loud voice, "Jesus, Master, have pity on us!"

14When he saw them, he said, "Go, show yourselves to the priests." And as they went, they were cleansed.

15One of them, when he saw he was healed, came back, praising God in a loud voice. 16He threw himself at Jesus' feet and thanked him — and he was a Samaritan.

17Jesus asked, "Were not all ten cleansed? Where are the other nine? 18Has no one returned to give praise to God except this foreigner?" 19Then he said to him, "Rise and go; your faith has made you well."

20Once, on being asked by the Pharisees when the kingdom of God would come, Jesus replied, "The coming of the kingdom of God is not something that can be observed, 21nor will people say, 'Here it is,' or 'There it is,' because the kingdom of God is in your midst."[c]

22Then he said to his disciples, "The time is coming when you will

---

[a] 3 The Greek word for *brother or sister* (*adelphos*) refers here to a fellow believer, whether man or woman.   [b] 12 The Greek word traditionally translated *leprosy* was used for various diseases affecting the skin.   [c] 21 Or *is within you*

long to see one of the days of the Son of Man, but you will not see it. 23 People will tell you, 'There he is!' or 'Here he is!' Do not go running off after them. 24 For the Son of Man in his day[a] will be like the lightning, which flashes and lights up the sky from one end to the other. 25 But first he must suffer many things and be rejected by this generation.

26 "Just as it was in the days of Noah, so also will it be in the days of the Son of Man. 27 People were eating, drinking, marrying and being given in marriage up to the day Noah entered the ark. Then the flood came and destroyed them all.

28 "It was the same in the days of Lot. People were eating and drinking, buying and selling, planting and building. 29 But the day Lot left Sodom, fire and sulfur rained down from heaven and destroyed them all.

30 "It will be just like this on the day the Son of Man is revealed. 31 On that day no one who is on the housetop, with possessions inside, should go down to get them. Likewise, no one in the field should go back for anything. 32 Remember Lot's wife! 33 Whoever tries to keep their life will lose it, and whoever loses their life will preserve it. 34 I tell you, on that night two people will be in one bed; one will be taken and the other left. 35 Two women will be grinding grain together; one will be taken and the other left." [36][b]

37 "Where, Lord?" they asked.

He replied, "Where there is a dead body, there the vultures will gather."

18 Then Jesus told his disciples a parable to show them that they should always pray and not give up. 2 He said: "In a certain town there was a judge who neither feared God nor cared what people thought. 3 And there was a widow in that town who kept coming to him with the plea, 'Grant me justice against my adversary.'

4 "For some time he refused. But finally he said to himself, 'Even though I don't fear God or care what people think, 5 yet because this widow keeps bothering me, I will see that she gets justice, so that she won't eventually come and attack me!'"

6 And the Lord said, "Listen to what the unjust judge says. 7 And will not God bring about justice for his chosen ones, who cry out to him day and night? Will he keep putting them off? 8 I tell you, he will see that they get justice, and quickly. However, when the Son of Man comes, will he find faith on the earth?"

9 To some who were confident of their own righteousness and looked down on everyone else, Jesus told this parable: 10 "Two men went up to the temple to pray, one a Pharisee and the other a tax collector. 11 The Pharisee stood by himself and prayed: 'God, I thank you that I am not like other people — robbers, evildoers, adulterers — or even like this tax collector. 12 I fast twice a week and give a tenth of all I get.'

13 "But the tax collector stood at a distance. He would not even look up to heaven, but beat his breast and said, 'God, have mercy on me, a sinner.'

14 "I tell you that this man, rather than the other, went home justified

---

[a] 24 Some manuscripts do not have *in his day*. similar to Matt. 24:40.

[b] 36 Some manuscripts include here words

before God. For all those who exalt themselves will be humbled, and those who humble themselves will be exalted."

15People were also bringing babies to Jesus for him to place his hands on them. When the disciples saw this, they rebuked them. 16But Jesus called the children to him and said, "Let the little children come to me, and do not hinder them, for the kingdom of God belongs to such as these. 17Truly I tell you, anyone who will not receive the kingdom of God like a little child will never enter it."

18A certain ruler asked him, "Good teacher, what must I do to inherit eternal life?"

19"Why do you call me good?" Jesus answered. "No one is good— except God alone. 20You know the commandments: 'You shall not commit adultery, you shall not murder, you shall not steal, you shall not give false testimony, honor your father and mother.'ᵃ"

21"All these I have kept since I was a boy," he said.

22When Jesus heard this, he said to him, "You still lack one thing. Sell everything you have and give to the poor, and you will have treasure in heaven. Then come, follow me."

23When he heard this, he became very sad, because he was very wealthy. 24Jesus looked at him and said, "How hard it is for the rich to enter the kingdom of God! 25Indeed, it is easier for a camel to go through the eye of a needle than for someone who is rich to enter the kingdom of God."

26Those who heard this asked, "Who then can be saved?"

27Jesus replied, "What is impos-

sible with man is possible with God."

28Peter said to him, "We have left all we had to follow you!"

29"Truly I tell you," Jesus said to them, "no one who has left home or wife or brothers or sisters or parents or children for the sake of the kingdom of God 30will fail to receive many times as much in this age, and in the age to come eternal life."

31Jesus took the Twelve aside and told them, "We are going up to Jerusalem, and everything that is written by the prophets about the Son of Man will be fulfilled. 32He will be delivered over to the Gentiles. They will mock him, insult him and spit on him; 33they will flog him and kill him. On the third day he will rise again."

34The disciples did not understand any of this. Its meaning was hidden from them, and they did not know what he was talking about.

35As Jesus approached Jericho, a blind man was sitting by the roadside begging. 36When he heard the crowd going by, he asked what was happening. 37They told him, "Jesus of Nazareth is passing by."

38He called out, "Jesus, Son of David, have mercy on me!"

39Those who led the way rebuked him and told him to be quiet, but he shouted all the more, "Son of David, have mercy on me!"

40Jesus stopped and ordered the man to be brought to him. When he came near, Jesus asked him, 41"What do you want me to do for you?"

"Lord, I want to see," he replied.

42Jesus said to him, "Receive your sight; your faith has healed you." 43Immediately he received

ᵃ 20 Exodus 20:12-16; Deut. 5:16-20

his sight and followed Jesus, praising God. When all the people saw it, they also praised God.

19 Jesus entered Jericho and was passing through. ²A man was there by the name of Zacchaeus; he was a chief tax collector and was wealthy. ³He wanted to see who Jesus was, but because he was short he could not see over the crowd. ⁴So he ran ahead and climbed a sycamore-fig tree to see him, since Jesus was coming that way.

⁵When Jesus reached the spot, he looked up and said to him, "Zacchaeus, come down immediately. I must stay at your house today." ⁶So he came down at once and welcomed him gladly.

⁷All the people saw this and began to mutter, "He has gone to be the guest of a sinner."

⁸But Zacchaeus stood up and said to the Lord, "Look, Lord! Here and now I give half of my possessions to the poor, and if I have cheated anybody out of anything, I will pay back four times the amount."

⁹Jesus said to him, "Today salvation has come to this house, because this man, too, is a son of Abraham. ¹⁰For the Son of Man came to seek and to save the lost."

¹¹While they were listening to this, he went on to tell them a parable, because he was near Jerusalem and the people thought that the kingdom of God was going to appear at once. ¹²He said: "A man of noble birth went to a distant country to have himself appointed king and then to return. ¹³So he called ten of his servants and gave them ten minas.ᵃ 'Put this money to work,' he said, 'until I come back.'

¹⁴"But his subjects hated him and sent a delegation after him to say, 'We don't want this man to be our king.'

¹⁵"He was made king, however, and returned home. Then he sent for the servants to whom he had given the money, in order to find out what they had gained with it.

¹⁶"The first one came and said, 'Sir, your mina has earned ten more.'

¹⁷"'Well done, my good servant!' his master replied. 'Because you have been trustworthy in a very small matter, take charge of ten cities.'

¹⁸"The second came and said, 'Sir, your mina has earned five more.'

¹⁹"His master answered, 'You take charge of five cities.'

²⁰"Then another servant came and said, 'Sir, here is your mina; I have kept it laid away in a piece of cloth. ²¹I was afraid of you, because you are a hard man. You take out what you did not put in and reap what you did not sow.'

²²"His master replied, 'I will judge you by your own words, you wicked servant! You knew, did you, that I am a hard man, taking out what I did not put in, and reaping what I did not sow? ²³Why then didn't you put my money on deposit, so that when I came back, I could have collected it with interest?'

²⁴"Then he said to those standing by, 'Take his mina away from him and give it to the one who has ten minas.'

²⁵"'Sir,' they said, 'he already has ten!'

²⁶"He replied, 'I tell you that to everyone who has, more will be given, but as for the one who has nothing, even what they have will be taken away. ²⁷But those enemies

---

ᵃ 13 A mina was about three months' wages.

of mine who did not want me to be king over them — bring them here and kill them in front of me.'"

28After Jesus had said this, he went on ahead, going up to Jerusalem. 29As he approached Bethphage and Bethany at the hill called the Mount of Olives, he sent two of his disciples, saying to them, 30"Go to the village ahead of you, and as you enter it, you will find a colt tied there, which no one has ever ridden. Untie it and bring it here. 31If anyone asks you, 'Why are you untying it?' say, 'The Lord needs it.'"

32Those who were sent ahead went and found it just as he had told them. 33As they were untying the colt, its owners asked them, "Why are you untying the colt?"

34They replied, "The Lord needs it."

35They brought it to Jesus, threw their cloaks on the colt and put Jesus on it. 36As he went along, people spread their cloaks on the road.

37When he came near the place where the road goes down the Mount of Olives, the whole crowd of disciples began joyfully to praise God in loud voices for all the miracles they had seen:

38"Blessed is the king who comes
        in the name of the Lord!"a

"Peace in heaven and glory in
        the highest!"

39Some of the Pharisees in the crowd said to Jesus, "Teacher, rebuke your disciples!"

40"I tell you," he replied, "if they keep quiet, the stones will cry out."

41As he approached Jerusalem and saw the city, he wept over it 42and said, "If you, even you, had

only known on this day what would bring you peace — but now it is hidden from your eyes. 43The days will come upon you when your enemies will build an embankment against you and encircle you and hem you in on every side. 44They will dash you to the ground, you and the children within your walls. They will not leave one stone on another, because you did not recognize the time of God's coming to you."

45When Jesus entered the temple courts, he began to drive out those who were selling. 46"It is written," he said to them, "'My house will be a house of prayer'b; but you have made it 'a den of robbers.'c"

47Every day he was teaching at the temple. But the chief priests, the teachers of the law and the leaders among the people were trying to kill him. 48Yet they could not find any way to do it, because all the people hung on his words.

20 One day as Jesus was teaching the people in the temple courts and proclaiming the good news, the chief priests and the teachers of the law, together with the elders, came up to him. 2"Tell us by what authority you are doing these things," they said. "Who gave you this authority?"

3He replied, "I will also ask you a question. Tell me: 4John's baptism — was it from heaven, or of human origin?"

5They discussed it among themselves and said, "If we say, 'From heaven,' he will ask, 'Why didn't you believe him?' 6But if we say, 'Of human origin,' all the people will stone us, because they are persuaded that John was a prophet."

7So they answered, "We don't know where it was from."

a 38 Psalm 118:26   b 46 Isaiah 56:7   c 46 Jer. 7:11

⁸Jesus said, "Neither will I tell you by what authority I am doing these things."

⁹He went on to tell the people this parable: "A man planted a vineyard, rented it to some farmers and went away for a long time. ¹⁰At harvest time he sent a servant to the tenants so they would give him some of the fruit of the vineyard. But the tenants beat him and sent him away empty-handed. ¹¹He sent another servant, but that one also they beat and treated shamefully and sent him away empty-handed. ¹²He sent still a third, and they wounded him and threw him out.

¹³"Then the owner of the vineyard said, 'What shall I do? I will send my son, whom I love; perhaps they will respect him.'

¹⁴"But when the tenants saw him, they talked the matter over. 'This is the heir,' they said. 'Let's kill him, and the inheritance will be ours.' ¹⁵So they threw him out of the vineyard and killed him.

"What then will the owner of the vineyard do to them? ¹⁶He will come and kill those tenants and give the vineyard to others."

When the people heard this, they said, "God forbid!"

¹⁷Jesus looked directly at them and asked, "Then what is the meaning of that which is written:

" 'The stone the builders rejected
    has become the cornerstone'ᵃ?

¹⁸Everyone who falls on that stone will be broken to pieces; anyone on whom it falls will be crushed."

¹⁹The teachers of the law and the chief priests looked for a way to arrest him immediately, because they knew he had spoken this parable against them. But they were afraid of the people.

²⁰Keeping a close watch on him, they sent spies, who pretended to be sincere. They hoped to catch Jesus in something he said, so that they might hand him over to the power and authority of the governor. ²¹So the spies questioned him: "Teacher, we know that you speak and teach what is right, and that you do not show partiality but teach the way of God in accordance with the truth. ²²Is it right for us to pay taxes to Caesar or not?"

²³He saw through their duplicity and said to them, ²⁴"Show me a denarius. Whose image and inscription are on it?"

"Caesar's," they replied.

²⁵He said to them, "Then give back to Caesar what is Caesar's, and to God what is God's."

²⁶They were unable to trap him in what he had said there in public. And astonished by his answer, they became silent.

²⁷Some of the Sadducees, who say there is no resurrection, came to Jesus with a question. ²⁸"Teacher," they said, "Moses wrote for us that if a man's brother dies and leaves a wife but no children, the man must marry the widow and raise up offspring for his brother. ²⁹Now there were seven brothers. The first one married a woman and died childless. ³⁰The second ³¹and then the third married her, and in the same way the seven died, leaving no children. ³²Finally, the woman died too. ³³Now then, at the resurrection whose wife will she be, since the seven were married to her?"

³⁴Jesus replied, "The people of this age marry and are given in marriage. ³⁵But those who are con-

ᵃ 17 Psalm 118:22

sidered worthy of taking part in the age to come and in the resurrection from the dead will neither marry nor be given in marriage, 36and they can no longer die; for they are like the angels. They are God's children, since they are children of the resurrection. 37But in the account of the burning bush, even Moses showed that the dead rise, for he calls the Lord 'the God of Abraham, and the God of Isaac, and the God of Jacob.'ᵃ 38He is not the God of the dead, but of the living, for to him all are alive."

39Some of the teachers of the law responded, "Well said, teacher!" 40And no one dared to ask him any more questions.

41Then Jesus said to them, "Why is it said that the Messiah is the son of David? 42David himself declares in the Book of Psalms:

"'The Lord said to my Lord:
    "Sit at my right hand
43until I make your enemies
    a footstool for your feet." 'ᵇ

44David calls him 'Lord.' How then can he be his son?"

45While all the people were listening, Jesus said to his disciples, 46"Beware of the teachers of the law. They like to walk around in flowing robes and love to be greeted with respect in the marketplaces and have the most important seats in the synagogues and the places of honor at banquets. 47They devour widows' houses and for a show make lengthy prayers. These men will be punished most severely."

21 As Jesus looked up, he saw the rich putting their gifts into the temple treasury. 2He also saw a poor widow put in two very small copper coins. 3"Truly I tell you," he said, "this poor widow has put in more than all the others. 4All these people gave their gifts out of their wealth; but she out of her poverty put in all she had to live on."

5Some of his disciples were remarking about how the temple was adorned with beautiful stones and with gifts dedicated to God. But Jesus said, 6"As for what you see here, the time will come when not one stone will be left on another; every one of them will be thrown down."

7"Teacher," they asked, "when will these things happen? And what will be the sign that they are about to take place?"

8He replied: "Watch out that you are not deceived. For many will come in my name, claiming, 'I am he,' and, 'The time is near.' Do not follow them. 9When you hear of wars and uprisings, do not be frightened. These things must happen first, but the end will not come right away."

10Then he said to them: "Nation will rise against nation, and kingdom against kingdom. 11There will be great earthquakes, famines and pestilences in various places, and fearful events and great signs from heaven.

12"But before all this, they will seize you and persecute you. They will hand you over to synagogues and put you in prison, and you will be brought before kings and governors, and all on account of my name. 13And so you will bear testimony to me. 14But make up your mind not to worry beforehand how you will defend yourselves. 15For I will give you words and wisdom that none of your adversaries will be able to resist or contradict. 16You

---

ᵃ 37 Exodus 3:6   ᵇ 43 Psalm 110:1

will be betrayed even by parents, brothers and sisters, relatives and friends, and they will put some of you to death. 17 Everyone will hate you because of me. 18 But not a hair of your head will perish. 19 Stand firm, and you will win life.

20 "When you see Jerusalem being surrounded by armies, you will know that its desolation is near. 21 Then let those who are in Judea flee to the mountains, let those in the city get out, and let those in the country not enter the city. 22 For this is the time of punishment in fulfillment of all that has been written. 23 How dreadful it will be in those days for pregnant women and nursing mothers! There will be great distress in the land and wrath against this people. 24 They will fall by the sword and will be taken as prisoners to all the nations. Jerusalem will be trampled on by the Gentiles until the times of the Gentiles are fulfilled.

25 "There will be signs in the sun, moon and stars. On the earth, nations will be in anguish and perplexity at the roaring and tossing of the sea. 26 People will faint from terror, apprehensive of what is coming on the world, for the heavenly bodies will be shaken. 27 At that time they will see the Son of Man coming in a cloud with power and great glory. 28 When these things begin to take place, stand up and lift up your heads, because your redemption is drawing near."

29 He told them this parable: "Look at the fig tree and all the trees. 30 When they sprout leaves, you can see for yourselves and know that summer is near. 31 Even so, when you see these things happening, you know that the kingdom of God is near.

32 "Truly I tell you, this generation will certainly not pass away until all these things have happened. 33 Heaven and earth will pass away, but my words will never pass away.

34 "Be careful, or your hearts will be weighed down with carousing, drunkenness and the anxieties of life, and that day will close on you suddenly like a trap. 35 For it will come on all those who live on the face of the whole earth. 36 Be always on the watch, and pray that you may be able to escape all that is about to happen, and that you may be able to stand before the Son of Man."

37 Each day Jesus was teaching at the temple, and each evening he went out to spend the night on the hill called the Mount of Olives, 38 and all the people came early in the morning to hear him at the temple.

22 Now the Festival of Unleavened Bread, called the Passover, was approaching, 2 and the chief priests and the teachers of the law were looking for some way to get rid of Jesus, for they were afraid of the people. 3 Then Satan entered Judas, called Iscariot, one of the Twelve. 4 And Judas went to the chief priests and the officers of the temple guard and discussed with them how he might betray Jesus. 5 They were delighted and agreed to give him money. 6 He consented, and watched for an opportunity to hand Jesus over to them when no crowd was present.

7 Then came the day of Unleavened Bread on which the Passover lamb had to be sacrificed. 8 Jesus sent Peter and John, saying, "Go and make preparations for us to eat the Passover."

9 "Where do you want us to prepare for it?" they asked.

¹⁰He replied, "As you enter the city, a man carrying a jar of water will meet you. Follow him to the house that he enters, ¹¹and say to the owner of the house, 'The Teacher asks: Where is the guest room, where I may eat the Passover with my disciples?' ¹²He will show you a large room upstairs, all furnished. Make preparations there."

¹³They left and found things just as Jesus had told them. So they prepared the Passover.

¹⁴When the hour came, Jesus and his apostles reclined at the table. ¹⁵And he said to them, "I have eagerly desired to eat this Passover with you before I suffer. ¹⁶For I tell you, I will not eat it again until it finds fulfillment in the kingdom of God."

¹⁷After taking the cup, he gave thanks and said, "Take this and divide it among you. ¹⁸For I tell you I will not drink again from the fruit of the vine until the kingdom of God comes."

¹⁹And he took bread, gave thanks and broke it, and gave it to them, saying, "This is my body given for you; do this in remembrance of me."

²⁰In the same way, after the supper he took the cup, saying, "This cup is the new covenant in my blood, which is poured out for you.ᵃ ²¹But the hand of him who is going to betray me is with mine on the table. ²²The Son of Man will go as it has been decreed. But woe to that man who betrays him!" ²³They began to question among themselves which of them it might be who would do this.

²⁴A dispute also arose among them as to which of them was considered to be greatest. ²⁵Jesus said to them, "The kings of the Gentiles lord it over them; and those who exercise authority over them call themselves Benefactors. ²⁶But you are not to be like that. Instead, the greatest among you should be like the youngest, and the one who rules like the one who serves. ²⁷For who is greater, the one who is at the table or the one who serves? Is it not the one who is at the table? But I am among you as one who serves. ²⁸You are those who have stood by me in my trials. ²⁹And I confer on you a kingdom, just as my Father conferred one on me, ³⁰so that you may eat and drink at my table in my kingdom and sit on thrones, judging the twelve tribes of Israel.

³¹"Simon, Simon, Satan has asked to sift all of you as wheat. ³²But I have prayed for you, Simon, that your faith may not fail. And when you have turned back, strengthen your brothers."

³³But he replied, "Lord, I am ready to go with you to prison and to death."

³⁴Jesus answered, "I tell you, Peter, before the rooster crows today, you will deny three times that you know me."

³⁵Then Jesus asked them, "When I sent you without purse, bag or sandals, did you lack anything?"

"Nothing," they answered.

³⁶He said to them, "But now if you have a purse, take it, and also a bag; and if you don't have a sword, sell your cloak and buy one. ³⁷It is written: 'And he was numbered with the transgressors'ᵇ; and I tell you that this must be fulfilled in me. Yes, what is written about me is reaching its fulfillment."

³⁸The disciples said, "See, Lord, here are two swords."

ᵃ 19,20 Some manuscripts do not have given for you . . . poured out for you.   ᵇ 37 Isaiah 53:12

"That's enough!" he replied.

³⁹ Jesus went out as usual to the Mount of Olives, and his disciples followed him. ⁴⁰ On reaching the place, he said to them, "Pray that you will not fall into temptation." ⁴¹ He withdrew about a stone's throw beyond them, knelt down and prayed, ⁴² "Father, if you are willing, take this cup from me; yet not my will, but yours be done." ⁴³ An angel from heaven appeared to him and strengthened him. ⁴⁴ And being in anguish, he prayed more earnestly, and his sweat was like drops of blood falling to the ground.ᵃ

⁴⁵ When he rose from prayer and went back to the disciples, he found them asleep, exhausted from sorrow. ⁴⁶ "Why are you sleeping?" he asked them. "Get up and pray so that you will not fall into temptation."

⁴⁷ While he was still speaking a crowd came up, and the man who was called Judas, one of the Twelve, was leading them. He approached Jesus to kiss him, ⁴⁸ but Jesus asked him, "Judas, are you betraying the Son of Man with a kiss?"

⁴⁹ When Jesus' followers saw what was going to happen, they said, "Lord, should we strike with our swords?" ⁵⁰ And one of them struck the servant of the high priest, cutting off his right ear.

⁵¹ But Jesus answered, "No more of this!" And he touched the man's ear and healed him.

⁵² Then Jesus said to the chief priests, the officers of the temple guard, and the elders, who had come for him, "Am I leading a rebellion, that you have come with swords and clubs? ⁵³ Every day I was with you in the temple courts, and you did not lay a hand on me. But this is your hour — when darkness reigns."

⁵⁴ Then seizing him, they led him away and took him into the house of the high priest. Peter followed at a distance. ⁵⁵ And when some there had kindled a fire in the middle of the courtyard and had sat down together, Peter sat down with them. ⁵⁶ A servant girl saw him seated there in the firelight. She looked closely at him and said, "This man was with him."

⁵⁷ But he denied it. "Woman, I don't know him," he said.

⁵⁸ A little later someone else saw him and said, "You also are one of them."

"Man, I am not!" Peter replied.

⁵⁹ About an hour later another asserted, "Certainly this fellow was with him, for he is a Galilean."

⁶⁰ Peter replied, "Man, I don't know what you're talking about!" Just as he was speaking, the rooster crowed. ⁶¹ The Lord turned and looked straight at Peter. Then Peter remembered the word the Lord had spoken to him: "Before the rooster crows today, you will disown me three times." ⁶² And he went outside and wept bitterly.

⁶³ The men who were guarding Jesus began mocking and beating him. ⁶⁴ They blindfolded him and demanded, "Prophesy! Who hit you?" ⁶⁵ And they said many other insulting things to him.

⁶⁶ At daybreak the council of the elders of the people, both the chief priests and the teachers of the law, met together, and Jesus was led before them. ⁶⁷ "If you are the Messiah," they said, "tell us."

Jesus answered, "If I tell you, you will not believe me, ⁶⁸ and if I asked

---

ᵃ 43,44 Many early manuscripts do not have verses 43 and 44.

you, you would not answer. ⁶⁹But from now on, the Son of Man will be seated at the right hand of the mighty God."

⁷⁰They all asked, "Are you then the Son of God?"

He replied, "You say that I am."

⁷¹Then they said, "Why do we need any more testimony? We have heard it from his own lips."

23 Then the whole assembly rose and led him off to Pilate. ²And they began to accuse him, saying, "We have found this man subverting our nation. He opposes payment of taxes to Caesar and claims to be Messiah, a king."

³So Pilate asked Jesus, "Are you the king of the Jews?"

"You have said so," Jesus replied.

⁴Then Pilate announced to the chief priests and the crowd, "I find no basis for a charge against this man."

⁵But they insisted, "He stirs up the people all over Judea by his teaching. He started in Galilee and has come all the way here."

⁶On hearing this, Pilate asked if the man was a Galilean. ⁷When he learned that Jesus was under Herod's jurisdiction, he sent him to Herod, who was also in Jerusalem at that time.

⁸When Herod saw Jesus, he was greatly pleased, because for a long time he had been wanting to see him. From what he had heard about him, he hoped to see him perform a sign of some sort. ⁹He plied him with many questions, but Jesus gave him no answer. ¹⁰The chief priests and the teachers of the law were standing there, vehemently accusing him. ¹¹Then Herod and his soldiers ridiculed and mocked him. Dressing him in an elegant robe, they sent him back to Pilate. ¹²That day Herod and Pilate became friends — before this they had been enemies.

¹³Pilate called together the chief priests, the rulers and the people, ¹⁴and said to them, "You brought me this man as one who was inciting the people to rebellion. I have examined him in your presence and have found no basis for your charges against him. ¹⁵Neither has Herod, for he sent him back to us; as you can see, he has done nothing to deserve death. ¹⁶Therefore, I will punish him and then release him." ⁽¹⁷⁾ᵃ

¹⁸But the whole crowd shouted, "Away with this man! Release Barabbas to us!" ¹⁹(Barabbas had been thrown into prison for an insurrection in the city, and for murder.)

²⁰Wanting to release Jesus, Pilate appealed to them again. ²¹But they kept shouting, "Crucify him! Crucify him!"

²²For the third time he spoke to them: "Why? What crime has this man committed? I have found in him no grounds for the death penalty. Therefore I will have him punished and then release him."

²³But with loud shouts they insistently demanded that he be crucified, and their shouts prevailed. ²⁴So Pilate decided to grant their demand. ²⁵He released the man who had been thrown into prison for insurrection and murder, the one they asked for, and surrendered Jesus to their will.

²⁶As the soldiers led him away, they seized Simon from Cyrene, who was on his way in from the country, and put the cross on him and made him carry it behind Jesus. ²⁷A large number of people

---

ᵃ 17 Some manuscripts include here words similar to Matt. 27:15 and Mark 15:6.

followed him, including women who mourned and wailed for him. 28Jesus turned and said to them, "Daughters of Jerusalem, do not weep for me; weep for yourselves and for your children. 29For the time will come when you will say, 'Blessed are the childless women, the wombs that never bore and the breasts that never nursed!' 30Then

> " 'they will say to the mountains,
>   "Fall on us!"
>   and to the hills, "Cover us!" ' a

31For if people do these things when the tree is green, what will happen when it is dry?"

32Two other men, both criminals, were also led out with him to be executed. 33When they came to the place called the Skull, they crucified him there, along with the criminals — one on his right, the other on his left. 34Jesus said, "Father, forgive them, for they do not know what they are doing." b And they divided up his clothes by casting lots.

35The people stood watching, and the rulers even sneered at him. They said, "He saved others; let him save himself if he is God's Messiah, the Chosen One."

36The soldiers also came up and mocked him. They offered him wine vinegar 37and said, "If you are the king of the Jews, save yourself."

38There was a written notice above him, which read: THIS IS THE KING OF THE JEWS.

39One of the criminals who hung there hurled insults at him: "Aren't you the Messiah? Save yourself and us!"

40But the other criminal rebuked him. "Don't you fear God," he said,

"since you are under the same sentence? 41We are punished justly, for we are getting what our deeds deserve. But this man has done nothing wrong."

42Then he said, "Jesus, remember me when you come into your kingdom.c "

43Jesus answered him, "Truly I tell you, today you will be with me in paradise."

44It was now about noon, and darkness came over the whole land until three in the afternoon, 45for the sun stopped shining. And the curtain of the temple was torn in two. 46Jesus called out with a loud voice, "Father, into your hands I commit my spirit."d When he had said this, he breathed his last.

47The centurion, seeing what had happened, praised God and said, "Surely this was a righteous man." 48When all the people who had gathered to witness this sight saw what took place, they beat their breasts and went away. 49But all those who knew him, including the women who had followed him from Galilee, stood at a distance, watching these things.

50Now there was a man named Joseph, a member of the Council, a good and upright man, 51who had not consented to their decision and action. He came from the Judean town of Arimathea, and he himself was waiting for the kingdom of God. 52Going to Pilate, he asked for Jesus' body. 53Then he took it down, wrapped it in linen cloth and placed it in a tomb cut in the rock, one in which no one had yet been laid. 54It was Preparation Day, and the Sabbath was about to begin.

55The women who had come

---

a 30 Hosea 10:8   b 34 Some early manuscripts do not have this sentence.   c 42 Some manuscripts come with your kingly power   d 46 Psalm 31:5

with Jesus from Galilee followed Joseph and saw the tomb and how his body was laid in it. 56Then they went home and prepared spices and perfumes. But they rested on the Sabbath in obedience to the commandment.

24 On the first day of the week, very early in the morning, the women took the spices they had prepared and went to the tomb. 2They found the stone rolled away from the tomb, 3but when they entered, they did not find the body of the Lord Jesus. 4While they were wondering about this, suddenly two men in clothes that gleamed like lightning stood beside them. 5In their fright the women bowed down with their faces to the ground, but the men said to them, "Why do you look for the living among the dead? 6He is not here; he has risen! Remember how he told you, while he was still with you in Galilee: 7'The Son of Man must be delivered over to the hands of sinners, be crucified and on the third day be raised again.'" 8Then they remembered his words.

9When they came back from the tomb, they told all these things to the Eleven and to all the others. 10It was Mary Magdalene, Joanna, Mary the mother of James, and the others with them who told this to the apostles. 11But they did not believe the women, because their words seemed to them like nonsense. 12Peter, however, got up and ran to the tomb. Bending over, he saw the strips of linen lying by themselves, and he went away, wondering to himself what had happened.

13Now that same day two of them were going to a village called Emmaus, about seven milesa from Je-

rusalem. 14They were talking with each other about everything that had happened. 15As they talked and discussed these things with each other, Jesus himself came up and walked along with them; 16but they were kept from recognizing him.

17He asked them, "What are you discussing together as you walk along?"

They stood still, their faces downcast. 18One of them, named Cleopas, asked him, "Are you the only one visiting Jerusalem who does not know the things that have happened there in these days?"

19"What things?" he asked.

"About Jesus of Nazareth," they replied. "He was a prophet, powerful in word and deed before God and all the people. 20The chief priests and our rulers handed him over to be sentenced to death, and they crucified him; 21but we had hoped that he was the one who was going to redeem Israel. And what is more, it is the third day since all this took place. 22In addition, some of our women amazed us. They went to the tomb early this morning 23but didn't find his body. They came and told us that they had seen a vision of angels, who said he was alive. 24Then some of our companions went to the tomb and found it just as the women had said, but they did not see Jesus."

25He said to them, "How foolish you are, and how slow to believe all that the prophets have spoken! 26Did not the Messiah have to suffer these things and then enter his glory?" 27And beginning with Moses and all the Prophets, he explained to them what was said in all the Scriptures concerning himself.

28As they approached the village

---

a 13 Or about 11 kilometers

to which they were going, Jesus continued on as if he were going farther. ²⁹But they urged him strongly, "Stay with us, for it is nearly evening; the day is almost over." So he went in to stay with them.

³⁰When he was at the table with them, he took bread, gave thanks, broke it and began to give it to them. ³¹Then their eyes were opened and they recognized him, and he disappeared from their sight. ³²They asked each other, "Were not our hearts burning within us while he talked with us on the road and opened the Scriptures to us?"

³³They got up and returned at once to Jerusalem. There they found the Eleven and those with them, assembled together ³⁴and saying, "It is true! The Lord has risen and has appeared to Simon." ³⁵Then the two told what had happened on the way, and how Jesus was recognized by them when he broke the bread.

³⁶While they were still talking about this, Jesus himself stood among them and said to them, "Peace be with you."

³⁷They were startled and frightened, thinking they saw a ghost. ³⁸He said to them, "Why are you troubled, and why do doubts rise in your minds? ³⁹Look at my hands and my feet. It is I myself! Touch me and see; a ghost does not have flesh and bones, as you see I have."

⁴⁰When he had said this, he showed them his hands and feet. ⁴¹And while they still did not believe it because of joy and amazement, he asked them, "Do you have anything here to eat?" ⁴²They gave him a piece of broiled fish, ⁴³and he took it and ate it in their presence.

⁴⁴He said to them, "This is what I told you while I was still with you: Everything must be fulfilled that is written about me in the Law of Moses, the Prophets and the Psalms."

⁴⁵Then he opened their minds so they could understand the Scriptures. ⁴⁶He told them, "This is what is written: The Messiah will suffer and rise from the dead on the third day, ⁴⁷and repentance for the forgiveness of sins will be preached in his name to all nations, beginning at Jerusalem. ⁴⁸You are witnesses of these things. ⁴⁹I am going to send you what my Father has promised; but stay in the city until you have been clothed with power from on high."

⁵⁰When he had led them out to the vicinity of Bethany, he lifted up his hands and blessed them. ⁵¹While he was blessing them, he left them and was taken up into heaven. ⁵²Then they worshiped him and returned to Jerusalem with great joy. ⁵³And they stayed continually at the temple, praising God.

JOHN

John closes his book by revealing his purpose in writing Jesus' story: *These are written that you may believe that Jesus is the Messiah, the Son of God, and that by believing you may have life in his name.*

John begins his book by echoing words from the Bible's creation story—*In the beginning*—showing his readers that this is a story of a new creation. Just as the first creation was completed in seven days, John uses the number seven to structure his book. For the Jews the number seven represented completeness and wholeness, a finished work of God revealing his purpose for the world.

The story is told in two main parts. The first describes Jesus' public ministry and has seven sections. Each section closes with a report on how people respond to Jesus, either in faith or unbelief. The second part is devoted to the Passover weekend, when Jesus gave his life for the world.

John records seven instances in which Jesus revealed his identity by using the phrase *I am*, the name by which God had revealed himself earlier. Similarly, John records seven miraculous signs that Jesus performed. John's narrative mentions twice that the resurrection of Jesus took place on the *first day of the week*. In this way he confirms that the power of a new creation has broken into our world.

---

1 In the beginning was the Word, and the Word was with God, and the Word was God. ²He was with God in the beginning. ³Through him all things were made; without him nothing was made that has been made. ⁴In him was life, and that life was the light of all mankind. ⁵The light shines in the darkness, and the darkness has not overcome[a] it.

⁶There was a man sent from God whose name was John. ⁷He came as a witness to testify concerning that light, so that through him all might believe. ⁸He himself was not the light; he came only as a witness to the light.

⁹The true light that gives light to everyone was coming into the world. ¹⁰He was in the world, and though the world was made through him, the world did not recognize him. ¹¹He came to that which was his own, but his own did not receive him. ¹²Yet to all who did receive him, to those who believed in his name, he gave the right to become children of God— ¹³children born not of natural descent, nor of human decision or a husband's will, but born of God.

¹⁴The Word became flesh and made his dwelling among us. We have seen his glory, the glory of the one and only Son, who came from the Father, full of grace and truth.

¹⁵(John testified concerning him. He cried out, saying, "This is the one I spoke about when I said, 'He who comes after me has surpassed me because he was before me.'") ¹⁶Out of his fullness we have all received grace in place of grace already given. ¹⁷For the law was given through Moses; grace and

a 5 Or understood

truth came through Jesus Christ. [18]No one has ever seen God, but the one and only Son, who is himself God and[a] is in closest relationship with the Father, has made him known.

[19]Now this was John's testimony when the Jewish leaders[b] in Jerusalem sent priests and Levites to ask him who he was. [20]He did not fail to confess, but confessed freely, "I am not the Messiah."

[21]They asked him, "Then who are you? Are you Elijah?"

He said, "I am not."

"Are you the Prophet?"

He answered, "No."

[22]Finally they said, "Who are you? Give us an answer to take back to those who sent us. What do you say about yourself?"

[23]John replied in the words of Isaiah the prophet, "I am the voice of one calling in the wilderness, 'Make straight the way for the Lord.'"[c]

[24]Now the Pharisees who had been sent [25]questioned him, "Why then do you baptize if you are not the Messiah, nor Elijah, nor the Prophet?"

[26]"I baptize with[d] water," John replied, "but among you stands one you do not know. [27]He is the one who comes after me, the straps of whose sandals I am not worthy to untie."

[28]This all happened at Bethany on the other side of the Jordan, where John was baptizing.

[29]The next day John saw Jesus coming toward him and said, "Look, the Lamb of God, who takes away the sin of the world! [30]This is the one I meant when I said, 'A man who comes after me has surpassed me because he was before me.' [31]I myself did not know him, but the reason I came baptizing with water was that he might be revealed to Israel."

[32]Then John gave this testimony: "I saw the Spirit come down from heaven as a dove and remain on him. [33]And I myself did not know him, but the one who sent me to baptize with water told me, 'The man on whom you see the Spirit come down and remain is the one who will baptize with the Holy Spirit.' [34]I have seen and I testify that this is God's Chosen One."[e]

[35]The next day John was there again with two of his disciples. [36]When he saw Jesus passing by, he said, "Look, the Lamb of God!"

[37]When the two disciples heard him say this, they followed Jesus. [38]Turning around, Jesus saw them following and asked, "What do you want?"

They said, "Rabbi" (which means "Teacher"), "where are you staying?"

[39]"Come," he replied, "and you will see."

So they went and saw where he was staying, and they spent that day with him. It was about four in the afternoon.

[40]Andrew, Simon Peter's brother, was one of the two who heard what John had said and who had followed Jesus. [41]The first thing Andrew did was to find his brother Simon and tell him, "We have found the Mes-

---

a 18 Some manuscripts *but the only Son, who* b 19 The Greek term traditionally translated *the Jews* (*hoi Ioudaioi*) refers here and elsewhere in John's Gospel to those Jewish leaders who opposed Jesus; also in 5:10, 15, 16; 7:1, 11, 13; 9:22; 18:14, 28, 36; 19:7, 12, 31, 38; 20:19. c 23 Isaiah 40:3 d 26 Or *in*; also in verses 31 and 33 (twice) e 34 See Isaiah 42:1; many manuscripts *is the Son of God.*

siah" (that is, the Christ). ⁴²And he brought him to Jesus.

Jesus looked at him and said, "You are Simon son of John. You will be called Cephas" (which, when translated, is Peterᵃ).

⁴³The next day Jesus decided to leave for Galilee. Finding Philip, he said to him, "Follow me."

⁴⁴Philip, like Andrew and Peter, was from the town of Bethsaida. ⁴⁵Philip found Nathanael and told him, "We have found the one Moses wrote about in the Law, and about whom the prophets also wrote—Jesus of Nazareth, the son of Joseph."

⁴⁶"Nazareth! Can anything good come from there?" Nathanael asked.

"Come and see," said Philip.

⁴⁷When Jesus saw Nathanael approaching, he said of him, "Here truly is an Israelite in whom there is no deceit."

⁴⁸"How do you know me?" Nathanael asked.

Jesus answered, "I saw you while you were still under the fig tree before Philip called you."

⁴⁹Then Nathanael declared, "Rabbi, you are the Son of God; you are the king of Israel."

⁵⁰Jesus said, "You believeᵇ because I told you I saw you under the fig tree. You will see greater things than that." ⁵¹He then added, "Very truly I tell you,ᶜ youᶜ will see 'heaven open, and the angels of God ascending and descending on'ᵈ the Son of Man."

2 On the third day a wedding took place at Cana in Galilee. Jesus' mother was there, ²and Jesus and his disciples had also been invited to the wedding. ³When the wine was gone, Jesus' mother said to him, "They have no more wine."

⁴"Woman,ᵉ why do you involve me?" Jesus replied. "My hour has not yet come."

⁵His mother said to the servants, "Do whatever he tells you."

⁶Nearby stood six stone water jars, the kind used by the Jews for ceremonial washing, each holding from twenty to thirty gallons.ᶠ

⁷Jesus said to the servants, "Fill the jars with water"; so they filled them to the brim.

⁸Then he told them, "Now draw some out and take it to the master of the banquet."

They did so, ⁹and the master of the banquet tasted the water that had been turned into wine. He did not realize where it had come from, though the servants who had drawn the water knew. Then he called the bridegroom aside ¹⁰and said, "Everyone brings out the choice wine first and then the cheaper wine after the guests have had too much to drink; but you have saved the best till now."

¹¹What Jesus did here in Cana of Galilee was the first of the signs through which he revealed his glory; and his disciples believed in him.

¹²After this he went down to Capernaum with his mother and brothers and his disciples. There they stayed for a few days.

¹³When it was almost time for the Jewish Passover, Jesus went up to Jerusalem. ¹⁴In the temple courts he found people selling cattle, sheep and doves, and others sitting

ᵃ 42 *Cephas* (Aramaic) and *Peter* (Greek) both mean *rock*.   ᵇ 50 Or *Do you believe...?*   ᶜ 51 The Greek is plural.   ᵈ 51 Gen. 28:12   ᵉ 4 The Greek for *Woman* does not denote any disrespect.   ᶠ 6 Or *from about 75 to about 115 liters*

at tables exchanging money. 15So he made a whip out of cords, and drove all from the temple courts, both sheep and cattle; he scattered the coins of the money changers and overturned their tables. 16To those who sold doves he said, "Get these out of here! Stop turning my Father's house into a market!" 17His disciples remembered that it is written: "Zeal for your house will consume me."[a]

18The Jews then responded to him, "What sign can you show us to prove your authority to do all this?"

19Jesus answered them, "Destroy this temple, and I will raise it again in three days."

20They replied, "It has taken forty-six years to build this temple, and you are going to raise it in three days?" 21But the temple he had spoken of was his body. 22After he was raised from the dead, his disciples recalled what he had said. Then they believed the scripture and the words that Jesus had spoken.

23Now while he was in Jerusalem at the Passover Festival, many people saw the signs he was performing and believed in his name.[b] 24But Jesus would not entrust himself to them, for he knew all people. 25He did not need any testimony about mankind, for he knew what was in each person.

3 Now there was a Pharisee, a man named Nicodemus who was a member of the Jewish ruling council. 2He came to Jesus at night and said, "Rabbi, we know that you are a teacher who has come from God. For no one could perform the signs you are doing if God were not with him."

3Jesus replied, "Very truly I tell you, no one can see the kingdom of God unless they are born again.[c]"

4"How can someone be born when they are old?" Nicodemus asked. "Surely they cannot enter a second time into their mother's womb to be born!"

5Jesus answered, "Very truly I tell you, no one can enter the kingdom of God unless they are born of water and the Spirit. 6Flesh gives birth to flesh, but the Spirit[d] gives birth to spirit. 7You should not be surprised at my saying, 'You[e] must be born again.' 8The wind blows wherever it pleases. You hear its sound, but you cannot tell where it comes from or where it is going. So it is with everyone born of the Spirit."[f]

9"How can this be?" Nicodemus asked.

10"You are Israel's teacher," said Jesus, "and do you not understand these things? 11Very truly I tell you, we speak of what we know, and we testify to what we have seen, but still you people do not accept our testimony. 12I have spoken to you of earthly things and you do not believe; how then will you believe if I speak of heavenly things? 13No one has ever gone into heaven except the one who came from heaven—the Son of Man.[g] 14Just as Moses lifted up the snake in the wilderness, so the Son of Man must be lifted up,[h] 15that everyone who believes may have eternal life in him."[i]

16For God so loved the world that he gave his one and only Son, that whoever believes in him shall not perish but have eternal life. 17For God did not send his Son into the world

---

[a] 17 Psalm 69:9   [b] 23 Or *in him*   [c] 3 The Greek for *again* also means *from above*; also in verse 7.   [d] 6 Or *but spirit*   [e] 7 The Greek is plural.   [f] 8 The Greek for *Spirit* is the same as that for *wind*.   [g] 13 Some manuscripts *Man, who is in heaven*   [h] 14 The Greek for *lifted up* also means *exalted*.   [i] 15 Some interpreters end the quotation with verse 21.

to condemn the world, but to save the world through him. [18]Whoever believes in him is not condemned, but whoever does not believe stands condemned already because they have not believed in the name of God's one and only Son. [19]This is the verdict: Light has come into the world, but people loved darkness instead of light because their deeds were evil. [20]Everyone who does evil hates the light, and will not come into the light for fear that their deeds will be exposed. [21]But whoever lives by the truth comes into the light, so that it may be seen plainly that what they have done has been done in the sight of God.

[22]After this, Jesus and his disciples went out into the Judean countryside, where he spent some time with them, and baptized. [23]Now John also was baptizing at Aenon near Salim, because there was plenty of water, and people were coming and being baptized. [24](This was before John was put in prison.) [25]An argument developed between some of John's disciples and a certain Jew over the matter of ceremonial washing. [26]They came to John and said to him, "Rabbi, that man who was with you on the other side of the Jordan—the one you testified about—look, he is baptizing, and everyone is going to him."

[27]To this John replied, "A person can receive only what is given them from heaven. [28]You yourselves can testify that I said, 'I am not the Messiah but am sent ahead of him.' [29]The bride belongs to the bridegroom. The friend who attends the bridegroom waits and listens for him, and is full of joy when he hears the bridegroom's voice. That joy is mine, and it is now complete. [30]He must become greater; I must become less."[a]

[31]The one who comes from above is above all; the one who is from the earth belongs to the earth, and speaks as one from the earth. The one who comes from heaven is above all. [32]He testifies to what he has seen and heard, but no one accepts his testimony. [33]Whoever has accepted it has certified that God is truthful. [34]For the one whom God has sent speaks the words of God, for God[b] gives the Spirit without limit. [35]The Father loves the Son and has placed everything in his hands. [36]Whoever believes in the Son has eternal life, but whoever rejects the Son will not see life, for God's wrath remains on them.

4 Now Jesus learned that the Pharisees had heard that he was gaining and baptizing more disciples than John— [2]although in fact it was not Jesus who baptized, but his disciples. [3]So he left Judea and went back once more to Galilee. [4]Now he had to go through Samaria. [5]So he came to a town in Samaria called Sychar, near the plot of ground Jacob had given to his son Joseph. [6]Jacob's well was there, and Jesus, tired as he was from the journey, sat down by the well. It was about noon.

[7]When a Samaritan woman came to draw water, Jesus said to her, "Will you give me a drink?" [8](His disciples had gone into the town to buy food.)

[9]The Samaritan woman said to him, "You are a Jew and I am a Samaritan woman. How can you ask me for a drink?" (For Jews do not associate with Samaritans.[c])

---

[a] 30 Some interpreters end the quotation with verse 36.   [b] 34 Greek he   [c] 9 Or do not use dishes Samaritans have used

¹⁰Jesus answered her, "If you knew the gift of God and who it is that asks you for a drink, you would have asked him and he would have given you living water."

¹¹"Sir," the woman said, "you have nothing to draw with and the well is deep. Where can you get this living water? ¹²Are you greater than our father Jacob, who gave us the well and drank from it himself, as did also his sons and his livestock?"

¹³Jesus answered, "Everyone who drinks this water will be thirsty again, ¹⁴but whoever drinks the water I give them will never thirst. Indeed, the water I give them will become in them a spring of water welling up to eternal life."

¹⁵The woman said to him, "Sir, give me this water so that I won't get thirsty and have to keep coming here to draw water."

¹⁶He told her, "Go, call your husband and come back."

¹⁷"I have no husband," she replied.

Jesus said to her, "You are right when you say you have no husband. ¹⁸The fact is, you have had five husbands, and the man you now have is not your husband. What you have just said is quite true."

¹⁹"Sir," the woman said, "I can see that you are a prophet. ²⁰Our ancestors worshiped on this mountain, but you Jews claim that the place where we must worship is in Jerusalem."

²¹"Woman," Jesus replied, "believe me, a time is coming when you will worship the Father neither on this mountain nor in Jerusalem. ²²You Samaritans worship what you do not know; we worship what we do know, for salvation is from the Jews. ²³Yet a time is coming and has now come when the true wor-

shipers will worship the Father in the Spirit and in truth, for they are the kind of worshipers the Father seeks. ²⁴God is spirit, and his worshipers must worship in the Spirit and in truth."

²⁵The woman said, "I know that Messiah" (called Christ) "is coming. When he comes, he will explain everything to us."

²⁶Then Jesus declared, "I, the one speaking to you — I am he."

²⁷Just then his disciples returned and were surprised to find him talking with a woman. But no one asked, "What do you want?" or "Why are you talking with her?"

²⁸Then, leaving her water jar, the woman went back to the town and said to the people, ²⁹"Come, see a man who told me everything I ever did. Could this be the Messiah?" ³⁰They came out of the town and made their way toward him.

³¹Meanwhile his disciples urged him, "Rabbi, eat something."

³²But he said to them, "I have food to eat that you know nothing about."

³³Then his disciples said to each other, "Could someone have brought him food?"

³⁴"My food," said Jesus, "is to do the will of him who sent me and to finish his work. ³⁵Don't you have a saying, 'It's still four months until harvest'? I tell you, open your eyes and look at the fields! They are ripe for harvest. ³⁶Even now the one who reaps draws a wage and harvests a crop for eternal life, so that the sower and the reaper may be glad together. ³⁷Thus the saying 'One sows and another reaps' is true. ³⁸I sent you to reap what you have not worked for. Others have done the hard work, and you have reaped the benefits of their labor."

³⁹Many of the Samaritans from that town believed in him because of the woman's testimony, "He told me everything I ever did." ⁴⁰So when the Samaritans came to him, they urged him to stay with them, and he stayed two days. ⁴¹And because of his words many more became believers.

⁴²They said to the woman, "We no longer believe just because of what you said; now we have heard for ourselves, and we know that this man really is the Savior of the world."

⁴³After the two days he left for Galilee. ⁴⁴(Now Jesus himself had pointed out that a prophet has no honor in his own country.) ⁴⁵When he arrived in Galilee, the Galileans welcomed him. They had seen all that he had done in Jerusalem at the Passover Festival, for they also had been there.

⁴⁶Once more he visited Cana in Galilee, where he had turned the water into wine. And there was a certain royal official whose son lay sick at Capernaum. ⁴⁷When this man heard that Jesus had arrived in Galilee from Judea, he went to him and begged him to come and heal his son, who was close to death.

⁴⁸"Unless you people see signs and wonders," Jesus told him, "you will never believe."

⁴⁹The royal official said, "Sir, come down before my child dies."

⁵⁰"Go," Jesus replied, "your son will live."

The man took Jesus at his word and departed. ⁵¹While he was still on the way, his servants met him with the news that his boy was living. ⁵²When he inquired as to the time when his son got better, they said to him, "Yesterday, at one in the afternoon, the fever left him."

⁵³Then the father realized that this was the exact time at which Jesus had said to him, "Your son will live." So he and his whole household believed.

⁵⁴This was the second sign Jesus performed after coming from Judea to Galilee.

5 Some time later, Jesus went up to Jerusalem for one of the Jewish festivals. ²Now there is in Jerusalem near the Sheep Gate a pool, which in Aramaic is called Bethesda[a] and which is surrounded by five covered colonnades. ³Here a great number of disabled people used to lie—the blind, the lame, the paralyzed. [4] [b] ⁵One who was there had been an invalid for thirty-eight years. ⁶When Jesus saw him lying there and learned that he had been in this condition for a long time, he asked him, "Do you want to get well?"

⁷"Sir," the invalid replied, "I have no one to help me into the pool when the water is stirred. While I am trying to get in, someone else goes down ahead of me."

⁸Then Jesus said to him, "Get up! Pick up your mat and walk." ⁹At once the man was cured; he picked up his mat and walked.

The day on which this took place was a Sabbath, ¹⁰and so the Jewish leaders said to the man who had been healed, "It is the Sabbath; the law forbids you to carry your mat."

¹¹But he replied, "The man who

---

a 2 Some manuscripts *Bethzatha*; other manuscripts *Bethsaida*   *b* 3,4 Some manuscripts include here, wholly or in part, *paralyzed—and they waited for the moving of the waters.* *⁴From time to time an angel of the Lord would come down and stir up the waters. The first one into the pool after each such disturbance would be cured of whatever disease they had.*

made me well said to me, 'Pick up your mat and walk.'"

¹²So they asked him, "Who is this fellow who told you to pick it up and walk?"

¹³The man who was healed had no idea who it was, for Jesus had slipped away into the crowd that was there.

¹⁴Later Jesus found him at the temple and said to him, "See, you are well again. Stop sinning or something worse may happen to you." ¹⁵The man went away and told the Jewish leaders that it was Jesus who had made him well.

¹⁶So, because Jesus was doing these things on the Sabbath, the Jewish leaders began to persecute him. ¹⁷In his defense Jesus said to them, "My Father is always at his work to this very day, and I too am working." ¹⁸For this reason they tried all the more to kill him; not only was he breaking the Sabbath, but he was even calling God his own Father, making himself equal with God.

¹⁹Jesus gave them this answer: "Very truly I tell you, the Son can do nothing by himself; he can do only what he sees his Father doing, because whatever the Father does the Son also does. ²⁰For the Father loves the Son and shows him all he does. Yes, and he will show him even greater works than these, so that you will be amazed. ²¹For just as the Father raises the dead and gives them life, even so the Son gives life to whom he is pleased to give it. ²²Moreover, the Father judges no one, but has entrusted all judgment to the Son, ²³that all may honor the Son just as they honor the Father. Whoever does not honor the Son does not honor the Father, who sent him.

²⁴"Very truly I tell you, whoever hears my word and believes him who sent me has eternal life and will not be judged but has crossed over from death to life. ²⁵Very truly I tell you, a time is coming and has now come when the dead will hear the voice of the Son of God and those who hear will live. ²⁶For as the Father has life in himself, so he has granted the Son also to have life in himself. ²⁷And he has given him authority to judge because he is the Son of Man.

²⁸"Do not be amazed at this, for a time is coming when all who are in their graves will hear his voice ²⁹and come out—those who have done what is good will rise to live, and those who have done what is evil will rise to be condemned. ³⁰By myself I can do nothing; I judge only as I hear, and my judgment is just, for I seek not to please myself but him who sent me.

³¹"If I testify about myself, my testimony is not true. ³²There is another who testifies in my favor, and I know that his testimony about me is true.

³³"You have sent to John and he has testified to the truth. ³⁴Not that I accept human testimony; but I mention it that you may be saved. ³⁵John was a lamp that burned and gave light, and you chose for a time to enjoy his light.

³⁶"I have testimony weightier than that of John. For the works that the Father has given me to finish—the very works that I am doing—testify that the Father has sent me. ³⁷And the Father who sent me has himself testified concerning me. You have never heard his voice nor seen his form, ³⁸nor does his word dwell in you, for you do not believe the one he sent. ³⁹You

study[a] the Scriptures diligently because you think that in them you have eternal life. These are the very Scriptures that testify about me, 40 yet you refuse to come to me to have life.

41 "I do not accept glory from human beings, 42 but I know you. I know that you do not have the love of God in your hearts. 43 I have come in my Father's name, and you do not accept me; but if someone else comes in his own name, you will accept him. 44 How can you believe since you accept glory from one another but do not seek the glory that comes from the only God[b]?

45 "But do not think I will accuse you before the Father. Your accuser is Moses, on whom your hopes are set. 46 If you believed Moses, you would believe me, for he wrote about me. 47 But since you do not believe what he wrote, how are you going to believe what I say?"

6 Some time after this, Jesus crossed to the far shore of the Sea of Galilee (that is, the Sea of Tiberias), 2 and a great crowd of people followed him because they saw the signs he had performed by healing the sick. 3 Then Jesus went up on a mountainside and sat down with his disciples. 4 The Jewish Passover Festival was near.

5 When Jesus looked up and saw a great crowd coming toward him, he said to Philip, "Where shall we buy bread for these people to eat?" 6 He asked this only to test him, for he already had in mind what he was going to do.

7 Philip answered him, "It would take more than half a year's wages[c]

to buy enough bread for each one to have a bite!"

8 Another of his disciples, Andrew, Simon Peter's brother, spoke up, 9 "Here is a boy with five small barley loaves and two small fish, but how far will they go among so many?"

10 Jesus said, "Have the people sit down." There was plenty of grass in that place, and they sat down (about five thousand men were there). 11 Jesus then took the loaves, gave thanks, and distributed to those who were seated as much as they wanted. He did the same with the fish.

12 When they had all had enough to eat, he said to his disciples, "Gather the pieces that are left over. Let nothing be wasted." 13 So they gathered them and filled twelve baskets with the pieces of the five barley loaves left over by those who had eaten.

14 After the people saw the sign Jesus performed, they began to say, "Surely this is the Prophet who is to come into the world." 15 Jesus, knowing that they intended to come and make him king by force, withdrew again to a mountain by himself.

16 When evening came, his disciples went down to the lake, 17 where they got into a boat and set off across the lake for Capernaum. By now it was dark, and Jesus had not yet joined them. 18 A strong wind was blowing and the waters grew rough. 19 When they had rowed about three or four miles,[d] they saw Jesus approaching the boat, walking on the water; and they were frightened. 20 But he said to them, "It is I; don't be afraid." 21 Then

a 39 Or 39 Study   b 44 Some early manuscripts the Only One   c 7 Greek take two hundred denarii   d 19 Or about 5 or 6 kilometers

they were willing to take him into the boat, and immediately the boat reached the shore where they were heading.

²²The next day the crowd that had stayed on the opposite shore of the lake realized that only one boat had been there, and that Jesus had not entered it with his disciples, but that they had gone away alone. ²³Then some boats from Tiberias landed near the place where the people had eaten the bread after the Lord had given thanks. ²⁴Once the crowd realized that neither Jesus nor his disciples were there, they got into the boats and went to Capernaum in search of Jesus.

²⁵When they found him on the other side of the lake, they asked him, "Rabbi, when did you get here?"

²⁶Jesus answered, "Very truly I tell you, you are looking for me, not because you saw the signs I performed but because you ate the loaves and had your fill. ²⁷Do not work for food that spoils, but for food that endures to eternal life, which the Son of Man will give you. For on him God the Father has placed his seal of approval."

²⁸Then they asked him, "What must we do to do the works God requires?"

²⁹Jesus answered, "The work of God is this: to believe in the one he has sent."

³⁰So they asked him, "What sign then will you give that we may see it and believe you? What will you do? ³¹Our ancestors ate the manna in the wilderness; as it is written: 'He gave them bread from heaven to eat.'ᵃ"

³²Jesus said to them, "Very truly I tell you, it is not Moses who has given you the bread from heaven, but it is my Father who gives you the true bread from heaven. ³³For the bread of God is the bread that comes down from heaven and gives life to the world."

³⁴"Sir," they said, "always give us this bread."

³⁵Then Jesus declared, "I am the bread of life. Whoever comes to me will never go hungry, and whoever believes in me will never be thirsty. ³⁶But as I told you, you have seen me and still you do not believe. ³⁷All those the Father gives me will come to me, and whoever comes to me I will never drive away. ³⁸For I have come down from heaven not to do my will but to do the will of him who sent me. ³⁹And this is the will of him who sent me, that I shall lose none of all those he has given me, but raise them up at the last day. ⁴⁰For my Father's will is that everyone who looks to the Son and believes in him shall have eternal life, and I will raise them up at the last day."

⁴¹At this the Jews there began to grumble about him because he said, "I am the bread that came down from heaven." ⁴²They said, "Is this not Jesus, the son of Joseph, whose father and mother we know? How can he now say, 'I came down from heaven'?"

⁴³"Stop grumbling among yourselves," Jesus answered. ⁴⁴"No one can come to me unless the Father who sent me draws them, and I will raise them up at the last day. ⁴⁵It is written in the Prophets: 'They will all be taught by God.'ᵇ Everyone who has heard the Father and learned from him comes to me. ⁴⁶No one has seen the Father except the one who is from God; only he has seen the Father. ⁴⁷Very truly

ᵃ 31 Exodus 16:4; Neh. 9:15; Psalm 78:24,25   ᵇ 45 Isaiah 54:13

I tell you, the one who believes has eternal life. ⁴⁸I am the bread of life. ⁴⁹Your ancestors ate the manna in the wilderness, yet they died. ⁵⁰But here is the bread that comes down from heaven, which anyone may eat and not die. ⁵¹I am the living bread that came down from heaven. Whoever eats this bread will live forever. This bread is my flesh, which I will give for the life of the world."

⁵²Then the Jews began to argue sharply among themselves, "How can this man give us his flesh to eat?"

⁵³Jesus said to them, "Very truly I tell you, unless you eat the flesh of the Son of Man and drink his blood, you have no life in you. ⁵⁴Whoever eats my flesh and drinks my blood has eternal life, and I will raise them up at the last day. ⁵⁵For my flesh is real food and my blood is real drink. ⁵⁶Whoever eats my flesh and drinks my blood remains in me, and I in them. ⁵⁷Just as the living Father sent me and I live because of the Father, so the one who feeds on me will live because of me. ⁵⁸This is the bread that came down from heaven. Your ancestors ate manna and died, but whoever feeds on this bread will live forever." ⁵⁹He said this while teaching in the synagogue in Capernaum.

⁶⁰On hearing it, many of his disciples said, "This is a hard teaching. Who can accept it?"

⁶¹Aware that his disciples were grumbling about this, Jesus said to them, "Does this offend you? ⁶²Then what if you see the Son of Man ascend to where he was before! ⁶³The Spirit gives life; the flesh counts for nothing. The words I have spoken to you—they are full of the Spirit[a]

and life. ⁶⁴Yet there are some of you who do not believe." For Jesus had known from the beginning which of them did not believe and who would betray him. ⁶⁵He went on to say, "This is why I told you that no one can come to me unless the Father has enabled them."

⁶⁶From this time many of his disciples turned back and no longer followed him.

⁶⁷"You do not want to leave too, do you?" Jesus asked the Twelve.

⁶⁸Simon Peter answered him, "Lord, to whom shall we go? You have the words of eternal life. ⁶⁹We have come to believe and to know that you are the Holy One of God."

⁷⁰Then Jesus replied, "Have I not chosen you, the Twelve? Yet one of you is a devil!" ⁷¹(He meant Judas, the son of Simon Iscariot, who, though one of the Twelve, was later to betray him.)

7 After this, Jesus went around in Galilee. He did not want[b] to go about in Judea because the Jewish leaders there were looking for a way to kill him. ²But when the Jewish Festival of Tabernacles was near, ³Jesus' brothers said to him, "Leave Galilee and go to Judea, so that your disciples there may see the works you do. ⁴No one who wants to become a public figure acts in secret. Since you are doing these things, show yourself to the world." ⁵For even his own brothers did not believe in him.

⁶Therefore Jesus told them, "My time is not yet here; for you any time will do. ⁷The world cannot hate you, but it hates me because I testify that its works are evil. ⁸You go to the festival. I am not[c] going up to this fes-

---

[a] 63 Or *are Spirit*; or *are spirit*   [b] 1 Some manuscripts *not have authority*   [c] 8 Some manuscripts *not yet*

tival, because my time has not yet fully come." ⁹After he had said this, he stayed in Galilee.

¹⁰However, after his brothers had left for the festival, he went also, not publicly, but in secret. ¹¹Now at the festival the Jewish leaders were watching for Jesus and asking, "Where is he?"

¹²Among the crowds there was widespread whispering about him. Some said, "He is a good man."

Others replied, "No, he deceives the people." ¹³But no one would say anything publicly about him for fear of the leaders.

¹⁴Not until halfway through the festival did Jesus go up to the temple courts and begin to teach. ¹⁵The Jews there were amazed and asked, "How did this man get such learning without having been taught?"

¹⁶Jesus answered, "My teaching is not my own. It comes from the one who sent me. ¹⁷Anyone who chooses to do the will of God will find out whether my teaching comes from God or whether I speak on my own. ¹⁸Whoever speaks on their own does so to gain personal glory, but he who seeks the glory of the one who sent him is a man of truth; there is nothing false about him. ¹⁹Has not Moses given you the law? Yet not one of you keeps the law. Why are you trying to kill me?"

²⁰"You are demon-possessed," the crowd answered. "Who is trying to kill you?"

²¹Jesus said to them, "I did one miracle, and you are all amazed. ²²Yet, because Moses gave you circumcision (though actually it did not come from Moses, but from the patriarchs), you circumcise a boy on the Sabbath. ²³Now if a boy can be circumcised on the Sabbath so that the law of Moses may not be broken, why are you angry with me for healing a man's whole body on the Sabbath? ²⁴Stop judging by mere appearances, but instead judge correctly."

²⁵At that point some of the people of Jerusalem began to ask, "Isn't this the man they are trying to kill? ²⁶Here he is, speaking publicly, and they are not saying a word to him. Have the authorities really concluded that he is the Messiah? ²⁷But we know where this man is from; when the Messiah comes, no one will know where he is from."

²⁸Then Jesus, still teaching in the temple courts, cried out, "Yes, you know me, and you know where I am from. I am not here on my own authority, but he who sent me is true. You do not know him, ²⁹but I know him because I am from him and he sent me."

³⁰At this they tried to seize him, but no one laid a hand on him, because his hour had not yet come. ³¹Still, many in the crowd believed in him. They said, "When the Messiah comes, will he perform more signs than this man?"

³²The Pharisees heard the crowd whispering such things about him. Then the chief priests and the Pharisees sent temple guards to arrest him.

³³Jesus said, "I am with you for only a short time, and then I am going to the one who sent me. ³⁴You will look for me, but you will not find me; and where I am, you cannot come."

³⁵The Jews said to one another, "Where does this man intend to go that we cannot find him? Will he go where our people live scattered among the Greeks, and teach the Greeks? ³⁶What did he mean when he said, 'You will look for me, but

you will not find me,' and 'Where I am, you cannot come'?"

37 On the last and greatest day of the festival, Jesus stood and said in a loud voice, "Let anyone who is thirsty come to me and drink. 38 Whoever believes in me, as Scripture has said, rivers of living water will flow from within them."*a* 39 By this he meant the Spirit, whom those who believed in him were later to receive. Up to that time the Spirit had not been given, since Jesus had not yet been glorified.

40 On hearing his words, some of the people said, "Surely this man is the Prophet."

41 Others said, "He is the Messiah."

Still others asked, "How can the Messiah come from Galilee? 42 Does not Scripture say that the Messiah will come from David's descendants and from Bethlehem, the town where David lived?" 43 Thus the people were divided because of Jesus. 44 Some wanted to seize him, but no one laid a hand on him.

45 Finally the temple guards went back to the chief priests and the Pharisees, who asked them, "Why didn't you bring him in?"

46 "No one ever spoke the way this man does," the guards replied.

47 "You mean he has deceived you also?" the Pharisees retorted. 48 "Have any of the rulers or of the Pharisees believed in him? 49 No! But this mob that knows nothing of the law—there is a curse on them."

50 Nicodemus, who had gone to Jesus earlier and who was one of their own number, asked, 51 "Does our law condemn a man without first hearing him to find out what he has been doing?"

52 They replied, "Are you from Galilee, too? Look into it, and you will find that a prophet does not come out of Galilee."

[The earliest manuscripts and many other ancient witnesses do not have John 7:53 — 8:11. A few manuscripts include these verses, wholly or in part, after John 7:36, John 21:25, Luke 21:38 or Luke 24:53.]

8 53 *Then they all went home, 1 but Jesus went to the Mount of Olives.*

2 *At dawn he appeared again in the temple courts, where all the people gathered around him, and he sat down to teach them. 3 The teachers of the law and the Pharisees brought in a woman caught in adultery. They made her stand before the group 4 and said to Jesus, "Teacher, this woman was caught in the act of adultery. 5 In the Law Moses commanded us to stone such women. Now what do you say?" 6 They were using this question as a trap, in order to have a basis for accusing him.*

But Jesus bent down and started to write on the ground with his finger. 7 When they kept on questioning him, he straightened up and said to them, "Let any one of you who is without sin be the first to throw a stone at her." 8 Again he stooped down and wrote on the ground.

9 *At this, those who heard began to go away one at a time, the older ones first, until only Jesus was left, with the woman still standing there. 10 Jesus straightened up and asked her, "Woman, where are they? Has no one condemned you?"*

11 *"No one, sir," she said.*

"Then neither do I condemn you," Jesus declared. "Go now and leave your life of sin."

---

a 37,38 Or me. And let anyone drink 38who believes in me." As Scripture has said, "Out of him (or them) will flow rivers of living water."

¹²When Jesus spoke again to the people, he said, "I am the light of the world. Whoever follows me will never walk in darkness, but will have the light of life."

¹³The Pharisees challenged him, "Here you are, appearing as your own witness; your testimony is not valid."

¹⁴Jesus answered, "Even if I testify on my own behalf, my testimony is valid, for I know where I came from and where I am going. But you have no idea where I come from or where I am going. ¹⁵You judge by human standards; I pass judgment on no one. ¹⁶But if I do judge, my decisions are true, because I am not alone. I stand with the Father, who sent me. ¹⁷In your own Law it is written that the testimony of two witnesses is true. ¹⁸I am one who testifies for myself; my other witness is the Father, who sent me."

¹⁹Then they asked him, "Where is your father?"

"You do not know me or my Father," Jesus replied. "If you knew me, you would know my Father also." ²⁰He spoke these words while teaching in the temple courts near the place where the offerings were put. Yet no one seized him, because his hour had not yet come.

²¹Once more Jesus said to them, "I am going away, and you will look for me, and you will die in your sin. Where I go, you cannot come."

²²This made the Jews ask, "Will he kill himself? Is that why he says, 'Where I go, you cannot come'?"

²³But he continued, "You are from below; I am from above. You are of this world; I am not of this world. ²⁴I told you that you would die in your sins; if you do not believe

that I am he, you will indeed die in your sins."

²⁵"Who are you?" they asked.

"Just what I have been telling you from the beginning," Jesus replied. ²⁶"I have much to say in judgment of you. But he who sent me is trustworthy, and what I have heard from him I tell the world."

²⁷They did not understand that he was telling them about his Father. ²⁸So Jesus said, "When you have lifted up^a the Son of Man, then you will know that I am he and that I do nothing on my own but speak just what the Father has taught me. ²⁹The one who sent me is with me; he has not left me alone, for I always do what pleases him." ³⁰Even as he spoke, many believed in him.

³¹To the Jews who had believed him, Jesus said, "If you hold to my teaching, you are really my disciples. ³²Then you will know the truth, and the truth will set you free."

³³They answered him, "We are Abraham's descendants and have never been slaves of anyone. How can you say that we shall be set free?"

³⁴Jesus replied, "Very truly I tell you, everyone who sins is a slave to sin. ³⁵Now a slave has no permanent place in the family, but a son belongs to it forever. ³⁶So if the Son sets you free, you will be free indeed. ³⁷I know that you are Abraham's descendants. Yet you are looking for a way to kill me, because you have no room for my word. ³⁸I am telling you what I have seen in the Father's presence, and you are doing what you have heard from your father.^b"

^a 28 The Greek for lifted up also means exalted, heard from the Father.

^b 38 Or presence. Therefore do what you have

³⁹"Abraham is our father," they answered.

"If you were Abraham's children," said Jesus, "then you would^a do what Abraham did. ⁴⁰As it is, you are looking for a way to kill me, a man who has told you the truth that I heard from God. Abraham did not do such things. ⁴¹You are doing the works of your own father."

"We are not illegitimate children," they protested. "The only Father we have is God himself."

⁴²Jesus said to them, "If God were your Father, you would love me, for I have come here from God. I have not come on my own; God sent me. ⁴³Why is my language not clear to you? Because you are unable to hear what I say. ⁴⁴You belong to your father, the devil, and you want to carry out your father's desires. He was a murderer from the beginning, not holding to the truth, for there is no truth in him. When he lies, he speaks his native language, for he is a liar and the father of lies. ⁴⁵Yet because I tell the truth, you do not believe me! ⁴⁶Can any of you prove me guilty of sin? If I am telling the truth, why don't you believe me? ⁴⁷Whoever belongs to God hears what God says. The reason you do not hear is that you do not belong to God."

⁴⁸The Jews answered him, "Aren't we right in saying that you are a Samaritan and demon-possessed?"

⁴⁹"I am not possessed by a demon," said Jesus, "but I honor my Father and you dishonor me. ⁵⁰I am not seeking glory for myself; but there is one who seeks it, and he is the judge. ⁵¹Very truly I tell you, whoever obeys my word will never see death."

⁵²At this they exclaimed, "Now we know that you are demon-possessed! Abraham died and so did the prophets, yet you say that whoever obeys your word will never taste death. ⁵³Are you greater than our father Abraham? He died, and so did the prophets. Who do you think you are?"

⁵⁴Jesus replied, "If I glorify myself, my glory means nothing. My Father, whom you claim as your God, is the one who glorifies me. ⁵⁵Though you do not know him, I know him. If I said I did not, I would be a liar like you, but I do know him and obey his word. ⁵⁶Your father Abraham rejoiced at the thought of seeing my day; he saw it and was glad."

⁵⁷"You are not yet fifty years old," they said to him, "and you have seen Abraham!"

⁵⁸"Very truly I tell you," Jesus answered, "before Abraham was born, I am!" ⁵⁹At this, they picked up stones to stone him, but Jesus hid himself, slipping away from the temple grounds.

9 As he went along, he saw a man blind from birth. ²His disciples asked him, "Rabbi, who sinned, this man or his parents, that he was born blind?"

³"Neither this man nor his parents sinned," said Jesus, "but this happened so that the works of God might be displayed in him. ⁴As long as it is day, we must do the works of him who sent me. Night is coming, when no one can work. ⁵While I am in the world, I am the light of the world."

⁶After saying this, he spit on the ground, made some mud with the saliva, and put it on the man's eyes. ⁷"Go," he told him, "wash in the

^a 39 Some early manuscripts *"If you are Abraham's children," said Jesus, "then*

Pool of Siloam" (this word means "Sent"). So the man went and washed, and came home seeing.

⁸His neighbors and those who had formerly seen him begging asked, "Isn't this the same man who used to sit and beg?" ⁹Some claimed that he was.

Others said, "No, he only looks like him."

But he himself insisted, "I am the man."

¹⁰"How then were your eyes opened?" they asked.

¹¹He replied, "The man they call Jesus made some mud and put it on my eyes. He told me to go to Siloam and wash. So I went and washed, and then I could see."

¹²"Where is this man?" they asked him.

"I don't know," he said.

¹³They brought to the Pharisees the man who had been blind. ¹⁴Now the day on which Jesus had made the mud and opened the man's eyes was a Sabbath. ¹⁵Therefore the Pharisees also asked him how he had received his sight. "He put mud on my eyes," the man replied, "and I washed, and now I see."

¹⁶Some of the Pharisees said, "This man is not from God, for he does not keep the Sabbath."

But others asked, "How can a sinner perform such signs?" So they were divided.

¹⁷Then they turned again to the blind man, "What have you to say about him? It was your eyes he opened."

The man replied, "He is a prophet."

¹⁸They still did not believe that he had been blind and had received his sight until they sent for the man's parents. ¹⁹"Is this your son?" they asked. "Is this the one you say was born blind? How is it that now he can see?"

²⁰"We know he is our son," the parents answered, "and we know he was born blind. ²¹But how he can see now, or who opened his eyes, we don't know. Ask him. He is of age; he will speak for himself." ²²His parents said this because they were afraid of the Jewish leaders, who already had decided that anyone who acknowledged that Jesus was the Messiah would be put out of the synagogue. ²³That was why his parents said, "He is of age; ask him."

²⁴A second time they summoned the man who had been blind. "Give glory to God by telling the truth," they said. "We know this man is a sinner."

²⁵He replied, "Whether he is a sinner or not, I don't know. One thing I do know. I was blind but now I see!"

²⁶Then they asked him, "What did he do to you? How did he open your eyes?"

²⁷He answered, "I have told you already and you did not listen. Why do you want to hear it again? Do you want to become his disciples too?"

²⁸Then they hurled insults at him and said, "You are this fellow's disciple! We are disciples of Moses! ²⁹We know that God spoke to Moses, but as for this fellow, we don't even know where he comes from."

³⁰The man answered, "Now that is remarkable! You don't know where he comes from, yet he opened my eyes. ³¹We know that God does not listen to sinners. He listens to the godly person who does his will. ³²Nobody has ever heard of opening the eyes of a man born blind. ³³If this man were not from God, he could do nothing."

³⁴To this they replied, "You were

steeped in sin at birth; how dare you lecture us!" And they threw him out.

35 Jesus heard that they had thrown him out, and when he found him, he said, "Do you believe in the Son of Man?"

36 "Who is he, sir?" the man asked. "Tell me so that I may believe in him."

37 Jesus said, "You have now seen him; in fact, he is the one speaking with you."

38 Then the man said, "Lord, I believe," and he worshiped him.

39 Jesus said,[a] "For judgment I have come into this world, so that the blind will see and those who see will become blind."

40 Some Pharisees who were with him heard him say this and asked, "What? Are we blind too?"

41 Jesus said, "If you were blind, you would not be guilty of sin; but now that you claim you can see, your guilt remains.

10 "Very truly I tell you Pharisees, anyone who does not enter the sheep pen by the gate, but climbs in by some other way, is a thief and a robber. 2 The one who enters by the gate is the shepherd of the sheep. 3 The gatekeeper opens the gate for him, and the sheep listen to his voice. He calls his own sheep by name and leads them out. 4 When he has brought out all his own, he goes on ahead of them, and his sheep follow him because they know his voice. 5 But they will never follow a stranger; in fact, they will run away from him because they do not recognize a stranger's voice." 6 Jesus used this figure of speech, but the Pharisees did not understand what he was telling them.

7 Therefore Jesus said again, "Very truly I tell you, I am the gate for the sheep. 8 All who have come before me are thieves and robbers, but the sheep have not listened to them. 9 I am the gate; whoever enters through me will be saved.[b] They will come in and go out, and find pasture. 10 The thief comes only to steal and kill and destroy; I have come that they may have life, and have it to the full.

11 "I am the good shepherd. The good shepherd lays down his life for the sheep. 12 The hired hand is not the shepherd and does not own the sheep. So when he sees the wolf coming, he abandons the sheep and runs away. Then the wolf attacks the flock and scatters it. 13 The man runs away because he is a hired hand and cares nothing for the sheep.

14 "I am the good shepherd; I know my sheep and my sheep know me— 15 just as the Father knows me and I know the Father—and I lay down my life for the sheep. 16 I have other sheep that are not of this sheep pen. I must bring them also. They too will listen to my voice, and there shall be one flock and one shepherd. 17 The reason my Father loves me is that I lay down my life—only to take it up again. 18 No one takes it from me, but I lay it down of my own accord. I have authority to lay it down and authority to take it up again. This command I received from my Father."

19 The Jews who heard these words were again divided. 20 Many of them said, "He is demon-possessed and raving mad. Why listen to him?"

21 But others said, "These are not the sayings of a man possessed by a

a 38,39 Some early manuscripts do not have Then the man said . . . 39 Jesus said.　　b 9 Or kept safe demon. Can a demon open the eyes of the blind?"

²²Then came the Festival of Dedication[a] at Jerusalem. It was winter, ²³and Jesus was in the temple courts walking in Solomon's Colonnade. ²⁴The Jews who were there gathered around him, saying, "How long will you keep us in suspense? If you are the Messiah, tell us plainly."

²⁵Jesus answered, "I did tell you, but you do not believe. The works I do in my Father's name testify about me, ²⁶but you do not believe because you are not my sheep. ²⁷My sheep listen to my voice; I know them, and they follow me. ²⁸I give them eternal life, and they shall never perish; no one will snatch them out of my hand. ²⁹My Father, who has given them to me, is greater than all[b]; no one can snatch them out of my Father's hand. ³⁰I and the Father are one."

³¹Again his Jewish opponents picked up stones to stone him, ³²but Jesus said to them, "I have shown you many good works from the Father. For which of these do you stone me?"

³³"We are not stoning you for any good work," they replied, "but for blasphemy, because you, a mere man, claim to be God."

³⁴Jesus answered them, "Is it not written in your Law, 'I have said you are "gods"'[c]? ³⁵If he called them 'gods,' to whom the word of God came — and Scripture cannot be set aside — ³⁶what about the one whom the Father set apart as his very own and sent into the world? Why then do you accuse me of blasphemy because I said, 'I am God's Son'? ³⁷Do not believe me unless I

do the works of my Father. ³⁸But if I do them, even though you do not believe me, believe the works, that you may know and understand that the Father is in me, and I in the Father." ³⁹Again they tried to seize him, but he escaped their grasp.

⁴⁰Then Jesus went back across the Jordan to the place where John had been baptizing in the early days. There he stayed, ⁴¹and many people came to him. They said, "Though John never performed a sign, all that John said about this man was true." ⁴²And in that place many believed in Jesus.

11 Now a man named Lazarus was sick. He was from Bethany, the village of Mary and her sister Martha. ²(This Mary, whose brother Lazarus now lay sick, was the same one who poured perfume on the Lord and wiped his feet with her hair.) ³So the sisters sent word to Jesus, "Lord, the one you love is sick."

⁴When he heard this, Jesus said, "This sickness will not end in death. No, it is for God's glory so that God's Son may be glorified through it." ⁵Now Jesus loved Martha and her sister and Lazarus. ⁶So when he heard that Lazarus was sick, he stayed where he was two more days, ⁷and then he said to his disciples, "Let us go back to Judea."

⁸"But Rabbi," they said, "a short while ago the Jews there tried to stone you, and yet you are going back?"

⁹Jesus answered, "Are there not twelve hours of daylight? Anyone who walks in the daytime will not stumble, for they see by this world's light. ¹⁰It is when a person walks at

---

[a] 22 That is, Hanukkah   [b] 29 Many early manuscripts What my Father has given me is greater than all   [c] 34 Psalm 82:6

night that they stumble, for they have no light."

¹¹After he had said this, he went on to tell them, "Our friend Lazarus has fallen asleep; but I am going there to wake him up."

¹²His disciples replied, "Lord, if he sleeps, he will get better." ¹³Jesus had been speaking of his death, but his disciples thought he meant natural sleep.

¹⁴So then he told them plainly, "Lazarus is dead, ¹⁵and for your sake I am glad I was not there, so that you may believe. But let us go to him."

¹⁶Then Thomas (also known as Didymus*ᵃ*) said to the rest of the disciples, "Let us also go, that we may die with him."

¹⁷On his arrival, Jesus found that Lazarus had already been in the tomb for four days. ¹⁸Now Bethany was less than two miles*ᵇ* from Jerusalem, ¹⁹and many Jews had come to Martha and Mary to comfort them in the loss of their brother. ²⁰When Martha heard that Jesus was coming, she went out to meet him, but Mary stayed at home.

²¹"Lord," Martha said to Jesus, "if you had been here, my brother would not have died. ²²But I know that even now God will give you whatever you ask."

²³Jesus said to her, "Your brother will rise again."

²⁴Martha answered, "I know he will rise again in the resurrection at the last day."

²⁵Jesus said to her, "I am the resurrection and the life. The one who believes in me will live, even though they die; ²⁶and whoever lives by believing in me will never die. Do you believe this?"

²⁷"Yes, Lord," she replied, "I believe that you are the Messiah, the Son of God, who is to come into the world."

²⁸After she had said this, she went back and called her sister Mary aside. "The Teacher is here," she said, "and is asking for you." ²⁹When Mary heard this, she got up quickly and went to him. ³⁰Now Jesus had not yet entered the village, but was still at the place where Martha had met him. ³¹When the Jews who had been with Mary in the house, comforting her, noticed how quickly she got up and went out, they followed her, supposing she was going to the tomb to mourn there.

³²When Mary reached the place where Jesus was and saw him, she fell at his feet and said, "Lord, if you had been here, my brother would not have died."

³³When Jesus saw her weeping, and the Jews who had come along with her also weeping, he was deeply moved in spirit and troubled. ³⁴"Where have you laid him?" he asked.

"Come and see, Lord," they replied.

³⁵Jesus wept.

³⁶Then the Jews said, "See how he loved him!"

³⁷But some of them said, "Could not he who opened the eyes of the blind man have kept this man from dying?"

³⁸Jesus, once more deeply moved, came to the tomb. It was a cave with a stone laid across the entrance. ³⁹"Take away the stone," he said.

"But, Lord," said Martha, the sister of the dead man, "by this time there is a bad odor, for he has been there four days."

⁴⁰Then Jesus said, "Did I not tell

ᵃ 16 Thomas (Aramaic) and Didymus (Greek) both mean twin.   *ᵇ 18 Or about 3 kilometers* you that if you believe, you will see the glory of God?"

41 So they took away the stone. Then Jesus looked up and said, "Father, I thank you that you have heard me. 42 I knew that you always hear me, but I said this for the benefit of the people standing here, that they may believe that you sent me."

43 When he had said this, Jesus called in a loud voice, "Lazarus, come out!" 44 The dead man came out, his hands and feet wrapped with strips of linen, and a cloth around his face.

Jesus said to them, "Take off the grave clothes and let him go."

45 Therefore many of the Jews who had come to visit Mary, and had seen what Jesus did, believed in him. 46 But some of them went to the Pharisees and told them what Jesus had done. 47 Then the chief priests and the Pharisees called a meeting of the Sanhedrin.

"What are we accomplishing?" they asked. "Here is this man performing many signs. 48 If we let him go on like this, everyone will believe in him, and then the Romans will come and take away both our temple and our nation."

49 Then one of them, named Caiaphas, who was high priest that year, spoke up, "You know nothing at all! 50 You do not realize that it is better for you that one man die for the people than that the whole nation perish."

51 He did not say this on his own, but as high priest that year he prophesied that Jesus would die for the Jewish nation, 52 and not only for that nation but also for the scattered children of God, to bring them together and make them one. 53 So

from that day on they plotted to take his life.

54 Therefore Jesus no longer moved about publicly among the people of Judea. Instead he withdrew to a region near the wilderness, to a village called Ephraim, where he stayed with his disciples.

55 When it was almost time for the Jewish Passover, many went up from the country to Jerusalem for their ceremonial cleansing before the Passover. 56 They kept looking for Jesus, and as they stood in the temple courts they asked one another, "What do you think? Isn't he coming to the festival at all?" 57 But the chief priests and the Pharisees had given orders that anyone who found out where Jesus was should report it so that they might arrest him.

12 Six days before the Passover, Jesus came to Bethany, where Lazarus lived, whom Jesus had raised from the dead. 2 Here a dinner was given in Jesus' honor. Martha served, while Lazarus was among those reclining at the table with him. 3 Then Mary took about a pint[a] of pure nard, an expensive perfume; she poured it on Jesus' feet and wiped his feet with her hair. And the house was filled with the fragrance of the perfume.

4 But one of his disciples, Judas Iscariot, who was later to betray him, objected, 5 "Why wasn't this perfume sold and the money given to the poor? It was worth a year's wages.[b]" 6 He did not say this because he cared about the poor but because he was a thief; as keeper of the money bag, he used to help himself to what was put into it.

7 "Leave her alone," Jesus replied. "It was intended that she should

___

[a] 3 Or about 0.5 liter   [b] 5 Greek *three hundred denarii*

save this perfume for the day of my burial. [8]You will always have the poor among you,[a] but you will not always have me."

[9]Meanwhile a large crowd of Jews found out that Jesus was there and came, not only because of him but also to see Lazarus, whom he had raised from the dead. [10]So the chief priests made plans to kill Lazarus as well, [11]for on account of him many of the Jews were going over to Jesus and believing in him.

[12]The next day the great crowd that had come for the festival heard that Jesus was on his way to Jerusalem. [13]They took palm branches and went out to meet him, shouting,

"Hosanna!"[b]

"Blessed is he who comes in the name of the Lord!"[c]

"Blessed is the king of Israel!"

[14]Jesus found a young donkey and sat on it, as it is written:

[15]"Do not be afraid, Daughter Zion;
see, your king is coming,
seated on a donkey's colt."[d]

[16]At first his disciples did not understand all this. Only after Jesus was glorified did they realize that these things had been written about him and that these things had been done to him.

[17]Now the crowd that was with him when he called Lazarus from the tomb and raised him from the dead continued to spread the word. [18]Many people, because they had heard that he had performed this sign, went out to meet him. [19]So the Pharisees said to one another, "See, this is getting us nowhere. Look how the whole world has gone after him!"

[20]Now there were some Greeks among those who went up to worship at the festival. [21]They came to Philip, who was from Bethsaida in Galilee, with a request. "Sir," they said, "we would like to see Jesus." [22]Philip went to tell Andrew; Andrew and Philip in turn told Jesus.

[23]Jesus replied, "The hour has come for the Son of Man to be glorified. [24]Very truly I tell you, unless a kernel of wheat falls to the ground and dies, it remains only a single seed. But if it dies, it produces many seeds. [25]Anyone who loves their life will lose it, while anyone who hates their life in this world will keep it for eternal life. [26]Whoever serves me must follow me; and where I am, my servant also will be. My Father will honor the one who serves me.

[27]"Now my soul is troubled, and what shall I say? 'Father, save me from this hour'? No, it was for this very reason I came to this hour. [28]Father, glorify your name!"

Then a voice came from heaven, "I have glorified it, and will glorify it again." [29]The crowd that was there and heard it said it had thundered; others said an angel had spoken to him.

[30]Jesus said, "This voice was for your benefit, not mine. [31]Now is the time for judgment on this world; now the prince of this world will be driven out. [32]And I, when I am lifted up[e] from the earth, will draw all people to myself." [33]He said this to show the kind of death he was going to die.

---

[a] 8 See Deut. 15:11. [b] 13 A Hebrew expression meaning "Save!" which became an exclamation of praise [c] 13 Psalm 118:25,26 [d] 15 Zech. 9:9 [e] 32 The Greek for lifted up also means exalted.

³⁴The crowd spoke up, "We have heard from the Law that the Messiah will remain forever, so how can you say, 'The Son of Man must be lifted up'? Who is this 'Son of Man'?"

³⁵Then Jesus told them, "You are going to have the light just a little while longer. Walk while you have the light, before darkness overtakes you. Whoever walks in the dark does not know where they are going. ³⁶Believe in the light while you have the light, so that you may become children of light." When he had finished speaking, Jesus left and hid himself from them.

³⁷Even after Jesus had performed so many signs in their presence, they still would not believe in him. ³⁸This was to fulfill the word of Isaiah the prophet:

"Lord, who has believed our
    message
and to whom has the arm of
    the Lord been revealed?"ᵃ

³⁹For this reason they could not believe, because, as Isaiah says elsewhere:

⁴⁰"He has blinded their eyes
    and hardened their hearts,
so they can neither see with their
    eyes,
    nor understand with their
        hearts,
    nor turn — and I would heal
        them."ᵇ

⁴¹Isaiah said this because he saw Jesus' glory and spoke about him.

⁴²Yet at the same time many even among the leaders believed in him. But because of the Pharisees they would not openly acknowledge their faith for fear they would be put out of the synagogue; ⁴³for they loved human praise more than praise from God.

⁴⁴Then Jesus cried out, "Whoever believes in me does not believe in me only, but in the one who sent me. ⁴⁵The one who looks at me is seeing the one who sent me. ⁴⁶I have come into the world as a light, so that no one who believes in me should stay in darkness.

⁴⁷"If anyone hears my words but does not keep them, I do not judge that person. For I did not come to judge the world, but to save the world. ⁴⁸There is a judge for the one who rejects me and does not accept my words; the very words I have spoken will condemn them at the last day. ⁴⁹For I did not speak on my own, but the Father who sent me commanded me to say all that I have spoken. ⁵⁰I know that his command leads to eternal life. So whatever I say is just what the Father has told me to say."

13 It was just before the Passover Festival. Jesus knew that the hour had come for him to leave this world and go to the Father. Having loved his own who were in the world, he loved them to the end.

²The evening meal was in progress, and the devil had already prompted Judas, the son of Simon Iscariot, to betray Jesus. ³Jesus knew that the Father had put all things under his power, and that he had come from God and was returning to God; ⁴so he got up from the meal, took off his outer clothing, and wrapped a towel around his waist. ⁵After that, he poured water into a basin and began to wash his disciples' feet, drying them with the towel that was wrapped around him.

ᵃ 38 Isaiah 53:1   ᵇ 40 Isaiah 6:10

⁶He came to Simon Peter, who said to him, "Lord, are you going to wash my feet?"

⁷Jesus replied, "You do not realize now what I am doing, but later you will understand."

⁸"No," said Peter, "you shall never wash my feet."

Jesus answered, "Unless I wash you, you have no part with me."

⁹"Then, Lord," Simon Peter replied, "not just my feet but my hands and my head as well!"

¹⁰Jesus answered, "Those who have had a bath need only to wash their feet; their whole body is clean. And you are clean, though not every one of you." ¹¹For he knew who was going to betray him, and that was why he said not every one was clean.

¹²When he had finished washing their feet, he put on his clothes and returned to his place. "Do you understand what I have done for you?" he asked them. ¹³"You call me 'Teacher' and 'Lord,' and rightly so, for that is what I am. ¹⁴Now that I, your Lord and Teacher, have washed your feet, you also should wash one another's feet. ¹⁵I have set you an example that you should do as I have done for you. ¹⁶Very truly I tell you, no servant is greater than his master, nor is a messenger greater than the one who sent him. ¹⁷Now that you know these things, you will be blessed if you do them.

¹⁸"I am not referring to all of you; I know those I have chosen. But this is to fulfill this passage of Scripture: 'He who shared my bread has turned[a] against me.'[b]

¹⁹"I am telling you now before it happens, so that when it does happen you will believe that I am who I am. ²⁰Very truly I tell you, whoever accepts anyone I send accepts me; and whoever accepts me accepts the one who sent me."

²¹After he had said this, Jesus was troubled in spirit and testified, "Very truly I tell you, one of you is going to betray me."

²²His disciples stared at one another, at a loss to know which of them he meant. ²³One of them, the disciple whom Jesus loved, was reclining next to him. ²⁴Simon Peter motioned to this disciple and said, "Ask him which one he means."

²⁵Leaning back against Jesus, he asked him, "Lord, who is it?"

²⁶Jesus answered, "It is the one to whom I will give this piece of bread when I have dipped it in the dish." Then, dipping the piece of bread, he gave it to Judas, the son of Simon Iscariot. ²⁷As soon as Judas took the bread, Satan entered into him.

So Jesus told him, "What you are about to do, do quickly." ²⁸But no one at the meal understood why Jesus said this to him. ²⁹Since Judas had charge of the money, some thought Jesus was telling him to buy what was needed for the festival, or to give something to the poor. ³⁰As soon as Judas had taken the bread, he went out. And it was night.

³¹When he was gone, Jesus said, "Now the Son of Man is glorified and God is glorified in him. ³²If God is glorified in him,[c] God will glorify the Son in himself, and will glorify him at once.

³³"My children, I will be with you only a little longer. You will look for me, and just as I told the Jews, so I tell you now: Where I am going, you cannot come.

³⁴"A new command I give you:

---

[a] 18 Greek *has lifted up his heel*   [b] 18 Psalm 41:9   [c] 32 Many early manuscripts do not have *If God is glorified in him.*

Love one another. As I have loved you, so you must love one another. ³⁵By this everyone will know that you are my disciples, if you love one another."

³⁶Simon Peter asked him, "Lord, where are you going?"

Jesus replied, "Where I am going, you cannot follow now, but you will follow later."

³⁷Peter asked, "Lord, why can't I follow you now? I will lay down my life for you."

³⁸Then Jesus answered, "Will you really lay down your life for me? Very truly I tell you, before the rooster crows, you will disown me three times!

14 "Do not let your hearts be troubled. You believe in God[a]; believe also in me. ²My Father's house has many rooms; if that were not so, would I have told you that I am going there to prepare a place for you? ³And if I go and prepare a place for you, I will come back and take you to be with me that you also may be where I am. ⁴You know the way to the place where I am going."

⁵Thomas said to him, "Lord, we don't know where you are going, so how can we know the way?"

⁶Jesus answered, "I am the way and the truth and the life. No one comes to the Father except through me. ⁷If you really know me, you will know[b] my Father as well. From now on, you do know him and have seen him."

⁸Philip said, "Lord, show us the Father and that will be enough for us."

⁹Jesus answered: "Don't you know me, Philip, even after I have been among you such a long time? Anyone who has seen me has seen the Father. How can you say, 'Show us the Father'? ¹⁰Don't you believe that I am in the Father, and that the Father is in me? The words I say to you I do not speak on my own authority. Rather, it is the Father, living in me, who is doing his work. ¹¹Believe me when I say that I am in the Father and the Father is in me; or at least believe on the evidence of the works themselves. ¹²Very truly I tell you, whoever believes in me will do the works I have been doing, and they will do even greater things than these, because I am going to the Father. ¹³And I will do whatever you ask in my name, so that the Father may be glorified in the Son. ¹⁴You may ask me for anything in my name, and I will do it.

¹⁵"If you love me, keep my commands. ¹⁶And I will ask the Father, and he will give you another advocate to help you and be with you forever— ¹⁷the Spirit of truth. The world cannot accept him, because it neither sees him nor knows him. But you know him, for he lives with you and will be[c] in you. ¹⁸I will not leave you as orphans; I will come to you. ¹⁹Before long, the world will not see me anymore, but you will see me. Because I live, you also will live. ²⁰On that day you will realize that I am in my Father, and you are in me, and I am in you. ²¹Whoever has my commands and keeps them is the one who loves me. The one who loves me will be loved by my Father, and I too will love them and show myself to them."

²²Then Judas (not Judas Iscariot) said, "But, Lord, why do you intend to show yourself to us and not to the world?"

²³Jesus replied, "Anyone who

---

loves me will obey my teaching. My Father will love them, and we will come to them and make our home with them. ²⁴Anyone who does not love me will not obey my teaching. These words you hear are not my own; they belong to the Father who sent me.

²⁵"All this I have spoken while still with you. ²⁶But the Advocate, the Holy Spirit, whom the Father will send in my name, will teach you all things and will remind you of everything I have said to you. ²⁷Peace I leave with you; my peace I give you. I do not give to you as the world gives. Do not let your hearts be troubled and do not be afraid.

²⁸"You heard me say, 'I am going away and I am coming back to you.' If you loved me, you would be glad that I am going to the Father, for the Father is greater than I. ²⁹I have told you now before it happens, so that when it does happen you will believe. ³⁰I will not say much more to you, for the prince of this world is coming. He has no hold over me, ³¹but he comes so that the world may learn that I love the Father and do exactly what my Father has commanded me.

"Come now; let us leave.

15 "I am the true vine, and my Father is the gardener. ²He cuts off every branch in me that bears no fruit, while every branch that does bear fruit he prunes*a* so that it will be even more fruitful. ³You are already clean because of the word I have spoken to you. ⁴Remain in me, as I also remain in you. No branch can bear fruit by itself; it must remain in the vine. Neither can you bear fruit unless you remain in me.

⁵"I am the vine; you are the branches. If you remain in me and

I in you, you will bear much fruit; apart from me you can do nothing. ⁶If you do not remain in me, you are like a branch that is thrown away and withers; such branches are picked up, thrown into the fire and burned. ⁷If you remain in me and my words remain in you, ask whatever you wish, and it will be done for you. ⁸This is to my Father's glory, that you bear much fruit, showing yourselves to be my disciples.

⁹"As the Father has loved me, so have I loved you. Now remain in my love. ¹⁰If you keep my commands, you will remain in my love, just as I have kept my Father's commands and remain in his love. ¹¹I have told you this so that my joy may be in you and that your joy may be complete. ¹²My command is this: Love each other as I have loved you. ¹³Greater love has no one than this: to lay down one's life for one's friends. ¹⁴You are my friends if you do what I command. ¹⁵I no longer call you servants, because a servant does not know his master's business. Instead, I have called you friends, for everything that I learned from my Father I have made known to you. ¹⁶You did not choose me, but I chose you and appointed you so that you might go and bear fruit—fruit that will last—and so that whatever you ask in my name the Father will give you. ¹⁷This is my command: Love each other.

¹⁸"If the world hates you, keep in mind that it hated me first. ¹⁹If you belonged to the world, it would love you as its own. As it is, you do not belong to the world, but I have chosen you out of the world. That is why the world hates you. ²⁰Remember what I told you: 'A servant is not greater than his master.'*b* If

---

a 2 The Greek for *he prunes* also means *he cleans.*   *b 20* John 13:16

they persecuted me, they will persecute you also. If they obeyed my teaching, they will obey yours also. [21]They will treat you this way because of my name, for they do not know the one who sent me. [22]If I had not come and spoken to them, they would not be guilty of sin; but now they have no excuse for their sin. [23]Whoever hates me hates my Father as well. [24]If I had not done among them the works no one else did, they would not be guilty of sin. As it is, they have seen, and yet they have hated both me and my Father. [25]But this is to fulfill what is written in their Law: 'They hated me without reason.'[a]

[26]"When the Advocate comes, whom I will send to you from the Father—the Spirit of truth who goes out from the Father—he will testify about me. [27]And you also must testify, for you have been with me from the beginning.

16 "All this I have told you so that you will not fall away. [2]They will put you out of the synagogue; in fact, the time is coming when anyone who kills you will think they are offering a service to God. [3]They will do such things because they have not known the Father or me. [4]I have told you this, so that when their time comes you will remember that I warned you about them. I did not tell you this from the beginning because I was with you, [5]but now I am going to him who sent me. None of you asks me, 'Where are you going?' [6]Rather, you are filled with grief because I have said these things. [7]But very truly I tell you, it is for your good that I am going away. Unless I go away, the Advocate will not come to you; but if I go, I will send him to you. [8]When he comes,

he will prove the world to be in the wrong about sin and righteousness and judgment: [9]about sin, because people do not believe in me; [10]about righteousness, because I am going to the Father, where you can see me no longer; [11]and about judgment, because the prince of this world now stands condemned.

[12]"I have much more to say to you, more than you can now bear. [13]But when he, the Spirit of truth, comes, he will guide you into all the truth. He will not speak on his own; he will speak only what he hears, and he will tell you what is yet to come. [14]He will glorify me because it is from me that he will receive what he will make known to you. [15]All that belongs to the Father is mine. That is why I said the Spirit will receive from me what he will make known to you."

[16]Jesus went on to say, "In a little while you will see me no more, and then after a little while you will see me."

[17]At this, some of his disciples said to one another, "What does he mean by saying, 'In a little while you will see me no more, and then after a little while you will see me,' and 'Because I am going to the Father'?" [18]They kept asking, "What does he mean by 'a little while'? We don't understand what he is saying."

[19]Jesus saw that they wanted to ask him about this, so he said to them, "Are you asking one another what I meant when I said, 'In a little while you will see me no more, and then after a little while you will see me'? [20]Very truly I tell you, you will weep and mourn while the world rejoices. You will grieve, but your grief will turn to joy. [21]A woman giving birth to a child has pain because her

---

[a] 25 Psalms 35:19; 69:4

time has come; but when her baby is born she forgets the anguish because of her joy that a child is born into the world. ²²So with you: Now is your time of grief, but I will see you again and you will rejoice, and no one will take away your joy. ²³In that day you will no longer ask me anything. Very truly I tell you, my Father will give you whatever you ask in my name. ²⁴Until now you have not asked for anything in my name. Ask and you will receive, and your joy will be complete.

²⁵"Though I have been speaking figuratively, a time is coming when I will no longer use this kind of language but will tell you plainly about my Father. ²⁶In that day you will ask in my name. I am not saying that I will ask the Father on your behalf. ²⁷No, the Father himself loves you because you have loved me and have believed that I came from God. ²⁸I came from the Father and entered the world; now I am leaving the world and going back to the Father."

²⁹Then Jesus' disciples said, "Now you are speaking clearly and without figures of speech. ³⁰Now we can see that you know all things and that you do not even need to have anyone ask you questions. This makes us believe that you came from God."

³¹"Do you now believe?" Jesus replied. ³²"A time is coming and in fact has come when you will be scattered, each to your own home. You will leave me all alone. Yet I am not alone, for my Father is with me.

³³"I have told you these things, so that in me you may have peace. In this world you will have trouble. But take heart! I have overcome the world."

17 After Jesus said this, he looked toward heaven and prayed:

"Father, the hour has come. Glorify your Son, that your Son may glorify you. ²For you granted him authority over all people that he might give eternal life to all those you have given him. ³Now this is eternal life: that they know you, the only true God, and Jesus Christ, whom you have sent. ⁴I have brought you glory on earth by finishing the work you gave me to do. ⁵And now, Father, glorify me in your presence with the glory I had with you before the world began.

⁶"I have revealed you[a] to those whom you gave me out of the world. They were yours; you gave them to me and they have obeyed your word. ⁷Now they know that everything you have given me comes from you. ⁸For I gave them the words you gave me and they accepted them. They knew with certainty that I came from you, and they believed that you sent me. ⁹I pray for them. I am not praying for the world, but for those you have given me, for they are yours. ¹⁰All I have is yours, and all you have is mine. And glory has come to me through them. ¹¹I will remain in the world no longer, but they are still in the world, and I am coming to you. Holy Father, protect them by the power of[b] your name, the name you gave me, so that they may be one as we are one. ¹²While I was with them, I protected them and kept them safe by[c] that name you gave me. None

---

[a] 6 Greek *your name*   [b] 11 Or *Father, keep them faithful to*   [c] 12 Or *kept them faithful to*

has been lost except the one doomed to destruction so that Scripture would be fulfilled.

¹³"I am coming to you now, but I say these things while I am still in the world, so that they may have the full measure of my joy within them. ¹⁴I have given them your word and the world has hated them, for they are not of the world any more than I am of the world. ¹⁵My prayer is not that you take them out of the world but that you protect them from the evil one. ¹⁶They are not of the world, even as I am not of it. ¹⁷Sanctify them by[a] the truth; your word is truth. ¹⁸As you sent me into the world, I have sent them into the world. ¹⁹For them I sanctify myself, that they too may be truly sanctified.

²⁰"My prayer is not for them alone. I pray also for those who will believe in me through their message, ²¹that all of them may be one, Father, just as you are in me and I am in you. May they also be in us so that the world may believe that you have sent me. ²²I have given them the glory that you gave me, that they may be one as we are one — ²³I in them and you in me — so that they may be brought to complete unity. Then the world will know that you sent me and have loved them even as you have loved me.

²⁴"Father, I want those you have given me to be with me where I am, and to see my glory, the glory you have given me because you loved me before the creation of the world.

²⁵"Righteous Father, though

the world does not know you, I know you, and they know that you have sent me. ²⁶I have made you[b] known to them, and will continue to make you known in order that the love you have for me may be in them and that I myself may be in them."

18 When he had finished praying, Jesus left with his disciples and crossed the Kidron Valley. On the other side there was a garden, and he and his disciples went into it.

²Now Judas, who betrayed him, knew the place, because Jesus had often met there with his disciples. ³So Judas came to the garden, guiding a detachment of soldiers and some officials from the chief priests and the Pharisees. They were carrying torches, lanterns and weapons.

⁴Jesus, knowing all that was going to happen to him, went out and asked them, "Who is it you want?"

⁵"Jesus of Nazareth," they replied.

"I am he," Jesus said. (And Judas the traitor was standing there with them.) ⁶When Jesus said, "I am he," they drew back and fell to the ground.

⁷Again he asked them, "Who is it you want?"

"Jesus of Nazareth," they said.

⁸Jesus answered, "I told you that I am he. If you are looking for me, then let these men go." ⁹This happened so that the words he had spoken would be fulfilled: "I have not lost one of those you gave me."[c]

¹⁰Then Simon Peter, who had a sword, drew it and struck the high priest's servant, cutting off his right ear. (The servant's name was Malchus.)

¹¹Jesus commanded Peter, "Put

---

a 17 Or *them to live in accordance with*   b 26 Greek *your name*   c 9 John 6:39

your sword away! Shall I not drink the cup the Father has given me?"

12Then the detachment of soldiers with its commander and the Jewish officials arrested Jesus. They bound him 13and brought him first to Annas, who was the father-in-law of Caiaphas, the high priest that year. 14Caiaphas was the one who had advised the Jewish leaders that it would be good if one man died for the people.

15Simon Peter and another disciple were following Jesus. Because this disciple was known to the high priest, he went with Jesus into the high priest's courtyard, 16but Peter had to wait outside at the door. The other disciple, who was known to the high priest, came back, spoke to the servant girl on duty there and brought Peter in.

17"You aren't one of this man's disciples too, are you?" she asked Peter.

He replied, "I am not."

18It was cold, and the servants and officials stood around a fire they had made to keep warm. Peter also was standing with them, warming himself.

19Meanwhile, the high priest questioned Jesus about his disciples and his teaching.

20"I have spoken openly to the world," Jesus replied. "I always taught in synagogues or at the temple, where all the Jews come together. I said nothing in secret. 21Why question me? Ask those who heard me. Surely they know what I said."

22When Jesus said this, one of the officials nearby slapped him in the face. "Is this the way you answer the high priest?" he demanded.

23"If I said something wrong," Jesus replied, "testify as to what is wrong. But if I spoke the truth, why did you strike me?" 24Then Annas sent him bound to Caiaphas the high priest.

25Meanwhile, Simon Peter was still standing there warming himself. So they asked him, "You aren't one of his disciples too, are you?"

He denied it, saying, "I am not."

26One of the high priest's servants, a relative of the man whose ear Peter had cut off, challenged him, "Didn't I see you with him in the garden?" 27Again Peter denied it, and at that moment a rooster began to crow.

28Then the Jewish leaders took Jesus from Caiaphas to the palace of the Roman governor. By now it was early morning, and to avoid ceremonial uncleanness they did not enter the palace, because they wanted to be able to eat the Passover. 29So Pilate came out to them and asked, "What charges are you bringing against this man?"

30"If he were not a criminal," they replied, "we would not have handed him over to you."

31Pilate said, "Take him yourselves and judge him by your own law."

"But we have no right to execute anyone," they objected. 32This took place to fulfill what Jesus had said about the kind of death he was going to die.

33Pilate then went back inside the palace, summoned Jesus and asked him, "Are you the king of the Jews?"

34"Is that your own idea," Jesus asked, "or did others talk to you about me?"

35"Am I a Jew?" Pilate replied. "Your own people and chief priests handed you over to me. What is it you have done?"

36Jesus said, "My kingdom is not

of this world. If it were, my servants would fight to prevent my arrest by the Jewish leaders. But now my kingdom is from another place."

37 "You are a king, then!" said Pilate.

Jesus answered, "You say that I am a king. In fact, the reason I was born and came into the world is to testify to the truth. Everyone on the side of truth listens to me."

38 "What is truth?" retorted Pilate. With this he went out again to the Jews gathered there and said, "I find no basis for a charge against him. 39 But it is your custom for me to release to you one prisoner at the time of the Passover. Do you want me to release 'the king of the Jews'?"

40 They shouted back, "No, not him! Give us Barabbas!" Now Barabbas had taken part in an uprising.

19 Then Pilate took Jesus and had him flogged. 2 The soldiers twisted together a crown of thorns and put it on his head. They clothed him in a purple robe 3 and went up to him again and again, saying, "Hail, king of the Jews!" And they slapped him in the face.

4 Once more Pilate came out and said to the Jews gathered there, "Look, I am bringing him out to you to let you know that I find no basis for a charge against him." 5 When Jesus came out wearing the crown of thorns and the purple robe, Pilate said to them, "Here is the man!"

6 As soon as the chief priests and their officials saw him, they shouted, "Crucify! Crucify!"

But Pilate answered, "You take him and crucify him. As for me, I find no basis for a charge against him."

7 The Jewish leaders insisted, "We have a law, and according to that law he must die, because he claimed to be the Son of God."

8 When Pilate heard this, he was even more afraid, 9 and he went back inside the palace. "Where do you come from?" he asked Jesus, but Jesus gave him no answer. 10 "Do you refuse to speak to me?" Pilate said. "Don't you realize I have power either to free you or to crucify you?"

11 Jesus answered, "You would have no power over me if it were not given to you from above. Therefore the one who handed me over to you is guilty of a greater sin."

12 From then on, Pilate tried to set Jesus free, but the Jewish leaders kept shouting, "If you let this man go, you are no friend of Caesar. Anyone who claims to be a king opposes Caesar."

13 When Pilate heard this, he brought Jesus out and sat down on the judge's seat at a place known as the Stone Pavement (which in Aramaic is Gabbatha). 14 It was the day of Preparation of the Passover; it was about noon.

"Here is your king," Pilate said to the Jews.

15 But they shouted, "Take him away! Take him away! Crucify him!"

"Shall I crucify your king?" Pilate asked.

"We have no king but Caesar," the chief priests answered.

16 Finally Pilate handed him over to them to be crucified.

So the soldiers took charge of Jesus. 17 Carrying his own cross, he went out to the place of the Skull (which in Aramaic is called Golgotha). 18 There they crucified him, and with him two others—one on each side and Jesus in the middle.

19 Pilate had a notice prepared

and fastened to the cross. It read: JESUS OF NAZARETH, THE KING OF THE JEWS. [20]Many of the Jews read this sign, for the place where Jesus was crucified was near the city, and the sign was written in Aramaic, Latin and Greek. [21]The chief priests of the Jews protested to Pilate, "Do not write 'The King of the Jews,' but that this man claimed to be king of the Jews."

[22]Pilate answered, "What I have written, I have written."

[23]When the soldiers crucified Jesus, they took his clothes, dividing them into four shares, one for each of them, with the undergarment remaining. This garment was seamless, woven in one piece from top to bottom.

[24]"Let's not tear it," they said to one another. "Let's decide by lot who will get it."

This happened that the scripture might be fulfilled that said,

"They divided my clothes among them
and cast lots for my garment."[a]

So this is what the soldiers did.

[25]Near the cross of Jesus stood his mother, his mother's sister, Mary the wife of Clopas, and Mary Magdalene. [26]When Jesus saw his mother there, and the disciple whom he loved standing nearby, he said to her, "Woman,[b] here is your son," [27]and to the disciple, "Here is your mother." From that time on, this disciple took her into his home.

[28]Later, knowing that everything had now been finished, and so that Scripture would be fulfilled, Jesus said, "I am thirsty." [29]A jar of wine vinegar was there, so they soaked a sponge in it, put the sponge on a stalk of the hyssop plant, and lifted it to Jesus' lips. [30]When he had received the drink, Jesus said, "It is finished." With that, he bowed his head and gave up his spirit.

[31]Now it was the day of Preparation, and the next day was to be a special Sabbath. Because the Jewish leaders did not want the bodies left on the crosses during the Sabbath, they asked Pilate to have the legs broken and the bodies taken down. [32]The soldiers therefore came and broke the legs of the first man who had been crucified with Jesus, and then those of the other. [33]But when they came to Jesus and found that he was already dead, they did not break his legs. [34]Instead, one of the soldiers pierced Jesus' side with a spear, bringing a sudden flow of blood and water. [35]The man who saw it has given testimony, and his testimony is true. He knows that he tells the truth, and he testifies so that you also may believe. [36]These things happened so that the scripture would be fulfilled: "Not one of his bones will be broken,"[c] [37]and, as another scripture says, "They will look on the one they have pierced."[d]

[38]Later, Joseph of Arimathea asked Pilate for the body of Jesus. Now Joseph was a disciple of Jesus, but secretly because he feared the Jewish leaders. With Pilate's permission, he came and took the body away. [39]He was accompanied by Nicodemus, the man who earlier had visited Jesus at night. Nicodemus brought a mixture of myrrh and aloes, about seventy-five pounds.[e] [40]Taking Jesus' body, the two of them wrapped it, with the spices, in strips of linen. This was in

---

[a] 24 Psalm 22:18   [b] 26 The Greek for Woman does not denote any disrespect.
[c] 36 Exodus 12:46; Num. 9:12; Psalm 34:20   [d] 37 Zech. 12:10   [e] 39 Or about 34 kilograms

accordance with Jewish burial customs. ⁴¹At the place where Jesus was crucified, there was a garden, and in the garden a new tomb, in which no one had ever been laid. ⁴²Because it was the Jewish day of Preparation and since the tomb was nearby, they laid Jesus there.

20 Early on the first day of the week, while it was still dark, Mary Magdalene went to the tomb and saw that the stone had been removed from the entrance. ²So she came running to Simon Peter and the other disciple, the one Jesus loved, and said, "They have taken the Lord out of the tomb, and we don't know where they have put him!"

³So Peter and the other disciple started for the tomb. ⁴Both were running, but the other disciple outran Peter and reached the tomb first. ⁵He bent over and looked in at the strips of linen lying there but did not go in. ⁶Then Simon Peter came along behind him and went straight into the tomb. He saw the strips of linen lying there, ⁷as well as the cloth that had been wrapped around Jesus' head. The cloth was still lying in its place, separate from the linen. ⁸Finally the other disciple, who had reached the tomb first, also went inside. He saw and believed. ⁹(They still did not understand from Scripture that Jesus had to rise from the dead.) ¹⁰Then the disciples went back to where they were staying.

¹¹Now Mary stood outside the tomb crying. As she wept, she bent over to look into the tomb ¹²and saw two angels in white, seated where Jesus' body had been, one at the head and the other at the foot.

¹³They asked her, "Woman, why are you crying?"

"They have taken my Lord away," she said, "and I don't know where they have put him." ¹⁴At this, she turned around and saw Jesus standing there, but she did not realize that it was Jesus.

¹⁵He asked her, "Woman, why are you crying? Who is it you are looking for?"

Thinking he was the gardener, she said, "Sir, if you have carried him away, tell me where you have put him, and I will get him."

¹⁶Jesus said to her, "Mary."

She turned toward him and cried out in Aramaic, "Rabboni!" (which means "Teacher").

¹⁷Jesus said, "Do not hold on to me, for I have not yet ascended to the Father. Go instead to my brothers and tell them, 'I am ascending to my Father and your Father, to my God and your God.'"

¹⁸Mary Magdalene went to the disciples with the news: "I have seen the Lord!" And she told them that he had said these things to her.

¹⁹On the evening of that first day of the week, when the disciples were together, with the doors locked for fear of the Jewish leaders, Jesus came and stood among them and said, "Peace be with you!" ²⁰After he said this, he showed them his hands and side. The disciples were overjoyed when they saw the Lord.

²¹Again Jesus said, "Peace be with you! As the Father has sent me, I am sending you." ²²And with that he breathed on them and said, "Receive the Holy Spirit. ²³If you forgive anyone's sins, their sins are forgiven; if you do not forgive them, they are not forgiven."

²⁴Now Thomas (also known as Didymusᵃ), one of the Twelve, was not with the disciples when Jesus

---

ᵃ 24 *Thomas* (Aramaic) and *Didymus* (Greek) both mean *twin*.

came. [25]So the other disciples told him, "We have seen the Lord!"

But he said to them, "Unless I see the nail marks in his hands and put my finger where the nails were, and put my hand into his side, I will not believe."

[26]A week later his disciples were in the house again, and Thomas was with them. Though the doors were locked, Jesus came and stood among them and said, "Peace be with you!" [27]Then he said to Thomas, "Put your finger here; see my hands. Reach out your hand and put it into my side. Stop doubting and believe."

[28]Thomas said to him, "My Lord and my God!"

[29]Then Jesus told him, "Because you have seen me, you have believed; blessed are those who have not seen and yet have believed."

[30]Jesus performed many other signs in the presence of his disciples, which are not recorded in this book. [31]But these are written that you may believe[a] that Jesus is the Messiah, the Son of God, and that by believing you may have life in his name.

21 Afterward Jesus appeared again to his disciples, by the Sea of Galilee.[b] It happened this way: [2]Simon Peter, Thomas (also known as Didymus[c]), Nathanael from Cana in Galilee, the sons of Zebedee, and two other disciples were together. [3]"I'm going out to fish," Simon Peter told them, and they said, "We'll go with you." So they went out and got into the boat, but that night they caught nothing.

[4]Early in the morning, Jesus stood on the shore, but the disciples did not realize that it was Jesus.

[5]He called out to them, "Friends, haven't you any fish?"

"No," they answered.

[6]He said, "Throw your net on the right side of the boat and you will find some." When they did, they were unable to haul the net in because of the large number of fish.

[7]Then the disciple whom Jesus loved said to Peter, "It is the Lord!" As soon as Simon Peter heard him say, "It is the Lord," he wrapped his outer garment around him (for he had taken it off) and jumped into the water. [8]The other disciples followed in the boat, towing the net full of fish, for they were not far from shore, about a hundred yards.[d] [9]When they landed, they saw a fire of burning coals there with fish on it, and some bread.

[10]Jesus said to them, "Bring some of the fish you have just caught." [11]So Simon Peter climbed back into the boat and dragged the net ashore. It was full of large fish, 153, but even with so many the net was not torn. [12]Jesus said to them, "Come and have breakfast." None of the disciples dared ask him, "Who are you?" They knew it was the Lord. [13]Jesus came, took the bread and gave it to them, and did the same with the fish. [14]This was now the third time Jesus appeared to his disciples after he was raised from the dead.

[15]When they had finished eating, Jesus said to Simon Peter, "Simon son of John, do you love me more than these?"

"Yes, Lord," he said, "you know that I love you."

Jesus said, "Feed my lambs."

---

[a] 31 Or *may continue to believe*   [b] 1 Greek *Tiberias*   [c] 2 *Thomas* (Aramaic) and *Didymus* (Greek) both mean *twin*.   [d] 8 Or about 90 meters

16Again Jesus said, "Simon son of John, do you love me?"

He answered, "Yes, Lord, you know that I love you."

Jesus said, "Take care of my sheep."

17The third time he said to him, "Simon son of John, do you love me?"

Peter was hurt because Jesus asked him the third time, "Do you love me?" He said, "Lord, you know all things; you know that I love you."

Jesus said, "Feed my sheep. 18Very truly I tell you, when you were younger you dressed yourself and went where you wanted; but when you are old you will stretch out your hands, and someone else will dress you and lead you where you do not want to go." 19Jesus said this to indicate the kind of death by which Peter would glorify God. Then he said to him, "Follow me!"

20Peter turned and saw that the disciple whom Jesus loved was following them. (This was the one who had leaned back against Jesus at the supper and had said, "Lord, who is going to betray you?") 21When Peter saw him, he asked, "Lord, what about him?"

22Jesus answered, "If I want him to remain alive until I return, what is that to you? You must follow me." 23Because of this, the rumor spread among the believers that this disciple would not die. But Jesus did not say that he would not die; he only said, "If I want him to remain alive until I return, what is that to you?"

24This is the disciple who testifies to these things and who wrote them down. We know that his testimony is true.

25Jesus did many other things as well. If every one of them were written down, I suppose that even the whole world would not have room for the books that would be written.

ACTS

Luke's second volume is known as the book of Acts (see p. 69 for the Invitation to Luke-Acts, and for more detailed information on the Gospel of Luke). The six parts of the book of Acts each describe a new phase in the expansion of the Messiah-following movement outward from Jerusalem. These sections are all marked by variations on the phrase *the word of God continued to spread and flourish*:

: First, the church is established in Jerusalem and becomes Greek-speaking, allowing it to spread its message throughout the empire.
: Next, the movement expands into the rest of Palestine.
: Third, Gentiles are included in the gathering of Jesus-followers alongside Jews.
: Fourth, messengers are sent west into the Roman province of Asia.
: Fifth, these messengers enter Europe.
: In the sixth and final phase, the movement reaches the capital city of Rome and into the highest levels of society; God's kingdom is thus announced to all nations.

---

1 In my former book, Theophilus, I wrote about all that Jesus began to do and to teach ²until the day he was taken up to heaven, after giving instructions through the Holy Spirit to the apostles he had chosen. ³After his suffering, he presented himself to them and gave many convincing proofs that he was alive. He appeared to them over a period of forty days and spoke about the kingdom of God. ⁴On one occasion, while he was eating with them, he gave them this command: "Do not leave Jerusalem, but wait for the gift my Father promised, which you have heard me speak about. ⁵For John baptized with*a* water, but in a few days you will be baptized with*a* the Holy Spirit."

⁶Then they gathered around him and asked him, "Lord, are you at this time going to restore the kingdom to Israel?"

⁷He said to them: "It is not for you to know the times or dates the Father has set by his own authority. ⁸But you will receive power when the Holy Spirit comes on you; and you will be my witnesses in Jerusalem, and in all Judea and Samaria, and to the ends of the earth."

⁹After he said this, he was taken up before their very eyes, and a cloud hid him from their sight.

¹⁰They were looking intently up into the sky as he was going, when suddenly two men dressed in white stood beside them. ¹¹"Men of Galilee," they said, "why do you stand here looking into the sky? This same Jesus, who has been taken from you into heaven, will come back in the same way you have seen him go into heaven."

¹²Then the apostles returned to Jerusalem from the hill called the Mount of Olives, a Sabbath day's walk*b* from the city. ¹³When they arrived, they went upstairs to the room where they were staying. Those present were Peter, John,

---

a 5 Or *in*   *b 12* That is, about 5/8 mile or about 1 kilometer

James and Andrew; Philip and Thomas, Bartholomew and Matthew; James son of Alphaeus and Simon the Zealot, and Judas son of James. ¹⁴They all joined together constantly in prayer, along with the women and Mary the mother of Jesus, and with his brothers.

¹⁵In those days Peter stood up among the believers (a group numbering about a hundred and twenty) ¹⁶and said, "Brothers and sisters,^a the Scripture had to be fulfilled in which the Holy Spirit spoke long ago through David concerning Judas, who served as guide for those who arrested Jesus. ¹⁷He was one of our number and shared in our ministry."

¹⁸(With the payment he received for his wickedness, Judas bought a field; there he fell headlong, his body burst open and all his intestines spilled out. ¹⁹Everyone in Jerusalem heard about this, so they called that field in their language Akeldama, that is, Field of Blood.)

²⁰"For," said Peter, "it is written in the Book of Psalms:

"'May his place be deserted;
    let there be no one to dwell
    in it,'^b

and,

"'May another take his place of
    leadership.'^c

²¹Therefore it is necessary to choose one of the men who have been with us the whole time the Lord Jesus was living among us, ²²beginning from John's baptism to the time when Jesus was taken up from us. For one of these must

become a witness with us of his resurrection."

²³So they nominated two men: Joseph called Barsabbas (also known as Justus) and Matthias. ²⁴Then they prayed, "Lord, you know everyone's heart. Show us which of these two you have chosen ²⁵to take over this apostolic ministry, which Judas left to go where he belongs." ²⁶Then they cast lots, and the lot fell to Matthias; so he was added to the eleven apostles.

2 When the day of Pentecost came, they were all together in one place. ²Suddenly a sound like the blowing of a violent wind came from heaven and filled the whole house where they were sitting. ³They saw what seemed to be tongues of fire that separated and came to rest on each of them. ⁴All of them were filled with the Holy Spirit and began to speak in other tongues^d as the Spirit enabled them.

⁵Now there were staying in Jerusalem God-fearing Jews from every nation under heaven. ⁶When they heard this sound, a crowd came together in bewilderment, because each one heard their own language being spoken. ⁷Utterly amazed, they asked: "Aren't all these who are speaking Galileans? ⁸Then how is it that each of us hears them in our native language? ⁹Parthians, Medes and Elamites; residents of Mesopotamia, Judea and Cappadocia, Pontus and Asia,^e ¹⁰Phrygia and Pamphylia, Egypt and the parts of Libya near Cyrene; visitors from Rome ¹¹(both Jews and converts to Judaism); Cretans and Arabs—we hear them declaring the wonders of God

---

^a 16 The Greek word for *brothers and sisters* (*adelphoi*) refers here to believers, both men and women, as part of God's family; also in 6:3; 11:29; 12:17; 16:40; 18:18, 27; 21:7, 17; 28:14, 15.
^b 20 Psalm 69:25   ^c 20 Psalm 109:8   ^d 4 Or *languages*; also in verse 11   ^e 9 That is, the Roman province by that name

in our own tongues!" [12]Amazed and perplexed, they asked one another, "What does this mean?"

[13]Some, however, made fun of them and said, "They have had too much wine."

[14]Then Peter stood up with the Eleven, raised his voice and addressed the crowd: "Fellow Jews and all of you who live in Jerusalem, let me explain this to you; listen carefully to what I say. [15]These people are not drunk, as you suppose. It's only nine in the morning! [16]No, this is what was spoken by the prophet Joel:

[17] " 'In the last days, God says,
I will pour out my Spirit on all people.
Your sons and daughters will prophesy,
your young men will see visions,
your old men will dream dreams.
[18]Even on my servants, both men and women,
I will pour out my Spirit in those days,
and they will prophesy.
[19]I will show wonders in the heavens above
and signs on the earth below,
blood and fire and billows of smoke.
[20]The sun will be turned to darkness
and the moon to blood
before the coming of the great and glorious day of the Lord.
[21]And everyone who calls
on the name of the Lord will be saved.'[a]

[22]"Fellow Israelites, listen to this: Jesus of Nazareth was a man accredited by God to you by miracles, wonders and signs, which God did among you through him, as you yourselves know. [23]This man was handed over to you by God's deliberate plan and foreknowledge; and you, with the help of wicked men,[b] put him to death by nailing him to the cross. [24]But God raised him from the dead, freeing him from the agony of death, because it was impossible for death to keep its hold on him. [25]David said about him:

" 'I saw the Lord always before me.
Because he is at my right hand, I will not be shaken.
[26]Therefore my heart is glad and my tongue rejoices;
my body also will rest in hope,
[27]because you will not abandon me to the realm of the dead,
you will not let your holy one see decay.
[28]You have made known to me the paths of life;
you will fill me with joy in your presence.'[c]

[29]"Fellow Israelites, I can tell you confidently that the patriarch David died and was buried, and his tomb is here to this day. [30]But he was a prophet and knew that God had promised him on oath that he would place one of his descendants on his throne. [31]Seeing what was to come, he spoke of the resurrection of the Messiah, that he was not abandoned to the realm of the dead, nor did his body see decay. [32]God has raised this Jesus to life, and we are all witnesses of it. [33]Exalted to the right hand of God, he has re-

---

[a] 21 Joel 2:28-32 (see Septuagint)   [b] 23 Or of those not having the law (that is, Gentiles)   [c] 28 Psalm 16:8-11

ceived from the Father the promised Holy Spirit and has poured out what you now see and hear. ³⁴For David did not ascend to heaven, and yet he said,

"'The Lord said to my Lord:
   "Sit at my right hand
³⁵until I make your enemies
   a footstool for your feet."'ᵃ

³⁶"Therefore let all Israel be assured of this: God has made this Jesus, whom you crucified, both Lord and Messiah."

³⁷When the people heard this, they were cut to the heart and said to Peter and the other apostles, "Brothers, what shall we do?"

³⁸Peter replied, "Repent and be baptized, every one of you, in the name of Jesus Christ for the forgiveness of your sins. And you will receive the gift of the Holy Spirit. ³⁹The promise is for you and your children and for all who are far off—for all whom the Lord our God will call."

⁴⁰With many other words he warned them; and he pleaded with them, "Save yourselves from this corrupt generation." ⁴¹Those who accepted his message were baptized, and about three thousand were added to their number that day.

⁴²They devoted themselves to the apostles' teaching and to fellowship, to the breaking of bread and to prayer. ⁴³Everyone was filled with awe at the many wonders and signs performed by the apostles. ⁴⁴All the believers were together and had everything in common. ⁴⁵They sold property and possessions to give to anyone who had need. ⁴⁶Every day they continued to meet together in the temple courts. They broke bread in their homes and ate together with glad and sincere hearts, ⁴⁷praising God and enjoying the favor of all the people. And the Lord added to their number daily those who were being saved.

3 One day Peter and John were going up to the temple at the time of prayer—at three in the afternoon. ²Now a man who was lame from birth was being carried to the temple gate called Beautiful, where he was put every day to beg from those going into the temple courts. ³When he saw Peter and John about to enter, he asked them for money. ⁴Peter looked straight at him, as did John. Then Peter said, "Look at us!" ⁵So the man gave them his attention, expecting to get something from them.

⁶Then Peter said, "Silver or gold I do not have, but what I do have I give you. In the name of Jesus Christ of Nazareth, walk." ⁷Taking him by the right hand, he helped him up, and instantly the man's feet and ankles became strong. ⁸He jumped to his feet and began to walk. Then he went with them into the temple courts, walking and jumping, and praising God. ⁹When all the people saw him walking and praising God, ¹⁰they recognized him as the same man who used to sit begging at the temple gate called Beautiful, and they were filled with wonder and amazement at what had happened to him.

¹¹While the man held on to Peter and John, all the people were astonished and came running to them in the place called Solomon's Colonnade. ¹²When Peter saw this, he said to them: "Fellow Israelites, why does this surprise you? Why do you stare at us as if by our own

ᵃ 35 Psalm 110:1

power or godliness we had made this man walk? [13] The God of Abraham, Isaac and Jacob, the God of our fathers, has glorified his servant Jesus. You handed him over to be killed, and you disowned him before Pilate, though he had decided to let him go. [14] You disowned the Holy and Righteous One and asked that a murderer be released to you. [15] You killed the author of life, but God raised him from the dead. We are witnesses of this. [16] By faith in the name of Jesus, this man whom you see and know was made strong. It is Jesus' name and the faith that comes through him that has completely healed him, as you can all see.

[17] "Now, fellow Israelites, I know that you acted in ignorance, as did your leaders. [18] But this is how God fulfilled what he had foretold through all the prophets, saying that his Messiah would suffer. [19] Repent, then, and turn to God, so that your sins may be wiped out, that times of refreshing may come from the Lord, [20] and that he may send the Messiah, who has been appointed for you — even Jesus. [21] Heaven must receive him until the time comes for God to restore everything, as he promised long ago through his holy prophets. [22] For Moses said, 'The Lord your God will raise up for you a prophet like me from among your own people; you must listen to everything he tells you. [23] Anyone who does not listen to him will be completely cut off from their people.'[a]

[24] "Indeed, beginning with Samuel, all the prophets who have spoken have foretold these days. [25] And you are heirs of the prophets and of the covenant God made with your fathers. He said to Abraham, 'Through your offspring all peoples on earth will be blessed.'[b] [26] When God raised up his servant, he sent him first to you to bless you by turning each of you from your wicked ways."

4 The priests and the captain of the temple guard and the Sadducees came up to Peter and John while they were speaking to the people. [2] They were greatly disturbed because the apostles were teaching the people, proclaiming in Jesus the resurrection of the dead. [3] They seized Peter and John, and because it was evening, they put them in jail until the next day. [4] But many who heard the message believed; so the number of men who believed grew to about five thousand.

[5] The next day the rulers, the elders and the teachers of the law met in Jerusalem. [6] Annas the high priest was there, and so were Caiaphas, John, Alexander and others of the high priest's family. [7] They had Peter and John brought before them and began to question them: "By what power or what name did you do this?"

[8] Then Peter, filled with the Holy Spirit, said to them: "Rulers and elders of the people! [9] If we are being called to account today for an act of kindness shown to a man who was lame and are being asked how he was healed, [10] then know this, you and all the people of Israel: It is by the name of Jesus Christ of Nazareth, whom you crucified but whom God raised from the dead, that this man stands before you healed. [11] Jesus is

" 'the stone you builders rejected,
    which has become the
        cornerstone.'[c]

a 23 Deut. 18:15,18,19   b 25 Gen. 22:18; 26:4   c 11 Psalm 118:22

¹²Salvation is found in no one else, for there is no other name under heaven given to mankind by which we must be saved."

¹³When they saw the courage of Peter and John and realized that they were unschooled, ordinary men, they were astonished and they took note that these men had been with Jesus. ¹⁴But since they could see the man who had been healed standing there with them, there was nothing they could say. ¹⁵So they ordered them to withdraw from the Sanhedrin and then conferred together. ¹⁶"What are we going to do with these men?" they asked. "Everyone living in Jerusalem knows they have performed a notable sign, and we cannot deny it. ¹⁷But to stop this thing from spreading any further among the people, we must warn them to speak no longer to anyone in this name."

¹⁸Then they called them in again and commanded them not to speak or teach at all in the name of Jesus. ¹⁹But Peter and John replied, "Which is right in God's eyes: to listen to you, or to him? You be the judges! ²⁰As for us, we cannot help speaking about what we have seen and heard."

²¹After further threats they let them go. They could not decide how to punish them, because all the people were praising God for what had happened. ²²For the man who was miraculously healed was over forty years old.

²³On their release, Peter and John went back to their own people and reported all that the chief priests and the elders had said to them. ²⁴When they heard this, they raised their voices together in prayer to God. "Sovereign Lord," they said,

"you made the heavens and the earth and the sea, and everything in them. ²⁵You spoke by the Holy Spirit through the mouth of your servant, our father David:

"'Why do the nations rage
    and the peoples plot in vain?
²⁶The kings of the earth rise up
    and the rulers band together
against the Lord
    and against his anointed
        one.ᵃᵇ

²⁷Indeed Herod and Pontius Pilate met together with the Gentiles and the people of Israel in this city to conspire against your holy servant Jesus, whom you anointed. ²⁸They did what your power and will had decided beforehand should happen. ²⁹Now, Lord, consider their threats and enable your servants to speak your word with great boldness. ³⁰Stretch out your hand to heal and perform signs and wonders through the name of your holy servant Jesus."

³¹After they prayed, the place where they were meeting was shaken. And they were all filled with the Holy Spirit and spoke the word of God boldly.

³²All the believers were one in heart and mind. No one claimed that any of their possessions was their own, but they shared everything they had. ³³With great power the apostles continued to testify to the resurrection of the Lord Jesus. And God's grace was so powerfully at work in them all ³⁴that there were no needy persons among them. For from time to time those who owned land or houses sold them, brought the money from the sales ³⁵and put it at the apostles' feet, and it was distributed to anyone who had need.

ᵃ 26 That is, Messiah or Christ   ᵇ 26 Psalm 2:1,2

³⁶Joseph, a Levite from Cyprus, whom the apostles called Barnabas (which means "son of encouragement"), ³⁷sold a field he owned and brought the money and put it at the apostles' feet.

5 Now a man named Ananias, together with his wife Sapphira, also sold a piece of property. ²With his wife's full knowledge he kept back part of the money for himself, but brought the rest and put it at the apostles' feet.

³Then Peter said, "Ananias, how is it that Satan has so filled your heart that you have lied to the Holy Spirit and have kept for yourself some of the money you received for the land? ⁴Didn't it belong to you before it was sold? And after it was sold, wasn't the money at your disposal? What made you think of doing such a thing? You have not lied just to human beings but to God."

⁵When Ananias heard this, he fell down and died. And great fear seized all who heard what had happened. ⁶Then some young men came forward, wrapped up his body, and carried him out and buried him.

⁷About three hours later his wife came in, not knowing what had happened. ⁸Peter asked her, "Tell me, is this the price you and Ananias got for the land?"

"Yes," she said, "that is the price."

⁹Peter said to her, "How could you conspire to test the Spirit of the Lord? Listen! The feet of the men who buried your husband are at the door, and they will carry you out also."

¹⁰At that moment she fell down at his feet and died. Then the young men came in and, finding her dead, carried her out and buried her beside her husband. ¹¹Great fear seized the whole church and all who heard about these events.

¹²The apostles performed many signs and wonders among the people. And all the believers used to meet together in Solomon's Colonnade. ¹³No one else dared join them, even though they were highly regarded by the people. ¹⁴Nevertheless, more and more men and women believed in the Lord and were added to their number. ¹⁵As a result, people brought the sick into the streets and laid them on beds and mats so that at least Peter's shadow might fall on some of them as he passed by. ¹⁶Crowds gathered also from the towns around Jerusalem, bringing their sick and those tormented by impure spirits, and all of them were healed.

¹⁷Then the high priest and all his associates, who were members of the party of the Sadducees, were filled with jealousy. ¹⁸They arrested the apostles and put them in the public jail. ¹⁹But during the night an angel of the Lord opened the doors of the jail and brought them out. ²⁰"Go, stand in the temple courts," he said, "and tell the people all about this new life."

²¹At daybreak they entered the temple courts, as they had been told, and began to teach the people.

When the high priest and his associates arrived, they called together the Sanhedrin — the full assembly of the elders of Israel — and sent to the jail for the apostles. ²²But on arriving at the jail, the officers did not find them there. So they went back and reported, ²³ "We found the jail securely locked, with the guards standing at the doors; but when we opened them, we found no one inside." ²⁴On hearing this report, the captain of the temple guard and the chief priests were at a loss, wondering what this might lead to.

25 Then someone came and said, "Look! The men you put in jail are standing in the temple courts teaching the people." 26 At that, the captain went with his officers and brought the apostles. They did not use force, because they feared that the people would stone them.

27 The apostles were brought in and made to appear before the Sanhedrin to be questioned by the high priest. 28 "We gave you strict orders not to teach in this name," he said. "Yet you have filled Jerusalem with your teaching and are determined to make us guilty of this man's blood."

29 Peter and the other apostles replied: "We must obey God rather than human beings! 30 The God of our ancestors raised Jesus from the dead—whom you killed by hanging him on a cross. 31 God exalted him to his own right hand as Prince and Savior that he might bring Israel to repentance and forgive their sins. 32 We are witnesses of these things, and so is the Holy Spirit, whom God has given to those who obey him."

33 When they heard this, they were furious and wanted to put them to death. 34 But a Pharisee named Gamaliel, a teacher of the law, who was honored by all the people, stood up in the Sanhedrin and ordered that the men be put outside for a little while. 35 Then he addressed the Sanhedrin: "Men of Israel, consider carefully what you intend to do to these men. 36 Some time ago Theudas appeared, claiming to be somebody, and about four hundred men rallied to him. He was killed, all his followers were dispersed, and it all

came to nothing. 37 After him, Judas the Galilean appeared in the days of the census and led a band of people in revolt. He too was killed, and all his followers were scattered. 38 Therefore, in the present case I advise you: Leave these men alone! Let them go! For if their purpose or activity is of human origin, it will fail. 39 But if it is from God, you will not be able to stop these men; you will only find yourselves fighting against God."

40 His speech persuaded them. They called the apostles in and had them flogged. Then they ordered them not to speak in the name of Jesus, and let them go.

41 The apostles left the Sanhedrin, rejoicing because they had been counted worthy of suffering disgrace for the Name. 42 Day after day, in the temple courts and from house to house, they never stopped teaching and proclaiming the good news that Jesus is the Messiah.

6 In those days when the number of disciples was increasing, the Hellenistic Jews[a] among them complained against the Hebraic Jews because their widows were being overlooked in the daily distribution of food. 2 So the Twelve gathered all the disciples together and said, "It would not be right for us to neglect the ministry of the word of God in order to wait on tables. 3 Brothers and sisters, choose seven men from among you who are known to be full of the Spirit and wisdom. We will turn this responsibility over to them 4 and will give our attention to prayer and the ministry of the word."

5 This proposal pleased the whole group. They chose Stephen, a man full of faith and of the Holy Spirit;

---

a 1 That is, Jews who had adopted the Greek language and culture

also Philip, Procorus, Nicanor, Timon, Parmenas, and Nicolas from Antioch, a convert to Judaism. [6]They presented these men to the apostles, who prayed and laid their hands on them.

[7]So the word of God spread. The number of disciples in Jerusalem increased rapidly, and a large number of priests became obedient to the faith.

[8]Now Stephen, a man full of God's grace and power, performed great wonders and signs among the people. [9]Opposition arose, however, from members of the Synagogue of the Freedmen (as it was called) — Jews of Cyrene and Alexandria as well as the provinces of Cilicia and Asia — who began to argue with Stephen. [10]But they could not stand up against the wisdom the Spirit gave him as he spoke.

[11]Then they secretly persuaded some men to say, "We have heard Stephen speak blasphemous words against Moses and against God."

[12]So they stirred up the people and the elders and the teachers of the law. They seized Stephen and brought him before the Sanhedrin. [13]They produced false witnesses, who testified, "This fellow never stops speaking against this holy place and against the law. [14]For we have heard him say that this Jesus of Nazareth will destroy this place and change the customs Moses handed down to us."

[15]All who were sitting in the Sanhedrin looked intently at Stephen, and they saw that his face was like the face of an angel.

7 Then the high priest asked Stephen, "Are these charges true?"
[2]To this he replied: "Brothers and

fathers, listen to me! The God of glory appeared to our father Abraham while he was still in Mesopotamia, before he lived in Harran. [3]'Leave your country and your people,' God said, 'and go to the land I will show you.'[a]

[4]"So he left the land of the Chaldeans and settled in Harran. After the death of his father, God sent him to this land where you are now living. [5]He gave him no inheritance here, not even enough ground to set his foot on. But God promised him that he and his descendants after him would possess the land, even though at that time Abraham had no child. [6]God spoke to him in this way: 'For four hundred years your descendants will be strangers in a country not their own, and they will be enslaved and mistreated. [7]But I will punish the nation they serve as slaves,' God said, 'and afterward they will come out of that country and worship me in this place.'[b] [8]Then he gave Abraham the covenant of circumcision. And Abraham became the father of Isaac and circumcised him eight days after his birth. Later Isaac became the father of Jacob, and Jacob became the father of the twelve patriarchs.

[9]"Because the patriarchs were jealous of Joseph, they sold him as a slave into Egypt. But God was with him [10]and rescued him from all his troubles. He gave Joseph wisdom and enabled him to gain the goodwill of Pharaoh king of Egypt. So Pharaoh made him ruler over Egypt and all his palace.

[11]"Then a famine struck all Egypt and Canaan, bringing great suffering, and our ancestors could not find food. [12]When Jacob heard that there was grain in Egypt, he sent

[a] 3 Gen. 12:1   [b] 7 Gen. 15:13,14

our forefathers on their first visit. [13]On their second visit, Joseph told his brothers who he was, and Pharaoh learned about Joseph's family. [14]After this, Joseph sent for his father Jacob and his whole family, seventy-five in all. [15]Then Jacob went down to Egypt, where he and our ancestors died. [16]Their bodies were brought back to Shechem and placed in the tomb that Abraham had bought from the sons of Hamor at Shechem for a certain sum of money.

[17]"As the time drew near for God to fulfill his promise to Abraham, the number of our people in Egypt had greatly increased. [18]Then 'a new king, to whom Joseph meant nothing, came to power in Egypt.'[a] [19]He dealt treacherously with our people and oppressed our ancestors by forcing them to throw out their newborn babies so that they would die.

[20]"At that time Moses was born, and he was no ordinary child.[b] For three months he was cared for by his family. [21]When he was placed outside, Pharaoh's daughter took him and brought him up as her own son. [22]Moses was educated in all the wisdom of the Egyptians and was powerful in speech and action.

[23]"When Moses was forty years old, he decided to visit his own people, the Israelites. [24]He saw one of them being mistreated by an Egyptian, so he went to his defense and avenged him by killing the Egyptian. [25]Moses thought that his own people would realize that God was using him to rescue them, but they did not. [26]The next day Moses came upon two Israelites who were fighting. He tried to reconcile them by saying, 'Men, you are brothers; why do you want to hurt each other?'

[27]"But the man who was mistreating the other pushed Moses aside and said, 'Who made you ruler and judge over us? [28]Are you thinking of killing me as you killed the Egyptian yesterday?'[c] [29]When Moses heard this, he fled to Midian, where he settled as a foreigner and had two sons.

[30]"After forty years had passed, an angel appeared to Moses in the flames of a burning bush in the desert near Mount Sinai. [31]When he saw this, he was amazed at the sight. As he went over to get a closer look, he heard the Lord say: [32]'I am the God of your fathers, the God of Abraham, Isaac and Jacob.'[d] Moses trembled with fear and did not dare to look.

[33]"Then the Lord said to him, 'Take off your sandals, for the place where you are standing is holy ground. [34]I have indeed seen the oppression of my people in Egypt. I have heard their groaning and have come down to set them free. Now come, I will send you back to Egypt.'[e]

[35]"This is the same Moses they had rejected with the words, 'Who made you ruler and judge?' He was sent to be their ruler and deliverer by God himself, through the angel who appeared to him in the bush. [36]He led them out of Egypt and performed wonders and signs in Egypt, at the Red Sea and for forty years in the wilderness.

[37]"This is the Moses who told the Israelites, 'God will raise up for you a prophet like me from your own people.'[f] [38]He was in the assembly in the wilderness, with the

---

[a] 18 Exodus 1:8   [b] 20 Or *was fair in the sight of God*   [c] 28 Exodus 2:14   [d] 32 Exodus 3:6
[e] 34 Exodus 3:5,7,8,10   [f] 37 Deut. 18:15

angel who spoke to him on Mount Sinai, and with our ancestors; and he received living words to pass on to us.

39 "But our ancestors refused to obey him. Instead, they rejected him and in their hearts turned back to Egypt. 40 They told Aaron, 'Make us gods who will go before us. As for this fellow Moses who led us out of Egypt—we don't know what has happened to him!'[a] 41 That was the time they made an idol in the form of a calf. They brought sacrifices to it and reveled in what their own hands had made. 42 But God turned away from them and gave them over to the worship of the sun, moon and stars. This agrees with what is written in the book of the prophets:

" 'Did you bring me sacrifices
        and offerings
    forty years in the wilderness,
        people of Israel?
43 You have taken up the tabernacle
        of Molek
    and the star of your god
        Rephan,
    the idols you made to worship.
Therefore I will send you into
        exile'[b] beyond Babylon.

44 "Our ancestors had the tabernacle of the covenant law with them in the wilderness. It had been made as God directed Moses, according to the pattern he had seen. 45 After receiving the tabernacle, our ancestors under Joshua brought it with them when they took the land from the nations God drove out before them. It remained in the land until the time of David, 46 who enjoyed God's favor and asked that he might provide a dwelling place for the God of Jacob.[c] 47 But it was Solomon who built a house for him.

48 "However, the Most High does not live in houses made by human hands. As the prophet says:

49 " 'Heaven is my throne,
        and the earth is my footstool.
    What kind of house will you
        build for me?
                    says the Lord.
    Or where will my resting place
        be?
50 Has not my hand made all these
        things?'[d]

51 "You stiff-necked people! Your hearts and ears are still uncircumcised. You are just like your ancestors: You always resist the Holy Spirit! 52 Was there ever a prophet your ancestors did not persecute? They even killed those who predicted the coming of the Righteous One. And now you have betrayed and murdered him— 53 you who have received the law that was given through angels but have not obeyed it."

54 When the members of the Sanhedrin heard this, they were furious and gnashed their teeth at him. 55 But Stephen, full of the Holy Spirit, looked up to heaven and saw the glory of God, and Jesus standing at the right hand of God. 56 "Look," he said, "I see heaven open and the Son of Man standing at the right hand of God."

57 At this they covered their ears and, yelling at the top of their voices, they all rushed at him, 58 dragged him out of the city and began to stone him. Meanwhile, the witnesses laid their coats at the feet of a young man named Saul.

59 While they were stoning him,

a 40 Exodus 32:1   b 43 Amos 5:25-27 (see Septuagint)   c 46 Some early manuscripts the house of Jacob   d 50 Isaiah 66:1,2

Stephen prayed, "Lord Jesus, receive my spirit." [60]Then he fell on his knees and cried out, "Lord, do not hold this sin against them." When he had said this, he fell asleep.

8 And Saul approved of their killing him.

On that day a great persecution broke out against the church in Jerusalem, and all except the apostles were scattered throughout Judea and Samaria. [2]Godly men buried Stephen and mourned deeply for him. [3]But Saul began to destroy the church. Going from house to house, he dragged off both men and women and put them in prison.

[4]Those who had been scattered preached the word wherever they went. [5]Philip went down to a city in Samaria and proclaimed the Messiah there. [6]When the crowds heard Philip and saw the signs he performed, they all paid close attention to what he said. [7]For with shrieks, impure spirits came out of many, and many who were paralyzed or lame were healed. [8]So there was great joy in that city.

[9]Now for some time a man named Simon had practiced sorcery in the city and amazed all the people of Samaria. He boasted that he was someone great, [10]and all the people, both high and low, gave him their attention and exclaimed, "This man is rightly called the Great Power of God." [11]They followed him because he had amazed them for a long time with his sorcery. [12]But when they believed Philip as he proclaimed the good news of the kingdom of God and the name of Jesus Christ, they were baptized, both men and women. [13]Simon himself believed and was baptized. And he followed Philip everywhere, astonished by

the great signs and miracles he saw.

[14]When the apostles in Jerusalem heard that Samaria had accepted the word of God, they sent Peter and John to Samaria. [15]When they arrived, they prayed for the new believers there that they might receive the Holy Spirit, [16]because the Holy Spirit had not yet come on any of them; they had simply been baptized in the name of the Lord Jesus. [17]Then Peter and John placed their hands on them, and they received the Holy Spirit.

[18]When Simon saw that the Spirit was given at the laying on of the apostles' hands, he offered them money [19]and said, "Give me also this ability so that everyone on whom I lay my hands may receive the Holy Spirit."

[20]Peter answered: "May your money perish with you, because you thought you could buy the gift of God with money! [21]You have no part or share in this ministry, because your heart is not right before God. [22]Repent of this wickedness and pray to the Lord in the hope that he may forgive you for having such a thought in your heart. [23]For I see that you are full of bitterness and captive to sin."

[24]Then Simon answered, "Pray to the Lord for me so that nothing you have said may happen to me."

[25]After they had further proclaimed the word of the Lord and testified about Jesus, Peter and John returned to Jerusalem, preaching the gospel in many Samaritan villages.

[26]Now an angel of the Lord said to Philip, "Go south to the road—the desert road—that goes down from Jerusalem to Gaza." [27]So he started out, and on his way he met an Ethi-

opian[a] eunuch, an important official in charge of all the treasury of the Kandake (which means "queen of the Ethiopians"). This man had gone to Jerusalem to worship, 28 and on his way home was sitting in his chariot reading the Book of Isaiah the prophet. 29 The Spirit told Philip, "Go to that chariot and stay near it."

30 Then Philip ran up to the chariot and heard the man reading Isaiah the prophet. "Do you understand what you are reading?" Philip asked.

31 "How can I," he said, "unless someone explains it to me?" So he invited Philip to come up and sit with him.

32 This is the passage of Scripture the eunuch was reading:

"He was led like a sheep to the
        slaughter,
    and as a lamb before its
        shearer is silent,
    so he did not open his mouth.
33 In his humiliation he was
        deprived of justice.
    Who can speak of his
        descendants?
    For his life was taken from the
        earth."[b]

34 The eunuch asked Philip, "Tell me, please, who is the prophet talking about, himself or someone else?" 35 Then Philip began with that very passage of Scripture and told him the good news about Jesus.

36 As they traveled along the road, they came to some water and the eunuch said, "Look, here is water. What can stand in the way of my being baptized?" [37][c] 38 And he gave orders to stop the chariot.

Then both Philip and the eunuch went down into the water and Philip baptized him. 39 When they came up out of the water, the Spirit of the Lord suddenly took Philip away, and the eunuch did not see him again, but went on his way rejoicing. 40 Philip, however, appeared at Azotus and traveled about, preaching the gospel in all the towns until he reached Caesarea.

9 Meanwhile, Saul was still breathing out murderous threats against the Lord's disciples. He went to the high priest 2 and asked him for letters to the synagogues in Damascus, so that if he found any there who belonged to the Way, whether men or women, he might take them as prisoners to Jerusalem. 3 As he neared Damascus on his journey, suddenly a light from heaven flashed around him. 4 He fell to the ground and heard a voice say to him, "Saul, Saul, why do you persecute me?"

5 "Who are you, Lord?" Saul asked.

"I am Jesus, whom you are persecuting," he replied. 6 "Now get up and go into the city, and you will be told what you must do."

7 The men traveling with Saul stood there speechless; they heard the sound but did not see anyone. 8 Saul got up from the ground, but when he opened his eyes he could see nothing. So they led him by the hand into Damascus. 9 For three days he was blind, and did not eat or drink anything.

10 In Damascus there was a disciple named Ananias. The Lord called to him in a vision, "Ananias!"

"Yes, Lord," he answered.

---

[a] 27 That is, from the southern Nile region   [b] 33 Isaiah 53:7,8 (see Septuagint)   [c] 37 Some manuscripts include here *Philip said, "If you believe with all your heart, you may." The eunuch answered, "I believe that Jesus Christ is the Son of God."*

11 The Lord told him, "Go to the house of Judas on Straight Street and ask for a man from Tarsus named Saul, for he is praying. 12 In a vision he has seen a man named Ananias come and place his hands on him to restore his sight."

13 "Lord," Ananias answered, "I have heard many reports about this man and all the harm he has done to your holy people in Jerusalem. 14 And he has come here with authority from the chief priests to arrest all who call on your name."

15 But the Lord said to Ananias, "Go! This man is my chosen instrument to proclaim my name to the Gentiles and their kings and to the people of Israel. 16 I will show him how much he must suffer for my name."

17 Then Ananias went to the house and entered it. Placing his hands on Saul, he said, "Brother Saul, the Lord—Jesus, who appeared to you on the road as you were coming here—has sent me so that you may see again and be filled with the Holy Spirit." 18 Immediately, something like scales fell from Saul's eyes, and he could see again. He got up and was baptized, 19 and after taking some food, he regained his strength.

Saul spent several days with the disciples in Damascus. 20 At once he began to preach in the synagogues that Jesus is the Son of God. 21 All those who heard him were astonished and asked, "Isn't he the man who raised havoc in Jerusalem among those who call on this name? And hasn't he come here to take them as prisoners to the chief priests?" 22 Yet Saul grew more and more powerful and baffled the Jews living in Damascus by proving that Jesus is the Messiah.

23 After many days had gone by, there was a conspiracy among the Jews to kill him, 24 but Saul learned of their plan. Day and night they kept close watch on the city gates in order to kill him. 25 But his followers took him by night and lowered him in a basket through an opening in the wall.

26 When he came to Jerusalem, he tried to join the disciples, but they were all afraid of him, not believing that he really was a disciple. 27 But Barnabas took him and brought him to the apostles. He told them how Saul on his journey had seen the Lord and that the Lord had spoken to him, and how in Damascus he had preached fearlessly in the name of Jesus. 28 So Saul stayed with them and moved about freely in Jerusalem, speaking boldly in the name of the Lord. 29 He talked and debated with the Hellenistic Jews,[a] but they tried to kill him. 30 When the believers learned of this, they took him down to Caesarea and sent him off to Tarsus.

31 Then the church throughout Judea, Galilee and Samaria enjoyed a time of peace and was strengthened. Living in the fear of the Lord and encouraged by the Holy Spirit, it increased in numbers.

32 As Peter traveled about the country, he went to visit the Lord's people who lived in Lydda. 33 There he found a man named Aeneas, who was paralyzed and had been bedridden for eight years. 34 "Aeneas," Peter said to him, "Jesus Christ heals you. Get up and roll up your mat." Immediately Aeneas got up. 35 All those who lived in Lydda and

a 29 That is, Jews who had adopted the Greek language and culture

Sharon saw him and turned to the Lord.

36In Joppa there was a disciple named Tabitha (in Greek her name is Dorcas); she was always doing good and helping the poor. 37About that time she became sick and died, and her body was washed and placed in an upstairs room. 38Lydda was near Joppa; so when the disciples heard that Peter was in Lydda, they sent two men to him and urged him, "Please come at once!"

39Peter went with them, and when he arrived he was taken upstairs to the room. All the widows stood around him, crying and showing him the robes and other clothing that Dorcas had made while she was still with them.

40Peter sent them all out of the room; then he got down on his knees and prayed. Turning toward the dead woman, he said, "Tabitha, get up." She opened her eyes, and seeing Peter she sat up. 41He took her by the hand and helped her to her feet. Then he called for the believers, especially the widows, and presented her to them alive. 42This became known all over Joppa, and many people believed in the Lord. 43Peter stayed in Joppa for some time with a tanner named Simon.

10 At Caesarea there was a man named Cornelius, a centurion in what was known as the Italian Regiment. 2He and all his family were devout and God-fearing; he gave generously to those in need and prayed to God regularly. 3One day at about three in the afternoon he had a vision. He distinctly saw an angel of God, who came to him and said, "Cornelius!"

4Cornelius stared at him in fear. "What is it, Lord?" he asked.

The angel answered, "Your prayers and gifts to the poor have come up as a memorial offering before God. 5Now send men to Joppa to bring back a man named Simon who is called Peter. 6He is staying with Simon the tanner, whose house is by the sea."

7When the angel who spoke to him had gone, Cornelius called two of his servants and a devout soldier who was one of his attendants. 8He told them everything that had happened and sent them to Joppa.

9About noon the following day as they were on their journey and approaching the city, Peter went up on the roof to pray. 10He became hungry and wanted something to eat, and while the meal was being prepared, he fell into a trance. 11He saw heaven opened and something like a large sheet being let down to earth by its four corners. 12It contained all kinds of four-footed animals, as well as reptiles and birds. 13Then a voice told him, "Get up, Peter. Kill and eat."

14"Surely not, Lord!" Peter replied. "I have never eaten anything impure or unclean."

15The voice spoke to him a second time, "Do not call anything impure that God has made clean."

16This happened three times, and immediately the sheet was taken back to heaven.

17While Peter was wondering about the meaning of the vision, the men sent by Cornelius found out where Simon's house was and stopped at the gate. 18They called out, asking if Simon who was known as Peter was staying there.

19While Peter was still thinking about the vision, the Spirit said to him, "Simon, three*a* men are

---

a 19 One early manuscript *two*; other manuscripts do not have the number.

looking for you. 20 So get up and go downstairs. Do not hesitate to go with them, for I have sent them."

21 Peter went down and said to the men, "I'm the one you're looking for. Why have you come?"

22 The men replied, "We have come from Cornelius the centurion. He is a righteous and God-fearing man, who is respected by all the Jewish people. A holy angel told him to ask you to come to his house so that he could hear what you have to say." 23 Then Peter invited the men into the house to be his guests.

The next day Peter started out with them, and some of the believers from Joppa went along. 24 The following day he arrived in Caesarea. Cornelius was expecting them and had called together his relatives and close friends. 25 As Peter entered the house, Cornelius met him and fell at his feet in reverence. 26 But Peter made him get up. "Stand up," he said, "I am only a man myself."

27 While talking with him, Peter went inside and found a large gathering of people. 28 He said to them: "You are well aware that it is against our law for a Jew to associate with or visit a Gentile. But God has shown me that I should not call anyone impure or unclean. 29 So when I was sent for, I came without raising any objection. May I ask why you sent for me?"

30 Cornelius answered: "Three days ago I was in my house praying at this hour, at three in the afternoon. Suddenly a man in shining clothes stood before me 31 and said, 'Cornelius, God has heard your prayer and remembered your gifts to the poor. 32 Send to Joppa for Simon who is called Peter. He is a guest in the home of Simon the tanner, who lives by the sea.' 33 So I sent for you immediately, and it was good of you to come. Now we are all here in the presence of God to listen to everything the Lord has commanded you to tell us."

34 Then Peter began to speak: "I now realize how true it is that God does not show favoritism 35 but accepts from every nation the one who fears him and does what is right. 36 You know the message God sent to the people of Israel, announcing the good news of peace through Jesus Christ, who is Lord of all. 37 You know what has happened throughout the province of Judea, beginning in Galilee after the baptism that John preached— 38 how God anointed Jesus of Nazareth with the Holy Spirit and power, and how he went around doing good and healing all who were under the power of the devil, because God was with him.

39 "We are witnesses of everything he did in the country of the Jews and in Jerusalem. They killed him by hanging him on a cross, 40 but God raised him from the dead on the third day and caused him to be seen. 41 He was not seen by all the people, but by witnesses whom God had already chosen—by us who ate and drank with him after he rose from the dead. 42 He commanded us to preach to the people and to testify that he is the one whom God appointed as judge of the living and the dead. 43 All the prophets testify about him that everyone who believes in him receives forgiveness of sins through his name."

44 While Peter was still speaking these words, the Holy Spirit came on all who heard the message. 45 The circumcised believers who had come with Peter were astonished

that the gift of the Holy Spirit had been poured out even on Gentiles. [46]For they heard them speaking in tongues[a] and praising God.

Then Peter said, [47]"Surely no one can stand in the way of their being baptized with water. They have received the Holy Spirit just as we have." [48]So he ordered that they be baptized in the name of Jesus Christ. Then they asked Peter to stay with them for a few days.

11 The apostles and the believers throughout Judea heard that the Gentiles also had received the word of God. [2]So when Peter went up to Jerusalem, the circumcised believers criticized him [3]and said, "You went into the house of uncircumcised men and ate with them."

[4]Starting from the beginning, Peter told them the whole story: [5]"I was in the city of Joppa praying, and in a trance I saw a vision. I saw something like a large sheet being let down from heaven by its four corners, and it came down to where I was. [6]I looked into it and saw fourfooted animals of the earth, wild beasts, reptiles and birds. [7]Then I heard a voice telling me, 'Get up, Peter. Kill and eat.'

[8]"I replied, 'Surely not, Lord! Nothing impure or unclean has ever entered my mouth.'

[9]"The voice spoke from heaven a second time, 'Do not call anything impure that God has made clean.' [10]This happened three times, and then it was all pulled up to heaven again.

[11]"Right then three men who had been sent to me from Caesarea stopped at the house where I was staying. [12]The Spirit told me to have no hesitation about going with them. These six brothers also went

with me, and we entered the man's house. [13]He told us how he had seen an angel appear in his house and say, 'Send to Joppa for Simon who is called Peter. [14]He will bring you a message through which you and all your household will be saved.'

[15]"As I began to speak, the Holy Spirit came on them as he had come on us at the beginning. [16]Then I remembered what the Lord had said: 'John baptized with[b] water, but you will be baptized with[b] the Holy Spirit.' [17]So if God gave them the same gift he gave us who believed in the Lord Jesus Christ, who was I to think that I could stand in God's way?"

[18]When they heard this, they had no further objections and praised God, saying, "So then, even to Gentiles God has granted repentance that leads to life."

[19]Now those who had been scattered by the persecution that broke out when Stephen was killed traveled as far as Phoenicia, Cyprus and Antioch, spreading the word only among Jews. [20]Some of them, however, men from Cyprus and Cyrene, went to Antioch and began to speak to Greeks also, telling them the good news about the Lord Jesus. [21]The Lord's hand was with them, and a great number of people believed and turned to the Lord.

[22]News of this reached the church in Jerusalem, and they sent Barnabas to Antioch. [23]When he arrived and saw what the grace of God had done, he was glad and encouraged them all to remain true to the Lord with all their hearts. [24]He was a good man, full of the Holy Spirit and faith, and a great number of people were brought to the Lord.

[25]Then Barnabas went to Tar-

sus to look for Saul, 26 and when he found him, he brought him to Antioch. So for a whole year Barnabas and Saul met with the church and taught great numbers of people. The disciples were called Christians first at Antioch.

27 During this time some prophets came down from Jerusalem to Antioch. 28 One of them, named Agabus, stood up and through the Spirit predicted that a severe famine would spread over the entire Roman world. (This happened during the reign of Claudius.) 29 The disciples, as each one was able, decided to provide help for the brothers and sisters living in Judea. 30 This they did, sending their gift to the elders by Barnabas and Saul.

12 It was about this time that King Herod arrested some who belonged to the church, intending to persecute them. 2 He had James, the brother of John, put to death with the sword. 3 When he saw that this met with approval among the Jews, he proceeded to seize Peter also. This happened during the Festival of Unleavened Bread. 4 After arresting him, he put him in prison, handing him over to be guarded by four squads of four soldiers each. Herod intended to bring him out for public trial after the Passover.

5 So Peter was kept in prison, but the church was earnestly praying to God for him.

6 The night before Herod was to bring him to trial, Peter was sleeping between two soldiers, bound with two chains, and sentries stood guard at the entrance. 7 Suddenly an angel of the Lord appeared and a light shone in the cell. He struck Peter on the side and woke him up. "Quick, get up!" he said, and the chains fell off Peter's wrists.

8 Then the angel said to him, "Put on your clothes and sandals." And Peter did so. "Wrap your cloak around you and follow me," the angel told him. 9 Peter followed him out of the prison, but he had no idea that what the angel was doing was really happening; he thought he was seeing a vision. 10 They passed the first and second guards and came to the iron gate leading to the city. It opened for them by itself, and they went through it. When they had walked the length of one street, suddenly the angel left him.

11 Then Peter came to himself and said, "Now I know without a doubt that the Lord has sent his angel and rescued me from Herod's clutches and from everything the Jewish people were hoping would happen."

12 When this had dawned on him, he went to the house of Mary the mother of John, also called Mark, where many people had gathered and were praying. 13 Peter knocked at the outer entrance, and a servant named Rhoda came to answer the door. 14 When she recognized Peter's voice, she was so overjoyed she ran back without opening it and exclaimed, "Peter is at the door!"

15 "You're out of your mind," they told her. When she kept insisting that it was so, they said, "It must be his angel."

16 But Peter kept on knocking, and when they opened the door and saw him, they were astonished. 17 Peter motioned with his hand for them to be quiet and described how the Lord had brought him out of prison. "Tell James and the other brothers and sisters about this," he said, and then he left for another place.

18 In the morning, there was no small commotion among the sol-

diers as to what had become of Peter. [19] After Herod had a thorough search made for him and did not find him, he cross-examined the guards and ordered that they be executed.

Then Herod went from Judea to Caesarea and stayed there. [20] He had been quarreling with the people of Tyre and Sidon; they now joined together and sought an audience with him. After securing the support of Blastus, a trusted personal servant of the king, they asked for peace, because they depended on the king's country for their food supply.

[21] On the appointed day Herod, wearing his royal robes, sat on his throne and delivered a public address to the people. [22] They shouted, "This is the voice of a god, not of a man." [23] Immediately, because Herod did not give praise to God, an angel of the Lord struck him down, and he was eaten by worms and died.

[24] But the word of God continued to spread and flourish.

[25] When Barnabas and Saul had finished their mission, they returned from[a] Jerusalem, taking with them John, also called Mark.

13 [1] Now in the church at Antioch there were prophets and teachers: Barnabas, Simeon called Niger, Lucius of Cyrene, Manaen (who had been brought up with Herod the tetrarch) and Saul. [2] While they were worshiping the Lord and fasting, the Holy Spirit said, "Set apart for me Barnabas and Saul for the work to which I have called them." [3] So after they had fasted and prayed, they placed their hands on them and sent them off.

[4] The two of them, sent on their way by the Holy Spirit, went down to Seleucia and sailed from there to Cyprus. [5] When they arrived at Salamis, they proclaimed the word of God in the Jewish synagogues. John was with them as their helper.

[6] They traveled through the whole island until they came to Paphos. There they met a Jewish sorcerer and false prophet named Bar-Jesus, [7] who was an attendant of the proconsul, Sergius Paulus. The proconsul, an intelligent man, sent for Barnabas and Saul because he wanted to hear the word of God. [8] But Elymas the sorcerer (for that is what his name means) opposed them and tried to turn the proconsul from the faith. [9] Then Saul, who was also called Paul, filled with the Holy Spirit, looked straight at Elymas and said, [10] "You are a child of the devil and an enemy of everything that is right! You are full of all kinds of deceit and trickery. Will you never stop perverting the right ways of the Lord? [11] Now the hand of the Lord is against you. You are going to be blind for a time, not even able to see the light of the sun."

Immediately mist and darkness came over him, and he groped about, seeking someone to lead him by the hand. [12] When the proconsul saw what had happened, he believed, for he was amazed at the teaching about the Lord.

[13] From Paphos, Paul and his companions sailed to Perga in Pamphylia, where John left them to return to Jerusalem. [14] From Perga they went on to Pisidian Antioch. On the Sabbath they entered the synagogue and sat down. [15] After the reading from the Law and the Prophets, the leaders of the synagogue sent word

---

a 25 Some manuscripts *to*

to them, saying, "Brothers, if you have a word of exhortation for the people, please speak."

16 Standing up, Paul motioned with his hand and said: "Fellow Israelites and you Gentiles who worship God, listen to me! 17 The God of the people of Israel chose our ancestors; he made the people prosper during their stay in Egypt; with mighty power he led them out of that country; 18 for about forty years he endured their conduct[a] in the wilderness; 19 and he overthrew seven nations in Canaan, giving their land to his people as their inheritance. 20 All this took about 450 years.

"After this, God gave them judges until the time of Samuel the prophet. 21 Then the people asked for a king, and he gave them Saul son of Kish, of the tribe of Benjamin, who ruled forty years. 22 After removing Saul, he made David their king. God testified concerning him: 'I have found David son of Jesse, a man after my own heart; he will do everything I want him to do.'

23 "From this man's descendants God has brought to Israel the Savior Jesus, as he promised. 24 Before the coming of Jesus, John preached repentance and baptism to all the people of Israel. 25 As John was completing his work, he said: 'Who do you suppose I am? I am not the one you are looking for. But there is one coming after me whose sandals I am not worthy to untie.'

26 "Fellow children of Abraham and you God-fearing Gentiles, it is to us that this message of salvation has been sent. 27 The people of Jerusalem and their rulers did not recognize Jesus, yet in condemn-ing him they fulfilled the words of the prophets that are read every Sabbath. 28 Though they found no proper ground for a death sentence, they asked Pilate to have him executed. 29 When they had carried out all that was written about him, they took him down from the cross and laid him in a tomb. 30 But God raised him from the dead, 31 and for many days he was seen by those who had traveled with him from Galilee to Jerusalem. They are now his witnesses to our people.

32 "We tell you the good news: What God promised our ancestors 33 he has fulfilled for us, their children, by raising up Jesus. As it is written in the second Psalm:

"'You are my son;
    today I have become your
        father.'[b]

34 God raised him from the dead so that he will never be subject to decay. As God has said,

"'I will give you the holy and
    sure blessings promised to
        David.'[c]

35 So it is also stated elsewhere:

"'You will not let your holy one
    see decay.'[d]

36 "Now when David had served God's purpose in his own generation, he fell asleep; he was buried with his ancestors and his body decayed. 37 But the one whom God raised from the dead did not see decay.

38 "Therefore, my friends, I want you to know that through Jesus the forgiveness of sins is proclaimed to you. 39 Through him everyone who believes is set free from every sin,

a 18 Some manuscripts he cared for them   b 33 Psalm 2:7   c 34 Isaiah 55:3
d 35 Psalm 16:10 (see Septuagint)

a justification you were not able to obtain under the law of Moses. ⁴⁰Take care that what the prophets have said does not happen to you:

⁴¹ " 'Look, you scoffers,
    wonder and perish,
for I am going to do something in
        your days
    that you would never believe,
        even if someone told you.'ᵃ"

⁴²As Paul and Barnabas were leaving the synagogue, the people invited them to speak further about these things on the next Sabbath. ⁴³When the congregation was dismissed, many of the Jews and devout converts to Judaism followed Paul and Barnabas, who talked with them and urged them to continue in the grace of God.

⁴⁴On the next Sabbath almost the whole city gathered to hear the word of the Lord. ⁴⁵When the Jews saw the crowds, they were filled with jealousy. They began to contradict what Paul was saying and heaped abuse on him.

⁴⁶Then Paul and Barnabas answered them boldly: "We had to speak the word of God to you first. Since you reject it and do not consider yourselves worthy of eternal life, we now turn to the Gentiles. ⁴⁷For this is what the Lord has commanded us:

" 'I have made youᵇ a light for the
        Gentiles,
    that youᵇ may bring salvation
        to the ends of the earth.'ᶜ"

⁴⁸When the Gentiles heard this, they were glad and honored the word of the Lord; and all who were appointed for eternal life believed.

⁴⁹The word of the Lord spread through the whole region. ⁵⁰But the Jewish leaders incited the God-fearing women of high standing and the leading men of the city. They stirred up persecution against Paul and Barnabas, and expelled them from their region. ⁵¹So they shook the dust off their feet as a warning to them and went to Iconium. ⁵²And the disciples were filled with joy and with the Holy Spirit.

14 At Iconium Paul and Barnabas went as usual into the Jewish synagogue. There they spoke so effectively that a great number of Jews and Greeks believed. ²But the Jews who refused to believe stirred up the other Gentiles and poisoned their minds against the brothers. ³So Paul and Barnabas spent considerable time there, speaking boldly for the Lord, who confirmed the message of his grace by enabling them to perform signs and wonders. ⁴The people of the city were divided; some sided with the Jews, others with the apostles. ⁵There was a plot afoot among both Gentiles and Jews, together with their leaders, to mistreat them and stone them. ⁶But they found out about it and fled to the Lycaonian cities of Lystra and Derbe and to the surrounding country, ⁷where they continued to preach the gospel.

⁸In Lystra there sat a man who was lame. He had been that way from birth and had never walked. ⁹He listened to Paul as he was speaking. Paul looked directly at him, saw that he had faith to be healed ¹⁰and called out, "Stand up on your feet!" At that, the man jumped up and began to walk.

¹¹When the crowd saw what Paul had done, they shouted in the Lycaonian language, "The gods have come down to us in human form!"

ᵃ 41 Hab. 1:5   ᵇ 47 The Greek is singular.   ᶜ 47 Isaiah 49:6

¹²Barnabas they called Zeus, and Paul they called Hermes because he was the chief speaker. ¹³The priest of Zeus, whose temple was just outside the city, brought bulls and wreaths to the city gates because he and the crowd wanted to offer sacrifices to them.

¹⁴But when the apostles Barnabas and Paul heard of this, they tore their clothes and rushed out into the crowd, shouting: ¹⁵"Friends, why are you doing this? We too are only human, like you. We are bringing you good news, telling you to turn from these worthless things to the living God, who made the heavens and the earth and the sea and everything in them. ¹⁶In the past, he let all nations go their own way. ¹⁷Yet he has not left himself without testimony: He has shown kindness by giving you rain from heaven and crops in their seasons; he provides you with plenty of food and fills your hearts with joy." ¹⁸Even with these words, they had difficulty keeping the crowd from sacrificing to them.

¹⁹Then some Jews came from Antioch and Iconium and won the crowd over. They stoned Paul and dragged him outside the city, thinking he was dead. ²⁰But after the disciples had gathered around him, he got up and went back into the city. The next day he and Barnabas left for Derbe.

²¹They preached the gospel in that city and won a large number of disciples. Then they returned to Lystra, Iconium and Antioch, ²²strengthening the disciples and encouraging them to remain true to the faith. "We must go through many hardships to enter the kingdom of God," they said. ²³Paul and Barnabas appointed elders[a] for them in each church and, with prayer and fasting, committed them to the Lord, in whom they had put their trust. ²⁴After going through Pisidia, they came into Pamphylia, ²⁵and when they had preached the word in Perga, they went down to Attalia.

²⁶From Attalia they sailed back to Antioch, where they had been committed to the grace of God for the work they had now completed. ²⁷On arriving there, they gathered the church together and reported all that God had done through them and how he had opened a door of faith to the Gentiles. ²⁸And they stayed there a long time with the disciples.

15 Certain people came down from Judea to Antioch and were teaching the believers: "Unless you are circumcised, according to the custom taught by Moses, you cannot be saved." ²This brought Paul and Barnabas into sharp dispute and debate with them. So Paul and Barnabas were appointed, along with some other believers, to go up to Jerusalem to see the apostles and elders about this question. ³The church sent them on their way, and as they traveled through Phoenicia and Samaria, they told how the Gentiles had been converted. This news made all the believers very glad. ⁴When they came to Jerusalem, they were welcomed by the church and the apostles and elders, to whom they reported everything God had done through them.

⁵Then some of the believers who belonged to the party of the Pharisees stood up and said, "The Gen-

---

ᵃ 23 Or *Barnabas ordained elders*; or *Barnabas had elders elected*

tiles must be circumcised and required to keep the law of Moses."

[6] The apostles and elders met to consider this question. [7] After much discussion, Peter got up and addressed them: "Brothers, you know that some time ago God made a choice among you that the Gentiles might hear from my lips the message of the gospel and believe. [8] God, who knows the heart, showed that he accepted them by giving the Holy Spirit to them, just as he did to us. [9] He did not discriminate between us and them, for he purified their hearts by faith. [10] Now then, why do you try to test God by putting on the necks of Gentiles a yoke that neither we nor our ancestors have been able to bear? [11] No! We believe it is through the grace of our Lord Jesus that we are saved, just as they are."

[12] The whole assembly became silent as they listened to Barnabas and Paul telling about the signs and wonders God had done among the Gentiles through them. [13] When they finished, James spoke up. "Brothers," he said, "listen to me. [14] Simon[a] has described to us how God first intervened to choose a people for his name from the Gentiles. [15] The words of the prophets are in agreement with this, as it is written:

[16] " 'After this I will return
      and rebuild David's fallen
      tent.
   Its ruins I will rebuild,
      and I will restore it,
[17] that the rest of mankind may
      seek the Lord,
      even all the Gentiles who bear
      my name,

says the Lord, who does these
      things'[b]—
[18]   things known from long ago.[c]

[19] "It is my judgment, therefore, that we should not make it difficult for the Gentiles who are turning to God. [20] Instead we should write to them, telling them to abstain from food polluted by idols, from sexual immorality, from the meat of strangled animals and from blood. [21] For the law of Moses has been preached in every city from the earliest times and is read in the synagogues on every Sabbath."

[22] Then the apostles and elders, with the whole church, decided to choose some of their own men and send them to Antioch with Paul and Barnabas. They chose Judas (called Barsabbas) and Silas, men who were leaders among the believers. [23] With them they sent the following letter:

The apostles and elders, your brothers,

To the Gentile believers in Antioch, Syria and Cilicia:

Greetings.

[24] We have heard that some went out from us without our authorization and disturbed you, troubling your minds by what they said. [25] So we all agreed to choose some men and send them to you with our dear friends Barnabas and Paul— [26] men who have risked their lives for the name of our Lord Jesus Christ. [27] Therefore we are sending Judas and Silas to confirm by word of mouth what we are writing. [28] It seemed good

---

[a] 14 Greek *Simeon*, a variant of *Simon*; that is, Peter   [b] 17 Amos 9:11,12 (see Septuagint)
[c] 17,18 Some manuscripts *things'* — / [18]*the Lord's work is known to him from long ago*

to the Holy Spirit and to us not to burden you with anything beyond the following requirements: ²⁹You are to abstain from food sacrificed to idols, from blood, from the meat of strangled animals and from sexual immorality. You will do well to avoid these things.

Farewell.

³⁰So the men were sent off and went down to Antioch, where they gathered the church together and delivered the letter. ³¹The people read it and were glad for its encouraging message. ³²Judas and Silas, who themselves were prophets, said much to encourage and strengthen the believers. ³³After spending some time there, they were sent off by the believers with the blessing of peace to return to those who had sent them. [³⁴]^a ³⁵But Paul and Barnabas remained in Antioch, where they and many others taught and preached the word of the Lord.

³⁶Some time later Paul said to Barnabas, "Let us go back and visit the believers in all the towns where we preached the word of the Lord and see how they are doing." ³⁷Barnabas wanted to take John, also called Mark, with them, ³⁸but Paul did not think it wise to take him, because he had deserted them in Pamphylia and had not continued with them in the work. ³⁹They had such a sharp disagreement that they parted company. Barnabas took Mark and sailed for Cyprus, ⁴⁰but Paul chose Silas and left, commended by the believers to the grace of the Lord. ⁴¹He went through Syria and Cilicia, strengthening the churches.

16 Paul came to Derbe and then to Lystra, where a disciple named Timothy lived, whose mother was Jewish and a believer but whose father was a Greek. ²The believers at Lystra and Iconium spoke well of him. ³Paul wanted to take him along on the journey, so he circumcised him because of the Jews who lived in that area, for they all knew that his father was a Greek. ⁴As they traveled from town to town, they delivered the decisions reached by the apostles and elders in Jerusalem for the people to obey. ⁵So the churches were strengthened in the faith and grew daily in numbers.

⁶Paul and his companions traveled throughout the region of Phrygia and Galatia, having been kept by the Holy Spirit from preaching the word in the province of Asia. ⁷When they came to the border of Mysia, they tried to enter Bithynia, but the Spirit of Jesus would not allow them to. ⁸So they passed by Mysia and went down to Troas. ⁹During the night Paul had a vision of a man of Macedonia standing and begging him, "Come over to Macedonia and help us." ¹⁰After Paul had seen the vision, we got ready at once to leave for Macedonia, concluding that God had called us to preach the gospel to them.

¹¹From Troas we put out to sea and sailed straight for Samothrace, and the next day we went on to Neapolis. ¹²From there we traveled to Philippi, a Roman colony and the leading city of that district^b of Macedonia. And we stayed there several days.

¹³On the Sabbath we went outside the city gate to the river, where we

---

^a 34 Some manuscripts include here *But Silas decided to remain there.*   ^b 12 The text and meaning of the Greek for *the leading city of that district* are uncertain.

expected to find a place of prayer. We sat down and began to speak to the women who had gathered there. ¹⁴One of those listening was a woman from the city of Thyatira named Lydia, a dealer in purple cloth. She was a worshiper of God. The Lord opened her heart to respond to Paul's message. ¹⁵When she and the members of her household were baptized, she invited us to her home. "If you consider me a believer in the Lord," she said, "come and stay at my house." And she persuaded us.

¹⁶Once when we were going to the place of prayer, we were met by a female slave who had a spirit by which she predicted the future. She earned a great deal of money for her owners by fortune-telling. ¹⁷She followed Paul and the rest of us, shouting, "These men are servants of the Most High God, who are telling you the way to be saved." ¹⁸She kept this up for many days. Finally Paul became so annoyed that he turned around and said to the spirit, "In the name of Jesus Christ I command you to come out of her!" At that moment the spirit left her.

¹⁹When her owners realized that their hope of making money was gone, they seized Paul and Silas and dragged them into the marketplace to face the authorities. ²⁰They brought them before the magistrates and said, "These men are Jews, and are throwing our city into an uproar ²¹by advocating customs unlawful for us Romans to accept or practice."

²²The crowd joined in the attack against Paul and Silas, and the magistrates ordered them to be stripped and beaten with rods. ²³After they had been severely flogged, they were thrown into prison, and the jailer was commanded to guard them carefully. ²⁴When he received these orders, he put them in the inner cell and fastened their feet in the stocks.

²⁵About midnight Paul and Silas were praying and singing hymns to God, and the other prisoners were listening to them. ²⁶Suddenly there was such a violent earthquake that the foundations of the prison were shaken. At once all the prison doors flew open, and everyone's chains came loose. ²⁷The jailer woke up, and when he saw the prison doors open, he drew his sword and was about to kill himself because he thought the prisoners had escaped. ²⁸But Paul shouted, "Don't harm yourself! We are all here!"

²⁹The jailer called for lights, rushed in and fell trembling before Paul and Silas. ³⁰He then brought them out and asked, "Sirs, what must I do to be saved?"

³¹They replied, "Believe in the Lord Jesus, and you will be saved—you and your household." ³²Then they spoke the word of the Lord to him and to all the others in his house. ³³At that hour of the night the jailer took them and washed their wounds; then immediately he and all his household were baptized. ³⁴The jailer brought them into his house and set a meal before them; he was filled with joy because he had come to believe in God—he and his whole household.

³⁵When it was daylight, the magistrates sent their officers to the jailer with the order: "Release those men." ³⁶The jailer told Paul, "The magistrates have ordered that you and Silas be released. Now you can leave. Go in peace."

³⁷But Paul said to the officers: "They beat us publicly without a tri-

al, even though we are Roman citizens, and threw us into prison. And now do they want to get rid of us quietly? No! Let them come themselves and escort us out."

³⁸The officers reported this to the magistrates, and when they heard that Paul and Silas were Roman citizens, they were alarmed. ³⁹They came to appease them and escorted them from the prison, requesting them to leave the city. ⁴⁰After Paul and Silas came out of the prison, they went to Lydia's house, where they met with the brothers and sisters and encouraged them. Then they left.

17 When Paul and his companions had passed through Amphipolis and Apollonia, they came to Thessalonica, where there was a Jewish synagogue. ²As was his custom, Paul went into the synagogue, and on three Sabbath days he reasoned with them from the Scriptures, ³explaining and proving that the Messiah had to suffer and rise from the dead. "This Jesus I am proclaiming to you is the Messiah," he said. ⁴Some of the Jews were persuaded and joined Paul and Silas, as did a large number of God-fearing Greeks and quite a few prominent women.

⁵But other Jews were jealous; so they rounded up some bad characters from the marketplace, formed a mob and started a riot in the city. They rushed to Jason's house in search of Paul and Silas in order to bring them out to the crowd.ᵃ ⁶But when they did not find them, they dragged Jason and some other believers before the city officials, shouting: "These men who have caused trouble all over the world have now come here, ⁷and Jason

has welcomed them into his house. They are all defying Caesar's decrees, saying that there is another king, one called Jesus." ⁸When they heard this, the crowd and the city officials were thrown into turmoil. ⁹Then they made Jason and the others post bond and let them go.

¹⁰As soon as it was night, the believers sent Paul and Silas away to Berea. On arriving there, they went to the Jewish synagogue. ¹¹Now the Berean Jews were of more noble character than those in Thessalonica, for they received the message with great eagerness and examined the Scriptures every day to see if what Paul said was true. ¹²As a result, many of them believed, as did also a number of prominent Greek women and many Greek men.

¹³But when the Jews in Thessalonica learned that Paul was preaching the word of God at Berea, some of them went there too, agitating the crowds and stirring them up. ¹⁴The believers immediately sent Paul to the coast, but Silas and Timothy stayed at Berea. ¹⁵Those who escorted Paul brought him to Athens and then left with instructions for Silas and Timothy to join him as soon as possible.

¹⁶While Paul was waiting for them in Athens, he was greatly distressed to see that the city was full of idols. ¹⁷So he reasoned in the synagogue with both Jews and God-fearing Greeks, as well as in the marketplace day by day with those who happened to be there. ¹⁸A group of Epicurean and Stoic philosophers began to debate with him. Some of them asked, "What is this babbler trying to say?" Others remarked, "He seems to be advocating foreign gods." They said this because Paul

---

ᵃ 5 Or *the assembly of the people*

was preaching the good news about Jesus and the resurrection. ¹⁹Then they took him and brought him to a meeting of the Areopagus, where they said to him, "May we know what this new teaching is that you are presenting? ²⁰You are bringing some strange ideas to our ears, and we would like to know what they mean." ²¹(All the Athenians and the foreigners who lived there spent their time doing nothing but talking about and listening to the latest ideas.)

²²Paul then stood up in the meeting of the Areopagus and said: "People of Athens! I see that in every way you are very religious. ²³For as I walked around and looked carefully at your objects of worship, I even found an altar with this inscription: TO AN UNKNOWN GOD. So you are ignorant of the very thing you worship—and this is what I am going to proclaim to you.

²⁴"The God who made the world and everything in it is the Lord of heaven and earth and does not live in temples built by human hands. ²⁵And he is not served by human hands, as if he needed anything. Rather, he himself gives everyone life and breath and everything else. ²⁶From one man he made all the nations, that they should inhabit the whole earth; and he marked out their appointed times in history and the boundaries of their lands. ²⁷God did this so that they would seek him and perhaps reach out for him and find him, though he is not far from any one of us. ²⁸'For in him we live and move and have our being.'ᵃ As some of your own poets have said, 'We are his offspring.'ᵇ

²⁹"Therefore since we are God's offspring, we should not think that the divine being is like gold or silver or stone—an image made by human design and skill. ³⁰In the past God overlooked such ignorance, but now he commands all people everywhere to repent. ³¹For he has set a day when he will judge the world with justice by the man he has appointed. He has given proof of this to everyone by raising him from the dead."

³²When they heard about the resurrection of the dead, some of them sneered, but others said, "We want to hear you again on this subject." ³³At that, Paul left the Council. ³⁴Some of the people became followers of Paul and believed. Among them was Dionysius, a member of the Areopagus, also a woman named Damaris, and a number of others.

18 After this, Paul left Athens and went to Corinth. ²There he met a Jew named Aquila, a native of Pontus, who had recently come from Italy with his wife Priscilla, because Claudius had ordered all Jews to leave Rome. Paul went to see them, ³and because he was a tentmaker as they were, he stayed and worked with them. ⁴Every Sabbath he reasoned in the synagogue, trying to persuade Jews and Greeks.

⁵When Silas and Timothy came from Macedonia, Paul devoted himself exclusively to preaching, testifying to the Jews that Jesus was the Messiah. ⁶But when they opposed Paul and became abusive, he shook out his clothes in protest and said to them, "Your blood be on your own heads! I am innocent of it. From now on I will go to the Gentiles."

⁷Then Paul left the synagogue and went next door to the house of

---

ᵃ 28 From the Cretan philosopher Epimenides   ᵇ 28 From the Cilician Stoic philosopher Aratus

Titius Justus, a worshiper of God. [8]Crispus, the synagogue leader, and his entire household believed in the Lord; and many of the Corinthians who heard Paul believed and were baptized.

[9]One night the Lord spoke to Paul in a vision: "Do not be afraid; keep on speaking, do not be silent. [10]For I am with you, and no one is going to attack and harm you, because I have many people in this city." [11]So Paul stayed in Corinth for a year and a half, teaching them the word of God.

[12]While Gallio was proconsul of Achaia, the Jews of Corinth made a united attack on Paul and brought him to the place of judgment. [13]"This man," they charged, "is persuading the people to worship God in ways contrary to the law."

[14]Just as Paul was about to speak, Gallio said to them, "If you Jews were making a complaint about some misdemeanor or serious crime, it would be reasonable for me to listen to you. [15]But since it involves questions about words and names and your own law—settle the matter yourselves. I will not be a judge of such things." [16]So he drove them off. [17]Then the crowd there turned on Sosthenes the synagogue leader and beat him in front of the proconsul; and Gallio showed no concern whatever.

[18]Paul stayed on in Corinth for some time. Then he left the brothers and sisters and sailed for Syria, accompanied by Priscilla and Aquila. Before he sailed, he had his hair cut off at Cenchreae because of a vow he had taken. [19]They arrived at Ephesus, where Paul left Priscilla and Aquila. He himself went into the synagogue and reasoned with the Jews. [20]When they asked him to spend more time with them, he declined. [21]But as he left, he promised, "I will come back if it is God's will." Then he set sail from Ephesus. [22]When he landed at Caesarea, he went up to Jerusalem and greeted the church and then went down to Antioch.

[23]After spending some time in Antioch, Paul set out from there and traveled from place to place throughout the region of Galatia and Phrygia, strengthening all the disciples.

[24]Meanwhile a Jew named Apollos, a native of Alexandria, came to Ephesus. He was a learned man, with a thorough knowledge of the Scriptures. [25]He had been instructed in the way of the Lord, and he spoke with great fervor[a] and taught about Jesus accurately, though he knew only the baptism of John. [26]He began to speak boldly in the synagogue. When Priscilla and Aquila heard him, they invited him to their home and explained to him the way of God more adequately.

[27]When Apollos wanted to go to Achaia, the brothers and sisters encouraged him and wrote to the disciples there to welcome him. When he arrived, he was a great help to those who by grace had believed. [28]For he vigorously refuted his Jewish opponents in public debate, proving from the Scriptures that Jesus was the Messiah.

19 While Apollos was at Corinth, Paul took the road through the interior and arrived at Ephesus. There he found some disciples [2]and asked them, "Did you receive the Holy Spirit when[b] you believed?"

They answered, "No, we have

---

[a] 25 Or *with fervor in the Spirit*   [b] 2 Or *after*

not even heard that there is a Holy Spirit."

³So Paul asked, "Then what baptism did you receive?"

"John's baptism," they replied.

⁴Paul said, "John's baptism was a baptism of repentance. He told the people to believe in the one coming after him, that is, in Jesus." ⁵On hearing this, they were baptized in the name of the Lord Jesus. ⁶When Paul placed his hands on them, the Holy Spirit came on them, and they spoke in tongues*ᵃ* and prophesied. ⁷There were about twelve men in all.

⁸Paul entered the synagogue and spoke boldly there for three months, arguing persuasively about the kingdom of God. ⁹But some of them became obstinate; they refused to believe and publicly maligned the Way. So Paul left them. He took the disciples with him and had discussions daily in the lecture hall of Tyrannus. ¹⁰This went on for two years, so that all the Jews and Greeks who lived in the province of Asia heard the word of the Lord.

¹¹God did extraordinary miracles through Paul, ¹²so that even handkerchiefs and aprons that had touched him were taken to the sick, and their illnesses were cured and the evil spirits left them.

¹³Some Jews who went around driving out evil spirits tried to invoke the name of the Lord Jesus over those who were demon-possessed. They would say, "In the name of the Jesus whom Paul preaches, I command you to come out." ¹⁴Seven sons of Sceva, a Jewish chief priest, were doing this. ¹⁵One day the evil spirit answered them, "Jesus I know, and Paul I know about, but

who are you?" ¹⁶Then the man who had the evil spirit jumped on them and overpowered them all. He gave them such a beating that they ran out of the house naked and bleeding.

¹⁷When this became known to the Jews and Greeks living in Ephesus, they were all seized with fear, and the name of the Lord Jesus was held in high honor. ¹⁸Many of those who believed now came and openly confessed what they had done. ¹⁹A number who had practiced sorcery brought their scrolls together and burned them publicly. When they calculated the value of the scrolls, the total came to fifty thousand drachmas.*ᵇ* ²⁰In this way the word of the Lord spread widely and grew in power.

²¹After all this had happened, Paul decided*ᶜ* to go to Jerusalem, passing through Macedonia and Achaia. "After I have been there," he said, "I must visit Rome also." ²²He sent two of his helpers, Timothy and Erastus, to Macedonia, while he stayed in the province of Asia a little longer.

²³About that time there arose a great disturbance about the Way. ²⁴A silversmith named Demetrius, who made silver shrines of Artemis, brought in a lot of business for the craftsmen there. ²⁵He called them together, along with the workers in related trades, and said: "You know, my friends, that we receive a good income from this business. ²⁶And you see and hear how this fellow Paul has convinced and led astray large numbers of people here in Ephesus and in practically the whole province of Asia. He says

---

ᵃ 6 Or *other languages*　　*ᵇ 19* A drachma was a silver coin worth about a day's wages.　　*ᶜ 21* Or *decided in the Spirit*

that gods made by human hands are no gods at all. ²⁷There is danger not only that our trade will lose its good name, but also that the temple of the great goddess Artemis will be discredited; and the goddess herself, who is worshiped throughout the province of Asia and the world, will be robbed of her divine majesty."

²⁸When they heard this, they were furious and began shouting: "Great is Artemis of the Ephesians!" ²⁹Soon the whole city was in an uproar. The people seized Gaius and Aristarchus, Paul's traveling companions from Macedonia, and all of them rushed into the theater together. ³⁰Paul wanted to appear before the crowd, but the disciples would not let him. ³¹Even some of the officials of the province, friends of Paul, sent him a message begging him not to venture into the theater.

³²The assembly was in confusion: Some were shouting one thing, some another. Most of the people did not even know why they were there. ³³The Jews in the crowd pushed Alexander to the front, and they shouted instructions to him. He motioned for silence in order to make a defense before the people. ³⁴But when they realized he was a Jew, they all shouted in unison for about two hours: "Great is Artemis of the Ephesians!"

³⁵The city clerk quieted the crowd and said: "Fellow Ephesians, doesn't all the world know that the city of Ephesus is the guardian of the temple of the great Artemis and of her image, which fell from heaven? ³⁶Therefore, since these facts are undeniable, you ought to calm down and not do anything rash. ³⁷You have brought these men here, though they have neither robbed temples nor blasphemed our goddess. ³⁸If, then, Demetrius and his fellow craftsmen have a grievance against anybody, the courts are open and there are proconsuls. They can press charges. ³⁹If there is anything further you want to bring up, it must be settled in a legal assembly. ⁴⁰As it is, we are in danger of being charged with rioting because of what happened today. In that case we would not be able to account for this commotion, since there is no reason for it." ⁴¹After he had said this, he dismissed the assembly.

20 When the uproar had ended, Paul sent for the disciples and, after encouraging them, said goodbye and set out for Macedonia. ²He traveled through that area, speaking many words of encouragement to the people, and finally arrived in Greece, ³where he stayed three months. Because some Jews had plotted against him just as he was about to sail for Syria, he decided to go back through Macedonia. ⁴He was accompanied by Sopater son of Pyrrhus from Berea, Aristarchus and Secundus from Thessalonica, Gaius from Derbe, Timothy also, and Tychicus and Trophimus from the province of Asia. ⁵These men went on ahead and waited for us at Troas. ⁶But we sailed from Philippi after the Festival of Unleavened Bread, and five days later joined the others at Troas, where we stayed seven days.

⁷On the first day of the week we came together to break bread. Paul spoke to the people and, because he intended to leave the next day, kept on talking until midnight. ⁸There were many lamps in the upstairs room where we were meeting. ⁹Seated in a window was a young

man named Eutychus, who was sinking into a deep sleep as Paul talked on and on. When he was sound asleep, he fell to the ground from the third story and was picked up dead. 10 Paul went down, threw himself on the young man and put his arms around him. "Don't be alarmed," he said. "He's alive!" 11 Then he went upstairs again and broke bread and ate. After talking until daylight, he left. 12 The people took the young man home alive and were greatly comforted.

13 We went on ahead to the ship and sailed for Assos, where we were going to take Paul aboard. He had made this arrangement because he was going there on foot. 14 When he met us at Assos, we took him aboard and went on to Mitylene. 15 The next day we set sail from there and arrived off Chios. The day after that we crossed over to Samos, and on the following day arrived at Miletus. 16 Paul had decided to sail past Ephesus to avoid spending time in the province of Asia, for he was in a hurry to reach Jerusalem, if possible, by the day of Pentecost.

17 From Miletus, Paul sent to Ephesus for the elders of the church. 18 When they arrived, he said to them: "You know how I lived the whole time I was with you, from the first day I came into the province of Asia. 19 I served the Lord with great humility and with tears, in the midst of severe testing by the plots of my Jewish opponents. 20 You know that I have not hesitated to preach anything that would be helpful to you but have taught you publicly and from house to house. 21 I have declared to both Jews and Greeks that they must turn to God

in repentance and have faith in our Lord Jesus.

22 "And now, compelled by the Spirit, I am going to Jerusalem, not knowing what will happen to me there. 23 I only know that in every city the Holy Spirit warns me that prison and hardships are facing me. 24 However, I consider my life worth nothing to me; my only aim is to finish the race and complete the task the Lord Jesus has given me — the task of testifying to the good news of God's grace.

25 "Now I know that none of you among whom I have gone about preaching the kingdom will ever see me again. 26 Therefore, I declare to you today that I am innocent of the blood of any of you. 27 For I have not hesitated to proclaim to you the whole will of God. 28 Keep watch over yourselves and all the flock of which the Holy Spirit has made you overseers. Be shepherds of the church of God,*a* which he bought with his own blood.*b* 29 I know that after I leave, savage wolves will come in among you and will not spare the flock. 30 Even from your own number men will arise and distort the truth in order to draw away disciples after them. 31 So be on your guard! Remember that for three years I never stopped warning each of you night and day with tears.

32 "Now I commit you to God and to the word of his grace, which can build you up and give you an inheritance among all those who are sanctified. 33 I have not coveted anyone's silver or gold or clothing. 34 You yourselves know that these hands of mine have supplied my own needs and the needs of my companions. 35 In everything I did, I showed you

a 28 Many manuscripts *of the Lord*   *b 28* Or *with the blood of his own Son.*

that by this kind of hard work we must help the weak, remembering the words the Lord Jesus himself said: 'It is more blessed to give than to receive.' "

36When Paul had finished speaking, he knelt down with all of them and prayed. 37They all wept as they embraced him and kissed him. 38What grieved them most was his statement that they would never see his face again. Then they accompanied him to the ship.

21 After we had torn ourselves away from them, we put out to sea and sailed straight to Kos. The next day we went to Rhodes and from there to Patara. 2We found a ship crossing over to Phoenicia, went on board and set sail. 3After sighting Cyprus and passing to the south of it, we sailed on to Syria. We landed at Tyre, where our ship was to unload its cargo. 4We sought out the disciples there and stayed with them seven days. Through the Spirit they urged Paul not to go on to Jerusalem. 5When it was time to leave, we left and continued on our way. All of them, including wives and children, accompanied us out of the city, and there on the beach we knelt to pray. 6After saying goodbye to each other, we went aboard the ship, and they returned home.

7We continued our voyage from Tyre and landed at Ptolemais, where we greeted the brothers and sisters and stayed with them for a day. 8Leaving the next day, we reached Caesarea and stayed at the house of Philip the evangelist, one of the Seven. 9He had four unmarried daughters who prophesied.

10After we had been there a number of days, a prophet named Agabus came down from Judea. 11Coming over to us, he took Paul's belt, tied his own hands and feet with it and said, "The Holy Spirit says, 'In this way the Jewish leaders in Jerusalem will bind the owner of this belt and will hand him over to the Gentiles.' "

12When we heard this, we and the people there pleaded with Paul not to go up to Jerusalem. 13Then Paul answered, "Why are you weeping and breaking my heart? I am ready not only to be bound, but also to die in Jerusalem for the name of the Lord Jesus." 14When he would not be dissuaded, we gave up and said, "The Lord's will be done."

15After this, we started on our way up to Jerusalem. 16Some of the disciples from Caesarea accompanied us and brought us to the home of Mnason, where we were to stay. He was a man from Cyprus and one of the early disciples.

17When we arrived at Jerusalem, the brothers and sisters received us warmly. 18The next day Paul and the rest of us went to see James, and all the elders were present. 19Paul greeted them and reported in detail what God had done among the Gentiles through his ministry.

20When they heard this, they praised God. Then they said to Paul: "You see, brother, how many thousands of Jews have believed, and all of them are zealous for the law. 21They have been informed that you teach all the Jews who live among the Gentiles to turn away from Moses, telling them not to circumcise their children or live according to our customs. 22What shall we do? They will certainly hear that you have come, 23so do what we tell you. There are four men with us who have made a vow. 24Take these men, join in their purification rites and pay their expenses, so that they can have their heads shaved. Then everyone will know there is no truth in these reports about you, but that you yourself are living in obedience to the law. 25 As for the Gentile believers, we have written to them our decision that they should abstain from food sacrificed to idols, from blood, from the meat of strangled animals and from sexual immorality."

26 The next day Paul took the men and purified himself along with them. Then he went to the temple to give notice of the date when the days of purification would end and the offering would be made for each of them.

27 When the seven days were nearly over, some Jews from the province of Asia saw Paul at the temple. They stirred up the whole crowd and seized him, 28 shouting, "Fellow Israelites, help us! This is the man who teaches everyone everywhere against our people and our law and this place. And besides, he has brought Greeks into the temple and defiled this holy place." 29 (They had previously seen Trophimus the Ephesian in the city with Paul and assumed that Paul had brought him into the temple.)

30 The whole city was aroused, and the people came running from all directions. Seizing Paul, they dragged him from the temple, and immediately the gates were shut. 31 While they were trying to kill him, news reached the commander of the Roman troops that the whole city of Jerusalem was in an uproar. 32 He at once took some officers and soldiers and ran down to the crowd. When the rioters saw the commander and his soldiers, they stopped beating Paul.

33 The commander came up and arrested him and ordered him to be bound with two chains. Then he asked who he was and what he had done. 34 Some in the crowd shouted one thing and some another, and since the commander could not get at the truth because of the uproar, he ordered that Paul be taken into the barracks. 35 When Paul reached the steps, the violence of the mob was so great he had to be carried by the soldiers. 36 The crowd that followed kept shouting, "Get rid of him!"

37 As the soldiers were about to take Paul into the barracks, he asked the commander, "May I say something to you?"

"Do you speak Greek?" he replied. 38 "Aren't you the Egyptian who started a revolt and led four thousand terrorists out into the wilderness some time ago?"

39 Paul answered, "I am a Jew, from Tarsus in Cilicia, a citizen of no ordinary city. Please let me speak to the people."

40 After receiving the commander's permission, Paul stood on the steps and motioned to the crowd. When they were all silent, he said to them in Aramaic: [a] 22 1 "Brothers and fathers, listen now to my defense."

2 When they heard him speak to them in Aramaic, they became very quiet.

Then Paul said: 3 "I am a Jew, born in Tarsus of Cilicia, but brought up in this city. I studied under Gamaliel and was thoroughly trained in the law of our ancestors. I was just as zealous for God as any of you are today. 4 I persecuted the followers of this Way to their death, arresting both men and women and throwing them into prison, 5 as the high priest and all the Council can themselves testify. I even obtained letters from them to their associates in Damascus, and went there to bring these people as prisoners to Jerusalem to be punished.

6 "About noon as I came near Damascus, suddenly a bright light from heaven flashed around me. 7 I fell to the ground and heard a voice say to me, 'Saul! Saul! Why do you persecute me?'

8 " 'Who are you, Lord?' I asked.

" 'I am Jesus of Nazareth, whom you are persecuting,' he replied. 9 My companions saw the light, but they did not understand the voice of him who was speaking to me.

10 " 'What shall I do, Lord?' I asked.

" 'Get up,' the Lord said, 'and go into Damascus. There you will be told all that you have been assigned to do.' 11 My companions led me by the hand into Damascus, because the brilliance of the light had blinded me.

12 "A man named Ananias came to see me. He was a devout observer of the law and highly respected by all the Jews living there. 13 He stood beside me and said, 'Brother Saul, receive your sight!' And at that very moment I was able to see him.

14 "Then he said: 'The God of our ancestors has chosen you to know his will and to see the Righteous One and to hear words from his mouth. 15 You will be his witness to all people of what you have seen and heard. 16 And now what are you waiting for? Get up, be baptized and wash your sins away, calling on his name.'

17 "When I returned to Jerusalem and was praying at the temple, I fell into a trance 18 and saw the Lord speaking to me. 'Quick!' he said. 'Leave Jerusalem immediately, because the people here will not accept your testimony about me.'

19 " 'Lord,' I replied, 'these people know that I went from one synagogue to another to imprison and beat those who believe in you. 20 And when the blood of your martyr[a] Stephen was shed, I stood there giving my approval and guarding the clothes of those who were killing him.'

21 "Then the Lord said to me, 'Go; I will send you far away to the Gentiles.' "

22 The crowd listened to Paul until he said this. Then they raised their voices and shouted, "Rid the earth of him! He's not fit to live!"

23 As they were shouting and throwing off their cloaks and flinging dust into the air, 24 the commander ordered that Paul be taken into the barracks. He directed that he be flogged and interrogated in order to find out why the people were shouting at him like this. 25 As they stretched him out to flog him, Paul said to the centurion standing there, "Is it legal for you to flog a Roman citizen who hasn't even been found guilty?"

26 When the centurion heard this, he went to the commander and reported it. "What are you going to do?" he asked. "This man is a Roman citizen."

27 The commander went to Paul and asked, "Tell me, are you a Roman citizen?"

"Yes, I am," he answered.

28 Then the commander said, "I had to pay a lot of money for my citizenship."

---

[a] 20 Or *witness*

"But I was born a citizen," Paul replied.

29 Those who were about to interrogate him withdrew immediately. The commander himself was alarmed when he realized that he had put Paul, a Roman citizen, in chains.

30 The commander wanted to find out exactly why Paul was being accused by the Jews. So the next day he released him and ordered the chief priests and all the members of the Sanhedrin to assemble. Then he brought Paul and had him stand before them.

23 Paul looked straight at the Sanhedrin and said, "My brothers, I have fulfilled my duty to God in all good conscience to this day." 2 At this the high priest Ananias ordered those standing near Paul to strike him on the mouth. 3 Then Paul said to him, "God will strike you, you whitewashed wall! You sit there to judge me according to the law, yet you yourself violate the law by commanding that I be struck!"

4 Those who were standing near Paul said, "How dare you insult God's high priest!"

5 Paul replied, "Brothers, I did not realize that he was the high priest; for it is written: 'Do not speak evil about the ruler of your people.'[a]"

6 Then Paul, knowing that some of them were Sadducees and the others Pharisees, called out in the Sanhedrin, "My brothers, I am a Pharisee, descended from Pharisees. I stand on trial because of the hope of the resurrection of the dead." 7 When he said this, a dispute broke out between the Pharisees and the Sadducees, and the assembly was divided. 8 (The Sadducees say that there is no resurrection, and that

there are neither angels nor spirits, but the Pharisees believe all these things.)

9 There was a great uproar, and some of the teachers of the law who were Pharisees stood up and argued vigorously. "We find nothing wrong with this man," they said. "What if a spirit or an angel has spoken to him?" 10 The dispute became so violent that the commander was afraid Paul would be torn to pieces by them. He ordered the troops to go down and take him away from them by force and bring him into the barracks.

11 The following night the Lord stood near Paul and said, "Take courage! As you have testified about me in Jerusalem, so you must also testify in Rome."

12 The next morning some Jews formed a conspiracy and bound themselves with an oath not to eat or drink until they had killed Paul. 13 More than forty men were involved in this plot. 14 They went to the chief priests and the elders and said, "We have taken a solemn oath not to eat anything until we have killed Paul. 15 Now then, you and the Sanhedrin petition the commander to bring him before you on the pretext of wanting more accurate information about his case. We are ready to kill him before he gets here."

16 But when the son of Paul's sister heard of this plot, he went into the barracks and told Paul.

17 Then Paul called one of the centurions and said, "Take this young man to the commander; he has something to tell him." 18 So he took him to the commander.

The centurion said, "Paul, the prisoner, sent for me and asked

a 5 Exodus 22:28

me to bring this young man to you because he has something to tell you."

[19] The commander took the young man by the hand, drew him aside and asked, "What is it you want to tell me?"

[20] He said: "Some Jews have agreed to ask you to bring Paul before the Sanhedrin tomorrow on the pretext of wanting more accurate information about him. [21] Don't give in to them, because more than forty of them are waiting in ambush for him. They have taken an oath not to eat or drink until they have killed him. They are ready now, waiting for your consent to their request."

[22] The commander dismissed the young man with this warning: "Don't tell anyone that you have reported this to me."

[23] Then he called two of his centurions and ordered them, "Get ready a detachment of two hundred soldiers, seventy horsemen and two hundred spearmen[a] to go to Caesarea at nine tonight. [24] Provide horses for Paul so that he may be taken safely to Governor Felix."

[25] He wrote a letter as follows:

[26] Claudius Lysias,

To His Excellency, Governor Felix:

Greetings.

[27] This man was seized by the Jews and they were about to kill him, but I came with my troops and rescued him, for I had learned that he is a Roman citizen. [28] I wanted to know why they were accusing him, so I brought him to their Sanhedrin. [29] I found that the accu-

sation had to do with questions about their law, but there was no charge against him that deserved death or imprisonment. [30] When I was informed of a plot to be carried out against the man, I sent him to you at once. I also ordered his accusers to present to you their case against him.

[31] So the soldiers, carrying out their orders, took Paul with them during the night and brought him as far as Antipatris. [32] The next day they let the cavalry go on with him, while they returned to the barracks. [33] When the cavalry arrived in Caesarea, they delivered the letter to the governor and handed Paul over to him. [34] The governor read the letter and asked what province he was from. Learning that he was from Cilicia, [35] he said, "I will hear your case when your accusers get here." Then he ordered that Paul be kept under guard in Herod's palace.

24 Five days later the high priest Ananias went down to Caesarea with some of the elders and a lawyer named Tertullus, and they brought their charges against Paul before the governor. [2] When Paul was called in, Tertullus presented his case before Felix: "We have enjoyed a long period of peace under you, and your foresight has brought about reforms in this nation. [3] Everywhere and in every way, most excellent Felix, we acknowledge this with profound gratitude. [4] But in order not to weary you further, I would request that you be kind enough to hear us briefly.

[5] "We have found this man to be a troublemaker, stirring up riots among the Jews all over the world.

---

[a] 23 The meaning of the Greek for this word is uncertain.

He is a ringleader of the Nazarene sect [6]and even tried to desecrate the temple; so we seized him. [7]a [8]By examining him yourself you will be able to learn the truth about all these charges we are bringing against him."

[9]The other Jews joined in the accusation, asserting that these things were true.

[10]When the governor motioned for him to speak, Paul replied: "I know that for a number of years you have been a judge over this nation; so I gladly make my defense. [11]You can easily verify that no more than twelve days ago I went up to Jerusalem to worship. [12]My accusers did not find me arguing with anyone at the temple, or stirring up a crowd in the synagogues or anywhere else in the city. [13]And they cannot prove to you the charges they are now making against me. [14]However, I admit that I worship the God of our ancestors as a follower of the Way, which they call a sect. I believe everything that is in accordance with the Law and that is written in the Prophets, [15]and I have the same hope in God as these men themselves have, that there will be a resurrection of both the righteous and the wicked. [16]So I strive always to keep my conscience clear before God and man.

[17]"After an absence of several years, I came to Jerusalem to bring my people gifts for the poor and to present offerings. [18]I was ceremonially clean when they found me in the temple courts doing this. There was no crowd with me, nor was I involved in any disturbance. [19]But there are some Jews from the province of Asia, who ought to be here before you and bring charges if they have anything against me. [20]Or these who are here should state what crime they found in me when I stood before the Sanhedrin— [21]unless it was this one thing I shouted as I stood in their presence: 'It is concerning the resurrection of the dead that I am on trial before you today.'"

[22]Then Felix, who was well acquainted with the Way, adjourned the proceedings. "When Lysias the commander comes," he said, "I will decide your case." [23]He ordered the centurion to keep Paul under guard but to give him some freedom and permit his friends to take care of his needs.

[24]Several days later Felix came with his wife Drusilla, who was Jewish. He sent for Paul and listened to him as he spoke about faith in Christ Jesus. [25]As Paul talked about righteousness, self-control and the judgment to come, Felix was afraid and said, "That's enough for now! You may leave. When I find it convenient, I will send for you." [26]At the same time he was hoping that Paul would offer him a bribe, so he sent for him frequently and talked with him.

[27]When two years had passed, Felix was succeeded by Porcius Festus, but because Felix wanted to grant a favor to the Jews, he left Paul in prison.

25 Three days after arriving in the province, Festus went up from Caesarea to Jerusalem, [2]where the chief priests and the Jewish leaders appeared before him and presented the charges against Paul. [3]They requested Festus, as a favor to them,

---

a 6-8 Some manuscripts include here him, and we would have judged him in accordance with our law. [7]But the commander Lysias came and took him from us with much violence, [8]ordering his accusers to come before you.

to have Paul transferred to Jerusalem, for they were preparing an ambush to kill him along the way. 4Festus answered, "Paul is being held at Caesarea, and I myself am going there soon. 5Let some of your leaders come with me, and if the man has done anything wrong, they can press charges against him there."

6After spending eight or ten days with them, Festus went down to Caesarea. The next day he convened the court and ordered that Paul be brought before him. 7When Paul came in, the Jews who had come down from Jerusalem stood around him. They brought many serious charges against him, but they could not prove them.

8Then Paul made his defense: "I have done nothing wrong against the Jewish law or against the temple or against Caesar."

9Festus, wishing to do the Jews a favor, said to Paul, "Are you willing to go up to Jerusalem and stand trial before me there on these charges?"

10Paul answered: "I am now standing before Caesar's court, where I ought to be tried. I have not done any wrong to the Jews, as you yourself know very well. 11If, however, I am guilty of doing anything deserving death, I do not refuse to die. But if the charges brought against me by these Jews are not true, no one has the right to hand me over to them. I appeal to Caesar!"

12After Festus had conferred with his council, he declared: "You have appealed to Caesar. To Caesar you will go!"

13A few days later King Agrippa and Bernice arrived at Caesarea to pay their respects to Festus. 14Since they were spending many days there, Festus discussed Paul's case with the king. He said: "There is a man here whom Felix left as a prisoner. 15When I went to Jerusalem, the chief priests and the elders of the Jews brought charges against him and asked that he be condemned.

16"I told them that it is not the Roman custom to hand over anyone before they have faced their accusers and have had an opportunity to defend themselves against the charges. 17When they came here with me, I did not delay the case, but convened the court the next day and ordered the man to be brought in. 18When his accusers got up to speak, they did not charge him with any of the crimes I had expected. 19Instead, they had some points of dispute with him about their own religion and about a dead man named Jesus who Paul claimed was alive. 20I was at a loss how to investigate such matters; so I asked if he would be willing to go to Jerusalem and stand trial there on these charges. 21But when Paul made his appeal to be held over for the Emperor's decision, I ordered him held until I could send him to Caesar."

22Then Agrippa said to Festus, "I would like to hear this man myself."

He replied, "Tomorrow you will hear him."

23The next day Agrippa and Bernice came with great pomp and entered the audience room with the high-ranking military officers and the prominent men of the city. At the command of Festus, Paul was brought in. 24Festus said: "King Agrippa, and all who are present with us, you see this man! The whole Jewish community has petitioned me about him in Jerusalem and here in Caesarea, shouting that he ought not to live any longer. 25I found he had done nothing deserving of death, but because he made his appeal to the Emperor I decided to send him to Rome. 26But I have nothing definite to write to His Majesty about him. Therefore I have brought him before all of you, and especially before you, King Agrippa, so that as a result of this investigation I may have something to write. 27For I think it is unreasonable to send a prisoner on to Rome without specifying the charges against him."

26 Then Agrippa said to Paul, "You have permission to speak for yourself."

So Paul motioned with his hand and began his defense: 2"King Agrippa, I consider myself fortunate to stand before you today as I make my defense against all the accusations of the Jews, 3and especially so because you are well acquainted with all the Jewish customs and controversies. Therefore, I beg you to listen to me patiently.

4"The Jewish people all know the way I have lived ever since I was a child, from the beginning of my life in my own country, and also in Jerusalem. 5They have known me for a long time and can testify, if they are willing, that I conformed to the strictest sect of our religion, living as a Pharisee. 6And now it is because of my hope in what God has promised our ancestors that I am on trial today. 7This is the promise our twelve tribes are hoping to see fulfilled as they earnestly serve God day and night. King Agrippa, it is because of this hope that these Jews are accusing me. 8Why should any of you consider it incredible that God raises the dead?

9"I too was convinced that I ought to do all that was possible to oppose the name of Jesus of Nazareth. 10And that is just what I did in Jerusalem. On the authority of the chief priests I put many of the Lord's people in prison, and when they were put to death, I cast my vote against them. 11Many a time I went from one synagogue to another to have them punished, and I tried to force them to blaspheme. I was so obsessed with persecuting them that I even hunted them down in foreign cities.

12"On one of these journeys I was going to Damascus with the authority and commission of the chief priests. 13About noon, King Agrippa, as I was on the road, I saw a light from heaven, brighter than the sun, blazing around me and my companions. 14We all fell to the ground, and I heard a voice saying to me in Aramaic,a 'Saul, Saul, why do you persecute me? It is hard for you to kick against the goads.'

15"Then I asked, 'Who are you, Lord?'

"'I am Jesus, whom you are persecuting,' the Lord replied. 16'Now get up and stand on your feet. I have appeared to you to appoint you as a servant and as a witness of what you have seen and will see of me. 17I will rescue you from your own people and from the Gentiles. I am sending you to them 18to open their eyes and turn them from darkness to light, and from the power of Satan to God, so that they may receive forgiveness of sins and a place among those who are sanctified by faith in me.'

19"So then, King Agrippa, I was not disobedient to the vision from heaven. 20First to those in Damas-

a 14 Or Hebrew

cus, then to those in Jerusalem and in all Judea, and then to the Gentiles, I preached that they should repent and turn to God and demonstrate their repentance by their deeds. [21]That is why some Jews seized me in the temple courts and tried to kill me. [22]But God has helped me to this very day; so I stand here and testify to small and great alike. I am saying nothing beyond what the prophets and Moses said would happen— [23]that the Messiah would suffer and, as the first to rise from the dead, would bring the message of light to his own people and to the Gentiles."

[24]At this point Festus interrupted Paul's defense. "You are out of your mind, Paul!" he shouted. "Your great learning is driving you insane."

[25]"I am not insane, most excellent Festus," Paul replied. "What I am saying is true and reasonable. [26]The king is familiar with these things, and I can speak freely to him. I am convinced that none of this has escaped his notice, because it was not done in a corner. [27]King Agrippa, do you believe the prophets? I know you do."

[28]Then Agrippa said to Paul, "Do you think that in such a short time you can persuade me to be a Christian?"

[29]Paul replied, "Short time or long—I pray to God that not only you but all who are listening to me today may become what I am, except for these chains."

[30]The king rose, and with him the governor and Bernice and those sitting with them. [31]After they left the room, they began saying to one another, "This man is not doing anything that deserves death or imprisonment."

[32]Agrippa said to Festus, "This man could have been set free if he had not appealed to Caesar."

27 When it was decided that we would sail for Italy, Paul and some other prisoners were handed over to a centurion named Julius, who belonged to the Imperial Regiment. [2]We boarded a ship from Adramyttium about to sail for ports along the coast of the province of Asia, and we put out to sea. Aristarchus, a Macedonian from Thessalonica, was with us.

[3]The next day we landed at Sidon; and Julius, in kindness to Paul, allowed him to go to his friends so they might provide for his needs. [4]From there we put out to sea again and passed to the lee of Cyprus because the winds were against us. [5]When we had sailed across the open sea off the coast of Cilicia and Pamphylia, we landed at Myra in Lycia. [6]There the centurion found an Alexandrian ship sailing for Italy and put us on board. [7]We made slow headway for many days and had difficulty arriving off Cnidus. When the wind did not allow us to hold our course, we sailed to the lee of Crete, opposite Salmone. [8]We moved along the coast with difficulty and came to a place called Fair Havens, near the town of Lasea.

[9]Much time had been lost, and sailing had already become dangerous because by now it was after the Day of Atonement.[a] So Paul warned them, [10]"Men, I can see that our voyage is going to be disastrous and bring great loss to ship and cargo, and to our own lives also." [11]But the centurion, instead of listening to what Paul said, followed the ad-

[a] 9 That is, Yom Kippur

vice of the pilot and of the owner of the ship. [12]Since the harbor was unsuitable to winter in, the majority decided that we should sail on, hoping to reach Phoenix and winter there. This was a harbor in Crete, facing both southwest and northwest.

[13]When a gentle south wind began to blow, they saw their opportunity; so they weighed anchor and sailed along the shore of Crete. [14]Before very long, a wind of hurricane force, called the Northeaster, swept down from the island. [15]The ship was caught by the storm and could not head into the wind; so we gave way to it and were driven along. [16]As we passed to the lee of a small island called Cauda, we were hardly able to make the lifeboat secure, [17]so the men hoisted it aboard. Then they passed ropes under the ship itself to hold it together. Because they were afraid they would run aground on the sandbars of Syrtis, they lowered the sea anchor[a] and let the ship be driven along. [18]We took such a violent battering from the storm that the next day they began to throw the cargo overboard. [19]On the third day, they threw the ship's tackle overboard with their own hands. [20]When neither sun nor stars appeared for many days and the storm continued raging, we finally gave up all hope of being saved.

[21]After they had gone a long time without food, Paul stood up before them and said: "Men, you should have taken my advice not to sail from Crete; then you would have spared yourselves this damage and loss. [22]But now I urge you to keep up your courage, because not one

of you will be lost; only the ship will be destroyed. [23]Last night an angel of the God to whom I belong and whom I serve stood beside me [24]and said, 'Do not be afraid, Paul. You must stand trial before Caesar; and God has graciously given you the lives of all who sail with you.' [25]So keep up your courage, men, for I have faith in God that it will happen just as he told me. [26]Nevertheless, we must run aground on some island."

[27]On the fourteenth night we were still being driven across the Adriatic[b] Sea, when about midnight the sailors sensed they were approaching land. [28]They took soundings and found that the water was a hundred and twenty feet[c] deep. A short time later they took soundings again and found it was ninety feet[d] deep. [29]Fearing that we would be dashed against the rocks, they dropped four anchors from the stern and prayed for daylight. [30]In an attempt to escape from the ship, the sailors let the lifeboat down into the sea, pretending they were going to lower some anchors from the bow. [31]Then Paul said to the centurion and the soldiers, "Unless these men stay with the ship, you cannot be saved." [32]So the soldiers cut the ropes that held the lifeboat and let it drift away.

[33]Just before dawn Paul urged them all to eat. "For the last fourteen days," he said, "you have been in constant suspense and have gone without food—you haven't eaten anything. [34]Now I urge you to take some food. You need it to survive. Not one of you will lose a single hair from his head." [35]After he said this, he took some bread and gave

---

[a] 17 Or the sails   [b] 27 In ancient times the name referred to an area extending well south of Italy.   [c] 28 Or about 37 meters   [d] 28 Or about 27 meters

thanks to God in front of them all. Then he broke it and began to eat. ³⁶They were all encouraged and ate some food themselves. ³⁷Altogether there were 276 of us on board. ³⁸When they had eaten as much as they wanted, they lightened the ship by throwing the grain into the sea.

³⁹When daylight came, they did not recognize the land, but they saw a bay with a sandy beach, where they decided to run the ship aground if they could. ⁴⁰Cutting loose the anchors, they left them in the sea and at the same time untied the ropes that held the rudders. Then they hoisted the foresail to the wind and made for the beach. ⁴¹But the ship struck a sandbar and ran aground. The bow stuck fast and would not move, and the stern was broken to pieces by the pounding of the surf.

⁴²The soldiers planned to kill the prisoners to prevent any of them from swimming away and escaping. ⁴³But the centurion wanted to spare Paul's life and kept them from carrying out their plan. He ordered those who could swim to jump overboard first and get to land. ⁴⁴The rest were to get there on planks or on other pieces of the ship. In this way everyone reached land safely.

28 Once safely on shore, we found out that the island was called Malta. ²The islanders showed us unusual kindness. They built a fire and welcomed us all because it was raining and cold. ³Paul gathered a pile of brushwood and, as he put it on the fire, a viper, driven out by the heat, fastened itself on his hand. ⁴When the islanders saw the snake hanging from his hand, they said to each other, "This man must be a murderer; for though he escaped from the sea, the goddess Justice has not allowed him to live." ⁵But Paul shook the snake off into the fire and suffered no ill effects. ⁶The people expected him to swell up or suddenly fall dead; but after waiting a long time and seeing nothing unusual happen to him, they changed their minds and said he was a god.

⁷There was an estate nearby that belonged to Publius, the chief official of the island. He welcomed us to his home and showed us generous hospitality for three days. ⁸His father was sick in bed, suffering from fever and dysentery. Paul went in to see him and, after prayer, placed his hands on him and healed him. ⁹When this had happened, the rest of the sick on the island came and were cured. ¹⁰They honored us in many ways; and when we were ready to sail, they furnished us with the supplies we needed.

¹¹After three months we put out to sea in a ship that had wintered in the island—it was an Alexandrian ship with the figurehead of the twin gods Castor and Pollux. ¹²We put in at Syracuse and stayed there three days. ¹³From there we set sail and arrived at Rhegium. The next day the south wind came up, and on the following day we reached Puteoli. ¹⁴There we found some brothers and sisters who invited us to spend a week with them. And so we came to Rome. ¹⁵The brothers and sisters there had heard that we were coming, and they traveled as far as the Forum of Appius and the Three Taverns to meet us. At the sight of these people Paul thanked God and was encouraged. ¹⁶When we got to Rome, Paul was allowed to live by himself, with a soldier to guard him.

¹⁷Three days later he called to-

gether the local Jewish leaders. When they had assembled, Paul said to them: "My brothers, although I have done nothing against our people or against the customs of our ancestors, I was arrested in Jerusalem and handed over to the Romans. [18] They examined me and wanted to release me, because I was not guilty of any crime deserving death. [19] The Jews objected, so I was compelled to make an appeal to Caesar. I certainly did not intend to bring any charge against my own people. [20] For this reason I have asked to see you and talk with you. It is because of the hope of Israel that I am bound with this chain."

[21] They replied, "We have not received any letters from Judea concerning you, and none of our people who have come from there has reported or said anything bad about you. [22] But we want to hear what your views are, for we know that people everywhere are talking against this sect."

[23] They arranged to meet Paul on a certain day, and came in even larger numbers to the place where he was staying. He witnessed to them from morning till evening, explaining about the kingdom of God, and from the Law of Moses and from the Prophets he tried to persuade them about Jesus. [24] Some

were convinced by what he said, but others would not believe. [25] They disagreed among themselves and began to leave after Paul had made this final statement: "The Holy Spirit spoke the truth to your ancestors when he said through Isaiah the prophet:

[26] "'Go to this people and say,
　"You will be ever hearing but
　　　　never understanding;
　you will be ever seeing but
　　　　never perceiving."
[27] For this people's heart has
　　　　become calloused;
　they hardly hear with their
　　　　ears,
　and they have closed their
　　　　eyes.
Otherwise they might see with
　　　　their eyes,
　hear with their ears,
　understand with their hearts
　and turn, and I would heal
　　　　them.'[a]

[28] "Therefore I want you to know that God's salvation has been sent to the Gentiles, and they will listen!" [29] [b]

[30] For two whole years Paul stayed there in his own rented house and welcomed all who came to see him. [31] He proclaimed the kingdom of God and taught about the Lord Jesus Christ — with all boldness and without hindrance!

---

[a] 27 Isaiah 6:9,10 (see Septuagint)　　[b] 29 Some manuscripts include here *After he said this, the Jews left, arguing vigorously among themselves.*

ROMANS

Addressing the believers in Rome, Paul writes what is most likely the meatiest missionary fundraising letter ever written. To Jesus-followers living directly under the shadow of Caesar, he is appealing for help to bring the gospel to the western part of the empire. As an apostle, Paul has been set apart to make the royal announcement about the Lordship of Jesus. God's plan for the world has been revealed through a descendant of king David—Jesus the Messiah. This message demonstrates that God has been faithful to his covenant with Israel.

The flow of the letter follows the pattern of the ancient Jewish story of slavery and rescue. Humanity is in exile due to the entrance of sin and death into the world. Even the Jewish law could not defeat death and bring life. But God has come to rescue both Jews and Gentiles through the death and resurrection of Jesus. A new worldwide family is being created. Baptism into Jesus breaks the power of evil and brings freedom. The Holy Spirit leads the way into this new life that will be complete in a new inheritance—a redeemed creation.

Although many in Israel had failed to believe in the Messiah, this ended up bringing life to the rest of the world. The offer of life through Jesus remains for all, however, and in the end God's mercy will triumph over judgment. The closing emphasis is on the practical shape of a redeemed humanity's new way of life.

---

1 Paul, a servant of Christ Jesus, called to be an apostle and set apart for the gospel of God — ²the gospel he promised beforehand through his prophets in the Holy Scriptures ³regarding his Son, who as to his earthly life[a] was a descendant of David, ⁴and who through the Spirit of holiness was appointed the Son of God in power[b] by his resurrection from the dead: Jesus Christ our Lord. ⁵Through him we received grace and apostleship to call all the Gentiles to the obedience that comes from[c] faith for his name's sake. ⁶And you also are among those Gentiles who are called to belong to Jesus Christ.

⁷To all in Rome who are loved by God and called to be his holy people:

Grace and peace to you from God our Father and from the Lord Jesus Christ.

⁸First, I thank my God through Jesus Christ for all of you, because your faith is being reported all over the world. ⁹God, whom I serve in my spirit in preaching the gospel of his Son, is my witness how constantly I remember you ¹⁰in my prayers at all times; and I pray that now at last by God's will the way may be opened for me to come to you.

¹¹I long to see you so that I may impart to you some spiritual gift to make you strong— ¹²that is, that you and I may be mutually encour-

---

[a] 3 Or who according to the flesh   [b] 4 Or was declared with power to be the Son of God
[c] 5 Or that is

aged by each other's faith. [13]I do not want you to be unaware, brothers and sisters,[a] that I planned many times to come to you (but have been prevented from doing so until now) in order that I might have a harvest among you, just as I have had among the other Gentiles.

[14]I am obligated both to Greeks and non-Greeks, both to the wise and the foolish. [15]That is why I am so eager to preach the gospel also to you who are in Rome.

[16]For I am not ashamed of the gospel, because it is the power of God that brings salvation to everyone who believes: first to the Jew, then to the Gentile. [17]For in the gospel the righteousness of God is revealed—a righteousness that is by faith from first to last,[b] just as it is written: "The righteous will live by faith."[c]

[18]The wrath of God is being revealed from heaven against all the godlessness and wickedness of people, who suppress the truth by their wickedness, [19]since what may be known about God is plain to them, because God has made it plain to them. [20]For since the creation of the world God's invisible qualities—his eternal power and divine nature—have been clearly seen, being understood from what has been made, so that people are without excuse.

[21]For although they knew God, they neither glorified him as God nor gave thanks to him, but their thinking became futile and their foolish hearts were darkened. [22]Although they claimed to be wise, they became fools [23]and ex-

changed the glory of the immortal God for images made to look like a mortal human being and birds and animals and reptiles.

[24]Therefore God gave them over in the sinful desires of their hearts to sexual impurity for the degrading of their bodies with one another. [25]They exchanged the truth about God for a lie, and worshiped and served created things rather than the Creator—who is forever praised. Amen.

[26]Because of this, God gave them over to shameful lusts. Even their women exchanged natural sexual relations for unnatural ones. [27]In the same way the men also abandoned natural relations with women and were inflamed with lust for one another. Men committed shameful acts with other men, and received in themselves the due penalty for their error.

[28]Furthermore, just as they did not think it worthwhile to retain the knowledge of God, so God gave them over to a depraved mind, so that they do what ought not to be done. [29]They have become filled with every kind of wickedness, evil, greed and depravity. They are full of envy, murder, strife, deceit and malice. They are gossips, [30]slanderers, God-haters, insolent, arrogant and boastful; they invent ways of doing evil; they disobey their parents; [31]they have no understanding, no fidelity, no love, no mercy. [32]Although they know God's righteous decree that those who do such things deserve death, they not only continue to do these very things but also approve of those who practice them.

---

[a] 13 The Greek word for *brothers and sisters (adelphoi)* refers here to believers, both men and women, as part of God's family; also in 7:1, 4; 8:12, 29; 10:1; 11:25; 12:1; 15:14, 30; 16:14, 17.
[b] 17 Or *is from faith to faith*   [c] 17 Hab. 2:4

2 You, therefore, have no excuse, you who pass judgment on someone else, for at whatever point you judge another, you are condemning yourself, because you who pass judgment do the same things. ²Now we know that God's judgment against those who do such things is based on truth. ³So when you, a mere human being, pass judgment on them and yet do the same things, do you think you will escape God's judgment? ⁴Or do you show contempt for the riches of his kindness, forbearance and patience, not realizing that God's kindness is intended to lead you to repentance?

⁵But because of your stubbornness and your unrepentant heart, you are storing up wrath against yourself for the day of God's wrath, when his righteous judgment will be revealed. ⁶God "will repay each person according to what they have done."ᵃ ⁷To those who by persistence in doing good seek glory, honor and immortality, he will give eternal life. ⁸But for those who are self-seeking and who reject the truth and follow evil, there will be wrath and anger. ⁹There will be trouble and distress for every human being who does evil: first for the Jew, then for the Gentile; ¹⁰but glory, honor and peace for everyone who does good: first for the Jew, then for the Gentile. ¹¹For God does not show favoritism.

¹²All who sin apart from the law will also perish apart from the law, and all who sin under the law will be judged by the law. ¹³For it is not those who hear the law who are righteous in God's sight, but it is those who obey the law who will be declared righteous. ¹⁴(Indeed, when Gentiles, who do not have the law, do by nature things required by the law, they are a law for themselves, even though they do not have the law. ¹⁵They show that the requirements of the law are written on their hearts, their consciences also bearing witness, and their thoughts sometimes accusing them and at other times even defending them.) ¹⁶This will take place on the day when God judges people's secrets through Jesus Christ, as my gospel declares.

¹⁷Now you, if you call yourself a Jew; if you rely on the law and boast in God; ¹⁸if you know his will and approve of what is superior because you are instructed by the law; ¹⁹if you are convinced that you are a guide for the blind, a light for those who are in the dark, ²⁰an instructor of the foolish, a teacher of little children, because you have in the law the embodiment of knowledge and truth — ²¹you, then, who teach others, do you not teach yourself? You who preach against stealing, do you steal? ²²You who say that people should not commit adultery, do you commit adultery? You who abhor idols, do you rob temples? ²³You who boast in the law, do you dishonor God by breaking the law? ²⁴As it is written: "God's name is blasphemed among the Gentiles because of you."ᵇ

²⁵Circumcision has value if you observe the law, but if you break the law, you have become as though you had not been circumcised. ²⁶So then, if those who are not circumcised keep the law's requirements, will they not be regarded as though they were circumcised? ²⁷The one who is not circumcised physically and yet obeys the law will condemn

ᵃ 6 Psalm 62:12; Prov. 24:12   ᵇ 24 Isaiah 52:5 (see Septuagint); Ezek. 36:20,22

you who, even though you have the[a] written code and circumcision, are a lawbreaker.

28 A person is not a Jew who is one only outwardly, nor is circumcision merely outward and physical. 29 No, a person is a Jew who is one inwardly; and circumcision is circumcision of the heart, by the Spirit, not by the written code. Such a person's praise is not from other people, but from God.

3 What advantage, then, is there in being a Jew, or what value is there in circumcision? 2 Much in every way! First of all, the Jews have been entrusted with the very words of God.

3 What if some were unfaithful? Will their unfaithfulness nullify God's faithfulness? 4 Not at all! Let God be true, and every human being a liar. As it is written:

"So that you may be proved right when you speak
and prevail when you judge."[b]

5 But if our unrighteousness brings out God's righteousness more clearly, what shall we say? That God is unjust in bringing his wrath on us? (I am using a human argument.) 6 Certainly not! If that were so, how could God judge the world? 7 Someone might argue, "If my falsehood enhances God's truthfulness and so increases his glory, why am I still condemned as a sinner?" 8 Why not say—as some slanderously claim that we say—"Let us do evil that good may result"? Their condemnation is just!

9 What shall we conclude then? Do we have any advantage? Not at all! For we have already made the charge that Jews and Gentiles alike are all under the power of sin. 10 As it is written:

"There is no one righteous, not even one;
11 there is no one who understands;
there is no one who seeks God.
12 All have turned away,
they have together become worthless;
there is no one who does good,
not even one."[c]
13 "Their throats are open graves;
their tongues practice deceit."[d]
"The poison of vipers is on their lips."[e]
14 "Their mouths are full of cursing and bitterness."[f]
15 "Their feet are swift to shed blood;
16 ruin and misery mark their ways,
17 and the way of peace they do not know."[g]
18 "There is no fear of God before their eyes."[h]

19 Now we know that whatever the law says, it says to those who are under the law, so that every mouth may be silenced and the whole world held accountable to God. 20 Therefore no one will be declared righteous in God's sight by the works of the law; rather, through the law we become conscious of our sin.

21 But now apart from the law the righteousness of God has been made known, to which the Law and the Prophets testify. 22 This righteousness is given through faith in[i] Jesus Christ to all who believe.

---

[a] 27 Or who, by means of a   [b] 4 Psalm 51:4   [c] 12 Psalms 14:1-3; 53:1-3; Eccles. 7:20
[d] 13 Psalm 5:9   [e] 13 Psalm 140:3   [f] 14 Psalm 10:7 (see Septuagint)   [g] 17 Isaiah 59:7,8
[h] 18 Psalm 36:1   [i] 22 Or through the faithfulness of

There is no difference between Jew and Gentile, [23] for all have sinned and fall short of the glory of God, [24] and all are justified freely by his grace through the redemption that came by Christ Jesus. [25] God presented Christ as a sacrifice of atonement,[a] through the shedding of his blood—to be received by faith. He did this to demonstrate his righteousness, because in his forbearance he had left the sins committed beforehand unpunished— [26] he did it to demonstrate his righteousness at the present time, so as to be just and the one who justifies those who have faith in Jesus.

[27] Where, then, is boasting? It is excluded. Because of what law? The law that requires works? No, because of the law that requires faith. [28] For we maintain that a person is justified by faith apart from the works of the law. [29] Or is God the God of Jews only? Is he not the God of Gentiles too? Yes, of Gentiles too, [30] since there is only one God, who will justify the circumcised by faith and the uncircumcised through that same faith. [31] Do we, then, nullify the law by this faith? Not at all! Rather, we uphold the law.

4 What then shall we say that Abraham, our forefather according to the flesh, discovered in this matter? [2] If, in fact, Abraham was justified by works, he had something to boast about—but not before God. [3] What does Scripture say? "Abraham believed God, and it was credited to him as righteousness."[b]

[4] Now to the one who works, wages are not credited as a gift but as an obligation. [5] However, to the one

who does not work but trusts God who justifies the ungodly, their faith is credited as righteousness. [6] David says the same thing when he speaks of the blessedness of the one to whom God credits righteousness apart from works:

[7] "Blessed are those
　　whose transgressions are
　　　forgiven,
　　whose sins are covered.
[8] Blessed is the one
　　whose sin the Lord will never
　　　count against them."[c]

[9] Is this blessedness only for the circumcised, or also for the uncircumcised? We have been saying that Abraham's faith was credited to him as righteousness. [10] Under what circumstances was it credited? Was it after he was circumcised, or before? It was not after, but before! [11] And he received circumcision as a sign, a seal of the righteousness that he had by faith while he was still uncircumcised. So then, he is the father of all who believe but have not been circumcised, in order that righteousness might be credited to them. [12] And he is then also the father of the circumcised who not only are circumcised but who also follow in the footsteps of the faith that our father Abraham had before he was circumcised.

[13] It was not through the law that Abraham and his offspring received the promise that he would be heir of the world, but through the righteousness that comes by faith. [14] For if those who depend on the law are heirs, faith means nothing and the promise is worthless, [15] because the law brings wrath.

---

[a] 25 The Greek for *sacrifice of atonement* refers to the atonement cover on the ark of the covenant (see Lev. 16:15,16).　　[b] 3 Gen. 15:6; also in verse 22　　[c] 8 Psalm 32:1,2

And where there is no law there is no transgression.

16Therefore, the promise comes by faith, so that it may be by grace and may be guaranteed to all Abraham's offspring—not only to those who are of the law but also to those who have the faith of Abraham. He is the father of us all. 17As it is written: "I have made you a father of many nations."*a* He is our father in the sight of God, in whom he believed—the God who gives life to the dead and calls into being things that were not.

18Against all hope, Abraham in hope believed and so became the father of many nations, just as it had been said to him, "So shall your offspring be."*b* 19Without weakening in his faith, he faced the fact that his body was as good as dead—since he was about a hundred years old—and that Sarah's womb was also dead. 20Yet he did not waver through unbelief regarding the promise of God, but was strengthened in his faith and gave glory to God, 21being fully persuaded that God had power to do what he had promised. 22This is why "it was credited to him as righteousness." 23The words "it was credited to him" were written not for him alone, 24but also for us, to whom God will credit righteousness—for us who believe in him who raised Jesus our Lord from the dead. 25He was delivered over to death for our sins and was raised to life for our justification.

5 Therefore, since we have been justified through faith, we*c* have peace with God through our Lord Jesus Christ, 2through whom we have gained access by faith into this grace in which we now stand. And we*d* boast in the hope of the glory of God. 3Not only so, but we*d* also glory in our sufferings, because we know that suffering produces perseverance; 4perseverance, character; and character, hope. 5And hope does not put us to shame, because God's love has been poured out into our hearts through the Holy Spirit, who has been given to us.

6You see, at just the right time, when we were still powerless, Christ died for the ungodly. 7Very rarely will anyone die for a righteous person, though for a good person someone might possibly dare to die. 8But God demonstrates his own love for us in this: While we were still sinners, Christ died for us.

9Since we have now been justified by his blood, how much more shall we be saved from God's wrath through him! 10For if, while we were God's enemies, we were reconciled to him through the death of his Son, how much more, having been reconciled, shall we be saved through his life! 11Not only is this so, but we also boast in God through our Lord Jesus Christ, through whom we have now received reconciliation.

12Therefore, just as sin entered the world through one man, and death through sin, and in this way death came to all people, because all sinned—

13To be sure, sin was in the world before the law was given, but sin is not charged against anyone's account where there is no law. 14Nevertheless, death reigned from the time of Adam to the time of Moses, even over those who did not sin by breaking a command, as did Adam, who is a pattern of the one to come.

a 17 Gen. 17:5   *b 18* Gen. 15:5   *c* Many manuscripts *let us*   *d 2,3* Or *let us*

15But the gift is not like the trespass. For if the many died by the trespass of the one man, how much more did God's grace and the gift that came by the grace of the one man, Jesus Christ, overflow to the many! 16Nor can the gift of God be compared with the result of one man's sin: The judgment followed one sin and brought condemnation, but the gift followed many trespasses and brought justification. 17For if, by the trespass of the one man, death reigned through that one man, how much more will those who receive God's abundant provision of grace and of the gift of righteousness reign in life through the one man, Jesus Christ!

18Consequently, just as one trespass resulted in condemnation for all people, so also one righteous act resulted in justification and life for all people. 19For just as through the disobedience of the one man the many were made sinners, so also through the obedience of the one man the many will be made righteous.

20The law was brought in so that the trespass might increase. But where sin increased, grace increased all the more, 21so that, just as sin reigned in death, so also grace might reign through righteousness to bring eternal life through Jesus Christ our Lord.

6 What shall we say, then? Shall we go on sinning so that grace may increase? 2By no means! We are those who have died to sin; how can we live in it any longer? 3Or don't you know that all of us who were baptized into Christ Jesus were baptized into his death? 4We were therefore buried with him through baptism into death in order that, just as Christ was raised from the dead through the glory of the Father, we too may live a new life.

5For if we have been united with him in a death like his, we will certainly also be united with him in a resurrection like his. 6For we know that our old self was crucified with him so that the body ruled by sin might be done away with,a that we should no longer be slaves to sin — 7because anyone who has died has been set free from sin.

8Now if we died with Christ, we believe that we will also live with him. 9For we know that since Christ was raised from the dead, he cannot die again; death no longer has mastery over him. 10The death he died, he died to sin once for all; but the life he lives, he lives to God.

11In the same way, count yourselves dead to sin but alive to God in Christ Jesus. 12Therefore do not let sin reign in your mortal body so that you obey its evil desires. 13Do not offer any part of yourself to sin as an instrument of wickedness, but rather offer yourselves to God as those who have been brought from death to life; and offer every part of yourself to him as an instrument of righteousness. 14For sin shall no longer be your master, because you are not under the law, but under grace.

15What then? Shall we sin because we are not under the law but under grace? By no means! 16Don't you know that when you offer yourselves to someone as obedient slaves, you are slaves of the one you obey—whether you are slaves to sin, which leads to death, or to obedience, which leads to righteousness? 17But thanks be to God that,

a 6 Or be rendered powerless

though you used to be slaves to sin, you have come to obey from your heart the pattern of teaching that has now claimed your allegiance. [18]You have been set free from sin and have become slaves to righteousness.

[19]I am using an example from everyday life because of your human limitations. Just as you used to offer yourselves as slaves to impurity and to ever-increasing wickedness, so now offer yourselves as slaves to righteousness leading to holiness. [20]When you were slaves to sin, you were free from the control of righteousness. [21]What benefit did you reap at that time from the things you are now ashamed of? Those things result in death! [22]But now that you have been set free from sin and have become slaves of God, the benefit you reap leads to holiness, and the result is eternal life. [23]For the wages of sin is death, but the gift of God is eternal life in[a] Christ Jesus our Lord.

7 Do you not know, brothers and sisters—for I am speaking to those who know the law—that the law has authority over someone only as long as that person lives? [2]For example, by law a married woman is bound to her husband as long as he is alive, but if her husband dies, she is released from the law that binds her to him. [3]So then, if she has sexual relations with another man while her husband is still alive, she is called an adulteress. But if her husband dies, she is released from that law and is not an adulteress if she marries another man.

[4]So, my brothers and sisters, you also died to the law through the body of Christ, that you might belong to another, to him who was raised from the dead, in order that we might bear fruit for God. [5]For when we were in the realm of the flesh,[b] the sinful passions aroused by the law were at work in us, so that we bore fruit for death. [6]But now, by dying to what once bound us, we have been released from the law so that we serve in the new way of the Spirit, and not in the old way of the written code.

[7]What shall we say, then? Is the law sinful? Certainly not! Nevertheless, I would not have known what sin was had it not been for the law. For I would not have known what coveting really was if the law had not said, "You shall not covet."[c] [8]But sin, seizing the opportunity afforded by the commandment, produced in me every kind of coveting. For apart from the law, sin was dead. [9]Once I was alive apart from the law; but when the commandment came, sin sprang to life and I died. [10]I found that the very commandment that was intended to bring life actually brought death. [11]For sin, seizing the opportunity afforded by the commandment, deceived me, and through the commandment put me to death. [12]So then, the law is holy, and the commandment is holy, righteous and good.

[13]Did that which is good, then, become death to me? By no means! Nevertheless, in order that sin might be recognized as sin, it used what is good to bring about my death, so that through the com-

---

[a] 23 Or through   [b] 5 In contexts like this, the Greek word for *flesh* (*sarx*) refers to the sinful state of human beings, often presented as a power in opposition to the Spirit.
[c] 7 Exodus 20:17; Deut. 5:21

mandment sin might become utterly sinful.

¹⁴We know that the law is spiritual; but I am unspiritual, sold as a slave to sin. ¹⁵I do not understand what I do. For what I want to do I do not do, but what I hate I do. ¹⁶And if I do what I do not want to do, I agree that the law is good. ¹⁷As it is, it is no longer I myself who do it, but it is sin living in me. ¹⁸For I know that good itself does not dwell in me, that is, in my sinful nature.ᵃ For I have the desire to do what is good, but I cannot carry it out. ¹⁹For I do not do the good I want to do, but the evil I do not want to do—this I keep on doing. ²⁰Now if I do what I do not want to do, it is no longer I who do it, but it is sin living in me that does it.

²¹So I find this law at work: Although I want to do good, evil is right there with me. ²²For in my inner being I delight in God's law; ²³but I see another law at work in me, waging war against the law of my mind and making me a prisoner of the law of sin at work within me. ²⁴What a wretched man I am! Who will rescue me from this body that is subject to death? ²⁵Thanks be to God, who delivers me through Jesus Christ our Lord!

So then, I myself in my mind am a slave to God's law, but in my sinful natureᵇ a slave to the law of sin.

8 Therefore, there is now no condemnation for those who are in Christ Jesus, ²because through Christ Jesus the law of the Spirit who gives life has set youᶜ free from the law of sin and death. ³For

what the law was powerless to do because it was weakened by the flesh,ᵈ God did by sending his own Son in the likeness of sinful flesh to be a sin offering.ᵉ And so he condemned sin in the flesh, ⁴in order that the righteous requirement of the law might be fully met in us, who do not live according to the flesh but according to the Spirit.

⁵Those who live according to the flesh have their minds set on what the flesh desires; but those who live in accordance with the Spirit have their minds set on what the Spirit desires. ⁶The mind governed by the flesh is death, but the mind governed by the Spirit is life and peace. ⁷The mind governed by the flesh is hostile to God; it does not submit to God's law, nor can it do so. ⁸Those who are in the realm of the flesh cannot please God.

⁹You, however, are not in the realm of the flesh but are in the realm of the Spirit, if indeed the Spirit of God lives in you. And if anyone does not have the Spirit of Christ, they do not belong to Christ. ¹⁰But if Christ is in you, then even though your body is subject to death because of sin, the Spirit gives lifeᶠ because of righteousness. ¹¹And if the Spirit of him who raised Jesus from the dead is living in you, he who raised Christ from the dead will also give life to your mortal bodies because ofᵍ his Spirit who lives in you.

¹²Therefore, brothers and sisters, we have an obligation—but it is not to the flesh, to live according to it. ¹³For if you live according to the

---

ᵃ 18 Or *my flesh*   ᵇ 25 Or *in the flesh*   ᶜ 2 The Greek is singular; some manuscripts *me*
ᵈ 3 In contexts like this, the Greek word for *flesh (sarx)* refers to the sinful state of human beings, often presented as a power in opposition to the Spirit; also in verses 4-13.   ᵉ 3 Or *flesh, for sin*
ᶠ 10 Or *you, your body is dead because of sin, yet your spirit is alive*   ᵍ 11 Some manuscripts *bodies through*

flesh, you will die; but if by the Spirit you put to death the misdeeds of the body, you will live.

14For those who are led by the Spirit of God are the children of God. 15The Spirit you received does not make you slaves, so that you live in fear again; rather, the Spirit you received brought about your adoption to sonship.[a] And by him we cry, "Abba,[b] Father." 16The Spirit himself testifies with our spirit that we are God's children. 17Now if we are children, then we are heirs—heirs of God and co-heirs with Christ, if indeed we share in his sufferings in order that we may also share in his glory.

18I consider that our present sufferings are not worth comparing with the glory that will be revealed in us. 19For the creation waits in eager expectation for the children of God to be revealed. 20For the creation was subjected to frustration, not by its own choice, but by the will of the one who subjected it, in hope 21that[c] the creation itself will be liberated from its bondage to decay and brought into the freedom and glory of the children of God.

22We know that the whole creation has been groaning as in the pains of childbirth right up to the present time. 23Not only so, but we ourselves, who have the firstfruits of the Spirit, groan inwardly as we wait eagerly for our adoption to sonship, the redemption of our bodies. 24For in this hope we were saved. But hope that is seen is no hope at all. Who hopes for what

they already have? 25But if we hope for what we do not yet have, we wait for it patiently.

26In the same way, the Spirit helps us in our weakness. We do not know what we ought to pray for, but the Spirit himself intercedes for us through wordless groans. 27And he who searches our hearts knows the mind of the Spirit, because the Spirit intercedes for God's people in accordance with the will of God.

28And we know that in all things God works for the good of those who love him, who[d] have been called according to his purpose. 29For those God foreknew he also predestined to be conformed to the image of his Son, that he might be the firstborn among many brothers and sisters. 30And those he predestined, he also called; those he called, he also justified; those he justified, he also glorified.

31What, then, shall we say in response to these things? If God is for us, who can be against us? 32He who did not spare his own Son, but gave him up for us all—how will he not also, along with him, graciously give us all things? 33Who will bring any charge against those whom God has chosen? It is God who justifies. 34Who then is the one who condemns? No one. Christ Jesus who died—more than that, who was raised to life—is at the right hand of God and is also interceding for us. 35Who shall separate us from the love of Christ? Shall trouble or hardship or persecution or famine or nakedness or danger or sword? 36As it is written:

---

[a] 15 The Greek word for *adoption to sonship* is a term referring to the full legal standing of an adopted male heir in Roman culture; also in verse 23.   [b] 15 Aramaic for *father*   [c] 20,21 Or *subjected it in hope.* 21For   [d] 28 Or *that all things work together for good to those who love God, who;* or *that in all things God works together with those who love him to bring about what is good—with those who*

"For your sake we face death all
    day long;
    we are considered as sheep to
        be slaughtered."[a]

[37] No, in all these things we are
more than conquerors through
him who loved us. [38] For I am convinced that neither death nor life,
neither angels nor demons,[b] neither the present nor the future,
nor any powers, [39] neither height
nor depth, nor anything else in all
creation, will be able to separate
us from the love of God that is in
Christ Jesus our Lord.

9 I speak the truth in Christ—I am
    not lying, my conscience con-
firms it through the Holy Spirit—
[2] I have great sorrow and unceasing
anguish in my heart. [3] For I could
wish that I myself were cursed and
cut off from Christ for the sake of
my people, those of my own race,
[4] the people of Israel. Theirs is the
adoption to sonship; theirs the divine glory, the covenants, the receiving of the law, the temple worship and the promises. [5] Theirs are
the patriarchs, and from them is
traced the human ancestry of the
Messiah, who is God over all, forever praised![c] Amen.

[6] It is not as though God's word
had failed. For not all who are descended from Israel are Israel. [7] Nor
because they are his descendants
are they all Abraham's children.
On the contrary, "It is through Isaac
that your offspring will be reckoned."[d] [8] In other words, it is not
the children by physical descent
who are God's children, but it is the
children of the promise who are

regarded as Abraham's offspring.
[9] For this was how the promise was
stated: "At the appointed time I
will return, and Sarah will have a
son."[e]

[10] Not only that, but Rebekah's
children were conceived at the
same time by our father Isaac. [11] Yet,
before the twins were born or had
done anything good or bad—in order that God's purpose in election
might stand: [12] not by works but
by him who calls—she was told,
"The older will serve the younger."[f]
[13] Just as it is written: "Jacob I loved,
but Esau I hated."[g]

[14] What then shall we say? Is God
unjust? Not at all! [15] For he says to
Moses,

"I will have mercy on whom I
    have mercy,
    and I will have compassion
        on whom I have
        compassion."[h]

[16] It does not, therefore, depend
on human desire or effort, but on
God's mercy. [17] For Scripture says
to Pharaoh: "I raised you up for this
very purpose, that I might display
my power in you and that my name
might be proclaimed in all the
earth."[i] [18] Therefore God has mercy
on whom he wants to have mercy,
and he hardens whom he wants to
harden.

[19] One of you will say to me:
"Then why does God still blame
us? For who is able to resist his
will?" [20] But who are you, a human
being, to talk back to God? "Shall
what is formed say to the one who
formed it, 'Why did you make me
like this?'"[j] [21] Does not the potter

---

[a] 36 Psalm 44:22   [b] 38 Or nor heavenly rulers
praised! Or Messiah. God who is over all be forever praised!   [c] 5 Or Messiah, who is over all. God be forever   [d] 7 Gen. 21:12   [e] 9 Gen. 18:10,14
[f] 12 Gen. 25:23   [g] 13 Mal. 1:2,3   [h] 15 Exodus 33:19   [i] 17 Exodus 9:16   [j] 20 Isaiah 29:16;
45:9

have the right to make out of the same lump of clay some pottery for special purposes and some for common use?

²²What if God, although choosing to show his wrath and make his power known, bore with great patience the objects of his wrath—prepared for destruction? ²³What if he did this to make the riches of his glory known to the objects of his mercy, whom he prepared in advance for glory— ²⁴even us, whom he also called, not only from the Jews but also from the Gentiles? ²⁵As he says in Hosea:

"I will call them 'my people' who
    are not my people;
and I will call her 'my loved
    one' who is not my loved
    one,"[a]

²⁶and,

"In the very place where it was
    said to them,
'You are not my people,'
    there they will be called
    'children of the living
    God.' "[b]

²⁷Isaiah cries out concerning Israel:

"Though the number of the
    Israelites be like the sand
    by the sea,
only the remnant will be
    saved.
²⁸For the Lord will carry out
    his sentence on earth with
    speed and finality."[c]

²⁹It is just as Isaiah said previously:

"Unless the Lord Almighty
    had left us descendants,

we would have become like
    Sodom,
we would have been like
    Gomorrah."[d]

³⁰What then shall we say? That the Gentiles, who did not pursue righteousness, have obtained it, a righteousness that is by faith; ³¹but the people of Israel, who pursued the law as the way of righteousness, have not attained their goal. ³²Why not? Because they pursued it not by faith but as if it were by works. They stumbled over the stumbling stone. ³³As it is written:

"See, I lay in Zion a stone that
    causes people to stumble
    and a rock that makes them
    fall,
and the one who believes in
    him will never be put to
    shame."[e]

10 Brothers and sisters, my heart's desire and prayer to God for the Israelites is that they may be saved. ²For I can testify about them that they are zealous for God, but their zeal is not based on knowledge. ³Since they did not know the righteousness of God and sought to establish their own, they did not submit to God's righteousness. ⁴Christ is the culmination of the law so that there may be righteousness for everyone who believes.

⁵Moses writes this about the righteousness that is by the law: "The person who does these things will live by them."[f] ⁶But the righteousness that is by faith says: "Do not say in your heart, 'Who will ascend into heaven?' "[g] (that is, to bring Christ down) ⁷or 'Who will descend into the deep?' "[h]

---

[a] 25 Hosea 2:23   [b] 26 Hosea 1:10   [c] 28 Isaiah 10:22,23 (see Septuagint)   [d] 29 Isaiah 1:9
[e] 33 Isaiah 8:14; 28:16   [f] 5 Lev. 18:5   [g] 6 Deut. 30:12   [h] 7 Deut. 30:13

(that is, to bring Christ up from the dead). [8]But what does it say? "The word is near you; it is in your mouth and in your heart,"[a] that is, the message concerning faith that we proclaim: [9]If you declare with your mouth, "Jesus is Lord," and believe in your heart that God raised him from the dead, you will be saved. [10]For it is with your heart that you believe and are justified, and it is with your mouth that you profess your faith and are saved. [11]As Scripture says, "Anyone who believes in him will never be put to shame."[b] [12]For there is no difference between Jew and Gentile — the same Lord is Lord of all and richly blesses all who call on him, [13]for, "Everyone who calls on the name of the Lord will be saved."[c]

[14]How, then, can they call on the one they have not believed in? And how can they believe in the one of whom they have not heard? And how can they hear without someone preaching to them? [15]And how can anyone preach unless they are sent? As it is written: "How beautiful are the feet of those who bring good news!"[d]

[16]But not all the Israelites accepted the good news. For Isaiah says, "Lord, who has believed our message?"[e] [17]Consequently, faith comes from hearing the message, and the message is heard through the word about Christ. [18]But I ask: Did they not hear? Of course they did:

"Their voice has gone out into all
    the earth,
    their words to the ends of the
    world."[f]

[19]Again I ask: Did Israel not understand? First, Moses says,

"I will make you envious by
    those who are not a
    nation;
I will make you angry by
    a nation that has no
    understanding."[g]

[20]And Isaiah boldly says,

"I was found by those who did
    not seek me;
I revealed myself to those who
    did not ask for me."[h]

[21]But concerning Israel he says,

"All day long I have held out my
    hands
    to a disobedient and obstinate
    people."[i]

11 I ask then: Did God reject his people? By no means! I am an Israelite myself, a descendant of Abraham, from the tribe of Benjamin. [2]God did not reject his people, whom he foreknew. Don't you know what Scripture says in the passage about Elijah — how he appealed to God against Israel: [3]"Lord, they have killed your prophets and torn down your altars; I am the only one left, and they are trying to kill me"[j]? [4]And what was God's answer to him? "I have reserved for myself seven thousand who have not bowed the knee to Baal."[k] [5]So too, at the present time there is a remnant chosen by grace. [6]And if by grace, then it cannot be based on works; if it were, grace would no longer be grace.

[7]What then? What the people of Israel sought so earnestly they did not obtain. The elect among them

---

[a] 8 Deut. 30:14   [b] 11 Isaiah 28:16 (see Septuagint)   [c] 13 Joel 2:32   [d] 15 Isaiah 52:7
[e] 16 Isaiah 53:1   [f] 18 Psalm 19:4   [g] 19 Deut. 32:21   [h] 20 Isaiah 65:1   [i] 21 Isaiah 65:2
[j] 3 1 Kings 19:10,14   [k] 4 1 Kings 19:18

did, but the others were hardened, [8]as it is written:

"God gave them a spirit of
   stupor,
eyes that could not see
   and ears that could not hear,
to this very day."[a]

[9]And David says:

"May their table become a snare
   and a trap,
a stumbling block and a
   retribution for them.
[10]May their eyes be darkened so
   they cannot see,
and their backs be bent
   forever."[b]

[11]Again I ask: Did they stumble so as to fall beyond recovery? Not at all! Rather, because of their transgression, salvation has come to the Gentiles to make Israel envious. [12]But if their transgression means riches for the world, and their loss means riches for the Gentiles, how much greater riches will their full inclusion bring!

[13]I am talking to you Gentiles. Inasmuch as I am the apostle to the Gentiles, I take pride in my ministry [14]in the hope that I may somehow arouse my own people to envy and save some of them. [15]For if their rejection brought reconciliation to the world, what will their acceptance be but life from the dead? [16]If the part of the dough offered as firstfruits is holy, then the whole batch is holy; if the root is holy, so are the branches.

[17]If some of the branches have been broken off, and you, though a wild olive shoot, have been grafted in among the others and now share in the nourishing sap from the olive root, [18]do not consider yourself to be superior to those other branches. If you do, consider this: You do not support the root, but the root supports you. [19]You will say then, "Branches were broken off so that I could be grafted in." [20]Granted. But they were broken off because of unbelief, and you stand by faith. Do not be arrogant, but tremble. [21]For if God did not spare the natural branches, he will not spare you either.

[22]Consider therefore the kindness and sternness of God: sternness to those who fell, but kindness to you, provided that you continue in his kindness. Otherwise, you also will be cut off. [23]And if they do not persist in unbelief, they will be grafted in, for God is able to graft them in again. [24]After all, if you were cut out of an olive tree that is wild by nature, and contrary to nature were grafted into a cultivated olive tree, how much more readily will these, the natural branches, be grafted into their own olive tree!

[25]I do not want you to be ignorant of this mystery, brothers and sisters, so that you may not be conceited: Israel has experienced a hardening in part until the full number of the Gentiles has come in, [26]and in this way[c] all Israel will be saved. As it is written:

"The deliverer will come from
   Zion;
he will turn godlessness away
   from Jacob.
[27]And this is[d] my covenant with
   them
when I take away their sins."[e]

[28]As far as the gospel is concerned, they are enemies for your

---

[a] 8 Deut. 29:4; Isaiah 29:10   [b] 10 Psalm 69:22,23   [c] 26 Or and so   [d] 27 Or will be
[e] 27 Isaiah 59:20,21; 27:9 (see Septuagint); Jer. 31:33,34

sake; but as far as election is concerned, they are loved on account of the patriarchs, 29for God's gifts and his call are irrevocable. 30Just as you who were at one time disobedient to God have now received mercy as a result of their disobedience, 31so they too have now become disobedient in order that they too may now[a] receive mercy as a result of God's mercy to you. 32For God has bound everyone over to disobedience so that he may have mercy on them all.

33Oh, the depth of the riches of the
     wisdom and[b] knowledge
     of God!
   How unsearchable his
     judgments,
   and his paths beyond tracing
     out!
34"Who has known the mind of the
     Lord?
   Or who has been his
     counselor?"[c]
35"Who has ever given to God,
     that God should repay them?"[d]
36For from him and through him
     and for him are all things.
   To him be the glory forever!
     Amen.

12 Therefore, I urge you, brothers and sisters, in view of God's mercy, to offer your bodies as a living sacrifice, holy and pleasing to God—this is your true and proper worship. 2Do not conform to the pattern of this world, but be transformed by the renewing of your mind. Then you will be able to test and approve what God's will is—his good, pleasing and perfect will.

3For by the grace given me I say to every one of you: Do not think

of yourself more highly than you ought, but rather think of yourself with sober judgment, in accordance with the faith God has distributed to each of you. 4For just as each of us has one body with many members, and these members do not all have the same function, 5so in Christ we, though many, form one body, and each member belongs to all the others. 6We have different gifts, according to the grace given to each of us. If your gift is prophesying, then prophesy in accordance with your[e] faith; 7if it is serving, then serve; if it is teaching, then teach; 8if it is to encourage, then give encouragement; if it is giving, then give generously; if it is to lead,[f] do it diligently; if it is to show mercy, do it cheerfully.

9Love must be sincere. Hate what is evil; cling to what is good. 10Be devoted to one another in love. Honor one another above yourselves. 11Never be lacking in zeal, but keep your spiritual fervor, serving the Lord. 12Be joyful in hope, patient in affliction, faithful in prayer. 13Share with the Lord's people who are in need. Practice hospitality.

14Bless those who persecute you; bless and do not curse. 15Rejoice with those who rejoice; mourn with those who mourn. 16Live in harmony with one another. Do not be proud, but be willing to associate with people of low position.[g] Do not be conceited.

17Do not repay anyone evil for evil. Be careful to do what is right in the eyes of everyone. 18If it is possible, as far as it depends on you, live at peace with everyone. 19Do not take revenge, my dear friends, but leave room for God's wrath, for it is written: "It is mine to avenge; I will repay,"[a] says the Lord. 20 On the contrary:

> "If your enemy is hungry, feed
> him;
> if he is thirsty, give him
> something to drink.
> In doing this, you will heap
> burning coals on his
> head."[b]

21 Do not be overcome by evil, but overcome evil with good.

13 Let everyone be subject to the governing authorities, for there is no authority except that which God has established. The authorities that exist have been established by God. 2 Consequently, whoever rebels against the authority is rebelling against what God has instituted, and those who do so will bring judgment on themselves. 3 For rulers hold no terror for those who do right, but for those who do wrong. Do you want to be free from fear of the one in authority? Then do what is right and you will be commended. 4 For the one in authority is God's servant for your good. But if you do wrong, be afraid, for they do not bear the sword for no reason. They are God's servants, agents of wrath to bring punishment on the wrongdoer. 5 Therefore, it is necessary to submit to the authorities, not only because of possible punishment but also as a matter of conscience.

6 This is also why you pay taxes, for the authorities are God's servants, who give their full time to governing. 7 Give to everyone what you owe them: If you owe taxes, pay taxes; if revenue, then revenue; if respect, then respect; if honor, then honor.

8 Let no debt remain outstanding, except the continuing debt to love one another, for whoever loves others has fulfilled the law. 9 The commandments, "You shall not commit adultery," "You shall not murder," "You shall not steal," "You shall not covet,"[c] and whatever other command there may be, are summed up in this one command: "Love your neighbor as yourself."[d] 10 Love does no harm to a neighbor. Therefore love is the fulfillment of the law.

11 And do this, understanding the present time: The hour has already come for you to wake up from your slumber, because our salvation is nearer now than when we first believed. 12 The night is nearly over; the day is almost here. So let us put aside the deeds of darkness and put on the armor of light. 13 Let us behave decently, as in the daytime, not in carousing and drunkenness, not in sexual immorality and debauchery, not in dissension and jealousy. 14 Rather, clothe yourselves with the Lord Jesus Christ, and do not think about how to gratify the desires of the flesh.[e]

14 Accept the one whose faith is weak, without quarreling over disputable matters. 2 One person's faith allows them to eat anything, but another, whose faith is weak, eats only vegetables. 3 The one who eats everything must not treat with contempt the one who does not, and the one who does not eat everything must not judge the one who

---

a 19 Deut. 32:35   b 20 Prov. 25:21,22   c 9 Exodus 20:13-15,17; Deut. 5:17-19,21
d 9 Lev. 19:18   e 14 In contexts like this, the Greek word for flesh (sarx) refers to the sinful state of human beings, often presented as a power in opposition to the Spirit.

does, for God has accepted them. [4]Who are you to judge someone else's servant? To their own master, servants stand or fall. And they will stand, for the Lord is able to make them stand.

[5]One person considers one day more sacred than another; another considers every day alike. Each of them should be fully convinced in their own mind. [6]Whoever regards one day as special does so to the Lord. Whoever eats meat does so to the Lord, for they give thanks to God; and whoever abstains does so to the Lord and gives thanks to God. [7]For none of us lives for ourselves alone, and none of us dies for ourselves alone. [8]If we live, we live for the Lord; and if we die, we die for the Lord. So, whether we live or die, we belong to the Lord. [9]For this very reason, Christ died and returned to life so that he might be the Lord of both the dead and the living.

[10]You, then, why do you judge your brother or sister[a]? Or why do you treat them with contempt? For we will all stand before God's judgment seat. [11]It is written:

"'As surely as I live,' says the
　　Lord,
'every knee will bow before me;
　　every tongue will acknowledge
　　God.'"[b]

[12]So then, each of us will give an account of ourselves to God.

[13]Therefore let us stop passing judgment on one another. Instead, make up your mind not to put any stumbling block or obstacle in the way of a brother or sister. [14]I am convinced, being fully persuaded in the Lord Jesus, that nothing is unclean in itself. But if anyone regards something as unclean, then for that person it is unclean. [15]If your brother or sister is distressed because of what you eat, you are no longer acting in love. Do not by your eating destroy someone for whom Christ died. [16]Therefore do not let what you know is good be spoken of as evil. [17]For the kingdom of God is not a matter of eating and drinking, but of righteousness, peace and joy in the Holy Spirit, [18]because anyone who serves Christ in this way is pleasing to God and receives human approval.

[19]Let us therefore make every effort to do what leads to peace and to mutual edification. [20]Do not destroy the work of God for the sake of food. All food is clean, but it is wrong for a person to eat anything that causes someone else to stumble. [21]It is better not to eat meat or drink wine or to do anything else that will cause your brother or sister to fall.

[22]So whatever you believe about these things keep between yourself and God. Blessed is the one who does not condemn himself by what he approves. [23]But whoever has doubts is condemned if they eat, because their eating is not from faith; and everything that does not come from faith is sin.[c]

15 We who are strong ought to bear with the failings of the weak and not to please ourselves. [2]Each of us should please our neighbors for their good, to build them up. [3]For even Christ did not please himself but, as it is written: "The insults of those who insult you have

---

[a] 10 The Greek word for *brother or sister* (*adelphos*) refers here to a believer, whether man or woman, as part of God's family; also in verses 13, 15 and 21.　　[b] 11 Isaiah 45:23　　[c] 23 Some manuscripts place 16:25-27 here; others after 15:33.

fallen on me."[a] [4]For everything that was written in the past was written to teach us, so that through the endurance taught in the Scriptures and the encouragement they provide we might have hope.

[5]May the God who gives endurance and encouragement give you the same attitude of mind toward each other that Christ Jesus had, [6]so that with one mind and one voice you may glorify the God and Father of our Lord Jesus Christ.

[7]Accept one another, then, just as Christ accepted you, in order to bring praise to God. [8]For I tell you that Christ has become a servant of the Jews[b] on behalf of God's truth, so that the promises made to the patriarchs might be confirmed [9]and, moreover, that the Gentiles might glorify God for his mercy. As it is written:

> "Therefore I will praise you
>   among the Gentiles;
>   I will sing the praises of your
>   name."[c]

[10]Again, it says,

> "Rejoice, you Gentiles, with his
>   people."[d]

[11]And again,

> "Praise the Lord, all you
>   Gentiles;
>   let all the peoples extol him."[e]

[12]And again, Isaiah says,

> "The Root of Jesse will spring up,
>   one who will arise to rule over
>   the nations;
>   in him the Gentiles will
>   hope."[f]

[13]May the God of hope fill you with all joy and peace as you trust in him, so that you may overflow with hope by the power of the Holy Spirit.

[14]I myself am convinced, my brothers and sisters, that you yourselves are full of goodness, filled with knowledge and competent to instruct one another. [15]Yet I have written you quite boldly on some points to remind you of them again, because of the grace God gave me [16]to be a minister of Christ Jesus to the Gentiles. He gave me the priestly duty of proclaiming the gospel of God, so that the Gentiles might become an offering acceptable to God, sanctified by the Holy Spirit.

[17]Therefore I glory in Christ Jesus in my service to God. [18]I will not venture to speak of anything except what Christ has accomplished through me in leading the Gentiles to obey God by what I have said and done— [19]by the power of signs and wonders, through the power of the Spirit of God. So from Jerusalem all the way around to Illyricum, I have fully proclaimed the gospel of Christ. [20]It has always been my ambition to preach the gospel where Christ was not known, so that I would not be building on someone else's foundation. [21]Rather, as it is written:

> "Those who were not told about
>   him will see,
>   and those who have not heard
>   will understand."[g]

[22]This is why I have often been hindered from coming to you.

[23]But now that there is no more place for me to work in these regions, and since I have been longing for many years to visit you, [24]I

---

[a] 3 Psalm 69:9   [b] 8 Greek *circumcision*   [c] 9 2 Samuel 22:50; Psalm 18:49   [d] 10 Deut. 32:43
[e] 11 Psalm 117:1   [f] 12 Isaiah 11:10 (see Septuagint)   [g] 21 Isaiah 52:15 (see Septuagint)

plan to do so when I go to Spain. I hope to see you while passing through and to have you assist me on my journey there, after I have enjoyed your company for a while. ²⁵Now, however, I am on my way to Jerusalem in the service of the Lord's people there. ²⁶For Macedonia and Achaia were pleased to make a contribution for the poor among the Lord's people in Jerusalem. ²⁷They were pleased to do it, and indeed they owe it to them. For if the Gentiles have shared in the Jews' spiritual blessings, they owe it to the Jews to share with them their material blessings. ²⁸So after I have completed this task and have made sure that they have received this contribution, I will go to Spain and visit you on the way. ²⁹I know that when I come to you, I will come in the full measure of the blessing of Christ.

³⁰I urge you, brothers and sisters, by our Lord Jesus Christ and by the love of the Spirit, to join me in my struggle by praying to God for me. ³¹Pray that I may be kept safe from the unbelievers in Judea and that the contribution I take to Jerusalem may be favorably received by the Lord's people there, ³²so that I may come to you with joy, by God's will, and in your company be refreshed. ³³The God of peace be with you all. Amen.

16 I commend to you our sister Phoebe, a deacon[a,b] of the church in Cenchreae. ²I ask you to receive her in the Lord in a way worthy of his people and to give her any help she may need from you, for she has been the benefactor of many people, including me.

³Greet Priscilla[c] and Aquila, my co-workers in Christ Jesus. ⁴They risked their lives for me. Not only I but all the churches of the Gentiles are grateful to them.

⁵Greet also the church that meets at their house.

Greet my dear friend Epenetus, who was the first convert to Christ in the province of Asia.

⁶Greet Mary, who worked very hard for you.

⁷Greet Andronicus and Junia, my fellow Jews who have been in prison with me. They are outstanding among[d] the apostles, and they were in Christ before I was.

⁸Greet Ampliatus, my dear friend in the Lord.

⁹Greet Urbanus, our co-worker in Christ, and my dear friend Stachys.

¹⁰Greet Apelles, whose fidelity to Christ has stood the test.

Greet those who belong to the household of Aristobulus.

¹¹Greet Herodion, my fellow Jew.

Greet those in the household of Narcissus who are in the Lord.

¹²Greet Tryphena and Tryphosa, those women who work hard in the Lord.

Greet my dear friend Persis, another woman who has worked very hard in the Lord.

¹³Greet Rufus, chosen in the Lord, and his mother, who has been a mother to me, too.

¹⁴Greet Asyncritus, Phlegon, Hermes, Patrobas, Hermas and the other brothers and sisters with them.

¹⁵Greet Philologus, Julia, Nereus

---

a 1 Or *servant*   *b 1* The word *deacon* refers here to a Christian designated to serve with the overseers/elders of the church in a variety of ways; similarly in Phil. 1:1 and 1 Tim. 3:8,12.
c 3 Greek *Prisca*, a variant of *Priscilla*   *d 7* Or *are esteemed by*

and his sister, and Olympas and all the Lord's people who are with them.

16 Greet one another with a holy kiss.

All the churches of Christ send greetings.

17 I urge you, brothers and sisters, to watch out for those who cause divisions and put obstacles in your way that are contrary to the teaching you have learned. Keep away from them. 18 For such people are not serving our Lord Christ, but their own appetites. By smooth talk and flattery they deceive the minds of naive people. 19 Everyone has heard about your obedience, so I rejoice because of you; but I want you to be wise about what is good, and innocent about what is evil.

20 The God of peace will soon crush Satan under your feet.

The grace of our Lord Jesus be with you.

21 Timothy, my co-worker, sends his greetings to you, as do Lucius, Jason and Sosipater, my fellow Jews.

22 I, Tertius, who wrote down this letter, greet you in the Lord.

23 Gaius, whose hospitality I and the whole church here enjoy, sends you his greetings.

Erastus, who is the city's director of public works, and our brother Quartus send you their greetings. [24] a

25 Now to him who is able to establish you in accordance with my gospel, the message I proclaim about Jesus Christ, in keeping with the revelation of the mystery hidden for long ages past, 26 but now revealed and made known through the prophetic writings by the command of the eternal God, so that all the Gentiles might come to the obedience that comes from b faith — 27 to the only wise God be glory forever through Jesus Christ! Amen.

a 24 Some manuscripts include here May the grace of our Lord Jesus Christ be with all of you. Amen.   b 26 Or that is

1 CORINTHIANS

The book of Acts describes how Paul brought the royal news about Jesus the Messiah to Macedonia (northern Greece), but then had to flee to Achaia (southern Greece) for his own safety. He visited the city of Corinth there, a wealthy and cosmopolitan commercial center. Many people became believers, so he stayed for a year and a half to teach them.

After he left, the Corinthians wrote to Paul (in a letter we no longer have) with some key questions. The Corinthians had adopted the common Greek idea that physical things are bad, so they wanted to free the human spirit from the body. This affected the way they saw such things as marriage, attendance at ceremonial meals for pagan gods, and even the resurrection of Jesus. In the letter we know as 1 Corinthians Paul addresses all of these concerns, as well as questions about worship.

Paul writes that *this world in its present form is passing away*, but the Corinthians can give themselves *fully to the work of the Lord* since their *labor in the Lord is not in vain*. The coming resurrection of the dead, and the new world that will accompany it, will show the value of all their current efforts. Paul's practical advice for how to consistently embody the new life of God's kingdom during a particular scene in the biblical drama gives us great insight as we seek to take up our roles today.

---

1 Paul, called to be an apostle of Christ Jesus by the will of God, and our brother Sosthenes,

2 To the church of God in Corinth, to those sanctified in Christ Jesus and called to be his holy people, together with all those everywhere who call on the name of our Lord Jesus Christ—their Lord and ours:

3 Grace and peace to you from God our Father and the Lord Jesus Christ.

4 I always thank my God for you because of his grace given you in Christ Jesus. 5 For in him you have been enriched in every way—with all kinds of speech and with all knowledge— 6 God thus confirming our testimony about Christ among you. 7 Therefore you do not lack any spiritual gift as you eagerly wait for our Lord Jesus Christ to be revealed. 8 He will also keep you firm to the end, so that you will be blameless on the day of our Lord Jesus Christ. 9 God is faithful, who has called you into fellowship with his Son, Jesus Christ our Lord.

10 I appeal to you, brothers and sisters,[a] in the name of our Lord Jesus Christ, that all of you agree with one another in what you say and that there be no divisions among you, but that you be perfectly united in mind and thought. 11 My brothers and sisters, some from Chloe's household have informed me that there are quarrels among you. 12 What I mean is this: One of you says, "I follow Paul"; another, "I follow Apollos"; another,

---

a 10 The Greek word for *brothers and sisters* (*adelphoi*) refers here to believers, both men and women, as part of God's family; also in verses 11 and 26; and in 2:1; 3:1; 4:6; 6:8; 7:24, 29; 10:1; 11:33; 12:1; 14:6, 20, 26, 39; 15:1, 6, 50, 58; 16:15, 20.

"I follow Cephas[a]"; still another, "I follow Christ."

13 Is Christ divided? Was Paul crucified for you? Were you baptized in the name of Paul? 14 I thank God that I did not baptize any of you except Crispus and Gaius, 15 so no one can say that you were baptized in my name. 16 (Yes, I also baptized the household of Stephanas; beyond that, I don't remember if I baptized anyone else.) 17 For Christ did not send me to baptize, but to preach the gospel—not with wisdom and eloquence, lest the cross of Christ be emptied of its power.

18 For the message of the cross is foolishness to those who are perishing, but to us who are being saved it is the power of God. 19 For it is written:

"I will destroy the wisdom of the
    wise;
the intelligence of the
    intelligent I will
    frustrate."[b]

20 Where is the wise person? Where is the teacher of the law? Where is the philosopher of this age? Has not God made foolish the wisdom of the world? 21 For since in the wisdom of God the world through its wisdom did not know him, God was pleased through the foolishness of what was preached to save those who believe. 22 Jews demand signs and Greeks look for wisdom, 23 but we preach Christ crucified: a stumbling block to Jews and foolishness to Gentiles, 24 but to those whom God has called, both Jews and Greeks, Christ the power of God and the wisdom of God. 25 For the foolishness of God is wiser than human wisdom, and

the weakness of God is stronger than human strength.

26 Brothers and sisters, think of what you were when you were called. Not many of you were wise by human standards; not many were influential; not many were of noble birth. 27 But God chose the foolish things of the world to shame the wise; God chose the weak things of the world to shame the strong. 28 God chose the lowly things of this world and the despised things—and the things that are not—to nullify the things that are, 29 so that no one may boast before him. 30 It is because of him that you are in Christ Jesus, who has become for us wisdom from God—that is, our righteousness, holiness and redemption. 31 Therefore, as it is written: "Let the one who boasts boast in the Lord."[c]

2 And so it was with me, brothers and sisters. When I came to you, I did not come with eloquence or human wisdom as I proclaimed to you the testimony about God.[d] 2 For I resolved to know nothing while I was with you except Jesus Christ and him crucified. 3 I came to you in weakness with great fear and trembling. 4 My message and my preaching were not with wise and persuasive words, but with a demonstration of the Spirit's power, 5 so that your faith might not rest on human wisdom, but on God's power.

6 We do, however, speak a message of wisdom among the mature, but not the wisdom of this age or of the rulers of this age, who are coming to nothing. 7 No, we declare God's wisdom, a mystery that has been hidden and that God destined for our glory before time be-

gan. [8]None of the rulers of this age understood it, for if they had, they would not have crucified the Lord of glory. [9]However, as it is written:

"What no eye has seen,
    what no ear has heard,
and what no human mind has
    conceived"[a] —
the things God has prepared
    for those who love him —

[10]these are the things God has revealed to us by his Spirit.

The Spirit searches all things, even the deep things of God. [11]For who knows a person's thoughts except their own spirit within them? In the same way no one knows the thoughts of God except the Spirit of God. [12]What we have received is not the spirit of the world, but the Spirit who is from God, so that we may understand what God has freely given us. [13]This is what we speak, not in words taught us by human wisdom but in words taught by the Spirit, explaining spiritual realities with Spirit-taught words.[b] [14]The person without the Spirit does not accept the things that come from the Spirit of God but considers them foolishness, and cannot understand them because they are discerned only through the Spirit. [15]The person with the Spirit makes judgments about all things, but such a person is not subject to merely human judgments, [16]for,

"Who has known the mind of the
    Lord
    so as to instruct him?"[c]

But we have the mind of Christ.

3 Brothers and sisters, I could not address you as people who live by the Spirit but as people who are still worldly—mere infants in Christ. [2]I gave you milk, not solid food, for you were not yet ready for it. Indeed, you are still not ready. [3]You are still worldly. For since there is jealousy and quarreling among you, are you not worldly? Are you not acting like mere humans? [4]For when one says, "I follow Paul," and another, "I follow Apollos," are you not mere human beings?

[5]What, after all, is Apollos? And what is Paul? Only servants, through whom you came to believe—as the Lord has assigned to each his task. [6]I planted the seed, Apollos watered it, but God has been making it grow. [7]So neither the one who plants nor the one who waters is anything, but only God, who makes things grow. [8]The one who plants and the one who waters have one purpose, and they will each be rewarded according to their own labor. [9]For we are co-workers in God's service; you are God's field, God's building.

[10]By the grace God has given me, I laid a foundation as a wise builder, and someone else is building on it. But each one should build with care. [11]For no one can lay any foundation other than the one already laid, which is Jesus Christ. [12]If anyone builds on this foundation using gold, silver, costly stones, wood, hay or straw, [13]their work will be shown for what it is, because the Day will bring it to light. It will be revealed with fire, and the fire will test the quality of each person's work. [14]If what has been built survives, the builder will receive a reward. [15]If it is burned up, the builder will suffer loss but yet will be saved—

---

[a] 9 Isaiah 64:4   [b] 13 Or Spirit, interpreting spiritual truths to those who are spiritual
[c] 16 Isaiah 40:13

even though only as one escaping through the flames.

16 Don't you know that you yourselves are God's temple and that God's Spirit dwells in your midst? 17 If anyone destroys God's temple, God will destroy that person; for God's temple is sacred, and you together are that temple.

18 Do not deceive yourselves. If any of you think you are wise by the standards of this age, you should become "fools" so that you may become wise. 19 For the wisdom of this world is foolishness in God's sight. As it is written: "He catches the wise in their craftiness"[a]; 20 and again, "The Lord knows that the thoughts of the wise are futile."[b] 21 So then, no more boasting about human leaders! All things are yours, 22 whether Paul or Apollos or Cephas[c] or the world or life or death or the present or the future — all are yours, 23 and you are of Christ, and Christ is of God.

4 This, then, is how you ought to regard us: as servants of Christ and as those entrusted with the mysteries God has revealed. 2 Now it is required that those who have been given a trust must prove faithful. 3 I care very little if I am judged by you or by any human court; indeed, I do not even judge myself. 4 My conscience is clear, but that does not make me innocent. It is the Lord who judges me. 5 Therefore judge nothing before the appointed time; wait until the Lord comes. He will bring to light what is hidden in darkness and will expose the motives of the heart. At that time each will receive their praise from God.

6 Now, brothers and sisters, I have applied these things to myself and Apollos for your benefit, so that you

may learn from us the meaning of the saying, "Do not go beyond what is written." Then you will not be puffed up in being a follower of one of us over against the other. 7 For who makes you different from anyone else? What do you have that you did not receive? And if you did receive it, why do you boast as though you did not?

8 Already you have all you want! Already you have become rich! You have begun to reign — and that without us! How I wish that you really had begun to reign so that we also might reign with you! 9 For it seems to me that God has put us apostles on display at the end of the procession, like those condemned to die in the arena. We have been made a spectacle to the whole universe, to angels as well as to human beings. 10 We are fools for Christ, but you are so wise in Christ! We are weak, but you are strong! You are honored, we are dishonored! 11 To this very hour we go hungry and thirsty, we are in rags, we are brutally treated, we are homeless. 12 We work hard with our own hands. When we are cursed, we bless; when we are persecuted, we endure it; 13 when we are slandered, we answer kindly. We have become the scum of the earth, the garbage of the world — right up to this moment.

14 I am writing this not to shame you but to warn you as my dear children. 15 Even if you had ten thousand guardians in Christ, you do not have many fathers, for in Christ Jesus I became your father through the gospel. 16 Therefore I urge you to imitate me. 17 For this reason I have sent to you Timothy, my son whom I love, who is faithful in the

a 19 Job 5:13   b 20 Psalm 94:11   c 22 That is, Peter

Lord. He will remind you of my way of life in Christ Jesus, which agrees with what I teach everywhere in every church.

¹⁸Some of you have become arrogant, as if I were not coming to you. ¹⁹But I will come to you very soon, if the Lord is willing, and then I will find out not only how these arrogant people are talking, but what power they have. ²⁰For the kingdom of God is not a matter of talk but of power. ²¹What do you prefer? Shall I come to you with a rod of discipline, or shall I come in love and with a gentle spirit?

5 It is actually reported that there is sexual immorality among you, and of a kind that even pagans do not tolerate: A man is sleeping with his father's wife. ²And you are proud! Shouldn't you rather have gone into mourning and have put out of your fellowship the man who has been doing this? ³For my part, even though I am not physically present, I am with you in spirit. As one who is present with you in this way, I have already passed judgment in the name of our Lord Jesus on the one who has been doing this. ⁴So when you are assembled and I am with you in spirit, and the power of our Lord Jesus is present, ⁵hand this man over to Satan for the destruction of the flesh,ᵃ,ᵇ so that his spirit may be saved on the day of the Lord.

⁶Your boasting is not good. Don't you know that a little yeast leavens the whole batch of dough? ⁷Get rid of the old yeast, so that you may be a new unleavened batch—as you really are. For Christ, our Passover lamb, has been sacrificed. ⁸Therefore let us keep the Festival, not with the old bread leavened with malice and wickedness, but with the unleavened bread of sincerity and truth.

⁹I wrote to you in my letter not to associate with sexually immoral people— ¹⁰not at all meaning the people of this world who are immoral, or the greedy and swindlers, or idolaters. In that case you would have to leave this world. ¹¹But now I am writing to you that you must not associate with anyone who claims to be a brother or sisterᶜ but is sexually immoral or greedy, an idolater or slanderer, a drunkard or swindler. Do not even eat with such people.

¹²What business is it of mine to judge those outside the church? Are you not to judge those inside? ¹³God will judge those outside. "Expel the wicked person from among you."ᵈ

6 If any of you has a dispute with another, do you dare to take it before the ungodly for judgment instead of before the Lord's people? ²Or do you not know that the Lord's people will judge the world? And if you are to judge the world, are you not competent to judge trivial cases? ³Do you not know that we will judge angels? How much more the things of this life! ⁴Therefore, if you have disputes about such matters, do you ask for a ruling from those whose way of life is scorned in the church? ⁵I say this to shame you. Is it possible that there is nobody

---

ᵃ 5 In contexts like this, the Greek word for *flesh* (*sarx*) refers to the sinful state of human beings, often presented as a power in opposition to the Spirit.   ᵇ 5 Or *of his body*   ᶜ 11 The Greek word for *brother or sister* (*adelphos*) refers here to a believer, whether man or woman, as part of God's family; also in 8:11, 13.   ᵈ 13 Deut. 13:5; 17:7; 19:19; 21:21; 22:21,24; 24:7

among you wise enough to judge a dispute between believers? ⁶But instead, one brother takes another to court—and this in front of unbelievers!

⁷The very fact that you have lawsuits among you means you have been completely defeated already. Why not rather be wronged? Why not rather be cheated? ⁸Instead, you yourselves cheat and do wrong, and you do this to your brothers and sisters. ⁹Or do you not know that wrongdoers will not inherit the kingdom of God? Do not be deceived: Neither the sexually immoral nor idolaters nor adulterers nor men who have sex with men[a] ¹⁰nor thieves nor the greedy nor drunkards nor slanderers nor swindlers will inherit the kingdom of God. ¹¹And that is what some of you were. But you were washed, you were sanctified, you were justified in the name of the Lord Jesus Christ and by the Spirit of our God.

¹²"I have the right to do anything," you say—but not everything is beneficial. "I have the right to do anything"—but I will not be mastered by anything. ¹³You say, "Food for the stomach and the stomach for food, and God will destroy them both." The body, however, is not meant for sexual immorality but for the Lord, and the Lord for the body. ¹⁴By his power God raised the Lord from the dead, and he will raise us also. ¹⁵Do you not know that your bodies are members of Christ himself? Shall I then take the members of Christ and unite them with a prostitute? Never! ¹⁶Do you not know that he who unites himself with a prostitute is one with her in body? For it is said, "The two will become one flesh."[b] ¹⁷But whoever is united with the Lord is one with him in spirit.[c]

¹⁸Flee from sexual immorality. All other sins a person commits are outside the body, but whoever sins sexually, sins against their own body. ¹⁹Do you not know that your bodies are temples of the Holy Spirit, who is in you, whom you have received from God? You are not your own; ²⁰you were bought at a price. Therefore honor God with your bodies.

7 Now for the matters you wrote about: "It is good for a man not to have sexual relations with a woman." ²But since sexual immorality is occurring, each man should have sexual relations with his own wife, and each woman with her own husband. ³The husband should fulfill his marital duty to his wife, and likewise the wife to her husband. ⁴The wife does not have authority over her own body but yields it to her husband. In the same way, the husband does not have authority over his own body but yields it to his wife. ⁵Do not deprive each other except perhaps by mutual consent and for a time, so that you may devote yourselves to prayer. Then come together again so that Satan will not tempt you because of your lack of self-control. ⁶I say this as a concession, not as a command. ⁷I wish that all of you were as I am. But each of you has your own gift from God; one has this gift, another has that.

⁸Now to the unmarried[d] and the

---

[a] 9 The words *men who have sex with men* translate two Greek words that refer to the passive and active participants in homosexual acts.   [b] 16 Gen. 2:24   [c] 17 Or *in the Spirit*
[d] 8 Or *widowers*

widows I say: It is good for them to stay unmarried, as I do. ⁹But if they cannot control themselves, they should marry, for it is better to marry than to burn with passion.

¹⁰To the married I give this command (not I, but the Lord): A wife must not separate from her husband. ¹¹But if she does, she must remain unmarried or else be reconciled to her husband. And a husband must not divorce his wife.

¹²To the rest I say this (I, not the Lord): If any brother has a wife who is not a believer and she is willing to live with him, he must not divorce her. ¹³And if a woman has a husband who is not a believer and he is willing to live with her, she must not divorce him. ¹⁴For the unbelieving husband has been sanctified through his wife, and the unbelieving wife has been sanctified through her believing husband. Otherwise your children would be unclean, but as it is, they are holy.

¹⁵But if the unbeliever leaves, let it be so. The brother or the sister is not bound in such circumstances; God has called us to live in peace. ¹⁶How do you know, wife, whether you will save your husband? Or, how do you know, husband, whether you will save your wife?

¹⁷Nevertheless, each person should live as a believer in whatever situation the Lord has assigned to them, just as God has called them. This is the rule I lay down in all the churches. ¹⁸Was a man already circumcised when he was called? He should not become uncircumcised. Was a man uncircumcised when he was called? He should not be circumcised. ¹⁹Circumcision is nothing and uncircumcision is nothing. Keeping God's commands is what counts. ²⁰Each person should remain in the situation they were in when God called them.

²¹Were you a slave when you were called? Don't let it trouble you — although if you can gain your freedom, do so. ²²For the one who was a slave when called to faith in the Lord is the Lord's freed person; similarly, the one who was free when called is Christ's slave. ²³You were bought at a price; do not become slaves of human beings. ²⁴Brothers and sisters, each person, as responsible to God, should remain in the situation they were in when God called them.

²⁵Now about virgins: I have no command from the Lord, but I give a judgment as one who by the Lord's mercy is trustworthy. ²⁶Because of the present crisis, I think that it is good for a man to remain as he is. ²⁷Are you pledged to a woman? Do not seek to be released. Are you free from such a commitment? Do not look for a wife. ²⁸But if you do marry, you have not sinned; and if a virgin marries, she has not sinned. But those who marry will face many troubles in this life, and I want to spare you this.

²⁹What I mean, brothers and sisters, is that the time is short. From now on those who have wives should live as if they do not; ³⁰those who mourn, as if they did not; those who are happy, as if they were not; those who buy something, as if it were not theirs to keep; ³¹those who use the things of the world, as if not engrossed in them. For this world in its present form is passing away.

³²I would like you to be free from concern. An unmarried man is concerned about the Lord's affairs — how he can please the Lord. ³³But

a married man is concerned about the affairs of this world—how he can please his wife— ³⁴and his interests are divided. An unmarried woman or virgin is concerned about the Lord's affairs: Her aim is to be devoted to the Lord in both body and spirit. But a married woman is concerned about the affairs of this world—how she can please her husband. ³⁵I am saying this for your own good, not to restrict you, but that you may live in a right way in undivided devotion to the Lord.

³⁶If anyone is worried that he might not be acting honorably toward the virgin he is engaged to, and if his passions are too strong*ᵃ* and he feels he ought to marry, he should do as he wants. He is not sinning. They should get married. ³⁷But the man who has settled the matter in his own mind, who is under no compulsion but has control over his own will, and who has made up his mind not to marry the virgin—this man also does the right thing. ³⁸So then, he who marries the virgin does right, but he who does not marry her does better.*ᵇ*

³⁹A woman is bound to her husband as long as he lives. But if her husband dies, she is free to marry anyone she wishes, but he must belong to the Lord. ⁴⁰In my judgment, she is happier if she stays as she is—and I think that I too have the Spirit of God.

8 Now about food sacrificed to idols: We know that "We all possess knowledge." But knowledge puffs up while love builds up. ²Those who think they know something do not yet know as they ought to know. ³But whoever loves God is known by God.*ᶜ*

⁴So then, about eating food sacrificed to idols: We know that "An idol is nothing at all in the world" and that "There is no God but one." ⁵For even if there are so-called gods, whether in heaven or on earth (as indeed there are many "gods" and many "lords"), ⁶yet for us there is but one God, the Father, from whom all things came and for whom we live; and there is but one Lord, Jesus Christ, through whom all things came and through whom we live.

⁷But not everyone possesses this knowledge. Some people are still so accustomed to idols that when they eat sacrificial food they think of it as having been sacrificed to a god, and since their conscience is weak, it is defiled. ⁸But food does not bring us near to God; we are no worse if we do not eat, and no better if we do.

⁹Be careful, however, that the exercise of your rights does not become a stumbling block to the weak. ¹⁰For if someone with a weak conscience sees you, with all your knowledge, eating in an idol's temple, won't that person be emboldened to eat what is sacrificed

---

ᵃ 36 Or if she is getting beyond the usual age for marriage   ᵇ 36-38 Or ³⁶If anyone thinks he is not treating his daughter properly, and if she is getting along in years (or if her passions are too strong), and he feels she ought to marry, he should do as he wants. He is not sinning. He should let her get married. ³⁷But the man who has settled the matter in his own mind, who is under no compulsion but has control over his own will, and who has made up his mind to keep the virgin unmarried—this man also does the right thing. ³⁸So then, he who gives his virgin in marriage does right, but he who does not give her in marriage does better.   ᶜ 2,3 An early manuscript and another ancient witness think they have knowledge do not yet know as they ought to know. ³But whoever loves truly knows.

to idols? [11]So this weak brother or sister, for whom Christ died, is destroyed by your knowledge. [12]When you sin against them in this way and wound their weak conscience, you sin against Christ. [13]Therefore, if what I eat causes my brother or sister to fall into sin, I will never eat meat again, so that I will not cause them to fall.

9 Am I not free? Am I not an apostle? Have I not seen Jesus our Lord? Are you not the result of my work in the Lord? [2]Even though I may not be an apostle to others, surely I am to you! For you are the seal of my apostleship in the Lord.

[3]This is my defense to those who sit in judgment on me. [4]Don't we have the right to food and drink? [5]Don't we have the right to take a believing wife along with us, as do the other apostles and the Lord's brothers and Cephas[a]? [6]Or is it only I and Barnabas who lack the right to not work for a living?

[7]Who serves as a soldier at his own expense? Who plants a vineyard and does not eat its grapes? Who tends a flock and does not drink the milk? [8]Do I say this merely on human authority? Doesn't the Law say the same thing? [9]For it is written in the Law of Moses: "Do not muzzle an ox while it is treading out the grain."[b] Is it about oxen that God is concerned? [10]Surely he says this for us, doesn't he? Yes, this was written for us, because whoever plows and threshes should be able to do so in the hope of sharing in the harvest. [11]If we have sown spiritual seed among you, is it too much if we reap a material harvest from you? [12]If others have this right of support from you, shouldn't we have it all the more?

But we did not use this right. On the contrary, we put up with anything rather than hinder the gospel of Christ.

[13]Don't you know that those who serve in the temple get their food from the temple, and that those who serve at the altar share in what is offered on the altar? [14]In the same way, the Lord has commanded that those who preach the gospel should receive their living from the gospel.

[15]But I have not used any of these rights. And I am not writing this in the hope that you will do such things for me, for I would rather die than allow anyone to deprive me of this boast. [16]For when I preach the gospel, I cannot boast, since I am compelled to preach. Woe to me if I do not preach the gospel! [17]If I preach voluntarily, I have a reward; if not voluntarily, I am simply discharging the trust committed to me. [18]What then is my reward? Just this: that in preaching the gospel I may offer it free of charge, and so not make full use of my rights as a preacher of the gospel.

[19]Though I am free and belong to no one, I have made myself a slave to everyone, to win as many as possible. [20]To the Jews I became like a Jew, to win the Jews. To those under the law I became like one under the law (though I myself am not under the law), so as to win those under the law. [21]To those not having the law I became like one not having the law (though I am not free from God's law but am under Christ's law), so as to win those not having the law. [22]To the weak I became weak, to win the weak. I have become all things to all people so that by all possible means I might save

---

[a] 5 That is, Peter   [b] 9 Deut. 25:4

some. ²³I do all this for the sake of the gospel, that I may share in its blessings.

²⁴Do you not know that in a race all the runners run, but only one gets the prize. Run in such a way as to get the prize. ²⁵Everyone who competes in the games goes into strict training. They do it to get a crown that will not last, but we do it to get a crown that will last forever. ²⁶Therefore I do not run like someone running aimlessly; I do not fight like a boxer beating the air. ²⁷No, I strike a blow to my body and make it my slave so that after I have preached to others, I myself will not be disqualified for the prize.

10 For I do not want you to be ignorant of the fact, brothers and sisters, that our ancestors were all under the cloud and that they all passed through the sea. ²They were all baptized into Moses in the cloud and in the sea. ³They all ate the same spiritual food ⁴and drank the same spiritual drink; for they drank from the spiritual rock that accompanied them, and that rock was Christ. ⁵Nevertheless, God was not pleased with most of them; their bodies were scattered in the wilderness.

⁶Now these things occurred as examples to keep us from setting our hearts on evil things as they did. ⁷Do not be idolaters, as some of them were; as it is written: "The people sat down to eat and drink and got up to indulge in revelry."ᵃ ⁸We should not commit sexual immorality, as some of them did — and in one day twenty-three thousand of them died. ⁹We should not test Christ,ᵇ as some of them did — and were killed by snakes.

¹⁰And do not grumble, as some of them did — and were killed by the destroying angel.

¹¹These things happened to them as examples and were written down as warnings for us, on whom the culmination of the ages has come. ¹²So, if you think you are standing firm, be careful that you don't fall! ¹³No temptationᶜ has overtaken you except what is common to mankind. And God is faithful; he will not let you be temptedᶜ beyond what you can bear. But when you are tempted,ᶜ he will also provide a way out so that you can endure it.

¹⁴Therefore, my dear friends, flee from idolatry. ¹⁵I speak to sensible people; judge for yourselves what I say. ¹⁶Is not the cup of thanksgiving for which we give thanks a participation in the blood of Christ? And is not the bread that we break a participation in the body of Christ? ¹⁷Because there is one loaf, we, who are many, are one body, for we all share the one loaf.

¹⁸Consider the people of Israel: Do not those who eat the sacrifices participate in the altar? ¹⁹Do I mean then that food sacrificed to an idol is anything, or that an idol is anything? ²⁰No, but the sacrifices of pagans are offered to demons, not to God, and I do not want you to be participants with demons. ²¹You cannot drink the cup of the Lord and the cup of demons too; you cannot have a part in both the Lord's table and the table of demons. ²²Are we trying to arouse the Lord's jealousy? Are we stronger than he?

²³"I have the right to do anything," you say — but not everything is beneficial. "I have the right

---

ᵃ 7 Exodus 32:6   ᵇ 9 Some manuscripts *test the Lord*   ᶜ 13 The Greek for *temptation* and *tempted* can also mean *testing* and *tested*.

to do anything"—but not everything is constructive. [24]No one should seek their own good, but the good of others.

[25]Eat anything sold in the meat market without raising questions of conscience, [26]for, "The earth is the Lord's, and everything in it."[a]

[27]If an unbeliever invites you to a meal and you want to go, eat whatever is put before you without raising questions of conscience. [28]But if someone says to you, "This has been offered in sacrifice," then do not eat it, both for the sake of the one who told you and for the sake of conscience. [29]I am referring to the other person's conscience, not yours. For why is my freedom being judged by another's conscience? [30]If I take part in the meal with thankfulness, why am I denounced because of something I thank God for?

[31]So whether you eat or drink or whatever you do, do it all for the glory of God. [32]Do not cause anyone to stumble, whether Jews, Greeks or the church of God— [33]even as I try to please everyone in every way. For I am not seeking my own good but the good of many, so that they may

11 be saved. [1]Follow my example, as I follow the example of Christ.

[2]I praise you for remembering me in everything and for holding to the traditions just as I passed them on to you. [3]But I want you to realize that the head of every man is Christ, and the head of the woman is man,[b] and the head of Christ is God. [4]Every man who prays or prophesies with his head covered dishonors his head. [5]But every woman who prays or prophesies with her head uncovered dishonors her head—it is the same as having her head shaved. [6]For if a woman does not cover her head, she might as well have her hair cut off; but if it is a disgrace for a woman to have her hair cut off or her head shaved, then she should cover her head.

[7]A man ought not to cover his head,[c] since he is the image and glory of God; but woman is the glory of man. [8]For man did not come from woman, but woman from man; [9]neither was man created for woman, but woman for man. [10]It is for this reason that a woman ought to have authority over her own[d] head, because of the angels. [11]Nevertheless, in the Lord woman is not independent of man, nor is man independent of woman. [12]For as woman came from man, so also man is born of woman. But everything comes from God.

[13]Judge for yourselves: Is it proper for a woman to pray to God with her head uncovered? [14]Does not the very nature of things teach you that if a man has long hair, it is a disgrace to him, [15]but that if a woman has long hair, it is her glory? For long hair is given to her as a covering. [16]If anyone wants to be contentious about this, we have no other practice—nor do the churches of God.

[17]In the following directives I have no praise for you, for your

meetings do more harm than good. 18In the first place, I hear that when you come together as a church, there are divisions among you, and to some extent I believe it. 19No doubt there have to be differences among you to show which of you have God's approval. 20So then, when you come together, it is not the Lord's Supper you eat, 21for when you are eating, some of you go ahead with your own private suppers. As a result, one person remains hungry and another gets drunk. 22Don't you have homes to eat and drink in? Or do you despise the church of God by humiliating those who have nothing? What shall I say to you? Shall I praise you? Certainly not in this matter!

23For I received from the Lord what I also passed on to you: The Lord Jesus, on the night he was betrayed, took bread, 24and when he had given thanks, he broke it and said, "This is my body, which is for you; do this in remembrance of me." 25In the same way, after supper he took the cup, saying, "This cup is the new covenant in my blood; do this, whenever you drink it, in remembrance of me." 26For whenever you eat this bread and drink this cup, you proclaim the Lord's death until he comes.

27So then, whoever eats the bread or drinks the cup of the Lord in an unworthy manner will be guilty of sinning against the body and blood of the Lord. 28Everyone ought to examine themselves before they eat of the bread and drink from the cup. 29For those who eat and drink without discerning the body of Christ eat and drink judgment on themselves. 30That is why many among you are weak and sick, and a number of you have fallen asleep.

31But if we were more discerning with regard to ourselves, we would not come under such judgment. 32Nevertheless, when we are judged in this way by the Lord, we are being disciplined so that we will not be finally condemned with the world.

33So then, my brothers and sisters, when you gather to eat, you should all eat together. 34Anyone who is hungry should eat something at home, so that when you meet together it may not result in judgment.

And when I come I will give further directions.

12 Now about the gifts of the Spirit, brothers and sisters, I do not want you to be uninformed. 2You know that when you were pagans, somehow or other you were influenced and led astray to mute idols. 3Therefore I want you to know that no one who is speaking by the Spirit of God says, "Jesus be cursed," and no one can say, "Jesus is Lord," except by the Holy Spirit.

4There are different kinds of gifts, but the same Spirit distributes them. 5There are different kinds of service, but the same Lord. 6There are different kinds of working, but in all of them and in everyone it is the same God at work.

7Now to each one the manifestation of the Spirit is given for the common good. 8To one there is given through the Spirit a message of wisdom, to another a message of knowledge by means of the same Spirit, 9to another faith by the same Spirit, to another gifts of healing by that one Spirit, 10to another miraculous powers, to another prophecy, to another distinguishing between spirits, to another speaking in different kinds of tongues,[a] and to still another the interpretation of tongues.[a] [11]All these are the work of one and the same Spirit, and he distributes them to each one, just as he determines.

[12]Just as a body, though one, has many parts, but all its many parts form one body, so it is with Christ. [13]For we were all baptized by[b] one Spirit so as to form one body— whether Jews or Gentiles, slave or free—and we were all given the one Spirit to drink. [14]Even so the body is not made up of one part but of many.

[15]Now if the foot should say, "Because I am not a hand, I do not belong to the body," it would not for that reason stop being part of the body. [16]And if the ear should say, "Because I am not an eye, I do not belong to the body," it would not for that reason stop being part of the body. [17]If the whole body were an eye, where would the sense of hearing be? If the whole body were an ear, where would the sense of smell be? [18]But in fact God has placed the parts in the body, every one of them, just as he wanted them to be. [19]If they were all one part, where would the body be? [20]As it is, there are many parts, but one body.

[21]The eye cannot say to the hand, "I don't need you!" And the head cannot say to the feet, "I don't need you!" [22]On the contrary, those parts of the body that seem to be weaker are indispensable, [23]and the parts that we think are less honorable we treat with special honor. And the parts that are unpresentable are treated with special modesty, [24]while our presentable parts need no special treatment. But

God has put the body together, giving greater honor to the parts that lacked it, [25]so that there should be no division in the body, but that its parts should have equal concern for each other. [26]If one part suffers, every part suffers with it; if one part is honored, every part rejoices with it.

[27]Now you are the body of Christ, and each one of you is a part of it. [28]And God has placed in the church first of all apostles, second prophets, third teachers, then miracles, then gifts of healing, of helping, of guidance, and of different kinds of tongues. [29]Are all apostles? Are all prophets? Are all teachers? Do all work miracles? [30]Do all have gifts of healing? Do all speak in tongues[c]? Do all interpret? [31]Now eagerly desire the greater gifts.

And yet I will show you the most excellent way.

13 If I speak in the tongues[d] of men or of angels, but do not have love, I am only a resounding gong or a clanging cymbal. [2]If I have the gift of prophecy and can fathom all mysteries and all knowledge, and if I have a faith that can move mountains, but do not have love, I am nothing. [3]If I give all I possess to the poor and give over my body to hardship that I may boast,[e] but do not have love, I gain nothing.

[4]Love is patient, love is kind. It does not envy, it does not boast, it is not proud. [5]It does not dishonor others, it is not self-seeking, it is not easily angered, it keeps no record of wrongs. [6]Love does not delight in evil but rejoices with the truth. [7]It always protects, always trusts, always hopes, always perseveres.

---

[a] 10 Or *languages;* also in verse 28   [b] 13 Or *with;* or in   [c] 30 Or *other languages*
[d] 1 Or *languages*   [e] 3 Some manuscripts *body to the flames*

[8]Love never fails. But where there are prophecies, they will cease; where there are tongues, they will be stilled; where there is knowledge, it will pass away. [9]For we know in part and we prophesy in part, [10]but when completeness comes, what is in part disappears. [11]When I was a child, I talked like a child, I thought like a child, I reasoned like a child. When I became a man, I put the ways of childhood behind me. [12]For now we see only a reflection as in a mirror; then we shall see face to face. Now I know in part; then I shall know fully, even as I am fully known.

[13]And now these three remain: faith, hope and love. But the greatest of these is love.

14 Follow the way of love and eagerly desire gifts of the Spirit, especially prophecy. [2]For anyone who speaks in a tongue[a] does not speak to people but to God. Indeed, no one understands them; they utter mysteries by the Spirit. [3]But the one who prophesies speaks to people for their strengthening, encouraging and comfort. [4]Anyone who speaks in a tongue edifies themselves, but the one who prophesies edifies the church. [5]I would like every one of you to speak in tongues,[b] but I would rather have you prophesy. The one who prophesies is greater than the one who speaks in tongues,[b] unless someone interprets, so that the church may be edified.

[6]Now, brothers and sisters, if I come to you and speak in tongues, what good will I be to you, unless I bring you some revelation or knowledge or prophecy or word of instruction? [7]Even in the case of lifeless things that make sounds, such as the pipe or harp, how will anyone know what tune is being played unless there is a distinction in the notes? [8]Again, if the trumpet does not sound a clear call, who will get ready for battle? [9]So it is with you. Unless you speak intelligible words with your tongue, how will anyone know what you are saying? You will just be speaking into the air. [10]Undoubtedly there are all sorts of languages in the world, yet none of them is without meaning. [11]If then I do not grasp the meaning of what someone is saying, I am a foreigner to the speaker, and the speaker is a foreigner to me. [12]So it is with you. Since you are eager for gifts of the Spirit, try to excel in those that build up the church.

[13]For this reason the one who speaks in a tongue should pray that they may interpret what they say. [14]For if I pray in a tongue, my spirit prays, but my mind is unfruitful. [15]So what shall I do? I will pray with my spirit, but I will also pray with my understanding; I will sing with my spirit, but I will also sing with my understanding. [16]Otherwise when you are praising God in the Spirit, how can someone else, who is now put in the position of an inquirer,[c] say "Amen" to your thanksgiving, since they do not know what you are saying? [17]You are giving thanks well enough, but no one else is edified.

[18]I thank God that I speak in tongues more than all of you. [19]But in the church I would rather speak five intelligible words to instruct others than ten thousand words in a tongue.

---

[a] 2 Or *in another language*; also in verses 4, 13, 14, 19, 26 and 27   [b] 5 Or *in other languages*; also in verses 6, 18, 22, 23 and 39   [c] 16 The Greek word for *inquirer* is a technical term for someone not fully initiated into a religion; also in verses 23 and 24.

²⁰Brothers and sisters, stop thinking like children. In regard to evil be infants, but in your thinking be adults. ²¹In the Law it is written:

"With other tongues
    and through the lips of
        foreigners
I will speak to this people,
    but even then they will not
        listen to me,
            says the Lord."ᵃ

²²Tongues, then, are a sign, not for believers but for unbelievers; prophecy, however, is not for unbelievers but for believers. ²³So if the whole church comes together and everyone speaks in tongues, and inquirers or unbelievers come in, will they not say that you are out of your mind? ²⁴But if an unbeliever or an inquirer comes in while everyone is prophesying, they are convicted of sin and are brought under judgment by all, ²⁵as the secrets of their hearts are laid bare. So they will fall down and worship God, exclaiming, "God is really among you!"

²⁶What then shall we say, brothers and sisters? When you come together, each of you has a hymn, or a word of instruction, a revelation, a tongue or an interpretation. Everything must be done so that the church may be built up. ²⁷If anyone speaks in a tongue, two—or at the most three—should speak, one at a time, and someone must interpret. ²⁸If there is no interpreter, the speaker should keep quiet in the church and speak to himself and to God.

²⁹Two or three prophets should speak, and the others should weigh carefully what is said. ³⁰And if a revelation comes to someone who is sitting down, the first speaker should stop. ³¹For you can all prophesy in turn so that everyone may be instructed and encouraged. ³²The spirits of prophets are subject to the control of prophets. ³³For God is not a God of disorder but of peace—as in all the congregations of the Lord's people.

³⁴Womenᵇ should remain silent in the churches. They are not allowed to speak, but must be in submission, as the law says. ³⁵If they want to inquire about something, they should ask their own husbands at home; for it is disgraceful for a woman to speak in the church.ᶜ

³⁶Or did the word of God originate with you? Or are you the only people it has reached? ³⁷If anyone thinks they are a prophet or otherwise gifted by the Spirit, let them acknowledge that what I am writing to you is the Lord's command. ³⁸But if anyone ignores this, they will themselves be ignored.ᵈ

³⁹Therefore, my brothers and sisters, be eager to prophesy, and do not forbid speaking in tongues. ⁴⁰But everything should be done in a fitting and orderly way.

15 Now, brothers and sisters, I want to remind you of the gospel I preached to you, which you received and on which you have taken your stand. ²By this gospel you are saved, if you hold firmly to the word I preached to you. Otherwise, you have believed in vain.

³For what I received I passed on to you as of first importanceᵉ: that Christ died for our sins according to the Scriptures, ⁴that he was bur-

ᵃ 21 Isaiah 28:11,12   ᵇ 33,34 Or peace. As in all the congregations of the Lord's people, ³⁴women   ᶜ 34,35 In a few manuscripts these verses come after verse 40.   ᵈ 38 Some manuscripts But anyone who is ignorant of this will be ignorant   ᵉ 3 Or you at the first

ied, that he was raised on the third day according to the Scriptures, [5]and that he appeared to Cephas,[a] and then to the Twelve. [6]After that, he appeared to more than five hundred of the brothers and sisters at the same time, most of whom are still living, though some have fallen asleep. [7]Then he appeared to James, then to all the apostles, [8]and last of all he appeared to me also, as to one abnormally born.

[9]For I am the least of the apostles and do not even deserve to be called an apostle, because I persecuted the church of God. [10]But by the grace of God I am what I am, and his grace to me was not without effect. No, I worked harder than all of them — yet not I, but the grace of God that was with me. [11]Whether, then, it is I or they, this is what we preach, and this is what you believed.

[12]But if it is preached that Christ has been raised from the dead, how can some of you say that there is no resurrection of the dead? [13]If there is no resurrection of the dead, then not even Christ has been raised. [14]And if Christ has not been raised, our preaching is useless and so is your faith. [15]More than that, we are then found to be false witnesses about God, for we have testified about God that he raised Christ from the dead. But he did not raise him if in fact the dead are not raised. [16]For if the dead are not raised, then Christ has not been raised either. [17]And if Christ has not been raised, your faith is futile; you are still in your sins. [18]Then those also who have fallen asleep in Christ are lost. [19]If only for this life we have hope in Christ, we are of all people most to be pitied.

[20]But Christ has indeed been raised from the dead, the firstfruits of those who have fallen asleep. [21]For since death came through a man, the resurrection of the dead comes also through a man. [22]For as in Adam all die, so in Christ all will be made alive. [23]But each in turn: Christ, the firstfruits; then, when he comes, those who belong to him. [24]Then the end will come, when he hands over the kingdom to God the Father after he has destroyed all dominion, authority and power. [25]For he must reign until he has put all his enemies under his feet. [26]The last enemy to be destroyed is death. [27]For he "has put everything under his feet."[b] Now when it says that "everything" has been put under him, it is clear that this does not include God himself, who put everything under Christ. [28]When he has done this, then the Son himself will be made subject to him who put everything under him, so that God may be all in all.

[29]Now if there is no resurrection, what will those do who are baptized for the dead? If the dead are not raised at all, why are people baptized for them? [30]And as for us, why do we endanger ourselves every hour? [31]I face death every day — yes, just as surely as I boast about you in Christ Jesus our Lord. [32]If I fought wild beasts in Ephesus with no more than human hopes, what have I gained? If the dead are not raised,

"Let us eat and drink,
    for tomorrow we die."[c]

[33]Do not be misled: "Bad company corrupts good character."[d] [34]Come back to your senses as you ought, and stop sinning; for there are

---

[a] 5 That is, Peter   [b] 27 Psalm 8:6   [c] 32 Isaiah 22:13   [d] 33 From the Greek poet Menander

some who are ignorant of God—I say this to your shame.

35 But someone will ask, "How are the dead raised? With what kind of body will they come?" 36 How foolish! What you sow does not come to life unless it dies. 37 When you sow, you do not plant the body that will be, but just a seed, perhaps of wheat or of something else. 38 But God gives it a body as he has determined, and to each kind of seed he gives its own body. 39 Not all flesh is the same: People have one kind of flesh, animals have another, birds another and fish another. 40 There are also heavenly bodies and there are earthly bodies; but the splendor of the heavenly bodies is one kind, and the splendor of the earthly bodies is another. 41 The sun has one kind of splendor, the moon another and the stars another; and star differs from star in splendor.

42 So will it be with the resurrection of the dead. The body that is sown is perishable, it is raised imperishable; 43 it is sown in dishonor, it is raised in glory; it is sown in weakness, it is raised in power; 44 it is sown a natural body, it is raised a spiritual body.

If there is a natural body, there is also a spiritual body. 45 So it is written: "The first man Adam became a living being"[a]; the last Adam, a life-giving spirit. 46 The spiritual did not come first, but the natural, and after that the spiritual. 47 The first man was of the dust of the earth; the second man is of heaven. 48 As was the earthly man, so are those who are of the earth; and as is the heavenly man, so also are those who are of heaven. 49 And just as we have borne the image of the earthly man, so shall we[b] bear the image of the heavenly man.

50 I declare to you, brothers and sisters, that flesh and blood cannot inherit the kingdom of God, nor does the perishable inherit the imperishable. 51 Listen, I tell you a mystery: We will not all sleep, but we will all be changed— 52 in a flash, in the twinkling of an eye, at the last trumpet. For the trumpet will sound, the dead will be raised imperishable, and we will be changed. 53 For the perishable must clothe itself with the imperishable, and the mortal with immortality. 54 When the perishable has been clothed with the imperishable, and the mortal with immortality, then the saying that is written will come true: "Death has been swallowed up in victory."[c]

55 "Where, O death, is your victory?
    Where, O death, is your
        sting?"[d]

56 The sting of death is sin, and the power of sin is the law. 57 But thanks be to God! He gives us the victory through our Lord Jesus Christ.

58 Therefore, my dear brothers and sisters, stand firm. Let nothing move you. Always give yourselves fully to the work of the Lord, because you know that your labor in the Lord is not in vain.

16 Now about the collection for the Lord's people: Do what I told the Galatian churches to do. 2 On the first day of every week, each one of you should set aside a sum of money in keeping with your income, saving it up, so that when I come no collections will have to be made. 3 Then, when I arrive, I will give letters of introduction to the

---

[a] 45 Gen. 2:7   [b] 49 Some early manuscripts *so let us*   [c] 54 Isaiah 25:8   [d] 55 Hosea 13:14

men you approve and send them with your gift to Jerusalem. [4]If it seems advisable for me to go also, they will accompany me.

[5]After I go through Macedonia, I will come to you—for I will be going through Macedonia. [6]Perhaps I will stay with you for a while, or even spend the winter, so that you can help me on my journey, wherever I go. [7]For I do not want to see you now and make only a passing visit; I hope to spend some time with you, if the Lord permits. [8]But I will stay on at Ephesus until Pentecost, [9]because a great door for effective work has opened to me, and there are many who oppose me.

[10]When Timothy comes, see to it that he has nothing to fear while he is with you, for he is carrying on the work of the Lord, just as I am. [11]No one, then, should treat him with contempt. Send him on his way in peace so that he may return to me. I am expecting him along with the brothers.

[12]Now about our brother Apollos: I strongly urged him to go to you with the brothers. He was quite unwilling to go now, but he will go when he has the opportunity.

[13]Be on your guard; stand firm in the faith; be courageous; be strong. [14]Do everything in love.

[15]You know that the household of Stephanas were the first converts in Achaia, and they have devoted themselves to the service of the Lord's people. I urge you, brothers and sisters, [16]to submit to such people and to everyone who joins in the work and labors at it. [17]I was glad when Stephanas, Fortunatus and Achaicus arrived, because they have supplied what was lacking from you. [18]For they refreshed my spirit and yours also. Such men deserve recognition.

[19]The churches in the province of Asia send you greetings. Aquila and Priscilla[a] greet you warmly in the Lord, and so does the church that meets at their house. [20]All the brothers and sisters here send you greetings. Greet one another with a holy kiss.

[21]I, Paul, write this greeting in my own hand.

[22]If anyone does not love the Lord, let that person be cursed! Come, Lord[b]!

[23]The grace of the Lord Jesus be with you.

[24]My love to all of you in Christ Jesus. Amen.[c]

---

[a] 19 Greek *Prisca*, a variant of *Priscilla*   [b] 22 The Greek for *Come, Lord* reproduces an Aramaic expression (*Marana tha*) used by early Christians.   [c] 24 Some manuscripts do not have *Amen*.

2 CORINTHIANS

Paul's first letter to the believers in Corinth gives us a glimpse into his deeply personal and tumultuous relationship with this gathering of Jesus-followers. The letter we know as 2 Corinthians further reveals the triumphs and struggles that result when life in the present age meets up with the in-breaking reality of God's kingdom. Here we see Paul working to repair relationships, explain various changes in travel plans, make practical arrangements for collecting a gift for the struggling believers in Jerusalem, and directly confront challenges to his own leadership by the self-proclaimed "super-apostles."

In the four main parts of the letter, each introduced by a reference to a place, Paul envisions himself in different locations, recalling or anticipating his relationship with the Corinthians. The single theme running through these sections is that God will comfort us in all our troubles, and we will offer this comfort to each other. This models the life of Jesus himself, who suffered first and then was comforted. Like the crucified Messiah, we are weak, yet we live in God's power.

In the final section, however, Paul feels he has no choice but to make the Corinthians uncomfortable, to help them face their present condition. But he ends the letter hopefully, calling on them to rejoice in God's grace, love and fellowship.

---

1 Paul, an apostle of Christ Jesus by the will of God, and Timothy our brother,

To the church of God in Corinth, together with all his holy people throughout Achaia:

2 Grace and peace to you from God our Father and the Lord Jesus Christ.

3 Praise be to the God and Father of our Lord Jesus Christ, the Father of compassion and the God of all comfort, 4 who comforts us in all our troubles, so that we can comfort those in any trouble with the comfort we ourselves receive from God. 5 For just as we share abundantly in the sufferings of Christ, so also our comfort abounds through Christ. 6 If we are distressed, it is for your comfort and salvation; if we are comforted, it is for your comfort, which produces in you patient endurance of the same sufferings we suffer. 7 And our hope for you is firm, because we know that just as you share in our sufferings, so also you share in our comfort.

8 We do not want you to be uninformed, brothers and sisters,[a] about the troubles we experienced in the province of Asia. We were under great pressure, far beyond our ability to endure, so that we despaired of life itself. 9 Indeed, we felt we had received the sentence of death. But this happened that we might not rely on ourselves but on God, who raises the dead. 10 He has delivered us from such a deadly peril, and he will deliver us again. On him we

a 8 The Greek word for *brothers and sisters* (*adelphoi*) refers here to believers, both men and women, as part of God's family; also in 8:1; 13:11.

have set our hope that he will continue to deliver us, [11] as you help us by your prayers. Then many will give thanks on our behalf for the gracious favor granted us in answer to the prayers of many.

[12] Now this is our boast: Our conscience testifies that we have conducted ourselves in the world, and especially in our relations with you, with integrity[a] and godly sincerity. We have done so, relying not on worldly wisdom but on God's grace. [13] For we do not write you anything you cannot read or understand. And I hope that, [14] as you have understood us in part, you will come to understand fully that you can boast of us just as we will boast of you in the day of the Lord Jesus.

[15] Because I was confident of this, I wanted to visit you first so that you might benefit twice. [16] I wanted to visit you on my way to Macedonia and to come back to you from Macedonia, and then to have you send me on my way to Judea. [17] Was I fickle when I intended to do this? Or do I make my plans in a worldly manner so that in the same breath I say both "Yes, yes" and "No, no"?

[18] But as surely as God is faithful, our message to you is not "Yes" and "No." [19] For the Son of God, Jesus Christ, who was preached among you by us—by me and Silas[b] and Timothy—was not "Yes" and "No," but in him it has always been "Yes." [20] For no matter how many promises God has made, they are "Yes" in Christ. And so through him the "Amen" is spoken by us to the glory of God. [21] Now it is God who makes both us and you stand firm in Christ. He anointed us, [22] set his seal of ownership on us, and put his Spirit in our hearts as a deposit, guaranteeing what is to come.

[23] I call God as my witness—and I stake my life on it—that it was in order to spare you that I did not return to Corinth. [24] Not that we lord it over your faith, but we work with you for your joy, because it is by faith you stand firm. 2 [1] So I made up my mind that I would not make another painful visit to you. [2] For if I grieve you, who is left to make me glad but you whom I have grieved? [3] I wrote as I did, so that when I came I would not be distressed by those who should have made me rejoice. I had confidence in all of you, that you would all share my joy. [4] For I wrote you out of great distress and anguish of heart and with many tears, not to grieve you but to let you know the depth of my love for you.

[5] If anyone has caused grief, he has not so much grieved me as he has grieved all of you to some extent—not to put it too severely. [6] The punishment inflicted on him by the majority is sufficient. [7] Now instead, you ought to forgive and comfort him, so that he will not be overwhelmed by excessive sorrow. [8] I urge you, therefore, to reaffirm your love for him. [9] Another reason I wrote you was to see if you would stand the test and be obedient in everything. [10] Anyone you forgive, I also forgive. And what I have forgiven—if there was anything to forgive—I have forgiven in the sight of Christ for your sake, [11] in order that Satan might not outwit us. For we are not unaware of his schemes.

[12] Now when I went to Troas to preach the gospel of Christ and found that the Lord had opened a

a 12 Many manuscripts holiness   b 19 Greek Silvanus, a variant of Silas

door for me, [13]I still had no peace of mind, because I did not find my brother Titus there. So I said goodbye to them and went on to Macedonia.

[14]But thanks be to God, who always leads us as captives in Christ's triumphal procession and uses us to spread the aroma of the knowledge of him everywhere. [15]For we are to God the pleasing aroma of Christ among those who are being saved and those who are perishing. [16]To the one we are an aroma that brings death; to the other, an aroma that brings life. And who is equal to such a task? [17]Unlike so many, we do not peddle the word of God for profit. On the contrary, in Christ we speak before God with sincerity, as those sent from God.

3 Are we beginning to commend ourselves again? Or do we need, like some people, letters of recommendation to you or from you? [2]You yourselves are our letter, written on our hearts, known and read by everyone. [3]You show that you are a letter from Christ, the result of our ministry, written not with ink but with the Spirit of the living God, not on tablets of stone but on tablets of human hearts.

[4]Such confidence we have through Christ before God. [5]Not that we are competent in ourselves to claim anything for ourselves, but our competence comes from God. [6]He has made us competent as ministers of a new covenant—not of the letter but of the Spirit; for the letter kills, but the Spirit gives life.

[7]Now if the ministry that brought death, which was engraved in letters on stone, came with glory, so that the Israelites could not look steadily at the face of Moses because of its glory, transitory though it was, [8]will not the ministry of the Spirit be even more glorious? [9]If the ministry that brought condemnation was glorious, how much more glorious is the ministry that brings righteousness! [10]For what was glorious has no glory now in comparison with the surpassing glory. [11]And if what was transitory came with glory, how much greater is the glory of that which lasts!

[12]Therefore, since we have such a hope, we are very bold. [13]We are not like Moses, who would put a veil over his face to prevent the Israelites from seeing the end of what was passing away. [14]But their minds were made dull, for to this day the same veil remains when the old covenant is read. It has not been removed, because only in Christ is it taken away. [15]Even to this day when Moses is read, a veil covers their hearts. [16]But whenever anyone turns to the Lord, the veil is taken away. [17]Now the Lord is the Spirit, and where the Spirit of the Lord is, there is freedom. [18]And we all, who with unveiled faces contemplate[a] the Lord's glory, are being transformed into his image with ever-increasing glory, which comes from the Lord, who is the Spirit.

4 Therefore, since through God's mercy we have this ministry, we do not lose heart. [2]Rather, we have renounced secret and shameful ways; we do not use deception, nor do we distort the word of God. On the contrary, by setting forth the truth plainly we commend ourselves to everyone's conscience in the sight of God. [3]And even if our gospel is veiled, it is veiled to those who are perishing. [4]The god of this age has blinded the minds of unbe-

a 18 Or reflect

lievers, so that they cannot see the light of the gospel that displays the glory of Christ, who is the image of God. ⁵For what we preach is not ourselves, but Jesus Christ as Lord, and ourselves as your servants for Jesus' sake. ⁶For God, who said, "Let light shine out of darkness,"[a] made his light shine in our hearts to give us the light of the knowledge of God's glory displayed in the face of Christ.

⁷But we have this treasure in jars of clay to show that this all-surpassing power is from God and not from us. ⁸We are hard pressed on every side, but not crushed; perplexed, but not in despair; ⁹persecuted, but not abandoned; struck down, but not destroyed. ¹⁰We always carry around in our body the death of Jesus, so that the life of Jesus may also be revealed in our body. ¹¹For we who are alive are always being given over to death for Jesus' sake, so that his life may also be revealed in our mortal body. ¹²So then, death is at work in us, but life is at work in you.

¹³It is written: "I believed; therefore I have spoken."[b] Since we have that same spirit of[c] faith, we also believe and therefore speak, ¹⁴because we know that the one who raised the Lord Jesus from the dead will also raise us with Jesus and present us with you to himself. ¹⁵All this is for your benefit, so that the grace that is reaching more and more people may cause thanksgiving to overflow to the glory of God.

¹⁶Therefore we do not lose heart. Though outwardly we are wasting away, yet inwardly we are being renewed day by day. ¹⁷For our light and momentary troubles are achieving for us an eternal glory that far outweighs them all. ¹⁸So we fix our eyes not on what is seen, but on what is unseen, since what is seen is temporary, but what is unseen is eternal.

5 For we know that if the earthly tent we live in is destroyed, we have a building from God, an eternal house in heaven, not built by human hands. ²Meanwhile we groan, longing to be clothed instead with our heavenly dwelling, ³because when we are clothed, we will not be found naked. ⁴For while we are in this tent, we groan and are burdened, because we do not wish to be unclothed but to be clothed instead with our heavenly dwelling, so that what is mortal may be swallowed up by life. ⁵Now the one who has fashioned us for this very purpose is God, who has given us the Spirit as a deposit, guaranteeing what is to come.

⁶Therefore we are always confident and know that as long as we are at home in the body we are away from the Lord. ⁷For we live by faith, not by sight. ⁸We are confident, I say, and would prefer to be away from the body and at home with the Lord. ⁹So we make it our goal to please him, whether we are at home in the body or away from it. ¹⁰For we must all appear before the judgment seat of Christ, so that each of us may receive what is due us for the things done while in the body, whether good or bad.

¹¹Since, then, we know what it is to fear the Lord, we try to persuade others. What we are is plain to God, and I hope it is also plain to your conscience. ¹²We are not trying to commend ourselves to you again, but are giving you an opportunity to take pride in us, so that you can

---

[a] 6 Gen. 1:3　　[b] 13 Psalm 116:10 (see Septuagint)　　[c] 13 Or Spirit-given

answer those who take pride in what is seen rather than in what is in the heart. [13]If we are "out of our mind," as some say, it is for God; if we are in our right mind, it is for you. [14]For Christ's love compels us, because we are convinced that one died for all, and therefore all died. [15]And he died for all, that those who live should no longer live for themselves but for him who died for them and was raised again.

[16]So from now on we regard no one from a worldly point of view. Though we once regarded Christ in this way, we do so no longer. [17]Therefore, if anyone is in Christ, the new creation has come:[a] The old has gone, the new is here! [18]All this is from God, who reconciled us to himself through Christ and gave us the ministry of reconciliation: [19]that God was reconciling the world to himself in Christ, not counting people's sins against them. And he has committed to us the message of reconciliation. [20]We are therefore Christ's ambassadors, as though God were making his appeal through us. We implore you on Christ's behalf: Be reconciled to God. [21]God made him who had no sin to be sin[b] for us, so that in him we might become the righteousness of God.

6 As God's co-workers we urge you not to receive God's grace in vain. [2]For he says,

"In the time of my favor I heard you,
    and in the day of salvation I helped you."[c]

I tell you, now is the time of God's favor, now is the day of salvation.

[3]We put no stumbling block in anyone's path, so that our ministry will not be discredited. [4]Rather, as servants of God we commend ourselves in every way: in great endurance; in troubles, hardships and distresses; [5]in beatings, imprisonments and riots; in hard work, sleepless nights and hunger; [6]in purity, understanding, patience and kindness; in the Holy Spirit and in sincere love; [7]in truthful speech and in the power of God; with weapons of righteousness in the right hand and in the left; [8]through glory and dishonor, bad report and good report; genuine, yet regarded as impostors; [9]known, yet regarded as unknown; dying, and yet we live on; beaten, and yet not killed; [10]sorrowful, yet always rejoicing; poor, yet making many rich; having nothing, and yet possessing everything.

[11]We have spoken freely to you, Corinthians, and opened wide our hearts to you. [12]We are not withholding our affection from you, but you are withholding yours from us. [13]As a fair exchange — I speak as to my children — open wide your hearts also.

[14]Do not be yoked together with unbelievers. For what do righteousness and wickedness have in common? Or what fellowship can light have with darkness? [15]What harmony is there between Christ and Belial[d]? Or what does a believer have in common with an unbeliever? [16]What agreement is there between the temple of God and idols? For we are the temple of the living God. As God has said:

"I will live with them
    and walk among them,

---

[a] 17 Or Christ, that person is a new creation. [b] 21 Or be a sin offering [c] 2 Isaiah 49:8
[d] 15 Greek Beliar, a variant of Belial

and I will be their God,
and they will be my people."[a]

[17]Therefore,

"Come out from them
and be separate,
says the Lord.
Touch no unclean thing,
and I will receive you."[b]

[18]And,

"I will be a Father to you,
and you will be my sons and
daughters,
says the Lord Almighty."[c]

7 Therefore, since we have these promises, dear friends, let us purify ourselves from everything that contaminates body and spirit, perfecting holiness out of reverence for God.

[2]Make room for us in your hearts. We have wronged no one, we have corrupted no one, we have exploited no one. [3]I do not say this to condemn you; I have said before that you have such a place in our hearts that we would live or die with you. [4]I have spoken to you with great frankness; I take great pride in you. I am greatly encouraged; in all our troubles my joy knows no bounds.

[5]For when we came into Macedonia, we had no rest, but we were harassed at every turn—conflicts on the outside, fears within. [6]But God, who comforts the downcast, comforted us by the coming of Titus, [7]and not only by his coming but also by the comfort you had given him. He told us about your longing for me, your deep sorrow, your ardent concern for me, so that my joy was greater than ever.

[8]Even if I caused you sorrow by my letter, I do not regret it. Though I did regret it—I see that my letter hurt you, but only for a little while— [9]yet now I am happy, not because you were made sorry, but because your sorrow led you to repentance. For you became sorrowful as God intended and so were not harmed in any way by us. [10]Godly sorrow brings repentance that leads to salvation and leaves no regret, but worldly sorrow brings death. [11]See what this godly sorrow has produced in you: what earnestness, what eagerness to clear yourselves, what indignation, what alarm, what longing, what concern, what readiness to see justice done. At every point you have proved yourselves to be innocent in this matter. [12]So even though I wrote to you, it was neither on account of the one who did the wrong nor on account of the injured party, but rather that before God you could see for yourselves how devoted to us you are. [13]By all this we are encouraged.

In addition to our own encouragement, we were especially delighted to see how happy Titus was, because his spirit has been refreshed by all of you. [14]I had boasted to him about you, and you have not embarrassed me. But just as everything we said to you was true, so our boasting about you to Titus has proved to be true as well. [15]And his affection for you is all the greater when he remembers that you were all obedient, receiving him with fear and trembling. [16]I am glad I can have complete confidence in you.

---

[a] 16 Lev. 26:12; Jer. 32:38; Ezek. 37:27   [b] 17 Isaiah 52:11; Ezek. 20:34,41   [c] 18 2 Samuel 7:14; 7:8

8 And now, brothers and sisters, we want you to know about the grace that God has given the Macedonian churches. ²In the midst of a very severe trial, their overflowing joy and their extreme poverty welled up in rich generosity. ³For I testify that they gave as much as they were able, and even beyond their ability. Entirely on their own, ⁴they urgently pleaded with us for the privilege of sharing in this service for the Lord's people. ⁵And they exceeded our expectations: They gave themselves first of all to the Lord, and then by the will of God also to us. ⁶So we urged Titus, just as he had earlier made a beginning, to bring also to completion this act of grace on your part. ⁷But since you excel in everything—in faith, in speech, in knowledge, in complete earnestness and in the love we have kindled in you[a]—see that you also excel in this grace of giving.

⁸I am not commanding you, but I want to test the sincerity of your love by comparing it with the earnestness of others. ⁹For you know the grace of our Lord Jesus Christ, that though he was rich, yet for your sake he became poor, so that you through his poverty might become rich.

¹⁰And here is my judgment about what is best for you in this matter. Last year you were the first not only to give but also to have the desire to do so. ¹¹Now finish the work, so that your eager willingness to do it may be matched by your completion of it, according to your means. ¹²For if the willingness is there, the gift is acceptable according to what one has, not according to what one does not have.

¹³Our desire is not that others might be relieved while you are hard pressed, but that there might be equality. ¹⁴At the present time your plenty will supply what they need, so that in turn their plenty will supply what you need. The goal is equality, ¹⁵as it is written: "The one who gathered much did not have too much, and the one who gathered little did not have too little."[b]

¹⁶Thanks be to God, who put into the heart of Titus the same concern I have for you. ¹⁷For Titus not only welcomed our appeal, but he is coming to you with much enthusiasm and on his own initiative. ¹⁸And we are sending along with him the brother who is praised by all the churches for his service to the gospel. ¹⁹What is more, he was chosen by the churches to accompany us as we carry the offering, which we administer in order to honor the Lord himself and to show our eagerness to help. ²⁰We want to avoid any criticism of the way we administer this liberal gift. ²¹For we are taking pains to do what is right, not only in the eyes of the Lord but also in the eyes of man.

²²In addition, we are sending with them our brother who has often proved to us in many ways that he is zealous, and now even more so because of his great confidence in you. ²³As for Titus, he is my partner and co-worker among you; as for our brothers, they are representatives of the churches and an honor to Christ. ²⁴Therefore show these men the proof of your love and the reason for our pride in you, so that the churches can see it.

9 There is no need for me to write to you about this service to the Lord's people. ²For I know your

---

[a] 7 Some manuscripts *and in your love for us*   [b] 15 Exodus 16:18

eagerness to help, and I have been boasting about it to the Macedonians, telling them that since last year you in Achaia were ready to give; and your enthusiasm has stirred most of them to action. [3]But I am sending the brothers in order that our boasting about you in this matter should not prove hollow, but that you may be ready, as I said you would be. [4]For if any Macedonians come with me and find you unprepared, we—not to say anything about you—would be ashamed of having been so confident. [5]So I thought it necessary to urge the brothers to visit you in advance and finish the arrangements for the generous gift you had promised. Then it will be ready as a generous gift, not as one grudgingly given.

[6]Remember this: Whoever sows sparingly will also reap sparingly, and whoever sows generously will also reap generously. [7]Each of you should give what you have decided in your heart to give, not reluctantly or under compulsion, for God loves a cheerful giver. [8]And God is able to bless you abundantly, so that in all things at all times, having all that you need, you will abound in every good work. [9]As it is written:

> "They have freely scattered their
>   gifts to the poor;
>   their righteousness endures
>   forever."[a]

[10]Now he who supplies seed to the sower and bread for food will also supply and increase your store of seed and will enlarge the harvest of your righteousness. [11]You will be enriched in every way so that you can be generous on every occasion, and through us your generosity will result in thanksgiving to God.

[12]This service that you perform is not only supplying the needs of the Lord's people but is also overflowing in many expressions of thanks to God. [13]Because of the service by which you have proved yourselves, others will praise God for the obedience that accompanies your confession of the gospel of Christ, and for your generosity in sharing with them and with everyone else. [14]And in their prayers for you their hearts will go out to you, because of the surpassing grace God has given you. [15]Thanks be to God for his indescribable gift!

10 By the humility and gentleness of Christ, I appeal to you—I, Paul, who am "timid" when face to face with you, but "bold" toward you when away! [2]I beg you that when I come I may not have to be as bold as I expect to be toward some people who think that we live by the standards of this world. [3]For though we live in the world, we do not wage war as the world does. [4]The weapons we fight with are not the weapons of the world. On the contrary, they have divine power to demolish strongholds. [5]We demolish arguments and every pretension that sets itself up against the knowledge of God, and we take captive every thought to make it obedient to Christ. [6]And we will be ready to punish every act of disobedience, once your obedience is complete.

[7]You are judging by appearances.[b] If anyone is confident that they belong to Christ, they should consider again that we belong to Christ just as much as they do. [8]So even if I boast somewhat freely about the authority the Lord gave us for

---

a 9 Psalm 112:9   b 7 Or *Look at the obvious facts*

building you up rather than tearing you down, I will not be ashamed of it. [9] I do not want to seem to be trying to frighten you with my letters. [10] For some say, "His letters are weighty and forceful, but in person he is unimpressive and his speaking amounts to nothing." [11] Such people should realize that what we are in our letters when we are absent, we will be in our actions when we are present.

[12] We do not dare to classify or compare ourselves with some who commend themselves. When they measure themselves by themselves and compare themselves with themselves, they are not wise. [13] We, however, will not boast beyond proper limits, but will confine our boasting to the sphere of service God himself has assigned to us, a sphere that also includes you. [14] We are not going too far in our boasting, as would be the case if we had not come to you, for we did get as far as you with the gospel of Christ. [15] Neither do we go beyond our limits by boasting of work done by others. Our hope is that, as your faith continues to grow, our sphere of activity among you will greatly expand, [16] so that we can preach the gospel in the regions beyond you. For we do not want to boast about work already done in someone else's territory. [17] But, "Let the one who boasts boast in the Lord."[a] [18] For it is not the one who commends himself who is approved, but the one whom the Lord commends.

11 I hope you will put up with me in a little foolishness. Yes, please put up with me! [2] I am jealous for you with a godly jealousy. I promised you to one husband, to Christ, so that I might present you as a pure virgin to him. [3] But I am afraid that just as Eve was deceived by the serpent's cunning, your minds may somehow be led astray from your sincere and pure devotion to Christ. [4] For if someone comes to you and preaches a Jesus other than the Jesus we preached, or if you receive a different spirit from the Spirit you received, or a different gospel from the one you accepted, you put up with it easily enough.

[5] I do not think I am in the least inferior to those "super-apostles."[b] [6] I may indeed be untrained as a speaker, but I do have knowledge. We have made this perfectly clear to you in every way. [7] Was it a sin for me to lower myself in order to elevate you by preaching the gospel of God to you free of charge? [8] I robbed other churches by receiving support from them so as to serve you. [9] And when I was with you and needed something, I was not a burden to anyone, for the brothers who came from Macedonia supplied what I needed. I have kept myself from being a burden to you in any way, and will continue to do so. [10] As surely as the truth of Christ is in me, nobody in the regions of Achaia will stop this boasting of mine. [11] Why? Because I do not love you? God knows I do!

[12] And I will keep on doing what I am doing in order to cut the ground from under those who want an opportunity to be considered equal with us in the things they boast about. [13] For such people are false apostles, deceitful workers, masquerading as apostles of Christ. [14] And no wonder, for Satan himself masquerades as an angel of

---

[a] 17 Jer. 9:24   [b] 5 Or to the most eminent apostles

light. 15 It is not surprising, then, if his servants also masquerade as servants of righteousness. Their end will be what their actions deserve.

16 I repeat: Let no one take me for a fool. But if you do, then tolerate me just as you would a fool, so that I may do a little boasting. 17 In this self-confident boasting I am not talking as the Lord would, but as a fool. 18 Since many are boasting in the way the world does, I too will boast. 19 You gladly put up with fools since you are so wise! 20 In fact, you even put up with anyone who enslaves you or exploits you or takes advantage of you or puts on airs or slaps you in the face. 21 To my shame I admit that we were too weak for that!

Whatever anyone else dares to boast about—I am speaking as a fool—I also dare to boast about. 22 Are they Hebrews? So am I. Are they Israelites? So am I. Are they Abraham's descendants? So am I. 23 Are they servants of Christ? (I am out of my mind to talk like this.) I am more. I have worked much harder, been in prison more frequently, been flogged more severely, and been exposed to death again and again. 24 Five times I received from the Jews the forty lashes minus one. 25 Three times I was beaten with rods, once I was pelted with stones, three times I was shipwrecked, I spent a night and a day in the open sea, 26 I have been constantly on the move. I have been in danger from rivers, in danger from bandits, in danger from my fellow Jews, in danger from Gentiles; in danger in the city, in danger in the country, in danger at sea; and in danger from false believers. 27 I have labored and toiled and have often gone without sleep; I have known hunger and thirst and have often gone without food; I have been cold and naked. 28 Besides everything else, I face daily the pressure of my concern for all the churches. 29 Who is weak, and I do not feel weak? Who is led into sin, and I do not inwardly burn?

30 If I must boast, I will boast of the things that show my weakness. 31 The God and Father of the Lord Jesus, who is to be praised forever, knows that I am not lying. 32 In Damascus the governor under King Aretas had the city of the Damascenes guarded in order to arrest me. 33 But I was lowered in a basket from a window in the wall and slipped through his hands.

12 I must go on boasting. Although there is nothing to be gained, I will go on to visions and revelations from the Lord. 2 I know a man in Christ who fourteen years ago was caught up to the third heaven. Whether it was in the body or out of the body I do not know—God knows. 3 And I know that this man—whether in the body or apart from the body I do not know, but God knows— 4 was caught up to paradise and heard inexpressible things, things that no one is permitted to tell. 5 I will boast about a man like that, but I will not boast about myself, except about my weaknesses. 6 Even if I should choose to boast, I would not be a fool, because I would be speaking the truth. But I refrain, so no one will think more of me than is warranted by what I do or say, 7 or because of these surpassingly great revelations. Therefore, in order to keep me from becoming conceited, I was given a thorn in my flesh, a messenger of Satan, to torment me. 8 Three times

I pleaded with the Lord to take it away from me. [9] But he said to me, "My grace is sufficient for you, for my power is made perfect in weakness." Therefore I will boast all the more gladly about my weaknesses, so that Christ's power may rest on me. [10] That is why, for Christ's sake, I delight in weaknesses, in insults, in hardships, in persecutions, in difficulties. For when I am weak, then I am strong.

[11] I have made a fool of myself, but you drove me to it. I ought to have been commended by you, for I am not in the least inferior to the "super-apostles,"[a] even though I am nothing. [12] I persevered in demonstrating among you the marks of a true apostle, including signs, wonders and miracles. [13] How were you inferior to the other churches, except that I was never a burden to you? Forgive me this wrong!

[14] Now I am ready to visit you for the third time, and I will not be a burden to you, because what I want is not your possessions but you. After all, children should not have to save up for their parents, but parents for their children. [15] So I will very gladly spend for you everything I have and expend myself as well. If I love you more, will you love me less? [16] Be that as it may, I have not been a burden to you. Yet, crafty fellow that I am, I caught you by trickery! [17] Did I exploit you through any of the men I sent to you? [18] I urged Titus to go to you and I sent our brother with him. Titus did not exploit you, did he? Did we not walk in the same footsteps by the same Spirit?

[19] Have you been thinking all along that we have been defending ourselves to you? We have been speaking in the sight of God as those in Christ; and everything we do, dear friends, is for your strengthening. [20] For I am afraid that when I come I may not find you as I want you to be, and you may not find me as you want me to be. I fear that there may be discord, jealousy, fits of rage, selfish ambition, slander, gossip, arrogance and disorder. [21] I am afraid that when I come again my God will humble me before you, and I will be grieved over many who have sinned earlier and have not repented of the impurity, sexual sin and debauchery in which they have indulged.

13 This will be my third visit to you. "Every matter must be established by the testimony of two or three witnesses."[b] [2] I already gave you a warning when I was with you the second time. I now repeat it while absent: On my return I will not spare those who sinned earlier or any of the others, [3] since you are demanding proof that Christ is speaking through me. He is not weak in dealing with you, but is powerful among you. [4] For to be sure, he was crucified in weakness, yet he lives by God's power. Likewise, we are weak in him, yet by God's power we will live with him in our dealing with you.

[5] Examine yourselves to see whether you are in the faith; test yourselves. Do you not realize that Christ Jesus is in you — unless, of course, you fail the test? [6] And I trust that you will discover that we have not failed the test. [7] Now we pray to God that you will not do anything wrong — not so that people will see that we have stood the test but so that you will do what is right even though we may seem to

---

[a] 11 Or *the most eminent apostles*   [b] 1 Deut. 19:15

have failed. 8 For we cannot do anything against the truth, but only for the truth. 9 We are glad whenever we are weak but you are strong; and our prayer is that you may be fully restored. 10 This is why I write these things when I am absent, that when I come I may not have to be harsh in my use of authority — the authority the Lord gave me for building you up, not for tearing you down.

11 Finally, brothers and sisters, rejoice! Strive for full restoration, encourage one another, be of one mind, live in peace. And the God of love and peace will be with you.

12 Greet one another with a holy kiss. 13 All God's people here send their greetings.

14 May the grace of the Lord Jesus Christ, and the love of God, and the fellowship of the Holy Spirit be with you all.

GALATIANS

Galatia was a Roman province in central Asia Minor. Paul traveled here on each of the three journeys he made to spread the message about Jesus. The Galatians received both Paul and his gospel announcement warmly. But later some people Paul calls *agitators* came and challenged Paul's leadership as well as the foundation of his teaching. So Paul wrote to answer the threat to his status as an apostle and to reaffirm the core message that faith in the Messiah is the basis of membership in God's new community.

Paul doesn't open his letter by appealing to the apostles in Jerusalem. Instead, he insists that *the gospel I preached is not of human origin . . . rather, I received it by revelation from Jesus Christ.* Paul is compelled to share this revelation, and he notes that the other apostles support him.

Paul then proceeds to his main argument, which is that Gentiles who have become followers of Jesus do not need to be circumcised. The new worldwide family which had been promised to Abraham is created by faith in Messiah Jesus, not by keeping the Jewish law (Torah). The biblical story had been pointing to this all along.

But if following Torah is not the basis of the gospel, won't there be anarchy? Paul answers by describing what Spirit-empowered life looks like in the community of Messiah-followers. Paul closes by emphasizing the main theme of his letter once more: *Neither circumcision nor uncircumcision means anything; what counts is the new creation.*

---

1 Paul, an apostle — sent not from men nor by a man, but by Jesus Christ and God the Father, who raised him from the dead — ²and all the brothers and sisters[a] with me,

To the churches in Galatia:

³Grace and peace to you from God our Father and the Lord Jesus Christ, ⁴who gave himself for our sins to rescue us from the present evil age, according to the will of our God and Father, ⁵to whom be glory for ever and ever. Amen.

⁶I am astonished that you are so quickly deserting the one who called you to live in the grace of Christ and are turning to a different gospel — ⁷which is really no gospel at all. Evidently some people are throwing you into confusion and are trying to pervert the gospel of Christ. ⁸But even if we or an angel from heaven should preach a gospel other than the one we preached to you, let them be under God's curse! ⁹As we have already said, so now I say again: If anybody is preaching to you a gospel other than what you accepted, let them be under God's curse!

¹⁰Am I now trying to win the approval of human beings, or of God? Or am I trying to please people? If I were still trying to please people, I would not be a servant of Christ.

¹¹I want you to know, broth-

---

a 2 The Greek word for *brothers and sisters* (*adelphoi*) refers here to believers, both men and women, as part of God's family; also in verse 11; and in 3:15; 4:12, 28, 31; 5:11, 13; 6:1, 18.

ers and sisters, that the gospel I preached is not of human origin. ¹²I did not receive it from any man, nor was I taught it; rather, I received it by revelation from Jesus Christ.

¹³For you have heard of my previous way of life in Judaism, how intensely I persecuted the church of God and tried to destroy it. ¹⁴I was advancing in Judaism beyond many of my own age among my people and was extremely zealous for the traditions of my fathers. ¹⁵But when God, who set me apart from my mother's womb and called me by his grace, was pleased ¹⁶to reveal his Son in me so that I might preach him among the Gentiles, my immediate response was not to consult any human being. ¹⁷I did not go up to Jerusalem to see those who were apostles before I was, but I went into Arabia. Later I returned to Damascus.

¹⁸Then after three years, I went up to Jerusalem to get acquainted with Cephas*a* and stayed with him fifteen days. ¹⁹I saw none of the other apostles — only James, the Lord's brother. ²⁰I assure you before God that what I am writing you is no lie.

²¹Then I went to Syria and Cilicia. ²²I was personally unknown to the churches of Judea that are in Christ. ²³They only heard the report: "The man who formerly persecuted us is now preaching the faith he once tried to destroy." ²⁴And they praised God because of me.

2 Then after fourteen years, I went up again to Jerusalem, this time with Barnabas. I took Titus along also. ²I went in response to a revelation and, meeting privately with those esteemed as leaders, I pre-

sented to them the gospel that I preach among the Gentiles. I wanted to be sure I was not running and had not been running my race in vain. ³Yet not even Titus, who was with me, was compelled to be circumcised, even though he was a Greek. ⁴This matter arose because some false believers had infiltrated our ranks to spy on the freedom we have in Christ Jesus and to make us slaves. ⁵We did not give in to them for a moment, so that the truth of the gospel might be preserved for you.

⁶As for those who were held in high esteem — whatever they were makes no difference to me; God does not show favoritism — they added nothing to my message. ⁷On the contrary, they recognized that I had been entrusted with the task of preaching the gospel to the uncircumcised,*b* just as Peter had been to the circumcised.*c* ⁸For God, who was at work in Peter as an apostle to the circumcised, was also at work in me as an apostle to the Gentiles. ⁹James, Cephas*d* and John, those esteemed as pillars, gave me and Barnabas the right hand of fellowship when they recognized the grace given to me. They agreed that we should go to the Gentiles, and they to the circumcised. ¹⁰All they asked was that we should continue to remember the poor, the very thing I had been eager to do all along.

¹¹When Cephas came to Antioch, I opposed him to his face, because he stood condemned. ¹²For before certain men came from James, he used to eat with the Gentiles. But when they arrived, he began to draw back and separate himself

---

a 18 That is, Peter   *b 7* That is, Gentiles   *c 7* That is, Jews; also in verses 8 and 9   *d 9* That is, Peter; also in verses 11 and 14

from the Gentiles because he was afraid of those who belonged to the circumcision group. [13]The other Jews joined him in his hypocrisy, so that by their hypocrisy even Barnabas was led astray.

[14]When I saw that they were not acting in line with the truth of the gospel, I said to Cephas in front of them all, "You are a Jew, yet you live like a Gentile and not like a Jew. How is it, then, that you force Gentiles to follow Jewish customs?

[15] "We who are Jews by birth and not sinful Gentiles [16]know that a person is not justified by the works of the law, but by faith in Jesus Christ. So we, too, have put our faith in Christ Jesus that we may be justified by faith in[a] Christ and not by the works of the law, because by the works of the law no one will be justified.

[17] "But if, in seeking to be justified in Christ, we Jews find ourselves also among the sinners, doesn't that mean that Christ promotes sin? Absolutely not! [18]If I rebuild what I destroyed, then I really would be a lawbreaker.

[19] "For through the law I died to the law so that I might live for God. [20]I have been crucified with Christ and I no longer live, but Christ lives in me. The life I now live in the body, I live by faith in the Son of God, who loved me and gave himself for me. [21]I do not set aside the grace of God, for if righteousness could be gained through the law, Christ died for nothing!"[b]

3 You foolish Galatians! Who has bewitched you? Before your very eyes Jesus Christ was clearly portrayed as crucified. [2]I would like to learn just one thing from you: Did you receive the Spirit by the works of the law, or by believing what you heard? [3]Are you so foolish? After beginning by means of the Spirit, are you now trying to finish by means of the flesh?[c] [4]Have you experienced[d] so much in vain—if it really was in vain? [5]So again I ask, does God give you his Spirit and work miracles among you by the works of the law, or by your believing what you heard? [6]So also Abraham "believed God, and it was credited to him as righteousness."[e]

[7]Understand, then, that those who have faith are children of Abraham. [8]Scripture foresaw that God would justify the Gentiles by faith, and announced the gospel in advance to Abraham: "All nations will be blessed through you."[f] [9]So those who rely on faith are blessed along with Abraham, the man of faith.

[10]For all who rely on the works of the law are under a curse, as it is written: "Cursed is everyone who does not continue to do everything written in the Book of the Law."[g] [11]Clearly no one who relies on the law is justified before God, because "the righteous will live by faith."[h] [12]The law is not based on faith; on the contrary, it says, "The person who does these things will live by them."[i] [13]Christ redeemed us from the curse of the law by becoming a curse for us, for it is written: "Cursed is everyone who is hung on a pole."[j] [14]He redeemed us in order

---

[a] 16 Or *but through the faithfulness of . . . justified on the basis of the faithfulness of*   [b] 21 Some interpreters end the quotation after verse 14.   [c] 3 In contexts like this, the Greek word for *flesh* (*sarx*) refers to the sinful state of human beings, often presented as a power in opposition to the Spirit.   [d] 4 Or *suffered*   [e] 6 Gen. 15:6   [f] 8 Gen. 12:3; 18:18; 22:18   [g] 10 Deut. 27:26   [h] 11 Hab. 2:4   [i] 12 Lev. 18:5   [j] 13 Deut. 21:23

that the blessing given to Abraham might come to the Gentiles through Christ Jesus, so that by faith we might receive the promise of the Spirit.

15Brothers and sisters, let me take an example from everyday life. Just as no one can set aside or add to a human covenant that has been duly established, so it is in this case. 16The promises were spoken to Abraham and to his seed. Scripture does not say "and to seeds," meaning many people, but "and to your seed,"[a] meaning one person, who is Christ. 17What I mean is this: The law, introduced 430 years later, does not set aside the covenant previously established by God and thus do away with the promise. 18For if the inheritance depends on the law, then it no longer depends on the promise; but God in his grace gave it to Abraham through a promise.

19Why, then, was the law given at all? It was added because of transgressions until the Seed to whom the promise referred had come. The law was given through angels and entrusted to a mediator. 20A mediator, however, implies more than one party; but God is one.

21Is the law, therefore, opposed to the promises of God? Absolutely not! For if a law had been given that could impart life, then righteousness would certainly have come by the law. 22But Scripture has locked up everything under the control of sin, so that what was promised, being given through faith in Jesus Christ, might be given to those who believe.

23Before the coming of this faith,[b] we were held in custody under the law, locked up until the faith that was to come would be revealed. 24So the law was our guardian until Christ came that we might be justified by faith. 25Now that this faith has come, we are no longer under a guardian.

26So in Christ Jesus you are all children of God through faith, 27for all of you who were baptized into Christ have clothed yourselves with Christ. 28There is neither Jew nor Gentile, neither slave nor free, nor is there male and female, for you are all one in Christ Jesus. 29If you belong to Christ, then you are Abraham's seed, and heirs according to the promise.

4 What I am saying is that as long as an heir is underage, he is no different from a slave, although he owns the whole estate. 2The heir is subject to guardians and trustees until the time set by his father. 3So also, when we were underage, we were in slavery under the elemental spiritual forces[c] of the world. 4But when the set time had fully come, God sent his Son, born of a woman, born under the law, 5to redeem those under the law, that we might receive adoption to sonship.[d] 6Because you are his sons, God sent the Spirit of his Son into our hearts, the Spirit who calls out, "Abba,[e] Father." 7So you are no longer a slave, but God's child; and since you are his child, God has made you also an heir.

8Formerly, when you did not know God, you were slaves to those who by nature are not gods. 9But

---

[a] 16 Gen. 12:7; 13:15; 24:7   [b] 22,23 Or through the faithfulness of Jesus . . . 23Before faith came   [c] 3 Or under the basic principles   [d] 5 The Greek word for adoption to sonship is a legal term referring to the full legal standing of an adopted male heir in Roman culture.   [e] 6 Aramaic for Father

now that you know God—or rather are known by God—how is it that you are turning back to those weak and miserable forces[a]? Do you wish to be enslaved by them all over again? [10]You are observing special days and months and seasons and years! [11]I fear for you, that somehow I have wasted my efforts on you.

[12]I plead with you, brothers and sisters, become like me, for I became like you. You did me no wrong. [13]As you know, it was because of an illness that I first preached the gospel to you, [14]and even though my illness was a trial to you, you did not treat me with contempt or scorn. Instead, you welcomed me as if I were an angel of God, as if I were Christ Jesus himself. [15]Where, then, is your blessing of me now? I can testify that, if you could have done so, you would have torn out your eyes and given them to me. [16]Have I now become your enemy by telling you the truth?

[17]Those people are zealous to win you over, but for no good. What they want is to alienate you from us, so that you may have zeal for them. [18]It is fine to be zealous, provided the purpose is good, and to be so always, not just when I am with you. [19]My dear children, for whom I am again in the pains of childbirth until Christ is formed in you, [20]how I wish I could be with you now and change my tone, because I am perplexed about you!

[21]Tell me, you who want to be under the law, are you not aware of what the law says? [22]For it is written that Abraham had two sons, one by the slave woman and the other by the free woman. [23]His son by the slave woman was born according to the flesh, but his son by the free woman was born as the result of a divine promise.

[24]These things are being taken figuratively: The women represent two covenants. One covenant is from Mount Sinai and bears children who are to be slaves: This is Hagar. [25]Now Hagar stands for Mount Sinai in Arabia and corresponds to the present city of Jerusalem, because she is in slavery with her children. [26]But the Jerusalem that is above is free, and she is our mother. [27]For it is written:

"Be glad, barren woman,
    you who never bore a child;
shout for joy and cry aloud,
    you who were never in labor;
because more are the children of
        the desolate woman
    than of her who has a
        husband."[b]

[28]Now you, brothers and sisters, like Isaac, are children of promise. [29]At that time the son born according to the flesh persecuted the son born by the power of the Spirit. It is the same now. [30]But what does Scripture say? "Get rid of the slave woman and her son, for the slave woman's son will never share in the inheritance with the free woman's son."[c] [31]Therefore, brothers and sisters, we are not children of the slave woman, but of the free woman.

5 It is for freedom that Christ has set us free. Stand firm, then, and do not let yourselves be burdened again by a yoke of slavery.

[2]Mark my words! I, Paul, tell you that if you let yourselves be circumcised, Christ will be of no value to you at all. [3]Again I declare to every man who lets himself be circum-

---

[a] 9 Or *principles*   [b] 27 Isaiah 54:1   [c] 30 Gen. 21:10

cised that he is obligated to obey the whole law. ⁴You who are trying to be justified by the law have been alienated from Christ; you have fallen away from grace. ⁵For through the Spirit we eagerly await by faith the righteousness for which we hope. ⁶For in Christ Jesus neither circumcision nor uncircumcision has any value. The only thing that counts is faith expressing itself through love.

⁷You were running a good race. Who cut in on you to keep you from obeying the truth? ⁸That kind of persuasion does not come from the one who calls you. ⁹"A little yeast works through the whole batch of dough." ¹⁰I am confident in the Lord that you will take no other view. The one who is throwing you into confusion, whoever that may be, will have to pay the penalty. ¹¹Brothers and sisters, if I am still preaching circumcision, why am I still being persecuted? In that case the offense of the cross has been abolished. ¹²As for those agitators, I wish they would go the whole way and emasculate themselves!

¹³You, my brothers and sisters, were called to be free. But do not use your freedom to indulge the flesh[a]; rather, serve one another humbly in love. ¹⁴For the entire law is fulfilled in keeping this one command: "Love your neighbor as yourself."[b] ¹⁵If you bite and devour each other, watch out or you will be destroyed by each other.

¹⁶So I say, walk by the Spirit, and you will not gratify the desires of the flesh. ¹⁷For the flesh desires what is contrary to the Spirit, and the Spirit what is contrary to the flesh. They are in conflict with each other, so that you are not to do whatever[c] you want. ¹⁸But if you are led by the Spirit, you are not under the law.

¹⁹The acts of the flesh are obvious: sexual immorality, impurity and debauchery; ²⁰idolatry and witchcraft; hatred, discord, jealousy, fits of rage, selfish ambition, dissensions, factions ²¹and envy; drunkenness, orgies, and the like. I warn you, as I did before, that those who live like this will not inherit the kingdom of God.

²²But the fruit of the Spirit is love, joy, peace, forbearance, kindness, goodness, faithfulness, ²³gentleness and self-control. Against such things there is no law. ²⁴Those who belong to Christ Jesus have crucified the flesh with its passions and desires. ²⁵Since we live by the Spirit, let us keep in step with the Spirit. ²⁶Let us not become conceited, provoking and envying each other.

6 Brothers and sisters, if someone is caught in a sin, you who live by the Spirit should restore that person gently. But watch yourselves, or you also may be tempted. ²Carry each other's burdens, and in this way you will fulfill the law of Christ. ³If anyone thinks they are something when they are not, they deceive themselves. ⁴Each one should test their own actions. Then they can take pride in themselves alone, without comparing themselves to someone else, ⁵for each one should carry their own load. ⁶Nevertheless, the one who receives instruction in the word should share all good things with their instructor.

---

[a] 13 In contexts like this, the Greek word for *flesh* (*sarx*) refers to the sinful state of human beings, often presented as a power in opposition to the Spirit; also in verses 16, 17, 19 and 24; and in 6:8.   [b] 14 Lev. 19:18   [c] 17 Or *you do not do what*

⁷Do not be deceived: God cannot be mocked. A man reaps what he sows. ⁸Whoever sows to please their flesh, from the flesh will reap destruction; whoever sows to please the Spirit, from the Spirit will reap eternal life. ⁹Let us not become weary in doing good, for at the proper time we will reap a harvest if we do not give up. ¹⁰Therefore, as we have opportunity, let us do good to all people, especially to those who belong to the family of believers.

¹¹See what large letters I use as I write to you with my own hand! ¹²Those who want to impress people by means of the flesh are trying to compel you to be circumcised. The only reason they do this is to avoid being persecuted for the cross of Christ. ¹³Not even those who are circumcised keep the law, yet they want you to be circumcised that they may boast about your circumcision in the flesh. ¹⁴May I never boast except in the cross of our Lord Jesus Christ, through whichᵃ the world has been crucified to me, and I to the world. ¹⁵Neither circumcision nor uncircumcision means anything; what counts is the new creation. ¹⁶Peace and mercy to all who follow this rule — toᵇ the Israel of God.

¹⁷From now on, let no one cause me trouble, for I bear on my body the marks of Jesus.

¹⁸The grace of our Lord Jesus Christ be with your spirit, brothers and sisters. Amen.

ᵃ 14 Or whom   ᵇ 16 Or rule and to

EPHESIANS

Traditionally named Ephesians, this letter may not actually have been written to the believers in Ephesus. Some of the best early copies of the letter don't include the phrase *in Ephesus* in the greeting. While Paul spent two years in Ephesus, this letter appears to address people Paul has never met.

Paul here presents a two-fold pattern, first explaining the new identity believers have in Christ and then bringing out the implications for their new way of life. God has brought everything together under the rule of the Messiah, exalting Jesus above all things. Paul echoes a phrase from Psalm 8—*God placed all things under his feet*—to show that Jesus is the truly human one. Jesus fulfills the original human calling to rule over the creation properly. Jews and Gentiles have been brought together into one body, with Jesus at the head. God is now creating *one new humanity* from all over the world through the reconciling work of the Messiah.

This means Jesus-followers must give up their former way of life and practice purity in daily living and integrity in their relationships. The reciprocal responsibilities of those in and under authority are used as key examples of the new kinds of relationships God is expecting. Paul cautions his readers that they are entering a spiritual battle. They must arm themselves with all the resources God has provided, until the Messiah brings *unity to all things in heaven and on earth.*

---

1 Paul, an apostle of Christ Jesus by the will of God,

To God's holy people in Ephesus,[a] the faithful in Christ Jesus:

[2] Grace and peace to you from God our Father and the Lord Jesus Christ.

[3] Praise be to the God and Father of our Lord Jesus Christ, who has blessed us in the heavenly realms with every spiritual blessing in Christ. [4] For he chose us in him before the creation of the world to be holy and blameless in his sight. In love [5] he[b] predestined us for adoption to sonship[c] through Jesus Christ, in accordance with his pleasure and will— [6] to the praise of his glorious grace, which he has freely given us in the One he loves. [7] In him we have redemption through his blood, the forgiveness of sins, in accordance with the riches of God's grace [8] that he lavished on us. With all wisdom and understanding, [9] he[d] made known to us the mystery of his will according to his good pleasure, which he purposed in Christ, [10] to be put into effect when the times reach their fulfillment—to bring unity to all things in heaven and on earth under Christ.

[11] In him we were also chosen,[e] having been predestined according to the plan of him who works

---

a 1 Some early manuscripts do not have *in Ephesus.*   *b 4,5* Or *sight in love. 5He*   *c 5* The Greek word for *adoption to sonship* is a legal term referring to the full legal standing of an adopted male heir in Roman culture.   *d 8,9* Or *us with all wisdom and understanding. 9And he*   *e 11* Or *were made heirs*

out everything in conformity with the purpose of his will, [12]in order that we, who were the first to put our hope in Christ, might be for the praise of his glory. [13]And you also were included in Christ when you heard the message of truth, the gospel of your salvation. When you believed, you were marked in him with a seal, the promised Holy Spirit, [14]who is a deposit guaranteeing our inheritance until the redemption of those who are God's possession — to the praise of his glory.

[15]For this reason, ever since I heard about your faith in the Lord Jesus and your love for all God's people, [16]I have not stopped giving thanks for you, remembering you in my prayers. [17]I keep asking that the God of our Lord Jesus Christ, the glorious Father, may give you the Spirit[a] of wisdom and revelation, so that you may know him better. [18]I pray that the eyes of your heart may be enlightened in order that you may know the hope to which he has called you, the riches of his glorious inheritance in his holy people, [19]and his incomparably great power for us who believe. That power is the same as the mighty strength [20]he exerted when he raised Christ from the dead and seated him at his right hand in the heavenly realms, [21]far above all rule and authority, power and dominion, and every name that is invoked, not only in the present age but also in the one to come. [22]And God placed all things under his feet and appointed him to be head over everything for the church, [23]which is his body, the fullness of him who fills everything in every way.

2 As for you, you were dead in your transgressions and sins, [2]in which you used to live when you followed the ways of this world and of the ruler of the kingdom of the air, the spirit who is now at work in those who are disobedient. [3]All of us also lived among them at one time, gratifying the cravings of our flesh[b] and following its desires and thoughts. Like the rest, we were by nature deserving of wrath. [4]But because of his great love for us, God, who is rich in mercy, [5]made us alive with Christ even when we were dead in transgressions — it is by grace you have been saved. [6]And God raised us up with Christ and seated us with him in the heavenly realms in Christ Jesus, [7]in order that in the coming ages he might show the incomparable riches of his grace, expressed in his kindness to us in Christ Jesus. [8]For it is by grace you have been saved, through faith — and this is not from yourselves, it is the gift of God — [9]not by works, so that no one can boast. [10]For we are God's handiwork, created in Christ Jesus to do good works, which God prepared in advance for us to do.

[11]Therefore, remember that formerly you who are Gentiles by birth and called "uncircumcised" by those who call themselves "the circumcision" (which is done in the body by human hands) — [12]remember that at that time you were separate from Christ, excluded from citizenship in Israel and foreigners to the covenants of the promise, without hope and without God in the world. [13]But now in Christ Jesus you who once were far away have been brought near by the blood of Christ.

[a] 17 Or *a spirit*   [b] 3 In contexts like this, the Greek word for *flesh (sarx)* refers to the sinful state of human beings, often presented as a power in opposition to the Spirit.

14For he himself is our peace, who has made the two groups one and has destroyed the barrier, the dividing wall of hostility, 15by setting aside in his flesh the law with its commands and regulations. His purpose was to create in himself one new humanity out of the two, thus making peace, 16and in one body to reconcile both of them to God through the cross, by which he put to death their hostility. 17He came and preached peace to you who were far away and peace to those who were near. 18For through him we both have access to the Father by one Spirit.

19Consequently, you are no longer foreigners and strangers, but fellow citizens with God's people and also members of his household, 20built on the foundation of the apostles and prophets, with Christ Jesus himself as the chief cornerstone. 21In him the whole building is joined together and rises to become a holy temple in the Lord. 22And in him you too are being built together to become a dwelling in which God lives by his Spirit.

3 For this reason I, Paul, the prisoner of Christ Jesus for the sake of you Gentiles —

2Surely you have heard about the administration of God's grace that was given to me for you, 3that is, the mystery made known to me by revelation, as I have already written briefly. 4In reading this, then, you will be able to understand my insight into the mystery of Christ, 5which was not made known to people in other generations as it has now been revealed by the Spirit to God's holy apostles and prophets. 6This mystery is that through the gospel the Gentiles are heirs together with Israel, members together of one body, and sharers together in the promise in Christ Jesus.

7I became a servant of this gospel by the gift of God's grace given me through the working of his power. 8Although I am less than the least of all the Lord's people, this grace was given me: to preach to the Gentiles the boundless riches of Christ, 9and to make plain to everyone the administration of this mystery, which for ages past was kept hidden in God, who created all things. 10His intent was that now, through the church, the manifold wisdom of God should be made known to the rulers and authorities in the heavenly realms, 11according to his eternal purpose that he accomplished in Christ Jesus our Lord. 12In him and through faith in him we may approach God with freedom and confidence. 13I ask you, therefore, not to be discouraged because of my sufferings for you, which are your glory.

14For this reason I kneel before the Father, 15from whom every family[a] in heaven and on earth derives its name. 16I pray that out of his glorious riches he may strengthen you with power through his Spirit in your inner being, 17so that Christ may dwell in your hearts through faith. And I pray that you, being rooted and established in love, 18may have power, together with all the Lord's holy people, to grasp how wide and long and high and deep is the love of Christ, 19and to know this love that surpasses knowledge — that you may be filled to the measure of all the fullness of God.

20Now to him who is able to do immeasurably more than all we ask

---

a 15 The Greek for family (patria) is derived from the Greek for father (pater).

or imagine, according to his power that is at work within us, 21 to him be glory in the church and in Christ Jesus throughout all generations, for ever and ever! Amen.

4 As a prisoner for the Lord, then, I urge you to live a life worthy of the calling you have received. 2 Be completely humble and gentle; be patient, bearing with one another in love. 3 Make every effort to keep the unity of the Spirit through the bond of peace. 4 There is one body and one Spirit, just as you were called to one hope when you were called; 5 one Lord, one faith, one baptism; 6 one God and Father of all, who is over all and through all and in all.

7 But to each one of us grace has been given as Christ apportioned it. 8 This is why it[a] says:

"When he ascended on high,
    he took many captives
    and gave gifts to his people."[b]

9 (What does "he ascended" mean except that he also descended to the lower, earthly regions[c]? 10 He who descended is the very one who ascended higher than all the heavens, in order to fill the whole universe.) 11 So Christ himself gave the apostles, the prophets, the evangelists, the pastors and teachers, 12 to equip his people for works of service, so that the body of Christ may be built up 13 until we all reach unity in the faith and in the knowledge of the Son of God and become mature, attaining to the whole measure of the fullness of Christ.

14 Then we will no longer be infants, tossed back and forth by the waves, and blown here and there by every wind of teaching and by the cunning and craftiness of people in their deceitful scheming. 15 Instead, speaking the truth in love, we will grow to become in every respect the mature body of him who is the head, that is, Christ. 16 From him the whole body, joined and held together by every supporting ligament, grows and builds itself up in love, as each part does its work.

17 So I tell you this, and insist on it in the Lord, that you must no longer live as the Gentiles do, in the futility of their thinking. 18 They are darkened in their understanding and separated from the life of God because of the ignorance that is in them due to the hardening of their hearts. 19 Having lost all sensitivity, they have given themselves over to sensuality so as to indulge in every kind of impurity, and they are full of greed.

20 That, however, is not the way of life you learned 21 when you heard about Christ and were taught in him in accordance with the truth that is in Jesus. 22 You were taught, with regard to your former way of life, to put off your old self, which is being corrupted by its deceitful desires; 23 to be made new in the attitude of your minds; 24 and to put on the new self, created to be like God in true righteousness and holiness.

25 Therefore each of you must put off falsehood and speak truthfully to your neighbor, for we are all members of one body. 26 "In your anger do not sin"[d]: Do not let the sun go down while you are still angry, 27 and do not give the devil a foothold. 28 Anyone who has been stealing must steal no longer, but

---

[a] 8 Or God   [b] 8 Psalm 68:18   [c] 9 Or The depths of the earth   [d] 26 Psalm 4:4 (see Septuagint)

must work, doing something useful with their own hands, that they may have something to share with those in need.

29 Do not let any unwholesome talk come out of your mouths, but only what is helpful for building others up according to their needs, that it may benefit those who listen. 30 And do not grieve the Holy Spirit of God, with whom you were sealed for the day of redemption. 31 Get rid of all bitterness, rage and anger, brawling and slander, along with every form of malice. 32 Be kind and compassionate to one another, forgiving each other, just as in Christ

5 God forgave you. 1 Follow God's example, therefore, as dearly loved children 2 and walk in the way of love, just as Christ loved us and gave himself up for us as a fragrant offering and sacrifice to God.

3 But among you there must not be even a hint of sexual immorality, or of any kind of impurity, or of greed, because these are improper for God's holy people. 4 Nor should there be obscenity, foolish talk or coarse joking, which are out of place, but rather thanksgiving. 5 For of this you can be sure: No immoral, impure or greedy person — such a person is an idolater — has any inheritance in the kingdom of Christ and of God.a 6 Let no one deceive you with empty words, for because of such things God's wrath comes on those who are disobedient. 7 Therefore do not be partners with them.

8 For you were once darkness, but now you are light in the Lord. Live as children of light 9 (for the fruit of the light consists in all goodness, righteousness and truth) 10 and find

out what pleases the Lord. 11 Have nothing to do with the fruitless deeds of darkness, but rather expose them. 12 It is shameful even to mention what the disobedient do in secret. 13 But everything exposed by the light becomes visible — and everything that is illuminated becomes a light. 14 This is why it is said:

> "Wake up, sleeper,
>   rise from the dead,
>   and Christ will shine on you."

15 Be very careful, then, how you live — not as unwise but as wise, 16 making the most of every opportunity, because the days are evil. 17 Therefore do not be foolish, but understand what the Lord's will is. 18 Do not get drunk on wine, which leads to debauchery. Instead, be filled with the Spirit, 19 speaking to one another with psalms, hymns, and songs from the Spirit. Sing and make music from your heart to the Lord, 20 always giving thanks to God the Father for everything, in the name of our Lord Jesus Christ.

21 Submit to one another out of reverence for Christ.

22 Wives, submit yourselves to your own husbands as you do to the Lord. 23 For the husband is the head of the wife as Christ is the head of the church, his body, of which he is the Savior. 24 Now as the church submits to Christ, so also wives should submit to their husbands in everything.

25 Husbands, love your wives, just as Christ loved the church and gave himself up for her 26 to make her holy, cleansingb her by the washing with water through the word, 27 and to present her to himself as a radiant church, without stain or

---

a 5 Or kingdom of the Messiah and God   b 26 Or having cleansed

wrinkle or any other blemish, but holy and blameless. 28 In this same way, husbands ought to love their wives as their own bodies. He who loves his wife loves himself. 29 After all, no one ever hated their own body, but they feed and care for their body, just as Christ does the church— 30 for we are members of his body. 31 "For this reason a man will leave his father and mother and be united to his wife, and the two will become one flesh." [a] 32 This is a profound mystery—but I am talking about Christ and the church. 33 However, each one of you also must love his wife as he loves himself, and the wife must respect her husband.

6 Children, obey your parents in the Lord, for this is right. 2 "Honor your father and mother"—which is the first commandment with a promise— 3 "so that it may go well with you and that you may enjoy long life on the earth." [b]

4 Fathers, [c] do not exasperate your children; instead, bring them up in the training and instruction of the Lord.

5 Slaves, obey your earthly masters with respect and fear, and with sincerity of heart, just as you would obey Christ. 6 Obey them not only to win their favor when their eye is on you, but as slaves of Christ, doing the will of God from your heart. 7 Serve wholeheartedly, as if you were serving the Lord, not people, 8 because you know that the Lord will reward each one for whatever good they do, whether they are slave or free.

9 And masters, treat your slaves in the same way. Do not threaten them, since you know that he who is both their Master and yours is in heaven, and there is no favoritism with him.

10 Finally, be strong in the Lord and in his mighty power. 11 Put on the full armor of God, so that you can take your stand against the devil's schemes. 12 For our struggle is not against flesh and blood, but against the rulers, against the authorities, against the powers of this dark world and against the spiritual forces of evil in the heavenly realms. 13 Therefore put on the full armor of God, so that when the day of evil comes, you may be able to stand your ground, and after you have done everything, to stand. 14 Stand firm then, with the belt of truth buckled around your waist, with the breastplate of righteousness in place, 15 and with your feet fitted with the readiness that comes from the gospel of peace. 16 In addition to all this, take up the shield of faith, with which you can extinguish all the flaming arrows of the evil one. 17 Take the helmet of salvation and the sword of the Spirit, which is the word of God.

18 And pray in the Spirit on all occasions with all kinds of prayers and requests. With this in mind, be alert and always keep on praying for all the Lord's people. 19 Pray also for me, that whenever I speak, words may be given me so that I will fearlessly make known the mystery of the gospel, 20 for which I am an ambassador in chains. Pray that I may declare it fearlessly, as I should.

21 Tychicus, the dear brother and faithful servant in the Lord, will tell you everything, so that you also may know how I am and what I am

[a] 31 Gen. 2:24   [b] 3 Deut. 5:16   [c] 4 Or Parents

doing. 22I am sending him to you for this very purpose, that you may know how we are, and that he may encourage you.

23Peace to the brothers and sisters,[a] and love with faith from God the Father and the Lord Jesus Christ. 24Grace to all who love our Lord Jesus Christ with an undying love.[b]

---

[a] 23 The Greek word for *brothers and sisters* (*adelphoi*) refers here to believers, both men and women, as part of God's family. [b] 24 Or *Grace and immortality to all who love our Lord Jesus Christ.*

PHILIPPIANS

On his second journey to bring the gospel to the Gentile world, the apostle Paul helped start a church in the city of Philippi (see pp. 171-173), a colony of retired Roman soldiers. The Philippians became Paul's friends and supporters for the rest of his life. When they heard that he was in Rome as a prisoner, they collected money to assist him and sent it with one of their members, a man named Epaphroditus. Later Paul sent him back with a letter to thank the Philippians for their friendship and support.

Paul knows the Philippians were experiencing a lot of opposition, so he appeals to his own life as an example of how to respond to hardship with joy. *Throughout the whole palace guard*—that is, right in the center of Caesar's realm—Paul is boldly making the royal announcement that Jesus is Lord. Paul's desire is that the Philippians will gain the same confidence and *dare all the more to proclaim the gospel without fear*.

In an amazing hymn, Paul urges the Philippians to have the servant attitude that Jesus had. He did not grasp his high position but humbled himself even to the point of death—all for the sake of others. This is the new way to be human that is revealed in God's kingdom. Our citizenship is in God's realm and so we eagerly await the Savior's return to us. Then he will transform our lowly bodies to become like his glorious resurrected body.

---

1 Paul and Timothy, servants of Christ Jesus,

To all God's holy people in Christ Jesus at Philippi, together with the overseers and deacons[a]:

2 Grace and peace to you from God our Father and the Lord Jesus Christ.

3 I thank my God every time I remember you. 4 In all my prayers for all of you, I always pray with joy 5 because of your partnership in the gospel from the first day until now, 6 being confident of this, that he who began a good work in you will carry it on to completion until the day of Christ Jesus.

7 It is right for me to feel this way about all of you, since I have you in my heart and, whether I am in chains or defending and confirming the gospel, all of you share in God's grace with me. 8 God can testify how I long for all of you with the affection of Christ Jesus.

9 And this is my prayer: that your love may abound more and more in knowledge and depth of insight, 10 so that you may be able to discern what is best and may be pure and blameless for the day of Christ, 11 filled with the fruit of righteousness that comes through Jesus Christ—to the glory and praise of God.

12 Now I want you to know, brothers and sisters,[b] that what has hap-

---

[a] 1 The word *deacons* refers here to Christians designated to serve with the overseers/elders of the church in a variety of ways; similarly in Romans 16:1 and 1 Tim. 3:8,12. [b] 12 The Greek word for *brothers and sisters* (*adelphoi*) refers here to believers, both men and women, as part of God's family; also in verse 14; and in 3:1, 13, 17; 4:1, 8, 21.

pened to me has actually served to advance the gospel. [13]As a result, it has become clear throughout the whole palace guard[a] and to everyone else that I am in chains for Christ. [14]And because of my chains, most of the brothers and sisters have become confident in the Lord and dare all the more to proclaim the gospel without fear.

[15]It is true that some preach Christ out of envy and rivalry, but others out of goodwill. [16]The latter do so out of love, knowing that I am put here for the defense of the gospel. [17]The former preach Christ out of selfish ambition, not sincerely, supposing that they can stir up trouble for me while I am in chains. [18]But what does it matter? The important thing is that in every way, whether from false motives or true, Christ is preached. And because of this I rejoice.

Yes, and I will continue to rejoice, [19]for I know that through your prayers and God's provision of the Spirit of Jesus Christ what has happened to me will turn out for my deliverance.[b] [20]I eagerly expect and hope that I will in no way be ashamed, but will have sufficient courage so that now as always Christ will be exalted in my body, whether by life or by death. [21]For to me, to live is Christ and to die is gain. [22]If I am to go on living in the body, this will mean fruitful labor for me. Yet what shall I choose? I do not know! [23]I am torn between the two: I desire to depart and be with Christ, which is better by far; [24]but it is more necessary for you that I remain in the body. [25]Convinced of this, I know that I will remain, and I will continue with all of you for your progress and joy in the faith, [26]so that through my being with you again your boasting in Christ Jesus will abound on account of me.

[27]Whatever happens, conduct yourselves in a manner worthy of the gospel of Christ. Then, whether I come and see you or only hear about you in my absence, I will know that you stand firm in the one Spirit,[c] striving together as one for the faith of the gospel [28]without being frightened in any way by those who oppose you. This is a sign to them that they will be destroyed, but that you will be saved — and that by God. [29]For it has been granted to you on behalf of Christ not only to believe in him, but also to suffer for him, [30]since you are going through the same struggle you saw I had, and now hear that I still have.

2 Therefore if you have any encouragement from being united with Christ, if any comfort from his love, if any common sharing in the Spirit, if any tenderness and compassion, [2]then make my joy complete by being like-minded, having the same love, being one in spirit and of one mind. [3]Do nothing out of selfish ambition or vain conceit. Rather, in humility value others above yourselves, [4]not looking to your own interests but each of you to the interests of the others.

[5]In your relationships with one another, have the same mindset as Christ Jesus:

[6]Who, being in very nature[d] God,
    did not consider equality with
        God something to be used
        to his own advantage;

---

[a] 13 Or *whole palace*   [b] 19 Or *vindication; or salvation*   [c] 27 Or *in one spirit*   [d] 6 Or *in the form of*

7 rather, he made himself nothing
by taking the very nature[a] of a
servant,
being made in human
likeness.
8 And being found in appearance
as a man,
he humbled himself
by becoming obedient to
death —
even death on a cross!

9 Therefore God exalted him to
the highest place
and gave him the name that is
above every name,
10 that at the name of Jesus every
knee should bow,
in heaven and on earth and
under the earth,
11 and every tongue acknowledge
that Jesus Christ is Lord,
to the glory of God the Father.

12 Therefore, my dear friends, as you have always obeyed—not only in my presence, but now much more in my absence—continue to work out your salvation with fear and trembling, 13 for it is God who works in you to will and to act in order to fulfill his good purpose.

14 Do everything without grumbling or arguing, 15 so that you may become blameless and pure, "children of God without fault in a warped and crooked generation."[b] Then you will shine among them like stars in the sky 16 as you hold firmly to the word of life. And then I will be able to boast on the day of Christ that I did not run or labor in vain. 17 But even if I am being poured out like a drink offering on the sacrifice and service coming from your faith, I am glad and rejoice with all of you. 18 So you too should be glad and rejoice with me.

19 I hope in the Lord Jesus to send Timothy to you soon, that I also may be cheered when I receive news about you. 20 I have no one else like him, who will show genuine concern for your welfare. 21 For everyone looks out for their own interests, not those of Jesus Christ. 22 But you know that Timothy has proved himself, because as a son with his father he has served with me in the work of the gospel. 23 I hope, therefore, to send him as soon as I see how things go with me. 24 And I am confident in the Lord that I myself will come soon.

25 But I think it is necessary to send back to you Epaphroditus, my brother, co-worker and fellow soldier, who is also your messenger, whom you sent to take care of my needs. 26 For he longs for all of you and is distressed because you heard he was ill. 27 Indeed he was ill, and almost died. But God had mercy on him, and not on him only but also on me, to spare me sorrow upon sorrow. 28 Therefore I am all the more eager to send him, so that when you see him again you may be glad and I may have less anxiety. 29 So then, welcome him in the Lord with great joy, and honor people like him, 30 because he almost died for the work of Christ. He risked his life to make up for the help you yourselves could not give me.

3 Further, my brothers and sisters, rejoice in the Lord! It is no trouble for me to write the same things to you again, and it is a safeguard for you. 2 Watch out for those dogs, those evildoers, those mutilators of the flesh. 3 For it is we who are the circumcision, we who serve God by

a 7 Or the form   b 15 Deut. 32:5

his Spirit, who boast in Christ Jesus, and who put no confidence in the flesh— [4]though I myself have reasons for such confidence.

If someone else thinks they have reasons to put confidence in the flesh, I have more: [5]circumcised on the eighth day, of the people of Israel, of the tribe of Benjamin, a Hebrew of Hebrews; in regard to the law, a Pharisee; [6]as for zeal, persecuting the church; as for righteousness based on the law, faultless.

[7]But whatever were gains to me I now consider loss for the sake of Christ. [8]What is more, I consider everything a loss because of the surpassing worth of knowing Christ Jesus my Lord, for whose sake I have lost all things. I consider them garbage, that I may gain Christ [9]and be found in him, not having a righteousness of my own that comes from the law, but that which is through faith in[a] Christ— the righteousness that comes from God on the basis of faith. [10]I want to know Christ—yes, to know the power of his resurrection and participation in his sufferings, becoming like him in his death, [11]and so, somehow, attaining to the resurrection from the dead.

[12]Not that I have already obtained all this, or have already arrived at my goal, but I press on to take hold of that for which Christ Jesus took hold of me. [13]Brothers and sisters, I do not consider myself yet to have taken hold of it. But one thing I do: Forgetting what is behind and straining toward what is ahead, [14]I press on toward the goal to win the prize for which God has called me heavenward in Christ Jesus.

[15]All of us, then, who are mature should take such a view of things.

And if on some point you think differently, that too God will make clear to you. [16]Only let us live up to what we have already attained.

[17]Join together in following my example, brothers and sisters, and just as you have us as a model, keep your eyes on those who live as we do. [18]For, as I have often told you before and now tell you again even with tears, many live as enemies of the cross of Christ. [19]Their destiny is destruction, their god is their stomach, and their glory is in their shame. Their mind is set on earthly things. [20]But our citizenship is in heaven. And we eagerly await a Savior from there, the Lord Jesus Christ, [21]who, by the power that enables him to bring everything under his control, will transform our lowly bodies so that they will be like his glorious body.

4 Therefore, my brothers and sisters, you whom I love and long for, my joy and crown, stand firm in the Lord in this way, dear friends!

[2]I plead with Euodia and I plead with Syntyche to be of the same mind in the Lord. [3]Yes, and I ask you, my true companion, help these women since they have contended at my side in the cause of the gospel, along with Clement and the rest of my co-workers, whose names are in the book of life.

[4]Rejoice in the Lord always. I will say it again: Rejoice! [5]Let your gentleness be evident to all. The Lord is near. [6]Do not be anxious about anything, but in every situation, by prayer and petition, with thanksgiving, present your requests to God. [7]And the peace of God, which transcends all understanding, will guard your hearts and your minds in Christ Jesus.

[a] 9 Or through the faithfulness of

[8]Finally, brothers and sisters, whatever is true, whatever is noble, whatever is right, whatever is pure, whatever is lovely, whatever is admirable—if anything is excellent or praiseworthy—think about such things. [9]Whatever you have learned or received or heard from me, or seen in me—put it into practice. And the God of peace will be with you.

[10]I rejoiced greatly in the Lord that at last you renewed your concern for me. Indeed, you were concerned, but you had no opportunity to show it. [11]I am not saying this because I am in need, for I have learned to be content whatever the circumstances. [12]I know what it is to be in need, and I know what it is to have plenty. I have learned the secret of being content in any and every situation, whether well fed or hungry, whether living in plenty or in want. [13]I can do all this through him who gives me strength.

[14]Yet it was good of you to share in my troubles. [15]Moreover, as you Philippians know, in the early days of your acquaintance with the gospel, when I set out from Macedonia, not one church shared with me in the matter of giving and receiving, except you only; [16]for even when I was in Thessalonica, you sent me aid more than once when I was in need. [17]Not that I desire your gifts; what I desire is that more be credited to your account. [18]I have received full payment and have more than enough. I am amply supplied, now that I have received from Epaphroditus the gifts you sent. They are a fragrant offering, an acceptable sacrifice, pleasing to God. [19]And my God will meet all your needs according to the riches of his glory in Christ Jesus.

[20]To our God and Father be glory for ever and ever. Amen.

[21]Greet all God's people in Christ Jesus. The brothers and sisters who are with me send greetings. [22]All God's people here send you greetings, especially those who belong to Caesar's household.

[23]The grace of the Lord Jesus Christ be with your spirit. Amen.[a]

---

[a] 23 Some manuscripts do not have *Amen*.

COLOSSIANS

While Paul was in prison in Rome, awaiting his upcoming trial before Caesar, one of the letters he wrote was to the gathering of believers in the city of Colossae. Paul had never met them, but they knew who he was and respected his leadership. Paul had worked with a man named Epaphras when he was in Ephesus. Epaphras was originally from Colossae, about 100 miles to the east. Paul sent him to bring the good news about Jesus to his city and to two other nearby cities, Laodicea and Hierapolis. Epaphras was later arrested and brought to Rome as a prisoner himself. Paul learned from him what was happening in those cities.

The Colossians were mostly Gentiles, but like the Galatians they were being pressured to follow the Jewish law and were adding extra rules and false teachings to the faith. Some of them were priding themselves on having visions and getting secret spiritual knowledge. So Paul wrote them a letter to say, "When you've got Jesus the Messiah, you've got it all!"

Paul emphasizes that all things in heaven and earth were created by the Son and were reconciled to God by the Son's death on the cross. Christ possesses the fullness of God's being. Since the Colossians have been brought into the new kingdom of light, they can live their faith to the fullest. They are to *put on the new self*, awaiting the time the Messiah will appear openly, revealing his glory.

---

1 Paul, an apostle of Christ Jesus by the will of God, and Timothy our brother,

2 To God's holy people in Colossae, the faithful brothers and sisters[a] in Christ:

Grace and peace to you from God our Father.[b]

3 We always thank God, the Father of our Lord Jesus Christ, when we pray for you, 4 because we have heard of your faith in Christ Jesus and of the love you have for all God's people— 5 the faith and love that spring from the hope stored up for you in heaven and about which you have already heard in the true message of the gospel 6 that has come to you. In the same way, the gospel is bearing fruit and growing throughout the whole world—just as it has been doing among you since the day you heard it and truly understood God's grace. 7 You learned it from Epaphras, our dear fellow servant,[c] who is a faithful minister of Christ on our[d] behalf, 8 and who also told us of your love in the Spirit.

9 For this reason, since the day we heard about you, we have not stopped praying for you. We continually ask God to fill you with the knowledge of his will through all the wisdom and understanding the Spirit gives,[e] 10 so that you may live a life worthy of the Lord and please him in every way:

---

[a] 2 The Greek word for *brothers and sisters* (*adelphoi*) refers here to believers, both men and women, as part of God's family; also in 4:15.   [b] 2 Some manuscripts *Father and the Lord Jesus Christ*   [c] 7 Or *slave*   [d] 7 Some manuscripts *your*   [e] 9 Or *all spiritual wisdom and understanding*

bearing fruit in every good work, growing in the knowledge of God, [11] being strengthened with all power according to his glorious might so that you may have great endurance and patience, [12] and giving joyful thanks to the Father, who has qualified you[a] to share in the inheritance of his holy people in the kingdom of light. [13] For he has rescued us from the dominion of darkness and brought us into the kingdom of the Son he loves, [14] in whom we have redemption, the forgiveness of sins.

[15] The Son is the image of the invisible God, the firstborn over all creation. [16] For in him all things were created: things in heaven and on earth, visible and invisible, whether thrones or powers or rulers or authorities; all things have been created through him and for him. [17] He is before all things, and in him all things hold together. [18] And he is the head of the body, the church; he is the beginning and the firstborn from among the dead, so that in everything he might have the supremacy. [19] For God was pleased to have all his fullness dwell in him, [20] and through him to reconcile to himself all things, whether things on earth or things in heaven, by making peace through his blood, shed on the cross.

[21] Once you were alienated from God and were enemies in your minds because of[b] your evil behavior. [22] But now he has reconciled you by Christ's physical body through death to present you holy in his sight, without blemish and free from accusation— [23] if you continue in your faith, established and firm, and do not move from the hope held out in the gospel. This is the gospel that you heard and that has been proclaimed to every creature under heaven, and of which I, Paul, have become a servant.

[24] Now I rejoice in what I am suffering for you, and I fill up in my flesh what is still lacking in regard to Christ's afflictions, for the sake of his body, which is the church. [25] I have become its servant by the commission God gave me to present to you the word of God in its fullness— [26] the mystery that has been kept hidden for ages and generations, but is now disclosed to the Lord's people. [27] To them God has chosen to make known among the Gentiles the glorious riches of this mystery, which is Christ in you, the hope of glory.

[28] He is the one we proclaim, admonishing and teaching everyone with all wisdom, so that we may present everyone fully mature in Christ. [29] To this end I strenuously contend with all the energy Christ so powerfully works in me.

2 I want you to know how hard I am contending for you and for those at Laodicea, and for all who have not met me personally. [2] My goal is that they may be encouraged in heart and united in love, so that they may have the full riches of complete understanding, in order that they may know the mystery of God, namely, Christ, [3] in whom are hidden all the treasures of wisdom and knowledge. [4] I tell you this so that no one may deceive you by fine-sounding arguments. [5] For though I am absent from you in body, I am present with you in spirit and delight to see how disciplined you are and how firm your faith in Christ is.

[6] So then, just as you received

---

[a] 12 Some manuscripts *us*   [b] 21 Or *minds, as shown by*

Christ Jesus as Lord, continue to live your lives in him, [7]rooted and built up in him, strengthened in the faith as you were taught, and overflowing with thankfulness.

[8]See to it that no one takes you captive through hollow and deceptive philosophy, which depends on human tradition and the elemental spiritual forces[a] of this world rather than on Christ.

[9]For in Christ all the fullness of the Deity lives in bodily form, [10]and in Christ you have been brought to fullness. He is the head over every power and authority. [11]In him you were also circumcised with a circumcision not performed by human hands. Your whole self ruled by the flesh[b] was put off when you were circumcised by[c] Christ, [12]having been buried with him in baptism, in which you were also raised with him through your faith in the working of God, who raised him from the dead.

[13]When you were dead in your sins and in the uncircumcision of your flesh, God made you[d] alive with Christ. He forgave us all our sins, [14]having canceled the charge of our legal indebtedness, which stood against us and condemned us; he has taken it away, nailing it to the cross. [15]And having disarmed the powers and authorities, he made a public spectacle of them, triumphing over them by the cross.[e]

[16]Therefore do not let anyone judge you by what you eat or drink, or with regard to a religious festival, a New Moon celebration or a Sabbath day. [17]These are a shadow of the things that were to come; the reality, however, is found in Christ. [18]Do not let anyone who delights in false humility and the worship of angels disqualify you. Such a person also goes into great detail about what they have seen; they are puffed up with idle notions by their unspiritual mind. [19]They have lost connection with the head, from whom the whole body, supported and held together by its ligaments and sinews, grows as God causes it to grow.

[20]Since you died with Christ to the elemental spiritual forces of this world, why, as though you still belonged to the world, do you submit to its rules: [21]"Do not handle! Do not taste! Do not touch!"? [22]These rules, which have to do with things that are all destined to perish with use, are based on merely human commands and teachings. [23]Such regulations indeed have an appearance of wisdom, with their self-imposed worship, their false humility and their harsh treatment of the body, but they lack any value in restraining sensual indulgence.

3 Since, then, you have been raised with Christ, set your hearts on things above, where Christ is, seated at the right hand of God. [2]Set your minds on things above, not on earthly things. [3]For you died, and your life is now hidden with Christ in God. [4]When Christ, who is your[f] life, appears, then you also will appear with him in glory.

[5]Put to death, therefore, whatever belongs to your earthly nature: sexual immorality, impurity, lust, evil desires and greed, which

---

[a] 8 Or *the basic principles*; also in verse 20   [b] 11 In contexts like this, the Greek word for *flesh* (*sarx*) refers to the sinful state of human beings, often presented as a power in opposition to the Spirit; also in verse 13.   [c] 11 Or *put off in the circumcision of*   [d] 13 Some manuscripts *us*
[e] 15 Or *them in him*   [f] 4 Some manuscripts *our*

is idolatry. ⁶Because of these, the wrath of God is coming.*ᵃ ⁷You used to walk in these ways, in the life you once lived. ⁸But now you must also rid yourselves of all such things as these: anger, rage, malice, slander, and filthy language from your lips. ⁹Do not lie to each other, since you have taken off your old self with its practices ¹⁰and have put on the new self, which is being renewed in knowledge in the image of its Creator. ¹¹Here there is no Gentile or Jew, circumcised or uncircumcised, barbarian, Scythian, slave or free, but Christ is all, and is in all.

¹²Therefore, as God's chosen people, holy and dearly loved, clothe yourselves with compassion, kindness, humility, gentleness and patience. ¹³Bear with each other and forgive one another if any of you has a grievance against someone. Forgive as the Lord forgave you. ¹⁴And over all these virtues put on love, which binds them all together in perfect unity.

¹⁵Let the peace of Christ rule in your hearts, since as members of one body you were called to peace. And be thankful. ¹⁶Let the message of Christ dwell among you richly as you teach and admonish one another with all wisdom through psalms, hymns, and songs from the Spirit, singing to God with gratitude in your hearts. ¹⁷And whatever you do, whether in word or deed, do it all in the name of the Lord Jesus, giving thanks to God the Father through him.

¹⁸Wives, submit yourselves to your husbands, as is fitting in the Lord. ¹⁹Husbands, love your wives and do not be harsh with them.

²⁰Children, obey your parents in everything, for this pleases the Lord.

²¹Fathers,ᵇ do not embitter your children, or they will become discouraged.

²²Slaves, obey your earthly masters in everything; and do it, not only when their eye is on you and to curry their favor, but with sincerity of heart and reverence for the Lord. ²³Whatever you do, work at it with all your heart, as working for the Lord, not for human masters, ²⁴since you know that you will receive an inheritance from the Lord as a reward. It is the Lord Christ you are serving. ²⁵Anyone who does wrong will be repaid for their wrongs, and there is no favoritism.

4 Masters, provide your slaves with what is right and fair, because you know that you also have a Master in heaven.

²Devote yourselves to prayer, being watchful and thankful. ³And pray for us, too, that God may open a door for our message, so that we may proclaim the mystery of Christ, for which I am in chains. ⁴Pray that I may proclaim it clearly, as I should. ⁵Be wise in the way you act toward outsiders; make the most of every opportunity. ⁶Let your conversation be always full of grace, seasoned with salt, so that you may know how to answer everyone.

⁷Tychicus will tell you all the news about me. He is a dear brother, a faithful minister and fellow servantᶜ in the Lord. ⁸I am sending him to you for the express purpose that you may know about ourᵈ circumstances and that he may encourage your hearts. ⁹He is coming

---

ᵃ 6 Some early manuscripts *coming on those who are disobedient*   ᵇ 21 Or *Parents*
ᶜ 7 Or *slave*; also in verse 12   ᵈ 8 Some manuscripts *that he may know about your*

with Onesimus, our faithful and dear brother, who is one of you. They will tell you everything that is happening here.

[10] My fellow prisoner Aristarchus sends you his greetings, as does Mark, the cousin of Barnabas. (You have received instructions about him; if he comes to you, welcome him.) [11] Jesus, who is called Justus, also sends greetings. These are the only Jews[a] among my co-workers for the kingdom of God, and they have proved a comfort to me. [12] Epaphras, who is one of you and a servant of Christ Jesus, sends greetings. He is always wrestling in prayer for you, that you may stand firm in all the will of God, mature

and fully assured. [13] I vouch for him that he is working hard for you and for those at Laodicea and Hierapolis. [14] Our dear friend Luke, the doctor, and Demas send greetings. [15] Give my greetings to the brothers and sisters at Laodicea, and to Nympha and the church in her house.

[16] After this letter has been read to you, see that it is also read in the church of the Laodiceans and that you in turn read the letter from Laodicea.

[17] Tell Archippus: "See to it that you complete the ministry you have received in the Lord."

[18] I, Paul, write this greeting in my own hand. Remember my chains. Grace be with you.

---

[a] 11 Greek *only ones of the circumcision group*

1 THESSALONIANS

Around AD 51, Paul, Silas and Timothy brought the message about Jesus the Messiah to the city of Thessalonica. Many people became believers, but there was a riot when Paul and Silas were accused of *defying Caesar's decrees, saying that there is another king, one called Jesus* (see p. 173). They narrowly escaped with their lives and had to flee.

A little later Paul became concerned that the believers in Thessalonica might fall away from the faith due to the opposition they were facing. So he sent Timothy to encourage them (as a Greek he could make the trip more safely). When Timothy returned to Achaia with the welcome news that the Thessalonians had remained faithful, Paul wrote to express his joy.

In this short letter, Paul first recalls his time in Thessalonica and gives thanks for their continuing faith, despite trials and challenges. He teaches them to avoid sexual immorality, to love one another sincerely, and to work hard to earn their own living.

Paul then addresses a key pastoral question: What is the Christian hope for those who have died? He explains that believers who die before the royal appearance of the Messiah are not lost, but will surely be raised from the dead when he comes. He reminds the Thessalonians that Jesus will appear suddenly and unexpectedly. They should therefore live in such a way that they would be unashamed to greet him. Throughout the letter Paul's basic message is, "Keep up the good work!"

1

Paul, Silas[a] and Timothy,

To the church of the Thessalonians in God the Father and the Lord Jesus Christ:

Grace and peace to you.

[2] We always thank God for all of you and continually mention you in our prayers. [3] We remember before our God and Father your work produced by faith, your labor prompted by love, and your endurance inspired by hope in our Lord Jesus Christ.

[4] For we know, brothers and sisters[b] loved by God, that he has chosen you, [5] because our gospel came to you not simply with words but also with power, with the Holy Spirit and deep conviction. You know how we lived among you for your sake. [6] You became imitators of us and of the Lord, for you welcomed the message in the midst of severe suffering with the joy given by the Holy Spirit. [7] And so you became a model to all the believers in Macedonia and Achaia. [8] The Lord's message rang out from you not only in Macedonia and Achaia—your faith in God has become known everywhere. Therefore we do not need to say anything about it, [9] for they themselves report what kind of reception you gave us. They tell how you turned to God from

---

[a] *1* Greek *Silvanus,* a variant of *Silas*   [b] *4* The Greek word for *brothers and sisters* (*adelphoi*) refers here to believers, both men and women, as part of God's family; also in 2:1, 9, 14, 17; 3:7; 4:1, 10, 13; 5:1, 4, 12, 14, 25, 27.

idols to serve the living and true God, [10] and to wait for his Son from heaven, whom he raised from the dead — Jesus, who rescues us from the coming wrath.

2 You know, brothers and sisters, that our visit to you was not without results. [2] We had previously suffered and been treated outrageously in Philippi, as you know, but with the help of our God we dared to tell you his gospel in the face of strong opposition. [3] For the appeal we make does not spring from error or impure motives, nor are we trying to trick you. [4] On the contrary, we speak as those approved by God to be entrusted with the gospel. We are not trying to please people but God, who tests our hearts. [5] You know we never used flattery, nor did we put on a mask to cover up greed — God is our witness. [6] We were not looking for praise from people, not from you or anyone else, even though as apostles of Christ we could have asserted our authority. [7] Instead, we were like young children[a] among you.

Just as a nursing mother cares for her children, [8] so we cared for you. Because we loved you so much, we were delighted to share with you not only the gospel of God but our lives as well. [9] Surely you remember, brothers and sisters, our toil and hardship; we worked night and day in order not to be a burden to anyone while we preached the gospel of God to you. [10] You are witnesses, and so is God, of how holy, righteous and blameless we were among you who believed. [11] For you know that we dealt with each of you as a father deals with his own children, [12] encouraging, comforting and urging you to live lives worthy of God, who calls you into his kingdom and glory.

[13] And we also thank God continually because, when you received the word of God, which you heard from us, you accepted it not as a human word, but as it actually is, the word of God, which is indeed at work in you who believe. [14] For you, brothers and sisters, became imitators of God's churches in Judea, which are in Christ Jesus: You suffered from your own people the same things those churches suffered from the Jews [15] who killed the Lord Jesus and the prophets and also drove us out. They displease God and are hostile to everyone [16] in their effort to keep us from speaking to the Gentiles so that they may be saved. In this way they always heap up their sins to the limit. The wrath of God has come upon them at last.[b]

[17] But, brothers and sisters, when we were orphaned by being separated from you for a short time (in person, not in thought), out of our intense longing we made every effort to see you. [18] For we wanted to come to you — certainly I, Paul, did, again and again — but Satan blocked our way. [19] For what is our hope, our joy, or the crown in which we will glory in the presence of our Lord Jesus when he comes? Is it not you? [20] Indeed, you are our glory and joy.

3 So when we could stand it no longer, we thought it best to be left by ourselves in Athens. [2] We sent Timothy, who is our brother and co-worker in God's service in spreading the gospel of Christ, to strengthen and encourage you in your faith, [3] so that no one would be unsettled by these trials. For

[a] 7 Some manuscripts were gentle   [b] 16 Or them fully

you know quite well that we are destined for them. ⁴In fact, when we were with you, we kept telling you that we would be persecuted. And it turned out that way, as you well know. ⁵For this reason, when I could stand it no longer, I sent to find out about your faith. I was afraid that in some way the tempter had tempted you and that our labors might have been in vain.

⁶But Timothy has just now come to us from you and has brought good news about your faith and love. He has told us that you always have pleasant memories of us and that you long to see us, just as we also long to see you. ⁷Therefore, brothers and sisters, in all our distress and persecution we were encouraged about you because of your faith. ⁸For now we really live, since you are standing firm in the Lord. ⁹How can we thank God enough for you in return for all the joy we have in the presence of our God because of you? ¹⁰Night and day we pray most earnestly that we may see you again and supply what is lacking in your faith.

¹¹Now may our God and Father himself and our Lord Jesus clear the way for us to come to you. ¹²May the Lord make your love increase and overflow for each other and for everyone else, just as ours does for you. ¹³May he strengthen your hearts so that you will be blameless and holy in the presence of our God and Father when our Lord Jesus comes with all his holy ones.

4 As for other matters, brothers and sisters, we instructed you how to live in order to please God, as in fact you are living. Now we ask you and urge you in the Lord Jesus to do this more and more. ²For you know what instructions we gave you by the authority of the Lord Jesus.

³It is God's will that you should be sanctified: that you should avoid sexual immorality; ⁴that each of you should learn to control your own body*ᵃ* in a way that is holy and honorable, ⁵not in passionate lust like the pagans, who do not know God; ⁶and that in this matter no one should wrong or take advantage of a brother or sister.*ᵇ* The Lord will punish all those who commit such sins, as we told you and warned you before. ⁷For God did not call us to be impure, but to live a holy life. ⁸Therefore, anyone who rejects this instruction does not reject a human being but God, the very God who gives you his Holy Spirit.

⁹Now about your love for one another we do not need to write to you, for you yourselves have been taught by God to love each other. ¹⁰And in fact, you do love all of God's family throughout Macedonia. Yet we urge you, brothers and sisters, to do so more and more, ¹¹and to make it your ambition to lead a quiet life: You should mind your own business and work with your hands, just as we told you, ¹²so that your daily life may win the respect of outsiders and so that you will not be dependent on anybody.

¹³Brothers and sisters, we do not want you to be uninformed about those who sleep in death, so that you do not grieve like the rest of mankind, who have no hope. ¹⁴For we believe that Jesus died and rose again, and so we believe that God

---

ᵃ 4 Or *learn to live with your own wife*; or *learn to acquire a wife*   *ᵇ 6* The Greek word for *brother or sister (adelphos)* refers here to a believer, whether man or woman, as part of God's family.

will bring with Jesus those who have fallen asleep in him. 15According to the Lord's word, we tell you that we who are still alive, who are left until the coming of the Lord, will certainly not precede those who have fallen asleep. 16For the Lord himself will come down from heaven, with a loud command, with the voice of the archangel and with the trumpet call of God, and the dead in Christ will rise first. 17After that, we who are still alive and are left will be caught up together with them in the clouds to meet the Lord in the air. And so we will be with the Lord forever. 18Therefore encourage one another with these words.

5 Now, brothers and sisters, about times and dates we do not need to write to you, 2for you know very well that the day of the Lord will come like a thief in the night. 3While people are saying, "Peace and safety," destruction will come on them suddenly, as labor pains on a pregnant woman, and they will not escape.

4But you, brothers and sisters, are not in darkness so that this day should surprise you like a thief. 5You are all children of the light and children of the day. We do not belong to the night or to the darkness. 6So then, let us not be like others, who are asleep, but let us be awake and sober. 7For those who sleep, sleep at night, and those who get drunk, get drunk at night. 8But since we belong to the day, let us be sober, putting on faith and love as a breastplate, and the hope of salvation as a helmet. 9For God did not appoint us to suffer wrath but to receive salvation through our

Lord Jesus Christ. 10He died for us so that, whether we are awake or asleep, we may live together with him. 11Therefore encourage one another and build each other up, just as in fact you are doing.

12Now we ask you, brothers and sisters, to acknowledge those who work hard among you, who care for you in the Lord and who admonish you. 13Hold them in the highest regard in love because of their work. Live in peace with each other. 14And we urge you, brothers and sisters, warn those who are idle and disruptive, encourage the disheartened, help the weak, be patient with everyone. 15Make sure that nobody pays back wrong for wrong, but always strive to do what is good for each other and for everyone else.

16Rejoice always, 17pray continually, 18give thanks in all circumstances; for this is God's will for you in Christ Jesus.

19Do not quench the Spirit. 20Do not treat prophecies with contempt 21but test them all; hold on to what is good, 22reject every kind of evil.

23May God himself, the God of peace, sanctify you through and through. May your whole spirit, soul and body be kept blameless at the coming of our Lord Jesus Christ. 24The one who calls you is faithful, and he will do it.

25Brothers and sisters, pray for us. 26Greet all God's people with a holy kiss. 27I charge you before the Lord to have this letter read to all the brothers and sisters.

28The grace of our Lord Jesus Christ be with you.

2 THESSALONIANS

Apparently only shortly after writing his first letter to the Thessalonians, Paul had to write again to correct a false report that he had said the day of the Lord had already come. The *day of the Lord* was a phrase from the Hebrew prophets to describe God's key victory over every opponent, when his faithful ones would be rewarded. The Thessalonians' concern seems to have been not that the day had come and gone and they had missed it, but that it was now present. That would mean nothing more was to be expected from God in terms of setting things right. Since they continued to suffer persecutions, this was a depressing prospect.

Even before he contradicts this false report, Paul reassures the Thessalonians that God will indeed pay back all those who were troubling them. He reminds them of the details he had discussed with them in person of how the day of the Lord would arrive. He then repeats some instruction from his earlier letter, urging them not to be idle but to work hard and earn their own livings.

At the end of the letter, most of which would have been written by a scribe, Paul adds a greeting in his own handwriting. He wants them to know for sure this teaching is really coming from him!

---

1 Paul, Silas[a] and Timothy,

To the church of the Thessalonians in God our Father and the Lord Jesus Christ:

[2] Grace and peace to you from God the Father and the Lord Jesus Christ.

[3] We ought always to thank God for you, brothers and sisters,[b] and rightly so, because your faith is growing more and more, and the love all of you have for one another is increasing. [4] Therefore, among God's churches we boast about your perseverance and faith in all the persecutions and trials you are enduring.

[5] All this is evidence that God's judgment is right, and as a result you will be counted worthy of the kingdom of God, for which you are suffering. [6] God is just: He will pay back trouble to those who trouble you [7] and give relief to you who are troubled, and to us as well. This will happen when the Lord Jesus is revealed from heaven in blazing fire with his powerful angels. [8] He will punish those who do not know God and do not obey the gospel of our Lord Jesus. [9] They will be punished with everlasting destruction and shut out from the presence of the Lord and from the glory of his might [10] on the day he comes to be glorified in his holy people and to be marveled at among all those who have believed. This includes you, because you believed our testimony to you.

[11] With this in mind, we constantly pray for you, that our God may make you worthy of his calling, and

---

[a] 1 Greek *Silvanus*, a variant of *Silas* [b] 3 The Greek word for *brothers and sisters (adelphoi)* refers here to believers, both men and women, as part of God's family; also in 2:1, 13, 15; 3:1, 6, 13.

that by his power he may bring to fruition your every desire for goodness and your every deed prompted by faith. 12We pray this so that the name of our Lord Jesus may be glorified in you, and you in him, according to the grace of our God and the Lord Jesus Christ.*a*

2 Concerning the coming of our Lord Jesus Christ and our being gathered to him, we ask you, brothers and sisters, 2not to become easily unsettled or alarmed by the teaching allegedly from us—whether by a prophecy or by word of mouth or by letter—asserting that the day of the Lord has already come. 3Don't let anyone deceive you in any way, for that day will not come until the rebellion occurs and the man of lawlessness*b* is revealed, the man doomed to destruction. 4He will oppose and will exalt himself over everything that is called God or is worshiped, so that he sets himself up in God's temple, proclaiming himself to be God.

5Don't you remember that when I was with you I used to tell you these things? 6And now you know what is holding him back, so that he may be revealed at the proper time. 7For the secret power of lawlessness is already at work; but the one who now holds it back will continue to do so till he is taken out of the way. 8And then the lawless one will be revealed, whom the Lord Jesus will overthrow with the breath of his mouth and destroy by the splendor of his coming. 9The coming of the lawless one will be in accordance with how Satan works. He will use all sorts of displays of power through signs and wonders that serve the lie, 10and all the ways

that wickedness deceives those who are perishing. They perish because they refused to love the truth and so be saved. 11For this reason God sends them a powerful delusion so that they will believe the lie 12and so that all will be condemned who have not believed the truth but have delighted in wickedness.

13But we ought always to thank God for you, brothers and sisters loved by the Lord, because God chose you as firstfruits*c* to be saved through the sanctifying work of the Spirit and through belief in the truth. 14He called you to this through our gospel, that you might share in the glory of our Lord Jesus Christ.

15So then, brothers and sisters, stand firm and hold fast to the teachings*d* we passed on to you, whether by word of mouth or by letter.

16May our Lord Jesus Christ himself and God our Father, who loved us and by his grace gave us eternal encouragement and good hope, 17encourage your hearts and strengthen you in every good deed and word.

3 As for other matters, brothers and sisters, pray for us that the message of the Lord may spread rapidly and be honored, just as it was with you. 2And pray that we may be delivered from wicked and evil people, for not everyone has faith. 3But the Lord is faithful, and he will strengthen you and protect you from the evil one. 4We have confidence in the Lord that you are doing and will continue to do the things we command. 5May the Lord direct your hearts into God's love and Christ's perseverance.

---

a 12 Or *God and Lord, Jesus Christ*   *b 3* Some manuscripts *sin*   *c 13* Some manuscripts
because from the beginning God chose you   *d 15* Or *traditions*

6In the name of the Lord Jesus Christ, we command you, brothers and sisters, to keep away from every believer who is idle and disruptive and does not live according to the teaching[a] you received from us. 7For you yourselves know how you ought to follow our example. We were not idle when we were with you, 8nor did we eat anyone's food without paying for it. On the contrary, we worked night and day, laboring and toiling so that we would not be a burden to any of you. 9We did this, not because we do not have the right to such help, but in order to offer ourselves as a model for you to imitate. 10For even when we were with you, we gave you this rule: "The one who is unwilling to work shall not eat."

11We hear that some among you are idle and disruptive. They are not busy; they are busybodies. 12Such people we command and urge in the Lord Jesus Christ to settle down and earn the food they eat. 13And as for you, brothers and sisters, never tire of doing what is good.

14Take special note of anyone who does not obey our instruction in this letter. Do not associate with them, in order that they may feel ashamed. 15Yet do not regard them as an enemy, but warn them as you would a fellow believer.

16Now may the Lord of peace himself give you peace at all times and in every way. The Lord be with all of you.

17I, Paul, write this greeting in my own hand, which is the distinguishing mark in all my letters. This is how I write.

18The grace of our Lord Jesus Christ be with you all.

a 6 Or tradition

1 TIMOTHY

After Paul was released from prison in Rome, he discovered that leaders in the Ephesian church had distorted the genuine message they had first heard from Paul himself. They had misapplied certain Jewish practices and borrowed some others from the philosophies of the day. They restricted certain foods, forbade marriage and stressed controversial speculations as the path to spiritual progress. At the same time, they tolerated immoral behavior. So Paul sent his co-worker Timothy to Ephesus and wrote him a letter, which he was expected to share with the church. He hoped it would give Timothy the power and influence to set things in order until Paul could get to Ephesus himself.

Paul's focus is on what true leadership in the church looks like. This would help the Ephesians reject those who weren't qualified and replace them with those who were. Paul includes a special warning toward the end of his letter about the dangers of greed, which seemed to be at the root of their problems.

Throughout the letter Paul uses the phrase *Christ Jesus*—that is, Messiah Jesus—which emphasizes the kingly rule of Jesus. This helped remind the church that Jesus is their real leader and is the clearest model of authentic leadership.

1 Paul, an apostle of Christ Jesus by the command of God our Savior and of Christ Jesus our hope,

2 To Timothy my true son in the faith:

Grace, mercy and peace from God the Father and Christ Jesus our Lord.

3 As I urged you when I went into Macedonia, stay there in Ephesus so that you may command certain people not to teach false doctrines any longer 4 or to devote themselves to myths and endless genealogies. Such things promote controversial speculations rather than advancing God's work—which is by faith. 5 The goal of this command is love, which comes from a pure heart and a good conscience and a sincere faith. 6 Some have departed from these and have turned to meaningless talk. 7 They want to be teachers of the law, but they do not know what they are talking about or what they so confidently affirm.

8 We know that the law is good if one uses it properly. 9 We also know that the law is made not for the righteous but for lawbreakers and rebels, the ungodly and sinful, the unholy and irreligious, for those who kill their fathers or mothers, for murderers, 10 for the sexually immoral, for those practicing homosexuality, for slave traders and liars and perjurers—and for whatever else is contrary to the sound doctrine 11 that conforms to the gospel concerning the glory of the blessed God, which he entrusted to me.

12 I thank Christ Jesus our Lord, who has given me strength, that he considered me trustworthy, appointing me to his service. 13 Even though I was once a blasphemer and a persecutor and a violent

man, I was shown mercy because I acted in ignorance and unbelief. [14]The grace of our Lord was poured out on me abundantly, along with the faith and love that are in Christ Jesus.

[15]Here is a trustworthy saying that deserves full acceptance: Christ Jesus came into the world to save sinners—of whom I am the worst. [16]But for that very reason I was shown mercy so that in me, the worst of sinners, Christ Jesus might display his immense patience as an example for those who would believe in him and receive eternal life. [17]Now to the King eternal, immortal, invisible, the only God, be honor and glory for ever and ever. Amen.

[18]Timothy, my son, I am giving you this command in keeping with the prophecies once made about you, so that by recalling them you may fight the battle well, [19]holding on to faith and a good conscience, which some have rejected and so have suffered shipwreck with regard to the faith. [20]Among them are Hymenaeus and Alexander, whom I have handed over to Satan to be taught not to blaspheme.

2 I urge, then, first of all, that petitions, prayers, intercession and thanksgiving be made for all people—[2]for kings and all those in authority, that we may live peaceful and quiet lives in all godliness and holiness. [3]This is good, and pleases God our Savior, [4]who wants all people to be saved and to come to a knowledge of the truth. [5]For there is one God and one mediator between God and mankind, the man Christ Jesus, [6]who gave himself as a ransom for all people. This has

now been witnessed to at the proper time. [7]And for this purpose I was appointed a herald and an apostle—I am telling the truth, I am not lying—and a true and faithful teacher of the Gentiles.

[8]Therefore I want the men everywhere to pray, lifting up holy hands without anger or disputing. [9]I also want the women to dress modestly, with decency and propriety, adorning themselves, not with elaborate hairstyles or gold or pearls or expensive clothes, [10]but with good deeds, appropriate for women who profess to worship God.

[11]A woman[a] should learn in quietness and full submission. [12]I do not permit a woman to teach or to assume authority over a man;[b] she must be quiet. [13]For Adam was formed first, then Eve. [14]And Adam was not the one deceived; it was the woman who was deceived and became a sinner. [15]But women[c] will be saved through childbearing—if they continue in faith, love and holiness with propriety.

3 Here is a trustworthy saying: Whoever aspires to be an overseer desires a noble task. [2]Now the overseer is to be above reproach, faithful to his wife, temperate, self-controlled, respectable, hospitable, able to teach, [3]not given to drunkenness, not violent but gentle, not quarrelsome, not a lover of money. [4]He must manage his own family well and see that his children obey him, and he must do so in a manner worthy of full[d] respect. [5](If anyone does not know how to manage his own family, how can he take care of God's church?) [6]He must not be a recent convert, or he may become conceited and fall under the same

---

[a] 11 Or wife; also in verse 12　[b] 12 Or over her husband　[c] 15 Greek she　[d] 4 Or him with proper

judgment as the devil. ⁷He must also be worthy of respect with outsiders, so that he will not fall into disgrace and into the devil's trap.

⁸In the same way, deacons*a* are to be worthy of respect, sincere, not indulging in much wine, and not pursuing dishonest gain. ⁹They must keep hold of the deep truths of the faith with a clear conscience. ¹⁰They must first be tested; and then if there is nothing against them, let them serve as deacons.

¹¹In the same way, the women*b* are to be worthy of respect, not malicious talkers but temperate and trustworthy in everything.

¹²A deacon must be faithful to his wife and must manage his children and his household well. ¹³Those who have served well gain an excellent standing and great assurance in their faith in Christ Jesus.

¹⁴Although I hope to come to you soon, I am writing you these instructions so that, ¹⁵if I am delayed, you will know how people ought to conduct themselves in God's household, which is the church of the living God, the pillar and foundation of the truth. ¹⁶Beyond all question, the mystery from which true godliness springs is great:

He appeared in the flesh,
    was vindicated by the Spirit,*c*
was seen by angels,
    was preached among the
        nations,
was believed on in the world,
    was taken up in glory.

4 The Spirit clearly says that in later times some will abandon the faith and follow deceiving spirits and things taught by demons. ²Such teachings come through hypocritical liars, whose consciences have been seared as with a hot iron. ³They forbid people to marry and order them to abstain from certain foods, which God created to be received with thanksgiving by those who believe and who know the truth. ⁴For everything God created is good, and nothing is to be rejected if it is received with thanksgiving, ⁵because it is consecrated by the word of God and prayer.

⁶If you point these things out to the brothers and sisters,*d* you will be a good minister of Christ Jesus, nourished on the truths of the faith and of the good teaching that you have followed. ⁷Have nothing to do with godless myths and old wives' tales; rather, train yourself to be godly. ⁸For physical training is of some value, but godliness has value for all things, holding promise for both the present life and the life to come. ⁹This is a trustworthy saying that deserves full acceptance. ¹⁰That is why we labor and strive, because we have put our hope in the living God, who is the Savior of all people, and especially of those who believe.

¹¹Command and teach these things. ¹²Don't let anyone look down on you because you are young, but set an example for the believers in speech, in conduct, in love, in faith and in purity. ¹³Until I come, devote yourself to the public reading of Scripture, to preaching

---

a 8 The word *deacons* refers here to Christians designated to serve with the overseers/elders of the church in a variety of ways; similarly in verse 12; and in Romans 16:1 and Phil. 1:1.   *b 11* Possibly deacons' wives or women who are deacons   *c 16* Or *vindicated in spirit*
d 6 The Greek word for *brothers and sisters* (*adelphoi*) refers here to believers, both men and women, as part of God's family.

and to teaching. 14Do not neglect your gift, which was given you through prophecy when the body of elders laid their hands on you.

15Be diligent in these matters; give yourself wholly to them, so that everyone may see your progress. 16Watch your life and doctrine closely. Persevere in them, because if you do, you will save both yourself and your hearers.

5 Do not rebuke an older man harshly, but exhort him as if he were your father. Treat younger men as brothers, 2older women as mothers, and younger women as sisters, with absolute purity.

3Give proper recognition to those widows who are really in need. 4But if a widow has children or grandchildren, these should learn first of all to put their religion into practice by caring for their own family and so repaying their parents and grandparents, for this is pleasing to God. 5The widow who is really in need and left all alone puts her hope in God and continues night and day to pray and to ask God for help. 6But the widow who lives for pleasure is dead even while she lives. 7Give the people these instructions, so that no one may be open to blame. 8Anyone who does not provide for his relatives, and especially for their own household, has denied the faith and is worse than an unbeliever.

9No widow may be put on the list of widows unless she is over sixty, has been faithful to her husband, 10and is well known for her good deeds, such as bringing up children, showing hospitality, washing the feet of the Lord's people, helping those in trouble and devoting herself to all kinds of good deeds.

11As for younger widows, do not put them on such a list. For when their sensual desires overcome their dedication to Christ, they want to marry. 12Thus they bring judgment on themselves, because they have broken their first pledge. 13Besides, they get into the habit of being idle and going about from house to house. And not only do they become idlers, but also busybodies who talk nonsense, saying things they ought not to. 14So I counsel younger widows to marry, to have children, to manage their homes and to give the enemy no opportunity for slander. 15Some have in fact already turned away to follow Satan.

16If any woman who is a believer has widows in her care, she should continue to help them and not let the church be burdened with them, so that the church can help those widows who are really in need.

17The elders who direct the affairs of the church well are worthy of double honor, especially those whose work is preaching and teaching. 18For Scripture says, "Do not muzzle an ox while it is treading out the grain,"[a] and "The worker deserves his wages."[b] 19Do not entertain an accusation against an elder unless it is brought by two or three witnesses. 20But those elders who are sinning you are to reprove before everyone, so that the others may take warning. 21I charge you, in the sight of God and Christ Jesus and the elect angels, to keep these instructions without partiality, and to do nothing out of favoritism.

22Do not be hasty in the laying on of hands, and do not share in

---

[a] 18 Deut. 25:4   [b] 18 Luke 10:7

the sins of others. Keep yourself pure.

23Stop drinking only water, and use a little wine because of your stomach and your frequent illnesses.

24The sins of some are obvious, reaching the place of judgment ahead of them; the sins of others trail behind them. 25In the same way, good deeds are obvious, and even those that are not obvious cannot remain hidden forever.

6 All who are under the yoke of slavery should consider their masters worthy of full respect, so that God's name and our teaching may not be slandered. 2Those who have believing masters should not show them disrespect just because they are fellow believers. Instead, they should serve them even better because their masters are dear to them as fellow believers and are devoted to the welfare*a* of their slaves.

These are the things you are to teach and insist on. 3If anyone teaches otherwise and does not agree to the sound instruction of our Lord Jesus Christ and to godly teaching, 4they are conceited and understand nothing. They have an unhealthy interest in controversies and quarrels about words that result in envy, strife, malicious talk, evil suspicions 5and constant friction between people of corrupt mind, who have been robbed of the truth and who think that godliness is a means to financial gain.

6But godliness with contentment is great gain. 7For we brought nothing into the world, and we can take nothing out of it. 8But if we have food and clothing, we will be content with that. 9Those who want

to get rich fall into temptation and a trap and into many foolish and harmful desires that plunge people into ruin and destruction. 10For the love of money is a root of all kinds of evil. Some people, eager for money, have wandered from the faith and pierced themselves with many griefs.

11But you, man of God, flee from all this, and pursue righteousness, godliness, faith, love, endurance and gentleness. 12Fight the good fight of the faith. Take hold of the eternal life to which you were called when you made your good confession in the presence of many witnesses. 13In the sight of God, who gives life to everything, and of Christ Jesus, who while testifying before Pontius Pilate made the good confession, I charge you 14to keep this command without spot or blame until the appearing of our Lord Jesus Christ, 15which God will bring about in his own time—God, the blessed and only Ruler, the King of kings and Lord of lords, 16who alone is immortal and who lives in unapproachable light, whom no one has seen or can see. To him be honor and might forever. Amen.

17Command those who are rich in this present world not to be arrogant nor to put their hope in wealth, which is so uncertain, but to put their hope in God, who richly provides us with everything for our enjoyment. 18Command them to do good, to be rich in good deeds, and to be generous and willing to share. 19In this way they will lay up treasure for themselves as a firm foundation for the coming age, so

---

a 2 Or and benefit from the service

that they may take hold of the life that is truly life.

[20]Timothy, guard what has been entrusted to your care. Turn away from godless chatter and the opposing ideas of what is falsely called knowledge, [21]which some have professed and in so doing have departed from the faith.

Grace be with you all.

2 TIMOTHY

Paul left his co-worker Timothy in the city of Ephesus to deal with some renegade leaders in the church there. When Timothy struggled, however, Paul went back to Ephesus. Once there, Paul suffered a *great deal of harm* from Alexander, one of these leaders, and he was once again imprisoned and taken to Rome. He expected that this time he would be tried and executed. Paul wrote to Timothy to ask him to come to Rome quickly.

Things in Ephesus had not gone as Paul or Timothy expected. Paul had ordered both Alexander and Hymenaeus to step down from leadership, but they were continuing to oppose Paul. Others had joined them, and they were still misdirecting people into a corrupted version of the faith that stressed debate and dissension rather than purity and obedience. Timothy was discouraged and intimidated. Paul's letter includes challenges to stay faithful to the true message—even if this meant suffering or death. Paul reminds Timothy that in the days before the open appearance of Jesus as king, there will be lots of trouble. False teachers, treacherous and insincere people, persecutions and more will all challenge the faithfulness of God's people.

Paul urges Timothy to remember the gospel message: *Jesus Christ, raised from the dead, descended from David*. He points out that the sacred writings Timothy has known since he was a child are God-breathed, and will help him continue in doing good work.

---

1 Paul, an apostle of Christ Jesus by the will of God, in keeping with the promise of life that is in Christ Jesus,

2 To Timothy, my dear son:

Grace, mercy and peace from God the Father and Christ Jesus our Lord.

3 I thank God, whom I serve, as my ancestors did, with a clear conscience, as night and day I constantly remember you in my prayers. 4 Recalling your tears, I long to see you, so that I may be filled with joy. 5 I am reminded of your sincere faith, which first lived in your grandmother Lois and in your mother Eunice and, I am persuaded, now lives in you also.

6 For this reason I remind you to fan into flame the gift of God, which is in you through the laying on of my hands. 7 For the Spirit God gave us does not make us timid, but gives us power, love and self-discipline. 8 So do not be ashamed of the testimony about our Lord or of me his prisoner. Rather, join with me in suffering for the gospel, by the power of God. 9 He has saved us and called us to a holy life — not because of anything we have done but because of his own purpose and grace. This grace was given us in Christ Jesus before the beginning of time, 10 but it has now been revealed through the appearing of our Savior, Christ Jesus, who has destroyed death and has brought life and immortality to light through the gospel. 11 And of this gospel I was appointed a herald and an apostle and a teacher. 12 That is why I am suffering as I am.

Yet this is no cause for shame, because I know whom I have believed, and am convinced that he is able to guard what I have entrusted to him until that day.

13 What you heard from me, keep as the pattern of sound teaching, with faith and love in Christ Jesus. 14 Guard the good deposit that was entrusted to you—guard it with the help of the Holy Spirit who lives in us.

15 You know that everyone in the province of Asia has deserted me, including Phygelus and Hermogenes.

16 May the Lord show mercy to the household of Onesiphorus, because he often refreshed me and was not ashamed of my chains. 17 On the contrary, when he was in Rome, he searched hard for me until he found me. 18 May the Lord grant that he will find mercy from the Lord on that day! You know very well in how many ways he helped me in Ephesus.

2 You then, my son, be strong in the grace that is in Christ Jesus. 2 And the things you have heard me say in the presence of many witnesses entrust to reliable people who will also be qualified to teach others. 3 Join with me in suffering, like a good soldier of Christ Jesus. 4 No one serving as a soldier gets entangled in civilian affairs, but rather tries to please his commanding officer. 5 Similarly, anyone who competes as an athlete does not receive the victor's crown except by competing according to the rules. 6 The hardworking farmer should be the first to receive a share of the crops. 7 Reflect on what I am saying, for the Lord will give you insight into all this.

8 Remember Jesus Christ, raised from the dead, descended from David. This is my gospel, 9 for which I am suffering even to the point of being chained like a criminal. But God's word is not chained. 10 Therefore I endure everything for the sake of the elect, that they too may obtain the salvation that is in Christ Jesus, with eternal glory.

11 Here is a trustworthy saying:

If we died with him,
  we will also live with him;
12 if we endure,
  we will also reign with him.
If we disown him,
  he will also disown us;
13 if we are faithless,
  he remains faithful,
  for he cannot disown himself.

14 Keep reminding God's people of these things. Warn them before God against quarreling about words; it is of no value, and only ruins those who listen. 15 Do your best to present yourself to God as one approved, a worker who does not need to be ashamed and who correctly handles the word of truth. 16 Avoid godless chatter, because those who indulge in it will become more and more ungodly. 17 Their teaching will spread like gangrene. Among them are Hymenaeus and Philetus, 18 who have departed from the truth. They say that the resurrection has already taken place, and they destroy the faith of some. 19 Nevertheless, God's solid foundation stands firm, sealed with this inscription: "The Lord knows those who are his," and, "Everyone who confesses the name of the Lord must turn away from wickedness."

20 In a large house there are articles not only of gold and silver, but also of wood and clay; some are for special purposes and some for

common use. 21 Those who cleanse themselves from the latter will be instruments for special purposes, made holy, useful to the Master and prepared to do any good work.

22 Flee the evil desires of youth and pursue righteousness, faith, love and peace, along with those who call on the Lord out of a pure heart. 23 Don't have anything to do with foolish and stupid arguments, because you know they produce quarrels. 24 And the Lord's servant must not be quarrelsome but must be kind to everyone, able to teach, not resentful. 25 Opponents must be gently instructed, in the hope that God will grant them repentance leading them to a knowledge of the truth, 26 and that they will come to their senses and escape from the trap of the devil, who has taken them captive to do his will.

3 But mark this: There will be terrible times in the last days. 2 People will be lovers of themselves, lovers of money, boastful, proud, abusive, disobedient to their parents, ungrateful, unholy, 3 without love, unforgiving, slanderous, without self-control, brutal, not lovers of the good, 4 treacherous, rash, conceited, lovers of pleasure rather than lovers of God— 5 having a form of godliness but denying its power. Have nothing to do with such people.

6 They are the kind who worm their way into homes and gain control over gullible women, who are loaded down with sins and are swayed by all kinds of evil desires, 7 always learning but never able to come to a knowledge of the truth. 8 Just as Jannes and Jambres opposed Moses, so also these teachers oppose the truth. They are men of depraved minds, who, as far as the faith is concerned, are rejected. 9 But they will not get very far because, as in the case of those men, their folly will be clear to everyone.

10 You, however, know all about my teaching, my way of life, my purpose, faith, patience, love, endurance, 11 persecutions, sufferings—what kinds of things happened to me in Antioch, Iconium and Lystra, the persecutions I endured. Yet the Lord rescued me from all of them. 12 In fact, everyone who wants to live a godly life in Christ Jesus will be persecuted, 13 while evildoers and impostors will go from bad to worse, deceiving and being deceived. 14 But as for you, continue in what you have learned and have become convinced of, because you know those from whom you learned it, 15 and how from infancy you have known the Holy Scriptures, which are able to make you wise for salvation through faith in Christ Jesus. 16 All Scripture is God-breathed and is useful for teaching, rebuking, correcting and training in righteousness, 17 so that the servant of God*a* may be thoroughly equipped for every good work.

4 In the presence of God and of Christ Jesus, who will judge the living and the dead, and in view of his appearing and his kingdom, I give you this charge: 2 Preach the word; be prepared in season and out of season; correct, rebuke and encourage—with great patience and careful instruction. 3 For the time will come when people will not put up with sound doctrine. Instead, to suit their own desires, they will gather around them a great number

---

a 17 Or that you, a man of God,

of teachers to say what their itching ears want to hear. [4] They will turn their ears away from the truth and turn aside to myths. [5] But you, keep your head in all situations, endure hardship, do the work of an evangelist, discharge all the duties of your ministry.

[6] For I am already being poured out like a drink offering, and the time for my departure is near. [7] I have fought the good fight, I have finished the race, I have kept the faith. [8] Now there is in store for me the crown of righteousness, which the Lord, the righteous Judge, will award to me on that day—and not only to me, but also to all who have longed for his appearing.

[9] Do your best to come to me quickly, [10] for Demas, because he loved this world, has deserted me and has gone to Thessalonica. Crescens has gone to Galatia, and Titus to Dalmatia. [11] Only Luke is with me. Get Mark and bring him with you, because he is helpful to me in my ministry. [12] I sent Tychicus to Ephesus. [13] When you come, bring the cloak that I left with Car-

pus at Troas, and my scrolls, especially the parchments.

[14] Alexander the metalworker did me a great deal of harm. The Lord will repay him for what he has done. [15] You too should be on your guard against him, because he strongly opposed our message.

[16] At my first defense, no one came to my support, but everyone deserted me. May it not be held against them. [17] But the Lord stood at my side and gave me strength, so that through me the message might be fully proclaimed and all the Gentiles might hear it. And I was delivered from the lion's mouth. [18] The Lord will rescue me from every evil attack and will bring me safely to his heavenly kingdom. To him be glory for ever and ever. Amen.

[19] Greet Priscilla[a] and Aquila and the household of Onesiphorus. [20] Erastus stayed in Corinth, and I left Trophimus sick in Miletus. [21] Do your best to get here before winter. Eubulus greets you, and so do Pudens, Linus, Claudia and all the brothers and sisters.[b]

[22] The Lord be with your spirit. Grace be with you all.

---

[a] 19 Greek Prisca, a variant of Priscilla   [b] 21 The Greek word for brothers and sisters (adelphoi) refers here to believers, both men and women, as part of God's family.

TITUS

After the apostle Paul was released from prison in Rome, he discovered that renegade leaders were preying on the people of the church he had founded in Ephesus. He therefore left his long-time co-worker Timothy in that city with a letter authorizing him to replace these leaders and restore order. A similar situation on the island of Crete required Paul to commission another long-time co-worker, Titus, to act as his representative there.

Paul's letter is addressed to Titus, but it is meant for the larger church as well. He confers his own authority on Titus and instructs him to appoint godly leaders. Paul's description of the false teaching matches that in Ephesus: a combination of selective Jewish observances (such as being circumcised and abstaining from certain foods) and the pursuit of controversial speculations. However, the teaching didn't help people live purer lives. Paul tells the community that *the grace of God has appeared that offers salvation to all people.* It is the true message about Jesus that helps God's people live a new kind of life.

Paul reveals his plan to spend the winter in Nicopolis, a city on the west coast of Macedonia. It would provide an excellent jumping-off point for bringing the gospel to the western part of the empire. He trusts that Titus will help restore order in Crete so he can accompany Paul on this new venture.

---

1 Paul, a servant of God and an apostle of Jesus Christ to further the faith of God's elect and their knowledge of the truth that leads to godliness — ²in the hope of eternal life, which God, who does not lie, promised before the beginning of time, ³and which now at his appointed season he has brought to light through the preaching entrusted to me by the command of God our Savior,

⁴To Titus, my true son in our common faith:

Grace and peace from God the Father and Christ Jesus our Savior.

⁵The reason I left you in Crete was that you might put in order what was left unfinished and appoint[a] elders in every town, as I directed you. ⁶An elder must be blameless, faithful to his wife, a man whose children believe[b] and are not open to the charge of being wild and disobedient. ⁷Since an overseer manages God's household, he must be blameless — not overbearing, not quick-tempered, not given to drunkenness, not violent, not pursuing dishonest gain. ⁸Rather, he must be hospitable, one who loves what is good, who is self-controlled, upright, holy and disciplined. ⁹He must hold firmly to the trustworthy message as it has been taught, so that he can encourage others by sound doctrine and refute those who oppose it.

¹⁰For there are many rebellious people, full of meaningless talk

---

and deception, especially those of the circumcision group. [11]They must be silenced, because they are disrupting whole households by teaching things they ought not to teach—and that for the sake of dishonest gain. [12]One of Crete's own prophets has said it: "Cretans are always liars, evil brutes, lazy gluttons."[a] [13]This saying is true. Therefore rebuke them sharply, so that they will be sound in the faith [14]and will pay no attention to Jewish myths or to the merely human commands of those who reject the truth. [15]To the pure, all things are pure, but to those who are corrupted and do not believe, nothing is pure. In fact, both their minds and consciences are corrupted. [16]They claim to know God, but by their actions they deny him. They are detestable, disobedient and unfit for doing anything good.

2 You, however, must teach what is appropriate to sound doctrine. [2]Teach the older men to be temperate, worthy of respect, self-controlled, and sound in faith, in love and in endurance.

[3]Likewise, teach the older women to be reverent in the way they live, not to be slanderers or addicted to much wine, but to teach what is good. [4]Then they can urge the younger women to love their husbands and children, [5]to be self-controlled and pure, to be busy at home, to be kind, and to be subject to their husbands, so that no one will malign the word of God.

[6]Similarly, encourage the young men to be self-controlled. [7]In everything set them an example by doing what is good. In your teaching show integrity, seriousness [8]and soundness of speech that can-

not be condemned, so that those who oppose you may be ashamed because they have nothing bad to say about us.

[9]Teach slaves to be subject to their masters in everything, to try to please them, not to talk back to them, [10]and not to steal from them, but to show that they can be fully trusted, so that in every way they will make the teaching about God our Savior attractive.

[11]For the grace of God has appeared that offers salvation to all people. [12]It teaches us to say "No" to ungodliness and worldly passions, and to live self-controlled, upright and godly lives in this present age, [13]while we wait for the blessed hope—the appearing of the glory of our great God and Savior, Jesus Christ, [14]who gave himself for us to redeem us from all wickedness and to purify for himself a people that are his very own, eager to do what is good.

[15]These, then, are the things you should teach. Encourage and rebuke with all authority. Do not let anyone despise you.

3 Remind the people to be subject to rulers and authorities, to be obedient, to be ready to do whatever is good, [2]to slander no one, to be peaceable and considerate, and always to be gentle toward everyone.

[3]At one time we too were foolish, disobedient, deceived and enslaved by all kinds of passions and pleasures. We lived in malice and envy, being hated and hating one another. [4]But when the kindness and love of God our Savior appeared, [5]he saved us, not because of righteous things we had done, but because of his mercy. He saved us through the washing of rebirth

---

[a] 12 From the Cretan philosopher Epimenides

and renewal by the Holy Spirit, ⁶whom he poured out on us generously through Jesus Christ our Savior, ⁷so that, having been justified by his grace, we might become heirs having the hope of eternal life. ⁸This is a trustworthy saying. And I want you to stress these things, so that those who have trusted in God may be careful to devote themselves to doing what is good. These things are excellent and profitable for everyone.

⁹But avoid foolish controversies and genealogies and arguments and quarrels about the law, because these are unprofitable and useless. ¹⁰Warn a divisive person once, and then warn them a second time. After that, have nothing to do with them. ¹¹You may be sure that such people are warped and sinful; they are self-condemned.

¹²As soon as I send Artemas or Tychicus to you, do your best to come to me at Nicopolis, because I have decided to winter there. ¹³Do everything you can to help Zenas the lawyer and Apollos on their way and see that they have everything they need. ¹⁴Our people must learn to devote themselves to doing what is good, in order to provide for urgent needs and not live unproductive lives.

¹⁵Everyone with me sends you greetings. Greet those who love us in the faith.

Grace be with you all.

PHILEMON

One of the people Paul chose to deliver the letters we know as Colossians and Ephesians was a man named Onesimus. Onesimus was originally from Colossae, and would have been known to the people there. But Paul was compelled to write a separate letter for him. This was because Onesimus had been the slave of a wealthy Colossian named Philemon, in whose home the church met. Onesimus had run away, probably robbing Philemon in the process. In Rome he had become a follower of Jesus. He'd been helping Paul in prison, but now Paul needed him to return to Colossae. Paul's hope was that Philemon would not only forgive Onesimus, but welcome him as a brother and no longer a slave.

Paul's brief letter to Philemon stresses the change in Onesimus's life. His name meant *useful* in Greek, and Paul tells Philemon that while he had formerly been *useless* (a servant Philemon couldn't count on), now he could be useful to both of them. Paul doesn't put Philemon under any obligation. His appeal is on the basis of love, and he promises to honor the demands of justice by making restitution himself if necessary.

Most likely Paul's appeal was successful, or this letter would not have been preserved. In the life of Onesimus we have a clear example of the kind of transformation that occurred in thousands of lives as the gospel message spread throughout the Roman Empire.

---

1 Paul, a prisoner of Christ Jesus, and Timothy our brother,

To Philemon our dear friend and fellow worker— 2 also to Apphia our sister and Archippus our fellow soldier—and to the church that meets in your home:

3 Grace and peace to you*a* from God our Father and the Lord Jesus Christ.

4 I always thank my God as I remember you in my prayers, 5 because I hear about your love for all his holy people and your faith in the Lord Jesus. 6 I pray that your partnership with us in the faith may be effective in deepening your understanding of every good thing we share for the sake of Christ. 7 Your love has given me great joy and encouragement, because you, brother, have refreshed the hearts of the Lord's people.

8 Therefore, although in Christ I could be bold and order you to do what you ought to do, 9 yet I prefer to appeal to you on the basis of love. It is as none other than Paul—an old man and now also a prisoner of Christ Jesus— 10 that I appeal to you for my son Onesimus,*b* who became my son while I was in chains. 11 Formerly he was useless to you, but now he has become useful both to you and to me.

12 I am sending him—who is my very heart—back to you. 13 I would have liked to keep him with me so that he could take your place in helping me while I am in chains for the gospel. 14 But I did not want to do anything without your consent,

a 3 The Greek is plural; also in verses 22 and 25; elsewhere in this letter "you" is singular.
b 10 Onesimus means useful.

so that any favor you do would not seem forced but would be voluntary. [15]Perhaps the reason he was separated from you for a little while was that you might have him back forever— [16]no longer as a slave, but better than a slave, as a dear brother. He is very dear to me but even dearer to you, both as a fellow man and as a brother in the Lord.

[17]So if you consider me a partner, welcome him as you would welcome me. [18]If he has done you any wrong or owes you anything, charge it to me. [19]I, Paul, am writing this with my own hand. I will pay it back—not to mention that you owe me your very self. [20]I do

wish, brother, that I may have some benefit from you in the Lord; refresh my heart in Christ. [21]Confident of your obedience, I write to you, knowing that you will do even more than I ask.

[22]And one thing more: Prepare a guest room for me, because I hope to be restored to you in answer to your prayers.

[23]Epaphras, my fellow prisoner in Christ Jesus, sends you greetings. [24]And so do Mark, Aristarchus, Demas and Luke, my fellow workers.

[25]The grace of the Lord Jesus Christ be with your spirit.

HEBREWS

Neither the author nor the audience of this book is specifically named, but the book itself reveals its nature and purpose. The recipients are Jesus-believing Jews who are in danger of falling away from the faith. They are likely in Italy, since the author passes on greetings to them from those who are from Italy—probably their friends who are traveling elsewhere. The goal of the whole book is to show the superiority of the final realities God has revealed in the new covenant to the temporary ones of the first covenant. Its readers are encouraged to respond to the threat of persecution by recommitting to the new reality brought by Jesus.

The book alternates between teachings—reviews of Israel's history or the temple worship arrangements—and challenges based on these teachings. There are four teaching-challenge pairs:

: Jesus and the salvation he brings are greater than the angels and the salvation they announced (the law of Moses).

: Jesus is our "apostle" (someone sent by God on a specific mission), and he brings us into a greater rest and promised land than Moses and Joshua brought Israel into.

: Jesus is a more effective high priest than the priests appointed by the law of Moses.

: As God's faithful people have done throughout the ages, we must continue living in light of God's unseen heavenly realities and stepping out in faith. Through the Messiah *we are receiving a kingdom that cannot be shaken.*

---

1 In the past God spoke to our ancestors through the prophets at many times and in various ways, ² but in these last days he has spoken to us by his Son, whom he appointed heir of all things, and through whom also he made the universe. ³ The Son is the radiance of God's glory and the exact representation of his being, sustaining all things by his powerful word. After he had provided purification for sins, he sat down at the right hand of the Majesty in heaven. ⁴ So he became as much superior to the angels as the name he has inherited is superior to theirs.

⁵ For to which of the angels did God ever say,

"You are my Son;
    today I have become your
        Father"ᵃ?

Or again,

"I will be his Father,
    and he will be my Son"ᵇ?

⁶ And again, when God brings his firstborn into the world, he says,

"Let all God's angels worship
    him."ᶜ

⁷ In speaking of the angels he says,

ᵃ 5 Psalm 2:7   ᵇ 5 2 Samuel 7:14; 1 Chron. 17:13   ᶜ 6 Deut. 32:43 (see Dead Sea Scrolls and Septuagint)

"He makes his angels spirits,
and his servants flames of
fire."[a]

8But about the Son he says,

"Your throne, O God, will last for
ever and ever;
a scepter of justice will be the
scepter of your kingdom.
9You have loved righteousness
and hated wickedness;
therefore God, your God,
has set you above your
companions
by anointing you with the oil
of joy."[b]

10He also says,

"In the beginning, Lord, you
laid the foundations of the
earth,
and the heavens are the work
of your hands.
11They will perish, but you
remain;
they will all wear out like a
garment.
12You will roll them up like a robe;
like a garment they will be
changed.
But you remain the same,
and your years will never
end."[c]

13To which of the angels did God
ever say,

"Sit at my right hand
until I make your enemies
a footstool for your feet"[d]?

14Are not all angels ministering
spirits sent to serve those who will
inherit salvation?

2 We must pay the most careful
attention, therefore, to what we
have heard, so that we do not drift
away. 2For since the message spoken through angels was binding,
and every violation and disobedience received its just punishment,
3how shall we escape if we ignore
so great a salvation? This salvation,
which was first announced by the
Lord, was confirmed to us by those
who heard him. 4God also testified
to it by signs, wonders and various
miracles, and by gifts of the Holy
Spirit distributed according to his
will.

5It is not to angels that he has
subjected the world to come, about
which we are speaking. 6But there
is a place where someone has testified:

"What is mankind that you are
mindful of them,
a son of man that you care for
him?
7You made them a little[e] lower
than the angels;
you crowned them with glory
and honor
8   and put everything under
their feet."[f,g]

In putting everything under them,[h]
God left nothing that is not subject
to them.[h] Yet at present we do not
see everything subject to them.[h]
9But we do see Jesus, who was
made lower than the angels for a
little while, now crowned with glory and honor because he suffered
death, so that by the grace of God
he might taste death for everyone.

10In bringing many sons and
daughters to glory, it was fitting
that God, for whom and through
whom everything exists, should
make the pioneer of their salvation
perfect through what he suffered.

a 7 Psalm 104:4   b 9 Psalm 45:6,7   c 12 Psalm 102:25-27   d 13 Psalm 110:1   e 7 Or them
for a little while   f 6-8 Psalm 8:4-6   g 7,8 Or "You made him a little lower than the angels;/
you crowned him with glory and honor/ 8and put everything under their feet."   h 8 Or him

¹¹Both the one who makes people holy and those who are made holy are of the same family. So Jesus is not ashamed to call them brothers and sisters.ᵃ ¹²He says,

"I will declare your name to my
    brothers and sisters;
in the assembly I will sing your
    praises."ᵇ

¹³And again,

"I will put my trust in him."ᶜ

And again he says,

"Here am I, and the children
    God has given me."ᵈ

¹⁴Since the children have flesh and blood, he too shared in their humanity so that by his death he might break the power of him who holds the power of death—that is, the devil— ¹⁵and free those who all their lives were held in slavery by their fear of death. ¹⁶For surely it is not angels he helps, but Abraham's descendants. ¹⁷For this reason he had to be made like them,ᵉ fully human in every way, in order that he might become a merciful and faithful high priest in service to God, and that he might make atonement for the sins of the people. ¹⁸Because he himself suffered when he was tempted, he is able to help those who are being tempted.

3 Therefore, holy brothers and sisters, who share in the heavenly calling, fix your thoughts on Jesus, whom we acknowledge as our apostle and high priest. ²He was faithful to the one who appointed him, just as Moses was faithful in all God's house. ³Jesus has been found worthy of greater honor than Moses, just as the builder of a house has greater honor than the house itself. ⁴For every house is built by someone, but God is the builder of everything. ⁵"Moses was faithful as a servant in all God's house,"ᶠ bearing witness to what would be spoken by God in the future. ⁶But Christ is faithful as the Son over God's house. And we are his house, if indeed we hold firmly to our confidence and the hope in which we glory.

⁷So, as the Holy Spirit says:

"Today, if you hear his voice,
⁸   do not harden your hearts
as you did in the rebellion,
    during the time of testing in
        the wilderness,
⁹where your ancestors tested and
        tried me,
    though for forty years they saw
        what I did.
¹⁰That is why I was angry with that
        generation;
    I said, 'Their hearts are always
        going astray,
    and they have not known my
        ways.'
¹¹So I declared on oath in my
        anger,
    'They shall never enter my
        rest.'"ᵍ

¹²See to it, brothers and sisters, that none of you has a sinful, unbelieving heart that turns away from the living God. ¹³But encourage one another daily, as long as it is called "Today," so that none of you may be hardened by sin's deceitfulness. ¹⁴We have come to share in Christ,

---

ᵃ 11 The Greek word for *brothers and sisters* (*adelphoi*) refers here to believers, both men and women, as part of God's family; also in verse 12; and in 3:1, 12; 10:19; 13:22.   ᵇ 12 Psalm 22:22
ᶜ 13 Isaiah 8:17   ᵈ 13 Isaiah 8:18   ᵉ 17 Or *like his brothers*   ᶠ 5 Num. 12:7
ᵍ 11 Psalm 95:7-11

if indeed we hold our original conviction firmly to the very end. [15]As has just been said:

"Today, if you hear his voice,
  do not harden your hearts
  as you did in the rebellion."[a]

[16]Who were they who heard and rebelled? Were they not all those Moses led out of Egypt? [17]And with whom was he angry for forty years? Was it not with those who sinned, whose bodies perished in the wilderness? [18]And to whom did God swear that they would never enter his rest if not to those who disobeyed? [19]So we see that they were not able to enter, because of their unbelief.

4 Therefore, since the promise of entering his rest still stands, let us be careful that none of you be found to have fallen short of it. [2]For we also have had the good news proclaimed to us, just as they did; but the message they heard was of no value to them, because they did not share the faith of those who obeyed.[b] [3]Now we who have believed enter that rest, just as God has said,

"So I declared on oath in my anger,
  'They shall never enter my rest.'"[c]

And yet his works have been finished since the creation of the world. [4]For somewhere he has spoken about the seventh day in these words: "On the seventh day God rested from all his works."[d] [5]And again in the passage above he says, "They shall never enter my rest."

[6]Therefore since it still remains for some to enter that rest, and since those who formerly had the good news proclaimed to them did not go in because of their disobedience, [7]God again set a certain day, calling it "Today." This he did when a long time later he spoke through David, as in the passage already quoted:

"Today, if you hear his voice,
  do not harden your hearts."[a]

[8]For if Joshua had given them rest, God would not have spoken later about another day. [9]There remains, then, a Sabbath-rest for the people of God; [10]for anyone who enters God's rest also rests from their works,[e] just as God did from his. [11]Let us, therefore, make every effort to enter that rest, so that no one will perish by following their example of disobedience.

[12]For the word of God is alive and active. Sharper than any double-edged sword, it penetrates even to dividing soul and spirit, joints and marrow; it judges the thoughts and attitudes of the heart. [13]Nothing in all creation is hidden from God's sight. Everything is uncovered and laid bare before the eyes of him to whom we must give account.

[14]Therefore, since we have a great high priest who has ascended into heaven,[f] Jesus the Son of God, let us hold firmly to the faith we profess. [15]For we do not have a high priest who is unable to empathize with our weaknesses, but we have one who has been tempted in every way, just as we are—yet he did not sin. [16]Let us then approach God's throne of grace with confidence,

---

a 15,7 Psalm 95:7,8   *b 2* Some manuscripts *because those who heard did not combine it with faith*   *c 3* Psalm 95:11; also in verse 5   *d 4* Gen. 2:2   *e 10* Or labor   *f 14* Greek *has gone through the heavens*

so that we may receive mercy and find grace to help us in our time of need.

5 Every high priest is selected from among the people and is appointed to represent the people in matters related to God, to offer gifts and sacrifices for sins. [2]He is able to deal gently with those who are ignorant and are going astray, since he himself is subject to weakness. [3]This is why he has to offer sacrifices for his own sins, as well as for the sins of the people. [4]And no one takes this honor on himself, but he receives it when called by God, just as Aaron was.

[5]In the same way, Christ did not take on himself the glory of becoming a high priest. But God said to him,

"You are my Son;
today I have become your
Father."[a]

[6]And he says in another place,

"You are a priest forever,
in the order of Melchizedek."[b]

[7]During the days of Jesus' life on earth, he offered up prayers and petitions with fervent cries and tears to the one who could save him from death, and he was heard because of his reverent submission. [8]Son though he was, he learned obedience from what he suffered [9]and, once made perfect, he became the source of eternal salvation for all who obey him [10]and was designated by God to be high priest in the order of Melchizedek.

[11]We have much to say about this, but it is hard to make it clear to you because you no longer try to understand. [12]In fact, though by

this time you ought to be teachers, you need someone to teach you the elementary truths of God's word all over again. You need milk, not solid food! [13]Anyone who lives on milk, being still an infant, is not acquainted with the teaching about righteousness. [14]But solid food is for the mature, who by constant use have trained themselves to distinguish good from evil.

6 Therefore let us move beyond the elementary teachings about Christ and be taken forward to maturity, not laying again the foundation of repentance from acts that lead to death,[c] and of faith in God, [2]instruction about cleansing rites,[d] the laying on of hands, the resurrection of the dead, and eternal judgment. [3]And God permitting, we will do so.

[4]It is impossible for those who have once been enlightened, who have tasted the heavenly gift, who have shared in the Holy Spirit, [5]who have tasted the goodness of the word of God and the powers of the coming age [6]and who have fallen[e] away, to be brought back to repentance. To their loss they are crucifying the Son of God all over again and subjecting him to public disgrace. [7]Land that drinks in the rain often falling on it and that produces a crop useful to those for whom it is farmed receives the blessing of God. [8]But land that produces thorns and thistles is worthless and is in danger of being cursed. In the end it will be burned.

[9]Even though we speak like this, dear friends, we are convinced of better things in your case—the things that have to do with salvation. [10]God is not unjust; he will

[a] 5 Psalm 2:7   [b] 6 Psalm 110:4   [c] 1 Or from useless rituals   [d] 2 Or about baptisms
[e] 6 Or age, [6]if they fall

not forget your work and the love you have shown him as you have helped his people and continue to help them. [11]We want each of you to show this same diligence to the very end, so that what you hope for may be fully realized. [12]We do not want you to become lazy, but to imitate those who through faith and patience inherit what has been promised.

[13]When God made his promise to Abraham, since there was no one greater for him to swear by, he swore by himself, [14]saying, "I will surely bless you and give you many descendants."[a] [15]And so after waiting patiently, Abraham received what was promised.

[16]People swear by someone greater than themselves, and the oath confirms what is said and puts an end to all argument. [17]Because God wanted to make the unchanging nature of his purpose very clear to the heirs of what was promised, he confirmed it with an oath. [18]God did this so that, by two unchangeable things in which it is impossible for God to lie, we who have fled to take hold of the hope set before us may be greatly encouraged. [19]We have this hope as an anchor for the soul, firm and secure. It enters the inner sanctuary behind the curtain, [20]where our forerunner, Jesus, has entered on our behalf. He has become a high priest forever, in the order of Melchizedek.

7 This Melchizedek was king of Salem and priest of God Most High. He met Abraham returning from the defeat of the kings and blessed him, [2]and Abraham gave him a tenth of everything. First, the name Melchizedek means "king of righteousness"; then also, "king of Salem" means "king of peace." [3]Without father or mother, without genealogy, without beginning of days or end of life, resembling the Son of God, he remains a priest forever.

[4]Just think how great he was: Even the patriarch Abraham gave him a tenth of the plunder! [5]Now the law requires the descendants of Levi who become priests to collect a tenth from the people—that is, from their fellow Israelites—even though they also are descended from Abraham. [6]This man, however, did not trace his descent from Levi, yet he collected a tenth from Abraham and blessed him who had the promises. [7]And without doubt the lesser is blessed by the greater. [8]In the one case, the tenth is collected by people who die; but in the other case, by him who is declared to be living. [9]One might even say that Levi, who collects the tenth, paid the tenth through Abraham, [10]because when Melchizedek met Abraham, Levi was still in the body of his ancestor.

[11]If perfection could have been attained through the Levitical priesthood—and indeed the law given to the people established that priesthood—why was there still need for another priest to come, one in the order of Melchizedek, not in the order of Aaron? [12]For when the priesthood is changed, the law must be changed also. [13]He of whom these things are said belonged to a different tribe, and no one from that tribe has ever served at the altar. [14]For it is clear that our Lord descended from Judah, and in regard to that tribe Moses said nothing about priests. [15]And what we have said is even more clear if

another priest like Melchizedek appears, ¹⁶one who has become a priest not on the basis of a regulation as to his ancestry but on the basis of the power of an indestructible life. ¹⁷For it is declared:

"You are a priest forever,
    in the order of Melchizedek."ᵃ

¹⁸The former regulation is set aside because it was weak and useless ¹⁹(for the law made nothing perfect), and a better hope is introduced, by which we draw near to God.

²⁰And it was not without an oath! Others became priests without any oath, ²¹but he became a priest with an oath when God said to him:

"The Lord has sworn
    and will not change his mind:
    'You are a priest forever.' "ᵃ

²²Because of this oath, Jesus has become the guarantor of a better covenant.

²³Now there have been many of those priests, since death prevented them from continuing in office; ²⁴but because Jesus lives forever, he has a permanent priesthood. ²⁵Therefore he is able to save completelyᵇ those who come to God through him, because he always lives to intercede for them.

²⁶Such a high priest truly meets our need—one who is holy, blameless, pure, set apart from sinners, exalted above the heavens. ²⁷Unlike the other high priests, he does not need to offer sacrifices day after day, first for his own sins, and then for the sins of the people. He sacrificed for their sins once for all when he offered himself. ²⁸For the law appoints as high priests men

in all their weakness; but the oath, which came after the law, appointed the Son, who has been made perfect forever.

8 Now the main point of what we are saying is this: We do have such a high priest, who sat down at the right hand of the throne of the Majesty in heaven, ²and who serves in the sanctuary, the true tabernacle set up by the Lord, not by a mere human being.

³Every high priest is appointed to offer both gifts and sacrifices, and so it was necessary for this one also to have something to offer. ⁴If he were on earth, he would not be a priest, for there are already priests who offer the gifts prescribed by the law. ⁵They serve at a sanctuary that is a copy and shadow of what is in heaven. This is why Moses was warned when he was about to build the tabernacle: "See to it that you make everything according to the pattern shown you on the mountain."ᶜ ⁶But in fact the ministry Jesus has received is as superior to theirs as the covenant of which he is mediator is superior to the old one, since the new covenant is established on better promises.

⁷For if there had been nothing wrong with that first covenant, no place would have been sought for another. ⁸But God found fault with the people and said ᵈ:

"The days are coming, declares
        the Lord,
    when I will make a new
        covenant
    with the people of Israel
    and with the people of Judah.
⁹It will not be like the covenant
    I made with their ancestors

ᵃ 17,21 Psalm 110:4   ᵇ 25 Or forever   ᶜ 5 Exodus 25:40   ᵈ 8 Some manuscripts may be translated fault and said to the people.

when I took them by the hand
    to lead them out of Egypt,
because they did not remain
    faithful to my covenant,
and I turned away from them,
              declares the Lord.
[10] This is the covenant I will
    establish with the people
    of Israel
    after that time, declares the
    Lord.
I will put my laws in their minds
    and write them on their
    hearts.
I will be their God,
    and they will be my people.
[11] No longer will they teach their
    neighbor,
    or say to one another, 'Know
        the Lord,'
because they will all know me,
    from the least of them to the
        greatest.
[12] For I will forgive their
        wickedness
    and will remember their sins
        no more."[a]

[13] By calling this covenant "new,"
he has made the first one obsolete;
and what is obsolete and outdated
will soon disappear.

9 Now the first covenant had reg-
    ulations for worship and also an
earthly sanctuary. [2] A tabernacle
was set up. In its first room were the
lampstand and the table with its
consecrated bread; this was called
the Holy Place. [3] Behind the second
curtain was a room called the Most
Holy Place, [4] which had the golden
altar of incense and the gold-cov-
ered ark of the covenant. This ark
contained the gold jar of manna,
Aaron's staff that had budded, and
the stone tablets of the covenant.
[5] Above the ark were the cherubim

of the Glory, overshadowing the
atonement cover. But we cannot
discuss these things in detail now.

[6] When everything had been
arranged like this, the priests entered regularly into the outer room
to carry on their ministry. [7] But only
the high priest entered the inner
room, and that only once a year,
and never without blood, which he
offered for himself and for the sins
the people had committed in ignorance. [8] The Holy Spirit was showing by this that the way into the
Most Holy Place had not yet been
disclosed as long as the first tabernacle was still functioning. [9] This
is an illustration for the present
time, indicating that the gifts and
sacrifices being offered were not
able to clear the conscience of the
worshiper. [10] They are only a matter of food and drink and various
ceremonial   washings — external
regulations applying until the time
of the new order.

[11] But when Christ came as high
priest of the good things that are
now already here,[b] he went through
the greater and more perfect tabernacle that is not made with human
hands, that is to say, is not a part
of this creation. [12] He did not enter
by means of the blood of goats and
calves; but he entered the Most Holy
Place once for all by his own blood,
thus obtaining[c] eternal redemption. [13] The blood of goats and bulls
and the ashes of a heifer sprinkled
on those who are ceremonially unclean sanctify them so that they
are outwardly clean. [14] How much
more, then, will the blood of Christ,
who through the eternal Spirit offered himself unblemished to God,
cleanse our consciences from acts

---

[a] 12 Jer. 31:31-34   [b] 11 Some early manuscripts *are to come*   [c] 12 Or *blood, having obtained*

that lead to death,[a] so that we may serve the living God!

15 For this reason Christ is the mediator of a new covenant, that those who are called may receive the promised eternal inheritance—now that he has died as a ransom to set them free from the sins committed under the first covenant.

16 In the case of a will,[b] it is necessary to prove the death of the one who made it, 17 because a will is in force only when somebody has died; it never takes effect while the one who made it is living. 18 This is why even the first covenant was not put into effect without blood. 19 When Moses had proclaimed every command of the law to all the people, he took the blood of calves, together with water, scarlet wool and branches of hyssop, and sprinkled the scroll and all the people. 20 He said, "This is the blood of the covenant, which God has commanded you to keep."[c] 21 In the same way, he sprinkled with the blood both the tabernacle and everything used in its ceremonies. 22 In fact, the law requires that nearly everything be cleansed with blood, and without the shedding of blood there is no forgiveness.

23 It was necessary, then, for the copies of the heavenly things to be purified with these sacrifices, but the heavenly things themselves with better sacrifices than these. 24 For Christ did not enter a sanctuary made with human hands that was only a copy of the true one; he entered heaven itself, now to appear for us in God's presence. 25 Nor did he enter heaven to offer himself again and again, the way the high priest enters the Most Holy Place every year with blood that is not his own. 26 Otherwise Christ would have had to suffer many times since the creation of the world. But he has appeared once for all at the culmination of the ages to do away with sin by the sacrifice of himself. 27 Just as people are destined to die once, and after that to face judgment, 28 so Christ was sacrificed once to take away the sins of many; and he will appear a second time, not to bear sin, but to bring salvation to those who are waiting for him.

10 The law is only a shadow of the good things that are coming—not the realities themselves. For this reason it can never, by the same sacrifices repeated endlessly year after year, make perfect those who draw near to worship. 2 Otherwise, would they not have stopped being offered? For the worshipers would have been cleansed once for all, and would no longer have felt guilty for their sins. 3 But those sacrifices are an annual reminder of sins. 4 It is impossible for the blood of bulls and goats to take away sins.

5 Therefore, when Christ came into the world, he said:

"Sacrifice and offering you did not desire,
    but a body you prepared for me;
6 with burnt offerings and sin offerings
    you were not pleased.
7 Then I said, 'Here I am—it is written about me in the scroll—
    I have come to do your will, my God.'"[d]

---

[a] 14 Or from useless rituals   [b] 16 Same Greek word as covenant; also in verse 17
[c] 20 Exodus 24:8   [d] 7 Psalm 40:6-8 (see Septuagint)

8First he said, "Sacrifices and offerings, burnt offerings and sin offerings you did not desire, nor were you pleased with them"—though they were offered in accordance with the law. 9Then he said, "Here I am, I have come to do your will." He sets aside the first to establish the second. 10And by that will, we have been made holy through the sacrifice of the body of Jesus Christ once for all.

11Day after day every priest stands and performs his religious duties; again and again he offers the same sacrifices, which can never take away sins. 12But when this priest had offered for all time one sacrifice for sins, he sat down at the right hand of God, 13and since that time he waits for his enemies to be made his footstool. 14For by one sacrifice he has made perfect forever those who are being made holy.

15The Holy Spirit also testifies to us about this. First he says:

16 "This is the covenant I will make
    with them
  after that time, says the Lord.
I will put my laws in their hearts,
    and I will write them on their
    minds."[a]

17Then he adds:

"Their sins and lawless acts
  I will remember no more."[b]

18And where these have been forgiven, sacrifice for sin is no longer necessary.

19Therefore, brothers and sisters, since we have confidence to enter the Most Holy Place by the blood of Jesus, 20by a new and living way opened for us through the curtain, that is, his body, 21and since we have a great priest over the house of God, 22let us draw near to God with a sincere heart and with the full assurance that faith brings, having our hearts sprinkled to cleanse us from a guilty conscience and having our bodies washed with pure water. 23Let us hold unswervingly to the hope we profess, for he who promised is faithful. 24And let us consider how we may spur one another on toward love and good deeds, 25not giving up meeting together, as some are in the habit of doing, but encouraging one another—and all the more as you see the Day approaching.

26If we deliberately keep on sinning after we have received the knowledge of the truth, no sacrifice for sins is left, 27but only a fearful expectation of judgment and of raging fire that will consume the enemies of God. 28Anyone who rejected the law of Moses died without mercy on the testimony of two or three witnesses. 29How much more severely do you think someone deserves to be punished who has trampled the Son of God underfoot, who has treated as an unholy thing the blood of the covenant that sanctified them, and who has insulted the Spirit of grace? 30For we know him who said, "It is mine to avenge; I will repay,"[c] and again, "The Lord will judge his people."[d] 31It is a dreadful thing to fall into the hands of the living God.

32Remember those earlier days after you had received the light, when you endured in a great conflict full of suffering. 33Sometimes you were publicly exposed to insult and persecution; at other times you stood side by side with those who were so treated. 34You suffered

---

a 16 Jer. 31:33   b 17 Jer. 31:34   c 30 Deut. 32:35   d 30 Deut. 32:36; Psalm 135:14

along with those in prison and joyfully accepted the confiscation of your property, because you knew that you yourselves had better and lasting possessions. ³⁵So do not throw away your confidence; it will be richly rewarded.

³⁶You need to persevere so that when you have done the will of God, you will receive what he has promised. ³⁷For,

"In just a little while,
    he who is coming will come
    and will not delay."ᵃ

³⁸And,

"But my righteousᵇ one will live
    by faith.
And I take no pleasure
    in the one who shrinks back."ᶜ

³⁹But we do not belong to those who shrink back and are destroyed, but to those who have faith and are saved.

11 Now faith is confidence in what we hope for and assurance about what we do not see. ²This is what the ancients were commended for.

³By faith we understand that the universe was formed at God's command, so that what is seen was not made out of what was visible.

⁴By faith Abel brought God a better offering than Cain did. By faith he was commended as righteous, when God spoke well of his offerings. And by faith Abel still speaks, even though he is dead.

⁵By faith Enoch was taken from this life, so that he did not experience death: "He could not be found, because God had taken him away."ᵈ For before he was taken, he was commended as one who pleased God. ⁶And without faith it is impossible to please God, because anyone who comes to him must believe that he exists and that he rewards those who earnestly seek him.

⁷By faith Noah, when warned about things not yet seen, in holy fear built an ark to save his family. By his faith he condemned the world and became heir of the righteousness that is in keeping with faith.

⁸By faith Abraham, when called to go to a place he would later receive as his inheritance, obeyed and went, even though he did not know where he was going. ⁹By faith he made his home in the promised land like a stranger in a foreign country; he lived in tents, as did Isaac and Jacob, who were heirs with him of the same promise. ¹⁰For he was looking forward to the city with foundations, whose architect and builder is God. ¹¹And by faith even Sarah, who was past childbearing age, was enabled to bear children because sheᵉ considered him faithful who had made the promise. ¹²And so from this one man, and he as good as dead, came descendants as numerous as the stars in the sky and as countless as the sand on the seashore.

¹³All these people were still living by faith when they died. They did not receive the things promised; they only saw them and welcomed them from a distance, admitting that they were foreigners

---

ᵃ 37 Isaiah 26:20; Hab. 2:3   ᵇ 38 Some early manuscripts But the righteous (see Septuagint)   ᶜ 38 Hab. 2:4   ᵈ 5 Gen. 5:24   ᵉ 11 Or By faith Abraham, even though he was too old to have children —and Sarah herself was not able to conceive —was enabled to become a father because he

and strangers on earth. 14People who say such things show that they are looking for a country of their own. 15If they had been thinking of the country they had left, they would have had opportunity to return. 16Instead, they were longing for a better country—a heavenly one. Therefore God is not ashamed to be called their God, for he has prepared a city for them.

17By faith Abraham, when God tested him, offered Isaac as a sacrifice. He who had embraced the promises was about to sacrifice his one and only son, 18even though God had said to him, "It is through Isaac that your offspring will be reckoned."[a] 19Abraham reasoned that God could even raise the dead, and so in a manner of speaking he did receive Isaac back from death.

20By faith Isaac blessed Jacob and Esau in regard to their future.

21By faith Jacob, when he was dying, blessed each of Joseph's sons, and worshiped as he leaned on the top of his staff.

22By faith Joseph, when his end was near, spoke about the exodus of the Israelites from Egypt and gave instructions concerning the burial of his bones.

23By faith Moses' parents hid him for three months after he was born, because they saw he was no ordinary child, and they were not afraid of the king's edict.

24By faith Moses, when he had grown up, refused to be known as the son of Pharaoh's daughter. 25He chose to be mistreated along with the people of God rather than to enjoy the fleeting pleasures of sin. 26He regarded disgrace for the sake of Christ as of greater value than the treasures of Egypt, because he was looking ahead to his reward. 27By faith he left Egypt, not fearing the king's anger; he persevered because he saw him who is invisible. 28By faith he kept the Passover and the application of blood, so that the destroyer of the firstborn would not touch the firstborn of Israel.

29By faith the people passed through the Red Sea as on dry land; but when the Egyptians tried to do so, they were drowned.

30By faith the walls of Jericho fell, after the army had marched around them for seven days.

31By faith the prostitute Rahab, because she welcomed the spies, was not killed with those who were disobedient.[b]

32And what more shall I say? I do not have time to tell about Gideon, Barak, Samson and Jephthah, about David and Samuel and the prophets, 33who through faith conquered kingdoms, administered justice, and gained what was promised; who shut the mouths of lions, 34quenched the fury of the flames, and escaped the edge of the sword; whose weakness was turned to strength; and who became powerful in battle and routed foreign armies. 35Women received back their dead, raised to life again. There were others who were tortured, refusing to be released so that they might gain an even better resurrection. 36Some faced jeers and flogging, and even chains and imprisonment. 37They were put to death by stoning;[c] they were sawed in two; they were killed by the sword. They went about in sheepskins and goatskins, destitute, persecuted and mistreated — 38the world was

---

[a] 18 Gen. 21:12   [b] 31 Or unbelieving   [c] 37 Some early manuscripts stoning; they were put to the test;

not worthy of them. They wandered in deserts and mountains, living in caves and in holes in the ground.

[39]These were all commended for their faith, yet none of them received what had been promised, [40]since God had planned something better for us so that only together with us would they be made perfect.

12 Therefore, since we are surrounded by such a great cloud of witnesses, let us throw off everything that hinders and the sin that so easily entangles. And let us run with perseverance the race marked out for us, [2]fixing our eyes on Jesus, the pioneer and perfecter of faith. For the joy set before him he endured the cross, scorning its shame, and sat down at the right hand of the throne of God. [3]Consider him who endured such opposition from sinners, so that you will not grow weary and lose heart.

[4]In your struggle against sin, you have not yet resisted to the point of shedding your blood. [5]And have you completely forgotten this word of encouragement that addresses you as a father addresses his son? It says,

"My son, do not make light of the
    Lord's discipline,
  and do not lose heart when he
    rebukes you,
[6]because the Lord disciplines the
    one he loves,
  and he chastens everyone he
    accepts as his son."[a]

[7]Endure hardship as discipline; God is treating you as his children. For what children are not disciplined by their father? [8]If you are not disciplined—and everyone undergoes discipline—then you

are not legitimate, not true sons and daughters at all. [9]Moreover, we have all had human fathers who disciplined us and we respected them for it. How much more should we submit to the Father of spirits and live! [10]They disciplined us for a little while as they thought best; but God disciplines us for our good, in order that we may share in his holiness. [11]No discipline seems pleasant at the time, but painful. Later on, however, it produces a harvest of righteousness and peace for those who have been trained by it.

[12]Therefore, strengthen your feeble arms and weak knees. [13]"Make level paths for your feet,"[b] so that the lame may not be disabled, but rather healed.

[14]Make every effort to live in peace with everyone and to be holy; without holiness no one will see the Lord. [15]See to it that no one falls short of the grace of God and that no bitter root grows up to cause trouble and defile many. [16]See that no one is sexually immoral, or is godless like Esau, who for a single meal sold his inheritance rights as the oldest son. [17]Afterward, as you know, when he wanted to inherit this blessing, he was rejected. Even though he sought the blessing with tears, he could not change what he had done.

[18]You have not come to a mountain that can be touched and that is burning with fire; to darkness, gloom and storm; [19]to a trumpet blast or to such a voice speaking words that those who heard it begged that no further word be spoken to them, [20]because they could not bear what was commanded: "If even an animal touches the moun-

---

[a] 5,6 Prov. 3:11,12 (see Septuagint)   [b] 13 Prov. 4:26

tain, it must be stoned to death."[a] [21]The sight was so terrifying that Moses said, "I am trembling with fear."[b]

[22]But you have come to Mount Zion, to the city of the living God, the heavenly Jerusalem. You have come to thousands upon thousands of angels in joyful assembly, [23]to the church of the firstborn, whose names are written in heaven. You have come to God, the Judge of all, to the spirits of the righteous made perfect, [24]to Jesus the mediator of a new covenant, and to the sprinkled blood that speaks a better word than the blood of Abel.

[25]See to it that you do not refuse him who speaks. If they did not escape when they refused him who warned them on earth, how much less will we, if we turn away from him who warns us from heaven? [26]At that time his voice shook the earth, but now he has promised, "Once more I will shake not only the earth but also the heavens."[c] [27]The words "once more" indicate the removing of what can be shaken—that is, created things—so that what cannot be shaken may remain.

[28]Therefore, since we are receiving a kingdom that cannot be shaken, let us be thankful, and so worship God acceptably with reverence and awe, [29]for our "God is a consuming fire."[d]

13 Keep on loving one another as brothers and sisters. [2]Do not forget to show hospitality to strangers, for by so doing some people have shown hospitality to angels without knowing it. [3]Continue to remember those in prison as if you were together with them in prison,

and those who are mistreated as if you yourselves were suffering.

[4]Marriage should be honored by all, and the marriage bed kept pure, for God will judge the adulterer and all the sexually immoral. [5]Keep your lives free from the love of money and be content with what you have, because God has said,

"Never will I leave you;
    never will I forsake you."[e]

[6]So we say with confidence,

"The Lord is my helper; I will not
    be afraid.
What can mere mortals do to
    me?"[f]

[7]Remember your leaders, who spoke the word of God to you. Consider the outcome of their way of life and imitate their faith. [8]Jesus Christ is the same yesterday and today and forever.

[9]Do not be carried away by all kinds of strange teachings. It is good for our hearts to be strengthened by grace, not by eating ceremonial foods, which is of no benefit to those who do so. [10]We have an altar from which those who minister at the tabernacle have no right to eat.

[11]The high priest carries the blood of animals into the Most Holy Place as a sin offering, but the bodies are burned outside the camp. [12]And so Jesus also suffered outside the city gate to make the people holy through his own blood. [13]Let us, then, go to him outside the camp, bearing the disgrace he bore. [14]For here we do not have an enduring city, but we are looking for the city that is to come.

[15]Through Jesus, therefore, let

[a] 20 Exodus 19:12,13   [b] 21 See Deut. 9:19.   [c] 26 Haggai 2:6   [d] 29 Deut. 4:24
[e] 5 Deut. 31:6   [f] 6 Psalm 118:6,7

us continually offer to God a sacrifice of praise — the fruit of lips that openly profess his name. [16]And do not forget to do good and to share with others, for with such sacrifices God is pleased.

[17]Have confidence in your leaders and submit to their authority, because they keep watch over you as those who must give an account. Do this so that their work will be a joy, not a burden, for that would be of no benefit to you.

[18]Pray for us. We are sure that we have a clear conscience and desire to live honorably in every way. [19]I particularly urge you to pray so that I may be restored to you soon.

[20]Now may the God of peace, who through the blood of the eternal covenant brought back from the dead our Lord Jesus, that great Shepherd of the sheep, [21]equip you with everything good for doing his will, and may he work in us what is pleasing to him, through Jesus Christ, to whom be glory for ever and ever. Amen.

[22]Brothers and sisters, I urge you to bear with my word of exhortation, for in fact I have written to you quite briefly.

[23]I want you to know that our brother Timothy has been released. If he arrives soon, I will come with him to see you.

[24]Greet all your leaders and all the Lord's people. Those from Italy send you their greetings.

[25]Grace be with you all.

JAMES

James, one of the brothers of Jesus, became a leader of the church in Jerusalem after Jesus' death and resurrection. He was respected for the advice he gave and for the wise decisions he helped the community of believers make (see p. 170). At one point he decided to write down some of his best teachings and advice and send them to other Jewish believers in Jesus who were scattered throughout the Roman Empire. What he wrote to them has become known as the book of James.

This book begins like a letter because it's being sent to people at a distance. But it is actually not very much like other letters of the time. It is a collection of short sayings and slightly longer discussions of practical topics. The conversational style, the short, pithy sayings and the interweaving of themes all make this book similar to the wisdom writing found in Proverbs and Ecclesiastes.

Like those wisdom books, James concentrates on questions of daily living in God's good creation. He considers such practical issues as concern for the poor, the responsible use of wealth, control of the tongue, purity of life, unity in the community of Christ-followers, and above all patience and endurance during times of trial. The godly wisdom here remains as valuable a guide to living fully human lives as when James first shared it centuries ago.

---

1 James, a servant of God and of the Lord Jesus Christ,

To the twelve tribes scattered among the nations:

Greetings.

2 Consider it pure joy, my brothers and sisters,[a] whenever you face trials of many kinds, 3 because you know that the testing of your faith produces perseverance. 4 Let perseverance finish its work so that you may be mature and complete, not lacking anything. 5 If any of you lacks wisdom, you should ask God, who gives generously to all without finding fault, and it will be given to you. 6 But when you ask, you must believe and not doubt, because the one who doubts is like a wave of the sea, blown and tossed by the wind. 7 That person should not expect to receive anything from the Lord. 8 Such a person is double-minded and unstable in all they do.

9 Believers in humble circumstances ought to take pride in their high position. 10 But the rich should take pride in their humiliation—since they will pass away like a wild flower. 11 For the sun rises with scorching heat and withers the plant; its blossom falls and its beauty is destroyed. In the same way, the rich will fade away even while they go about their business.

12 Blessed is the one who perseveres under trial because, having stood the test, that person will receive the crown of life that the Lord

---

[a] 2 The Greek word for *brothers and sisters* (*adelphoi*) refers here to believers, both men and women, as part of God's family; also in verses 16 and 19; and in 2:1, 5, 14; 3:10, 12; 4:11; 5:7, 9, 10, 12, 19.

has promised to those who love him.

[13] When tempted, no one should say, "God is tempting me." For God cannot be tempted by evil, nor does he tempt anyone; [14] but each person is tempted when they are dragged away by their own evil desire and enticed. [15] Then, after desire has conceived, it gives birth to sin; and sin, when it is full-grown, gives birth to death.

[16] Don't be deceived, my dear brothers and sisters. [17] Every good and perfect gift is from above, coming down from the Father of the heavenly lights, who does not change like shifting shadows. [18] He chose to give us birth through the word of truth, that we might be a kind of firstfruits of all he created.

[19] My dear brothers and sisters, take note of this: Everyone should be quick to listen, slow to speak and slow to become angry, [20] because human anger does not produce the righteousness that God desires. [21] Therefore, get rid of all moral filth and the evil that is so prevalent and humbly accept the word planted in you, which can save you.

[22] Do not merely listen to the word, and so deceive yourselves. Do what it says. [23] Anyone who listens to the word but does not do what it says is like someone who looks at his face in a mirror [24] and, after looking at himself, goes away and immediately forgets what he looks like. [25] But whoever looks intently into the perfect law that gives freedom, and continues in it — not forgetting what they have heard, but doing it — they will be blessed in what they do.

[26] Those who consider themselves religious and yet do not keep a tight rein on their tongues deceive themselves, and their religion is worthless. [27] Religion that God our Father accepts as pure and faultless is this: to look after orphans and widows in their distress and to keep oneself from being polluted by the world.

2 My brothers and sisters, believers in our glorious Lord Jesus Christ must not show favoritism. [2] Suppose a man comes into your meeting wearing a gold ring and fine clothes, and a poor man in filthy old clothes also comes in. [3] If you show special attention to the man wearing fine clothes and say, "Here's a good seat for you," but say to the poor man, "You stand there" or "Sit on the floor by my feet," [4] have you not discriminated among yourselves and become judges with evil thoughts?

[5] Listen, my dear brothers and sisters: Has not God chosen those who are poor in the eyes of the world to be rich in faith and to inherit the kingdom he promised those who love him? [6] But you have dishonored the poor. Is it not the rich who are exploiting you? Are they not the ones who are dragging you into court? [7] Are they not the ones who are blaspheming the noble name of him to whom you belong?

[8] If you really keep the royal law found in Scripture, "Love your neighbor as yourself,"[a] you are doing right. [9] But if you show favoritism, you sin and are convicted by the law as lawbreakers. [10] For whoever keeps the whole law and yet stumbles at just one point is guilty of breaking all of it. [11] For he who said, "You shall not commit adultery,"[b] also said, "You shall not murder."[c] If you do not commit

_a 8_ Lev. 19:18   _b 11_ Exodus 20:14; Deut. 5:18   _c 11_ Exodus 20:13; Deut. 5:17

adultery but do commit murder, you have become a lawbreaker.

¹²Speak and act as those who are going to be judged by the law that gives freedom, ¹³because judgment without mercy will be shown to anyone who has not been merciful. Mercy triumphs over judgment.

¹⁴What good is it, my brothers and sisters, if someone claims to have faith but has no deeds? Can such faith save them? ¹⁵Suppose a brother or a sister is without clothes and daily food. ¹⁶If one of you says to them, "Go in peace; keep warm and well fed," but does nothing about their physical needs, what good is it? ¹⁷In the same way, faith by itself, if it is not accompanied by action, is dead.

¹⁸But someone will say, "You have faith; I have deeds."

Show me your faith without deeds, and I will show you my faith by my deeds. ¹⁹You believe that there is one God. Good! Even the demons believe that—and shudder.

²⁰You foolish person, do you want evidence that faith without deeds is useless*a*? ²¹Was not our father Abraham considered righteous for what he did when he offered his son Isaac on the altar? ²²You see that his faith and his actions were working together, and his faith was made complete by what he did. ²³And the scripture was fulfilled that says, "Abraham believed God, and it was credited to him as righteousness,"*b* and he was called God's friend. ²⁴You see that a person is considered righteous by what they do and not by faith alone.

²⁵In the same way, was not even Rahab the prostitute considered righteous for what she did when she gave lodging to the spies and sent them off in a different direction? ²⁶As the body without the spirit is dead, so faith without deeds is dead.

3 Not many of you should become teachers, my fellow believers, because you know that we who teach will be judged more strictly. ²We all stumble in many ways. Anyone who is never at fault in what they say is perfect, able to keep their whole body in check.

³When we put bits into the mouths of horses to make them obey us, we can turn the whole animal. ⁴Or take ships as an example. Although they are so large and are driven by strong winds, they are steered by a very small rudder wherever the pilot wants to go. ⁵Likewise, the tongue is a small part of the body, but it makes great boasts. Consider what a great forest is set on fire by a small spark. ⁶The tongue also is a fire, a world of evil among the parts of the body. It corrupts the whole body, sets the whole course of one's life on fire, and is itself set on fire by hell.

⁷All kinds of animals, birds, reptiles and sea creatures are being tamed and have been tamed by mankind, ⁸but no human being can tame the tongue. It is a restless evil, full of deadly poison.

⁹With the tongue we praise our Lord and Father, and with it we curse human beings, who have been made in God's likeness. ¹⁰Out of the same mouth come praise and cursing. My brothers and sisters, this should not be. ¹¹Can both fresh water and salt water flow from the same spring? ¹²My brothers and sisters, can a fig tree bear

a 20 Some early manuscripts *dead*   *b 23* Gen. 15:6

olives, or a grapevine bear figs? Neither can a salt spring produce fresh water.

13 Who is wise and understanding among you? Let them show it by their good life, by deeds done in the humility that comes from wisdom. 14 But if you harbor bitter envy and selfish ambition in your hearts, do not boast about it or deny the truth. 15 Such "wisdom" does not come down from heaven but is earthly, unspiritual, demonic. 16 For where you have envy and selfish ambition, there you find disorder and every evil practice.

17 But the wisdom that comes from heaven is first of all pure; then peace-loving, considerate, submissive, full of mercy and good fruit, impartial and sincere. 18 Peacemakers who sow in peace reap a harvest of righteousness.

4 What causes fights and quarrels among you? Don't they come from your desires that battle within you? 2 You desire but do not have, so you kill. You covet but you cannot get what you want, so you quarrel and fight. You do not have because you do not ask God. 3 When you ask, you do not receive, because you ask with wrong motives, that you may spend what you get on your pleasures.

4 You adulterous people,[a] don't you know that friendship with the world means enmity against God? Therefore, anyone who chooses to be a friend of the world becomes an enemy of God. 5 Or do you think Scripture says without reason that he jealously longs for the spirit he has caused to dwell in us[b]? 6 But he

gives us more grace. That is why Scripture says:

"God opposes the proud
    but shows favor to the
    humble."[c]

7 Submit yourselves, then, to God. Resist the devil, and he will flee from you. 8 Come near to God and he will come near to you. Wash your hands, you sinners, and purify your hearts, you double-minded. 9 Grieve, mourn and wail. Change your laughter to mourning and your joy to gloom. 10 Humble yourselves before the Lord, and he will lift you up.

11 Brothers and sisters, do not slander one another. Anyone who speaks against a brother or sister[d] or judges them speaks against the law and judges it. When you judge the law, you are not keeping it, but sitting in judgment on it. 12 There is only one Lawgiver and Judge, the one who is able to save and destroy. But you—who are you to judge your neighbor?

13 Now listen, you who say, "Today or tomorrow we will go to this or that city, spend a year there, carry on business and make money." 14 Why, you do not even know what will happen tomorrow. What is your life? You are a mist that appears for a little while and then vanishes. 15 Instead, you ought to say, "If it is the Lord's will, we will live and do this or that." 16 As it is, you boast in your arrogant schemes. All such boasting is evil. 17 If anyone, then, knows the good they ought to do and doesn't do it, it is sin for them.

---

[a] 4 An allusion to covenant unfaithfulness; see Hosea 3:1.   [b] 5 Or that the spirit he caused to dwell in us envies intensely; or that the Spirit he caused to dwell in us longs jealously   [c] 6 Prov. 3:34   [d] 11 The Greek word for brother or sister (adelphos) refers here to a believer, whether man or woman, as part of God's family.

5 Now listen, you rich people, weep and wail because of the misery that is coming on you. ²Your wealth has rotted, and moths have eaten your clothes. ³Your gold and silver are corroded. Their corrosion will testify against you and eat your flesh like fire. You have hoarded wealth in the last days. ⁴Look! The wages you failed to pay the workers who mowed your fields are crying out against you. The cries of the harvesters have reached the ears of the Lord Almighty. ⁵You have lived on earth in luxury and self-indulgence. You have fattened yourselves in the day of slaughter.ᵃ ⁶You have condemned and murdered the innocent one, who was not opposing you.

⁷Be patient, then, brothers and sisters, until the Lord's coming. See how the farmer waits for the land to yield its valuable crop, patiently waiting for the autumn and spring rains. ⁸You too, be patient and stand firm, because the Lord's coming is near. ⁹Don't grumble against one another, brothers and sisters, or you will be judged. The Judge is standing at the door!

¹⁰Brothers and sisters, as an example of patience in the face of suffering, take the prophets who spoke in the name of the Lord. ¹¹As you know, we count as blessed those who have persevered. You have heard of Job's perseverance and have seen what the Lord finally brought about. The Lord is full of compassion and mercy.

¹²Above all, my brothers and sisters, do not swear — not by heaven or by earth or by anything else. All you need to say is a simple "Yes" or "No." Otherwise you will be condemned.

¹³Is anyone among you in trouble? Let them pray. Is anyone happy? Let them sing songs of praise. ¹⁴Is anyone among you sick? Let them call the elders of the church to pray over them and anoint them with oil in the name of the Lord. ¹⁵And the prayer offered in faith will make the sick person well; the Lord will raise them up. If they have sinned, they will be forgiven. ¹⁶Therefore confess your sins to each other and pray for each other so that you may be healed. The prayer of a righteous person is powerful and effective.

¹⁷Elijah was a human being, even as we are. He prayed earnestly that it would not rain, and it did not rain on the land for three and a half years. ¹⁸Again he prayed, and the heavens gave rain, and the earth produced its crops.

¹⁹My brothers and sisters, if one of you should wander from the truth and someone should bring that person back, ²⁰remember this: Whoever turns a sinner from the error of their way will save them from death and cover over a multitude of sins.

ᵃ 5 Or yourselves as in a day of feasting

1 PETER

The apostle Peter was one of the twelve disciples Jesus appointed and taught during his time on earth. Peter spent the final years of his life and ministry—in the early 60s AD—as a leader of the church in Rome. When he learned that churches in other Roman provinces (all located in what is now Turkey) were experiencing persecution, he wrote to urge them to remain faithful to Jesus. Peter's letter was delivered by Silas, a man who also worked with the apostle Paul (see pp. 170-173). Peter introduces Silas and explains that he helped to compose the letter.

After the opening, the letter has three main sections:

: Peter first tells his readers to *be holy in all you do*. As Gentiles they once lived in ignorance (they did not know the ways of God). But they are now a holy nation, part of God's own people, and are called to a new way of life.
: Peter then explains how this way of life will impress those who might accuse and persecute them without just cause.
: Finally, Peter acknowledges that his readers are suffering for their faith, but he explains that this is only to be expected. The Messiah himself suffered, and believers all over the world are facing the same challenge. The followers of Jesus are waiting for the day God will visit them, and even in their suffering they can show they belong to God.

---

1 Peter, an apostle of Jesus Christ,

To God's elect, exiles scattered throughout the provinces of Pontus, Galatia, Cappadocia, Asia and Bithynia, 2who have been chosen according to the foreknowledge of God the Father, through the sanctifying work of the Spirit, to be obedient to Jesus Christ and sprinkled with his blood:

Grace and peace be yours in abundance.

3Praise be to the God and Father of our Lord Jesus Christ! In his great mercy he has given us new birth into a living hope through the resurrection of Jesus Christ from the dead, 4and into an inheritance that can never perish, spoil or fade. This inheritance is kept in heaven for you, 5who through faith are shielded by God's power until the coming of the salvation that is ready to be revealed in the last time. 6In all this you greatly rejoice, though now for a little while you may have had to suffer grief in all kinds of trials. 7These have come so that the proven genuineness of your faith—of greater worth than gold, which perishes even though refined by fire—may result in praise, glory and honor when Jesus Christ is revealed. 8Though you have not seen him, you love him; and even though you do not see him now, you believe in him and are filled with an inexpressible and glorious joy, 9for you are receiving the end result of your faith, the salvation of your souls.

10Concerning this salvation, the prophets, who spoke of the grace that was to come to you, searched intently and with the greatest care,

11 trying to find out the time and circumstances to which the Spirit of Christ in them was pointing when he predicted the sufferings of the Messiah and the glories that would follow. 12 It was revealed to them that they were not serving themselves but you, when they spoke of the things that have now been told you by those who have preached the gospel to you by the Holy Spirit sent from heaven. Even angels long to look into these things.

13 Therefore, with minds that are alert and fully sober, set your hope on the grace to be brought to you when Jesus Christ is revealed at his coming. 14 As obedient children, do not conform to the evil desires you had when you lived in ignorance. 15 But just as he who called you is holy, so be holy in all you do; 16 for it is written: "Be holy, because I am holy."[a]

17 Since you call on a Father who judges each person's work impartially, live out your time as foreigners here in reverent fear. 18 For you know that it was not with perishable things such as silver or gold that you were redeemed from the empty way of life handed down to you from your ancestors, 19 but with the precious blood of Christ, a lamb without blemish or defect. 20 He was chosen before the creation of the world, but was revealed in these last times for your sake. 21 Through him you believe in God, who raised him from the dead and glorified him, and so your faith and hope are in God.

22 Now that you have purified yourselves by obeying the truth so that you have sincere love for each other, love one another deeply, from the heart.[b] 23 For you have been born again, not of perishable seed, but of imperishable, through the living and enduring word of God. 24 For,

> "All people are like grass,
>   and all their glory is like the
>   flowers of the field;
> the grass withers and the flowers
>   fall,
> 25 but the word of the Lord
>   endures forever."[c]

And this is the word that was preached to you.

2 Therefore, rid yourselves of all malice and all deceit, hypocrisy, envy, and slander of every kind. 2 Like newborn babies, crave pure spiritual milk, so that by it you may grow up in your salvation, 3 now that you have tasted that the Lord is good.

4 As you come to him, the living Stone—rejected by humans but chosen by God and precious to him— 5 you also, like living stones, are being built into a spiritual house[d] to be a holy priesthood, offering spiritual sacrifices acceptable to God through Jesus Christ. 6 For in Scripture it says:

> "See, I lay a stone in Zion,
>   a chosen and precious
>   cornerstone,
> and the one who trusts in him
>   will never be put to shame."[e]

7 Now to you who believe, this stone is precious. But to those who do not believe,

> "The stone the builders rejected
>   has become the cornerstone,"[f]

8 and,

---

[a] 16 Lev. 11:44,45; 19:2   [b] 22 Some early manuscripts *from a pure heart*   [c] 25 Isaiah 40:6-8 (see Septuagint)   [d] 5 Or *into a temple of the Spirit*   [e] 6 Isaiah 28:16   [f] 7 Psalm 118:22

"A stone that causes people to
stumble
and a rock that makes them
fall."[a]

They stumble because they disobey
the message—which is also what
they were destined for.

9But you are a chosen people,
a royal priesthood, a holy nation,
God's special possession, that you
may declare the praises of him who
called you out of darkness into his
wonderful light. 10Once you were
not a people, but now you are the
people of God; once you had not
received mercy, but now you have
received mercy.

11Dear friends, I urge you, as
foreigners and exiles, to abstain
from sinful desires, which wage
war against your soul. 12Live such
good lives among the pagans that,
though they accuse you of doing
wrong, they may see your good
deeds and glorify God on the day
he visits us.

13Submit yourselves for the Lord's
sake to every human authority:
whether to the emperor, as the supreme authority, 14or to governors,
who are sent by him to punish those
who do wrong and to commend
those who do right. 15For it is God's
will that by doing good you should
silence the ignorant talk of foolish
people. 16Live as free people, but do
not use your freedom as a cover-up
for evil; live as God's slaves. 17Show
proper respect to everyone, love the
family of believers, fear God, honor
the emperor.

18Slaves, in reverent fear of God
submit yourselves to your masters,
not only to those who are good and
considerate, but also to those who
are harsh. 19For it is commendable

if someone bears up under the pain
of unjust suffering because they are
conscious of God. 20But how is it to
your credit if you receive a beating
for doing wrong and endure it? But
if you suffer for doing good and you
endure it, this is commendable before God. 21To this you were called,
because Christ suffered for you,
leaving you an example, that you
should follow in his steps.

22"He committed no sin,
and no deceit was found in his
mouth."[b]

23When they hurled their insults at
him, he did not retaliate; when he
suffered, he made no threats. Instead, he entrusted himself to him
who judges justly. 24"He himself
bore our sins" in his body on the
cross, so that we might die to sins
and live for righteousness; "by his
wounds you have been healed."
25For "you were like sheep going
astray,"[c] but now you have returned
to the Shepherd and Overseer of
your souls.

3 Wives, in the same way submit
yourselves to your own husbands so that, if any of them do not
believe the word, they may be won
over without words by the behavior
of their wives, 2when they see the
purity and reverence of your lives.
3Your beauty should not come from
outward adornment, such as elaborate hairstyles and the wearing of
gold jewelry or fine clothes. 4Rath-
er, it should be that of your inner
self, the unfading beauty of a gentle and quiet spirit, which is of great
worth in God's sight. 5For this is the
way the holy women of the past who
put their hope in God used to adorn
themselves. They submitted themselves to their own husbands, 6like

---

[a] 8 Isaiah 8:14   [b] 22 Isaiah 53:9   [c] 24,25 Isaiah 53:4,5,6 (see Septuagint)

Sarah, who obeyed Abraham and called him her lord. You are her daughters if you do what is right and do not give way to fear.

⁷Husbands, in the same way be considerate as you live with your wives, and treat them with respect as the weaker partner and as heirs with you of the gracious gift of life, so that nothing will hinder your prayers.

⁸Finally, all of you, be like-minded, be sympathetic, love one another, be compassionate and humble. ⁹Do not repay evil with evil or insult with insult. On the contrary, repay evil with blessing, because to this you were called so that you may inherit a blessing. ¹⁰For,

"Whoever would love life
    and see good days
must keep their tongue from evil
    and their lips from deceitful
        speech.
¹¹They must turn from evil and do
        good;
    they must seek peace and
        pursue it.
¹²For the eyes of the Lord are on
        the righteous
    and his ears are attentive to
        their prayer,
but the face of the Lord is against
    those who do evil."ᵃ

¹³Who is going to harm you if you are eager to do good? ¹⁴But even if you should suffer for what is right, you are blessed. "Do not fear their threatsᵇ; do not be frightened."ᶜ ¹⁵But in your hearts revere Christ as Lord. Always be prepared to give an answer to everyone who asks you to give the reason for the hope that you have. But do this with gentleness and respect, ¹⁶keeping a

clear conscience, so that those who speak maliciously against your good behavior in Christ may be ashamed of their slander. ¹⁷For it is better, if it is God's will, to suffer for doing good than for doing evil. ¹⁸For Christ also suffered once for sins, the righteous for the unrighteous, to bring you to God. He was put to death in the body but made alive in the Spirit. ¹⁹After being made alive,ᵈ he went and made proclamation to the imprisoned spirits— ²⁰to those who were disobedient long ago when God waited patiently in the days of Noah while the ark was being built. In it only a few people, eight in all, were saved through water, ²¹and this water symbolizes baptism that now saves you also—not the removal of dirt from the body but the pledge of a clear conscience toward God.ᵉ It saves you by the resurrection of Jesus Christ, ²²who has gone into heaven and is at God's right hand—with angels, authorities and powers in submission to him.

4 Therefore, since Christ suffered in his body, arm yourselves also with the same attitude, because whoever suffers in the body is done with sin. ²As a result, they do not live the rest of their earthly lives for evil human desires, but rather for the will of God. ³For you have spent enough time in the past doing what pagans choose to do—living in debauchery, lust, drunkenness, orgies, carousing and detestable idolatry. ⁴They are surprised that you do not join them in their reckless, wild living, and they heap abuse on you. ⁵But they will have to give account to him who is ready to judge the living and the dead. ⁶For this is

---

ᵃ 12 Psalm 34:12-16   ᵇ 14 Or fear what they fear   ᶜ 14 Isaiah 8:12   ᵈ 18,19 Or but made alive in the spirit, ¹⁹in which also   ᵉ 21 Or but an appeal to God for a clear conscience

the reason the gospel was preached even to those who are now dead, so that they might be judged according to human standards in regard to the body, but live according to God in regard to the spirit.

⁷The end of all things is near. Therefore be alert and of sober mind so that you may pray. ⁸Above all, love each other deeply, because love covers over a multitude of sins. ⁹Offer hospitality to one another without grumbling. ¹⁰Each of you should use whatever gift you have received to serve others, as faithful stewards of God's grace in its various forms. ¹¹If anyone speaks, they should do so as one who speaks the very words of God. If anyone serves, they should do so with the strength God provides, so that in all things God may be praised through Jesus Christ. To him be the glory and the power for ever and ever. Amen.

¹²Dear friends, do not be surprised at the fiery ordeal that has come on you to test you, as though something strange were happening to you. ¹³But rejoice inasmuch as you participate in the sufferings of Christ, so that you may be overjoyed when his glory is revealed. ¹⁴If you are insulted because of the name of Christ, you are blessed, for the Spirit of glory and of God rests on you. ¹⁵If you suffer, it should not be as a murderer or thief or any other kind of criminal, or even as a meddler. ¹⁶However, if you suffer as a Christian, do not be ashamed, but praise God that you bear that name. ¹⁷For it is time for judgment to begin with God's household; and if it begins with us, what will the outcome be for those who do not obey the gospel of God? ¹⁸And,

"If it is hard for the righteous to
        be saved,
    what will become of the
        ungodly and the sinner?"[a]

¹⁹So then, those who suffer according to God's will should commit themselves to their faithful Creator and continue to do good.

5 To the elders among you, I appeal as a fellow elder and a witness of Christ's sufferings who also will share in the glory to be revealed: ²Be shepherds of God's flock that is under your care, watching over them — not because you must, but because you are willing, as God wants you to be; not pursuing dishonest gain, but eager to serve; ³not lording it over those entrusted to you, but being examples to the flock. ⁴And when the Chief Shepherd appears, you will receive the crown of glory that will never fade away.

⁵In the same way, you who are younger, submit yourselves to your elders. All of you, clothe yourselves with humility toward one another, because,

"God opposes the proud
    but shows favor to the
        humble."[b]

⁶Humble yourselves, therefore, under God's mighty hand, that he may lift you up in due time. ⁷Cast all your anxiety on him because he cares for you.

⁸Be alert and of sober mind. Your enemy the devil prowls around like a roaring lion looking for someone to devour. ⁹Resist him, standing firm in the faith, because you know that the family of believers throughout the world is undergoing the same kind of sufferings.

---

a 18 Prov. 11:31 (see Septuagint)   b 5 Prov. 3:34

[10]And the God of all grace, who called you to his eternal glory in Christ, after you have suffered a little while, will himself restore you and make you strong, firm and steadfast. [11]To him be the power for ever and ever. Amen.

[12]With the help of Silas,[a] whom I regard as a faithful brother, I have written to you briefly, encouraging you and testifying that this is the true grace of God. Stand fast in it.

[13]She who is in Babylon, chosen together with you, sends you her greetings, and so does my son Mark. [14]Greet one another with a kiss of love.

Peace to all of you who are in Christ.

---

[a] 12 Greek *Silvanus*, a variant of *Silas*

2 PETER

Around AD 65 the apostle Peter was imprisoned in Rome by the emperor Nero, and he realized that he would soon be executed. Since he was an eyewitness of the ministry of Jesus, he decided to write another letter to the believers he had written to before, confirming what they had been taught about Jesus. False teachers were proposing that, since Jesus hadn't returned already, his return couldn't be expected at all. Because they didn't expect any future judgment, they were living immoral lives. (Peter likely learned about the threat of these teachers from a letter sent by Jude, a brother of Jesus, to warn believers against them. Peter's letter echoes Jude's, but in shorter form. See p. 324.)

Peter answers the false teachers by stressing that he personally saw the glory and majesty of Jesus *on the sacred mountain* (see p. 55). Everyone will see this glory when Jesus returns. In powerful imagery Peter describes the false teachers' destructive effect on the community and the judgment that awaits them. In the final section of his letter, Peter explains that the Messiah's return has been delayed because God wants everyone to repent. Our proper response is to live good lives filled with hope, since we are looking forward to a new heaven and a new earth, where righteousness dwells.

---

1 Simon Peter, a servant and apostle of Jesus Christ,

To those who through the righteousness of our God and Savior Jesus Christ have received a faith as precious as ours:

2 Grace and peace be yours in abundance through the knowledge of God and of Jesus our Lord.

3 His divine power has given us everything we need for a godly life through our knowledge of him who called us by his own glory and goodness. 4 Through these he has given us his very great and precious promises, so that through them you may participate in the divine nature, having escaped the corruption in the world caused by evil desires. 5 For this very reason, make every effort to add to your faith goodness; and to goodness, knowledge; 6 and to knowledge, self-control; and to self-control, perseverance; and to perseverance, godliness; 7 and to godliness, mutual affection; and to mutual affection, love. 8 For if you possess these qualities in increasing measure, they will keep you from being ineffective and unproductive in your knowledge of our Lord Jesus Christ. 9 But whoever does not have them is nearsighted and blind, forgetting that they have been cleansed from their past sins.

10 Therefore, my brothers and sisters,[a] make every effort to confirm your calling and election. For if you do these things, you will never stumble, 11 and you will receive a rich welcome into the eternal kingdom of our Lord and Savior Jesus Christ.

---

[a] 10 The Greek word for *brothers and sisters* (*adelphoi*) refers here to believers, both men and women, as part of God's family.

¹²So I will always remind you of these things, even though you know them and are firmly established in the truth you now have. ¹³I think it is right to refresh your memory as long as I live in the tent of this body, ¹⁴because I know that I will soon put it aside, as our Lord Jesus Christ has made clear to me. ¹⁵And I will make every effort to see that after my departure you will always be able to remember these things.

¹⁶For we did not follow cleverly devised stories when we told you about the coming of our Lord Jesus Christ in power, but we were eyewitnesses of his majesty. ¹⁷He received honor and glory from God the Father when the voice came to him from the Majestic Glory, saying, "This is my Son, whom I love; with him I am well pleased."ᵃ ¹⁸We ourselves heard this voice that came from heaven when we were with him on the sacred mountain.

¹⁹We also have the prophetic message as something completely reliable, and you will do well to pay attention to it, as to a light shining in a dark place, until the day dawns and the morning star rises in your hearts. ²⁰Above all, you must understand that no prophecy of Scripture came about by the prophet's own interpretation of things. ²¹For prophecy never had its origin in the human will, but prophets, though human, spoke from God as they were carried along by the Holy Spirit.

2 But there were also false prophets among the people, just as there will be false teachers among you. They will secretly introduce destructive heresies, even denying the sovereign Lord who bought them—bringing swift destruction on themselves. ²Many will follow their depraved conduct and will bring the way of truth into disrepute. ³In their greed these teachers will exploit you with fabricated stories. Their condemnation has long been hanging over them, and their destruction has not been sleeping.

⁴For if God did not spare angels when they sinned, but sent them to hell,ᵇ putting them in chains of darknessᶜ to be held for judgment; ⁵if he did not spare the ancient world when he brought the flood on its ungodly people, but protected Noah, a preacher of righteousness, and seven others; ⁶if he condemned the cities of Sodom and Gomorrah by burning them to ashes, and made them an example of what is going to happen to the ungodly; ⁷and if he rescued Lot, a righteous man, who was distressed by the depraved conduct of the lawless ⁸(for that righteous man, living among them day after day, was tormented in his righteous soul by the lawless deeds he saw and heard)— ⁹if this is so, then the Lord knows how to rescue the godly from trials and to hold the unrighteous for punishment on the day of judgment. ¹⁰This is especially true of those who follow the corrupt desire of the fleshᵈ and despise authority.

Bold and arrogant, they are not afraid to heap abuse on celestial beings; ¹¹yet even angels, although they are stronger and more powerful, do not heap abuse on such beings when bringing judgment on

---

ᵃ 17 Matt. 17:5; Mark 9:7; Luke 9:35   ᵇ 4 Greek *Tartarus*   ᶜ 4 Some manuscripts *in gloomy dungeons*   ᵈ 10 In contexts like this, the Greek word for *flesh (sarx)* refers to the sinful state of human beings, often presented as a power in opposition to the Spirit; also in verse 18.

them from[a] the Lord. 12But these people blaspheme in matters they do not understand. They are like unreasoning animals, creatures of instinct, born only to be caught and destroyed, and like animals they too will perish.

13They will be paid back with harm for the harm they have done. Their idea of pleasure is to carouse in broad daylight. They are blots and blemishes, reveling in their pleasures while they feast with you.[b] 14With eyes full of adultery, they never stop sinning; they seduce the unstable; they are experts in greed—an accursed brood! 15They have left the straight way and wandered off to follow the way of Balaam son of Bezer,[c] who loved the wages of wickedness. 16But he was rebuked for his wrongdoing by a donkey—an animal without speech—who spoke with a human voice and restrained the prophet's madness.

17These people are springs without water and mists driven by a storm. Blackest darkness is reserved for them. 18For they mouth empty, boastful words and, by appealing to the lustful desires of the flesh, they entice people who are just escaping from those who live in error. 19They promise them freedom, while they themselves are slaves of depravity—for "people are slaves to whatever has mastered them." 20If they have escaped the corruption of the world by knowing our Lord and Savior Jesus Christ and are again entangled in it and are overcome, they are worse off at the end than they were at the beginning. 21It would have been better for them not to

have known the way of righteousness, than to have known it and then to turn their backs on the sacred command that was passed on to them. 22Of them the proverbs are true: "A dog returns to its vomit,"[d] and, "A sow that is washed returns to her wallowing in the mud."

3 Dear friends, this is now my second letter to you. I have written both of them as reminders to stimulate you to wholesome thinking. 2I want you to recall the words spoken in the past by the holy prophets and the command given by our Lord and Savior through your apostles.

3Above all, you must understand that in the last days scoffers will come, scoffing and following their own evil desires. 4They will say, "Where is this 'coming' he promised? Ever since our ancestors died, everything goes on as it has since the beginning of creation." 5But they deliberately forget that long ago by God's word the heavens came into being and the earth was formed out of water and by water. 6By these waters also the world of that time was deluged and destroyed. 7By the same word the present heavens and earth are reserved for fire, being kept for the day of judgment and destruction of the ungodly.

8But do not forget this one thing, dear friends: With the Lord a day is like a thousand years, and a thousand years are like a day. 9The Lord is not slow in keeping his promise, as some understand slowness. Instead he is patient with you, not wanting anyone to perish, but everyone to come to repentance.

10But the day of the Lord will come like a thief. The heavens will

---

[a] 11 Many manuscripts *beings in the presence of*   [b] 13 Some manuscripts *in their love feasts*
[c] 15 Greek *Bosor*   [d] 22 Prov. 26:11

disappear with a roar; the elements will be destroyed by fire, and the earth and everything done in it will be laid bare.^a

¹¹Since everything will be destroyed in this way, what kind of people ought you to be? You ought to live holy and godly lives ¹²as you look forward to the day of God and speed its coming.^b That day will bring about the destruction of the heavens by fire, and the elements will melt in the heat. ¹³But in keeping with his promise we are looking forward to a new heaven and a new earth, where righteousness dwells.

¹⁴So then, dear friends, since you are looking forward to this, make every effort to be found spotless, blameless and at peace with him.

¹⁵Bear in mind that our Lord's patience means salvation, just as our dear brother Paul also wrote you with the wisdom that God gave him. ¹⁶He writes the same way in all his letters, speaking in them of these matters. His letters contain some things that are hard to understand, which ignorant and unstable people distort, as they do the other Scriptures, to their own destruction.

¹⁷Therefore, dear friends, since you have been forewarned, be on your guard so that you may not be carried away by the error of the lawless and fall from your secure position. ¹⁸But grow in the grace and knowledge of our Lord and Savior Jesus Christ. To him be glory both now and forever! Amen.

---

^a 10 Some manuscripts be burned up   ^b 12 Or as you wait eagerly for the day of God to come

1 JOHN

The letter known as 1 John was sent to a group of believers who were in
the midst of an unsettling situation. Some of them had abandoned faith in
Jesus the Messiah as it had first been taught to them. They found the proclamation that God had come in a human body impossible to reconcile
with the common Greek idea that the flesh is evil and only spirit is good.
But despite their denial of the Messiah, their immoral lives and their lack
of practical love, they claimed to know God and belong to God. They
asserted that their spiritual insight put them above the rest of the group,
which they demonstrated by deserting the fellowship. Those left behind
were deeply shaken, uncertain about everything they had been taught.

Someone who was close to this community and who had been an eyewitness of Jesus wrote to reassure them of what they had heard *from the
beginning*. The author doesn't identify himself, but very likely he was
the apostle John. Much of the language is similar to the Gospel of John.
The letter testifies to the reality of the Messiah's coming in the flesh, reas-
suring the believers that they have full access to the truth. It emphasizes
godly living and practical caring as the signs of those who genuinely
know God.

---

1 That which was from the beginning, which we have heard,
which we have seen with our eyes,
which we have looked at and our
hands have touched—this we proclaim concerning the Word of life.
²The life appeared; we have seen it
and testify to it, and we proclaim to
you the eternal life, which was with
the Father and has appeared to us.
³We proclaim to you what we have
seen and heard, so that you also
may have fellowship with us. And
our fellowship is with the Father and
with his Son, Jesus Christ. ⁴We write
this to make our*ᵃ* joy complete.

⁵This is the message we have
heard from him and declare to
you: God is light; in him there is no
darkness at all. ⁶If we claim to have
fellowship with him and yet walk in
the darkness, we lie and do not live
out the truth. ⁷But if we walk in the
light, as he is in the light, we have

fellowship with one another, and
the blood of Jesus, his Son, purifies
us from all*ᵇ* sin.

⁸If we claim to be without sin, we
deceive ourselves and the truth is
not in us. ⁹If we confess our sins, he
is faithful and just and will forgive
us our sins and purify us from all
unrighteousness. ¹⁰If we claim we
have not sinned, we make him out
to be a liar and his word is not in us.

2 My dear children, I write this to
you so that you will not sin. But if
anybody does sin, we have an advocate with the Father — Jesus Christ,
the Righteous One. ²He is the atoning sacrifice for our sins, and not
only for ours but also for the sins of
the whole world.

³We know that we have come
to know him if we keep his commands. ⁴Whoever says, "I know
him," but does not do what he commands is a liar, and the truth is

---

ᵃ 4 Some manuscripts *your*   *ᵇ 7* Or *every*

not in that person. [5]But if anyone obeys his word, love for God[a] is truly made complete in them. This is how we know we are in him: [6]Whoever claims to live in him must live as Jesus did.

[7]Dear friends, I am not writing you a new command but an old one, which you have had since the beginning. This old command is the message you have heard. [8]Yet I am writing you a new command; its truth is seen in him and in you, because the darkness is passing and the true light is already shining.

[9]Anyone who claims to be in the light but hates a brother or sister[b] is still in the darkness. [10]Anyone who loves their brother and sister[c] lives in the light, and there is nothing in them to make them stumble. [11]But anyone who hates a brother or sister is in the darkness and walks around in the darkness. They do not know where they are going, because the darkness has blinded them.

[12]I am writing to you, dear children,
    because your sins have been forgiven on account of his name.
[13]I am writing to you, fathers,
    because you know him who is from the beginning.
I am writing to you, young men,
    because you have overcome the evil one.

[14]I write to you, dear children,
    because you know the Father.
I write to you, fathers,
    because you know him who is from the beginning.

I write to you, young men,
    because you are strong,
    and the word of God lives in you,
    and you have overcome the evil one.

[15]Do not love the world or anything in the world. If anyone loves the world, love for the Father[d] is not in them. [16]For everything in the world—the lust of the flesh, the lust of the eyes, and the pride of life—comes not from the Father but from the world. [17]The world and its desires pass away, but whoever does the will of God lives forever.

[18]Dear children, this is the last hour; and as you have heard that the antichrist is coming, even now many antichrists have come. This is how we know it is the last hour. [19]They went out from us, but they did not really belong to us. For if they had belonged to us, they would have remained with us; but their going showed that none of them belonged to us.

[20]But you have an anointing from the Holy One, and all of you know the truth.[e] [21]I do not write to you because you do not know the truth, but because you do know it and because no lie comes from the truth. [22]Who is the liar? It is whoever denies that Jesus is the Christ. Such a person is the antichrist—denying the Father and the Son. [23]No one who denies the Son has the Father; whoever acknowledges the Son has the Father also.

[24]As for you, see that what you have heard from the beginning remains in you. If it does, you also

---

a 5 Or *word, God's love*   *b 9* The Greek word for *brother or sister* (*adelphos*) refers here to a believer, whether man or woman, as part of God's family; also in verse 11; and in 3:15, 17; 4:20; 5:16.   *c 10* The Greek word for *brother and sister* (*adelphos*) refers here to a believer, whether man or woman, as part of God's family; also in 3:10; 4:20, 21.   *d 15* Or *world, the Father's love*
e 20 Some manuscripts *and you know all things*

will remain in the Son and in the Father. 25 And this is what he promised us — eternal life.

26 I am writing these things to you about those who are trying to lead you astray. 27 As for you, the anointing you received from him remains in you, and you do not need anyone to teach you. But as his anointing teaches you about all things and as that anointing is real, not counterfeit — just as it has taught you, remain in him.

28 And now, dear children, continue in him, so that when he appears we may be confident and unashamed before him at his coming.

29 If you know that he is righteous, you know that everyone who does what is right has been born of him.

3 See what great love the Father has lavished on us, that we should be called children of God! And that is what we are! The reason the world does not know us is that it did not know him. 2 Dear friends, now we are children of God, and what we will be has not yet been made known. But we know that when Christ appears,[a] we shall be like him, for we shall see him as he is. 3 All who have this hope in him purify themselves, just as he is pure.

4 Everyone who sins breaks the law; in fact, sin is lawlessness. 5 But you know that he appeared so that he might take away our sins. And in him is no sin. 6 No one who lives in him keeps on sinning. No one who continues to sin has either seen him or known him.

7 Dear children, do not let anyone lead you astray. The one who does what is right is righteous, just as he is righteous. 8 The one who does what is sinful is of the devil, because the devil has been sinning from the beginning. The reason the Son of God appeared was to destroy the devil's work. 9 No one who is born of God will continue to sin, because God's seed remains in them; they cannot go on sinning, because they have been born of God. 10 This is how we know who the children of God are and who the children of the devil are: Anyone who does not do what is right is not God's child, nor is anyone who does not love their brother and sister.

11 For this is the message you heard from the beginning: We should love one another. 12 Do not be like Cain, who belonged to the evil one and murdered his brother. And why did he murder him? Because his own actions were evil and his brother's were righteous. 13 Do not be surprised, my brothers and sisters,[b] if the world hates you. 14 We know that we have passed from death to life, because we love each other. Anyone who does not love remains in death. 15 Anyone who hates a brother or sister is a murderer, and you know that no murderer has eternal life residing in him.

16 This is how we know what love is: Jesus Christ laid down his life for us. And we ought to lay down our lives for our brothers and sisters. 17 If anyone has material possessions and sees a brother or sister in need but has no pity on them, how can the love of God be in that person? 18 Dear children, let us not love with words or speech but with actions and in truth.

19 This is how we know that we

a 2 Or when it is made known   b 13 The Greek word for brothers and sisters (adelphoi) refers here to believers, both men and women, as part of God's family; also in verse 16.

belong to the truth and how we set our hearts at rest in his presence: 20 If our hearts condemn us, we know that God is greater than our hearts, and he knows everything. 21 Dear friends, if our hearts do not condemn us, we have confidence before God 22 and receive from him anything we ask, because we keep his commands and do what pleases him. 23 And this is his command: to believe in the name of his Son, Jesus Christ, and to love one another as he commanded us. 24 The one who keeps God's commands lives in him, and he in them. And this is how we know that he lives in us: We know it by the Spirit he gave us.

4 Dear friends, do not believe every spirit, but test the spirits to see whether they are from God, because many false prophets have gone out into the world. 2 This is how you can recognize the Spirit of God: Every spirit that acknowledges that Jesus Christ has come in the flesh is from God, 3 but every spirit that does not acknowledge Jesus is not from God. This is the spirit of the antichrist, which you have heard is coming and even now is already in the world.

4 You, dear children, are from God and have overcome them, because the one who is in you is greater than the one who is in the world. 5 They are from the world and therefore speak from the viewpoint of the world, and the world listens to them. 6 We are from God, and whoever knows God listens to us; but whoever is not from God does not listen to us. This is how we recognize the Spirit[a] of truth and the spirit of falsehood.

7 Dear friends, let us love one another, for love comes from God. Everyone who loves has been born of God and knows God. 8 Whoever does not love does not know God, because God is love. 9 This is how God showed his love among us: He sent his one and only Son into the world that we might live through him. 10 This is love: not that we loved God, but that he loved us and sent his Son as an atoning sacrifice for our sins. 11 Dear friends, since God so loved us, we also ought to love one another. 12 No one has ever seen God; but if we love one another, God lives in us and his love is made complete in us.

13 This is how we know that we live in him and he in us: He has given us of his Spirit. 14 And we have seen and testify that the Father has sent his Son to be the Savior of the world. 15 If anyone acknowledges that Jesus is the Son of God, God lives in them and they in God. 16 And so we know and rely on the love God has for us.

God is love. Whoever lives in love lives in God, and God in them. 17 This is how love is made complete among us so that we will have confidence on the day of judgment: In this world we are like Jesus. 18 There is no fear in love. But perfect love drives out fear, because fear has to do with punishment. The one who fears is not made perfect in love.

19 We love because he first loved us. 20 Whoever claims to love God yet hates a brother or sister is a liar. For whoever does not love their brother and sister, whom they have seen, cannot love God, whom they have not seen. 21 And he has given us this command: Anyone who loves God must also love their brother and sister.

a 6 Or spirit

5 Everyone who believes that Jesus is the Christ is born of God, and everyone who loves the father loves his child as well. ²This is how we know that we love the children of God: by loving God and carrying out his commands. ³In fact, this is love for God: to keep his commands. And his commands are not burdensome, ⁴for everyone born of God overcomes the world. This is the victory that has overcome the world, even our faith. ⁵Who is it that overcomes the world? Only the one who believes that Jesus is the Son of God.

⁶This is the one who came by water and blood—Jesus Christ. He did not come by water only, but by water and blood. And it is the Spirit who testifies, because the Spirit is the truth. ⁷For there are three that testify: ⁸the[a] Spirit, the water and the blood; and the three are in agreement. ⁹We accept human testimony, but God's testimony is greater because it is the testimony of God, which he has given about his Son. ¹⁰Whoever believes in the Son of God accepts this testimony. Whoever does not believe God has made him out to be a liar, because they have not believed the testimony God has given about his Son. ¹¹And this is the testimony: God has given us eternal life, and this life is in his Son. ¹²Whoever has the Son has life; whoever does not have the Son of God does not have life.

¹³I write these things to you who believe in the name of the Son of God so that you may know that you have eternal life. ¹⁴This is the confidence we have in approaching God: that if we ask anything according to his will, he hears us. ¹⁵And if we know that he hears us—whatever we ask—we know that we have what we asked of him.

¹⁶If you see any brother or sister commit a sin that does not lead to death, you should pray and God will give them life. I refer to those whose sin does not lead to death. There is a sin that leads to death. I am not saying that you should pray about that. ¹⁷All wrongdoing is sin, and there is sin that does not lead to death.

¹⁸We know that anyone born of God does not continue to sin; the One who was born of God keeps them safe, and the evil one cannot harm them. ¹⁹We know that we are children of God, and that the whole world is under the control of the evil one. ²⁰We know also that the Son of God has come and has given us understanding, so that we may know him who is true. And we are in him who is true by being in his Son Jesus Christ. He is the true God and eternal life.

²¹Dear children, keep yourselves from idols.

---

[a] 7,8 Late manuscripts of the Vulgate *testify in heaven: the Father, the Word and the Holy Spirit, and these three are one.* ⁸*And there are three that testify on earth: the* (not found in any Greek manuscript before the fourteenth century)

2 JOHN

The same person who wrote 1 John to encourage believers also found it necessary to write to other churches where the false teachers might go to spread their ideas and practices. The letter of 2 John addresses one such gathering, referring to the church as a *lady* and its members as her *children*. The author describes the members of his own community as *the children of your sister*. (This was apparently typical of early followers of Jesus; there is a similar greeting at the end of 1 Peter.) He identifies himself as a church leader by using the title *elder*.

Apparently some people from this church had just come to visit him and he was pleased to learn that they were walking in the truth. He warns the church not to support the false teachers in any way. Despite its brevity, this letter expresses all of the themes that receive deeper development in 1 John.

¹ The elder,

To the lady chosen by God and to her children, whom I love in the truth—and not I only, but also all who know the truth— ² because of the truth, which lives in us and will be with us forever:

³ Grace, mercy and peace from God the Father and from Jesus Christ, the Father's Son, will be with us in truth and love.

⁴ It has given me great joy to find some of your children walking in the truth, just as the Father commanded us. ⁵ And now, dear lady, I am not writing you a new command but one we have had from the beginning. I ask that we love one another. ⁶ And this is love: that we walk in obedience to his commands. As you have heard from the beginning, his command is that you walk in love.

⁷ I say this because many deceivers, who do not acknowledge Jesus Christ as coming in the flesh, have gone out into the world. Any such person is the deceiver and the antichrist. ⁸ Watch out that you do not lose what we[a] have worked for, but that you may be rewarded fully. ⁹ Anyone who runs ahead and does not continue in the teaching of Christ does not have God; whoever continues in the teaching has both the Father and the Son. ¹⁰ If anyone comes to you and does not bring this teaching, do not take them into your house or welcome them. ¹¹ Anyone who welcomes them shares in their wicked work.

¹² I have much to write to you, but I do not want to use paper and ink. Instead, I hope to visit you and talk with you face to face, so that our joy may be complete.

¹³ The children of your sister, who is chosen by God, send their greetings.

---

a 8 Some manuscripts *you*

3 JOHN

This letter is a note of thanks and encouragement to an individual named Gaius. John had sent a letter to the church of which Gaius was a member, introducing and commending certain individuals, but a leader named Diotrephes refused to accommodate them. He opposed John's authority to the point of actually expelling anyone who supported the people he had sent. Gaius, however, put these preachers up in his own home, enabling them to carry out their mission. John's gratitude makes it clear that the church should provide a base of operations for traveling preachers who were walking in the truth. John also promises to come soon to set matters right.

¹The elder,

To my dear friend Gaius, whom I love in the truth.

²Dear friend, I pray that you may enjoy good health and that all may go well with you, even as your soul is getting along well. ³It gave me great joy when some believers came and testified about your faithfulness to the truth, telling how you continue to walk in it. ⁴I have no greater joy than to hear that my children are walking in the truth.

⁵Dear friend, you are faithful in what you are doing for the brothers and sisters,ᵃ even though they are strangers to you. ⁶They have told the church about your love. Please send them on their way in a manner that honors God. ⁷It was for the sake of the Name that they went out, receiving no help from the pagans. ⁸We ought therefore to show hospitality to such people so that we may work together for the truth.

⁹I wrote to the church, but Diotrephes, who loves to be first, will not welcome us. ¹⁰So when I come, I will call attention to what he is doing, spreading malicious nonsense about us. Not satisfied with that, he even refuses to welcome other believers. He also stops those who want to do so and puts them out of the church.

¹¹Dear friend, do not imitate what is evil but what is good. Anyone who does what is good is from God. Anyone who does what is evil has not seen God. ¹²Demetrius is well spoken of by everyone — and even by the truth itself. We also speak well of him, and you know that our testimony is true.

¹³I have much to write you, but I do not want to do so with pen and ink. ¹⁴I hope to see you soon, and we will talk face to face.

Peace to you. The friends here send their greetings. Greet the friends there by name.

ᵃ 5 The Greek word for *brothers and sisters* (*adelphoi*) refers here to believers, both men and women, as part of God's family.

JUDE

Jesus had several brothers, two of whom were James and Jude. Much less is known about Jude than James (see p. 302), but he was clearly a church leader, since he wrote to believers with authority in this letter that bears his name. It cannot be determined exactly who was meant to receive the letter, although the references to angels, to Israel's history and to specific writings indicate that Jewish Christians were in view.

Jude addresses the problem of false teachers who have come and are now threatening *the faith that was once for all entrusted to God's holy people*. On the basis of supposedly inspired dreams, they reject authority and pollute their own bodies. Even though they claim to be bringing God's message, they really *follow mere natural instincts and do not have the Spirit*. The believers must actively resist them and cleanse their community by rejecting both the teaching and the example of these ungodly men.

It seems that the apostle Peter received a copy of Jude's letter and wrote a similar one of his own to show that it faithfully presented the teaching of the apostles of the Lord Jesus Christ (see p. 313).

---

[1] Jude, a servant of Jesus Christ and a brother of James,

To those who have been called, who are loved in God the Father and kept for[a] Jesus Christ:

[2] Mercy, peace and love be yours in abundance.

[3] Dear friends, although I was very eager to write to you about the salvation we share, I felt compelled to write and urge you to contend for the faith that was once for all entrusted to God's holy people. [4] For certain individuals whose condemnation was written about[b] long ago have secretly slipped in among you. They are ungodly people, who pervert the grace of our God into a license for immorality and deny Jesus Christ our only Sovereign and Lord.

[5] Though you already know all this, I want to remind you that the Lord[c] at one time delivered his people out of Egypt, but later destroyed those who did not believe. [6] And the angels who did not keep their positions of authority but abandoned their proper dwelling—these he has kept in darkness, bound with everlasting chains for judgment on the great Day. [7] In a similar way, Sodom and Gomorrah and the surrounding towns gave themselves up to sexual immorality and perversion. They serve as an example of those who suffer the punishment of eternal fire.

[8] In the very same way, on the strength of their dreams these ungodly people pollute their own bodies, reject authority and heap abuse on celestial beings. [9] But even the archangel Michael, when he was disputing with the devil about the body of Moses, did not himself dare to condemn him for slander but said, "The Lord rebuke

---

a 1 Or by; or in   b 4 Or individuals who were marked out for condemnation   c 5 Some early manuscripts Jesus

you!" [a] ¹⁰Yet these people slander whatever they do not understand, and the very things they do understand by instinct—as irrational animals do—will destroy them.

¹¹Woe to them! They have taken the way of Cain; they have rushed for profit into Balaam's error; they have been destroyed in Korah's rebellion.

¹²These people are blemishes at your love feasts, eating with you without the slightest qualm— shepherds who feed only themselves. They are clouds without rain, blown along by the wind; autumn trees, without fruit and uprooted—twice dead. ¹³They are wild waves of the sea, foaming up their shame; wandering stars, for whom blackest darkness has been reserved forever.

¹⁴Enoch, the seventh from Adam, prophesied about them: "See, the Lord is coming with thousands upon thousands of his holy ones ¹⁵to judge everyone, and to convict all of them of all the ungodly acts they have committed in their ungodliness, and of all the defiant words ungodly sinners have spoken against him." [b] ¹⁶These people are grumblers and faultfinders; they follow their own evil desires; they boast about themselves and flatter others for their own advantage.

¹⁷But, dear friends, remember what the apostles of our Lord Jesus Christ foretold. ¹⁸They said to you, "In the last times there will be scoffers who will follow their own ungodly desires." ¹⁹These are the people who divide you, who follow mere natural instincts and do not have the Spirit.

²⁰But you, dear friends, by building yourselves up in your most holy faith and praying in the Holy Spirit, ²¹keep yourselves in God's love as you wait for the mercy of our Lord Jesus Christ to bring you to eternal life.

²²Be merciful to those who doubt; ²³save others by snatching them from the fire; to others show mercy, mixed with fear—hating even the clothing stained by corrupted flesh. [c]

²⁴To him who is able to keep you from stumbling and to present you before his glorious presence without fault and with great joy— ²⁵to the only God our Savior be glory, majesty, power and authority, through Jesus Christ our Lord, before all ages, now and forevermore! Amen.

---

[a] 9 Jude is alluding to the Jewish *Testament of Moses* (approximately the first century A.D.)
[b] 14,15 From the Jewish *First Book of Enoch* (approximately the first century B.C.) [c] 22,23 The Greek manuscripts of these verses vary at several points.

REVELATION

The ancient Roman Empire defended its economic and political control in spiritual terms, calling its gospel the *Pax Romana*, or Roman Peace. While in exile on the island of Patmos, a Jewish Christian prophet named John received a vision showing that the cult of emperor worship would soon become deadly to followers of the Messiah. The book of Revelation (or Apocalypse, meaning *unveiling*) is a warning, circulated to seven cities in the Roman province of Asia Minor. John's main point is to challenge and encourage the believers in the midst of their opposition and persecution.

Revelation is an apocalypse, a literary form well known in John's day. In an apocalypse a visitor from heaven reveals the secrets of the unseen world and the future through vivid symbols. While the symbols may appear strange at first, they become more clear when seen in their first-century setting and in light of other Bible imagery.

John's vision has four main parts, each marked by the phrase *in the Spirit*. After words of warning and encouragement to each of the seven churches, John's visions then center on Jesus—his role in redemption and the judgments he brings to the world. The immoral political and economic forces that rebel against God will be destroyed, and the Messiah will triumph over all his enemies. The vision closes with the promise that God's faithful servants will reign over the new creation.

Revelation also functions as the appropriate conclusion to the entire drama of the Bible. John concludes with images from the garden of Eden, the first story in the Bible. The world will experience a fresh beginning: *He who was seated on the throne said, "I am making everything new!"*

---

1 The revelation from Jesus Christ, which God gave him to show his servants what must soon take place. He made it known by sending his angel to his servant John, ²who testifies to everything he saw — that is, the word of God and the testimony of Jesus Christ. ³Blessed is the one who reads aloud the words of this prophecy, and blessed are those who hear it and take to heart what is written in it, because the time is near.

⁴John,

To the seven churches in the province of Asia:

Grace and peace to you from him who is, and who was, and who is to come, and from the seven spirits[a] before his throne, ⁵and from Jesus Christ, who is the faithful witness, the firstborn from the dead, and the ruler of the kings of the earth.

To him who loves us and has freed us from our sins by his blood, ⁶and has made us to be a kingdom and priests to serve his God and Father—to him be glory and power for ever and ever! Amen.

⁷ "Look, he is coming with the clouds,"[b]
and "every eye will see him,
even those who pierced him";

---

[a] 4 That is, the sevenfold Spirit   [b] 7 Daniel 7:13

and all peoples on earth "will mourn because of him."[a]

So shall it be! Amen.

[8]"I am the Alpha and the Omega," says the Lord God, "who is, and who was, and who is to come, the Almighty."

[9]I, John, your brother and companion in the suffering and kingdom and patient endurance that are ours in Jesus, was on the island of Patmos because of the word of God and the testimony of Jesus. [10]On the Lord's Day I was in the Spirit, and I heard behind me a loud voice like a trumpet, [11]which said: "Write on a scroll what you see and send it to the seven churches: to Ephesus, Smyrna, Pergamum, Thyatira, Sardis, Philadelphia and Laodicea."

[12]I turned around to see the voice that was speaking to me. And when I turned I saw seven golden lampstands, [13]and among the lampstands was someone like a son of man,[b] dressed in a robe reaching down to his feet and with a golden sash around his chest. [14]The hair on his head was white like wool, as white as snow, and his eyes were like blazing fire. [15]His feet were like bronze glowing in a furnace, and his voice was like the sound of rushing waters. [16]In his right hand he held seven stars, and coming out of his mouth was a sharp, double-edged sword. His face was like the sun shining in all its brilliance.

[17]When I saw him, I fell at his feet as though dead. Then he placed his right hand on me and said: "Do not be afraid. I am the First and the Last. [18]I am the Living One; I was dead, and now look, I am alive for ever and ever! And I hold the keys of death and Hades.

[19]"Write, therefore, what you have seen, what is now and what will take place later. [20]The mystery of the seven stars that you saw in my right hand and of the seven golden lampstands is this: The seven stars are the angels[c] of the seven churches, and the seven lampstands are the seven churches.

2 "To the angel[d] of the church in Ephesus write:

These are the words of him who holds the seven stars in his right hand and walks among the seven golden lampstands. [2]I know your deeds, your hard work and your perseverance. I know that you cannot tolerate wicked people, that you have tested those who claim to be apostles but are not, and have found them false. [3]You have persevered and have endured hardships for my name, and have not grown weary.

[4]Yet I hold this against you: You have forsaken the love you had at first. [5]Consider how far you have fallen! Repent and do the things you did at first. If you do not repent, I will come to you and remove your lampstand from its place. [6]But you have this in your favor: You hate the practices of the Nicolaitans, which I also hate.

[7]Whoever has ears, let them hear what the Spirit says to the churches. To the one who is victorious, I will give the right to eat from the tree of life, which is in the paradise of God.

---

[a] 7 Zech. 12:10   [b] 13 See Daniel 7:13.   [c] 20 Or messengers   [d] 1 Or messenger; also in verses 8, 12 and 18

8"To the angel of the church in Smyrna write:

These are the words of him who is the First and the Last, who died and came to life again. 9I know your afflictions and your poverty — yet you are rich! I know about the slander of those who say they are Jews and are not, but are a synagogue of Satan. 10Do not be afraid of what you are about to suffer. I tell you, the devil will put some of you in prison to test you, and you will suffer persecution for ten days. Be faithful, even to the point of death, and I will give you life as your victor's crown.

11Whoever has ears, let them hear what the Spirit says to the churches. The one who is victorious will not be hurt at all by the second death.

12"To the angel of the church in Pergamum write:

These are the words of him who has the sharp, double-edged sword. 13I know where you live — where Satan has his throne. Yet you remain true to my name. You did not renounce your faith in me, not even in the days of Antipas, my faithful witness, who was put to death in your city — where Satan lives.

14Nevertheless, I have a few things against you: There are some among you who hold to the teaching of Balaam, who taught Balak to entice the Israelites to sin so that they ate food sacrificed to idols and committed sexual immorality. 15Likewise, you also have those who hold to the teaching of the Nicolaitans. 16Repent therefore! Otherwise, I will soon come to you and will fight against them with the sword of my mouth.

17Whoever has ears, let them hear what the Spirit says to the churches. To the one who is victorious, I will give some of the hidden manna. I will also give that person a white stone with a new name written on it, known only to the one who receives it.

18"To the angel of the church in Thyatira write:

These are the words of the Son of God, whose eyes are like blazing fire and whose feet are like burnished bronze. 19I know your deeds, your love and faith, your service and perseverance, and that you are now doing more than you did at first.

20Nevertheless, I have this against you: You tolerate that woman Jezebel, who calls herself a prophet. By her teaching she misleads my servants into sexual immorality and the eating of food sacrificed to idols. 21I have given her time to repent of her immorality, but she is unwilling. 22So I will cast her on a bed of suffering, and I will make those who commit adultery with her suffer intensely, unless they repent of her ways. 23I will strike her children dead. Then all the churches will know that I am he who searches hearts and minds, and I will repay each of you according to your deeds.

24Now I say to the rest of you in Thyatira, to you who do not hold to her teaching and have not learned Satan's so-called deep secrets, 'I will not impose any other burden on you, 25except to hold on to what you have until I come.'

26To the one who is victorious and does my will to the end, I will give authority over the nations— 27that one 'will rule them with an iron scepter and will dash them to pieces like pottery'*a*—just as I have received authority from my Father. 28I will also give that one the morning star. 29Whoever has ears, let them hear what the Spirit says to the churches.

3 "To the angel*b* of the church in Sardis write:

These are the words of him who holds the seven spirits*c* of God and the seven stars. I know your deeds; you have a reputation of being alive, but you are dead. 2Wake up! Strengthen what remains and is about to die, for I have found your deeds unfinished in the sight of my God. 3Remember, therefore, what you have received and heard; hold it fast, and repent. But if you do not wake up, I will come like a thief, and you will not know at what time I will come to you.

4Yet you have a few people in Sardis who have not soiled their clothes. They will walk with me, dressed in white, for they are worthy. 5The one who is victorious will, like them, be dressed in white. I will never blot out the name of that person from the book of life, but will acknowledge that name

before my Father and his angels. 6Whoever has ears, let them hear what the Spirit says to the churches.

7"To the angel of the church in Philadelphia write:

These are the words of him who is holy and true, who holds the key of David. What he opens no one can shut, and what he shuts no one can open. 8I know your deeds. See, I have placed before you an open door that no one can shut. I know that you have little strength, yet you have kept my word and have not denied my name. 9I will make those who are of the synagogue of Satan, who claim to be Jews though they are not, but are liars—I will make them come and fall down at your feet and acknowledge that I have loved you. 10Since you have kept my command to endure patiently, I will also keep you from the hour of trial that is going to come on the whole world to test the inhabitants of the earth.

11I am coming soon. Hold on to what you have, so that no one will take your crown. 12The one who is victorious I will make a pillar in the temple of my God. Never again will they leave it. I will write on them the name of my God and the name of the city of my God, the new Jerusalem, which is coming down out of heaven from my God; and I will also write on them my new name. 13Whoever has ears, let them hear what the Spirit says to the churches.

a 27 Psalm 2:9   *b 1* Or *messenger*; also in verses 7 and 14   *c 1* That is, the sevenfold Spirit

¹⁴ "To the angel of the church in Laodicea write:

These are the words of the Amen, the faithful and true witness, the ruler of God's creation. ¹⁵ I know your deeds, that you are neither cold nor hot. I wish you were either one or the other! ¹⁶ So, because you are lukewarm—neither hot nor cold—I am about to spit you out of my mouth. ¹⁷ You say, 'I am rich; I have acquired wealth and do not need a thing.' But you do not realize that you are wretched, pitiful, poor, blind and naked. ¹⁸ I counsel you to buy from me gold refined in the fire, so you can become rich; and white clothes to wear, so you can cover your shameful nakedness; and salve to put on your eyes, so you can see.

¹⁹ Those whom I love I rebuke and discipline. So be earnest and repent. ²⁰ Here I am! I stand at the door and knock. If anyone hears my voice and opens the door, I will come in and eat with that person, and they with me.

²¹ To the one who is victorious, I will give the right to sit with me on my throne, just as I was victorious and sat down with my Father on his throne. ²² Whoever has ears, let them hear what the Spirit says to the churches."

4 After this I looked, and there before me was a door standing open in heaven. And the voice I had first heard speaking to me like a trumpet said, "Come up here, and I will show you what must take place after this." ² At once I was in the Spirit, and there before me was a throne in heaven with someone sitting on it. ³ And the one who sat there had the appearance of jasper and ruby. A rainbow that shone like an emerald encircled the throne. ⁴ Surrounding the throne were twenty-four other thrones, and seated on them were twenty-four elders. They were dressed in white and had crowns of gold on their heads. ⁵ From the throne came flashes of lightning, rumblings and peals of thunder. In front of the throne, seven lamps were blazing. These are the seven spirits[a] of God. ⁶ Also in front of the throne there was what looked like a sea of glass, clear as crystal.

In the center, around the throne, were four living creatures, and they were covered with eyes, in front and in back. ⁷ The first living creature was like a lion, the second was like an ox, the third had a face like a man, the fourth was like a flying eagle. ⁸ Each of the four living creatures had six wings and was covered with eyes all around, even under its wings. Day and night they never stop saying:

" 'Holy, holy, holy
is the Lord God Almighty,'[b]
who was, and is, and is to come."

⁹ Whenever the living creatures give glory, honor and thanks to him who sits on the throne and who lives for ever and ever, ¹⁰ the twenty-four elders fall down before him who sits on the throne and worship him who lives for ever and ever. They lay their crowns before the throne and say:

ᵃ 5 That is, the sevenfold Spirit   ᵇ 8 Isaiah 6:3

11 "You are worthy, our Lord and God,
> to receive glory and honor and power,
> for you created all things,
> and by your will they were created
> and have their being."

5 Then I saw in the right hand of him who sat on the throne a scroll with writing on both sides and sealed with seven seals. ²And I saw a mighty angel proclaiming in a loud voice, "Who is worthy to break the seals and open the scroll?" ³But no one in heaven or on earth or under the earth could open the scroll or even look inside it. ⁴I wept and wept because no one was found who was worthy to open the scroll or look inside. ⁵Then one of the elders said to me, "Do not weep! See, the Lion of the tribe of Judah, the Root of David, has triumphed. He is able to open the scroll and its seven seals."

⁶Then I saw a Lamb, looking as if it had been slain, standing at the center of the throne, encircled by the four living creatures and the elders. The Lamb had seven horns and seven eyes, which are the seven spirits[a] of God sent out into all the earth. ⁷He went and took the scroll from the right hand of him who sat on the throne. ⁸And when he had taken it, the four living creatures and the twenty-four elders fell down before the Lamb. Each one had a harp and they were holding golden bowls full of incense, which are the prayers of God's people. ⁹And they sang a new song, saying:

> "You are worthy to take the scroll
> and to open its seals,
> because you were slain,
> and with your blood you purchased for God
> persons from every tribe and language and people and nation.
10 You have made them to be a kingdom and priests to serve our God,
> and they will reign[b] on the earth."

11 Then I looked and heard the voice of many angels, numbering thousands upon thousands, and ten thousand times ten thousand. They encircled the throne and the living creatures and the elders. ¹²In a loud voice they were saying:

> "Worthy is the Lamb, who was slain,
> to receive power and wealth and wisdom and strength and honor and glory and praise!"

¹³Then I heard every creature in heaven and on earth and under the earth and on the sea, and all that is in them, saying:

> "To him who sits on the throne and to the Lamb
> be praise and honor and glory and power,
> for ever and ever!"

¹⁴The four living creatures said, "Amen," and the elders fell down and worshiped.

6 I watched as the Lamb opened the first of the seven seals. Then I heard one of the four living creatures say in a voice like thunder, "Come!" ²I looked, and there before me was a white horse! Its rider held a bow, and he was given a crown,

---

[a] 6 That is, the sevenfold Spirit   [b] 10 Some manuscripts *they reign*

and he rode out as a conqueror bent on conquest.

3 When the Lamb opened the second seal, I heard the second living creature say, "Come!" 4 Then another horse came out, a fiery red one. Its rider was given power to take peace from the earth and to make people kill each other. To him was given a large sword.

5 When the Lamb opened the third seal, I heard the third living creature say, "Come!" I looked, and there before me was a black horse! Its rider was holding a pair of scales in his hand. 6 Then I heard what sounded like a voice among the four living creatures, saying, "Two pounds*a* of wheat for a day's wages,*b* and six pounds*c* of barley for a day's wages,*b* and do not damage the oil and the wine!"

7 When the Lamb opened the fourth seal, I heard the voice of the fourth living creature say, "Come!" 8 I looked, and there before me was a pale horse! Its rider was named Death, and Hades was following close behind him. They were given power over a fourth of the earth to kill by sword, famine and plague, and by the wild beasts of the earth.

9 When he opened the fifth seal, I saw under the altar the souls of those who had been slain because of the word of God and the testimony they had maintained. 10 They called out in a loud voice, "How long, Sovereign Lord, holy and true, until you judge the inhabitants of the earth and avenge our blood?" 11 Then each of them was given a white robe, and they were told to wait a little longer, until the full number of their fellow servants,

their brothers and sisters,*d* were killed just as they had been.

12 I watched as he opened the sixth seal. There was a great earthquake. The sun turned black like sackcloth made of goat hair, the whole moon turned blood red, 13 and the stars in the sky fell to earth, as figs drop from a fig tree when shaken by a strong wind. 14 The heavens receded like a scroll being rolled up, and every mountain and island was removed from its place.

15 Then the kings of the earth, the princes, the generals, the rich, the mighty, and everyone else, both slave and free, hid in caves and among the rocks of the mountains. 16 They called to the mountains and the rocks, "Fall on us and hide us*e* from the face of him who sits on the throne and from the wrath of the Lamb! 17 For the great day of their*f* wrath has come, and who can withstand it?"

7 After this I saw four angels standing at the four corners of the earth, holding back the four winds of the earth to prevent any wind from blowing on the land or on the sea or on any tree. 2 Then I saw another angel coming up from the east, having the seal of the living God. He called out in a loud voice to the four angels who had been given power to harm the land and the sea: 3 "Do not harm the land or the sea or the trees until we put a seal on the foreheads of the servants of our God." 4 Then I heard the number of those who were sealed: 144,000 from all the tribes of Israel.

5 From the tribe of Judah 12,000 were sealed,

---

a 6 Or about 1 kilogram   *b 6* Greek *a denarius*   *c 6* Or about 3 kilograms   *d 11* The Greek word for *brothers and sisters* (*adelphoi*) refers here to believers, both men and women, as part of God's family; also in 12:10; 19:10.   *e 16* See Hosea 10:8.   *f 17* Some manuscripts *his*

from the tribe of Reuben 12,000,

from the tribe of Gad 12,000,

⁶from the tribe of Asher 12,000,

from the tribe of Naphtali 12,000,

from the tribe of Manasseh 12,000,

⁷from the tribe of Simeon 12,000,

from the tribe of Levi 12,000,

from the tribe of Issachar 12,000,

⁸from the tribe of Zebulun 12,000,

from the tribe of Joseph 12,000,

from the tribe of Benjamin 12,000.

⁹After this I looked, and there before me was a great multitude that no one could count, from every nation, tribe, people and language, standing before the throne and before the Lamb. They were wearing white robes and were holding palm branches in their hands. ¹⁰And they cried out in a loud voice:

"Salvation belongs to our God,
who sits on the throne,
and to the Lamb."

¹¹All the angels were standing around the throne and around the elders and the four living creatures. They fell down on their faces before the throne and worshiped God, ¹²saying:

"Amen!
Praise and glory
and wisdom and thanks and honor
and power and strength
be to our God for ever and ever.
Amen!"

¹³Then one of the elders asked me, "These in white robes—who are they, and where did they come from?"

¹⁴I answered, "Sir, you know."

And he said, "These are they who have come out of the great tribulation; they have washed their robes and made them white in the blood of the Lamb. ¹⁵Therefore,

"they are before the throne of God
and serve him day and night in his temple;
and he who sits on the throne will shelter them with his presence.
¹⁶ 'Never again will they hunger; never again will they thirst.
The sun will not beat down on them,'ᵃ
nor any scorching heat.
¹⁷For the Lamb at the center of the throne
will be their shepherd;
'he will lead them to springs of living water.'ᵃ
'And God will wipe away every tear from their eyes.'ᵇ"

8 When he opened the seventh seal, there was silence in heaven for about half an hour.

²And I saw the seven angels who stand before God, and seven trumpets were given to them.

³Another angel, who had a golden censer, came and stood at the altar. He was given much incense to offer, with the prayers of all God's people, on the golden altar in front of the throne. ⁴The smoke of the incense, together with the prayers of God's people, went up before God from the angel's hand. ⁵Then the angel took the censer, filled it with fire from the altar, and hurled it on

ᵃ 16,17 Isaiah 49:10   ᵇ 17 Isaiah 25:8

the earth; and there came peals of thunder, rumblings, flashes of lightning and an earthquake.

6Then the seven angels who had the seven trumpets prepared to sound them.

7The first angel sounded his trumpet, and there came hail and fire mixed with blood, and it was hurled down on the earth. A third of the earth was burned up, a third of the trees were burned up, and all the green grass was burned up.

8The second angel sounded his trumpet, and something like a huge mountain, all ablaze, was thrown into the sea. A third of the sea turned into blood, 9a third of the living creatures in the sea died, and a third of the ships were destroyed.

10The third angel sounded his trumpet, and a great star, blazing like a torch, fell from the sky on a third of the rivers and on the springs of water— 11the name of the star is Wormwood.[a] A third of the waters turned bitter, and many people died from the waters that had become bitter.

12The fourth angel sounded his trumpet, and a third of the sun was struck, a third of the moon, and a third of the stars, so that a third of them turned dark. A third of the day was without light, and also a third of the night.

13As I watched, I heard an eagle that was flying in midair call out in a loud voice: "Woe! Woe! Woe to the inhabitants of the earth, because of the trumpet blasts about to be sounded by the other three angels!"

9 The fifth angel sounded his trumpet, and I saw a star that had fallen from the sky to the earth. The star was given the key to the shaft of the Abyss. 2When he opened the Abyss, smoke rose from it like the smoke from a gigantic furnace. The sun and sky were darkened by the smoke from the Abyss. 3And out of the smoke locusts came down on the earth and were given power like that of scorpions of the earth. 4They were told not to harm the grass of the earth or any plant or tree, but only those people who did not have the seal of God on their foreheads. 5They were not allowed to kill them but only to torture them for five months. And the agony they suffered was like that of the sting of a scorpion when it strikes. 6During those days people will seek death but will not find it; they will long to die, but death will elude them.

7The locusts looked like horses prepared for battle. On their heads they wore something like crowns of gold, and their faces resembled human faces. 8Their hair was like women's hair, and their teeth were like lions' teeth. 9They had breastplates like breastplates of iron, and the sound of their wings was like the thundering of many horses and chariots rushing into battle. 10They had tails with stingers, like scorpions, and in their tails they had power to torment people for five months. 11They had as king over them the angel of the Abyss, whose name in Hebrew is Abaddon and in Greek is Apollyon (that is, Destroyer).

12The first woe is past; two other woes are yet to come.

13The sixth angel sounded his trumpet, and I heard a voice coming from the four horns of the golden altar that is before God. 14It

---

[a] 11 Wormwood is a bitter substance.

said to the sixth angel who had the trumpet, "Release the four angels who are bound at the great river Euphrates." 15And the four angels who had been kept ready for this very hour and day and month and year were released to kill a third of mankind. 16The number of the mounted troops was twice ten thousand times ten thousand. I heard their number.

17The horses and riders I saw in my vision looked like this: Their breastplates were fiery red, dark blue, and yellow as sulfur. The heads of the horses resembled the heads of lions, and out of their mouths came fire, smoke and sulfur. 18A third of mankind was killed by the three plagues of fire, smoke and sulfur that came out of their mouths. 19The power of the horses was in their mouths and in their tails; for their tails were like snakes, having heads with which they inflict injury.

20The rest of mankind who were not killed by these plagues still did not repent of the work of their hands; they did not stop worshiping demons, and idols of gold, silver, bronze, stone and wood—idols that cannot see or hear or walk. 21Nor did they repent of their murders, their magic arts, their sexual immorality or their thefts.

10 Then I saw another mighty angel coming down from heaven. He was robed in a cloud, with a rainbow above his head; his face was like the sun, and his legs were like fiery pillars. 2He was holding a little scroll, which lay open in his hand. He planted his right foot on the sea and his left foot on the land, 3and he gave a loud shout like the roar of a lion. When he shouted,

the voices of the seven thunders spoke. 4And when the seven thunders spoke, I was about to write; but I heard a voice from heaven say, "Seal up what the seven thunders have said and do not write it down."

5Then the angel I had seen standing on the sea and on the land raised his right hand to heaven. 6And he swore by him who lives for ever and ever, who created the heavens and all that is in them, the earth and all that is in it, and the sea and all that is in it, and said, "There will be no more delay! 7But in the days when the seventh angel is about to sound his trumpet, the mystery of God will be accomplished, just as he announced to his servants the prophets."

8Then the voice that I had heard from heaven spoke to me once more: "Go, take the scroll that lies open in the hand of the angel who is standing on the sea and on the land."

9So I went to the angel and asked him to give me the little scroll. He said to me, "Take it and eat it. It will turn your stomach sour, but 'in your mouth it will be as sweet as honey.'a" 10I took the little scroll from the angel's hand and ate it. It tasted as sweet as honey in my mouth, but when I had eaten it, my stomach turned sour. 11Then I was told, "You must prophesy again about many peoples, nations, languages and kings."

11 I was given a reed like a measuring rod and was told, "Go and measure the temple of God and the altar, with its worshipers. 2But exclude the outer court; do not measure it, because it has been given to the Gentiles. They

a 9 Ezek. 3:3

will trample on the holy city for 42 months. ³And I will appoint my two witnesses, and they will prophesy for 1,260 days, clothed in sackcloth." ⁴They are "the two olive trees" and the two lampstands, and "they stand before the Lord of the earth."ᵃ ⁵If anyone tries to harm them, fire comes from their mouths and devours their enemies. This is how anyone who wants to harm them must die. ⁶They have power to shut up the heavens so that it will not rain during the time they are prophesying; and they have power to turn the waters into blood and to strike the earth with every kind of plague as often as they want.

⁷Now when they have finished their testimony, the beast that comes up from the Abyss will attack them, and overpower and kill them. ⁸Their bodies will lie in the public square of the great city—which is figuratively called Sodom and Egypt—where also their Lord was crucified. ⁹For three and a half days some from every people, tribe, language and nation will gaze on their bodies and refuse them burial. ¹⁰The inhabitants of the earth will gloat over them and will celebrate by sending each other gifts, because these two prophets had tormented those who live on the earth.

¹¹But after the three and a half days the breathᵇ of life from God entered them, and they stood on their feet, and terror struck those who saw them. ¹²Then they heard a loud voice from heaven saying to them, "Come up here." And they went up to heaven in a cloud, while their enemies looked on.

¹³At that very hour there was a severe earthquake and a tenth of the city collapsed. Seven thousand people were killed in the earthquake, and the survivors were terrified and gave glory to the God of heaven.

¹⁴The second woe has passed; the third woe is coming soon.

¹⁵The seventh angel sounded his trumpet, and there were loud voices in heaven, which said:

> "The kingdom of the world has
> become
>   the kingdom of our Lord and
>   of his Messiah,
>   and he will reign for ever and
>   ever."

¹⁶And the twenty-four elders, who were seated on their thrones before God, fell on their faces and worshiped God, ¹⁷saying:

> "We give thanks to you, Lord
>   God Almighty,
>   the One who is and who was,
> because you have taken your
>   great power
>   and have begun to reign.
> ¹⁸The nations were angry,
>   and your wrath has come.
> The time has come for judging
>   the dead,
>   and for rewarding your
>   servants the prophets
> and your people who revere your
>   name,
>   both great and small—
> and for destroying those who
>   destroy the earth."

¹⁹Then God's temple in heaven was opened, and within his temple was seen the ark of his covenant. And there came flashes of lightning, rumblings, peals of thunder, an earthquake and a severe hailstorm.

ᵃ 4 See Zech. 4:3,11,14.   ᵇ 11 Or *Spirit* (see Ezek. 37:5,14)

12 A great sign appeared in heaven: a woman clothed with the sun, with the moon under her feet and a crown of twelve stars on her head. ²She was pregnant and cried out in pain as she was about to give birth. ³Then another sign appeared in heaven: an enormous red dragon with seven heads and ten horns and seven crowns on its heads. ⁴Its tail swept a third of the stars out of the sky and flung them to the earth. The dragon stood in front of the woman who was about to give birth, so that it might devour her child the moment he was born. ⁵She gave birth to a son, a male child, who "will rule all the nations with an iron scepter."[a] And her child was snatched up to God and to his throne. ⁶The woman fled into the wilderness to a place prepared for her by God, where she might be taken care of for 1,260 days.

⁷Then war broke out in heaven. Michael and his angels fought against the dragon, and the dragon and his angels fought back. ⁸But he was not strong enough, and they lost their place in heaven. ⁹The great dragon was hurled down — that ancient serpent called the devil, or Satan, who leads the whole world astray. He was hurled to the earth, and his angels with him.

¹⁰Then I heard a loud voice in heaven say:

"Now have come the salvation
        and the power
    and the kingdom of our God,
    and the authority of his
        Messiah.
For the accuser of our brothers
        and sisters,
    who accuses them before our
        God day and night,
has been hurled down.
¹¹They triumphed over him
    by the blood of the Lamb
    and by the word of their
        testimony;
they did not love their lives so
        much
    as to shrink from death.
¹²Therefore rejoice, you heavens
    and you who dwell in them!
But woe to the earth and the sea,
    because the devil has gone
        down to you!
He is filled with fury,
    because he knows that his
        time is short."

¹³When the dragon saw that he had been hurled to the earth, he pursued the woman who had given birth to the male child. ¹⁴The woman was given the two wings of a great eagle, so that she might fly to the place prepared for her in the wilderness, where she would be taken care of for a time, times and half a time, out of the serpent's reach. ¹⁵Then from his mouth the serpent spewed water like a river, to overtake the woman and sweep her away with the torrent. ¹⁶But the earth helped the woman by opening its mouth and swallowing the river that the dragon had spewed out of his mouth. ¹⁷Then the dragon was enraged at the woman and went off to wage war against the rest of her offspring — those who keep God's commands and hold fast their testimony about Jesus.

13 The dragon[b] stood on the shore of the sea. And I saw a beast coming out of the sea. It had ten horns and seven heads, with ten crowns on its horns, and on each head a blasphemous name. ²The beast I saw resembled a leopard,

---

[a] 5 Psalm 2:9   [b] 1 Some manuscripts *And I*

but had feet like those of a bear and a mouth like that of a lion. The dragon gave the beast his power and his throne and great authority. ³One of the heads of the beast seemed to have had a fatal wound, but the fatal wound had been healed. The whole world was filled with wonder and followed the beast. ⁴People worshiped the dragon because he had given authority to the beast, and they also worshiped the beast and asked, "Who is like the beast? Who can wage war against it?"

⁵The beast was given a mouth to utter proud words and blasphemies and to exercise its authority for forty-two months. ⁶It opened its mouth to blaspheme God, and to slander his name and his dwelling place and those who live in heaven. ⁷It was given power to wage war against God's holy people and to conquer them. And it was given authority over every tribe, people, language and nation. ⁸All inhabitants of the earth will worship the beast—all whose names have not been written in the Lamb's book of life, the Lamb who was slain from the creation of the world.ᵃ

⁹Whoever has ears, let them hear.

¹⁰ "If anyone is to go into captivity,
    into captivity they will go.
If anyone is to be killedᵇ with the
        sword,
    with the sword they will be
        killed."ᶜ

This calls for patient endurance and faithfulness on the part of God's people.

¹¹Then I saw a second beast, coming out of the earth. It had two horns like a lamb, but it spoke like a dragon. ¹²It exercised all the authority of the first beast on its behalf, and made the earth and its inhabitants worship the first beast, whose fatal wound had been healed. ¹³And it performed great signs, even causing fire to come down from heaven to the earth in full view of the people. ¹⁴Because of the signs it was given power to perform on behalf of the first beast, it deceived the inhabitants of the earth. It ordered them to set up an image in honor of the beast who was wounded by the sword and yet lived. ¹⁵The second beast was given power to give breath to the image of the first beast, so that the image could speak and cause all who refused to worship the image to be killed. ¹⁶It also forced all people, great and small, rich and poor, free and slave, to receive a mark on their right hands or on their foreheads, ¹⁷so that they could not buy or sell unless they had the mark, which is the name of the beast or the number of its name.

¹⁸This calls for wisdom. Let the person who has insight calculate the number of the beast, for it is the number of a man.ᵈ That number is 666.

14 Then I looked, and there before me was the Lamb, standing on Mount Zion, and with him 144,000 who had his name and his Father's name written on their foreheads. ²And I heard a sound from heaven like the roar of rushing waters and like a loud peal of thunder. The sound I heard was like that of harpists playing their harps. ³And they sang a new song before the throne and before the four living creatures and the elders. No one

---

ᵃ 8 Or *written from the creation of the world in the book of life belonging to the Lamb who was slain*   ᵇ 10 Some manuscripts *anyone kills*   ᶜ 10 Jer. 15:2   ᵈ 18 Or *is humanity's number*

could learn the song except the 144,000 who had been redeemed from the earth. [4]These are those who did not defile themselves with women, for they remained virgins. They follow the Lamb wherever he goes. They were purchased from among mankind and offered as firstfruits to God and the Lamb. [5]No lie was found in their mouths; they are blameless.

[6]Then I saw another angel flying in midair, and he had the eternal gospel to proclaim to those who live on the earth—to every nation, tribe, language and people. [7]He said in a loud voice, "Fear God and give him glory, because the hour of his judgment has come. Worship him who made the heavens, the earth, the sea and the springs of water."

[8]A second angel followed and said, "'Fallen! Fallen is Babylon the Great,'[a] which made all the nations drink the maddening wine of her adulteries."

[9]A third angel followed them and said in a loud voice: "If anyone worships the beast and its image and receives its mark on their forehead or on their hand, [10]they, too, will drink the wine of God's fury, which has been poured full strength into the cup of his wrath. They will be tormented with burning sulfur in the presence of the holy angels and of the Lamb. [11]And the smoke of their torment will rise for ever and ever. There will be no rest day or night for those who worship the beast and its image, or for anyone who receives the mark of its name." [12]This calls for patient endurance on the part of the people of God who keep his commands and remain faithful to Jesus.

[13]Then I heard a voice from heaven say, "Write this: Blessed are the dead who die in the Lord from now on."

"Yes," says the Spirit, "they will rest from their labor, for their deeds will follow them."

[14]I looked, and there before me was a white cloud, and seated on the cloud was one like a son of man[b] with a crown of gold on his head and a sharp sickle in his hand. [15]Then another angel came out of the temple and called in a loud voice to him who was sitting on the cloud, "Take your sickle and reap, because the time to reap has come, for the harvest of the earth is ripe." [16]So he who was seated on the cloud swung his sickle over the earth, and the earth was harvested.

[17]Another angel came out of the temple in heaven, and he too had a sharp sickle. [18]Still another angel, who had charge of the fire, came from the altar and called in a loud voice to him who had the sharp sickle, "Take your sharp sickle and gather the clusters of grapes from the earth's vine, because its grapes are ripe." [19]The angel swung his sickle on the earth, gathered its grapes and threw them into the great winepress of God's wrath. [20]They were trampled in the winepress outside the city, and blood flowed out of the press, rising as high as the horses' bridles for a distance of 1,600 stadia.[c]

15 I saw in heaven another great and marvelous sign: seven angels with the seven last plagues—last, because with them God's wrath is completed. [2]And I saw what looked like a sea of glass glowing with fire and, standing beside the sea, those who had been

---

[a] 8 Isaiah 21:9   [b] 14 See Daniel 7:13.   [c] 20 That is, about 180 miles or about 300 kilometers

victorious over the beast and its image and over the number of its name. They held harps given them by God [3] and sang the song of God's servant Moses and of the Lamb:

"Great and marvelous are your deeds,
    Lord God Almighty.
Just and true are your ways,
    King of the nations.[a]
[4] Who will not fear you, Lord,
    and bring glory to your name?
For you alone are holy.
All nations will come
    and worship before you,
for your righteous acts have
    been revealed."[b]

[5] After this I looked, and I saw in heaven the temple — that is, the tabernacle of the covenant law — and it was opened. [6] Out of the temple came the seven angels with the seven plagues. They were dressed in clean, shining linen and wore golden sashes around their chests. [7] Then one of the four living creatures gave to the seven angels seven golden bowls filled with the wrath of God, who lives for ever and ever. [8] And the temple was filled with smoke from the glory of God and from his power, and no one could enter the temple until the seven plagues of the seven angels were completed.

16 Then I heard a loud voice from the temple saying to the seven angels, "Go, pour out the seven bowls of God's wrath on the earth."

[2] The first angel went and poured out his bowl on the land, and ugly, festering sores broke out on the people who had the mark of the beast and worshiped its image.

[3] The second angel poured out his bowl on the sea, and it turned into blood like that of a dead person, and every living thing in the sea died.

[4] The third angel poured out his bowl on the rivers and springs of water, and they became blood. [5] Then I heard the angel in charge of the waters say:

"You are just in these judgments,
    O Holy One,
you who are and who were;
[6] for they have shed the blood of
    your holy people and your
    prophets,
    and you have given them
    blood to drink as they
    deserve."

[7] And I heard the altar respond:

"Yes, Lord God Almighty,
    true and just are your
    judgments."

[8] The fourth angel poured out his bowl on the sun, and the sun was allowed to scorch people with fire. [9] They were seared by the intense heat and they cursed the name of God, who had control over these plagues, but they refused to repent and glorify him.

[10] The fifth angel poured out his bowl on the throne of the beast, and its kingdom was plunged into darkness. People gnawed their tongues in agony [11] and cursed the God of heaven because of their pains and their sores, but they refused to repent of what they had done.

[12] The sixth angel poured out his bowl on the great river Euphrates, and its water was dried up to prepare the way for the kings from the East. [13] Then I saw three impure spirits that looked like frogs; they

---

[a] 3 Some manuscripts *ages* [b] 3,4 Phrases in this song are drawn from Psalm 111:2,3; Deut. 32:4; Jer. 10:7; Psalms 86:9; 98:2.

came out of the mouth of the dragon, out of the mouth of the beast and out of the mouth of the false prophet. 14They are demonic spirits that perform signs, and they go out to the kings of the whole world, to gather them for the battle on the great day of God Almighty.

15"Look, I come like a thief! Blessed is the one who stays awake and remains clothed, so as not to go naked and be shamefully exposed."

16Then they gathered the kings together to the place that in Hebrew is called Armageddon.

17The seventh angel poured out his bowl into the air, and out of the temple came a loud voice from the throne, saying, "It is done!" 18Then there came flashes of lightning, rumblings, peals of thunder and a severe earthquake. No earthquake like it has ever occurred since mankind has been on earth, so tremendous was the quake. 19The great city split into three parts, and the cities of the nations collapsed. God remembered Babylon the Great and gave her the cup filled with the wine of the fury of his wrath. 20Every island fled away and the mountains could not be found. 21From the sky huge hailstones, each weighing about a hundred pounds,a fell on people. And they cursed God on account of the plague of hail, because the plague was so terrible.

17 One of the seven angels who had the seven bowls came and said to me, "Come, I will show you the punishment of the great prostitute, who sits by many waters. 2With her the kings of the earth committed adultery, and the inhabitants of the earth were intoxicated with the wine of her adulteries."

3Then the angel carried me away in the Spirit into a wilderness. There I saw a woman sitting on a scarlet beast that was covered with blasphemous names and had seven heads and ten horns. 4The woman was dressed in purple and scarlet, and was glittering with gold, precious stones and pearls. She held a golden cup in her hand, filled with abominable things and the filth of her adulteries. 5The name written on her forehead was a mystery:

BABYLON THE GREAT
THE MOTHER OF PROSTITUTES
AND OF THE ABOMINATIONS
OF THE EARTH.

6I saw that the woman was drunk with the blood of God's holy people, the blood of those who bore testimony to Jesus.

When I saw her, I was greatly astonished. 7Then the angel said to me: "Why are you astonished? I will explain to you the mystery of the woman and of the beast she rides, which has the seven heads and ten horns. 8The beast, which you saw, once was, now is not, and yet will come up out of the Abyss and go to its destruction. The inhabitants of the earth whose names have not been written in the book of life from the creation of the world will be astonished when they see the beast, because it once was, now is not, and yet will come.

9"This calls for a mind with wisdom. The seven heads are seven hills on which the woman sits. 10They are also seven kings. Five have fallen, one is, the other has not yet come; but when he does come, he must remain for only a little

a 21 Or about 45 kilograms

while. ¹¹The beast who once was, and now is not, is an eighth king. He belongs to the seven and is going to his destruction.

¹²"The ten horns you saw are ten kings who have not yet received a kingdom, but who for one hour will receive authority as kings along with the beast. ¹³They have one purpose and will give their power and authority to the beast. ¹⁴They will wage war against the Lamb, but the Lamb will triumph over them because he is Lord of lords and King of kings—and with him will be his called, chosen and faithful followers."

¹⁵Then the angel said to me, "The waters you saw, where the prostitute sits, are peoples, multitudes, nations and languages. ¹⁶The beast and the ten horns you saw will hate the prostitute. They will bring her to ruin and leave her naked; they will eat her flesh and burn her with fire. ¹⁷For God has put it into their hearts to accomplish his purpose by agreeing to hand over to the beast their royal authority, until God's words are fulfilled. ¹⁸The woman you saw is the great city that rules over the kings of the earth."

18 After this I saw another angel coming down from heaven. He had great authority, and the earth was illuminated by his splendor. ²With a mighty voice he shouted:

" 'Fallen! Fallen is Babylon the Great!'ᵃ
She has become a dwelling for demons
and a haunt for every impure spirit,
 a haunt for every unclean bird,
 a haunt for every unclean and detestable animal.
³ For all the nations have drunk the maddening wine of her adulteries.
The kings of the earth committed adultery with her,
 and the merchants of the earth grew rich from her excessive luxuries."

⁴Then I heard another voice from heaven say:

" 'Come out of her, my people,'ᵇ
so that you will not share in her sins,
 so that you will not receive any of her plagues;
⁵ for her sins are piled up to heaven,
 and God has remembered her crimes.
⁶ Give back to her as she has given;
 pay her back double for what she has done.
Pour her a double portion from her own cup.
⁷ Give her as much torment and grief
 as the glory and luxury she gave herself.
In her heart she boasts,
 'I sit enthroned as queen.
I am not a widow;ᶜ
I will never mourn.'
⁸ Therefore in one day her plagues will overtake her:
 death, mourning and famine.
She will be consumed by fire,
 for mighty is the Lord God who judges her.

⁹ "When the kings of the earth who committed adultery with her and shared her luxury see the smoke of her burning, they will

---

ᵃ 2 Isaiah 21:9   ᵇ 4 Jer. 51:45   ᶜ 7 See Isaiah 47:7,8.

weep and mourn over her. ¹⁰Terrified at her torment, they will stand far off and cry:

"'Woe! Woe to you, great city,
    you mighty city of Babylon!
In one hour your doom has
    come!'

¹¹ "The merchants of the earth will weep and mourn over her because no one buys their cargoes anymore— ¹²cargoes of gold, silver, precious stones and pearls; fine linen, purple, silk and scarlet cloth; every sort of citron wood, and articles of every kind made of ivory, costly wood, bronze, iron and marble; ¹³cargoes of cinnamon and spice, of incense, myrrh and frankincense, of wine and olive oil, of fine flour and wheat; cattle and sheep; horses and carriages; and human beings sold as slaves.

¹⁴"They will say, 'The fruit you longed for is gone from you. All your luxury and splendor have vanished, never to be recovered.' ¹⁵The merchants who sold these things and gained their wealth from her will stand far off, terrified at her torment. They will weep and mourn ¹⁶and cry out:

"'Woe! Woe to you, great city,
    dressed in fine linen, purple
        and scarlet,
    and glittering with gold,
        precious stones and
        pearls!
¹⁷In one hour such great wealth
    has been brought to ruin!'

"Every sea captain, and all who travel by ship, the sailors, and all who earn their living from the sea, will stand far off. ¹⁸When they see the smoke of her burning, they will exclaim, 'Was there ever a city like this great city?' ¹⁹They will throw

dust on their heads, and with weeping and mourning cry out:

"'Woe! Woe to you, great city,
    where all who had ships on the
        sea
    became rich through her
        wealth!
In one hour she has been
    brought to ruin!'

²⁰"Rejoice over her, you heavens!
    Rejoice, you people of God!
    Rejoice, apostles and
        prophets!
For God has judged her
    with the judgment she
        imposed on you."

²¹Then a mighty angel picked up a boulder the size of a large millstone and threw it into the sea, and said:

"With such violence
    the great city of Babylon will
        be thrown down,
    never to be found again.
²²The music of harpists and
        musicians, pipers and
        trumpeters,
    will never be heard in you
        again.
No worker of any trade
    will ever be found in you
        again.
The sound of a millstone
    will never be heard in you
        again.
²³The light of a lamp
    will never shine in you again.
The voice of bridegroom and
        bride
    will never be heard in you
        again.
Your merchants were the world's
        important people.
By your magic spell all the
        nations were led astray.
²⁴In her was found the blood of

prophets and of God's holy people,
of all who have been
  slaughtered on the earth."

19

After this I heard what sounded like the roar of a great multitude in heaven shouting:

"Hallelujah!
Salvation and glory and power
  belong to our God,
2 for true and just are his
  judgments.
He has condemned the great
  prostitute
who corrupted the earth by
  her adulteries.
He has avenged on her the blood
  of his servants."

3 And again they shouted:

"Hallelujah!
The smoke from her goes up for
  ever and ever."

4 The twenty-four elders and the four living creatures fell down and worshiped God, who was seated on the throne. And they cried:

"Amen, Hallelujah!"

5 Then a voice came from the throne, saying:

"Praise our God,
  all you his servants,
you who fear him,
  both great and small!"

6 Then I heard what sounded like a great multitude, like the roar of rushing waters and like loud peals of thunder, shouting:

"Hallelujah!
  For our Lord God Almighty
  reigns.
7 Let us rejoice and be glad
  and give him glory!

For the wedding of the Lamb has
  come,
  and his bride has made herself
  ready.
8 Fine linen, bright and clean,
  was given her to wear."
(Fine linen stands for the righteous acts of God's holy people.)

9 Then the angel said to me, "Write this: Blessed are those who are invited to the wedding supper of the Lamb!" And he added, "These are the true words of God."

10 At this I fell at his feet to worship him. But he said to me, "Don't do that! I am a fellow servant with you and with your brothers and sisters who hold to the testimony of Jesus. Worship God! For it is the Spirit of prophecy who bears testimony to Jesus."

11 I saw heaven standing open and there before me was a white horse, whose rider is called Faithful and True. With justice he judges and wages war. 12 His eyes are like blazing fire, and on his head are many crowns. He has a name written on him that no one knows but he himself. 13 He is dressed in a robe dipped in blood, and his name is the Word of God. 14 The armies of heaven were following him, riding on white horses and dressed in fine linen, white and clean. 15 Coming out of his mouth is a sharp sword with which to strike down the nations. "He will rule them with an iron scepter."[a] He treads the winepress of the fury of the wrath of God Almighty. 16 On his robe and on his thigh he has this name written:

KING OF KINGS AND LORD OF LORDS.

a 15 Psalm 2:9

[17]And I saw an angel standing in the sun, who cried in a loud voice to all the birds flying in midair, "Come, gather together for the great supper of God, [18]so that you may eat the flesh of kings, generals, and the mighty, of horses and their riders, and the flesh of all people, free and slave, great and small."

[19]Then I saw the beast and the kings of the earth and their armies gathered together to wage war against the rider on the horse and his army. [20]But the beast was captured, and with it the false prophet who had performed the signs on its behalf. With these signs he had deluded those who had received the mark of the beast and worshiped its image. The two of them were thrown alive into the fiery lake of burning sulfur. [21]The rest were killed with the sword coming out of the mouth of the rider on the horse, and all the birds gorged themselves on their flesh.

20 And I saw an angel coming down out of heaven, having the key to the Abyss and holding in his hand a great chain. [2]He seized the dragon, that ancient serpent, who is the devil, or Satan, and bound him for a thousand years. [3]He threw him into the Abyss, and locked and sealed it over him, to keep him from deceiving the nations anymore until the thousand years were ended. After that, he must be set free for a short time.

[4]I saw thrones on which were seated those who had been given authority to judge. And I saw the souls of those who had been beheaded because of their testimony about Jesus and because of the word of God. They[a] had not worshiped the beast or its image and had not received its mark on their foreheads or their hands. They came to life and reigned with Christ a thousand years. [5](The rest of the dead did not come to life until the thousand years were ended.) This is the first resurrection. [6]Blessed and holy are those who share in the first resurrection. The second death has no power over them, but they will be priests of God and of Christ and will reign with him for a thousand years.

[7]When the thousand years are over, Satan will be released from his prison [8]and will go out to deceive the nations in the four corners of the earth—Gog and Magog—and to gather them for battle. In number they are like the sand on the seashore. [9]They marched across the breadth of the earth and surrounded the camp of God's people, the city he loves. But fire came down from heaven and devoured them. [10]And the devil, who deceived them, was thrown into the lake of burning sulfur, where the beast and the false prophet had been thrown. They will be tormented day and night for ever and ever.

[11]Then I saw a great white throne and him who was seated on it. The earth and the heavens fled from his presence, and there was no place for them. [12]And I saw the dead, great and small, standing before the throne, and books were opened. Another book was opened, which is the book of life. The dead were judged according to what they had done as recorded in the books. [13]The sea gave up the dead that were in it, and death and Hades gave up the dead that were in them, and each person was judged according to what

---

[a] 4 Or God; I also saw those who

they had done. [14]Then death and Hades were thrown into the lake of fire. The lake of fire is the second death. [15]Anyone whose name was not found written in the book of life was thrown into the lake of fire.

21 Then I saw "a new heaven and a new earth,"[a] for the first heaven and the first earth had passed away, and there was no longer any sea. [2]I saw the Holy City, the new Jerusalem, coming down out of heaven from God, prepared as a bride beautifully dressed for her husband. [3]And I heard a loud voice from the throne saying, "Look! God's dwelling place is now among the people, and he will dwell with them. They will be his people, and God himself will be with them and be their God. [4]'He will wipe every tear from their eyes. There will be no more death'[b] or mourning or crying or pain, for the old order of things has passed away."

[5]He who was seated on the throne said, "I am making everything new!" Then he said, "Write this down, for these words are trustworthy and true."

[6]He said to me: "It is done. I am the Alpha and the Omega, the Beginning and the End. To the thirsty I will give water without cost from the spring of the water of life. [7]Those who are victorious will inherit all this, and I will be their God and they will be my children. [8]But the cowardly, the unbelieving, the vile, the murderers, the sexually immoral, those who practice magic arts, the idolaters and all liars— they will be consigned to the fiery lake of burning sulfur. This is the second death."

[9]One of the seven angels who had the seven bowls full of the seven last plagues came and said to me, "Come, I will show you the bride, the wife of the Lamb." [10]And he carried me away in the Spirit to a mountain great and high, and showed me the Holy City, Jerusalem, coming down out of heaven from God. [11]It shone with the glory of God, and its brilliance was like that of a very precious jewel, like a jasper, clear as crystal. [12]It had a great, high wall with twelve gates, and with twelve angels at the gates. On the gates were written the names of the twelve tribes of Israel. [13]There were three gates on the east, three on the north, three on the south and three on the west. [14]The wall of the city had twelve foundations, and on them were the names of the twelve apostles of the Lamb.

[15]The angel who talked with me had a measuring rod of gold to measure the city, its gates and its walls. [16]The city was laid out like a square, as long as it was wide. He measured the city with the rod and found it to be 12,000 stadia[c] in length, and as wide and high as it is long. [17]The angel measured the wall using human measurement, and it was 144 cubits[d] thick.[e] [18]The wall was made of jasper, and the city of pure gold, as pure as glass. [19]The foundations of the city walls were decorated with every kind of precious stone. The first foundation was jasper, the second sapphire, the third agate, the fourth emerald, [20]the fifth onyx, the sixth ruby, the seventh chrysolite, the eighth beryl, the ninth topaz, the tenth turquoise, the eleventh jacinth, and

---

a 1 Isaiah 65:17   *b 4* Isaiah 25:8   *c 16* That is, about 1,400 miles or about 2,200 kilometers   *d 17* That is, about 200 feet or about 65 meters   *e 17* Or *high*

the twelfth amethyst.[a] 21 The twelve gates were twelve pearls, each gate made of a single pearl. The great street of the city was of gold, as pure as transparent glass.

22 I did not see a temple in the city, because the Lord God Almighty and the Lamb are its temple. 23 The city does not need the sun or the moon to shine on it, for the glory of God gives it light, and the Lamb is its lamp. 24 The nations will walk by its light, and the kings of the earth will bring their splendor into it. 25 On no day will its gates ever be shut, for there will be no night there. 26 The glory and honor of the nations will be brought into it. 27 Nothing impure will ever enter it, nor will anyone who does what is shameful or deceitful, but only those whose names are written in the Lamb's book of life.

22 Then the angel showed me the river of the water of life, as clear as crystal, flowing from the throne of God and of the Lamb 2 down the middle of the great street of the city. On each side of the river stood the tree of life, bearing twelve crops of fruit, yielding its fruit every month. And the leaves of the tree are for the healing of the nations. 3 No longer will there be any curse. The throne of God and of the Lamb will be in the city, and his servants will serve him. 4 They will see his face, and his name will be on their foreheads. 5 There will be no more night. They will not need the light of a lamp or the light of the sun, for the Lord God will give them light. And they will reign for ever and ever.

6 The angel said to me, "These words are trustworthy and true. The Lord, the God who inspires the prophets, sent his angel to show his servants the things that must soon take place."

7 "Look, I am coming soon! Blessed is the one who keeps the words of the prophecy written in this scroll."

8 I, John, am the one who heard and saw these things. And when I had heard and seen them, I fell down to worship at the feet of the angel who had been showing them to me. 9 But he said to me, "Don't do that! I am a fellow servant with you and with your fellow prophets and with all who keep the words of this scroll. Worship God!"

10 Then he told me, "Do not seal up the words of the prophecy of this scroll, because the time is near. 11 Let the one who does wrong continue to do wrong; let the vile person continue to be vile; let the one who does right continue to do right; and let the holy person continue to be holy."

12 "Look, I am coming soon! My reward is with me, and I will give to each person according to what they have done. 13 I am the Alpha and the Omega, the First and the Last, the Beginning and the End.

14 "Blessed are those who wash their robes, that they may have the right to the tree of life and may go through the gates into the city. 15 Outside are the dogs, those who practice magic arts, the sexually immoral, the murderers, the idolaters and everyone who loves and practices falsehood.

16 "I, Jesus, have sent my angel to give you[b] this testimony for the

---

[a] 20 The precise identification of some of these precious stones is uncertain. [b] 16 The Greek is plural.

churches. I am the Root and the Offspring of David, and the bright Morning Star."

17The Spirit and the bride say, "Come!" And let the one who hears say, "Come!" Let the one who is thirsty come; and let the one who wishes take the free gift of the water of life.

18I warn everyone who hears the words of the prophecy of this scroll: If anyone adds anything to them, God will add to that person the plagues described in this scroll. 19And if anyone takes words away from this scroll of prophecy, God will take away from that person any share in the tree of life and in the Holy City, which are described in this scroll.

20He who testifies to these things says, "Yes, I am coming soon."

Amen. Come, Lord Jesus.

21The grace of the Lord Jesus be with God's people. Amen.

A collection of Israel's songs that
CELEBRATE, LAMENT AND REFLECT
ON VICTORIES AND STRUGGLES,
together with a gathering of
ISRAEL'S WISDOM SAYINGS,
guiding us on our journey
in God's story
OF OVERCOMING EVIL AND BRINGING
THE NEW CREATION,

PRESENTED
IN THE BOOKS OF **PSALMS**
AND PROVERBS

PSALMS

The book of Psalms is a collection of song lyrics. Like many songs, they were first written in response to events in the lives of their authors. Later, the whole community used them in worship. When Israel returned from exile in Babylon many of the songs from over the centuries were collected in the book of Psalms.

The book is structured into five parts marked off by the phrase, *Praise be to the LORD . . . Amen and Amen!* These five "books" remind the reader of the five books of Moses. Like the law, these song lyrics can be read and studied for instruction. Psalm 1 emphasizes such meditation and seems to have been placed first to make this point.

The five books also tell a three-part story of Israel's redemption: monarchy, exile and return. The psalms of King David dominate books one and two. The beginning and ending of book three highlight Israel's exile. The fourth book ends with a plea that God bring the exiled people home. The fifth book declares that God has done just that. Now the reason for the group of praise psalms at the end of the book is apparent: God has been faithful, judging Israel in exile but then bringing the nation home again.

The book of Psalms thus operates at two levels: individually the songs explore a wide variety of honest spiritual responses to God, while the overall collection tells, and celebrates, the work of God in history to save his people.

BOOK I

Psalms 1–41

Psalm 1

1 Blessed is the one
  who does not walk in step with
    the wicked
 or stand in the way that sinners
    take
 or sit in the company of
    mockers,
2 but whose delight is in the law of
    the LORD,
  and who meditates on his law
    day and night.
3 That person is like a tree planted
    by streams of water,
  which yields its fruit in season
  and whose leaf does not wither—
    whatever they do prospers.

4 Not so the wicked!
  They are like chaff
    that the wind blows away.
5 Therefore the wicked will not
    stand in the judgment,
  nor sinners in the assembly of
    the righteous.

6 For the LORD watches over the
    way of the righteous,
  but the way of the wicked leads
    to destruction.

Psalm 2

1 Why do the nations conspire[a]
  and the peoples plot in vain?
2 The kings of the earth rise up
  and the rulers band
    together
 against the LORD and against
    his anointed, saying,

---

[a] 1 Hebrew; Septuagint *rage*

3 "Let us break their chains
    and throw off their shackles."

4 The One enthroned in heaven
    laughs;
    the Lord scoffs at them.
5 He rebukes them in his anger
    and terrifies them in his
    wrath, saying,
6 "I have installed my king
    on Zion, my holy mountain."

7 I will proclaim the LORD's decree:

    He said to me, "You are my son;
    today I have become your father.
8 Ask me,
    and I will make the nations
    your inheritance,
    the ends of the earth your
    possession.
9 You will break them with a rod of
    iron[a];
    you will dash them to pieces
    like pottery."

10 Therefore, you kings, be wise;
    be warned, you rulers of the
    earth.
11 Serve the LORD with fear
    and celebrate his rule with
    trembling.
12 Kiss his son, or he will be angry
    and your way will lead to your
    destruction,
    for his wrath can flare up in a
    moment.
    Blessed are all who take refuge
    in him.

Psalm 3[b]

*A psalm of David. When he fled from his
son Absalom.*

1 LORD, how many are my foes!
    How many rise up against me!

2 Many are saying of me,
    "God will not deliver him."[c]

3 But you, LORD, are a shield
    around me,
    my glory, the One who lifts my
    head high.
4 I call out to the LORD,
    and he answers me from his
    holy mountain.

5 I lie down and sleep;
    I wake again, because the
    LORD sustains me.
6 I will not fear though tens of
    thousands
    assail me on every side.

7 Arise, LORD!
    Deliver me, my God!
    Strike all my enemies on the
    jaw;
    break the teeth of the wicked.

8 From the LORD comes
    deliverance.
    May your blessing be on your
    people.

Psalm 4[d]

*For the director of music. With stringed
instruments. A psalm of David.*

1 Answer me when I call to you,
    my righteous God.
    Give me relief from my distress;
    have mercy on me and hear my
    prayer.

2 How long will you people turn
    my glory into shame?
    How long will you love
    delusions and seek false
    gods[e]?[f]
3 Know that the LORD has set
    apart his faithful servant
    for himself;

---

a 9 Or will rule them with an iron scepter (see Septuagint and Syriac)   *b* In Hebrew texts 3:1-8
is numbered 3:2-9.   *c 2* The Hebrew has *Selah* (a word of uncertain meaning) here and at the
end of verses 4 and 8.   *d* In Hebrew texts 4:1-8 is numbered 4:2-9.   *e 2* Or *seek lies*   *f 2* The
Hebrew has *Selah* (a word of uncertain meaning) here and at the end of verse 4.

the LORD hears when I call to
him.

4 Tremble and[a] do not sin;
   when you are on your beds,
   search your hearts and be
   silent.
5 Offer the sacrifices of the
   righteous
   and trust in the LORD.

6 Many, LORD, are asking, "Who
   will bring us prosperity?"
   Let the light of your face shine
   on us.
7 Fill my heart with joy
   when their grain and new
   wine abound.

8 In peace I will lie down and
   sleep,
   for you alone, LORD,
   make me dwell in safety.

Psalm 5[b]

*For the director of music. For pipes.
A psalm of David.*

1 Listen to my words, LORD,
   consider my lament.
2 Hear my cry for help,
   my King and my God,
   for to you I pray.

3 In the morning, LORD, you hear
   my voice;
   in the morning I lay my
   requests before you
   and wait expectantly.
4 For you are not a God who is
   pleased with wickedness;
   with you, evil people are not
   welcome.
5 The arrogant cannot stand
   in your presence.
   You hate all who do wrong;
6   you destroy those who tell lies.
   The bloodthirsty and deceitful

you, LORD, detest.
7 But I, by your great love,
   can come into your house;
   in reverence I bow down
   toward your holy temple.

8 Lead me, LORD, in your
   righteousness
   because of my enemies—
   make your way straight before
   me.
9 Not a word from their mouth can
   be trusted;
   their heart is filled with
   malice.
   Their throat is an open grave;
   with their tongues they tell
   lies.
10 Declare them guilty, O God!
   Let their intrigues be their
   downfall.
   Banish them for their many sins,
   for they have rebelled against
   you.
11 But let all who take refuge in you
   be glad;
   let them ever sing for joy.
   Spread your protection over
   them,
   that those who love your name
   may rejoice in you.

12 Surely, LORD, you bless the
   righteous;
   you surround them with your
   favor as with a shield.

Psalm 6[c]

*For the director of music. With stringed
instruments. According to* sheminith.[d]
A psalm of David.

1 LORD, do not rebuke me in your
   anger
   or discipline me in your wrath.
2 Have mercy on me, LORD, for I
   am faint;

---

[a] 4 Or *In your anger* (see Septuagint)   [b] In Hebrew texts 5:1-12 is numbered 5:2-13.   [c] In Hebrew texts 6:1-10 is numbered 6:2-11.   [d] Title: Probably a musical term

heal me, LORD, for my bones
　　are in agony.
[3] My soul is in deep anguish.
　　How long, LORD, how long?

[4] Turn, LORD, and deliver me;
　　save me because of your
　　　unfailing love.
[5] Among the dead no one
　　　proclaims your name.
　　Who praises you from the
　　　grave?

[6] I am worn out from my groaning.

　　All night long I flood my bed
　　　with weeping
　　and drench my couch with
　　　tears.
[7] My eyes grow weak with sorrow;
　　they fail because of all my foes.

[8] Away from me, all you who do
　　　evil,
　　for the LORD has heard my
　　　weeping.
[9] The LORD has heard my cry for
　　　mercy;
　　the LORD accepts my prayer.
[10] All my enemies will be
　　　overwhelmed with shame
　　　and anguish;
　　they will turn back and
　　　suddenly be put to shame.

Psalm 7[a]

*A shiggaion[b] of David, which he sang to
the LORD concerning Cush, a Benjamite.*

[1] LORD my God, I take refuge in
　　　you;
　　save and deliver me from all
　　　who pursue me,
[2] or they will tear me apart like a
　　　lion
　　and rip me to pieces with no
　　　one to rescue me.

[3] LORD my God, if I have done this
　　　and there is guilt on my
　　　hands —
[4] if I have repaid my ally with evil
　　　or without cause have robbed
　　　my foe —
[5] then let my enemy pursue and
　　　overtake me;
　　let him trample my life to the
　　　ground
　　and make me sleep in the
　　　dust.[c]

[6] Arise, LORD, in your anger;
　　rise up against the rage of my
　　　enemies.
　　Awake, my God; decree
　　　justice.
[7] Let the assembled peoples
　　　gather around you,
　　while you sit enthroned over
　　　them on high.
[8]　　Let the LORD judge the
　　　peoples.
　　Vindicate me, LORD, according
　　　to my righteousness,
　　according to my integrity,
　　　O Most High.
[9] Bring to an end the violence of
　　　the wicked
　　and make the righteous
　　　secure —
　　you, the righteous God
　　who probes minds and hearts.

[10] My shield[d] is God Most High,
　　who saves the upright in heart.
[11] God is a righteous judge,
　　a God who displays his wrath
　　　every day.
[12] If he does not relent,
　　he[e] will sharpen his sword;
　　he will bend and string his
　　　bow.
[13] He has prepared his deadly
　　　weapons;

---

a In Hebrew texts 7:1-17 is numbered 7:2-18.   *b* Title: Probably a literary or musical term
c 5 The Hebrew has *Selah* (a word of uncertain meaning) here.   *d* 10 Or *sovereign*   *e* 12 Or *If
anyone does not repent, / God*

he makes ready his flaming
arrows.

14 Whoever is pregnant with evil
conceives trouble and gives
birth to disillusionment.
15 Whoever digs a hole and scoops
it out
falls into the pit they have
made.
16 The trouble they cause recoils
on them;
their violence comes down on
their own heads.

17 I will give thanks to the
LORD because of his
righteousness;
I will sing the praises of the
name of the LORD Most
High.

Psalm 8[a]

*For the director of music. According to
gittith.[b] A psalm of David.*

1 LORD, our Lord,
how majestic is your name in
all the earth!

You have set your glory
in the heavens.
2 Through the praise of children
and infants
you have established a
stronghold against your
enemies,
to silence the foe and the
avenger.
3 When I consider your
heavens,
the work of your fingers,
the moon and the stars,
which you have set in place,

4 what is mankind that you are
mindful of them,
human beings that you care
for them?[c]

5 You have made them[d] a little
lower than the angels[e]
and crowned them[d] with glory
and honor.
6 You made them rulers over the
works of your hands;
you put everything under
their[f] feet:
7 all flocks and herds,
and the animals of the wild,
8 the birds in the sky,
and the fish in the sea,
all that swim the paths of the
seas.

9 LORD, our Lord,
how majestic is your name in
all the earth!

Psalm 9[g,h]

*For the director of music. To the tune
of "The Death of the Son." A psalm
of David.*

1 I will give thanks to you, LORD,
with all my heart;
I will tell of all your wonderful
deeds.
2 I will be glad and rejoice in you;
I will sing the praises of your
name, O Most High.

3 My enemies turn back;
they stumble and perish
before you.
4 For you have upheld my right
and my cause,
sitting enthroned as the
righteous judge.

---

[a] In Hebrew texts 8:1-9 are numbered 8:2-10.   [b] Title: Probably a musical term   [c] 4 Or *what
is a human being that you are mindful of him, / a son of man that you care for him?*   [d] 5 Or *him*
[e] 5 Or *than God*   [f] 6 Or *made him ruler . . . ; / . . . his*   [g] Psalms 9 and 10 may originally have
been a single acrostic poem in which alternating lines began with the successive letters of the
Hebrew alphabet. In the Septuagint they constitute one psalm.   [h] In Hebrew texts 9:1-20 are
numbered 9:2-21.

⁵You have rebuked the nations
    and destroyed the wicked;
  you have blotted out their
    name for ever and ever.
⁶Endless ruin has overtaken my
    enemies,
  you have uprooted their
    cities;
  even the memory of them has
    perished.

⁷The Lord reigns forever;
  he has established his throne
    for judgment.
⁸He rules the world in
    righteousness
  and judges the peoples with
    equity.
⁹The Lord is a refuge for the
    oppressed,
  a stronghold in times of
    trouble.
¹⁰Those who know your name
    trust in you,
  for you, Lord, have never
    forsaken those who seek
    you.

¹¹Sing the praises of the Lord,
    enthroned in Zion;
  proclaim among the nations
    what he has done.
¹²For he who avenges blood
    remembers;
  he does not ignore the cries of
    the afflicted.

¹³Lord, see how my enemies
    persecute me!
  Have mercy and lift me up
    from the gates of death,
¹⁴that I may declare your praises
  in the gates of Daughter Zion,
    and there rejoice in your
    salvation.

¹⁵The nations have fallen into the
    pit they have dug;
  their feet are caught in the net
    they have hidden.
¹⁶The Lord is known by his acts of
    justice;
  the wicked are ensnared by
    the work of their hands.ᵃ

¹⁷The wicked go down to the
    realm of the dead,
  all the nations that forget God.
¹⁸But God will never forget the
    needy;
  the hope of the afflicted will
    never perish.

¹⁹Arise, Lord, do not let mortals
    triumph;
  let the nations be judged in
    your presence.
²⁰Strike them with terror, Lord;
  let the nations know they are
    only mortal.

Psalm 10ᵇ

¹Why, Lord, do you stand far off?
  Why do you hide yourself in
    times of trouble?

²In his arrogance the wicked man
    hunts down the weak,
  who are caught in the schemes
    he devises.
³He boasts about the cravings of
    his heart;
  he blesses the greedy and
    reviles the Lord.
⁴In his pride the wicked man
    does not seek him;
  in all his thoughts there is no
    room for God.
⁵His ways are always prosperous;
  your laws are rejected byᶜ him;
  he sneers at all his enemies.

ᵃ 16 The Hebrew has *Higgaion* and *Selah* (words of uncertain meaning) here; *Selah* occurs also
at the end of verse 20.   ᵇ Psalms 9 and 10 may originally have been a single acrostic poem
in which alternating lines began with the successive letters of the Hebrew alphabet. In the
Septuagint they constitute one psalm.   ᶜ 5 See Septuagint; Hebrew / *they are haughty, and
your laws are far from*

6 He says to himself, "Nothing will
　　ever shake me."
　He swears, "No one will ever
　　do me harm."

7 His mouth is full of lies and
　　threats;
　trouble and evil are under his
　　tongue.
8 He lies in wait near the villages;
　from ambush he murders the
　　innocent.
　His eyes watch in secret for his
　　victims;
9 　like a lion in cover he lies in
　　wait.
　He lies in wait to catch the
　　helpless;
　he catches the helpless and
　　drags them off in his net.
10 His victims are crushed, they
　　collapse;
　they fall under his strength.
11 He says to himself, "God will
　　never notice;
　he covers his face and never
　　sees."

12 Arise, LORD! Lift up your hand,
　　O God.
　Do not forget the helpless.
13 Why does the wicked man revile
　　God?
　Why does he say to himself,
　　"He won't call me to account"?
14 But you, God, see the trouble of
　　the afflicted;
　you consider their grief and
　　take it in hand.
　The victims commit themselves
　　to you;
　you are the helper of the
　　fatherless.
15 Break the arm of the wicked
　　man;
　call the evildoer to account for
　　his wickedness
　that would not otherwise be
　　found out.

16 The LORD is King for ever and
　　ever;
　the nations will perish from
　　his land.
17 You, LORD, hear the desire of the
　　afflicted;
　you encourage them, and you
　　listen to their cry,
18 defending the fatherless and the
　　oppressed,
　so that mere earthly mortals
　　will never again strike terror.

Psalm 11

For the director of music. Of David.

1 In the LORD I take refuge.
　How then can you say to me:
　"Flee like a bird to your
　　mountain.
2 For look, the wicked bend their
　　bows;
　they set their arrows against
　　the strings
　to shoot from the shadows
　at the upright in heart.
3 When the foundations are being
　　destroyed,
　what can the righteous do?"

4 The LORD is in his holy temple;
　the LORD is on his heavenly
　　throne.
　He observes everyone on earth;
　his eyes examine them.
5 The LORD examines the
　　righteous,
　but the wicked, those who love
　　violence,
　he hates with a passion.
6 On the wicked he will rain
　fiery coals and burning
　　sulfur;
　a scorching wind will be their
　　lot.

7 For the LORD is righteous,
　he loves justice;
　the upright will see his face.

Psalm 12[a]

For the director of music. According to
sheminith.[b] A psalm of David.

[1] Help, Lord, for no one is faithful
anymore;
those who are loyal have
vanished from the human
race.
[2] Everyone lies to their neighbor;
they flatter with their lips
but harbor deception in their
hearts.

[3] May the Lord silence all
flattering lips
and every boastful tongue —
[4] those who say,
"By our tongues we will prevail;
our own lips will defend us —
who is lord over us?"

[5] "Because the poor are plundered
and the needy groan,
I will now arise," says the Lord.
"I will protect them from those
who malign them."
[6] And the words of the Lord are
flawless,
like silver purified in a crucible,
like gold[c] refined seven times.

[7] You, Lord, will keep the needy
safe
and will protect us forever
from the wicked,
[8] who freely strut about
when what is vile is honored
by the human race.

Psalm 13[d]

For the director of music. A psalm
of David.

[1] How long, Lord? Will you forget
me forever?
How long will you hide your
face from me?
[2] How long must I wrestle with my
thoughts
and day after day have sorrow
in my heart?
How long will my enemy
triumph over me?

[3] Look on me and answer, Lord
my God.
Give light to my eyes, or I will
sleep in death,
[4] and my enemy will say, "I have
overcome him,"
and my foes will rejoice when I
fall.

[5] But I trust in your unfailing love;
my heart rejoices in your
salvation.
[6] I will sing the Lord's praise,
for he has been good to me.

Psalm 14

For the director of music. Of David.

[1] The fool[e] says in his heart,
"There is no God."
They are corrupt, their deeds are
vile;
there is no one who does good.

[2] The Lord looks down from
heaven
on all mankind
to see if there are any who
understand,
any who seek God.
[3] All have turned away, all have
become corrupt;
there is no one who does good,
not even one.

[4] Do all these evildoers know
nothing?

---

[a] In Hebrew texts 12:1-8 is numbered 12:2-9.   [b] Title: Probably a musical term   [c] 6 Probable
reading of the original Hebrew text; Masoretic Text *earth*   [d] In Hebrew texts 13:1-6 is
numbered 13:2-6.   [e] 1 The Hebrew words rendered *fool* in Psalms denote one who is morally
deficient.

They devour my people as
 though eating bread;
 they never call on the LORD.
⁵ But there they are, overwhelmed
 with dread,
 for God is present in the
 company of the righteous.
⁶ You evildoers frustrate the plans
 of the poor,
 but the LORD is their refuge.

⁷ Oh, that salvation for Israel
 would come out of Zion!
 When the LORD restores his
 people,
 let Jacob rejoice and Israel be
 glad!

Psalm 15

A psalm of David.

¹ LORD, who may dwell in your
 sacred tent?
 Who may live on your holy
 mountain?

² The one whose walk is blameless,
 who does what is righteous,
 who speaks the truth from
 their heart;
³ whose tongue utters no slander,
 who does no wrong to a
 neighbor,
 and casts no slur on others;
⁴ who despises a vile person
 but honors those who fear the
 LORD;
 who keeps an oath even when it
 hurts,
 and does not change their
 mind;
⁵ who lends money to the poor
 without interest;
 who does not accept a bribe
 against the innocent.

 Whoever does these things
 will never be shaken.

Psalm 16

*A miktam*ᵃ *of David.*

¹ Keep me safe, my God,
 for in you I take refuge.

² I say to the LORD, "You are my
 Lord;
 apart from you I have no good
 thing."
³ I say of the holy people who are
 in the land,
 "They are the noble ones in
 whom is all my delight."
⁴ Those who run after other gods
 will suffer more and
 more.
 I will not pour out libations of
 blood to such gods
 or take up their names on my
 lips.

⁵ LORD, you alone are my portion
 and my cup;
 you make my lot secure.
⁶ The boundary lines have fallen
 for me in pleasant places;
 surely I have a delightful
 inheritance.
⁷ I will praise the LORD, who
 counsels me;
 even at night my heart
 instructs me.
⁸ I keep my eyes always on the
 LORD.
 With him at my right hand, I
 will not be shaken.

⁹ Therefore my heart is glad and
 my tongue rejoices;
 my body also will rest secure,
¹⁰ because you will not abandon
 me to the realm of the
 dead,
 nor will you let your faithfulᵇ
 one see decay.
¹¹ You make known to me the path
 of life;

ᵃ Title: Probably a literary or musical term   ᵇ 10 Or *holy*

you will fill me with joy in your
     presence,
   with eternal pleasures at your
     right hand.

Psalm 17

A prayer of David.

¹ Hear me, LORD, my plea is just;
   listen to my cry.
 Hear my prayer —
   it does not rise from deceitful
     lips.
² Let my vindication come from
     you;
   may your eyes see what is right.

³ Though you probe my heart,
   though you examine me at
     night and test me,
 you will find that I have planned
     no evil;
   my mouth has not transgressed.
⁴ Though people tried to bribe me,
   I have kept myself from the
     ways of the violent
   through what your lips have
     commanded.
⁵ My steps have held to your paths;
   my feet have not stumbled.

⁶ I call on you, my God, for you
     will answer me;
   turn your ear to me and hear
     my prayer.
⁷ Show me the wonders of your
     great love,
   you who save by your right
     hand
   those who take refuge in you
     from their foes.
⁸ Keep me as the apple of your eye;
   hide me in the shadow of your
     wings
⁹ from the wicked who are out to
     destroy me,
   from my mortal enemies who
     surround me.

¹⁰ They close up their callous
     hearts,
   and their mouths speak with
     arrogance.
¹¹ They have tracked me down,
   they now surround me,
   with eyes alert, to throw me to
     the ground.
¹² They are like a lion hungry for
     prey,
   like a fierce lion crouching in
     cover.

¹³ Rise up, LORD, confront them,
     bring them down;
   with your sword rescue me
     from the wicked.
¹⁴ By your hand save me from such
     people, LORD,
   from those of this world whose
     reward is in this life.
 May what you have stored up for
     the wicked fill their bellies;
   may their children gorge
     themselves on it,
   and may there be leftovers for
     their little ones.

¹⁵ As for me, I will be vindicated
   and will see your face;
 when I awake, I will be
     satisfied with seeing your
     likeness.

Psalm 18 [a]

*For the director of music. Of David the
servant of the LORD. He sang to the LORD
the words of this song when the LORD
delivered him from the hand of all his
enemies and from the hand of Saul.
He said:*

¹ I love you, LORD, my strength.

² The LORD is my rock, my fortress
     and my deliverer;
   my God is my rock, in whom I
     take refuge,

---

[a] In Hebrew texts 18:1-50 is numbered 18:2-51.

my shield[a] and the horn[b] of my
salvation, my stronghold.

3 I called to the LORD, who is
worthy of praise,
and I have been saved from my
enemies.

4 The cords of death entangled
me;
the torrents of destruction
overwhelmed me.

5 The cords of the grave coiled
around me;
the snares of death confronted
me.

6 In my distress I called to the
LORD;
I cried to my God for help.
From his temple he heard my
voice;
my cry came before him, into
his ears.

7 The earth trembled and quaked,
and the foundations of the
mountains shook;
they trembled because he was
angry.

8 Smoke rose from his nostrils;
consuming fire came from his
mouth,
burning coals blazed out of it.

9 He parted the heavens and came
down;
dark clouds were under his
feet.

10 He mounted the cherubim and
flew;
he soared on the wings of the
wind.

11 He made darkness his covering,
his canopy around him —
the dark rain clouds of the sky.

12 Out of the brightness of
his presence clouds
advanced,

with hailstones and bolts of
lightning.

13 The LORD thundered from
heaven;
the voice of the Most High
resounded.[c]

14 He shot his arrows and scattered
the enemy,
with great bolts of lightning he
routed them.

15 The valleys of the sea were
exposed
and the foundations of the
earth laid bare
at your rebuke, LORD,
at the blast of breath from your
nostrils.

16 He reached down from on high
and took hold of me;
he drew me out of deep waters.

17 He rescued me from my
powerful enemy,
from my foes, who were too
strong for me.

18 They confronted me in the day of
my disaster,
but the LORD was my support.

19 He brought me out into a
spacious place;
he rescued me because he
delighted in me.

20 The LORD has dealt with
me according to my
righteousness;
according to the cleanness of
my hands he has rewarded
me.

21 For I have kept the ways of the
LORD;
I am not guilty of turning from
my God.

22 All his laws are before me;
I have not turned away from
his decrees.

---

[a] 2 Or sovereign   [b] 2 Horn here symbolizes strength.   [c] 13 Some Hebrew manuscripts and
Septuagint (see also 2 Samuel 22:14); most Hebrew manuscripts resounded, / amid hailstones
and bolts of lightning

²³I have been blameless before
       him
    and have kept myself from
       sin.
²⁴The LORD has rewarded
       me according to my
       righteousness,
    according to the cleanness of
       my hands in his sight.

²⁵To the faithful you show yourself
       faithful,
    to the blameless you show
       yourself blameless,
²⁶to the pure you show yourself
       pure,
    but to the devious you show
       yourself shrewd.
²⁷You save the humble
    but bring low those whose
       eyes are haughty.
²⁸You, LORD, keep my lamp
       burning;
    my God turns my darkness
       into light.
²⁹With your help I can advance
       against a troopᵃ;
    with my God I can scale a wall.

³⁰As for God, his way is perfect:
       The LORD's word is flawless;
    he shields all who take refuge
       in him.
³¹For who is God besides the
       LORD?
    And who is the Rock except
       our God?
³²It is God who arms me with
       strength
    and keeps my way secure.
³³He makes my feet like the feet of
       a deer;
    he causes me to stand on the
       heights.
³⁴He trains my hands for battle;
    my arms can bend a bow of
       bronze.

³⁵You make your saving help my
       shield,
    and your right hand sustains
       me;
    your help has made me great.
³⁶You provide a broad path for my
       feet,
    so that my ankles do not give
       way.

³⁷I pursued my enemies and
       overtook them;
    I did not turn back till they
       were destroyed.
³⁸I crushed them so that they
       could not rise;
    they fell beneath my feet.
³⁹You armed me with strength for
       battle;
    you humbled my adversaries
       before me.
⁴⁰You made my enemies turn their
       backs in flight,
    and I destroyed my foes.
⁴¹They cried for help, but there
       was no one to save them —
    to the LORD, but he did not
       answer.
⁴²I beat them as fine as windblown
       dust;
    I trampled themᵇ like mud in
       the streets.

⁴³You have delivered me from the
       attacks of the people;
    you have made me the head of
       nations.
    People I did not know now serve
       me,
⁴⁴   foreigners cower before me;
    as soon as they hear of me,
       they obey me.
⁴⁵They all lose heart;
    they come trembling from
       their strongholds.

⁴⁶The LORD lives! Praise be to my
       Rock!

ᵃ 29 Or can run through a barricade   ᵇ 42 Many Hebrew manuscripts, Septuagint, Syriac and
Targum (see also 2 Samuel 22:43); Masoretic Text I poured them out

Exalted be God my Savior!
47 He is the God who avenges me,
    who subdues nations under
        me,
48   who saves me from my
        enemies.
You exalted me above my foes;
    from a violent man you
        rescued me.
49 Therefore I will praise you,
        LORD, among the nations;
    I will sing the praises of your
        name.

50 He gives his king great victories;
    he shows unfailing love to his
        anointed,
    to David and to his
        descendants forever.

Psalm 19[a]

*For the director of music. A psalm
of David.*

1 The heavens declare the glory of
        God;
    the skies proclaim the work of
        his hands.
2 Day after day they pour forth
        speech;
    night after night they reveal
        knowledge.
3 They have no speech, they use
        no words;
    no sound is heard from them.
4 Yet their voice[b] goes out into all
        the earth,
    their words to the ends of the
        world.
In the heavens God has pitched
        a tent for the sun.
5   It is like a bridegroom coming
        out of his chamber,
    like a champion rejoicing to
        run his course.
6 It rises at one end of the heavens

and makes its circuit to the
        other;
    nothing is deprived of its
        warmth.

7 The law of the LORD is perfect,
    refreshing the soul.
The statutes of the LORD are
        trustworthy,
    making wise the simple.
8 The precepts of the LORD are
        right,
    giving joy to the heart.
The commands of the LORD are
        radiant,
    giving light to the eyes.
9 The fear of the LORD is pure,
    enduring forever.
The decrees of the LORD are
        firm,
    and all of them are righteous.

10 They are more precious than
        gold,
    than much pure gold;
    they are sweeter than honey,
        than honey from the
        honeycomb.
11 By them your servant is warned;
    in keeping them there is great
        reward.
12 But who can discern their own
        errors?
    Forgive my hidden faults.
13 Keep your servant also from
        willful sins;
    may they not rule over me.
Then I will be blameless,
    innocent of great
        transgression.

14 May these words of my mouth
        and this meditation of my
        heart
    be pleasing in your sight,
    LORD, my Rock and my
        Redeemer.

---

a In Hebrew texts 19:1-14 is numbered 19:2-15.
measuring line

b 4 Septuagint, Jerome and Syriac; Hebrew

Psalm 20[a]

For the director of music. A psalm of David.

1 May the LORD answer you when
    you are in distress;
  may the name of the God of
    Jacob protect you.
2 May he send you help from the
    sanctuary
  and grant you support from
    Zion.
3 May he remember all your
    sacrifices
  and accept your burnt
    offerings.[b]
4 May he give you the desire of
    your heart
  and make all your plans
    succeed.
5 May we shout for joy over your
    victory
  and lift up our banners in the
    name of our God.

  May the LORD grant all your
    requests.

6 Now this I know:
    The LORD gives victory to his
      anointed.
  He answers him from his
    heavenly sanctuary
  with the victorious power of
    his right hand.
7 Some trust in chariots and some
    in horses,
  but we trust in the name of the
    LORD our God.
8 They are brought to their knees
    and fall,
  but we rise up and stand
    firm.
9 LORD, give victory to the king!
  Answer us when we call!

Psalm 21[c]

For the director of music. A psalm of David.

1 The king rejoices in your
    strength, LORD.
  How great is his joy in the
    victories you give!
2 You have granted him his heart's
    desire
  and have not withheld the
    request of his lips.[b]
3 You came to greet him with rich
    blessings
  and placed a crown of pure
    gold on his head.
4 He asked you for life, and you
    gave it to him—
  length of days, for ever and
    ever.
5 Through the victories you gave,
    his glory is great;
  you have bestowed on him
    splendor and majesty.
6 Surely you have granted him
    unending blessings
  and made him glad with the
    joy of your presence.
7 For the king trusts in the LORD;
  through the unfailing love of
    the Most High
  he will not be shaken.
8 Your hand will lay hold on all
    your enemies;
  your right hand will seize your
    foes.
9 When you appear for battle,
  you will burn them up as in a
    blazing furnace.
  The LORD will swallow them up
    in his wrath,
  and his fire will consume
    them.

---

a In Hebrew texts 20:1-9 is numbered 20:2-10.   b 3,2 The Hebrew has *Selah* (a word of uncertain meaning) here.   c In Hebrew texts 21:1-13 is numbered 21:2-14.

¹⁰ You will destroy their
        descendants from the
        earth,
    their posterity from mankind.
¹¹ Though they plot evil against
        you
    and devise wicked schemes,
        they cannot succeed.
¹² You will make them turn their
        backs
    when you aim at them with
        drawn bow.

¹³ Be exalted in your strength, LORD;
    we will sing and praise your
        might.

Psalm 22ᵃ

*For the director of music. To the tune
of "The Doe of the Morning." A psalm
of David.*

¹ My God, my God, why have you
        forsaken me?
    Why are you so far from saving
        me,
    so far from my cries of anguish?
² My God, I cry out by day, but you
        do not answer,
    by night, but I find no rest.ᵇ

³ Yet you are enthroned as the
        Holy One;
    you are the one Israel praises.ᶜ
⁴ In you our ancestors put their
        trust;
    they trusted and you delivered
        them.
⁵ To you they cried out and were
        saved;
    in you they trusted and were
        not put to shame.

⁶ But I am a worm and not a man,
    scorned by everyone, despised
        by the people.

⁷ All who see me mock me;
    they hurl insults, shaking their
        heads.
⁸ "He trusts in the LORD," they say,
    "let the LORD rescue him.
    Let him deliver him,
    since he delights in him."

⁹ Yet you brought me out of the
        womb;
    you made me trust in you,
    even at my mother's
        breast.
¹⁰ From birth I was cast on you;
    from my mother's womb you
        have been my God.

¹¹ Do not be far from me,
    for trouble is near
    and there is no one to help.

¹² Many bulls surround me;
    strong bulls of Bashan encircle
        me.
¹³ Roaring lions that tear their prey
    open their mouths wide
        against me.

¹⁴ I am poured out like water,
    and all my bones are out of
        joint.
    My heart has turned to wax;
    it has melted within me.
¹⁵ My mouthᵈ is dried up like a
        potsherd,
    and my tongue sticks to the
        roof of my mouth;
    you lay me in the dust of
        death.

¹⁶ Dogs surround me,
    a pack of villains encircles me;
    they pierceᵉ my hands and my
        feet.
¹⁷ All my bones are on display;
    people stare and gloat over
        me.

ᵃ In Hebrew texts 22:1-31 is numbered 22:2-32.   ᵇ 2 Or *night, and am not silent*   ᶜ 3 Or *Yet
you are holy, / enthroned on the praises of Israel*   ᵈ 15 Probable reading of the original Hebrew
text; Masoretic Text *strength*   ᵉ 16 Dead Sea Scrolls and some manuscripts of the Masoretic
Text, Septuagint and Syriac; most manuscripts of the Masoretic Text *me, / like a lion*

18 They divide my clothes among
them
and cast lots for my garment.

19 But you, LORD, do not be far from
me.
You are my strength; come
quickly to help me.
20 Deliver me from the sword,
my precious life from the
power of the dogs.
21 Rescue me from the mouth of
the lions;
save me from the horns of the
wild oxen.

22 I will declare your name to my
people;
in the assembly I will praise
you.
23 You who fear the LORD, praise
him!
All you descendants of Jacob,
honor him!
Revere him, all you
descendants of Israel!
24 For he has not despised or
scorned
the suffering of the afflicted
one;
he has not hidden his face from
him
but has listened to his cry for
help.

25 From you comes the theme of
my praise in the great
assembly;
before those who fear you[a] I
will fulfill my vows.
26 The poor will eat and be
satisfied;
those who seek the LORD will
praise him —
may your hearts live forever!

27 All the ends of the earth
will remember and turn to the
LORD,
and all the families of the
nations
will bow down before him,
28 for dominion belongs to the
LORD
and he rules over the nations.

29 All the rich of the earth will feast
and worship;
all who go down to the dust
will kneel before him —
those who cannot keep
themselves alive.
30 Posterity will serve him;
future generations will be told
about the Lord.
31 They will proclaim his
righteousness,
declaring to a people yet
unborn:
He has done it!

Psalm 23

A psalm of David.

1 The LORD is my shepherd, I lack
nothing.
2   He makes me lie down in
green pastures,
he leads me beside quiet waters,
3   he refreshes my soul.
He guides me along the right
paths
for his name's sake.
4 Even though I walk
through the darkest valley,[b]
I will fear no evil,
for you are with me;
your rod and your staff,
they comfort me.

5 You prepare a table before me
in the presence of my enemies.
You anoint my head with oil;
my cup overflows.
6 Surely your goodness and love
will follow me
all the days of my life,

---

[a] 25 Hebrew *him*   [b] 4 Or *the valley of the shadow of death*

and I will dwell in the house of
    the LORD
    forever.

Psalm 24

Of David. A psalm.

[1] The earth is the LORD's, and
    everything in it,
  the world, and all who live in
    it;
[2] for he founded it on the seas
  and established it on the
    waters.

[3] Who may ascend the mountain
    of the LORD?
  Who may stand in his holy
    place?
[4] The one who has clean hands
    and a pure heart,
  who does not trust in an idol
    or swear by a false god.[a]

[5] They will receive blessing from
    the LORD
  and vindication from God
    their Savior.
[6] Such is the generation of those
    who seek him,
  who seek your face, God of
    Jacob.[b,c]

[7] Lift up your heads, you gates;
  be lifted up, you ancient doors,
  that the King of glory may
    come in.
[8] Who is this King of glory?
  The LORD strong and mighty,
  the LORD mighty in battle.
[9] Lift up your heads, you gates;
  lift them up, you ancient
    doors,
  that the King of glory may
    come in.
[10] Who is he, this King of glory?

The LORD Almighty—
  he is the King of glory.

Psalm 25[d]

Of David.

[1] In you, LORD my God,
  I put my trust.

[2] I trust in you;
  do not let me be put to shame,
  nor let my enemies triumph
    over me.
[3] No one who hopes in you
  will ever be put to shame,
  but shame will come on those
  who are treacherous without
    cause.

[4] Show me your ways, LORD,
  teach me your paths.
[5] Guide me in your truth and
    teach me,
  for you are God my Savior,
  and my hope is in you all day
    long.
[6] Remember, LORD, your great
    mercy and love,
  for they are from of old.
[7] Do not remember the sins of my
    youth
  and my rebellious ways;
according to your love
  remember me,
  for you, LORD, are good.

[8] Good and upright is the LORD;
  therefore he instructs sinners
    in his ways.
[9] He guides the humble in what is
    right
  and teaches them his way.
[10] All the ways of the LORD are
    loving and faithful
  toward those who keep the
    demands of his covenant.

---

a 4 Or *swear falsely* *b 6* Two Hebrew manuscripts and Syriac (see also Septuagint); most
Hebrew manuscripts *face, Jacob* *c 6* The Hebrew has *Selah* (a word of uncertain meaning)
here and at the end of verse 10.   *d* This psalm is an acrostic poem, the verses of which begin
with the successive letters of the Hebrew alphabet.

11 For the sake of your name, LORD,
    forgive my iniquity, though it
    is great.

12 Who, then, are those who fear
    the LORD?
    He will instruct them in the
    ways they should choose.[a]

13 They will spend their days in
    prosperity,
    and their descendants will
    inherit the land.

14 The LORD confides in those who
    fear him;
    he makes his covenant known
    to them.

15 My eyes are ever on the LORD,
    for only he will release my feet
    from the snare.

16 Turn to me and be gracious to me,
    for I am lonely and afflicted.

17 Relieve the troubles of my heart
    and free me from my anguish.

18 Look on my affliction and my
    distress
    and take away all my sins.

19 See how numerous are my
    enemies
    and how fiercely they hate me!

20 Guard my life and rescue me;
    do not let me be put to shame,
    for I take refuge in you.

21 May integrity and uprightness
    protect me,
    because my hope, LORD,[b] is in
    you.

22 Deliver Israel, O God,
    from all their troubles!

Psalm 26

Of David.

1 Vindicate me, LORD,
    for I have led a blameless life;
    I have trusted in the LORD
    and have not faltered.

2 Test me, LORD, and try me,
    examine my heart and my mind;

3 for I have always been mindful
    of your unfailing love
    and have lived in reliance on
    your faithfulness.

4 I do not sit with the deceitful,
    nor do I associate with
    hypocrites.

5 I abhor the assembly of evildoers
    and refuse to sit with the
    wicked.

6 I wash my hands in innocence,
    and go about your altar, LORD,

7 proclaiming aloud your praise
    and telling of all your
    wonderful deeds.

8 LORD, I love the house where you
    live,
    the place where your glory
    dwells.

9 Do not take away my soul along
    with sinners,
    my life with those who are
    bloodthirsty,

10 in whose hands are wicked
    schemes,
    whose right hands are full of
    bribes.

11 I lead a blameless life;
    deliver me and be merciful to
    me.

12 My feet stand on level ground;
    in the great congregation I will
    praise the LORD.

Psalm 27

Of David.

1 The LORD is my light and my
    salvation —
    whom shall I fear?
    The LORD is the stronghold of
    my life —
    of whom shall I be afraid?

---

a 12 Or *ways he chooses*   b 21 Septuagint; Hebrew does not have LORD.

2 When the wicked advance
      against me
   to devour[a] me,
it is my enemies and my foes
   who will stumble and fall.
3 Though an army besiege me,
   my heart will not fear;
though war break out against
      me,
   even then I will be confident.

4 One thing I ask from the LORD,
   this only do I seek:
that I may dwell in the house of
      the LORD
   all the days of my life,
to gaze on the beauty of the LORD
   and to seek him in his temple.

5 For in the day of trouble
   he will keep me safe in his
      dwelling;
he will hide me in the shelter of
      his sacred tent
   and set me high upon a rock.

6 Then my head will be exalted
      above the enemies who
      surround me;
at his sacred tent I will sacrifice
      with shouts of joy;
   I will sing and make music to
      the LORD.

7 Hear my voice when I call, LORD;
   be merciful to me and answer
      me.
8 My heart says of you, "Seek his
      face!"
   Your face, LORD, I will seek.
9 Do not hide your face from me,
   do not turn your servant away
      in anger;
   you have been my helper.
Do not reject me or forsake me,
   God my Savior.
10 Though my father and mother
      forsake me,
   the LORD will receive me.

11 Teach me your way, LORD;
   lead me in a straight path
   because of my oppressors.
12 Do not turn me over to the desire
      of my foes,
   for false witnesses rise up
      against me,
   spouting malicious
      accusations.

13 I remain confident of this:
   I will see the goodness of the
      LORD
   in the land of the living.
14 Wait for the LORD;
   be strong and take heart
   and wait for the LORD.

Psalm 28

Of David.

1 To you, LORD, I call;
   you are my Rock,
   do not turn a deaf ear to me.
For if you remain silent,
   I will be like those who go
      down to the pit.
2 Hear my cry for mercy
   as I call to you for help,
as I lift up my hands
   toward your Most Holy Place.

3 Do not drag me away with the
      wicked,
   with those who do evil,
who speak cordially with their
      neighbors
   but harbor malice in their
      hearts.
4 Repay them for their deeds
   and for their evil work;
repay them for what their hands
      have done
   and bring back on them what
      they deserve.
5 Because they have no regard for
      the deeds of the LORD

and what his hands have done,
he will tear them down
   and never build them up
   again.

6 Praise be to the LORD,
   for he has heard my cry for
    mercy.
7 The LORD is my strength and my
   shield;
   my heart trusts in him, and he
    helps me.
My heart leaps for joy,
   and with my song I praise him.

8 The LORD is the strength of his
   people,
   a fortress of salvation for his
    anointed one.
9 Save your people and bless your
   inheritance;
   be their shepherd and carry
    them forever.

Psalm 29

A psalm of David.

1 Ascribe to the LORD, you
   heavenly beings,
   ascribe to the LORD glory and
    strength.
2 Ascribe to the LORD the glory
   due his name;
   worship the LORD in the
    splendor of his[a] holiness.

3 The voice of the LORD is over the
   waters;
   the God of glory thunders,
   the LORD thunders over the
    mighty waters.
4 The voice of the LORD is
   powerful;
   the voice of the LORD is
    majestic.
5 The voice of the LORD breaks the
   cedars;

the LORD breaks in pieces the
   cedars of Lebanon.
6 He makes Lebanon leap like a
   calf,
   Sirion[b] like a young wild ox.
7 The voice of the LORD strikes
   with flashes of lightning.
8 The voice of the LORD shakes the
   desert;
   the LORD shakes the Desert of
    Kadesh.
9 The voice of the LORD twists the
   oaks[c]
   and strips the forests bare.
And in his temple all cry,
   "Glory!"

10 The LORD sits enthroned over
   the flood;
   the LORD is enthroned as King
    forever.
11 The LORD gives strength to his
   people;
   the LORD blesses his people
    with peace.

Psalm 30[d]

*A psalm. A song. For the dedication of
the temple.[e] Of David.*

1 I will exalt you, LORD,
   for you lifted me out of the
    depths
   and did not let my enemies
    gloat over me.
2 LORD my God, I called to you for
   help,
   and you healed me.
3 You, LORD, brought me up from
   the realm of the dead;
   you spared me from going
    down to the pit.

4 Sing the praises of the LORD, you
   his faithful people;
   praise his holy name.

---

a 2 Or *LORD with the splendor of*   *b 6* That is, Mount Hermon   *c 9* Or *LORD makes the deer give birth*   *d* In Hebrew texts 30:1-12 is numbered 30:2-13.   *e Title:* Or *palace*

5 For his anger lasts only a
        moment,
    but his favor lasts a lifetime;
weeping may stay for the night,
    but rejoicing comes in the
        morning.

6 When I felt secure, I said,
    "I will never be shaken."
7 LORD, when you favored me,
    you made my royal mountain*a*
        stand firm;
but when you hid your face,
    I was dismayed.

8 To you, LORD, I called;
    to the Lord I cried for mercy:
9 "What is gained if I am silenced,
    if I go down to the pit?
Will the dust praise you?
    Will it proclaim your
        faithfulness?
10 Hear, LORD, and be merciful to
        me;
    LORD, be my help."

11 You turned my wailing into
        dancing;
    you removed my sackcloth and
        clothed me with joy,
12 that my heart may sing your
        praises and not be silent.
    LORD my God, I will praise you
        forever.

Psalm 31*b*

*For the director of music. A psalm
of David.*

1 In you, LORD, I have taken
        refuge;
    let me never be put to shame;
    deliver me in your
        righteousness.
2 Turn your ear to me,
    come quickly to my rescue;
    be my rock of refuge,
        a strong fortress to save me.

3 Since you are my rock and my
        fortress,
    for the sake of your name lead
        and guide me.
4 Keep me free from the trap that
        is set for me,
    for you are my refuge.
5 Into your hands I commit my
        spirit;
    deliver me, LORD, my faithful
        God.

6 I hate those who cling to
        worthless idols;
    as for me, I trust in the LORD.
7 I will be glad and rejoice in your
        love,
    for you saw my affliction
    and knew the anguish of my
        soul.
8 You have not given me into the
        hands of the enemy
    but have set my feet in a
        spacious place.

9 Be merciful to me, LORD, for I am
        in distress;
    my eyes grow weak with
        sorrow,
    my soul and body with grief.
10 My life is consumed by anguish
        and my years by groaning;
    my strength fails because of my
        affliction,*c*
    and my bones grow weak.
11 Because of all my enemies,
    I am the utter contempt of my
        neighbors
    and an object of dread to my
        closest friends—
    those who see me on the street
        flee from me.
12 I am forgotten as though I were
        dead;
    I have become like broken
        pottery.
13 For I hear many whispering,
    "Terror on every side!"

a 7 That is, Mount Zion   *b* In Hebrew texts 31:1-24 is numbered 31:2-25.   *c* 10 Or guilt

They conspire against me
and plot to take my life.
[14] But I trust in you, LORD;
I say, "You are my God."
[15] My times are in your hands;
deliver me from the hands of
my enemies,
from those who pursue me.
[16] Let your face shine on your
servant;
save me in your unfailing love.
[17] Let me not be put to shame,
LORD,
for I have cried out to you;
but let the wicked be put to
shame
and be silent in the realm of
the dead.
[18] Let their lying lips be silenced,
for with pride and contempt
they speak arrogantly against
the righteous.

[19] How abundant are the good
things
that you have stored up for
those who fear you,
that you bestow in the sight of all,
on those who take refuge in
you.
[20] In the shelter of your presence
you hide them
from all human intrigues;
you keep them safe in your
dwelling
from accusing tongues.

[21] Praise be to the LORD,
for he showed me the wonders
of his love
when I was in a city under
siege.
[22] In my alarm I said,
"I am cut off from your sight!"
Yet you heard my cry for mercy
when I called to you for help.

[23] Love the LORD, all his faithful
people!
The LORD preserves those who
are true to him,
but the proud he pays back in
full.
[24] Be strong and take heart,
all you who hope in the LORD.

Psalm 32

Of David. A maskil.[a]

[1] Blessed is the one
whose transgressions are
forgiven,
whose sins are covered.
[2] Blessed is the one
whose sin the LORD does not
count against them
and in whose spirit is no
deceit.

[3] When I kept silent,
my bones wasted away
through my groaning all day
long.
[4] For day and night
your hand was heavy on me;
my strength was sapped
as in the heat of summer.[b]

[5] Then I acknowledged my sin to
you
and did not cover up my
iniquity.
I said, "I will confess
my transgressions to the
LORD."
And you forgave
the guilt of my sin.

[6] Therefore let all the faithful pray
to you
while you may be found;
surely the rising of the mighty
waters
will not reach them.

---

a Title: Probably a literary or musical term meaning) here and at the end of verses 5 and 7.   *b* 4 The Hebrew has *Selah* (a word of uncertain

⁷You are my hiding place;
  you will protect me from
      trouble
  and surround me with songs of
      deliverance.

⁸I will instruct you and teach you
      in the way you should go;
  I will counsel you with my
      loving eye on you.

⁹Do not be like the horse or the
      mule,
  which have no understanding
  but must be controlled by bit and
      bridle
  or they will not come to you.

¹⁰Many are the woes of the wicked,
  but the Lord's unfailing love
      surrounds the one who trusts
      in him.

¹¹Rejoice in the Lord and be glad,
      you righteous;
  sing, all you who are upright in
      heart!

Psalm 33

¹Sing joyfully to the Lord, you
      righteous;
  it is fitting for the upright to
      praise him.

²Praise the Lord with the harp;
  make music to him on the ten-
      stringed lyre.

³Sing to him a new song;
  play skillfully, and shout for
      joy.

⁴For the word of the Lord is right
      and true;
  he is faithful in all he does.

⁵The Lord loves righteousness
      and justice;
  the earth is full of his unfailing
      love.

⁶By the word of the Lord the
      heavens were made,

their starry host by the breath
    of his mouth.

⁷He gathers the waters of the sea
    into jars[a];
  he puts the deep into
      storehouses.

⁸Let all the earth fear the Lord;
  let all the people of the world
      revere him.

⁹For he spoke, and it came to be;
  he commanded, and it stood
      firm.

¹⁰The Lord foils the plans of the
      nations;
  he thwarts the purposes of the
      peoples.

¹¹But the plans of the Lord stand
      firm forever,
  the purposes of his heart
      through all generations.

¹²Blessed is the nation whose God
      is the Lord,
  the people he chose for his
      inheritance.

¹³From heaven the Lord looks
      down
  and sees all mankind;

¹⁴from his dwelling place he
      watches
  all who live on earth—

¹⁵he who forms the hearts of all,
  who considers everything they
      do.

¹⁶No king is saved by the size of his
      army;
  no warrior escapes by his great
      strength.

¹⁷A horse is a vain hope for
      deliverance;
  despite all its great strength it
      cannot save.

¹⁸But the eyes of the Lord are on
      those who fear him,
  on those whose hope is in his
      unfailing love,

---

[a] 7 Or *sea as into a heap*

19 to deliver them from death
  and keep them alive in famine.

20 We wait in hope for the LORD;
  he is our help and our shield.
21 In him our hearts rejoice,
  for we trust in his holy name.
22 May your unfailing love be with
    us, LORD,
  even as we put our hope in
    you.

Psalm 34 [a,b]

*Of David. When he pretended to be
insane before Abimelek, who drove him
away, and he left.*

1 I will extol the LORD at all times;
  his praise will always be on my
    lips.
2 I will glory in the LORD;
  let the afflicted hear and
    rejoice.
3 Glorify the LORD with me;
  let us exalt his name together.

4 I sought the LORD, and he
    answered me;
  he delivered me from all my
    fears.
5 Those who look to him are
    radiant;
  their faces are never covered
    with shame.
6 This poor man called, and the
    LORD heard him;
  he saved him out of all his
    troubles.
7 The angel of the LORD encamps
    around those who fear
    him,
  and he delivers them.

8 Taste and see that the LORD is
    good;
  blessed is the one who takes
    refuge in him.

9 Fear the LORD, you his holy
    people,
  for those who fear him lack
    nothing.
10 The lions may grow weak and
    hungry,
  but those who seek the LORD
    lack no good thing.
11 Come, my children, listen to me;
  I will teach you the fear of the
    LORD.
12 Whoever of you loves life
  and desires to see many good
    days,
13 keep your tongue from evil
  and your lips from telling
    lies.
14 Turn from evil and do good;
  seek peace and pursue it.

15 The eyes of the LORD are on the
    righteous,
  and his ears are attentive to
    their cry;
16 but the face of the LORD is
    against those who do evil,
  to blot out their name from the
    earth.

17 The righteous cry out, and the
    LORD hears them;
  he delivers them from all their
    troubles.
18 The LORD is close to the
    brokenhearted
  and saves those who are
    crushed in spirit.

19 The righteous person may have
    many troubles,
  but the LORD delivers him
    from them all;
20 he protects all his bones,
  not one of them will be broken.

21 Evil will slay the wicked;
  the foes of the righteous will
    be condemned.

---

[a] This psalm is an acrostic poem, the verses of which begin with the successive letters of the
Hebrew alphabet.   [b] In Hebrew texts 34:1-22 is numbered 34:2-23.

22 The LORD will rescue his
       servants;
    no one who takes refuge in
       him will be condemned.

Psalm 35

Of David.

1 Contend, LORD, with those who
       contend with me;
    fight against those who fight
       against me.
2 Take up shield and armor;
    arise and come to my aid.
3 Brandish spear and javelin[a]
       against those who pursue me.
    Say to me,
    "I am your salvation."

4 May those who seek my life
       be disgraced and put to
       shame;
    may those who plot my ruin
       be turned back in dismay.
5 May they be like chaff before the
       wind,
    with the angel of the LORD
       driving them away;
6 may their path be dark and
       slippery,
    with the angel of the LORD
       pursuing them.

7 Since they hid their net for me
       without cause
    and without cause dug a pit for
       me,
8 may ruin overtake them by
       surprise—
    may the net they hid entangle
       them,
    may they fall into the pit, to
       their ruin.
9 Then my soul will rejoice in the
       LORD
    and delight in his salvation.
10 My whole being will exclaim,

"Who is like you, LORD?
    You rescue the poor from those
       too strong for them,
    the poor and needy from those
       who rob them."

11 Ruthless witnesses come
       forward;
    they question me on things I
       know nothing about.
12 They repay me evil for good
    and leave me like one
       bereaved.
13 Yet when they were ill, I put on
       sackcloth
    and humbled myself with
       fasting.
    When my prayers returned to me
       unanswered,
14   I went about mourning
       as though for my friend or
       brother.
    I bowed my head in grief
       as though weeping for my
       mother.
15 But when I stumbled, they
       gathered in glee;
    assailants gathered against me
       without my knowledge.
    They slandered me without
       ceasing.
16 Like the ungodly they
       maliciously mocked;[b]
    they gnashed their teeth at me.

17 How long, Lord, will you look
       on?
    Rescue me from their ravages,
    my precious life from these
       lions.
18 I will give you thanks in the
       great assembly;
    among the throngs I will
       praise you.
19 Do not let those gloat over me
    who are my enemies without
       cause;

---

[a] 3 Or *and block the way*   [b] 16 Septuagint; Hebrew may mean *Like an ungodly circle of mockers,*

do not let those who hate me
  without reason
    maliciously wink the eye.
20 They do not speak peaceably,
    but devise false accusations
      against those who live quietly
        in the land.
21 They sneer at me and say, "Aha!
  Aha!
    With our own eyes we have
      seen it."

22 Lord, you have seen this; do not
    be silent.
  Do not be far from me, Lord.
23 Awake, and rise to my defense!
    Contend for me, my God and
      Lord.
24 Vindicate me in your
    righteousness, Lord my
      God;
  do not let them gloat over
    me.
25 Do not let them think, "Aha, just
    what we wanted!"
  or say, "We have swallowed
    him up."

26 May all who gloat over my
    distress
  be put to shame and
    confusion;
  may all who exalt themselves
    over me
  be clothed with shame and
    disgrace.
27 May those who delight in my
    vindication
  shout for joy and gladness;
  may they always say, "The Lord
    be exalted,
  who delights in the well-being
    of his servant."

28 My tongue will proclaim your
    righteousness,
  your praises all day long.

Psalm 36[a]

*For the director of music. Of David the
    servant of the Lord.*

1 I have a message from God in my
    heart
  concerning the sinfulness of
    the wicked:[b]
  There is no fear of God
    before their eyes.

2 In their own eyes they flatter
    themselves
  too much to detect or hate
    their sin.
3 The words of their mouths are
    wicked and deceitful;
  they fail to act wisely or do
    good.
4 Even on their beds they plot
    evil;
  they commit themselves to a
    sinful course
  and do not reject what is
    wrong.

5 Your love, Lord, reaches to the
    heavens,
  your faithfulness to the
    skies.
6 Your righteousness is like the
    highest mountains,
  your justice like the great
    deep.
  You, Lord, preserve both
    people and animals.
7 How priceless is your unfailing
    love, O God!
  People take refuge in the
    shadow of your wings.
8 They feast on the abundance of
    your house;
  you give them drink from your
    river of delights.
9 For with you is the fountain of
    life;
  in your light we see light.

---

a In Hebrew texts 36:1-12 is numbered 36:2-13.
  of the wicked / resides in their hearts.   b 1 Or *A message from God: The transgression*

¹⁰ Continue your love to those who
know you,
your righteousness to the
upright in heart.
¹¹ May the foot of the proud not
come against me,
nor the hand of the wicked
drive me away.
¹² See how the evildoers lie
fallen—
thrown down, not able to rise!

Psalm 37[a]

Of David.

¹ Do not fret because of those who
are evil
or be envious of those who do
wrong;
² for like the grass they will soon
wither,
like green plants they will
soon die away.

³ Trust in the LORD and do good;
dwell in the land and enjoy
safe pasture.
⁴ Take delight in the LORD,
and he will give you the
desires of your heart.

⁵ Commit your way to the LORD;
trust in him and he will do this:
⁶ He will make your righteous
reward shine like the
dawn,
your vindication like the
noonday sun.

⁷ Be still before the LORD
and wait patiently for him;
do not fret when people succeed
in their ways,
when they carry out their
wicked schemes.

⁸ Refrain from anger and turn
from wrath;

do not fret—it leads only to
evil.
⁹ For those who are evil will be
destroyed,
but those who hope in the
LORD will inherit the
land.

¹⁰ A little while, and the wicked
will be no more;
though you look for them, they
will not be found.
¹¹ But the meek will inherit the
land
and enjoy peace and
prosperity.

¹² The wicked plot against the
righteous
and gnash their teeth at them;
¹³ but the Lord laughs at the
wicked,
for he knows their day is
coming.

¹⁴ The wicked draw the sword
and bend the bow
to bring down the poor and
needy,
to slay those whose ways are
upright.
¹⁵ But their swords will pierce their
own hearts,
and their bows will be broken.

¹⁶ Better the little that the
righteous have
than the wealth of many
wicked;
¹⁷ for the power of the wicked will
be broken,
but the LORD upholds the
righteous.

¹⁸ The blameless spend their days
under the LORD's care,
and their inheritance will
endure forever.

---

[a] This psalm is an acrostic poem, the stanzas of which begin with the successive letters of the Hebrew alphabet.

¹⁹ In times of disaster they will not
       wither;
    in days of famine they will
       enjoy plenty.

²⁰ But the wicked will perish:
    Though the LORD's enemies
       are like the flowers of the
       field,
    they will be consumed, they
       will go up in smoke.

²¹ The wicked borrow and do not
       repay,
    but the righteous give
       generously;
²² those the LORD blesses will
       inherit the land,
    but those he curses will be
       destroyed.

²³ The LORD makes firm the steps
    of the one who delights in him;
²⁴ though he may stumble, he will
       not fall,
    for the LORD upholds him with
       his hand.

²⁵ I was young and now I am old,
    yet I have never seen the
       righteous forsaken
    or their children begging
       bread.
²⁶ They are always generous and
       lend freely;
    their children will be a
       blessing.ᵃ

²⁷ Turn from evil and do good;
    then you will dwell in the land
       forever.
²⁸ For the LORD loves the just
    and will not forsake his
       faithful ones.

    Wrongdoers will be completely
       destroyedᵇ;

the offspring of the wicked will
       perish.
²⁹ The righteous will inherit the
       land
    and dwell in it forever.

³⁰ The mouths of the righteous
       utter wisdom,
    and their tongues speak what
       is just.
³¹ The law of their God is in their
       hearts;
    their feet do not slip.

³² The wicked lie in wait for the
       righteous,
    intent on putting them to
       death;
³³ but the LORD will not leave
       them in the power of the
       wicked
    or let them be condemned
       when brought to trial.

³⁴ Hope in the LORD
    and keep his way.
    He will exalt you to inherit the
       land;
    when the wicked are
       destroyed, you will see it.

³⁵ I have seen a wicked and
       ruthless man
    flourishing like a luxuriant
       native tree,
³⁶ but he soon passed away and
       was no more;
    though I looked for him, he
       could not be found.

³⁷ Consider the blameless, observe
       the upright;
    a future awaits those who seek
       peace.ᶜ
³⁸ But all sinners will be destroyed;
    there will be no futureᵈ for the
       wicked.

ᵃ 26 Or freely; / the names of their children will be used in blessings (see Gen. 48:20); or
freely; / others will see that their children are blessed   ᵇ 28 See Septuagint; Hebrew They
will be protected forever   ᶜ 37 Or upright; / those who seek peace will have posterity
ᵈ 38 Or posterity

39 The salvation of the righteous
    comes from the LORD;
  he is their stronghold in time
    of trouble.
40 The LORD helps them and
    delivers them;
  he delivers them from the
    wicked and saves them,
    because they take refuge in
    him.

Psalm 38[a]

A psalm of David. A petition.

1 LORD, do not rebuke me in your
    anger
  or discipline me in your
    wrath.
2 Your arrows have pierced me,
    and your hand has come down
    on me.
3 Because of your wrath there is
    no health in my body;
  there is no soundness in my
    bones because of my sin.
4 My guilt has overwhelmed me
    like a burden too heavy to
    bear.

5 My wounds fester and are
    loathsome
  because of my sinful folly.
6 I am bowed down and brought
    very low;
  all day long I go about
    mourning.
7 My back is filled with searing
    pain;
  there is no health in my body.
8 I am feeble and utterly
    crushed;
  I groan in anguish of heart.

9 All my longings lie open before
    you, Lord;
  my sighing is not hidden from
    you.

10 My heart pounds, my strength
    fails me;
  even the light has gone from
    my eyes.
11 My friends and companions
    avoid me because of my
    wounds;
  my neighbors stay far away.
12 Those who want to kill me set
    their traps,
  those who would harm me talk
    of my ruin;
  all day long they scheme and
    lie.

13 I am like the deaf, who cannot
    hear,
  like the mute, who cannot
    speak;
14 I have become like one who does
    not hear,
  whose mouth can offer no
    reply.

15 LORD, I wait for you;
  you will answer, Lord my God.
16 For I said, "Do not let them gloat
  or exalt themselves over me
    when my feet slip."

17 For I am about to fall,
    and my pain is ever with me.
18 I confess my iniquity;
  I am troubled by my sin.
19 Many have become my enemies
    without cause[b];
  those who hate me without
    reason are numerous.
20 Those who repay my good with
    evil
  lodge accusations against me,
    though I seek only to do what
    is good.

21 LORD, do not forsake me;
  do not be far from me, my God.
22 Come quickly to help me,
  my Lord and my Savior.

---

a In Hebrew texts 38:1-22 is numbered 38:2-23.
Masoretic Text *my vigorous enemies*   b 19 One Dead Sea Scrolls manuscript;

Psalm 39[a]

For the director of music. For Jeduthun.
A psalm of David.

1 I said, "I will watch my ways
    and keep my tongue from sin;
I will put a muzzle on my mouth
    while in the presence of the
      wicked."
2 So I remained utterly silent,
    not even saying anything
      good.
But my anguish increased;
3   my heart grew hot within me.
While I meditated, the fire
    burned;
    then I spoke with my tongue:

4 "Show me, LORD, my life's end
    and the number of my days;
let me know how fleeting my
    life is.
5 You have made my days a mere
    handbreadth;
    the span of my years is as
      nothing before you.
Everyone is but a breath,
    even those who seem secure.[b]

6 "Surely everyone goes around
    like a mere phantom;
in vain they rush about,
    heaping up wealth
    without knowing whose it will
      finally be.

7 "But now, Lord, what do I look
    for?
My hope is in you.
8 Save me from all my
    transgressions;
    do not make me the scorn of
      fools.
9 I was silent; I would not open my
    mouth,
    for you are the one who has
      done this.

10 Remove your scourge from me;
    I am overcome by the blow of
      your hand.
11 When you rebuke and discipline
    anyone for their sin,
you consume their wealth like
    a moth—
    surely everyone is but a
      breath.

12 "Hear my prayer, LORD,
    listen to my cry for help;
    do not be deaf to my weeping.
I dwell with you as a foreigner,
    a stranger, as all my ancestors
      were.
13 Look away from me, that I may
    enjoy life again
    before I depart and am no
      more."

Psalm 40[c]

For the director of music. Of David.
A psalm.

1 I waited patiently for the LORD;
    he turned to me and heard my
      cry.
2 He lifted me out of the slimy pit,
    out of the mud and mire;
he set my feet on a rock
    and gave me a firm place to
      stand.
3 He put a new song in my mouth,
    a hymn of praise to our God.
Many will see and fear the LORD
    and put their trust in him.

4 Blessed is the one
    who trusts in the LORD,
who does not look to the proud,
    to those who turn aside to
      false gods.[d]
5 Many, LORD my God,
    are the wonders you have
      done,

---

[a] In Hebrew texts 39:1-13 is numbered 39:2-14.
uncertain meaning) here and at the end of verse 11.
40:2-18.   [d] 4 Or *to lies*

[b] 5 The Hebrew has *Selah* (a word of
[c] In Hebrew texts 40:1-17 is numbered

the things you planned for
   us.
None can compare with you;
   were I to speak and tell of your
     deeds,
   they would be too many to
     declare.

6 Sacrifice and offering you did
     not desire—
   but my ears you have
     opened[a]—
   burnt offerings and sin
     offerings[b] you did not
     require.
7 Then I said, "Here I am, I have
     come—
   it is written about me in the
     scroll.[c]
8 I desire to do your will, my
     God;
   your law is within my heart."

9 I proclaim your saving acts in
     the great assembly;
   I do not seal my lips, LORD,
     as you know.
10 I do not hide your righteousness
     in my heart;
   I speak of your faithfulness
     and your saving help.
   I do not conceal your love and
     your faithfulness
   from the great assembly.

11 Do not withhold your mercy
     from me, LORD;
   may your love and faithfulness
     always protect me.
12 For troubles without number
     surround me;
   my sins have overtaken me,
     and I cannot see.
They are more than the hairs of
     my head,
   and my heart fails within me.
13 Be pleased to save me, LORD;

come quickly, LORD, to help
   me.

14 May all who want to take my
     life
   be put to shame and
     confusion;
   may all who desire my ruin
     be turned back in disgrace.
15 May those who say to me, "Aha!
     Aha!"
   be appalled at their own
     shame.
16 But may all who seek you
     rejoice and be glad in you;
   may those who long for your
     saving help always say,
   "The LORD is great!"

17 But as for me, I am poor and
     needy;
   may the Lord think of me.
You are my help and my
     deliverer;
   you are my God, do not delay.

Psalm 41 [d]

*For the director of music. A psalm
of David.*

1 Blessed are those who have
     regard for the weak;
   the LORD delivers them in
     times of trouble.
2 The LORD protects and preserves
     them—
   they are counted among the
     blessed in the land—
   he does not give them over to
     the desire of their foes.
3 The LORD sustains them on their
     sickbed
   and restores them from their
     bed of illness.

4 I said, "Have mercy on me,
     LORD;

---

[a] 6 Hebrew; some Septuagint manuscripts *but a body you have prepared for me*
[b] 6 Or *purification offerings*   [c] 7 Or *come / with the scroll written for me*   [d] In Hebrew texts
41:1-13 is numbered 41:2-14.

heal me, for I have sinned
    against you."
5 My enemies say of me in
        malice,
    "When will he die and his
        name perish?"
6 When one of them comes to see
        me,
    he speaks falsely, while his
        heart gathers slander;
    then he goes out and spreads it
        around.

7 All my enemies whisper together
        against me;
    they imagine the worst for me,
        saying,
8 "A vile disease has afflicted
        him;
    he will never get up from the
        place where he lies."
9 Even my close friend,
        someone I trusted,
    one who shared my bread,
        has turned[a] against me.

10 But may you have mercy on me,
        LORD;
    raise me up, that I may repay
        them.
11 I know that you are pleased with
        me,
    for my enemy does not
        triumph over me.
12 Because of my integrity you
        uphold me
    and set me in your presence
        forever.

13 Praise be to the LORD, the God of
        Israel,
    from everlasting to
        everlasting.
            Amen and Amen.

BOOK II

Psalms 42–72

Psalm 42[b,c]

*For the director of music. A maskil[d] of
    the Sons of Korah.*

1 As the deer pants for streams of
        water,
    so my soul pants for you, my
        God.
2 My soul thirsts for God, for the
        living God.
    When can I go and meet with
        God?
3 My tears have been my food
        day and night,
    while people say to me all day
        long,
    "Where is your God?"
4 These things I remember
    as I pour out my soul:
    how I used to go to the house of
        God
    under the protection of the
        Mighty One[e]
    with shouts of joy and praise
        among the festive throng.

5 Why, my soul, are you downcast?
    Why so disturbed within me?
    Put your hope in God,
    for I will yet praise him,
        my Savior and my God.

6 My soul is downcast within me;
    therefore I will remember you
    from the land of the Jordan,
    the heights of Hermon — from
        Mount Mizar.
7 Deep calls to deep
    in the roar of your waterfalls;
    all your waves and breakers
        have swept over me.

---

[a] 9 Hebrew *has lifted up his heel*   [b] In many Hebrew manuscripts Psalms 42 and 43 constitute one psalm.   [c] In Hebrew texts 42:1-11 is numbered 42:2-12.   [d] Title: Probably a literary or musical term   [e] 4 See Septuagint and Syriac; the meaning of the Hebrew for this line is uncertain.

8 By day the LORD directs his love,
    at night his song is with me —
  a prayer to the God of my life.

9 I say to God my Rock,
    "Why have you forgotten me?
  Why must I go about mourning,
    oppressed by the enemy?"
10 My bones suffer mortal agony
    as my foes taunt me,
  saying to me all day long,
    "Where is your God?"

11 Why, my soul, are you downcast?
    Why so disturbed within me?
  Put your hope in God,
    for I will yet praise him,
    my Savior and my God.

Psalm 43[a]

1 Vindicate me, my God,
    and plead my cause
    against an unfaithful nation.
  Rescue me from those who are
    deceitful and wicked.
2 You are God my stronghold.
    Why have you rejected me?
  Why must I go about mourning,
    oppressed by the enemy?
3 Send me your light and your
    faithful care,
    let them lead me;
  let them bring me to your holy
    mountain,
  to the place where you dwell.
4 Then I will go to the altar of God,
    to God, my joy and my delight.
  I will praise you with the lyre,
    O God, my God.

5 Why, my soul, are you downcast?
    Why so disturbed within me?
  Put your hope in God,
    for I will yet praise him,
    my Savior and my God.

Psalm 44[b]

*For the director of music. Of the Sons of
    Korah. A maskil.[c]*

1 We have heard it with our ears,
    O God;
  our ancestors have told us
    what you did in their days,
    in days long ago.
2 With your hand you drove out
    the nations
    and planted our ancestors;
  you crushed the peoples
    and made our ancestors
    flourish.
3 It was not by their sword that
    they won the land,
  nor did their arm bring them
    victory;
  it was your right hand, your
    arm,
  and the light of your face, for
    you loved them.

4 You are my King and my God,
    who decrees[d] victories for
    Jacob.
5 Through you we push back our
    enemies;
  through your name we
    trample our foes.
6 I put no trust in my bow,
    my sword does not bring me
    victory;
7 but you give us victory over our
    enemies,
  you put our adversaries to
    shame.
8 In God we make our boast all
    day long,
  and we will praise your name
    forever.[e]

9 But now you have rejected and
    humbled us;

---

a In many Hebrew manuscripts Psalms 42 and 43 constitute one psalm.   b In Hebrew texts 44:1-26 is numbered 44:2-27.   c Title: Probably a literary or musical term   d 4 Septuagint, Aquila and Syriac; Hebrew *King, O God; / command*   e 8 The Hebrew has *Selah* (a word of uncertain meaning) here.

you no longer go out with our
    armies.
10 You made us retreat before the
    enemy,
    and our adversaries have
        plundered us.
11 You gave us up to be devoured
    like sheep
    and have scattered us among
        the nations.
12 You sold your people for a
    pittance,
    gaining nothing from their
        sale.

13 You have made us a reproach to
    our neighbors,
    the scorn and derision of those
        around us.
14 You have made us a byword
    among the nations;
    the peoples shake their heads
        at us.
15 I live in disgrace all day long,
    and my face is covered with
        shame
16 at the taunts of those who
    reproach and revile me,
    because of the enemy, who is
        bent on revenge.

17 All this came upon us,
    though we had not forgotten
        you;
    we had not been false to your
        covenant.
18 Our hearts had not turned back;
    our feet had not strayed from
        your path.
19 But you crushed us and made us
    a haunt for jackals;
    you covered us over with deep
        darkness.

20 If we had forgotten the name of
    our God
    or spread out our hands to a
        foreign god,

21 would not God have discovered
    it,
    since he knows the secrets of
        the heart?
22 Yet for your sake we face death
    all day long;
    we are considered as sheep to
        be slaughtered.

23 Awake, Lord! Why do you sleep?
    Rouse yourself! Do not reject
        us forever.
24 Why do you hide your face
    and forget our misery and
        oppression?

25 We are brought down to the
    dust;
    our bodies cling to the ground.
26 Rise up and help us;
    rescue us because of your
        unfailing love.

Psalm 45[a]

*For the director of music. To the tune of
"Lilies." Of the Sons of Korah. A maskil.[b]
A wedding song.*

1 My heart is stirred by a noble
    theme
    as I recite my verses for the
        king;
    my tongue is the pen of a
        skillful writer.

2 You are the most excellent of
    men
    and your lips have been
        anointed with grace,
    since God has blessed you
        forever.

3 Gird your sword on your side,
    you mighty one;
    clothe yourself with splendor
        and majesty.
4 In your majesty ride forth
    victoriously

---

a In Hebrew texts 45:1-17 is numbered 45:2-18.   b Title: Probably a literary or musical term

in the cause of truth, humility
and justice;
let your right hand achieve
awesome deeds.
5 Let your sharp arrows pierce
the hearts of the king's
enemies;
let the nations fall beneath
your feet.
6 Your throne, O God,[a] will last for
ever and ever;
a scepter of justice will be
the scepter of your
kingdom.
7 You love righteousness and hate
wickedness;
therefore God, your God,
has set you above your
companions
by anointing you with the oil
of joy.
8 All your robes are fragrant with
myrrh and aloes and
cassia;
from palaces adorned with
ivory
the music of the strings makes
you glad.
9 Daughters of kings are among
your honored women;
at your right hand is the royal
bride in gold of Ophir.
10 Listen, daughter, and pay careful
attention:
Forget your people and your
father's house.
11 Let the king be enthralled by
your beauty;
honor him, for he is your lord.
12 The city of Tyre will come with a
gift,[b]
people of wealth will seek your
favor.
13 All glorious is the princess
within her chamber;

her gown is interwoven with
gold.
14 In embroidered garments she is
led to the king;
her virgin companions follow
her —
those brought to be with her.
15 Led in with joy and gladness,
they enter the palace of the
king.
16 Your sons will take the place of
your fathers;
you will make them princes
throughout the land.
17 I will perpetuate your memory
through all generations;
therefore the nations will
praise you for ever and
ever.

Psalm 46[c]

*For the director of music. Of the Sons of
Korah. According to* alamoth.[d] *A song.*

1 God is our refuge and strength,
an ever-present help in
trouble.
2 Therefore we will not fear,
though the earth give way
and the mountains fall into
the heart of the sea,
3 though its waters roar and foam
and the mountains quake with
their surging.[e]

4 There is a river whose streams
make glad the city of God,
the holy place where the Most
High dwells.
5 God is within her, she will not
fall;
God will help her at break of
day.
6 Nations are in uproar, kingdoms
fall;

---

[a] 6 Here the king is addressed as God's representative.   [b] 12 Or *A Tyrian robe is among the
gifts*   [c] In Hebrew texts 46:1-11 is numbered 46:2-12.   [d] Title: Probably a musical term
[e] 3 The Hebrew has *Selah* (a word of uncertain meaning) here and at the end of verses 7 and 11.

he lifts his voice, the earth
    melts.

[7] The LORD Almighty is with us;
    the God of Jacob is our
        fortress.

[8] Come and see what the LORD has
    done,
    the desolations he has brought
        on the earth.

[9] He makes wars cease
    to the ends of the earth.
He breaks the bow and shatters
    the spear;
    he burns the shields[a] with
        fire.

[10] He says, "Be still, and know that
    I am God;
I will be exalted among the
    nations,
I will be exalted in the earth."

[11] The LORD Almighty is with us;
    the God of Jacob is our
        fortress.

Psalm 47[b]

*For the director of music. Of the Sons of
Korah. A psalm.*

[1] Clap your hands, all you nations;
    shout to God with cries of joy.

[2] For the LORD Most High is
    awesome,
    the great King over all the
        earth.

[3] He subdued nations under us,
    peoples under our feet.

[4] He chose our inheritance for us,
    the pride of Jacob, whom he
        loved.[c]

[5] God has ascended amid shouts
    of joy,
    the LORD amid the sounding
        of trumpets.

[6] Sing praises to God, sing
    praises;
    sing praises to our King, sing
        praises.

[7] For God is the King of all the
    earth;
    sing to him a psalm of praise.

[8] God reigns over the nations;
    God is seated on his holy
        throne.

[9] The nobles of the nations
    assemble
    as the people of the God of
        Abraham,
for the kings[d] of the earth belong
    to God;
    he is greatly exalted.

Psalm 48[e]

A song. A psalm of the Sons of Korah.

[1] Great is the LORD, and most
    worthy of praise,
    in the city of our God, his holy
        mountain.

[2] Beautiful in its loftiness,
    the joy of the whole earth,
    like the heights of Zaphon[f] is
        Mount Zion,
    the city of the Great King.

[3] God is in her citadels;
    he has shown himself to be her
        fortress.

[4] When the kings joined forces,
    when they advanced together,

[5] they saw her and were
    astounded;
    they fled in terror.

[6] Trembling seized them there,
    pain like that of a woman in
        labor.

[7] You destroyed them like ships of
    Tarshish
    shattered by an east wind.

---

[a] 9 Or *chariots* [b] In Hebrew texts 47:1-9 is numbered 47:2-10. [c] 4 The Hebrew has *Selah*
(a word of uncertain meaning) here. [d] 9 Or *shields* [e] In Hebrew texts 48:1-14 is numbered
48:2-15. [f] 2 *Zaphon* was the most sacred mountain of the Canaanites.

[8] As we have heard,
    so we have seen
in the city of the LORD Almighty,
    in the city of our God:
God makes her secure
    forever.[a]

[9] Within your temple, O God,
    we meditate on your unfailing
        love.
[10] Like your name, O God,
    your praise reaches to the ends
        of the earth;
    your right hand is filled with
        righteousness.
[11] Mount Zion rejoices,
    the villages of Judah are glad
because of your judgments.

[12] Walk about Zion, go around
        her,
    count her towers,
[13] consider well her ramparts,
    view her citadels,
    that you may tell of them
        to the next generation.

[14] For this God is our God for ever
        and ever;
    he will be our guide even to
        the end.

Psalm 49[b]

*For the director of music. Of the Sons of
    Korah. A psalm.*

[1] Hear this, all you peoples;
    listen, all who live in this
        world,
[2] both low and high,
    rich and poor alike:
[3] My mouth will speak words of
        wisdom;
    the meditation of my heart will
        give you understanding.
[4] I will turn my ear to a proverb;

with the harp I will expound
        my riddle:

[5] Why should I fear when evil days
        come,
    when wicked deceivers
        surround me—
[6] those who trust in their wealth
    and boast of their great riches?
[7] No one can redeem the life of
        another
    or give to God a ransom for
        them—
[8] the ransom for a life is costly,
    no payment is ever enough—
[9] so that they should live on
        forever
    and not see decay.

[10] For all can see that the wise die,
    that the foolish and the
        senseless also perish,
    leaving their wealth to others.
[11] Their tombs will remain their
        houses[c] forever,
    their dwellings for endless
        generations,
    though they had[d] named
        lands after themselves.

[12] People, despite their wealth, do
        not endure;
    they are like the beasts that
        perish.

[13] This is the fate of those who trust
        in themselves,
    and of their followers, who
        approve their sayings.[e]
[14] They are like sheep and are
        destined to die;
    death will be their shepherd
    (but the upright will prevail
        over them in the
        morning).
    Their forms will decay in the
        grave,

---

a 8 The Hebrew has *Selah* (a word of uncertain meaning) here.   *b* In Hebrew texts 49:1-20
is numbered 49:2-21.   *c 11* Septuagint and Syriac; Hebrew *In their thoughts their houses
will remain*   *d 11* Or *generations, / for they have*   *e 13* The Hebrew has *Selah* (a word of
uncertain meaning) here and at the end of verse 15.

far from their princely
mansions.
15 But God will redeem me from
the realm of the dead;
he will surely take me to
himself.
16 Do not be overawed when others
grow rich,
when the splendor of their
houses increases;
17 for they will take nothing with
them when they die,
their splendor will not
descend with them.
18 Though while they live they
count themselves
blessed—
and people praise you when
you prosper—
19 they will join those who have
gone before them,
who will never again see the
light of life.

20 People who have wealth but lack
understanding
are like the beasts that perish.

Psalm 50

A psalm of Asaph.

1 The Mighty One, God, the LORD,
speaks and summons the
earth
from the rising of the sun to
where it sets.
2 From Zion, perfect in beauty,
God shines forth.
3 Our God comes
and will not be silent;
a fire devours before him,
and around him a tempest
rages.
4 He summons the heavens above,
and the earth, that he may
judge his people:

5 "Gather to me this consecrated
people,
who made a covenant with me
by sacrifice."
6 And the heavens proclaim his
righteousness,
for he is a God of justice.*a,b*

7 "Listen, my people, and I will
speak;
I will testify against you,
Israel:
I am God, your God.
8 I bring no charges against you
concerning your sacrifices
or concerning your burnt
offerings, which are ever
before me.
9 I have no need of a bull from
your stall
or of goats from your pens,
10 for every animal of the forest is
mine,
and the cattle on a thousand
hills.
11 I know every bird in the
mountains,
and the insects in the fields
are mine.
12 If I were hungry I would not tell
you,
for the world is mine, and all
that is in it.
13 Do I eat the flesh of bulls
or drink the blood of goats?

14 "Sacrifice thank offerings to
God,
fulfill your vows to the Most
High,
15 and call on me in the day of
trouble;
I will deliver you, and you will
honor me."

16 But to the wicked person, God
says:

---

a 6 With a different word division of the Hebrew; Masoretic Text *for God himself is judge*
b 6 The Hebrew has *Selah* (a word of uncertain meaning) here.

"What right have you to recite
        my laws
    or take my covenant on your
        lips?
17 You hate my instruction
    and cast my words behind you.
18 When you see a thief, you join
        with him;
    you throw in your lot with
        adulterers.
19 You use your mouth for evil
    and harness your tongue to
        deceit.
20 You sit and testify against your
        brother
    and slander your own
        mother's son.
21 When you did these things and I
        kept silent,
    you thought I was exactly[a] like
        you.
    But I now arraign you
    and set my accusations before
        you.

22 "Consider this, you who forget
        God,
    or I will tear you to pieces,
        with no one to rescue you:
23 Those who sacrifice thank
        offerings honor me,
    and to the blameless[b] I will
        show my salvation."

Psalm 51[c]

*For the director of music. A psalm
of David. When the prophet Nathan
came to him after David had committed
adultery with Bathsheba.*

1 Have mercy on me, O God,
        according to your unfailing
        love;
    according to your great
        compassion
    blot out my transgressions.

2 Wash away all my iniquity
    and cleanse me from my sin.

3 For I know my transgressions,
    and my sin is always before
        me.
4 Against you, you only, have I
        sinned
    and done what is evil in your
        sight;
    so you are right in your verdict
    and justified when you judge.
5 Surely I was sinful at birth,
    sinful from the time my
        mother conceived me.
6 Yet you desired faithfulness
        even in the womb;
    you taught me wisdom in that
        secret place.

7 Cleanse me with hyssop, and I
        will be clean;
    wash me, and I will be whiter
        than snow.
8 Let me hear joy and gladness;
    let the bones you have crushed
        rejoice.
9 Hide your face from my sins
    and blot out all my iniquity.

10 Create in me a pure heart,
        O God,
    and renew a steadfast spirit
        within me.
11 Do not cast me from your
        presence
    or take your Holy Spirit from
        me.
12 Restore to me the joy of your
        salvation
    and grant me a willing spirit,
        to sustain me.
13 Then I will teach transgressors
        your ways,
    so that sinners will turn back
        to you.

a 21 Or *thought the 'I AM' was*   *b 23* Probable reading of the original Hebrew text; the meaning
of the Masoretic Text for this phrase is uncertain.   *c* In Hebrew texts 51:1-19 is numbered
51:3-21.

14 Deliver me from the guilt of
   bloodshed, O God,
      you who are God my Savior,
   and my tongue will sing of
      your righteousness.
15 Open my lips, Lord,
   and my mouth will declare
      your praise.
16 You do not delight in sacrifice, or
      I would bring it;
   you do not take pleasure in
      burnt offerings.
17 My sacrifice, O God, is[a] a broken
      spirit;
   a broken and contrite heart
   you, God, will not despise.

18 May it please you to prosper
      Zion,
   to build up the walls of
      Jerusalem.
19 Then you will delight in the
      sacrifices of the righteous,
   in burnt offerings offered
      whole;
   then bulls will be offered on
      your altar.

Psalm 52[b]

*For the director of music. A maskil[c]
of David. When Doeg the Edomite had
gone to Saul and told him: "David has
gone to the house of Ahimelek."*

1 Why do you boast of evil, you
      mighty hero?
   Why do you boast all day long,
   you who are a disgrace in the
      eyes of God?
2 You who practice deceit,
   your tongue plots destruction;
   it is like a sharpened razor.
3 You love evil rather than good,
   falsehood rather than
      speaking the truth.[d]

4 You love every harmful word,
   you deceitful tongue!

5 Surely God will bring you down
      to everlasting ruin:
   He will snatch you up and
   pluck you from your tent;
   he will uproot you from the
      land of the living.
6 The righteous will see and fear;
   they will laugh at you,
      saying,
7 "Here now is the man
   who did not make God his
      stronghold
   but trusted in his great wealth
   and grew strong by destroying
      others!"

8 But I am like an olive tree
   flourishing in the house of
      God;
   I trust in God's unfailing love
   for ever and ever.
9 For what you have done I will
   always praise you
   in the presence of your faithful
      people.
   And I will hope in your name,
   for your name is good.

Psalm 53[e]

*For the director of music. According to
mahalath.[f] A maskil[c] of David.*

1 The fool says in his heart,
   "There is no God."
   They are corrupt, and their ways
      are vile;
   there is no one who does good.

2 God looks down from heaven
   on all mankind
   to see if there are any who
      understand,
   any who seek God.

---

a 17 Or *The sacrifices of God are*   b In Hebrew texts 52:1-9 is numbered 52:3-11.   c Title:
Probably a literary or musical term   d 3 The Hebrew has *Selah* (a word of uncertain meaning)
here and at the end of verse 5.   e In Hebrew texts 53:1-6 is numbered 53:2-7.   f Title:
Probably a musical term

3 Everyone has turned away, all
        have become corrupt;
    there is no one who does good,
        not even one.

4 Do all these evildoers know
        nothing?

    They devour my people as
        though eating bread;
    they never call on God.

5 But there they are, overwhelmed
        with dread,
    where there was nothing to
        dread.
    God scattered the bones of those
        who attacked you;
    you put them to shame, for
        God despised them.

6 Oh, that salvation for Israel
        would come out of Zion!
    When God restores his people,
        let Jacob rejoice and Israel be
        glad!

Psalm 54[a]

*For the director of music. With stringed
instruments. A maskil[b] of David. When
the Ziphites had gone to Saul and said,
"Is not David hiding among us?"*

1 Save me, O God, by your name;
    vindicate me by your might.
2 Hear my prayer, O God;
    listen to the words of my
        mouth.

3 Arrogant foes are attacking me;
    ruthless people are trying to
        kill me —
    people without regard for
        God.[c]

4 Surely God is my help;
    the Lord is the one who
        sustains me.

5 Let evil recoil on those who
        slander me;
    in your faithfulness destroy
        them.

6 I will sacrifice a freewill offering
        to you;
    I will praise your name, LORD,
        for it is good.
7 You have delivered me from all
        my troubles,
    and my eyes have looked in
        triumph on my foes.

Psalm 55[d]

*For the director of music. With stringed
instruments. A maskil[b] of David.*

1 Listen to my prayer, O God,
    do not ignore my plea;
2   hear me and answer me.
    My thoughts trouble me and I
        am distraught
3   because of what my enemy is
        saying,
    because of the threats of the
        wicked;
    for they bring down suffering on
        me
    and assail me in their anger.

4 My heart is in anguish within
        me;
    the terrors of death have fallen
        on me.
5 Fear and trembling have beset
        me;
    horror has overwhelmed me.
6 I said, "Oh, that I had the wings
        of a dove!
    I would fly away and be at rest.
7 I would flee far away
    and stay in the desert;[e]
8 I would hurry to my place of
        shelter,

---

[a] In Hebrew texts 54:1-7 is numbered 54:3-9.   [b] Title: Probably a literary or musical term
[c] 3 The Hebrew has *Selah* (a word of uncertain meaning) here.   [d] In Hebrew texts 55:1-23 is
numbered 55:2-24.   [e] 7 The Hebrew has *Selah* (a word of uncertain meaning) here and in the
middle of verse 19.

far from the tempest and
      storm."

9 Lord, confuse the wicked,
      confound their words,
   for I see violence and strife in
      the city.
10 Day and night they prowl about
      on its walls;
   malice and abuse are within it.
11 Destructive forces are at work in
      the city;
   threats and lies never leave its
      streets.

12 If an enemy were insulting me,
      I could endure it;
   if a foe were rising against me,
      I could hide.
13 But it is you, a man like myself,
      my companion, my close
      friend,
14 with whom I once enjoyed sweet
      fellowship
   at the house of God,
   as we walked about
      among the worshipers.

15 Let death take my enemies by
      surprise;
   let them go down alive to the
      realm of the dead,
   for evil finds lodging among
      them.

16 As for me, I call to God,
   and the LORD saves me.
17 Evening, morning and noon
   I cry out in distress,
   and he hears my voice.
18 He rescues me unharmed
   from the battle waged against
      me,
   even though many oppose
      me.
19 God, who is enthroned from of
      old,
   who does not change —

he will hear them and humble
      them,
   because they have no fear of
      God.
20 My companion attacks his
      friends;
   he violates his covenant.
21 His talk is smooth as butter,
      yet war is in his heart;
   his words are more soothing
      than oil,
      yet they are drawn swords.

22 Cast your cares on the LORD
   and he will sustain you;
   he will never let
      the righteous be shaken.
23 But you, God, will bring down
      the wicked
   into the pit of decay;
   the bloodthirsty and deceitful
   will not live out half their days.

But as for me, I trust in you.

Psalm 56[a]

*For the director of music. To the tune
of "A Dove on Distant Oaks." Of David.
A miktam.[b] When the Philistines had
seized him in Gath.*

1 Be merciful to me, my God,
   for my enemies are in hot
      pursuit;
   all day long they press their
      attack.
2 My adversaries pursue me all
      day long;
   in their pride many are
      attacking me.

3 When I am afraid, I put my trust
      in you.
4   In God, whose word I praise —
   in God I trust and am not afraid.
   What can mere mortals do
      to me?

---

a In Hebrew texts 56:1-13 is numbered 56:2-14.   b Title: Probably a literary or musical term

5 All day long they twist my words;
   all their schemes are for my
      ruin.
6 They conspire, they lurk,
   they watch my steps,
      hoping to take my life.
7 Because of their wickedness do
      not[a] let them escape;
   in your anger, God, bring the
      nations down.

8 Record my misery;
   list my tears on your scroll[b]—
      are they not in your record?
9 Then my enemies will turn back
      when I call for help.
   By this I will know that God is
      for me.

10 In God, whose word I praise,
   in the LORD, whose word I
      praise—
11 in God I trust and am not afraid.
   What can man do to me?

12 I am under vows to you, my God;
   I will present my thank
      offerings to you.
13 For you have delivered me from
      death
   and my feet from stumbling,
   that I may walk before God
      in the light of life.

Psalm 57[c]

*For the director of music. To the tune of
"Do Not Destroy." Of David. A miktam.[d]
When he had fled from Saul into the
cave.*

1 Have mercy on me, my God,
   have mercy on me,
   for in you I take refuge.
   I will take refuge in the shadow
      of your wings
   until the disaster has passed.

2 I cry out to God Most High,
   to God, who vindicates me.
3 He sends from heaven and saves
      me,
   rebuking those who hotly
      pursue me— [e]
   God sends forth his love and
      his faithfulness.

4 I am in the midst of lions;
   I am forced to dwell among
      ravenous beasts—
   men whose teeth are spears and
      arrows,
   whose tongues are sharp
      swords.

5 Be exalted, O God, above the
      heavens;
   let your glory be over all the
      earth.

6 They spread a net for my feet—
   I was bowed down in
      distress.
   They dug a pit in my path—
   but they have fallen into it
      themselves.

7 My heart, O God, is steadfast,
   my heart is steadfast;
   I will sing and make music.
8 Awake, my soul!
   Awake, harp and lyre!
   I will awaken the dawn.

9 I will praise you, Lord, among
      the nations;
   I will sing of you among the
      peoples.
10 For great is your love, reaching
      to the heavens;
   your faithfulness reaches to
      the skies.

11 Be exalted, O God, above the
      heavens;

---

[a] 7 Probable reading of the original Hebrew text; Masoretic Text does not have *do not*.
[b] 8 Or *misery; / put my tears in your wineskin*
[c] In Hebrew texts 57:1-11 is numbered 57:2-12.
[d] Title: Probably a literary or musical term here and at the end of verse 6.
[e] 3 The Hebrew has *Selah* (a word of uncertain meaning)

let your glory be over all the
earth.

Psalm 58[a]

*For the director of music. To the tune
of "Do Not Destroy." Of David.
A miktam.[b]*

[1] Do you rulers indeed speak
justly?
Do you judge people with
equity?
[2] No, in your heart you devise
injustice,
and your hands mete out
violence on the earth.

[3] Even from birth the wicked go
astray;
from the womb they are
wayward, spreading
lies.
[4] Their venom is like the venom of
a snake,
like that of a cobra that has
stopped its ears,
[5] that will not heed the tune of the
charmer,
however skillful the enchanter
may be.

[6] Break the teeth in their mouths,
O God;
Lord, tear out the fangs of
those lions!
[7] Let them vanish like water that
flows away;
when they draw the bow, let
their arrows fall short.
[8] May they be like a slug that melts
away as it moves along,
like a stillborn child that never
sees the sun.

[9] Before your pots can feel the
heat of the thorns—

whether they be green or
dry—the wicked will be
swept away.[c]
[10] The righteous will be glad when
they are avenged,
when they dip their feet in the
blood of the wicked.
[11] Then people will say,
"Surely the righteous still are
rewarded;
surely there is a God who
judges the earth."

Psalm 59[d]

*For the director of music. To the tune of
"Do Not Destroy." Of David. A miktam.[b]
When Saul had sent men to watch
David's house in order to kill him.*

[1] Deliver me from my enemies,
O God;
be my fortress against those
who are attacking me.
[2] Deliver me from evildoers
and save me from those who
are after my blood.

[3] See how they lie in wait for me!
Fierce men conspire against me
for no offense or sin of mine,
Lord.
[4] I have done no wrong, yet they
are ready to attack me.
Arise to help me; look on my
plight!
[5] You, Lord God Almighty,
you who are the God of Israel,
rouse yourself to punish all the
nations;
show no mercy to wicked
traitors.[e]

[6] They return at evening,
snarling like dogs,
and prowl about the city.

---

[a] In Hebrew texts 58:1-11 is numbered 58:2-12.   [b] Title: Probably a literary or musical term
[c] 9 The meaning of the Hebrew for this verse is uncertain.   [d] In Hebrew texts 59:1-17 is
numbered 59:2-18.   [e] 5 The Hebrew has *Selah* (a word of uncertain meaning) here and at the
end of verse 13.

7 See what they spew from their
       mouths—
   the words from their lips are
       sharp as swords,
   and they think, "Who can hear
       us?"

8 But you laugh at them, LORD;
   you scoff at all those nations.

9 You are my strength, I watch for
       you;
   you, God, are my fortress,
10   my God on whom I can rely.

   God will go before me
   and will let me gloat over those
       who slander me.
11 But do not kill them, Lord our
       shield,[a]
   or my people will forget.
   In your might uproot them
   and bring them down.
12 For the sins of their mouths,
   for the words of their lips,
   let them be caught in their
       pride.
   For the curses and lies they
       utter,
13   consume them in your
           wrath,
   consume them till they are no
       more.
   Then it will be known to the
       ends of the earth
   that God rules over Jacob.

14 They return at evening,
   snarling like dogs,
   and prowl about the city.
15 They wander about for food
   and howl if not satisfied.
16 But I will sing of your strength,
   in the morning I will sing of
       your love;
   for you are my fortress,
   my refuge in times of trouble.

17 You are my strength, I sing
       praise to you;
   you, God, are my fortress,
   my God on whom I can rely.

Psalm 60[b]

*For the director of music. To the tune of
"The Lily of the Covenant." A miktam[c]
of David. For teaching. When he fought
Aram Naharaim[d] and Aram Zobah,[e]
and when Joab returned and struck
down twelve thousand Edomites in the
Valley of Salt.*

1 You have rejected us, God, and
       burst upon us;
   you have been angry—now
       restore us!
2 You have shaken the land and
       torn it open;
   mend its fractures, for it is
       quaking.
3 You have shown your people
       desperate times;
   you have given us wine that
       makes us stagger.
4 But for those who fear you, you
       have raised a banner
   to be unfurled against the
       bow.[f]

5 Save us and help us with your
       right hand,
   that those you love may be
       delivered.
6 God has spoken from his
       sanctuary:
   "In triumph I will parcel out
       Shechem
   and measure off the Valley of
       Sukkoth.
7 Gilead is mine, and Manasseh is
       mine;
   Ephraim is my helmet,
   Judah is my scepter.

---

a 11 Or *sovereign*   b In Hebrew texts 60:1-12 is numbered 60:3-14.   c Title: Probably a
literary or musical term   d Title: That is, Arameans of Northwest Mesopotamia   e Title:
That is, Arameans of central Syria   f 4 The Hebrew has *Selah* (a word of uncertain meaning)
here.

⁸Moab is my washbasin,
on Edom I toss my sandal;
over Philistia I shout in
triumph."

⁹Who will bring me to the
fortified city?
Who will lead me to Edom?
¹⁰Is it not you, God, you who have
now rejected us
and no longer go out with our
armies?
¹¹Give us aid against the enemy,
for human help is worthless.
¹²With God we will gain the
victory,
and he will trample down our
enemies.

Psalm 61 [a]

*For the director of music. With stringed
instruments. Of David.*

¹Hear my cry, O God;
listen to my prayer.

²From the ends of the earth I call
to you,
I call as my heart grows faint;
lead me to the rock that is
higher than I.

³For you have been my refuge,
a strong tower against the foe.

⁴I long to dwell in your tent
forever
and take refuge in the shelter
of your wings. [b]

⁵For you, God, have heard my
vows;
you have given me the heritage
of those who fear your
name.

⁶Increase the days of the king's
life,

his years for many
generations.
⁷May he be enthroned in God's
presence forever;
appoint your love and
faithfulness to protect
him.

⁸Then I will ever sing in praise of
your name
and fulfill my vows day after
day.

Psalm 62 [c]

*For the director of music. For Jeduthun.
A psalm of David.*

¹Truly my soul finds rest in God;
my salvation comes from
him.
²Truly he is my rock and my
salvation;
he is my fortress, I will never
be shaken.

³How long will you assault me?
Would all of you throw me
down—
this leaning wall, this tottering
fence?
⁴Surely they intend to topple me
from my lofty place;
they take delight in lies.
With their mouths they bless,
but in their hearts they curse. [d]

⁵Yes, my soul, find rest in God;
my hope comes from him.
⁶Truly he is my rock and my
salvation;
he is my fortress, I will not be
shaken.
⁷My salvation and my honor
depend on God [e];
he is my mighty rock, my
refuge.

---

a In Hebrew texts 61:1-8 is numbered 61:2-9.   *b 4* The Hebrew has *Selah* (a word of uncertain meaning) here.   *c* In Hebrew texts 62:1-12 is numbered 62:2-13.   *d 4* The Hebrew has *Selah* (a word of uncertain meaning) here and at the end of verse 8.   *e 7* Or / *God Most High is my salvation and my honor*

8 Trust in him at all times, you
people;
pour out your hearts to him,
for God is our refuge.

9 Surely the lowborn are but a
breath,
the highborn are but a lie.
If weighed on a balance, they are
nothing;
together they are only a
breath.

10 Do not trust in extortion
or put vain hope in stolen
goods;
though your riches increase,
do not set your heart on them.

11 One thing God has spoken,
two things I have heard:
"Power belongs to you, God,
12   and with you, Lord, is
unfailing love";
and, "You reward everyone
according to what they have
done."

Psalm 63[a]

*A psalm of David. When he was in the
Desert of Judah.*

1 You, God, are my God,
earnestly I seek you;
I thirst for you,
my whole being longs for you,
in a dry and parched land
where there is no water.

2 I have seen you in the
sanctuary
and beheld your power and
your glory.

3 Because your love is better than
life,
my lips will glorify you.

4 I will praise you as long as I live,
and in your name I will lift up
my hands.

5 I will be fully satisfied as with
the richest of foods;
with singing lips my mouth
will praise you.

6 On my bed I remember you;
I think of you through the
watches of the night.

7 Because you are my help,
I sing in the shadow of your
wings.

8 I cling to you;
your right hand upholds me.

9 Those who want to kill me will
be destroyed;
they will go down to the
depths of the earth.

10 They will be given over to the
sword
and become food for jackals.

11 But the king will rejoice in God;
all who swear by God will
glory in him,
while the mouths of liars will
be silenced.

Psalm 64[b]

*For the director of music. A psalm
of David.*

1 Hear me, my God, as I voice my
complaint;
protect my life from the threat
of the enemy.

2 Hide me from the conspiracy of
the wicked,
from the plots of evildoers.

3 They sharpen their tongues like
swords
and aim cruel words like
deadly arrows.

4 They shoot from ambush at the
innocent;
they shoot suddenly, without
fear.

---

a In Hebrew texts 63:1-11 is numbered 63:2-12.   b In Hebrew texts 64:1-10 is numbered 64:2-11.

⁵ They encourage each other in
  evil plans,
    they talk about hiding their
      snares;
    they say, "Who will see it*a*?"
⁶ They plot injustice and say,
  "We have devised a perfect
      plan!"
    Surely the human mind and
      heart are cunning.

⁷ But God will shoot them with his
  arrows;
    they will suddenly be struck
      down.
⁸ He will turn their own tongues
  against them
    and bring them to ruin;
    all who see them will shake
      their heads in scorn.
⁹ All people will fear;
    they will proclaim the works of
      God
    and ponder what he has done.

¹⁰ The righteous will rejoice in the
  LORD
    and take refuge in him;
    all the upright in heart will
      glory in him!

Psalm 65*b*

*For the director of music. A psalm
of David. A song.*

¹ Praise awaits*c* you, our God, in
  Zion;
    to you our vows will be
      fulfilled.
² You who answer prayer,
    to you all people will come.
³ When we were overwhelmed by
  sins,
    you forgave*d* our
      transgressions.
⁴ Blessed are those you choose

and bring near to live in your
  courts!
We are filled with the good
  things of your house,
    of your holy temple.

⁵ You answer us with awesome
  and righteous deeds,
    God our Savior,
    the hope of all the ends of the
      earth
    and of the farthest seas,
⁶ who formed the mountains by
  your power,
    having armed yourself with
      strength,
⁷ who stilled the roaring of the
  seas,
    the roaring of their waves,
    and the turmoil of the nations.
⁸ The whole earth is filled with
  awe at your wonders;
    where morning dawns, where
      evening fades,
    you call forth songs of joy.

⁹ You care for the land and water
  it;
    you enrich it abundantly.
    The streams of God are filled
      with water
    to provide the people with
      grain,
    for so you have ordained it.*e*
¹⁰ You drench its furrows and level
  its ridges;
    you soften it with showers and
      bless its crops.
¹¹ You crown the year with your
  bounty,
    and your carts overflow with
      abundance.
¹² The grasslands of the wilderness
  overflow;
    the hills are clothed with
      gladness.

---

a 5 Or *us*   *b* In Hebrew texts 65:1-13 is numbered 65:2-14.   *c 1* Or *befits; the meaning of the
Hebrew for this word is uncertain.*   *d 3* Or *made atonement for*   *e 9* Or *for that is how you
prepare the land*

13 The meadows are covered with
    flocks
  and the valleys are mantled
    with grain;
  they shout for joy and sing.

Psalm 66

For the director of music. A song.
A psalm.

1 Shout for joy to God, all the
    earth!
2   Sing the glory of his name;
  make his praise glorious.
3 Say to God, "How awesome are
    your deeds!
  So great is your power
  that your enemies cringe
    before you.
4 All the earth bows down to you;
  they sing praise to you,
  they sing the praises of your
    name."[a]

5 Come and see what God has
    done,
  his awesome deeds for
    mankind!
6 He turned the sea into dry land,
  they passed through the
    waters on foot—
  come, let us rejoice in him.
7 He rules forever by his power,
  his eyes watch the nations—
  let not the rebellious rise up
    against him.

8 Praise our God, all peoples,
  let the sound of his praise be
    heard;
9 he has preserved our lives
  and kept our feet from
    slipping.
10 For you, God, tested us;
  you refined us like silver.
11 You brought us into prison

and laid burdens on our backs.
12 You let people ride over our
    heads;
  we went through fire and
    water,
  but you brought us to a place
    of abundance.

13 I will come to your temple with
    burnt offerings
  and fulfill my vows to you—
14 vows my lips promised and my
    mouth spoke
  when I was in trouble.
15 I will sacrifice fat animals to you
  and an offering of rams;
  I will offer bulls and goats.

16 Come and hear, all you who fear
    God;
  let me tell you what he has
    done for me.
17 I cried out to him with my
    mouth;
  his praise was on my tongue.
18 If I had cherished sin in my
    heart,
  the Lord would not have
    listened;
19 but God has surely listened
  and has heard my prayer.
20 Praise be to God,
  who has not rejected my
    prayer
  or withheld his love from me!

Psalm 67[b]

For the director of music. With stringed
instruments. A psalm. A song.

1 May God be gracious to us and
    bless us
  and make his face shine on
    us—[c]
2 so that your ways may be known
    on earth,

---

a 4 The Hebrew has *Selah* (a word of uncertain meaning) here and at the end of verses 7 and 15.
b In Hebrew texts 67:1-7 is numbered 67:2-8.   c 1 The Hebrew has *Selah* (a word of uncertain
meaning) here and at the end of verse 4.

your salvation among all
nations.

³ May the peoples praise you,
God;
may all the peoples praise you.
⁴ May the nations be glad and sing
for joy,
for you rule the peoples with
equity
and guide the nations of the
earth.
⁵ May the peoples praise you,
God;
may all the peoples praise you.

⁶ The land yields its harvest;
God, our God, blesses us.
⁷ May God bless us still,
so that all the ends of the earth
will fear him.

Psalm 68ᵃ

*For the director of music. Of David.
A psalm. A song.*

¹ May God arise, may his enemies
be scattered;
may his foes flee before him.
² May you blow them away like
smoke—
as wax melts before the fire,
may the wicked perish before
God.
³ But may the righteous be glad
and rejoice before God;
may they be happy and joyful.

⁴ Sing to God, sing in praise of his
name,
extol him who rides on the
cloudsᵇ;
rejoice before him—his name
is the LORD.
⁵ A father to the fatherless, a
defender of widows,

is God in his holy dwelling.
⁶ God sets the lonely in families,ᶜ
he leads out the prisoners with
singing;
but the rebellious live in a sun-
scorched land.

⁷ When you, God, went out before
your people,
when you marched through
the wilderness,ᵈ
⁸ the earth shook, the heavens
poured down rain,
before God, the One of Sinai,
before God, the God of Israel.
⁹ You gave abundant showers,
O God;
you refreshed your weary
inheritance.
¹⁰ Your people settled in it,
and from your bounty, God,
you provided for the poor.

¹¹ The Lord announces the word,
and the women who proclaim
it are a mighty throng:
¹² "Kings and armies flee in haste;
the women at home divide the
plunder.
¹³ Even while you sleep among the
sheep pens,ᵉ
the wings of my dove are
sheathed with silver,
its feathers with shining
gold."
¹⁴ When the Almightyᶠ scattered
the kings in the land,
it was like snow fallen on
Mount Zalmon.

¹⁵ Mount Bashan, majestic
mountain,
Mount Bashan, rugged
mountain,
¹⁶ why gaze in envy, you rugged
mountain,

ᵃ In Hebrew texts 68:1-35 is numbered 68:2-36.   ᵇ 4 Or *name, / prepare the way for him who
rides through the deserts*   ᶜ 6 Or *the desolate in a homeland*   ᵈ 7 The Hebrew has *Selah* (a
word of uncertain meaning) here and at the end of verses 19 and 32.   ᵉ 13 Or *the campfires;* or
the saddlebags   ᶠ 14 Hebrew *Shaddai*

at the mountain where God
chooses to reign,
where the LORD himself will
dwell forever?

¹⁷ The chariots of God are tens of
thousands
and thousands of thousands;
the Lord has come from Sinai
into his sanctuary.[a]

¹⁸ When you ascended on high,
you took many captives;
you received gifts from
people,
even from[b] the rebellious —
that you,[c] LORD God, might
dwell there.

¹⁹ Praise be to the Lord, to God our
Savior,
who daily bears our burdens.

²⁰ Our God is a God who saves;
from the Sovereign LORD
comes escape from death.

²¹ Surely God will crush the heads
of his enemies,
the hairy crowns of those who
go on in their sins.

²² The Lord says, "I will bring them
from Bashan;
I will bring them from the
depths of the sea,

²³ that your feet may wade in the
blood of your foes,
while the tongues of your dogs
have their share."

²⁴ Your procession, God, has come
into view,
the procession of my God and
King into the sanctuary.

²⁵ In front are the singers, after
them the musicians;
with them are the young
women playing the
timbrels.

²⁶ Praise God in the great
congregation;
praise the LORD in the
assembly of Israel.

²⁷ There is the little tribe of
Benjamin, leading them,
there the great throng of
Judah's princes,
and there the princes of
Zebulun and of Naphtali.

²⁸ Summon your power, God[d];
show us your strength, our God,
as you have done before.

²⁹ Because of your temple at
Jerusalem
kings will bring you gifts.

³⁰ Rebuke the beast among the
reeds,
the herd of bulls among the
calves of the nations.
Humbled, may the beast bring
bars of silver.
Scatter the nations who
delight in war.

³¹ Envoys will come from Egypt;
Cush[e] will submit herself to
God.

³² Sing to God, you kingdoms of the
earth,
sing praise to the Lord,

³³ to him who rides across the
highest heavens, the
ancient heavens,
who thunders with mighty
voice.

³⁴ Proclaim the power of God,
whose majesty is over Israel,
whose power is in the heavens.

³⁵ You, God, are awesome in your
sanctuary;
the God of Israel gives power
and strength to his people.

Praise be to God!

---

[a] 17 Probable reading of the original Hebrew text; Masoretic Text *Lord is among them at Sinai in holiness*   [b] 18 Or *gifts for people, / even*   [c] 18 Or *they*   [d] 28 Many Hebrew manuscripts *Your God has summoned power for you*
[e] 31 That is, the upper Nile region

Psalm 69[a]

For the director of music. To the tune of "Lilies." Of David.

¹ Save me, O God,
    for the waters have come up to
        my neck.
² I sink in the miry depths,
    where there is no foothold.
  I have come into the deep
        waters;
    the floods engulf me.
³ I am worn out calling for help;
    my throat is parched.
  My eyes fail,
    looking for my God.
⁴ Those who hate me without
        reason
    outnumber the hairs of my
        head;
  many are my enemies without
        cause,
    those who seek to destroy me.
  I am forced to restore
    what I did not steal.

⁵ You, God, know my folly;
    my guilt is not hidden from
        you.
⁶ Lord, the LORD Almighty,
    may those who hope in you
    not be disgraced because of
        me;
  God of Israel,
    may those who seek you
    not be put to shame because of
        me.
⁷ For I endure scorn for your sake,
    and shame covers my face.
⁸ I am a foreigner to my own
        family,
    a stranger to my own mother's
        children;
⁹ for zeal for your house consumes
        me,
    and the insults of those who
        insult you fall on me.

¹⁰ When I weep and fast,
    I must endure scorn;
¹¹ when I put on sackcloth,
    people make sport of me.
¹² Those who sit at the gate mock
        me,
    and I am the song of the
        drunkards.

¹³ But I pray to you, LORD,
    in the time of your favor;
  in your great love, O God,
    answer me with your sure
        salvation.
¹⁴ Rescue me from the mire,
    do not let me sink;
  deliver me from those who hate
        me,
    from the deep waters.
¹⁵ Do not let the floodwaters engulf
        me
    or the depths swallow me up
    or the pit close its mouth over
        me.

¹⁶ Answer me, LORD, out of the
        goodness of your love;
    in your great mercy turn to
        me.
¹⁷ Do not hide your face from your
        servant;
    answer me quickly, for I am in
        trouble.
¹⁸ Come near and rescue me;
    deliver me because of my foes.

¹⁹ You know how I am scorned,
        disgraced and shamed;
    all my enemies are before you.
²⁰ Scorn has broken my heart
    and has left me helpless;
  I looked for sympathy, but there
        was none,
    for comforters, but I found
        none.
²¹ They put gall in my food
    and gave me vinegar for my
        thirst.

---

[a] In Hebrew texts 69:1-36 is numbered 69:2-37.

22 May the table set before them
become a snare;
may it become retribution
and[a] a trap.
23 May their eyes be darkened so
they cannot see,
and their backs be bent
forever.
24 Pour out your wrath on them;
let your fierce anger overtake
them.
25 May their place be deserted;
let there be no one to dwell in
their tents.
26 For they persecute those you
wound
and talk about the pain of
those you hurt.
27 Charge them with crime upon
crime;
do not let them share in your
salvation.
28 May they be blotted out of the
book of life
and not be listed with the
righteous.
29 But as for me, afflicted and in
pain —
may your salvation, God,
protect me.

30 I will praise God's name in song
and glorify him with
thanksgiving.
31 This will please the LORD more
than an ox,
more than a bull with its horns
and hooves.
32 The poor will see and be glad —
you who seek God, may your
hearts live!
33 The LORD hears the needy
and does not despise his
captive people.
34 Let heaven and earth praise
him,

the seas and all that move in
them,
35 for God will save Zion
and rebuild the cities of
Judah.
Then people will settle there and
possess it;
36   the children of his servants
will inherit it,
and those who love his name
will dwell there.

Psalm 70[b]

For the director of music. Of David.
A petition.

1 Hasten, O God, to save me;
come quickly, LORD, to help
me.

2 May those who want to take my
life
be put to shame and
confusion;
may all who desire my ruin
be turned back in disgrace.
3 May those who say to me, "Aha!
Aha!"
turn back because of their
shame.
4 But may all who seek you
rejoice and be glad in you;
may those who long for your
saving help always say,
"The LORD is great!"

5 But as for me, I am poor and
needy;
come quickly to me, O God.
You are my help and my
deliverer;
LORD, do not delay.

Psalm 71

1 In you, LORD, I have taken
refuge;
let me never be put to shame.

---

a 22 Or *snare / and their fellowship become*   b In Hebrew texts 70:1-5 is numbered 70:2-6.

² In your righteousness, rescue
        me and deliver me;
    turn your ear to me and save
        me.
³ Be my rock of refuge,
    to which I can always go;
    give the command to save me,
    for you are my rock and my
        fortress.
⁴ Deliver me, my God, from the
        hand of the wicked,
    from the grasp of those who
        are evil and cruel.

⁵ For you have been my hope,
        Sovereign LORD,
    my confidence since my
        youth.
⁶ From birth I have relied on you;
    you brought me forth from my
        mother's womb.
    I will ever praise you.
⁷ I have become a sign to many;
    you are my strong refuge.
⁸ My mouth is filled with your
        praise,
    declaring your splendor all
        day long.

⁹ Do not cast me away when I am
        old;
    do not forsake me when my
        strength is gone.
¹⁰ For my enemies speak against
        me;
    those who wait to kill me
        conspire together.
¹¹ They say, "God has forsaken
        him;
    pursue him and seize him,
    for no one will rescue him."
¹² Do not be far from me, my God;
    come quickly, God, to help me.
¹³ May my accusers perish in
        shame;
    may those who want to harm
        me
    be covered with scorn and
        disgrace.

¹⁴ As for me, I will always have
        hope;
    I will praise you more and
        more.
¹⁵ My mouth will tell of your
        righteous deeds,
    of your saving acts all day
        long—
    though I know not how to
        relate them all.
¹⁶ I will come and proclaim your
        mighty acts, Sovereign
        LORD;
    I will proclaim your righteous
        deeds, yours alone.
¹⁷ Since my youth, God, you have
        taught me,
    and to this day I declare your
        marvelous deeds.
¹⁸ Even when I am old and gray,
    do not forsake me, my God,
    till I declare your power to the
        next generation,
    your mighty acts to all who are
        to come.

¹⁹ Your righteousness, God,
        reaches to the heavens,
    you who have done great
        things.
    Who is like you, God?
²⁰ Though you have made me see
        troubles,
    many and bitter,
    you will restore my life again;
    from the depths of the earth
    you will again bring me up.
²¹ You will increase my honor
    and comfort me once more.

²² I will praise you with the harp
    for your faithfulness, my
        God;
    I will sing praise to you with the
        lyre,
    Holy One of Israel.
²³ My lips will shout for joy
    when I sing praise to you—
    I whom you have delivered.

24 My tongue will tell of your
righteous acts
all day long,
for those who wanted to harm me
have been put to shame and
confusion.

Psalm 72

Of Solomon.

1 Endow the king with your
justice, O God,
the royal son with your
righteousness.
2 May he judge your people in
righteousness,
your afflicted ones with
justice.

3 May the mountains bring
prosperity to the people,
the hills the fruit of
righteousness.
4 May he defend the afflicted
among the people
and save the children of the
needy;
may he crush the oppressor.
5 May he endure*a* as long as the
sun,
as long as the moon, through
all generations.
6 May he be like rain falling on a
mown field,
like showers watering the
earth.
7 In his days may the righteous
flourish
and prosperity abound till the
moon is no more.

8 May he rule from sea to sea
and from the River*b* to the
ends of the earth.
9 May the desert tribes bow before
him

and his enemies lick the dust.
10 May the kings of Tarshish and of
distant shores
bring tribute to him.
May the kings of Sheba and Seba
present him gifts.
11 May all kings bow down to him
and all nations serve him.

12 For he will deliver the needy who
cry out,
the afflicted who have no one
to help.
13 He will take pity on the weak
and the needy
and save the needy from
death.
14 He will rescue them from
oppression and violence,
for precious is their blood in
his sight.

15 Long may he live!
May gold from Sheba be given
him.
May people ever pray for him
and bless him all day long.
16 May grain abound throughout
the land;
on the tops of the hills may it
sway.
May the crops flourish like
Lebanon
and thrive*c* like the grass of
the field.
17 May his name endure forever;
may it continue as long as the
sun.

Then all nations will be blessed
through him,*d*
and they will call him blessed.

18 Praise be to the LORD God, the
God of Israel,
who alone does marvelous
deeds.

---

a 5 Septuagint; Hebrew *You will be feared*   *b 8* That is, the Euphrates   *c 16* Probable
reading of the original Hebrew text; Masoretic Text *Lebanon, / from the city*   *d 17* Or *will use
his name in blessings* (see Gen. 48:20)

¹⁹ Praise be to his glorious name
forever;
   may the whole earth be filled
   with his glory.
      Amen and Amen.

²⁰ This concludes the prayers
of David son of Jesse.

BOOK III

Psalms 73–89

Psalm 73

A psalm of Asaph.

¹ Surely God is good to Israel,
   to those who are pure in heart.

² But as for me, my feet had almost
   slipped;
   I had nearly lost my foothold.

³ For I envied the arrogant
   when I saw the prosperity of
   the wicked.

⁴ They have no struggles;
   their bodies are healthy and
   strong.[a]

⁵ They are free from common
   human burdens;
   they are not plagued by
   human ills.

⁶ Therefore pride is their
   necklace;
   they clothe themselves with
   violence.

⁷ From their callous hearts comes
   iniquity[b];
   their evil imaginations have
   no limits.

⁸ They scoff, and speak with
   malice;
   with arrogance they threaten
   oppression.

⁹ Their mouths lay claim to
   heaven,

and their tongues take
possession of the earth.

¹⁰ Therefore their people turn to
them
   and drink up waters in
   abundance.[c]

¹¹ They say, "How would God know?
Does the Most High know
anything?"

¹² This is what the wicked are like—
always free of care, they go on
amassing wealth.

¹³ Surely in vain I have kept my
heart pure
   and have washed my hands in
   innocence.

¹⁴ All day long I have been
afflicted,
   and every morning brings new
   punishments.

¹⁵ If I had spoken out like that,
   I would have betrayed your
   children.

¹⁶ When I tried to understand all
this,
   it troubled me deeply

¹⁷ till I entered the sanctuary of
God;
   then I understood their final
   destiny.

¹⁸ Surely you place them on
slippery ground;
   you cast them down to ruin.

¹⁹ How suddenly are they destroyed,
completely swept away by
terrors!

²⁰ They are like a dream when one
awakes;
   when you arise, Lord,
   you will despise them as
   fantasies.

²¹ When my heart was grieved
and my spirit embittered,

---

[a] 4 With a different word division of the Hebrew; Masoretic Text *struggles at their death; /
their bodies are healthy*   [b] 7 Syriac (see also Septuagint); Hebrew *Their eyes bulge with fat*
[c] 10 The meaning of the Hebrew for this verse is uncertain.

22 I was senseless and ignorant;
     I was a brute beast before you.

23 Yet I am always with you;
     you hold me by my right hand.
24 You guide me with your counsel,
     and afterward you will take
       me into glory.
25 Whom have I in heaven but you?
     And earth has nothing I desire
       besides you.
26 My flesh and my heart may fail,
     but God is the strength of my
       heart
     and my portion forever.

27 Those who are far from you will
       perish;
     you destroy all who are
       unfaithful to you.
28 But as for me, it is good to be
       near God.
     I have made the Sovereign
       Lord my refuge;
     I will tell of all your deeds.

Psalm 74

A maskil[a] of Asaph.

1 O God, why have you rejected us
       forever?
     Why does your anger smolder
       against the sheep of your
       pasture?
2 Remember the nation you
       purchased long ago,
     the people of your inheritance,
       whom you redeemed —
     Mount Zion, where you dwelt.
3 Turn your steps toward these
       everlasting ruins,
     all this destruction the enemy
       has brought on the
       sanctuary.

4 Your foes roared in the place
       where you met with us;
     they set up their standards as
       signs.
5 They behaved like men wielding
       axes
     to cut through a thicket of
       trees.
6 They smashed all the carved
       paneling
     with their axes and hatchets.
7 They burned your sanctuary to
       the ground;
     they defiled the dwelling place
       of your Name.
8 They said in their hearts,
     "We will crush them
       completely!"
     They burned every place
       where God was worshiped
       in the land.

9 We are given no signs from God;
     no prophets are left,
     and none of us knows how
       long this will be.
10 How long will the enemy mock
       you, God?
     Will the foe revile your name
       forever?
11 Why do you hold back your
       hand, your right hand?
     Take it from the folds of your
       garment and destroy
       them!

12 But God is my King from long
       ago;
     he brings salvation on the
       earth.

13 It was you who split open the sea
       by your power;
     you broke the heads of the
       monster in the waters.
14 It was you who crushed the
       heads of Leviathan
     and gave it as food to the
       creatures of the desert.

---

a Title: Probably a literary or musical term

15 It was you who opened up
        springs and streams;
    you dried up the ever-flowing
        rivers.
16 The day is yours, and yours also
        the night;
    you established the sun and
        moon.
17 It was you who set all the
        boundaries of the earth;
    you made both summer and
        winter.

18 Remember how the enemy has
        mocked you, LORD,
    how foolish people have
        reviled your name.
19 Do not hand over the life of your
        dove to wild beasts;
    do not forget the lives of your
        afflicted people forever.
20 Have regard for your covenant,
    because haunts of violence
        fill the dark places of the
        land.
21 Do not let the oppressed retreat
        in disgrace;
    may the poor and needy praise
        your name.
22 Rise up, O God, and defend your
        cause;
    remember how fools mock you
        all day long.
23 Do not ignore the clamor of your
        adversaries,
    the uproar of your enemies,
        which rises continually.

Psalm 75[a]

*For the director of music. To the tune
of "Do Not Destroy." A psalm of Asaph.
A song.*

1 We praise you, God,
    we praise you, for your Name
        is near;

people tell of your wonderful
        deeds.

2 You say, "I choose the appointed
        time;
    it is I who judge with equity.
3 When the earth and all its
        people quake,
    it is I who hold its pillars firm.[b]
4 To the arrogant I say, 'Boast no
        more,'
    and to the wicked, 'Do not lift
        up your horns.[c]
5 Do not lift your horns against
        heaven;
    do not speak so defiantly.' "

6 No one from the east or the west
    or from the desert can exalt
        themselves.
7 It is God who judges:
    He brings one down, he exalts
        another.
8 In the hand of the LORD is a cup
        full of foaming wine mixed
        with spices;
    he pours it out, and all the
        wicked of the earth
        drink it down to its very dregs.

9 As for me, I will declare this
        forever;
    I will sing praise to the God of
        Jacob.
10 who says, "I will cut off the horns
        of all the wicked,
    but the horns of the righteous
        will be lifted up."

Psalm 76[d]

*For the director of music. With stringed
instruments. A psalm of Asaph. A song.*

1 God is renowned in Judah;
    in Israel his name is great.
2 His tent is in Salem,
    his dwelling place in Zion.

---

[a] In Hebrew texts 75:1-10 is numbered 75:2-11.
meaning) here.   [c] 4 *Horns* here symbolize strength; also in verses 5 and 10.   [b] 3 The Hebrew has *Selah* (a word of uncertain   [d] In Hebrew
texts 76:1-12 is numbered 76:2-13.

3 There he broke the flashing
  arrows,
    the shields and the swords, the
    weapons of war.[a]

4 You are radiant with light,
    more majestic than mountains
    rich with game.

5 The valiant lie plundered,
    they sleep their last sleep;
  not one of the warriors
    can lift his hands.

6 At your rebuke, God of Jacob,
    both horse and chariot lie still.

7 It is you alone who are to be
  feared.
    Who can stand before you
    when you are angry?

8 From heaven you pronounced
  judgment,
    and the land feared and was
    quiet—

9 when you, God, rose up to judge,
    to save all the afflicted of the
    land.

10 Surely your wrath against
    mankind brings you praise,
    and the survivors of your
    wrath are restrained.[b]

11 Make vows to the LORD your God
    and fulfill them;
  let all the neighboring lands
    bring gifts to the One to be
    feared.

12 He breaks the spirit of rulers;
    he is feared by the kings of the
    earth.

Psalm 77[c]

*For the director of music. For Jeduthun.
Of Asaph. A psalm.*

1 I cried out to God for help;
    I cried out to God to hear me.

2 When I was in distress, I sought
    the Lord;
  at night I stretched out
    untiring hands,
    and I would not be comforted.

3 I remembered you, God, and I
    groaned;
  I meditated, and my spirit
    grew faint.[d]

4 You kept my eyes from closing;
    I was too troubled to speak.

5 I thought about the former days,
    the years of long ago;

6 I remembered my songs in the
    night.
  My heart meditated and my
    spirit asked:

7 "Will the Lord reject forever?
    Will he never show his favor
    again?

8 Has his unfailing love vanished
    forever?
  Has his promise failed for all
    time?

9 Has God forgotten to be merciful?
    Has he in anger withheld his
    compassion?"

10 Then I thought, "To this I will
    appeal:
    the years when the Most High
    stretched out his right
    hand.

11 I will remember the deeds of the
    LORD;
  yes, I will remember your
    miracles of long ago.

12 I will consider all your works
    and meditate on all your
    mighty deeds."

13 Your ways, God, are holy.
    What god is as great as our
    God?

---

[a] 3 The Hebrew has *Selah* (a word of uncertain meaning) here and at the end of verse 9.
[b] 10 Or *Surely the wrath of mankind brings you praise, / and with the remainder of wrath you arm yourself*   [c] In Hebrew texts 77:1-20 is numbered 77:2-21.   [d] 3 The Hebrew has *Selah* (a word of uncertain meaning) here and at the end of verses 9 and 15.

14 You are the God who performs
    miracles;
    you display your power among
      the peoples.
15 With your mighty arm you
    redeemed your people,
    the descendants of Jacob and
      Joseph.

16 The waters saw you, God,
    the waters saw you and
      writhed;
    the very depths were
      convulsed.
17 The clouds poured down water,
    the heavens resounded with
      thunder;
    your arrows flashed back and
      forth.
18 Your thunder was heard in the
      whirlwind,
    your lightning lit up the world;
    the earth trembled and
      quaked.
19 Your path led through the sea,
    your way through the mighty
      waters,
    though your footprints were
      not seen.
20 You led your people like a flock
    by the hand of Moses and
      Aaron.

Psalm 78

A maskil[a] of Asaph.

1 My people, hear my teaching;
    listen to the words of my
      mouth.
2 I will open my mouth with a
      parable;
    I will utter hidden things,
      things from of old —
3 things we have heard and
      known,
    things our ancestors have told
      us.

4 We will not hide them from their
      descendants;
    we will tell the next generation
    the praiseworthy deeds of the
      LORD,
    his power, and the wonders he
      has done.
5 He decreed statutes for Jacob
    and established the law in
      Israel,
    which he commanded our
      ancestors
    to teach their children,
6 so the next generation would
      know them,
    even the children yet to be
      born,
    and they in turn would tell
      their children.
7 Then they would put their trust
      in God
    and would not forget his deeds
    but would keep his
      commands.
8 They would not be like their
      ancestors —
    a stubborn and rebellious
      generation,
    whose hearts were not loyal to
      God,
    whose spirits were not faithful
      to him.

9 The men of Ephraim, though
      armed with bows,
    turned back on the day of
      battle;
10 they did not keep God's
      covenant
    and refused to live by his law.
11 They forgot what he had done,
    the wonders he had shown
      them.
12 He did miracles in the sight of
      their ancestors
    in the land of Egypt, in the
      region of Zoan.

---

a Title: Probably a literary or musical term

¹³ He divided the sea and led them
through;
　he made the water stand up
　　like a wall.
¹⁴ He guided them with the cloud
by day
　and with light from the fire all
　　night.
¹⁵ He split the rocks in the
wilderness
　and gave them water as
　　abundant as the seas;
¹⁶ he brought streams out of a
rocky crag
　and made water flow down
　　like rivers.

¹⁷ But they continued to sin against
him,
　rebelling in the wilderness
　　against the Most High.
¹⁸ They willfully put God to the
test
　by demanding the food they
　　craved.
¹⁹ They spoke against God;
　they said, "Can God really
　　spread a table in the
　　wilderness?
²⁰ True, he struck the rock,
　and water gushed out,
　　streams flowed abundantly,
　but can he also give us bread?
　　Can he supply meat for his
　　people?"
²¹ When the LORD heard them, he
was furious;
　his fire broke out against
　　Jacob,
　and his wrath rose against
　　Israel,
²² for they did not believe in God
　or trust in his deliverance.
²³ Yet he gave a command to the
skies above
　and opened the doors of the
　　heavens;
²⁴ he rained down manna for the
people to eat,

he gave them the grain of
heaven.
²⁵ Human beings ate the bread of
angels;
　he sent them all the food they
　　could eat.
²⁶ He let loose the east wind from
the heavens
　and by his power made the
　　south wind blow.
²⁷ He rained meat down on them
like dust,
　birds like sand on the
　　seashore.
²⁸ He made them come down
inside their camp,
　all around their tents.
²⁹ They ate till they were gorged —
　he had given them what they
　　craved.
³⁰ But before they turned from
what they craved,
　even while the food was still in
　　their mouths,
³¹ God's anger rose against them;
　he put to death the sturdiest
　　among them,
　cutting down the young men
　　of Israel.

³² In spite of all this, they kept on
sinning;
　in spite of his wonders, they
　　did not believe.
³³ So he ended their days in
futility
　and their years in terror.
³⁴ Whenever God slew them, they
would seek him;
　they eagerly turned to him
　　again.
³⁵ They remembered that God was
their Rock,
　that God Most High was their
　　Redeemer.
³⁶ But then they would flatter him
with their mouths,
　lying to him with their
　　tongues;

37 their hearts were not loyal to
        him,
    they were not faithful to his
        covenant.
38 Yet he was merciful;
    he forgave their iniquities
        and did not destroy them.
    Time after time he restrained his
        anger
        and did not stir up his full
            wrath.
39 He remembered that they were
        but flesh,
    a passing breeze that does not
        return.

40 How often they rebelled against
        him in the wilderness
    and grieved him in the
        wasteland!
41 Again and again they put God to
        the test;
    they vexed the Holy One of
        Israel.
42 They did not remember his
        power —
    the day he redeemed them
        from the oppressor,
43 the day he displayed his signs in
        Egypt,
    his wonders in the region of
        Zoan.
44 He turned their river into
        blood;
    they could not drink from
        their streams.
45 He sent swarms of flies that
        devoured them,
    and frogs that devastated
        them.
46 He gave their crops to the
        grasshopper,
    their produce to the locust.
47 He destroyed their vines with
        hail
    and their sycamore-figs with
        sleet.
48 He gave over their cattle to the
        hail,

their livestock to bolts of
        lightning.
49 He unleashed against them his
        hot anger,
    his wrath, indignation and
        hostility —
    a band of destroying angels.
50 He prepared a path for his anger;
    he did not spare them from
        death
    but gave them over to the
        plague.
51 He struck down all the firstborn
        of Egypt,
    the firstfruits of manhood in
        the tents of Ham.
52 But he brought his people out
        like a flock;
    he led them like sheep
        through the wilderness.
53 He guided them safely, so they
        were unafraid;
    but the sea engulfed their
        enemies.
54 And so he brought them to the
        border of his holy land,
    to the hill country his right
        hand had taken.
55 He drove out nations before
        them
    and allotted their lands to
        them as an inheritance;
    he settled the tribes of Israel in
        their homes.
56 But they put God to the test
    and rebelled against the Most
        High;
    they did not keep his statutes.
57 Like their ancestors they were
        disloyal and faithless,
    as unreliable as a faulty bow.
58 They angered him with their
        high places;
    they aroused his jealousy with
        their idols.
59 When God heard them, he was
        furious;
    he rejected Israel completely.

60 He abandoned the tabernacle of
      Shiloh,
   the tent he had set up among
      humans.
61 He sent the ark of his might into
      captivity,
   his splendor into the hands of
      the enemy.
62 He gave his people over to the
      sword;
   he was furious with his
      inheritance.
63 Fire consumed their young men,
   and their young women had
      no wedding songs;
64 their priests were put to the
      sword,
   and their widows could not
      weep.

65 Then the Lord awoke as from
      sleep,
   as a warrior wakes from the
      stupor of wine.
66 He beat back his enemies;
   he put them to everlasting
      shame.
67 Then he rejected the tents of
      Joseph,
   he did not choose the tribe of
      Ephraim;
68 but he chose the tribe of Judah,
   Mount Zion, which he loved.
69 He built his sanctuary like the
      heights,
   like the earth that he
      established forever.

70 He chose David his servant
   and took him from the sheep
      pens;
71 from tending the sheep he
      brought him
   to be the shepherd of his
      people Jacob,
   of Israel his inheritance.
72 And David shepherded them
      with integrity of heart;
   with skillful hands he led
      them.

Psalm 79

A psalm of Asaph.

1 O God, the nations have invaded
      your inheritance;
   they have defiled your holy
      temple,
   they have reduced Jerusalem
      to rubble.
2 They have left the dead bodies of
      your servants
   as food for the birds of the sky,
   the flesh of your own people
      for the animals of the wild.
3 They have poured out blood like
      water
   all around Jerusalem,
   and there is no one to bury the
      dead.
4 We are objects of contempt to
      our neighbors,
   of scorn and derision to those
      around us.

5 How long, Lord? Will you be
      angry forever?
   How long will your jealousy
      burn like fire?
6 Pour out your wrath on the
      nations
   that do not acknowledge you,
   on the kingdoms
   that do not call on your name;
7 for they have devoured Jacob
   and devastated his homeland.

8 Do not hold against us the sins of
      past generations;
   may your mercy come quickly
      to meet us,
   for we are in desperate need.
9 Help us, God our Savior,
   for the glory of your name;
   deliver us and forgive our sins
   for your name's sake.
10 Why should the nations say,
   "Where is their God?"

Before our eyes, make known
      among the nations

that you avenge the outpoured
  blood of your servants.
11 May the groans of the prisoners
   come before you;
   with your strong arm preserve
     those condemned to die.
12 Pay back into the laps of our
   neighbors seven times
   the contempt they have hurled
     at you, Lord.
13 Then we your people, the sheep
   of your pasture,
   will praise you forever;
   from generation to generation
   we will proclaim your praise.

Psalm 80[a]

A psalm.

*For the director of music. To the tune of
"The Lilies of the Covenant." Of Asaph.
A psalm.*

1 Hear us, Shepherd of Israel,
  you who lead Joseph like a
    flock.
  You who sit enthroned between
    the cherubim,
  shine forth 2 before Ephraim,
    Benjamin and Manasseh.
  Awaken your might;
  come and save us.

3 Restore us, O God;
  make your face shine on us,
  that we may be saved.

4 How long, LORD God Almighty,
  will your anger smolder
  against the prayers of your
    people?
5 You have fed them with the
    bread of tears;
  you have made them drink
    tears by the bowlful.
6 You have made us an object of
    derision[b] to our neighbors,
  and our enemies mock us.

7 Restore us, God Almighty;
  make your face shine on us,
  that we may be saved.

8 You transplanted a vine from
    Egypt;
  you drove out the nations and
    planted it.
9 You cleared the ground for it,
  and it took root and filled the
    land.
10 The mountains were covered
     with its shade,
   the mighty cedars with its
     branches.
11 Its branches reached as far as
     the Sea,[c]
   its shoots as far as the River.[d]
12 Why have you broken down its
     walls
   so that all who pass by pick its
     grapes?
13 Boars from the forest ravage it,
   and insects from the fields
     feed on it.
14 Return to us, God Almighty!
   Look down from heaven and
     see!
   Watch over this vine,
15   the root your right hand has
       planted,
   the son[e] you have raised up for
     yourself.
16 Your vine is cut down, it is
     burned with fire;
   at your rebuke your people
     perish.
17 Let your hand rest on the man at
     your right hand,
   the son of man you have raised
     up for yourself.
18 Then we will not turn away from
     you;
   revive us, and we will call on
     your name.

---

a In Hebrew texts 80:1-19 is numbered 80:2-20.   *b* 6 Probable reading of the original Hebrew
text; Masoretic Text *contention*   *c* 11 Probably the Mediterranean   *d* 11 That is, the
Euphrates   *e* 15 Or *branch*

19 Restore us, LORD God Almighty;
   make your face shine on us,
   that we may be saved.

Psalm 81ᵃ

*For the director of music. According to
gittith.ᵇ Of Asaph.*

1 Sing for joy to God our strength;
   shout aloud to the God of
      Jacob!
2 Begin the music, strike the
      timbrel,
   play the melodious harp and
      lyre.
3 Sound the ram's horn at the New
      Moon,
   and when the moon is full, on
      the day of our festival;
4 this is a decree for Israel,
   an ordinance of the God of
      Jacob.
5 When God went out against
      Egypt,
   he established it as a statute
      for Joseph.

   I heard an unknown voice say:

6 "I removed the burden from
      their shoulders;
   their hands were set free from
      the basket.
7 In your distress you called and I
      rescued you,
   I answered you out of a
      thundercloud;
   I tested you at the waters of
      Meribah.ᶜ
8 Hear me, my people, and I will
      warn you —
   if you would only listen to me,
      Israel!
9 You shall have no foreign god
      among you;

you shall not worship any god
      other than me.
10 I am the LORD your God,
   who brought you up out of
      Egypt.
   Open wide your mouth and I will
      fill it.
11 "But my people would not listen
      to me;
   Israel would not submit to me.
12 So I gave them over to their
      stubborn hearts
   to follow their own devices.
13 "If my people would only listen
      to me,
   if Israel would only follow my
      ways,
14 how quickly I would subdue
      their enemies
   and turn my hand against
      their foes!
15 Those who hate the LORD would
      cringe before him,
   and their punishment would
      last forever.
16 But you would be fed with the
      finest of wheat;
   with honey from the rock I
      would satisfy you."

Psalm 82

A psalm of Asaph.

1 God presides in the great
      assembly;
   he renders judgment among
      the "gods":

2 "How long will youᵈ defend the
      unjust
   and show partiality to the
      wicked?ᶜ
3 Defend the weak and the
      fatherless;

ᵃ In Hebrew texts 81:1-16 is numbered 81:2-17.   ᵇ Title: Probably a musical term   ᶜ 7,2 The
Hebrew has *Selah* (a word of uncertain meaning) here.   ᵈ 2 The Hebrew is plural.

uphold the cause of the poor
    and the oppressed.
4 Rescue the weak and the
    needy;
  deliver them from the hand of
    the wicked.

5 "The 'gods' know nothing, they
    understand nothing.
They walk about in darkness;
  all the foundations of the
    earth are shaken.

6 "I said, 'You are "gods";
  you are all sons of the Most
    High.'
7 But you will die like mere
    mortals;
  you will fall like every other
    ruler."

8 Rise up, O God, judge the
    earth,
  for all the nations are your
    inheritance.

Psalm 83[a]

A song. A psalm of Asaph.

1 O God, do not remain silent;
  do not turn a deaf ear,
  do not stand aloof, O God.
2 See how your enemies growl,
  how your foes rear their
    heads.
3 With cunning they conspire
    against your people;
  they plot against those you
    cherish.
4 "Come," they say, "let us destroy
    them as a nation,
  so that Israel's name is
    remembered no more."

5 With one mind they plot
    together;
  they form an alliance against
    you—

6 the tents of Edom and the
    Ishmaelites,
  of Moab and the Hagrites,
7 Byblos, Ammon and Amalek,
  Philistia, with the people of
    Tyre.
8 Even Assyria has joined them
  to reinforce Lot's
    descendants.[b]

9 Do to them as you did to
    Midian,
  as you did to Sisera and Jabin
    at the river Kishon,
10 who perished at Endor
  and became like dung on the
    ground.
11 Make their nobles like Oreb and
    Zeeb,
  all their princes like Zebah
    and Zalmunna,
12 who said, "Let us take
    possession
  of the pasturelands of God."

13 Make them like tumbleweed, my
    God,
  like chaff before the wind.
14 As fire consumes the forest
  or a flame sets the mountains
    ablaze,
15 so pursue them with your
    tempest
  and terrify them with your
    storm.
16 Cover their faces with shame,
    Lord,
  so that they will seek your
    name.

17 May they ever be ashamed and
    dismayed;
  may they perish in disgrace.
18 Let them know that you, whose
    name is the Lord—
  that you alone are the Most
    High over all the earth.

---

[a] In Hebrew texts 83:1-18 is numbered 83:2-19. uncertain meaning) here.

[b] 8 The Hebrew has *Selah* (a word of

Psalm 84[a]

For the director of music. According to gittith.[b] Of the Sons of Korah. A psalm.

[1] How lovely is your dwelling place,
   LORD Almighty!
[2] My soul yearns, even faints,
   for the courts of the LORD;
my heart and my flesh cry out
   for the living God.
[3] Even the sparrow has found a
   home,
   and the swallow a nest for
      herself,
   where she may have her
      young—
a place near your altar,
   LORD Almighty, my King and
      my God.
[4] Blessed are those who dwell in
   your house;
   they are ever praising you.[c]

[5] Blessed are those whose
      strength is in you,
   whose hearts are set on
      pilgrimage.
[6] As they pass through the Valley
      of Baka,
   they make it a place of springs;
   the autumn rains also cover it
      with pools.[d]
[7] They go from strength to
      strength,
   till each appears before God in
      Zion.

[8] Hear my prayer, LORD God
   Almighty;
   listen to me, God of Jacob.
[9] Look on our shield,[e] O God;
   look with favor on your
      anointed one.

[10] Better is one day in your courts
   than a thousand elsewhere;

I would rather be a doorkeeper
   in the house of my God
than dwell in the tents of the
   wicked.
[11] For the LORD God is a sun and
      shield;
   the LORD bestows favor and
      honor;
no good thing does he withhold
   from those whose walk is
      blameless.

[12] LORD Almighty,
   blessed is the one who trusts
      in you.

Psalm 85[f]

For the director of music. Of the Sons of Korah. A psalm.

[1] You, LORD, showed favor to your
   land;
   you restored the fortunes of
      Jacob.
[2] You forgave the iniquity of your
      people
   and covered all their sins.[g]
[3] You set aside all your wrath
   and turned from your fierce
      anger.

[4] Restore us again, God our
      Savior,
   and put away your displeasure
      toward us.
[5] Will you be angry with us
      forever?
   Will you prolong your anger
      through all generations?
[6] Will you not revive us again,
   that your people may rejoice in
      you?
[7] Show us your unfailing love,
   LORD,
   and grant us your salvation.

---

[a] In Hebrew texts 84:1-12 is numbered 84:2-13.   [b] Title: Probably a musical term
[c] 4 The Hebrew has *Selah* (a word of uncertain meaning) here and at the end of verse 8.   [d] 6 Or *blessings*   [e] 9 Or *sovereign*   [f] In Hebrew texts 85:1-13 is numbered 85:2-14.   [g] 2 The Hebrew has *Selah* (a word of uncertain meaning) here.

8 I will listen to what God the
    LORD says;
  he promises peace to his
      people, his faithful
      servants —
  but let them not turn to folly.
9 Surely his salvation is near those
      who fear him,
  that his glory may dwell in our
      land.
10 Love and faithfulness meet
      together;
  righteousness and peace kiss
      each other.
11 Faithfulness springs forth from
      the earth,
  and righteousness looks down
      from heaven.
12 The LORD will indeed give what
      is good,
  and our land will yield its
      harvest.
13 Righteousness goes before him
  and prepares the way for his
      steps.

Psalm 86

A prayer of David.

1 Hear me, LORD, and answer
    me,
  for I am poor and needy.
2 Guard my life, for I am faithful to
      you;
  save your servant who trusts
      in you.
  You are my God; 3 have mercy on
      me, Lord,
  for I call to you all day long.
4 Bring joy to your servant, Lord,
  for I put my trust in you.

5 You, Lord, are forgiving and
      good,
  abounding in love to all who
      call to you.
6 Hear my prayer, LORD;
  listen to my cry for mercy.

7 When I am in distress, I call to
      you,
  because you answer me.
8 Among the gods there is none
      like you, Lord;
  no deeds can compare with
      yours.
9 All the nations you have made
  will come and worship before
      you, Lord;
  they will bring glory to your
      name.
10 For you are great and do
      marvelous deeds;
  you alone are God.
11 Teach me your way, LORD,
  that I may rely on your
      faithfulness;
  give me an undivided heart,
  that I may fear your name.
12 I will praise you, Lord my God,
      with all my heart;
  I will glorify your name
      forever.
13 For great is your love toward me;
  you have delivered me from
      the depths,
  from the realm of the dead.

14 Arrogant foes are attacking me,
      O God;
  ruthless people are trying to
      kill me —
  they have no regard for you.
15 But you, Lord, are a
      compassionate and
      gracious God,
  slow to anger, abounding in
      love and faithfulness.
16 Turn to me and have mercy on
      me;
  show your strength in behalf
      of your servant;
  save me, because I serve you
  just as my mother did.
17 Give me a sign of your goodness,
  that my enemies may see it
      and be put to shame,

for you, LORD, have helped me
and comforted me.

Psalm 87

Of the Sons of Korah. A psalm. A song.

¹ He has founded his city on the
holy mountain.
² The LORD loves the gates of Zion
more than all the other
dwellings of Jacob.

³ Glorious things are said of you,
city of God:[a]
⁴ "I will record Rahab[b] and
Babylon
among those who
acknowledge me —
Philistia too, and Tyre, along
with Cush[c] —
and will say, 'This one was
born in Zion.'"[d]
⁵ Indeed, of Zion it will be said,
"This one and that one were
born in her,
and the Most High himself will
establish her."
⁶ The LORD will write in the
register of the peoples:
"This one was born in Zion."

⁷ As they make music they will
sing,
"All my fountains are in you."

Psalm 88[e]

*A song. A psalm of the Sons of Korah.
For the director of music. According
to* mahalath leannoth.[f] *A* maskil[g] *of
Heman the Ezrahite.*

¹ LORD, you are the God who saves
me;
day and night I cry out to you.
² May my prayer come before you;
turn your ear to my cry.

³ I am overwhelmed with troubles
and my life draws near to
death.
⁴ I am counted among those who
go down to the pit;
I am like one without
strength.
⁵ I am set apart with the dead,
like the slain who lie in the
grave,
whom you remember no more,
who are cut off from your care.

⁶ You have put me in the lowest
pit,
in the darkest depths.
⁷ Your wrath lies heavily on me;
you have overwhelmed me
with all your waves.[h]
⁸ You have taken from me my
closest friends
and have made me repulsive
to them.
I am confined and cannot
escape;
⁹   my eyes are dim with grief.

I call to you, LORD, every day;
I spread out my hands to you.
¹⁰ Do you show your wonders to
the dead?
Do their spirits rise up and
praise you?
¹¹ Is your love declared in the
grave,
your faithfulness in
Destruction[i]?
¹² Are your wonders known in the
place of darkness,

---

^a 3 The Hebrew has *Selah* (a word of uncertain meaning) here and at the end of verse 6.
^b 4 A poetic name for Egypt   ^c 4 That is, the upper Nile region   ^d 4 Or *"I will record
concerning those who acknowledge me: / 'This one was born in Zion.' / Hear this, Rahab and
Babylon, / and you too, Philistia, Tyre and Cush."*   ^e In Hebrew texts 88:1-18 is numbered
88:2-19.   ^f Title: Possibly a tune, "The Suffering of Affliction"   ^g Title: Probably a literary or
musical term   ^h 7 The Hebrew has *Selah* (a word of uncertain meaning) here and at the end of
verse 10.   ⁱ 11 Hebrew *Abaddon*

or your righteous deeds in the
    land of oblivion?

13 But I cry to you for help, LORD;
    in the morning my prayer
       comes before you.
14 Why, LORD, do you reject me
    and hide your face from me?

15 From my youth I have suffered
    and been close to death;
    I have borne your terrors and
       am in despair.
16 Your wrath has swept over me;
    your terrors have destroyed
       me.
17 All day long they surround me
    like a flood;
    they have completely engulfed
       me.
18 You have taken from me friend
    and neighbor—
    darkness is my closest friend.

Psalm 89[a]

A maskil[b] of Ethan the Ezrahite.

1 I will sing of the LORD's great
    love forever;
    with my mouth I will make
       your faithfulness known
       through all generations.
2 I will declare that your love
    stands firm forever,
    that you have established your
       faithfulness in heaven
       itself.
3 You said, "I have made a
    covenant with my chosen
       one,
    I have sworn to David my
       servant,
4 'I will establish your line
    forever
    and make your throne firm
       through all generations.' "[c]

5 The heavens praise your
    wonders, LORD,
    your faithfulness too, in the
       assembly of the holy
       ones.
6 For who in the skies above can
    compare with the LORD?
    Who is like the LORD among
       the heavenly beings?
7 In the council of the holy ones
    God is greatly feared;
    he is more awesome than all
       who surround him.
8 Who is like you, LORD God
    Almighty?
    You, LORD, are mighty,
    and your faithfulness
       surrounds you.

9 You rule over the surging sea;
    when its waves mount up, you
       still them.
10 You crushed Rahab like one of
    the slain;
    with your strong arm you
       scattered your enemies.
11 The heavens are yours, and
    yours also the earth;
    you founded the world and all
       that is in it.
12 You created the north and the
    south;
    Tabor and Hermon sing for joy
       at your name.
13 Your arm is endowed with
    power;
    your hand is strong, your right
       hand exalted.

14 Righteousness and justice are
    the foundation of your
       throne;
    love and faithfulness go before
       you.
15 Blessed are those who have
    learned to acclaim you,

---

[a] In Hebrew texts 89:1-52 is numbered 89:2-53.   [b] Title: Probably a literary or musical term
[c] 4 The Hebrew has *Selah* (a word of uncertain meaning) here and at the end of verses 37, 45
and 48.

who walk in the light of your
  presence, LORD.
16 They rejoice in your name all
    day long;
  they celebrate your
    righteousness.
17 For you are their glory and
    strength,
  and by your favor you exalt our
    horn.[a]
18 Indeed, our shield[b] belongs to
    the LORD,
  our king to the Holy One of
    Israel.

19 Once you spoke in a vision,
  to your faithful people you said:
  "I have bestowed strength on a
    warrior;
  I have raised up a young man
    from among the people.
20 I have found David my servant;
  with my sacred oil I have
    anointed him.
21 My hand will sustain him;
  surely my arm will strengthen
    him.
22 The enemy will not get the better
    of him;
  the wicked will not oppress
    him.
23 I will crush his foes before him
  and strike down his
    adversaries.
24 My faithful love will be with him,
  and through my name his
    horn[c] will be exalted.
25 I will set his hand over the sea,
  his right hand over the rivers.
26 He will call out to me, 'You are
    my Father,
  my God, the Rock my Savior.'
27 And I will appoint him to be my
    firstborn,
  the most exalted of the kings of
    the earth.

28 I will maintain my love to him
    forever,
  and my covenant with him
    will never fail.
29 I will establish his line forever,
  his throne as long as the
    heavens endure.

30 "If his sons forsake my law
  and do not follow my statutes,
31 if they violate my decrees
  and fail to keep my
    commands,
32 I will punish their sin with the
    rod,
  their iniquity with flogging;
33 but I will not take my love from
    him,
  nor will I ever betray my
    faithfulness.
34 I will not violate my covenant
  or alter what my lips have
    uttered.
35 Once for all, I have sworn by my
    holiness—
  and I will not lie to David—
36 that his line will continue
    forever
  and his throne endure before
    me like the sun;
37 it will be established forever like
    the moon,
  the faithful witness in the sky."

38 But you have rejected, you have
    spurned,
  you have been very angry with
    your anointed one.
39 You have renounced the
    covenant with your
    servant
  and have defiled his crown in
    the dust.
40 You have broken through all his
    walls
  and reduced his strongholds
    to ruins.

---

[a] 17 Horn here symbolizes strong one.   [b] 18 Or sovereign   [c] 24 Horn here symbolizes
strength.

⁴¹ All who pass by have plundered
 him;
  he has become the scorn of his
   neighbors.
⁴² You have exalted the right hand
 of his foes;
  you have made all his enemies
   rejoice.
⁴³ Indeed, you have turned back
 the edge of his sword
  and have not supported him in
   battle.
⁴⁴ You have put an end to his
 splendor
  and cast his throne to the
   ground.
⁴⁵ You have cut short the days of
 his youth;
  you have covered him with a
   mantle of shame.
⁴⁶ How long, LORD? Will you hide
 yourself forever?
  How long will your wrath burn
   like fire?
⁴⁷ Remember how fleeting is my
 life.
  For what futility you have
   created all humanity!
⁴⁸ Who can live and not see death,
  or who can escape the power
   of the grave?
⁴⁹ Lord, where is your former great
 love,
  which in your faithfulness you
   swore to David?
⁵⁰ Remember, Lord, how your
 servant hasᵃ been
  mocked,
  how I bear in my heart the
   taunts of all the nations,
⁵¹ the taunts with which your
 enemies, LORD, have
  mocked,
  with which they have mocked
   every step of your
    anointed one.

⁵² Praise be to the LORD forever!
 Amen and Amen.

BOOK IV

Psalms 90–106

Psalm 90

A prayer of Moses the man of God.

¹ Lord, you have been our
 dwelling place
  throughout all generations.
² Before the mountains were born
 or you brought forth the whole
  world,
  from everlasting to everlasting
   you are God.
³ You turn people back to dust,
 saying, "Return to dust, you
  mortals."
⁴ A thousand years in your sight
 are like a day that has just
  gone by,
  or like a watch in the night.
⁵ Yet you sweep people away in
 the sleep of death—
  they are like the new grass of
   the morning:
⁶ In the morning it springs up
 new,
  but by evening it is dry and
   withered.
⁷ We are consumed by your anger
 and terrified by your
  indignation.
⁸ You have set our iniquities
 before you,
  our secret sins in the light of
   your presence.
⁹ All our days pass away under
 your wrath;
  we finish our years with a
   moan.
¹⁰ Our days may come to seventy
 years,

ᵃ 50 Or *your servants have*

or eighty, if our strength
  endures;
yet the best of them are but
  trouble and sorrow,
for they quickly pass, and we
  fly away.
[11] If only we knew the power of
  your anger!
Your wrath is as great as the
  fear that is your due.
[12] Teach us to number our days,
  that we may gain a heart of
  wisdom.

[13] Relent, LORD! How long will it be?
  Have compassion on your
  servants.
[14] Satisfy us in the morning with
  your unfailing love,
that we may sing for joy and be
  glad all our days.
[15] Make us glad for as many days as
  you have afflicted us,
for as many years as we have
  seen trouble.
[16] May your deeds be shown to
  your servants,
  your splendor to their
  children.

[17] May the favor[a] of the Lord our
  God rest on us;
establish the work of our
  hands for us —
yes, establish the work of our
  hands.

Psalm 91

[1] Whoever dwells in the shelter of
  the Most High
will rest in the shadow of the
  Almighty.[b]
[2] I will say of the LORD, "He is my
  refuge and my fortress,
my God, in whom I trust."

[3] Surely he will save you
  from the fowler's snare

and from the deadly
  pestilence.
[4] He will cover you with his
  feathers,
and under his wings you will
  find refuge;
his faithfulness will be your
  shield and rampart.
[5] You will not fear the terror of
  night,
  nor the arrow that flies by
  day,
[6] nor the pestilence that stalks in
  the darkness,
  nor the plague that destroys at
  midday.
[7] A thousand may fall at your side,
  ten thousand at your right
  hand,
but it will not come near you.
[8] You will only observe with your
  eyes
and see the punishment of the
  wicked.

[9] If you say, "The LORD is my
  refuge,"
and you make the Most High
  your dwelling,
[10] no harm will overtake you,
  no disaster will come near
  your tent.
[11] For he will command his angels
  concerning you
  to guard you in all your ways;
[12] they will lift you up in their
  hands,
so that you will not strike your
  foot against a stone.
[13] You will tread on the lion and
  the cobra;
you will trample the great lion
  and the serpent.

[14] "Because he[c] loves me," says the
  LORD, "I will rescue him;
I will protect him, for he
  acknowledges my name.

---

[a] 17 Or *beauty*   [b] 1 Hebrew *Shaddai*   [c] 14 That is, probably the king

15 He will call on me, and I will
　　answer him;
　　I will be with him in trouble,
　　I will deliver him and honor
　　him.
16 With long life I will satisfy him
　　and show him my salvation."

Psalm 92[a]

A psalm. A song. For the Sabbath day.

1 It is good to praise the LORD
　　and make music to your name,
　　O Most High,
2 proclaiming your love in the
　　morning
　　and your faithfulness at night,
3 to the music of the ten-stringed
　　lyre
　　and the melody of the harp.

4 For you make me glad by your
　　deeds, LORD;
　　I sing for joy at what your
　　hands have done.
5 How great are your works,
　　LORD,
　　how profound your thoughts!
6 Senseless people do not know,
　　fools do not understand,
7 that though the wicked spring
　　up like grass
　　and all evildoers flourish,
　　they will be destroyed forever.

8 But you, LORD, are forever
　　exalted.

9 For surely your enemies, LORD,
　　surely your enemies will
　　perish;
　　all evildoers will be scattered.
10 You have exalted my horn[b] like
　　that of a wild ox;
　　fine oils have been poured on
　　me.
11 My eyes have seen the defeat of
　　my adversaries;

my ears have heard the rout of
　　my wicked foes.

12 The righteous will flourish like a
　　palm tree,
　　they will grow like a cedar of
　　Lebanon;
13 planted in the house of the
　　LORD,
　　they will flourish in the courts
　　of our God.
14 They will still bear fruit in old
　　age,
　　they will stay fresh and
　　green,
15 proclaiming, "The LORD is
　　upright;
　　he is my Rock, and there is no
　　wickedness in him."

Psalm 93

1 The LORD reigns, he is robed in
　　majesty;
　　the LORD is robed in majesty
　　and armed with strength;
　　indeed, the world is
　　established, firm and
　　secure.
2 Your throne was established
　　long ago;
　　you are from all eternity.

3 The seas have lifted up, LORD,
　　the seas have lifted up their
　　voice;
　　the seas have lifted up their
　　pounding waves.
4 Mightier than the thunder of the
　　great waters,
　　mightier than the breakers of
　　the sea—
　　the LORD on high is mighty.

5 Your statutes, LORD, stand
　　firm;
　　holiness adorns your house
　　for endless days.

---

a In Hebrew texts 92:1-15 is numbered 92:2-16.　　*b* 10 *Horn* here symbolizes strength.

Psalm 94

¹ The LORD is a God who avenges.
    O God who avenges, shine
        forth.
² Rise up, Judge of the earth;
    pay back to the proud what
        they deserve.
³ How long, LORD, will the wicked,
    how long will the wicked be
        jubilant?

⁴ They pour out arrogant words;
    all the evildoers are full of
        boasting.
⁵ They crush your people, LORD;
    they oppress your inheritance.
⁶ They slay the widow and the
        foreigner;
    they murder the fatherless.
⁷ They say, "The LORD does not
        see;
    the God of Jacob takes no
        notice."

⁸ Take notice, you senseless ones
        among the people;
    you fools, when will you
        become wise?
⁹ Does he who fashioned the ear
        not hear?
    Does he who formed the eye
        not see?
¹⁰ Does he who disciplines nations
        not punish?
    Does he who teaches mankind
        lack knowledge?
¹¹ The LORD knows all human
        plans;
    he knows that they are futile.

¹² Blessed is the one you discipline,
        LORD,
    the one you teach from your
        law;
¹³ you grant them relief from days
        of trouble,
    till a pit is dug for the wicked.
¹⁴ For the LORD will not reject his
        people;

he will never forsake his
        inheritance.
¹⁵ Judgment will again be founded
        on righteousness,
    and all the upright in heart
        will follow it.

¹⁶ Who will rise up for me against
        the wicked?
    Who will take a stand for me
        against evildoers?
¹⁷ Unless the LORD had given me
        help,
    I would soon have dwelt in the
        silence of death.
¹⁸ When I said, "My foot is
        slipping,"
    your unfailing love, LORD,
        supported me.
¹⁹ When anxiety was great within
        me,
    your consolation brought me
        joy.

²⁰ Can a corrupt throne be allied
        with you—
    a throne that brings on misery
        by its decrees?
²¹ The wicked band together
        against the righteous
    and condemn the innocent to
        death.
²² But the LORD has become my
        fortress,
    and my God the rock in whom
        I take refuge.
²³ He will repay them for their sins
    and destroy them for their
        wickedness;
    the LORD our God will destroy
        them.

Psalm 95

¹ Come, let us sing for joy to the
        LORD;
    let us shout aloud to the Rock
        of our salvation.
² Let us come before him with
        thanksgiving

and extol him with music and
song.

3 For the LORD is the great God,
the great King above all gods.
4 In his hand are the depths of the
earth,
and the mountain peaks
belong to him.
5 The sea is his, for he made it,
and his hands formed the dry
land.

6 Come, let us bow down in
worship,
let us kneel before the LORD
our Maker;
7 for he is our God
and we are the people of his
pasture,
the flock under his care.

Today, if only you would hear his
voice,
8 "Do not harden your hearts as
you did at Meribah,[a]
as you did that day at Massah[b]
in the wilderness,
9 where your ancestors tested me;
they tried me, though they had
seen what I did.
10 For forty years I was angry with
that generation;
I said, 'They are a people
whose hearts go astray,
and they have not known my
ways.'
11 So I declared on oath in my anger,
'They shall never enter my
rest.' "

Psalm 96

1 Sing to the LORD a new song;
sing to the LORD, all the earth.
2 Sing to the LORD, praise his
name;
proclaim his salvation day
after day.

3 Declare his glory among the
nations,
his marvelous deeds among
all peoples.
4 For great is the LORD and most
worthy of praise;
he is to be feared above all
gods.
5 For all the gods of the nations
are idols,
but the LORD made the
heavens.
6 Splendor and majesty are before
him;
strength and glory are in his
sanctuary.

7 Ascribe to the LORD, all you
families of nations,
ascribe to the LORD glory and
strength.
8 Ascribe to the LORD the glory
due his name;
bring an offering and come
into his courts.
9 Worship the LORD in the
splendor of his[c] holiness;
tremble before him, all the
earth.
10 Say among the nations, "The
LORD reigns."
The world is firmly
established, it cannot be
moved;
he will judge the peoples with
equity.

11 Let the heavens rejoice, let the
earth be glad;
let the sea resound, and all
that is in it.
12 Let the fields be jubilant, and
everything in them;
let all the trees of the forest
sing for joy.
13 Let all creation rejoice before the
LORD, for he comes,

---

[a] 8 *Meribah* means *quarreling.*   [b] 8 *Massah* means *testing.*   [c] 9 Or LORD *with the splendor of*

he comes to judge the earth.
He will judge the world in
righteousness
and the peoples in his
faithfulness.

Psalm 97

¹ The LORD reigns, let the earth be
glad;
let the distant shores rejoice.
² Clouds and thick darkness
surround him;
righteousness and justice
are the foundation of his
throne.
³ Fire goes before him
and consumes his foes on
every side.
⁴ His lightning lights up the world;
the earth sees and trembles.
⁵ The mountains melt like wax
before the LORD,
before the Lord of all the
earth.
⁶ The heavens proclaim his
righteousness,
and all peoples see his glory.

⁷ All who worship images are put
to shame,
those who boast in idols —
worship him, all you gods!

⁸ Zion hears and rejoices
and the villages of Judah are
glad
because of your judgments,
LORD.
⁹ For you, LORD, are the Most High
over all the earth;
you are exalted far above all
gods.
¹⁰ Let those who love the LORD
hate evil,
for he guards the lives of his
faithful ones

and delivers them from the
hand of the wicked.
¹¹ Light shines*a* on the righteous
and joy on the upright in
heart.
¹² Rejoice in the LORD, you who are
righteous,
and praise his holy name.

Psalm 98

A psalm.

¹ Sing to the LORD a new song,
for he has done marvelous
things;
his right hand and his holy arm
have worked salvation for him.
² The LORD has made his salvation
known
and revealed his righteousness
to the nations.
³ He has remembered his love
and his faithfulness to Israel;
all the ends of the earth have
seen
the salvation of our God.

⁴ Shout for joy to the LORD, all the
earth,
burst into jubilant song with
music;
⁵ make music to the LORD with the
harp,
with the harp and the sound of
singing,
⁶ with trumpets and the blast of
the ram's horn —
shout for joy before the LORD,
the King.

⁷ Let the sea resound, and
everything in it,
the world, and all who live in
it.
⁸ Let the rivers clap their hands,
let the mountains sing
together for joy;

---

a 11 One Hebrew manuscript and ancient versions (see also 112:4); most Hebrew manuscripts
Light is sown

⁹ let them sing before the LORD,
  for he comes to judge the
    earth.
He will judge the world in
    righteousness
  and the peoples with equity.

Psalm 99

¹ The LORD reigns,
  let the nations tremble;
he sits enthroned between the
    cherubim,
  let the earth shake.
² Great is the LORD in Zion;
  he is exalted over all the
    nations.
³ Let them praise your great and
    awesome name—
  he is holy.

⁴ The King is mighty, he loves
    justice—
  you have established equity;
in Jacob you have done
  what is just and right.
⁵ Exalt the LORD our God
  and worship at his footstool;
  he is holy.

⁶ Moses and Aaron were among
    his priests,
  Samuel was among those who
    called on his name;
they called on the LORD
  and he answered them.
⁷ He spoke to them from the pillar
    of cloud;
  they kept his statutes and the
    decrees he gave them.

⁸ LORD our God,
  you answered them;
you were to Israel a forgiving
    God,
  though you punished their
    misdeeds.ᵃ
⁹ Exalt the LORD our God

and worship at his holy
    mountain,
  for the LORD our God is holy.

Psalm 100

A psalm. For giving grateful praise.

¹ Shout for joy to the LORD, all the
    earth.
² Worship the LORD with
    gladness;
  come before him with joyful
    songs.
³ Know that the LORD is God.
  It is he who made us, and we
    are hisᵇ;
  we are his people, the sheep of
    his pasture.

⁴ Enter his gates with
    thanksgiving
  and his courts with praise;
  give thanks to him and praise
    his name.
⁵ For the LORD is good and his love
    endures forever;
  his faithfulness continues
    through all generations.

Psalm 101

Of David. A psalm.

¹ I will sing of your love and justice;
  to you, LORD, I will sing praise.
² I will be careful to lead a
    blameless life—
  when will you come to me?

I will conduct the affairs of my
    house
  with a blameless heart.
³ I will not look with approval
  on anything that is vile.

I hate what faithless people do;
  I will have no part in it.
⁴ The perverse of heart shall be far
    from me;

---

a 8 Or God, / an avenger of the wrongs done to them   *b 3 Or and not we ourselves*

I will have nothing to do with
    what is evil.

5 Whoever slanders their neighbor
    in secret,
  I will put to silence;
whoever has haughty eyes and a
    proud heart,
  I will not tolerate.

6 My eyes will be on the faithful in
    the land,
  that they may dwell with me;
the one whose walk is blameless
  will minister to me.

7 No one who practices deceit
  will dwell in my house;
no one who speaks falsely
  will stand in my presence.

8 Every morning I will put to
    silence
  all the wicked in the land;
I will cut off every evildoer
  from the city of the LORD.

Psalm 102[a]

A prayer of an afflicted person who has
grown weak and pours out a lament
before the LORD.

1 Hear my prayer, LORD;
  let my cry for help come to you.
2 Do not hide your face from me
    when I am in distress.
  Turn your ear to me;
    when I call, answer me
    quickly.

3 For my days vanish like smoke;
  my bones burn like glowing
    embers.
4 My heart is blighted and
    withered like grass;
  I forget to eat my food.
5 In my distress I groan aloud
  and am reduced to skin and
    bones.

6 I am like a desert owl,
  like an owl among the ruins.
7 I lie awake; I have become
  like a bird alone on a roof.
8 All day long my enemies taunt
    me;
  those who rail against me use
    my name as a curse.
9 For I eat ashes as my food
  and mingle my drink with tears
10 because of your great wrath,
  for you have taken me up and
    thrown me aside.
11 My days are like the evening
    shadow;
  I wither away like grass.

12 But you, LORD, sit enthroned
    forever;
  your renown endures through
    all generations.
13 You will arise and have
    compassion on Zion,
  for it is time to show favor to
    her;
  the appointed time has come.
14 For her stones are dear to your
    servants;
  her very dust moves them to
    pity.
15 The nations will fear the name of
    the LORD,
  all the kings of the earth will
    revere your glory.
16 For the LORD will rebuild Zion
  and appear in his glory.
17 He will respond to the prayer of
    the destitute;
  he will not despise their plea.

18 Let this be written for a future
    generation,
  that a people not yet created
    may praise the LORD:
19 "The LORD looked down from
    his sanctuary on high,
  from heaven he viewed the
    earth,

---

a In Hebrew texts 102:1-28 is numbered 102:2-29.

²⁰to hear the groans of the
prisoners
and release those condemned
to death."
²¹So the name of the LORD will be
declared in Zion
and his praise in Jerusalem
²²when the peoples and the
kingdoms
assemble to worship the LORD.

²³In the course of my life ͣ he broke
my strength;
he cut short my days.
²⁴So I said:
"Do not take me away, my God,
in the midst of my days;
your years go on through all
generations.
²⁵In the beginning you laid the
foundations of the earth,
and the heavens are the work
of your hands.
²⁶They will perish, but you
remain;
they will all wear out like a
garment.
Like clothing you will change
them
and they will be discarded.
²⁷But you remain the same,
and your years will never
end.
²⁸The children of your servants
will live in your presence;
their descendants will be
established before you."

Psalm 103

Of David.

¹Praise the LORD, my soul;
all my inmost being, praise his
holy name.
²Praise the LORD, my soul,
and forget not all his
benefits—

³who forgives all your sins
and heals all your diseases,
⁴who redeems your life from the
pit
and crowns you with love and
compassion,
⁵who satisfies your desires with
good things
so that your youth is renewed
like the eagle's.

⁶The LORD works righteousness
and justice for all the
oppressed.

⁷He made known his ways to
Moses,
his deeds to the people of
Israel:
⁸The LORD is compassionate and
gracious,
slow to anger, abounding in
love.
⁹He will not always accuse,
nor will he harbor his anger
forever;
¹⁰he does not treat us as our sins
deserve
or repay us according to our
iniquities.
¹¹For as high as the heavens are
above the earth,
so great is his love for those
who fear him;
¹²as far as the east is from the west,
so far has he removed our
transgressions from us.

¹³As a father has compassion on
his children,
so the LORD has compassion
on those who fear him;
¹⁴for he knows how we are formed,
he remembers that we are
dust.
¹⁵The life of mortals is like grass,
they flourish like a flower of
the field;

ͣ *23 Or By his power*

16 the wind blows over it and it is
gone,
   and its place remembers it no
   more.
17 But from everlasting to
everlasting
   the LORD's love is with those
   who fear him,
   and his righteousness with
   their children's children —
18 with those who keep his covenant
   and remember to obey his
   precepts.

19 The LORD has established his
throne in heaven,
   and his kingdom rules over all.

20 Praise the LORD, you his angels,
   you mighty ones who do his
   bidding,
   who obey his word.
21 Praise the LORD, all his heavenly
hosts,
   you his servants who do his
   will.
22 Praise the LORD, all his works
   everywhere in his dominion.

   Praise the LORD, my soul.

Psalm 104

1 Praise the LORD, my soul.

LORD my God, you are very
great;
   you are clothed with splendor
   and majesty.

2 The LORD wraps himself in light
   as with a garment;
   he stretches out the heavens
   like a tent
3 and lays the beams of his
   upper chambers on their
   waters.
   He makes the clouds his chariot
   and rides on the wings of the
   wind.

4 He makes winds his
messengers,[a]
   flames of fire his servants.

5 He set the earth on its
foundations;
   it can never be moved.
6 You covered it with the watery
   depths as with a garment;
   the waters stood above the
   mountains.
7 But at your rebuke the waters
fled,
   at the sound of your thunder
   they took to flight;
8 they flowed over the mountains,
   they went down into the
   valleys,
   to the place you assigned for
   them.
9 You set a boundary they cannot
cross;
   never again will they cover the
   earth.

10 He makes springs pour water
   into the ravines;
   it flows between the
   mountains.
11 They give water to all the beasts
   of the field;
   the wild donkeys quench their
   thirst.
12 The birds of the sky nest by the
waters;
   they sing among the branches.
13 He waters the mountains from
   his upper chambers;
   the land is satisfied by the fruit
   of his work.
14 He makes grass grow for the
cattle,
   and plants for people to
   cultivate —
   bringing forth food from the
   earth:
15 wine that gladdens human
hearts,

a 4 Or angels

oil to make their faces shine,
and bread that sustains their
hearts.

16 The trees of the LORD are well
watered,
the cedars of Lebanon that he
planted.

17 There the birds make their
nests;
the stork has its home in the
junipers.

18 The high mountains belong to
the wild goats;
the crags are a refuge for the
hyrax.

19 He made the moon to mark the
seasons,
and the sun knows when to go
down.

20 You bring darkness, it becomes
night,
and all the beasts of the forest
prowl.

21 The lions roar for their prey
and seek their food from God.

22 The sun rises, and they steal
away;
they return and lie down in
their dens.

23 Then people go out to their
work,
to their labor until evening.

24 How many are your works,
LORD!
In wisdom you made them all;
the earth is full of your
creatures.

25 There is the sea, vast and
spacious,
teeming with creatures
beyond number—
living things both large and
small.

26 There the ships go to and fro,
and Leviathan, which you
formed to frolic there.

27 All creatures look to you
to give them their food at the
proper time.

28 When you give it to them,
they gather it up;
when you open your hand,
they are satisfied with good
things.

29 When you hide your face,
they are terrified;
when you take away their breath,
they die and return to the dust.

30 When you send your Spirit,
they are created,
and you renew the face of the
ground.

31 May the glory of the LORD
endure forever;
may the LORD rejoice in his
works—

32 he who looks at the earth, and it
trembles,
who touches the mountains,
and they smoke.

33 I will sing to the LORD all my life;
I will sing praise to my God as
long as I live.

34 May my meditation be pleasing
to him,
as I rejoice in the LORD.

35 But may sinners vanish from the
earth
and the wicked be no more.

Praise the LORD, my soul.

Praise the LORD.[a]

Psalm 105

1 Give praise to the LORD,
proclaim his name;
make known among the
nations what he has done.

2 Sing to him, sing praise to him;
tell of all his wonderful acts.

3 Glory in his holy name;

---

a 35 Hebrew *Hallelu Yah*; in the Septuagint this line stands at the beginning of Psalm 105.

let the hearts of those who
        seek the LORD rejoice.
4 Look to the LORD and his
        strength;
    seek his face always.

5 Remember the wonders he has
        done,
    his miracles, and the
        judgments he
        pronounced,
6 you his servants, the
        descendants of Abraham,
    his chosen ones, the children
        of Jacob.

7 He is the LORD our God;
    his judgments are in all the
        earth.

8 He remembers his covenant
        forever,
    the promise he made, for a
        thousand generations,
9 the covenant he made with
        Abraham,
    the oath he swore to Isaac.
10 He confirmed it to Jacob as a
        decree,
    to Israel as an everlasting
        covenant:
11 "To you I will give the land of
        Canaan
    as the portion you will
        inherit."

12 When they were but few in
        number,
    few indeed, and strangers in it,
13 they wandered from nation to
        nation,
    from one kingdom to another.
14 He allowed no one to oppress
        them;
    for their sake he rebuked
        kings:
15 "Do not touch my anointed ones;
    do my prophets no harm."

16 He called down famine on the
        land

and destroyed all their
        supplies of food;
17 and he sent a man before
        them—
    Joseph, sold as a slave.
18 They bruised his feet with
        shackles,
    his neck was put in irons,
19 till what he foretold came to
        pass,
    till the word of the LORD
        proved him true.
20 The king sent and released him,
    the ruler of peoples set him
        free.
21 He made him master of his
        household,
    ruler over all he possessed,
22 to instruct his princes as he
        pleased
    and teach his elders wisdom.

23 Then Israel entered Egypt;
    Jacob resided as a foreigner in
        the land of Ham.
24 The LORD made his people very
        fruitful;
    he made them too numerous
        for their foes,
25 whose hearts he turned to hate
        his people,
    to conspire against his
        servants.
26 He sent Moses his servant,
    and Aaron, whom he had
        chosen.
27 They performed his signs among
        them,
    his wonders in the land of Ham.
28 He sent darkness and made the
        land dark—
    for had they not rebelled
        against his words?
29 He turned their waters into
        blood,
    causing their fish to die.
30 Their land teemed with frogs,
    which went up into the
        bedrooms of their rulers.

31 He spoke, and there came
    swarms of flies,
    and gnats throughout their
    country.
32 He turned their rain into hail,
    with lightning throughout
    their land;
33 he struck down their vines and
    fig trees
    and shattered the trees of their
    country.
34 He spoke, and the locusts came,
    grasshoppers without number;
35 they ate up every green thing in
    their land,
    ate up the produce of their
    soil.
36 Then he struck down all the
    firstborn in their land,
    the firstfruits of all their
    manhood.
37 He brought out Israel, laden with
    silver and gold,
    and from among their tribes
    no one faltered.
38 Egypt was glad when they left,
    because dread of Israel had
    fallen on them.
39 He spread out a cloud as a
    covering,
    and a fire to give light at
    night.
40 They asked, and he brought
    them quail;
    he fed them well with the
    bread of heaven.
41 He opened the rock, and water
    gushed out;
    it flowed like a river in the
    desert.
42 For he remembered his holy
    promise
    given to his servant Abraham.
43 He brought out his people with
    rejoicing,

his chosen ones with shouts of
    joy;
44 he gave them the lands of the
    nations,
    and they fell heir to what
    others had toiled for —
45 that they might keep his
    precepts
    and observe his laws.

Praise the LORD.[a]

Psalm 106

1 Praise the LORD.[b]

Give thanks to the LORD, for he is
    good;
    his love endures forever.

2 Who can proclaim the mighty
    acts of the LORD
    or fully declare his praise?
3 Blessed are those who act justly,
    who always do what is right.

4 Remember me, LORD, when you
    show favor to your people,
    come to my aid when you save
    them,
5 that I may enjoy the prosperity of
    your chosen ones,
    that I may share in the joy of
    your nation
    and join your inheritance in
    giving praise.

6 We have sinned, even as our
    ancestors did;
    we have done wrong and acted
    wickedly.
7 When our ancestors were in
    Egypt,
    they gave no thought to your
    miracles;
    they did not remember your
    many kindnesses,
    and they rebelled by the sea,
    the Red Sea.[c]

a 45 Hebrew Hallelu Yah;   b 1 Hebrew Hallelu Yah; also in verse 48   c 7 Or the Sea of Reeds;
also in verses 9 and 22

8 Yet he saved them for his name's sake,
   to make his mighty power known.
9 He rebuked the Red Sea, and it dried up;
   he led them through the depths as through a desert.
10 He saved them from the hand of the foe;
   from the hand of the enemy he redeemed them.
11 The waters covered their adversaries;
   not one of them survived.
12 Then they believed his promises
   and sang his praise.

13 But they soon forgot what he had done
   and did not wait for his plan to unfold.
14 In the desert they gave in to their craving;
   in the wilderness they put God to the test.
15 So he gave them what they asked for,
   but sent a wasting disease among them.
16 In the camp they grew envious of Moses
   and of Aaron, who was consecrated to the LORD.
17 The earth opened up and swallowed Dathan;
   it buried the company of Abiram.
18 Fire blazed among their followers;
   a flame consumed the wicked.
19 At Horeb they made a calf
   and worshiped an idol cast from metal.
20 They exchanged their glorious God
   for an image of a bull, which eats grass.
21 They forgot the God who saved them,
   who had done great things in Egypt,
22 miracles in the land of Ham
   and awesome deeds by the Red Sea.
23 So he said he would destroy them—
   had not Moses, his chosen one,
   stood in the breach before him
   to keep his wrath from destroying them.

24 Then they despised the pleasant land;
   they did not believe his promise.
25 They grumbled in their tents
   and did not obey the LORD.
26 So he swore to them with uplifted hand
   that he would make them fall in the wilderness,
27 make their descendants fall among the nations
   and scatter them throughout the lands.

28 They yoked themselves to the Baal of Peor
   and ate sacrifices offered to lifeless gods;
29 they aroused the LORD's anger by their wicked deeds,
   and a plague broke out among them.
30 But Phinehas stood up and intervened,
   and the plague was checked.
31 This was credited to him as righteousness
   for endless generations to come.
32 By the waters of Meribah they angered the LORD,

and trouble came to Moses
because of them;
³³ for they rebelled against the
Spirit of God,
and rash words came from
Moses' lips.*a*

³⁴ They did not destroy the
peoples
as the LORD had commanded
them,
³⁵ but they mingled with the
nations
and adopted their customs.
³⁶ They worshiped their idols,
which became a snare to
them.
³⁷ They sacrificed their sons
and their daughters to false
gods.
³⁸ They shed innocent blood,
the blood of their sons and
daughters,
whom they sacrificed to the idols
of Canaan,
and the land was desecrated
by their blood.
³⁹ They defiled themselves by what
they did;
by their deeds they prostituted
themselves.

⁴⁰ Therefore the LORD was angry
with his people
and abhorred his inheritance.
⁴¹ He gave them into the hands of
the nations,
and their foes ruled over them.
⁴² Their enemies oppressed them
and subjected them to their
power.
⁴³ Many times he delivered them,
but they were bent on
rebellion
and they wasted away in their
sin.
⁴⁴ Yet he took note of their distress
when he heard their cry;

⁴⁵ for their sake he remembered his
covenant
and out of his great love he
relented.
⁴⁶ He caused all who held them
captive
to show them mercy.

⁴⁷ Save us, LORD our God,
and gather us from the
nations,
that we may give thanks to your
holy name
and glory in your praise.

⁴⁸ Praise be to the LORD, the God of
Israel,
from everlasting to
everlasting.

Let all the people say, "Amen!"

Praise the LORD.

BOOK V

Psalms 107–150

Psalm 107

¹ Give thanks to the LORD, for he is
good;
his love endures forever.

² Let the redeemed of the LORD
tell their story—
those he redeemed from the
hand of the foe,
³ those he gathered from the
lands,
from east and west, from north
and south.*b*

⁴ Some wandered in desert
wastelands,
finding no way to a city where
they could settle.
⁵ They were hungry and thirsty,
and their lives ebbed away.
⁶ Then they cried out to the LORD
in their trouble,

---

a 33 Or against his spirit, / and rash words came from his lips   *b 3 Hebrew north and the sea*

and he delivered them from their distress.

7 He led them by a straight way to a city where they could settle.

8 Let them give thanks to the LORD for his unfailing love and his wonderful deeds for mankind,

9 for he satisfies the thirsty and fills the hungry with good things.

10 Some sat in darkness, in utter darkness, prisoners suffering in iron chains,

11 because they rebelled against God's commands and despised the plans of the Most High.

12 So he subjected them to bitter labor; they stumbled, and there was no one to help.

13 Then they cried to the LORD in their trouble, and he saved them from their distress.

14 He brought them out of darkness, the utter darkness, and broke away their chains.

15 Let them give thanks to the LORD for his unfailing love and his wonderful deeds for mankind,

16 for he breaks down gates of bronze and cuts through bars of iron.

17 Some became fools through their rebellious ways and suffered affliction because of their iniquities.

18 They loathed all food and drew near the gates of death.

19 Then they cried to the LORD in their trouble, and he saved them from their distress.

20 He sent out his word and healed them; he rescued them from the grave.

21 Let them give thanks to the LORD for his unfailing love and his wonderful deeds for mankind.

22 Let them sacrifice thank offerings and tell of his works with songs of joy.

23 Some went out on the sea in ships; they were merchants on the mighty waters.

24 They saw the works of the LORD, his wonderful deeds in the deep.

25 For he spoke and stirred up a tempest that lifted high the waves.

26 They mounted up to the heavens and went down to the depths; in their peril their courage melted away.

27 They reeled and staggered like drunkards; they were at their wits' end.

28 Then they cried out to the LORD in their trouble, and he brought them out of their distress.

29 He stilled the storm to a whisper; the waves of the sea[a] were hushed.

30 They were glad when it grew calm, and he guided them to their desired haven.

---

[a] 29 Dead Sea Scrolls; Masoretic Text / their waves

31 Let them give thanks to the
LORD for his unfailing love
and his wonderful deeds for
mankind.
32 Let them exalt him in the
assembly of the people
and praise him in the council
of the elders.

33 He turned rivers into a desert,
flowing springs into thirsty
ground,
34 and fruitful land into a salt
waste,
because of the wickedness of
those who lived there.
35 He turned the desert into pools
of water
and the parched ground into
flowing springs;
36 there he brought the hungry to
live,
and they founded a city where
they could settle.
37 They sowed fields and planted
vineyards
that yielded a fruitful harvest;
38 he blessed them, and their
numbers greatly
increased,
and he did not let their herds
diminish.

39 Then their numbers decreased,
and they were humbled
by oppression, calamity and
sorrow;
40 he who pours contempt on
nobles
made them wander in a
trackless waste.
41 But he lifted the needy out of
their affliction
and increased their families
like flocks.
42 The upright see and rejoice,
but all the wicked shut their
mouths.

43 Let the one who is wise heed
these things
and ponder the loving deeds of
the LORD.

Psalm 108[a]

A song. A psalm of David.

1 My heart, O God, is steadfast;
I will sing and make music
with all my soul.
2 Awake, harp and lyre!
I will awaken the dawn.
3 I will praise you, LORD, among
the nations;
I will sing of you among the
peoples.
4 For great is your love, higher
than the heavens;
your faithfulness reaches to
the skies.
5 Be exalted, O God, above the
heavens;
let your glory be over all the
earth.

6 Save us and help us with your
right hand,
that those you love may be
delivered.
7 God has spoken from his
sanctuary:
"In triumph I will parcel out
Shechem
and measure off the Valley of
Sukkoth.
8 Gilead is mine, Manasseh is
mine;
Ephraim is my helmet,
Judah is my scepter.
9 Moab is my washbasin,
on Edom I toss my sandal;
over Philistia I shout in
triumph."

10 Who will bring me to the
fortified city?
Who will lead me to Edom?

---

a In Hebrew texts 108:1-13 is numbered 108:2-14.

¹¹ Is it not you, God, you who have
     rejected us
   and no longer go out with our
     armies?
¹² Give us aid against the enemy,
   for human help is worthless.
¹³ With God we will gain the
     victory,
   and he will trample down our
     enemies.

Psalm 109

*For the director of music. Of David.
A psalm.*

¹ My God, whom I praise,
   do not remain silent,
² for people who are wicked and
     deceitful
   have opened their mouths
     against me;
   they have spoken against me
     with lying tongues.
³ With words of hatred they
     surround me;
   they attack me without cause.
⁴ In return for my friendship they
     accuse me,
   but I am a man of prayer.
⁵ They repay me evil for good,
   and hatred for my friendship.

⁶ Appoint someone evil to oppose
     my enemy;
   let an accuser stand at his
     right hand.
⁷ When he is tried, let him be
     found guilty,
   and may his prayers condemn
     him.
⁸ May his days be few;
   may another take his place of
     leadership.
⁹ May his children be fatherless
   and his wife a widow.
¹⁰ May his children be wandering
     beggars;

may they be driven[a] from their
   ruined homes.
¹¹ May a creditor seize all he has;
   may strangers plunder the
     fruits of his labor.
¹² May no one extend kindness to
     him
   or take pity on his fatherless
     children.
¹³ May his descendants be cut off,
   their names blotted out from
     the next generation.
¹⁴ May the iniquity of his fathers
   be remembered before the
     LORD;
   may the sin of his mother
     never be blotted out.
¹⁵ May their sins always remain
   before the LORD,
   that he may blot out their
     name from the earth.

¹⁶ For he never thought of doing a
     kindness,
   but hounded to death the poor
     and the needy and the
     brokenhearted.
¹⁷ He loved to pronounce a curse—
   may it come back on him.
   He found no pleasure in
     blessing—
   may it be far from him.
¹⁸ He wore cursing as his garment;
   it entered into his body like
     water,
   into his bones like oil.
¹⁹ May it be like a cloak wrapped
     about him,
   like a belt tied forever around
     him.
²⁰ May this be the LORD's payment
     to my accusers,
   to those who speak evil of me.
²¹ But you, Sovereign LORD,
   help me for your name's sake;
   out of the goodness of your
     love, deliver me.

---

a 10 Septuagint; Hebrew sought

22 For I am poor and needy,
   and my heart is wounded
      within me.
23 I fade away like an evening
      shadow;
   I am shaken off like a locust.
24 My knees give way from fasting;
   my body is thin and gaunt.
25 I am an object of scorn to my
      accusers;
   when they see me, they shake
      their heads.

26 Help me, LORD my God;
   save me according to your
      unfailing love.
27 Let them know that it is your
      hand,
   that you, LORD, have done it.
28 While they curse, may you
      bless;
   may those who attack me be
      put to shame,
   but may your servant rejoice.
29 May my accusers be clothed
      with disgrace
   and wrapped in shame as in a
      cloak.

30 With my mouth I will greatly
      extol the LORD;
   in the great throng of
      worshipers I will praise
      him.
31 For he stands at the right hand of
      the needy,
   to save their lives from those
      who would condemn
      them.

Psalm 110

Of David. A psalm.

1 The LORD says to my lord:[a]

   "Sit at my right hand

until I make your enemies
      a footstool for your feet."

2 The LORD will extend your
      mighty scepter from Zion,
      saying,
   "Rule in the midst of your
      enemies!"

3 Your troops will be willing
      on your day of battle.
   Arrayed in holy splendor,
      your young men will come to
         you
      like dew from the morning's
         womb.[b]

4 The LORD has sworn
   and will not change his mind:
   "You are a priest forever,
      in the order of Melchizedek."

5 The Lord is at your right hand;[c]
   he will crush kings on the day
      of his wrath.
6 He will judge the nations,
   heaping up the dead
      and crushing the rulers of the
         whole earth.
7 He will drink from a brook along
      the way,[d]
   and so he will lift his head
      high.

Psalm 111[e]

1 Praise the LORD.[f]

   I will extol the LORD with all my
      heart
   in the council of the upright
      and in the assembly.

2 Great are the works of the LORD;
   they are pondered by all who
      delight in them.
3 Glorious and majestic are his
      deeds,

---

a 1 Or *Lord*   b 3 The meaning of the Hebrew for this sentence is uncertain.   c 5 Or *My lord is at your right hand, LORD*   d 7 The meaning of the Hebrew for this clause is uncertain.
e This psalm is an acrostic poem, the lines of which begin with the successive letters of the Hebrew alphabet.   f 1 Hebrew *Hallelu Yah*

and his righteousness endures
    forever.
4 He has caused his wonders to be
    remembered;
    the LORD is gracious and
    compassionate.
5 He provides food for those who
    fear him;
    he remembers his covenant
    forever.

6 He has shown his people the
    power of his works,
    giving them the lands of other
    nations.
7 The works of his hands are
    faithful and just;
    all his precepts are
    trustworthy.
8 They are established for ever
    and ever,
    enacted in faithfulness and
    uprightness.
9 He provided redemption for his
    people;
    he ordained his covenant
    forever —
    holy and awesome is his name.

10 The fear of the LORD is the
    beginning of wisdom;
    all who follow his precepts
    have good understanding.
    To him belongs eternal praise.

Psalm 112a

1 Praise the LORD.b

Blessed are those who fear the
    LORD,
    who find great delight in his
    commands.
2 Their children will be mighty in
    the land;
    the generation of the upright
    will be blessed.

3 Wealth and riches are in their
    houses,
    and their righteousness
    endures forever.
4 Even in darkness light dawns for
    the upright,
    for those who are gracious
    and compassionate and
    righteous.
5 Good will come to those who are
    generous and lend freely,
    who conduct their affairs with
    justice.

6 Surely the righteous will never
    be shaken;
    they will be remembered
    forever.
7 They will have no fear of bad
    news;
    their hearts are steadfast,
    trusting in the LORD.
8 Their hearts are secure, they will
    have no fear;
    in the end they will look in
    triumph on their foes.
9 They have freely scattered their
    gifts to the poor,
    their righteousness endures
    forever;
    their hornc will be lifted high
    in honor.

10 The wicked will see and be
    vexed,
    they will gnash their teeth and
    waste away;
    the longings of the wicked will
    come to nothing.

Psalm 113

1 Praise the LORD.d

Praise the LORD, you his
    servants;
    praise the name of the LORD.

---

a This psalm is an acrostic poem, the lines of which begin with the successive letters of
the Hebrew alphabet.   b 1 Hebrew Hallelu Yah   c 9 Horn here symbolizes dignity.
d 1 Hebrew Hallelu Yah; also in verse 9

² Let the name of the LORD be
  praised,
    both now and forevermore.
³ From the rising of the sun to the
  place where it sets,
    the name of the LORD is to be
      praised.

⁴ The LORD is exalted over all the
  nations,
    his glory above the heavens.
⁵ Who is like the LORD our God,
  the One who sits enthroned on
    high,
⁶ who stoops down to look
  on the heavens and the earth?

⁷ He raises the poor from the dust
  and lifts the needy from the
    ash heap;
⁸ he seats them with princes,
  with the princes of his people.
⁹ He settles the childless woman
  in her home
    as a happy mother of children.

Praise the LORD.

Psalm 114

¹ When Israel came out of Egypt,
  Jacob from a people of foreign
    tongue,
² Judah became God's sanctuary,
  Israel his dominion.

³ The sea looked and fled,
  the Jordan turned back;
⁴ the mountains leaped like rams,
  the hills like lambs.

⁵ Why was it, sea, that you fled?
  Why, Jordan, did you turn
    back?
⁶ Why, mountains, did you leap
  like rams,
    you hills, like lambs?

⁷ Tremble, earth, at the presence
  of the Lord,
    at the presence of the God of
      Jacob,

⁸ who turned the rock into a pool,
  the hard rock into springs of
    water.

Psalm 115

¹ Not to us, LORD, not to us
  but to your name be the glory,
    because of your love and
      faithfulness.

² Why do the nations say,
  "Where is their God?"
³ Our God is in heaven;
  he does whatever pleases
    him.
⁴ But their idols are silver and
  gold,
    made by human hands.
⁵ They have mouths, but cannot
  speak,
    eyes, but cannot see.
⁶ They have ears, but cannot
  hear,
    noses, but cannot smell.
⁷ They have hands, but cannot
  feel,
    feet, but cannot walk,
    nor can they utter a sound
      with their throats.
⁸ Those who make them will be
  like them,
    and so will all who trust in
      them.

⁹ All you Israelites, trust in the
  LORD —
    he is their help and shield.
¹⁰ House of Aaron, trust in the
  LORD —
    he is their help and shield.
¹¹ You who fear him, trust in the
  LORD —
    he is their help and shield.

¹² The LORD remembers us and
  will bless us:
    He will bless his people Israel,
    he will bless the house of
      Aaron,

13 he will bless those who fear the
    LORD—
      small and great alike.

14 May the LORD cause you to
    flourish,
      both you and your children.

15 May you be blessed by the LORD,
    the Maker of heaven and
    earth.

16 The highest heavens belong to
    the LORD,
      but the earth he has given to
      mankind.

17 It is not the dead who praise the
    LORD,
      those who go down to the
      place of silence;

18 it is we who extol the LORD,
    both now and forevermore.

Praise the LORD.[a]

Psalm 116

1 I love the LORD, for he heard my
    voice;
      he heard my cry for mercy.

2 Because he turned his ear to me,
    I will call on him as long as I
    live.

3 The cords of death entangled
    me,
      the anguish of the grave came
      over me;
      I was overcome by distress and
      sorrow.

4 Then I called on the name of the
    LORD:
      "LORD, save me!"

5 The LORD is gracious and
    righteous;
      our God is full of compassion.

6 The LORD protects the unwary;
    when I was brought low, he
    saved me.

7 Return to your rest, my soul,
    for the LORD has been good to
    you.

8 For you, LORD, have delivered
    me from death,
      my eyes from tears,
      my feet from stumbling,

9 that I may walk before the LORD
    in the land of the living.

10 I trusted in the LORD when I
    said,
      "I am greatly afflicted";

11 in my alarm I said,
      "Everyone is a liar."

12 What shall I return to the LORD
    for all his goodness to me?

13 I will lift up the cup of salvation
    and call on the name of the
    LORD.

14 I will fulfill my vows to the LORD
    in the presence of all his
    people.

15 Precious in the sight of the
    LORD
      is the death of his faithful
      servants.

16 Truly I am your servant, LORD;
    I serve you just as my mother
    did;
      you have freed me from my
      chains.

17 I will sacrifice a thank offering
    to you
      and call on the name of the
      LORD.

18 I will fulfill my vows to the
    LORD
      in the presence of all his
      people,

19 in the courts of the house of the
    LORD—
      in your midst, Jerusalem.

Praise the LORD.[a]

---

a 18,19 Hebrew Hallelu Yah

Psalm 117

¹ Praise the LORD, all you nations;
  extol him, all you peoples.
² For great is his love toward us,
  and the faithfulness of the
  LORD endures forever.

Praise the LORD.ᵃ

Psalm 118

¹ Give thanks to the LORD, for he is
  good;
  his love endures forever.

² Let Israel say:
  "His love endures forever."
³ Let the house of Aaron say:
  "His love endures forever."
⁴ Let those who fear the LORD
  say:
  "His love endures forever."

⁵ When hard pressed, I cried to
  the LORD;
  he brought me into a spacious
  place.
⁶ The LORD is with me; I will not
  be afraid.
  What can mere mortals do to
  me?
⁷ The LORD is with me; he is my
  helper.
  I look in triumph on my
  enemies.

⁸ It is better to take refuge in the
  LORD
  than to trust in humans.
⁹ It is better to take refuge in the
  LORD
  than to trust in princes.
¹⁰ All the nations surrounded me,
  but in the name of the LORD I
  cut them down.
¹¹ They surrounded me on every
  side,
  but in the name of the LORD I
  cut them down.

¹² They swarmed around me like
  bees,
  but they were consumed as
  quickly as burning thorns;
  in the name of the LORD I cut
  them down.
¹³ I was pushed back and about to
  fall,
  but the LORD helped me.
¹⁴ The LORD is my strength and my
  defenseᵇ;
  he has become my salvation.

¹⁵ Shouts of joy and victory
  resound in the tents of the
  righteous:
  "The LORD's right hand has done
  mighty things!
¹⁶ The LORD's right hand is lifted
  high;
  the LORD's right hand has
  done mighty things!"

¹⁷ I will not die but live,
  and will proclaim what the
  LORD has done.
¹⁸ The LORD has chastened me
  severely,
  but he has not given me over to
  death.
¹⁹ Open for me the gates of the
  righteous;
  I will enter and give thanks to
  the LORD.
²⁰ This is the gate of the LORD
  through which the righteous
  may enter.
²¹ I will give you thanks, for you
  answered me;
  you have become my
  salvation.

²² The stone the builders rejected
  has become the cornerstone;
²³ the LORD has done this,
  and it is marvelous in our
  eyes.
²⁴ The LORD has done it this very
  day;

ᵃ 2 Hebrew *Hallelu Yah*   ᵇ 14 Or *song*

let us rejoice today and be
glad.
²⁵ LORD, save us!
LORD, grant us success!

²⁶ Blessed is he who comes in the
name of the LORD.
From the house of the LORD we
bless you.ᵃ
²⁷ The LORD is God,
and he has made his light
shine on us.
With boughs in hand, join in the
festal procession
upᵇ to the horns of the altar.
²⁸ You are my God, and I will praise
you;
you are my God, and I will
exalt you.
²⁹ Give thanks to the LORD, for he is
good;
his love endures forever.

Psalm 119ᶜ

א Aleph

¹ Blessed are those whose ways
are blameless,
who walk according to the
law of the LORD.
² Blessed are those who keep his
statutes
and seek him with all their
heart—
³ they do no wrong
but follow his ways.
⁴ You have laid down precepts
that are to be fully obeyed.
⁵ Oh, that my ways were
steadfast
in obeying your decrees!
⁶ Then I would not be put to
shame

when I consider all your
commands.
⁷ I will praise you with an upright
heart
as I learn your righteous laws.
⁸ I will obey your decrees;
do not utterly forsake me.

ב Beth

⁹ How can a young person stay on
the path of purity?
By living according to your
word.
¹⁰ I seek you with all my heart;
do not let me stray from your
commands.
¹¹ I have hidden your word in my
heart
that I might not sin against
you.
¹² Praise be to you, LORD;
teach me your decrees.
¹³ With my lips I recount
all the laws that come from
your mouth.
¹⁴ I rejoice in following your
statutes
as one rejoices in great
riches.
¹⁵ I meditate on your precepts
and consider your ways.
¹⁶ I delight in your decrees;
I will not neglect your word.

ג Gimel

¹⁷ Be good to your servant while I
live,
that I may obey your word.
¹⁸ Open my eyes that I may see
wonderful things in your law.
¹⁹ I am a stranger on earth;
do not hide your commands
from me.

ᵃ 26 The Hebrew is plural.   ᵇ 27 Or Bind the festal sacrifice with ropes / and take it   ᶜ This
psalm is an acrostic poem, the stanzas of which begin with successive letters of the Hebrew
alphabet; moreover, the verses of each stanza begin with the same letter of the Hebrew
alphabet.

²⁰My soul is consumed with longing
for your laws at all times.
²¹You rebuke the arrogant, who are accursed,
those who stray from your commands.
²²Remove from me their scorn and contempt,
for I keep your statutes.
²³Though rulers sit together and slander me,
your servant will meditate on your decrees.
²⁴Your statutes are my delight;
they are my counselors.

ד Daleth

²⁵I am laid low in the dust;
preserve my life according to your word.
²⁶I gave an account of my ways and you answered me;
teach me your decrees.
²⁷Cause me to understand the way of your precepts,
that I may meditate on your wonderful deeds.
²⁸My soul is weary with sorrow;
strengthen me according to your word.
²⁹Keep me from deceitful ways;
be gracious to me and teach me your law.
³⁰I have chosen the way of faithfulness;
I have set my heart on your laws.
³¹I hold fast to your statutes, LORD;
do not let me be put to shame.
³²I run in the path of your commands,
for you have broadened my understanding.

ה He

³³Teach me, LORD, the way of your decrees,
that I may follow it to the end.ᵃ
³⁴Give me understanding, so that I may keep your law
and obey it with all my heart.
³⁵Direct me in the path of your commands,
for there I find delight.
³⁶Turn my heart toward your statutes
and not toward selfish gain.
³⁷Turn my eyes away from worthless things;
preserve my life according to your word.ᵇ
³⁸Fulfill your promise to your servant,
so that you may be feared.
³⁹Take away the disgrace I dread,
for your laws are good.
⁴⁰How I long for your precepts!
In your righteousness preserve my life.

ו Waw

⁴¹May your unfailing love come to me, LORD,
your salvation, according to your promise;
⁴²then I can answer anyone who taunts me,
for I trust in your word.
⁴³Never take your word of truth from my mouth,
for I have put my hope in your laws.
⁴⁴I will always obey your law,
for ever and ever.
⁴⁵I will walk about in freedom,
for I have sought out your precepts.
⁴⁶I will speak of your statutes before kings

ᵃ 33 Or *follow it for its reward*   ᵇ 37 Two manuscripts of the Masoretic Text and Dead Sea Scrolls; most manuscripts of the Masoretic Text *life in your way*

and will not be put to shame,
⁴⁷for I delight in your commands
　　because I love them.
⁴⁸I reach out for your commands,
　　which I love,
　　that I may meditate on your
　　　decrees.

ℸ Zayin

⁴⁹Remember your word to your
　　servant,
　　for you have given me hope.
⁵⁰My comfort in my suffering is
　　this:
　　Your promise preserves my
　　　life.
⁵¹The arrogant mock me
　　unmercifully,
　　but I do not turn from your
　　　law.
⁵²I remember, LORD, your ancient
　　laws,
　　and I find comfort in them.
⁵³Indignation grips me because of
　　the wicked,
　　who have forsaken your law.
⁵⁴Your decrees are the theme of
　　my song
　　wherever I lodge.
⁵⁵In the night, LORD, I remember
　　your name,
　　that I may keep your law.
⁵⁶This has been my practice:
　　I obey your precepts.

ℸ Heth

⁵⁷You are my portion, LORD;
　　I have promised to obey your
　　　words.
⁵⁸I have sought your face with all
　　my heart;
　　be gracious to me according to
　　　your promise.
⁵⁹I have considered my ways
　　and have turned my steps to
　　　your statutes.
⁶⁰I will hasten and not delay

to obey your commands.
⁶¹Though the wicked bind me with
　　ropes,
　　I will not forget your law.
⁶²At midnight I rise to give you
　　thanks
　　for your righteous laws.
⁶³I am a friend to all who fear you,
　　to all who follow your
　　　precepts.
⁶⁴The earth is filled with your love,
　　LORD;
　　teach me your decrees.

ℸ Teth

⁶⁵Do good to your servant
　　according to your word, LORD.
⁶⁶Teach me knowledge and good
　　judgment,
　　for I trust your commands.
⁶⁷Before I was afflicted I went
　　astray,
　　but now I obey your word.
⁶⁸You are good, and what you do is
　　good;
　　teach me your decrees.
⁶⁹Though the arrogant have
　　smeared me with lies,
　　I keep your precepts with all
　　　my heart.
⁷⁰Their hearts are callous and
　　unfeeling,
　　but I delight in your law.
⁷¹It was good for me to be
　　afflicted
　　so that I might learn your
　　　decrees.
⁷²The law from your mouth is
　　more precious to me
　　than thousands of pieces of
　　　silver and gold.

ℸ Yodh

⁷³Your hands made me and
　　formed me;
　　give me understanding to
　　　learn your commands.

⁷⁴ May those who fear you rejoice
      when they see me,
   for I have put my hope in your
      word.
⁷⁵ I know, LORD, that your laws are
      righteous,
   and that in faithfulness you
      have afflicted me.
⁷⁶ May your unfailing love be my
      comfort,
   according to your promise to
      your servant.
⁷⁷ Let your compassion come to me
      that I may live,
   for your law is my delight.
⁷⁸ May the arrogant be put to
      shame for wronging me
      without cause;
   but I will meditate on your
      precepts.
⁷⁹ May those who fear you turn to
      me,
   those who understand your
      statutes.
⁸⁰ May I wholeheartedly follow
      your decrees,
   that I may not be put to shame.

כ Kaph

⁸¹ My soul faints with longing for
      your salvation,
   but I have put my hope in your
      word.
⁸² My eyes fail, looking for your
      promise;
   I say, "When will you comfort
      me?"
⁸³ Though I am like a wineskin in
      the smoke,
   I do not forget your decrees.
⁸⁴ How long must your servant
      wait?
   When will you punish my
      persecutors?
⁸⁵ The arrogant dig pits to trap me,
      contrary to your law.
⁸⁶ All your commands are
      trustworthy;

help me, for I am being
      persecuted without cause.
⁸⁷ They almost wiped me from the
      earth,
   but I have not forsaken your
      precepts.
⁸⁸ In your unfailing love preserve
      my life,
   that I may obey the statutes of
      your mouth.

ל Lamedh

⁸⁹ Your word, LORD, is eternal;
   it stands firm in the heavens.
⁹⁰ Your faithfulness continues
      through all generations;
   you established the earth, and
      it endures.
⁹¹ Your laws endure to this day,
   for all things serve you.
⁹² If your law had not been my
      delight,
   I would have perished in my
      affliction.
⁹³ I will never forget your precepts,
   for by them you have
      preserved my life.
⁹⁴ Save me, for I am yours;
   I have sought out your
      precepts.
⁹⁵ The wicked are waiting to
      destroy me,
   but I will ponder your statutes.
⁹⁶ To all perfection I see a limit,
   but your commands are
      boundless.

מ Mem

⁹⁷ Oh, how I love your law!
   I meditate on it all day long.
⁹⁸ Your commands are always
      with me
   and make me wiser than my
      enemies.
⁹⁹ I have more insight than all my
      teachers,
   for I meditate on your statutes.

100I have more understanding
than the elders,
for I obey your precepts.
101I have kept my feet from every
evil path
so that I might obey your
word.
102I have not departed from your
laws,
for you yourself have taught
me.
103How sweet are your words to my
taste,
sweeter than honey to my
mouth!
104I gain understanding from your
precepts;
therefore I hate every wrong
path.

ב Nun

105Your word is a lamp for my feet,
a light on my path.
106I have taken an oath and
confirmed it,
that I will follow your
righteous laws.
107I have suffered much;
preserve my life, LORD,
according to your word.
108Accept, LORD, the willing praise
of my mouth,
and teach me your laws.
109Though I constantly take my life
in my hands,
I will not forget your law.
110The wicked have set a snare
for me,
but I have not strayed from
your precepts.
111Your statutes are my heritage
forever;
they are the joy of my heart.
112My heart is set on keeping your
decrees
to the very end.a

ס Samekh

113I hate double-minded people,
but I love your law.
114You are my refuge and my
shield;
I have put my hope in your
word.
115Away from me, you evildoers,
that I may keep the commands
of my God!
116Sustain me, my God, according
to your promise, and I will
live;
do not let my hopes be dashed.
117Uphold me, and I will be
delivered;
I will always have regard for
your decrees.
118You reject all who stray from
your decrees,
for their delusions come to
nothing.
119All the wicked of the earth you
discard like dross;
therefore I love your statutes.
120My flesh trembles in fear of
you;
I stand in awe of your laws.

ע Ayin

121I have done what is righteous
and just;
do not leave me to my
oppressors.
122Ensure your servant's well-
being;
do not let the arrogant oppress
me.
123My eyes fail, looking for your
salvation,
looking for your righteous
promise.
124Deal with your servant
according to your love
and teach me your decrees.

a 112 Or decrees / for their enduring reward

¹²⁵I am your servant; give me
discernment
that I may understand your
statutes.
¹²⁶It is time for you to act, LORD;
your law is being broken.
¹²⁷Because I love your commands
more than gold, more than
pure gold,
¹²⁸and because I consider all your
precepts right,
I hate every wrong path.

פ Pe

¹²⁹Your statutes are wonderful;
therefore I obey them.
¹³⁰The unfolding of your words
gives light;
it gives understanding to the
simple.
¹³¹I open my mouth and pant,
longing for your commands.
¹³²Turn to me and have mercy
on me,
as you always do to those who
love your name.
¹³³Direct my footsteps according
to your word;
let no sin rule over me.
¹³⁴Redeem me from human
oppression,
that I may obey your
precepts.
¹³⁵Make your face shine on your
servant
and teach me your decrees.
¹³⁶Streams of tears flow from my
eyes,
for your law is not obeyed.

צ Tsadhe

¹³⁷You are righteous, LORD,
and your laws are right.
¹³⁸The statutes you have laid down
are righteous;
they are fully trustworthy.
¹³⁹My zeal wears me out,
for my enemies ignore your
words.
¹⁴⁰Your promises have been
thoroughly tested,
and your servant loves them.
¹⁴¹Though I am lowly and
despised,
I do not forget your precepts.
¹⁴²Your righteousness is
everlasting
and your law is true.
¹⁴³Trouble and distress have come
upon me,
but your commands give me
delight.
¹⁴⁴Your statutes are always
righteous;
give me understanding that I
may live.

ק Qoph

¹⁴⁵I call with all my heart; answer
me, LORD,
and I will obey your decrees.
¹⁴⁶I call out to you; save me
and I will keep your statutes.
¹⁴⁷I rise before dawn and cry for
help;
I have put my hope in your
word.
¹⁴⁸My eyes stay open through the
watches of the night,
that I may meditate on your
promises.
¹⁴⁹Hear my voice in accordance
with your love;
preserve my life, LORD,
according to your laws.
¹⁵⁰Those who devise wicked
schemes are near,
but they are far from your law.
¹⁵¹Yet you are near, LORD,
and all your commands are
true.
¹⁵²Long ago I learned from your
statutes
that you established them to
last forever.

ר Resh

153Look on my suffering and
    deliver me,
  for I have not forgotten your
    law.
154Defend my cause and
    redeem me;
  preserve my life according to
    your promise.
155Salvation is far from the wicked,
  for they do not seek out your
    decrees.
156Your compassion, LORD, is
    great;
  preserve my life according to
    your laws.
157Many are the foes who
    persecute me,
  but I have not turned from
    your statutes.
158I look on the faithless with
    loathing,
  for they do not obey your
    word.
159See how I love your precepts;
  preserve my life, LORD, in
    accordance with your
    love.
160All your words are true;
  all your righteous laws are
    eternal.

ש Sin and Shin

161Rulers persecute me without
    cause,
  but my heart trembles at your
    word.
162I rejoice in your promise
  like one who finds great spoil.
163I hate and detest falsehood
  but I love your law.
164Seven times a day I praise you
  for your righteous laws.
165Great peace have those who
    love your law,
  and nothing can make them
    stumble.

166I wait for your salvation, LORD,
  and I follow your commands.
167I obey your statutes,
  for I love them greatly.
168I obey your precepts and your
    statutes,
  for all my ways are known to
    you.

ת Taw

169May my cry come before you,
    LORD;
  give me understanding
    according to your word.
170May my supplication come
    before you;
  deliver me according to your
    promise.
171May my lips overflow with
    praise,
  for you teach me your
    decrees.
172May my tongue sing of your
    word,
  for all your commands are
    righteous.
173May your hand be ready to
    help me,
  for I have chosen your
    precepts.
174I long for your salvation, LORD,
  and your law gives me delight.
175Let me live that I may praise
    you,
  and may your laws sustain me.
176I have strayed like a lost sheep.
  Seek your servant,
  for I have not forgotten your
    commands.

Psalm 120

A song of ascents.

1 I call on the LORD in my distress,
  and he answers me.
2 Save me, LORD,
  from lying lips
  and from deceitful tongues.

3 What will he do to you,
and what more besides,
you deceitful tongue?
4 He will punish you with a
warrior's sharp arrows,
with burning coals of the
broom bush.

5 Woe to me that I dwell in
Meshek,
that I live among the tents of
Kedar!
6 Too long have I lived
among those who hate peace.
7 I am for peace;
but when I speak, they are for
war.

Psalm 121

A song of ascents.

1 I lift up my eyes to the
mountains—
where does my help come
from?
2 My help comes from the LORD,
the Maker of heaven and
earth.

3 He will not let your foot slip—
he who watches over you will
not slumber;
4 indeed, he who watches over
Israel
will neither slumber nor
sleep.

5 The LORD watches over you—
the LORD is your shade at your
right hand;
6 the sun will not harm you by
day,
nor the moon by night.

7 The LORD will keep you from all
harm—
he will watch over your life;
8 the LORD will watch over your
coming and going
both now and forevermore.

Psalm 122

A song of ascents. Of David.

1 I rejoiced with those who said to
me,
"Let us go to the house of the
LORD."
2 Our feet are standing
in your gates, Jerusalem.

3 Jerusalem is built like a city
that is closely compacted
together.
4 That is where the tribes go
up—
the tribes of the LORD—
to praise the name of the
LORD
according to the statute given
to Israel.
5 There stand the thrones for
judgment,
the thrones of the house
of David.

6 Pray for the peace of
Jerusalem:
"May those who love you be
secure.
7 May there be peace within your
walls
and security within your
citadels."
8 For the sake of my family and
friends,
I will say, "Peace be within
you."
9 For the sake of the house of the
LORD our God,
I will seek your prosperity.

Psalm 123

A song of ascents.

1 I lift up my eyes to you,
to you who sit enthroned in
heaven.
2 As the eyes of slaves look to the
hand of their master,

as the eyes of a female slave
  look to the hand of her
  mistress,
so our eyes look to the LORD our
  God,
  till he shows us his mercy.

3 Have mercy on us, LORD, have
  mercy on us,
  for we have endured no end of
    contempt.
4 We have endured no end
  of ridicule from the
    arrogant,
  of contempt from the proud.

Psalm 124

A song of ascents. Of David.

1 If the LORD had not been on our
  side—
  let Israel say—
2 if the LORD had not been on our
  side
  when people attacked us,
3 they would have swallowed us
  alive
  when their anger flared
    against us;
4 the flood would have engulfed
  us,
  the torrent would have swept
    over us,
5 the raging waters
  would have swept us away.

6 Praise be to the LORD,
  who has not let us be torn by
    their teeth.
7 We have escaped like a bird
  from the fowler's snare;
  the snare has been broken,
  and we have escaped.
8 Our help is in the name of the
  LORD,
  the Maker of heaven and
    earth.

Psalm 125

A song of ascents.

1 Those who trust in the LORD are
  like Mount Zion,
  which cannot be shaken but
    endures forever.
2 As the mountains surround
  Jerusalem,
  so the LORD surrounds his
    people
  both now and forevermore.

3 The scepter of the wicked will
  not remain
  over the land allotted to the
    righteous,
  for then the righteous might use
    their hands to do evil.

4 LORD, do good to those who are
  good,
  to those who are upright in
    heart.
5 But those who turn to crooked
  ways
  the LORD will banish with the
    evildoers.

Peace be on Israel.

Psalm 126

A song of ascents.

1 When the LORD restored the
  fortunes of[a] Zion,
  we were like those who
    dreamed.[b]
2 Our mouths were filled with
  laughter,
  our tongues with songs of joy.
Then it was said among the
  nations,
  "The LORD has done great
    things for them."
3 The LORD has done great things
  for us,
  and we are filled with joy.

a 1 Or LORD brought back the captives to   *b 1 Or those restored to health*

4 Restore our fortunes,[a] LORD,
 like streams in the Negev.
5 Those who sow with tears
 will reap with songs of joy.
6 Those who go out weeping,
 carrying seed to sow,
 will return with songs of joy,
 carrying sheaves with them.

Psalm 127

A song of ascents. Of Solomon.

1 Unless the LORD builds the
 house,
 the builders labor in vain.
 Unless the LORD watches over
 the city,
 the guards stand watch in
 vain.
2 In vain you rise early
 and stay up late,
 toiling for food to eat—
 for he grants sleep to[b] those he
 loves.

3 Children are a heritage from the
 LORD,
 offspring a reward from him.
4 Like arrows in the hands of a
 warrior
 are children born in one's
 youth.
5 Blessed is the man
 whose quiver is full of them.
 They will not be put to shame
 when they contend with their
 opponents in court.

Psalm 128

A song of ascents.

1 Blessed are all who fear the
 LORD,
 who walk in obedience to
 him.
2 You will eat the fruit of your
 labor;

blessings and prosperity will
 be yours.
3 Your wife will be like a fruitful
 vine
 within your house;
 your children will be like olive
 shoots
 around your table.
4 Yes, this will be the blessing
 for the man who fears the
 LORD.

5 May the LORD bless you from
 Zion;
 may you see the prosperity of
 Jerusalem
 all the days of your life.
6 May you live to see your
 children's children—
 peace be on Israel.

Psalm 129

A song of ascents.

1 "They have greatly oppressed
 me from my youth,"
 let Israel say;
2 "they have greatly oppressed me
 from my youth,
 but they have not gained the
 victory over me.
3 Plowmen have plowed my
 back
 and made their furrows long.
4 But the LORD is righteous;
 he has cut me free from the
 cords of the wicked."

5 May all who hate Zion
 be turned back in shame.
6 May they be like grass on the
 roof,
 which withers before it can
 grow;
7 a reaper cannot fill his hands
 with it,
 nor one who gathers fill his
 arms.

---

[a] 4 Or *Bring back our captives*   [b] 2 Or *eat—/ for while they sleep he provides for*

8 May those who pass by not say to
   them,
      "The blessing of the LORD be
         on you;
      we bless you in the name of the
         LORD."

Psalm 130

A song of ascents.

1 Out of the depths I cry to you,
      LORD;
2   Lord, hear my voice.
   Let your ears be attentive
      to my cry for mercy.

3 If you, LORD, kept a record of
      sins,
   Lord, who could stand?
4 But with you there is
      forgiveness,
   so that we can, with reverence,
      serve you.

5 I wait for the LORD, my whole
      being waits,
   and in his word I put my hope.
6 I wait for the Lord
      more than watchmen wait for
         the morning,
   more than watchmen wait for
      the morning.

7 Israel, put your hope in the
      LORD,
   for with the LORD is unfailing
      love
   and with him is full
      redemption.
8 He himself will redeem Israel
      from all their sins.

Psalm 131

A song of ascents. Of David.

1 My heart is not proud, LORD,
   my eyes are not haughty;

I do not concern myself with
      great matters
   or things too wonderful for
      me.
2 But I have calmed and quieted
      myself,
   I am like a weaned child with
      its mother;
   like a weaned child I am
      content.

3 Israel, put your hope in the
      LORD
   both now and forevermore.

Psalm 132

A song of ascents.

1 LORD, remember David
   and all his self-denial.

2 He swore an oath to the LORD,
   he made a vow to the Mighty
      One of Jacob:
3 "I will not enter my house
   or go to my bed,
4 I will allow no sleep to my eyes
   or slumber to my eyelids,
5 till I find a place for the LORD,
   a dwelling for the Mighty One
      of Jacob."

6 We heard it in Ephrathah,
   we came upon it in the fields of
      Jaar:[a]
7 "Let us go to his dwelling place,
   let us worship at his footstool,
      saying,
8 'Arise, LORD, and come to your
      resting place,
   you and the ark of your might.
9 May your priests be clothed with
      your righteousness;
   may your faithful people sing
      for joy.' "

10 For the sake of your servant
      David,

---

[a] 6 Or *heard of it in Ephrathah, / we found it in the fields of Jearim.* (See 1 Chron. 13:5,6) (And no
quotation marks around verses 7-9)

do not reject your anointed
one.

[11] The LORD swore an oath to
David,
a sure oath he will not revoke:
"One of your own descendants
I will place on your throne.
[12] If your sons keep my covenant
and the statutes I teach them,
then their sons will sit
on your throne for ever and
ever."

[13] For the LORD has chosen Zion,
he has desired it for his
dwelling, saying,
[14] "This is my resting place for ever
and ever;
here I will sit enthroned, for I
have desired it.
[15] I will bless her with abundant
provisions;
her poor I will satisfy with food.
[16] I will clothe her priests with
salvation,
and her faithful people will
ever sing for joy.

[17] "Here I will make a horn[a] grow
for David
and set up a lamp for my
anointed one.
[18] I will clothe his enemies with
shame,
but his head will be adorned
with a radiant crown."

Psalm 133

A song of ascents. Of David.

[1] How good and pleasant it is
when God's people live
together in unity!

[2] It is like precious oil poured on
the head,
running down on the beard,

running down on Aaron's beard,
down on the collar of his robe.
[3] It is as if the dew of Hermon
were falling on Mount Zion.
For there the LORD bestows his
blessing,
even life forevermore.

Psalm 134

A song of ascents.

[1] Praise the LORD, all you servants
of the LORD
who minister by night in the
house of the LORD.
[2] Lift up your hands in the
sanctuary
and praise the LORD.

[3] May the LORD bless you from
Zion,
he who is the Maker of heaven
and earth.

Psalm 135

[1] Praise the LORD.[b]

Praise the name of the LORD;
praise him, you servants of the
LORD,
[2] you who minister in the house of
the LORD,
in the courts of the house of
our God.

[3] Praise the LORD, for the LORD is
good;
sing praise to his name, for
that is pleasant.
[4] For the LORD has chosen Jacob
to be his own,
Israel to be his treasured
possession.

[5] I know that the LORD is great,
that our Lord is greater than
all gods.

---

a 17 Horn here symbolizes strong one, that is, king.
3 and 21   *b 1* Hebrew *Hallelu Yah;* also in verses

⁶ The LORD does whatever pleases
    him,
    in the heavens and on the
        earth,
    in the seas and all their
        depths.
⁷ He makes clouds rise from the
        ends of the earth;
    he sends lightning with the
        rain
    and brings out the wind from
        his storehouses.

⁸ He struck down the firstborn of
        Egypt,
    the firstborn of people and
        animals.
⁹ He sent his signs and wonders
        into your midst, Egypt,
    against Pharaoh and all his
        servants.
¹⁰ He struck down many nations
    and killed mighty kings —
¹¹ Sihon king of the Amorites,
    Og king of Bashan,
    and all the kings of
        Canaan —
¹² and he gave their land as an
        inheritance,
    an inheritance to his people
        Israel.

¹³ Your name, LORD, endures
        forever,
    your renown, LORD, through
        all generations.
¹⁴ For the LORD will vindicate his
        people
    and have compassion on his
        servants.

¹⁵ The idols of the nations are silver
        and gold,
    made by human hands.
¹⁶ They have mouths, but cannot
        speak,
    eyes, but cannot see.
¹⁷ They have ears, but cannot hear,
    nor is there breath in their
        mouths.

¹⁸ Those who make them will be
        like them,
    and so will all who trust in
        them.

¹⁹ All you Israelites, praise the
        LORD;
    house of Aaron, praise the
        LORD;
²⁰ house of Levi, praise the LORD;
    you who fear him, praise the
        LORD.
²¹ Praise be to the LORD from Zion,
    to him who dwells in
        Jerusalem.

Praise the LORD.

Psalm 136

¹ Give thanks to the LORD, for he is
        good.
    His love endures forever.
² Give thanks to the God of gods.
    His love endures forever.
³ Give thanks to the Lord of lords:
    His love endures forever.

⁴ to him who alone does great
        wonders,
    His love endures forever.
⁵ who by his understanding made
        the heavens,
    His love endures forever.
⁶ who spread out the earth upon
        the waters,
    His love endures forever.
⁷ who made the great lights —
    His love endures forever.
⁸ the sun to govern the day,
    His love endures forever.
⁹ the moon and stars to govern the
        night;
    His love endures forever.

¹⁰ to him who struck down the
        firstborn of Egypt
    His love endures forever.
¹¹ and brought Israel out from
        among them
    His love endures forever.

¹²with a mighty hand and
outstretched arm;
His love endures forever.

¹³to him who divided the Red Sea[a]
asunder
His love endures forever.

¹⁴and brought Israel through the
midst of it,
His love endures forever.

¹⁵but swept Pharaoh and his army
into the Red Sea;
His love endures forever.

¹⁶to him who led his people
through the wilderness;
His love endures forever.

¹⁷to him who struck down great
kings,
His love endures forever.

¹⁸and killed mighty kings —
His love endures forever.

¹⁹Sihon king of the Amorites
His love endures forever.

²⁰and Og king of Bashan —
His love endures forever.

²¹and gave their land as an
inheritance,
His love endures forever.

²²an inheritance to his servant
Israel.
His love endures forever.

²³He remembered us in our low
estate
His love endures forever.

²⁴and freed us from our enemies.
His love endures forever.

²⁵He gives food to every creature.
His love endures forever.

²⁶Give thanks to the God of
heaven.
His love endures forever.

Psalm 137

¹By the rivers of Babylon we sat
and wept
when we remembered Zion.

²There on the poplars
we hung our harps,

³for there our captors asked us for
songs,
our tormentors demanded
songs of joy;
they said, "Sing us one of the
songs of Zion!"

⁴How can we sing the songs of the
LORD
while in a foreign land?

⁵If I forget you, Jerusalem,
may my right hand forget its
skill.

⁶May my tongue cling to the roof
of my mouth
if I do not remember you,
if I do not consider Jerusalem
my highest joy.

⁷Remember, LORD, what the
Edomites did
on the day Jerusalem fell.
"Tear it down," they cried,
"tear it down to its
foundations!"

⁸Daughter Babylon, doomed to
destruction,
happy is the one who repays
you
according to what you have
done to us.

⁹Happy is the one who seizes your
infants
and dashes them against the
rocks.

Psalm 138

Of David.

¹I will praise you, LORD, with all
my heart;
before the "gods" I will sing
your praise.

²I will bow down toward your
holy temple

---

a 13 Or the Sea of Reeds; also in verse 15

and will praise your name
  for your unfailing love and
    your faithfulness,
for you have so exalted your
    solemn decree
  that it surpasses your fame.
3 When I called, you answered
    me;
  you greatly emboldened me.

4 May all the kings of the earth
    praise you, LORD,
  when they hear what you have
    decreed.
5 May they sing of the ways of the
    LORD,
  for the glory of the LORD is
    great.

6 Though the LORD is exalted, he
    looks kindly on the lowly;
  though lofty, he sees them
    from afar.
7 Though I walk in the midst of
    trouble,
  you preserve my life.
You stretch out your hand
    against the anger of my
    foes;
  with your right hand you save
    me.
8 The LORD will vindicate me;
  your love, LORD, endures
    forever—
  do not abandon the works of
    your hands.

Psalm 139

*For the director of music. Of David.
A psalm.*

1 You have searched me, LORD,
  and you know me.
2 You know when I sit and when I
    rise;
  you perceive my thoughts
    from afar.
3 You discern my going out and
    my lying down;

you are familiar with all my
    ways.
4 Before a word is on my tongue
  you, LORD, know it
    completely.
5 You hem me in behind and
    before,
  and you lay your hand upon
    me.
6 Such knowledge is too
    wonderful for me,
  too lofty for me to attain.

7 Where can I go from your
    Spirit?
  Where can I flee from your
    presence?
8 If I go up to the heavens, you are
    there;
  if I make my bed in the depths,
    you are there.
9 If I rise on the wings of the
    dawn,
  if I settle on the far side of the
    sea,
10 even there your hand will guide
    me,
  your right hand will hold me
    fast.
11 If I say, "Surely the darkness will
    hide me
  and the light become night
    around me,"
12 even the darkness will not be
    dark to you;
  the night will shine like the
    day,
  for darkness is as light to
    you.

13 For you created my inmost
    being;
  you knit me together in my
    mother's womb.
14 I praise you because I am
    fearfully and wonderfully
    made;
  your works are wonderful,
  I know that full well.

15 My frame was not hidden from you
  when I was made in the secret place,
  when I was woven together in the depths of the earth.
16 Your eyes saw my unformed body;
  all the days ordained for me were written in your book
  before one of them came to be.
17 How precious to me are your thoughts,[a] God!
  How vast is the sum of them!
18 Were I to count them,
  they would outnumber the grains of sand—
  when I awake, I am still with you.
19 If only you, God, would slay the wicked!
  Away from me, you who are bloodthirsty!
20 They speak of you with evil intent;
  your adversaries misuse your name.
21 Do I not hate those who hate you, LORD,
  and abhor those who are in rebellion against you?
22 I have nothing but hatred for them;
  I count them my enemies.
23 Search me, God, and know my heart;
  test me and know my anxious thoughts.
24 See if there is any offensive way in me,
  and lead me in the way everlasting.

Psalm 140[b]

For the director of music. A psalm of David.

1 Rescue me, LORD, from evildoers;
  protect me from the violent,
2 who devise evil plans in their hearts
  and stir up war every day.
3 They make their tongues as sharp as a serpent's;
  the poison of vipers is on their lips.[c]

4 Keep me safe, LORD, from the hands of the wicked;
  protect me from the violent,
  who devise ways to trip my feet.
5 The arrogant have hidden a snare for me;
  they have spread out the cords of their net
  and have set traps for me along my path.

6 I say to the LORD, "You are my God."
  Hear, LORD, my cry for mercy.
7 Sovereign LORD, my strong deliverer,
  you shield my head in the day of battle.
8 Do not grant the wicked their desires, LORD;
  do not let their plans succeed.

9 Those who surround me proudly rear their heads;
  may the mischief of their lips engulf them.
10 May burning coals fall on them;
  may they be thrown into the fire,
  into miry pits, never to rise.

---

a 17 Or *How amazing are your thoughts concerning me*   b In Hebrew texts 140:1-13 is numbered 140:2-14.   c 3 The Hebrew has *Selah* (a word of uncertain meaning) here and at the end of verses 5 and 8.

¹¹ May slanderers not be
established in the land;
may disaster hunt down the
violent.

¹² I know that the LORD secures
justice for the poor
and upholds the cause of the
needy.
¹³ Surely the righteous will praise
your name,
and the upright will live in
your presence.

Psalm 141

A psalm of David.

¹ I call to you, LORD, come quickly
to me;
hear me when I call to you.
² May my prayer be set before you
like incense;
may the lifting up of my
hands be like the evening
sacrifice.

³ Set a guard over my mouth,
LORD;
keep watch over the door of my
lips.
⁴ Do not let my heart be drawn to
what is evil
so that I take part in wicked
deeds
along with those who are
evildoers;
do not let me eat their
delicacies.

⁵ Let a righteous man strike me —
that is a kindness;
let him rebuke me — that is oil
on my head.
My head will not refuse it,
for my prayer will still be
against the deeds of
evildoers.

⁶ Their rulers will be thrown
down from the cliffs,
and the wicked will learn
that my words were well
spoken.
⁷ They will say, "As one plows and
breaks up the earth,
so our bones have been
scattered at the mouth of
the grave."

⁸ But my eyes are fixed on you,
Sovereign LORD;
in you I take refuge — do not
give me over to death.
⁹ Keep me safe from the traps set
by evildoers,
from the snares they have laid
for me.
¹⁰ Let the wicked fall into their own
nets,
while I pass by in safety.

Psalm 142ᵃ

*A maskilᵇ of David. When he was in the
cave. A prayer.*

¹ I cry aloud to the LORD;
I lift up my voice to the LORD
for mercy.
² I pour out before him my
complaint;
before him I tell my trouble.

³ When my spirit grows faint
within me,
it is you who watch over my
way.
In the path where I walk
people have hidden a snare for
me.
⁴ Look and see, there is no one at
my right hand;
no one is concerned for me.
I have no refuge;
no one cares for my life.

ᵃ In Hebrew texts 142:1-7 is numbered 142:2-8.   ᵇ Title: Probably a literary or musical term

⁵ I cry to you, LORD;
  I say, "You are my refuge,
  my portion in the land of the
    living."

⁶ Listen to my cry,
  for I am in desperate need;
  rescue me from those who
    pursue me,
  for they are too strong for me.
⁷ Set me free from my prison,
  that I may praise your name.
  Then the righteous will gather
    about me
  because of your goodness to
    me.

Psalm 143

A psalm of David.

¹ LORD, hear my prayer,
  listen to my cry for mercy;
  in your faithfulness and
    righteousness
  come to my relief.
² Do not bring your servant into
    judgment,
  for no one living is righteous
    before you.
³ The enemy pursues me,
  he crushes me to the ground;
  he makes me dwell in the
    darkness
  like those long dead.
⁴ So my spirit grows faint within
    me;
  my heart within me is
    dismayed.
⁵ I remember the days of long
    ago;
  I meditate on all your works
  and consider what your hands
    have done.
⁶ I spread out my hands to you;
  I thirst for you like a parched
    land.ᵃ

⁷ Answer me quickly, LORD;
  my spirit fails.
  Do not hide your face from me
  or I will be like those who go
    down to the pit.
⁸ Let the morning bring me word
    of your unfailing love,
  for I have put my trust in you.
  Show me the way I should go,
  for to you I entrust my life.
⁹ Rescue me from my enemies,
    LORD,
  for I hide myself in you.
¹⁰ Teach me to do your will,
  for you are my God;
  may your good Spirit
  lead me on level ground.

¹¹ For your name's sake, LORD,
    preserve my life;
  in your righteousness, bring
    me out of trouble.
¹² In your unfailing love, silence
    my enemies;
  destroy all my foes,
  for I am your servant.

Psalm 144

Of David.

¹ Praise be to the LORD my Rock,
  who trains my hands for war,
  my fingers for battle.
² He is my loving God and my
    fortress,
  my stronghold and my
    deliverer,
  my shield, in whom I take
    refuge,
  who subdues peoplesᵇ under
    me.

³ LORD, what are human beings
  that you care for them,
  mere mortals that you think of
    them?

ᵃ 6 The Hebrew has *Selah* (a word of uncertain meaning) here.   ᵇ 2 Many manuscripts of the
Masoretic Text, Dead Sea Scrolls, Aquila, Jerome and Syriac; most manuscripts of the Masoretic
Text *subdues my people*

4 They are like a breath;
  their days are like a fleeting
    shadow.

5 Part your heavens, LORD, and
    come down;
  touch the mountains, so that
    they smoke.
6 Send forth lightning and scatter
    the enemy;
  shoot your arrows and rout
    them.
7 Reach down your hand from on
    high;
  deliver me and rescue me
  from the mighty waters,
    from the hands of foreigners
8 whose mouths are full of lies,
  whose right hands are
    deceitful.

9 I will sing a new song to you, my
    God;
  on the ten-stringed lyre I will
    make music to you,
10 to the One who gives victory to
    kings,
  who delivers his servant
    David.

From the deadly sword 11 deliver
    me;
  rescue me from the hands of
    foreigners
  whose mouths are full of lies,
  whose right hands are
    deceitful.

12 Then our sons in their youth
  will be like well-nurtured
    plants,
and our daughters will be like
    pillars
  carved to adorn a palace.
13 Our barns will be filled
  with every kind of provision.

Our sheep will increase by
    thousands,
  by tens of thousands in our
    fields;
14   our oxen will draw heavy
    loads.[a]
There will be no breaching of
    walls,
  no going into captivity,
  no cry of distress in our
    streets.
15 Blessed is the people of whom
    this is true;
  blessed is the people whose
    God is the LORD.

Psalm 145[b]

A psalm of praise. Of David.

1 I will exalt you, my God the
    King;
  I will praise your name for
    ever and ever.
2 Every day I will praise you
  and extol your name for ever
    and ever.

3 Great is the LORD and most
    worthy of praise;
  his greatness no one can
    fathom.
4 One generation commends your
    works to another;
  they tell of your mighty acts.
5 They speak of the glorious
    splendor of your
    majesty—
  and I will meditate on your
    wonderful works.[c]
6 They tell of the power of your
    awesome works—
  and I will proclaim your great
    deeds.
7 They celebrate your abundant
    goodness

---

[a] 14 Or *our chieftains will be firmly established
of which (including verse 13b) begin with the successive letters of the Hebrew alphabet.*   [b] This psalm is an acrostic poem, the verses
[c] 5 Dead Sea Scrolls and Syriac (see also Septuagint); Masoretic Text *On the glorious splendor of
your majesty / and on your wonderful works I will meditate*

and joyfully sing of your
righteousness.

⁸ The LORD is gracious and
compassionate,
slow to anger and rich in love.

⁹ The LORD is good to all;
he has compassion on all he
has made.

¹⁰ All your works praise you, LORD;
your faithful people extol you.

¹¹ They tell of the glory of your
kingdom
and speak of your might,

¹² so that all people may know of
your mighty acts
and the glorious splendor of
your kingdom.

¹³ Your kingdom is an everlasting
kingdom,
and your dominion endures
through all generations.

The LORD is trustworthy in all he
promises
and faithful in all he does.^a

¹⁴ The LORD upholds all who fall
and lifts up all who are bowed
down.

¹⁵ The eyes of all look to you,
and you give them their food
at the proper time.

¹⁶ You open your hand
and satisfy the desires of every
living thing.

¹⁷ The LORD is righteous in all his
ways
and faithful in all he does.

¹⁸ The LORD is near to all who call
on him,
to all who call on him in truth.

¹⁹ He fulfills the desires of those
who fear him;
he hears their cry and saves
them.

²⁰ The LORD watches over all who
love him,
but all the wicked he will
destroy.

²¹ My mouth will speak in praise of
the LORD.
Let every creature praise his
holy name
for ever and ever.

Psalm 146

¹ Praise the LORD.^b

Praise the LORD, my soul.

² I will praise the LORD all my life;
I will sing praise to my God as
long as I live.

³ Do not put your trust in princes,
in human beings, who cannot
save.

⁴ When their spirit departs, they
return to the ground;
on that very day their plans
come to nothing.

⁵ Blessed are those whose help is
the God of Jacob,
whose hope is in the LORD
their God.

⁶ He is the Maker of heaven and
earth,
the sea, and everything in
them—
he remains faithful forever.

⁷ He upholds the cause of the
oppressed
and gives food to the hungry.
The LORD sets prisoners free,

⁸ the LORD gives sight to the
blind,
the LORD lifts up those who are
bowed down,
the LORD loves the righteous.

⁹ The LORD watches over the
foreigner

and sustains the fatherless
and the widow,
but he frustrates the ways of
the wicked.
¹⁰ The LORD reigns forever,
your God, O Zion, for all
generations.

Praise the LORD.

Psalm 147

¹ Praise the LORD.ᵃ

How good it is to sing praises to
our God,
how pleasant and fitting to
praise him!

² The LORD builds up Jerusalem;
he gathers the exiles of Israel.
³ He heals the brokenhearted
and binds up their wounds.
⁴ He determines the number of
the stars
and calls them each by name.
⁵ Great is our Lord and mighty in
power;
his understanding has no
limit.
⁶ The LORD sustains the humble
but casts the wicked to the
ground.

⁷ Sing to the LORD with grateful
praise;
make music to our God on the
harp.

⁸ He covers the sky with clouds;
he supplies the earth with rain
and makes grass grow on the
hills.
⁹ He provides food for the cattle
and for the young ravens when
they call.

¹⁰ His pleasure is not in the
strength of the horse,

nor his delight in the legs of
the warrior;
¹¹ the LORD delights in those who
fear him,
who put their hope in his
unfailing love.

¹² Extol the LORD, Jerusalem;
praise your God, Zion.
¹³ He strengthens the bars of your
gates
and blesses your people
within you.
¹⁴ He grants peace to your
borders
and satisfies you with the
finest of wheat.

¹⁵ He sends his command to the
earth;
his word runs swiftly.
¹⁶ He spreads the snow like wool
and scatters the frost like
ashes.
¹⁷ He hurls down his hail like
pebbles.
Who can withstand his icy
blast?
¹⁸ He sends his word and melts
them;
he stirs up his breezes, and the
waters flow.

¹⁹ He has revealed his word to
Jacob,
his laws and decrees to Israel.
²⁰ He has done this for no other
nation;
they do not know his laws.ᵇ

Praise the LORD.

Psalm 148

¹ Praise the LORD.ᶜ

Praise the LORD from the
heavens;

ᵃ 1 Hebrew *Hallelu Yah*; also in verse 20   ᵇ 20 Masoretic Text; Dead Sea Scrolls and Septuagint
nation; / he has not made his laws known to them   ᶜ 1 Hebrew *Hallelu Yah*; also in verse 14

praise him in the heights
above.
2 Praise him, all his angels;
praise him, all his heavenly
hosts.
3 Praise him, sun and moon;
praise him, all you shining
stars.
4 Praise him, you highest
heavens
and you waters above the
skies.

5 Let them praise the name of the
LORD,
for at his command they were
created,
6 and he established them for ever
and ever—
he issued a decree that will
never pass away.

7 Praise the LORD from the earth,
you great sea creatures and all
ocean depths,
8 lightning and hail, snow and
clouds,
stormy winds that do his
bidding,
9 you mountains and all hills,
fruit trees and all cedars,
10 wild animals and all cattle,
small creatures and flying
birds,
11 kings of the earth and all
nations,
you princes and all rulers on
earth,
12 young men and women,
old men and children.

13 Let them praise the name of the
LORD,
for his name alone is exalted;
his splendor is above the earth
and the heavens.
14 And he has raised up for his
people a horn,[a]

the praise of all his faithful
servants,
of Israel, the people close to
his heart.

Praise the LORD.

Psalm 149

1 Praise the LORD.[b]

Sing to the LORD a new song,
his praise in the assembly of
his faithful people.

2 Let Israel rejoice in their
Maker;
let the people of Zion be glad
in their King.
3 Let them praise his name with
dancing
and make music to him with
timbrel and harp.
4 For the LORD takes delight in his
people;
he crowns the humble with
victory.
5 Let his faithful people rejoice in
this honor
and sing for joy on their beds.

6 May the praise of God be in their
mouths
and a double-edged sword in
their hands,
7 to inflict vengeance on the
nations
and punishment on the
peoples,
8 to bind their kings with
fetters,
their nobles with shackles of
iron,
9 to carry out the sentence written
against them—
this is the glory of all his
faithful people.

Praise the LORD.

---

a 14 *Horn* here symbolizes strength.   *b* 1 Hebrew *Hallelu Yah*; also in verse 9

Psalm 150

[1] Praise the LORD.[a]

Praise God in his sanctuary;
  praise him in his mighty
    heavens.
[2] Praise him for his acts of power;
  praise him for his surpassing
    greatness.
[3] Praise him with the sounding of
    the trumpet,
  praise him with the harp and
    lyre,

[4] praise him with timbrel and
    dancing,
  praise him with the strings
    and pipe,
[5] praise him with the clash of
    cymbals,
  praise him with resounding
    cymbals.

[6] Let everything that has breath
    praise the LORD.

Praise the LORD.

---

[a] 1 Hebrew *Hallelu Yah*; also in verse 6

PROVERBS

Israel understood that the Creator had placed an order in his world that could be discovered. The book of Proverbs captures these lessons in compact, memorable sayings passed down from the wisest among their elders. Many of them are from Solomon, a king renowned for his wisdom. These proverbs are especially designed to help younger people avoid common pitfalls and find the path to prosperity, health and security.

After a short section of teaching, wisdom itself, personified as a woman, calls out to the simple and invites them to grow in knowledge. This section ends by presenting two banquets, one hosted by Wisdom and one by Folly, illustrating the essential choice to be made in life. A collection of 375 proverbs of Solomon follows, reflecting the numerical value of his name in Hebrew. (Hebrew letters were also used as numbers, so words had a value equal to the sum of their letters.) After some "sayings of the wise," next is a collection of Solomon's wisdom compiled by the men of Hezekiah, king of Judah. Here the count is 130, equaling the value of Hezekiah's name. The book closes with sayings from Agur and Lemuel, ending with a poem whose 22 parts begin with consecutive letters of the Hebrew alphabet. The character qualities praised throughout the book are seen in a description of the ideal wife.

This rich book of short, pithy wisdom presents a consistent theme: *the fear of the LORD is the beginning of knowledge.*

---

1 The proverbs of Solomon son of David, king of Israel:

2 for gaining wisdom and
    instruction;
  for understanding words of
    insight;
3 for receiving instruction in
    prudent behavior,
  doing what is right and just
    and fair;
4 for giving prudence to those who
    are simple,*a*
  knowledge and discretion to
    the young —
5 let the wise listen and add to
    their learning,
  and let the discerning get
    guidance —

6 for understanding proverbs and
    parables,
  the sayings and riddles of the
    wise.*b*

7 The fear of the LORD is the
    beginning of knowledge,
  but fools*c* despise wisdom and
    instruction.

8 Listen, my son, to your father's
    instruction
  and do not forsake your
    mother's teaching.
9 They are a garland to grace your
    head
  and a chain to adorn your
    neck.

10 My son, if sinful men entice you,
   do not give in to them.

---

a 4 The Hebrew word rendered *simple* in Proverbs denotes a person who is gullible, without moral direction and inclined to evil.   *b 6* Or *understanding a proverb, namely, a parable, / and the sayings of the wise, their riddles*   *c 7* The Hebrew words rendered *fool* in Proverbs, and often elsewhere in the Old Testament, denote a person who is morally deficient.

11 If they say, "Come along with us;
    let's lie in wait for innocent
        blood,
    let's ambush some harmless
        soul;
12 let's swallow them alive, like the
        grave,
    and whole, like those who go
        down to the pit;
13 we will get all sorts of valuable
        things
    and fill our houses with
        plunder;
14 cast lots with us;
    we will all share the loot" —
15 my son, do not go along with
        them,
    do not set foot on their paths;
16 for their feet rush into evil,
    they are swift to shed blood.
17 How useless to spread a net
    where every bird can see it!
18 These men lie in wait for their
        own blood;
    they ambush only
        themselves!
19 Such are the paths of all who go
        after ill-gotten gain;
    it takes away the life of those
        who get it.

20 Out in the open wisdom calls
        aloud,
    she raises her voice in the
        public square;
21 on top of the wall[a] she cries out,
    at the city gate she makes her
        speech:

22 "How long will you who are
        simple love your simple
        ways?
    How long will mockers delight
        in mockery
    and fools hate knowledge?
23 Repent at my rebuke!
    Then I will pour out my
        thoughts to you,

I will make known to you my
        teachings.
24 But since you refuse to listen
        when I call
    and no one pays attention
        when I stretch out my
        hand,
25 since you disregard all my
        advice
    and do not accept my rebuke,
26 I in turn will laugh when
        disaster strikes you;
    I will mock when calamity
        overtakes you —
27 when calamity overtakes you
        like a storm,
    when disaster sweeps over you
        like a whirlwind,
    when distress and trouble
        overwhelm you.

28 "Then they will call to me but I
        will not answer;
    they will look for me but will
        not find me,
29 since they hated knowledge
    and did not choose to fear the
        LORD.
30 Since they would not accept my
        advice
    and spurned my rebuke,
31 they will eat the fruit of their
        ways
    and be filled with the fruit of
        their schemes.
32 For the waywardness of the
        simple will kill them,
    and the complacency of fools
        will destroy them;
33 but whoever listens to me will
        live in safety
    and be at ease, without fear of
        harm."

2 My son, if you accept my words
    and store up my commands
        within you,
2 turning your ear to wisdom

---

a 21 Septuagint; Hebrew / at noisy street corners

and applying your heart to
　　understanding—
³ indeed, if you call out for insight
　　and cry aloud for
　　understanding,
⁴ and if you look for it as for silver
　　and search for it as for hidden
　　treasure,
⁵ then you will understand the
　　fear of the LORD
　　and find the knowledge of
　　God.
⁶ For the LORD gives wisdom;
　　from his mouth come
　　knowledge and
　　understanding.
⁷ He holds success in store for the
　　upright,
　　he is a shield to those whose
　　walk is blameless,
⁸ for he guards the course of the
　　just
　　and protects the way of his
　　faithful ones.
⁹ Then you will understand what
　　is right and just
　　and fair—every good path.
¹⁰ For wisdom will enter your
　　heart,
　　and knowledge will be
　　pleasant to your soul.
¹¹ Discretion will protect you,
　　and understanding will guard
　　you.
¹² Wisdom will save you from the
　　ways of wicked men,
　　from men whose words are
　　perverse,
¹³ who have left the straight paths
　　to walk in dark ways,
¹⁴ who delight in doing wrong
　　and rejoice in the perverseness
　　of evil,
¹⁵ whose paths are crooked
　　and who are devious in their
　　ways.

¹⁶ Wisdom will save you also from
　　the adulterous woman,
　　from the wayward woman
　　with her seductive words,
¹⁷ who has left the partner of her
　　youth
　　and ignored the covenant she
　　made before God.ᵃ
¹⁸ Surely her house leads down to
　　death
　　and her paths to the spirits of
　　the dead.
¹⁹ None who go to her return
　　or attain the paths of life.
²⁰ Thus you will walk in the ways of
　　the good
　　and keep to the paths of the
　　righteous.
²¹ For the upright will live in the
　　land,
　　and the blameless will remain
　　in it;
²² but the wicked will be cut off
　　from the land,
　　and the unfaithful will be torn
　　from it.

3 My son, do not forget my
　　teaching,
　　but keep my commands in
　　your heart,
² for they will prolong your life
　　many years
　　and bring you peace and
　　prosperity.

³ Let love and faithfulness never
　　leave you;
　　bind them around your neck,
　　write them on the tablet of
　　your heart.
⁴ Then you will win favor and a
　　good name
　　in the sight of God and man.

⁵ Trust in the LORD with all your
　　heart

ᵃ 17 Or *covenant of her God*

and lean not on your own
   understanding;
6 in all your ways submit to him,
   and he will make your paths
   straight.*a*

7 Do not be wise in your own
   eyes;
   fear the LORD and shun evil.
8 This will bring health to your
   body
   and nourishment to your
   bones.

9 Honor the LORD with your
   wealth,
   with the firstfruits of all your
   crops;
10 then your barns will be filled to
   overflowing,
   and your vats will brim over
   with new wine.

11 My son, do not despise the
   LORD's discipline,
   and do not resent his rebuke,
12 because the LORD disciplines
   those he loves,
   as a father the son he delights
   in.*b*

13 Blessed are those who find
   wisdom,
   those who gain
   understanding,
14 for she is more profitable than
   silver
   and yields better returns than
   gold.
15 She is more precious than
   rubies;
   nothing you desire can
   compare with her.
16 Long life is in her right hand;
   in her left hand are riches and
   honor.
17 Her ways are pleasant ways,
   and all her paths are peace.

18 She is a tree of life to those who
   take hold of her;
   those who hold her fast will be
   blessed.

19 By wisdom the LORD laid the
   earth's foundations,
   by understanding he set the
   heavens in place;
20 by his knowledge the watery
   depths were divided,
   and the clouds let drop the
   dew.

21 My son, do not let wisdom and
   understanding out of your
   sight,
   preserve sound judgment and
   discretion;
22 they will be life for you,
   an ornament to grace your
   neck.
23 Then you will go on your way in
   safety,
   and your foot will not stumble.
24 When you lie down, you will not
   be afraid;
   when you lie down, your sleep
   will be sweet.
25 Have no fear of sudden disaster
   or of the ruin that overtakes
   the wicked,
26 for the LORD will be at your side
   and will keep your foot from
   being snared.

27 Do not withhold good from
   those to whom it is due,
   when it is in your power to act.
28 Do not say to your neighbor,
   "Come back tomorrow and I'll
   give it to you" —
   when you already have it with
   you.
29 Do not plot harm against your
   neighbor,
   who lives trustfully near you.

---

a 6 Or *will direct your paths*   *b* 12 Hebrew; Septuagint *loves, / and he chastens everyone he
accepts as his child*

30 Do not accuse anyone for no
reason—
   when they have done you no
harm.

31 Do not envy the violent
   or choose any of their ways.

32 For the LORD detests the
perverse
   but takes the upright into his
confidence.

33 The LORD's curse is on the house
of the wicked,
   but he blesses the home of the
righteous.

34 He mocks proud mockers
   but shows favor to the humble
and oppressed.

35 The wise inherit honor,
   but fools get only shame.

4 Listen, my sons, to a father's
instruction;
   pay attention and gain
understanding.

2 I give you sound learning,
   so do not forsake my teaching.

3 For I too was a son to my father,
   still tender, and cherished by
my mother.

4 Then he taught me, and he said
to me,
   "Take hold of my words with
all your heart;
   keep my commands, and you
will live.

5 Get wisdom, get understanding;
   do not forget my words or turn
away from them.

6 Do not forsake wisdom, and she
will protect you;
   love her, and she will watch
over you.

7 The beginning of wisdom is this:
Get[a] wisdom.
   Though it cost all you have,[b]
get understanding.

8 Cherish her, and she will exalt
you;
   embrace her, and she will
honor you.

9 She will give you a garland to
grace your head
   and present you with a
glorious crown."

10 Listen, my son, accept what I say,
   and the years of your life will
be many.

11 I instruct you in the way of
wisdom
   and lead you along straight
paths.

12 When you walk, your steps will
not be hampered;
   when you run, you will not
stumble.

13 Hold on to instruction, do not let
it go;
   guard it well, for it is your life.

14 Do not set foot on the path of the
wicked
   or walk in the way of evildoers.

15 Avoid it, do not travel on it;
   turn from it and go on your
way.

16 For they cannot rest until they
do evil;
   they are robbed of sleep till
they make someone
stumble.

17 They eat the bread of wickedness
   and drink the wine of violence.

18 The path of the righteous is like
the morning sun,
   shining ever brighter till the
full light of day.

19 But the way of the wicked is like
deep darkness;
   they do not know what makes
them stumble.

20 My son, pay attention to what I
say;

---

a 7 Or *Wisdom is supreme; therefore get*   b 7 Or *wisdom. / Whatever else you get*

turn your ear to my words.

21 Do not let them out of your sight,
keep them within your heart;

22 for they are life to those who find
them
and health to one's whole
body.

23 Above all else, guard your heart,
for everything you do flows
from it.

24 Keep your mouth free of
perversity;
keep corrupt talk far from your
lips.

25 Let your eyes look straight
ahead;
fix your gaze directly before
you.

26 Give careful thought to the[a]
paths for your feet
and be steadfast in all your
ways.

27 Do not turn to the right or the
left;
keep your foot from evil.

5 My son, pay attention to my
wisdom,
turn your ear to my words of
insight,

2 that you may maintain
discretion
and your lips may preserve
knowledge.

3 For the lips of the adulterous
woman drip honey,
and her speech is smoother
than oil;

4 but in the end she is bitter as
gall,
sharp as a double-edged
sword.

5 Her feet go down to death;
her steps lead straight to the
grave.

6 She gives no thought to the way
of life;

her paths wander aimlessly,
but she does not know it.

7 Now then, my sons, listen to me;
do not turn aside from what I
say.

8 Keep to a path far from her,
do not go near the door of her
house,

9 lest you lose your honor to others
and your dignity[b] to one who
is cruel,

10 lest strangers feast on your
wealth
and your toil enrich the house
of another.

11 At the end of your life you will
groan,
when your flesh and body are
spent.

12 You will say, "How I hated
discipline!
How my heart spurned
correction!

13 I would not obey my teachers
or turn my ear to my
instructors.

14 And I was soon in serious
trouble
in the assembly of God's
people."

15 Drink water from your own
cistern,
running water from your own
well.

16 Should your springs overflow in
the streets,
your streams of water in the
public squares?

17 Let them be yours alone,
never to be shared with
strangers.

18 May your fountain be blessed,
and may you rejoice in the
wife of your youth.

19 A loving doe, a graceful deer—

[a] 26 Or *Make level*   [b] 9 Or *years*

may her breasts satisfy you
always,
may you ever be intoxicated
with her love.
²⁰ Why, my son, be intoxicated
with another man's wife?
Why embrace the bosom of a
wayward woman?

²¹ For your ways are in full view of
the LORD,
and he examines all your
paths.
²² The evil deeds of the wicked
ensnare them;
the cords of their sins hold
them fast.
²³ For lack of discipline they will
die,
led astray by their own great
folly.

6 My son, if you have put up
security for your neighbor,
if you have shaken hands in
pledge for a stranger,
² you have been trapped by what
you said,
ensnared by the words of your
mouth.
³ So do this, my son, to free
yourself,
since you have fallen into your
neighbor's hands:
Go — to the point of
exhaustion — ^a
and give your neighbor no rest!
⁴ Allow no sleep to your eyes,
no slumber to your eyelids.
⁵ Free yourself, like a gazelle from
the hand of the hunter,
like a bird from the snare of
the fowler.

⁶ Go to the ant, you sluggard;
consider its ways and be wise!
⁷ It has no commander,
no overseer or ruler,

⁸ yet it stores its provisions in
summer
and gathers its food at harvest.

⁹ How long will you lie there, you
sluggard?
When will you get up from
your sleep?
¹⁰ A little sleep, a little slumber,
a little folding of the hands to
rest —
¹¹ and poverty will come on you
like a thief
and scarcity like an armed
man.

¹² A troublemaker and a villain,
who goes about with a corrupt
mouth,
¹³   who winks maliciously with
his eye,
signals with his feet
and motions with his fingers,
¹⁴   who plots evil with deceit in
his heart —
he always stirs up conflict.
¹⁵ Therefore disaster will overtake
him in an instant;
he will suddenly be
destroyed — without
remedy.

¹⁶ There are six things the LORD
hates,
seven that are detestable to
him:
¹⁷   haughty eyes,
a lying tongue,
hands that shed innocent
blood,
¹⁸   a heart that devises wicked
schemes,
feet that are quick to rush
into evil,
¹⁹   a false witness who pours
out lies
and a person who stirs up
conflict in the community.

^a 3 Or *Go and humble yourself,*

20 My son, keep your father's
command
and do not forsake your
mother's teaching.
21 Bind them always on your heart;
fasten them around your neck.
22 When you walk, they will guide
you;
when you sleep, they will
watch over you;
when you awake, they will
speak to you.
23 For this command is a lamp,
this teaching is a light,
and correction and instruction
are the way to life,
24 keeping you from your
neighbor's wife,
from the smooth talk of a
wayward woman.

25 Do not lust in your heart after
her beauty
or let her captivate you with
her eyes.
26 For a prostitute can be had for a
loaf of bread,
but another man's wife preys
on your very life.
27 Can a man scoop fire into his
lap
without his clothes being
burned?
28 Can a man walk on hot coals
without his feet being
scorched?
29 So is he who sleeps with another
man's wife;
no one who touches her will go
unpunished.

30 People do not despise a thief if
he steals
to satisfy his hunger when he
is starving.
31 Yet if he is caught, he must pay
sevenfold,
though it costs him all the
wealth of his house.

32 But a man who commits
adultery has no sense;
whoever does so destroys
himself.
33 Blows and disgrace are his lot,
and his shame will never be
wiped away.
34 For jealousy arouses a husband's
fury,
and he will show no mercy
when he takes revenge.
35 He will not accept any
compensation;
he will refuse a bribe, however
great it is.

7 My son, keep my words
and store up my commands
within you.
2 Keep my commands and you
will live;
guard my teachings as the
apple of your eye.
3 Bind them on your fingers;
write them on the tablet of
your heart.
4 Say to wisdom, "You are my
sister,"
and to insight, "You are my
relative."
5 They will keep you from the
adulterous woman,
from the wayward woman
with her seductive words.

6 At the window of my house
I looked down through the
lattice.
7 I saw among the simple,
I noticed among the young
men,
a youth who had no sense.
8 He was going down the street
near her corner,
walking along in the direction
of her house
9 at twilight, as the day was
fading,
as the dark of night set in.

¹⁰ Then out came a woman to meet him,
   dressed like a prostitute and with crafty intent.
¹¹ (She is unruly and defiant,
   her feet never stay at home;
¹² now in the street, now in the squares,
   at every corner she lurks.)
¹³ She took hold of him and kissed him
   and with a brazen face she said:

¹⁴ "Today I fulfilled my vows,
   and I have food from my fellowship offering at home.
¹⁵ So I came out to meet you;
   I looked for you and have found you!
¹⁶ I have covered my bed
   with colored linens from Egypt.
¹⁷ I have perfumed my bed
   with myrrh, aloes and cinnamon.
¹⁸ Come, let's drink deeply of love till morning;
   let's enjoy ourselves with love!
¹⁹ My husband is not at home;
   he has gone on a long journey.
²⁰ He took his purse filled with money
   and will not be home till full moon."

²¹ With persuasive words she led him astray;
   she seduced him with her smooth talk.
²² All at once he followed her
   like an ox going to the slaughter,
   like a deer[a] stepping into a noose[b]

²³ till an arrow pierces his liver,
   like a bird darting into a snare,
   little knowing it will cost him his life.

²⁴ Now then, my sons, listen to me;
   pay attention to what I say.
²⁵ Do not let your heart turn to her ways
   or stray into her paths.
²⁶ Many are the victims she has brought down;
   her slain are a mighty throng.
²⁷ Her house is a highway to the grave,
   leading down to the chambers of death.

8 Does not wisdom call out?
   Does not understanding raise her voice?
² At the highest point along the way,
   where the paths meet, she takes her stand;
³ beside the gate leading into the city,
   at the entrance, she cries aloud:
⁴ "To you, O people, I call out;
   I raise my voice to all mankind.
⁵ You who are simple, gain prudence;
   you who are foolish, set your hearts on it.[c]
⁶ Listen, for I have trustworthy things to say;
   I open my lips to speak what is right.
⁷ My mouth speaks what is true,
   for my lips detest wickedness.
⁸ All the words of my mouth are just;
   none of them is crooked or perverse.

---

a 22 Syriac (see also Septuagint); Hebrew *fool*   b 22 The meaning of the Hebrew for this line is uncertain.   c 5 Septuagint; Hebrew *foolish, instruct your minds*

⁹ To the discerning all of them are
     right;
  they are upright to those who
     have found knowledge.
¹⁰ Choose my instruction instead
     of silver,
  knowledge rather than choice
     gold,
¹¹ for wisdom is more precious
     than rubies,
  and nothing you desire can
     compare with her.

¹² "I, wisdom, dwell together with
     prudence;
  I possess knowledge and
     discretion.
¹³ To fear the LORD is to hate evil;
  I hate pride and arrogance,
     evil behavior and perverse
     speech.
¹⁴ Counsel and sound judgment
     are mine;
  I have insight, I have power.
¹⁵ By me kings reign
  and rulers issue decrees that
     are just;
¹⁶ by me princes govern,
  and nobles — all who rule on
     earth.ᵃ
¹⁷ I love those who love me,
  and those who seek me find
     me.
¹⁸ With me are riches and honor,
  enduring wealth and
     prosperity.
¹⁹ My fruit is better than fine gold;
  what I yield surpasses choice
     silver.
²⁰ I walk in the way of
     righteousness,
  along the paths of justice,
²¹ bestowing a rich inheritance on
     those who love me
  and making their treasuries
     full.

²² "The LORD brought me forth as
     the first of his works,ᵇ,ᶜ
  before his deeds of old;
²³ I was formed long ages ago,
  at the very beginning, when
     the world came to be.
²⁴ When there were no watery
     depths, I was given birth,
  when there were no springs
     overflowing with water;
²⁵ before the mountains were
     settled in place,
  before the hills, I was given
     birth,
²⁶ before he made the world or its
     fields
  or any of the dust of the
     earth.
²⁷ I was there when he set the
     heavens in place,
  when he marked out the
     horizon on the face of the
     deep,
²⁸ when he established the clouds
     above
  and fixed securely the
     fountains of the deep,
²⁹ when he gave the sea its
     boundary
  so the waters would not
     overstep his command,
  and when he marked out the
     foundations of the earth.
³⁰   Then I was constantlyᵈ at his
       side.
  I was filled with delight day after
     day,
  rejoicing always in his
     presence,
³¹ rejoicing in his whole world
  and delighting in mankind.

³² "Now then, my children, listen
     to me;
  blessed are those who keep my
     ways.

ᵃ 16 Some Hebrew manuscripts and Septuagint; other Hebrew manuscripts *all righteous rulers*
ᵇ 22 Or *way; or dominion*   ᶜ 22 Or *The LORD possessed me at the beginning of his work;* or *The LORD brought me forth at the beginning of his work*   ᵈ 30 Or *was the artisan;* or *was a little child*

33 Listen to my instruction and be
    wise;
    do not disregard it.
34 Blessed are those who listen to
    me,
    watching daily at my doors,
    waiting at my doorway.
35 For those who find me find life
    and receive favor from the
    LORD.
36 But those who fail to find me
    harm themselves;
    all who hate me love death."

9 Wisdom has built her house;
    she has set up[a] its seven
    pillars.
2 She has prepared her meat and
    mixed her wine;
    she has also set her table.
3 She has sent out her servants,
    and she calls
    from the highest point of the
    city,
4   "Let all who are simple come
    to my house!"
    To those who have no sense she
    says,
5   "Come, eat my food
    and drink the wine I have
    mixed.
6 Leave your simple ways and you
    will live;
    walk in the way of insight."

7 Whoever corrects a mocker
    invites insults;
    whoever rebukes the wicked
    incurs abuse.
8 Do not rebuke mockers or they
    will hate you;
    rebuke the wise and they will
    love you.
9 Instruct the wise and they will
    be wiser still;
    teach the righteous and they
    will add to their learning.

10 The fear of the LORD is the
    beginning of wisdom,
    and knowledge of the Holy
    One is understanding.
11 For through wisdom[b] your days
    will be many,
    and years will be added to
    your life.
12 If you are wise, your wisdom will
    reward you;
    if you are a mocker, you alone
    will suffer.

13 Folly is an unruly woman;
    she is simple and knows
    nothing.
14 She sits at the door of her house,
    on a seat at the highest point of
    the city,
15 calling out to those who pass
    by,
    who go straight on their way,
16 "Let all who are simple come
    to my house!"
    To those who have no sense she
    says,
17 "Stolen water is sweet;
    food eaten in secret is
    delicious!"
18 But little do they know that the
    dead are there,
    that her guests are deep in the
    realm of the dead.

10 The proverbs of Solomon:

    A wise son brings joy to his
    father,
    but a foolish son brings grief to
    his mother.

2 Ill-gotten treasures have no
    lasting value,
    but righteousness delivers
    from death.

3 The LORD does not let the
    righteous go hungry,

---

[a] 1 Septuagint, Syriac and Targum; Hebrew *has hewn out*   [b] 11 Septuagint, Syriac and Targum; Hebrew *me*

but he thwarts the craving of
the wicked.

4 Lazy hands make for poverty,
but diligent hands bring
wealth.

5 He who gathers crops in summer
is a prudent son,
but he who sleeps during
harvest is a disgraceful
son.

6 Blessings crown the head of the
righteous,
but violence overwhelms the
mouth of the wicked.[a]

7 The name of the righteous is
used in blessings,[b]
but the name of the wicked
will rot.

8 The wise in heart accept
commands,
but a chattering fool comes to
ruin.

9 Whoever walks in integrity
walks securely,
but whoever takes crooked
paths will be found out.

10 Whoever winks maliciously
causes grief,
and a chattering fool comes to
ruin.

11 The mouth of the righteous is a
fountain of life,
but the mouth of the wicked
conceals violence.

12 Hatred stirs up conflict,
but love covers over all
wrongs.

13 Wisdom is found on the lips of
the discerning,
but a rod is for the back of one
who has no sense.

14 The wise store up knowledge,
but the mouth of a fool invites
ruin.

15 The wealth of the rich is their
fortified city,
but poverty is the ruin of the
poor.

16 The wages of the righteous is
life,
but the earnings of the wicked
are sin and death.

17 Whoever heeds discipline shows
the way to life,
but whoever ignores
correction leads others
astray.

18 Whoever conceals hatred with
lying lips
and spreads slander is a fool.

19 Sin is not ended by multiplying
words,
but the prudent hold their
tongues.

20 The tongue of the righteous is
choice silver,
but the heart of the wicked is
of little value.

21 The lips of the righteous nourish
many,
but fools die for lack of sense.

22 The blessing of the LORD brings
wealth,
without painful toil for it.

23 A fool finds pleasure in wicked
schemes,
but a person of understanding
delights in wisdom.

24 What the wicked dread will
overtake them;
what the righteous desire will
be granted.

---

a 6 Or righteous, / but the mouth of the wicked conceals violence   b 7 See Gen. 48:20.

25 When the storm has swept by,
       the wicked are gone,
   but the righteous stand firm
       forever.

26 As vinegar to the teeth and
       smoke to the eyes,
   so are sluggards to those who
       send them.

27 The fear of the LORD adds length
       to life,
   but the years of the wicked are
       cut short.

28 The prospect of the righteous is
       joy,
   but the hopes of the wicked
       come to nothing.

29 The way of the LORD is a refuge
       for the blameless,
   but it is the ruin of those who
       do evil.

30 The righteous will never be
       uprooted,
   but the wicked will not remain
       in the land.

31 From the mouth of the righteous
       comes the fruit of
       wisdom,
   but a perverse tongue will be
       silenced.

32 The lips of the righteous know
       what finds favor,
   but the mouth of the wicked
       only what is perverse.

11 The LORD detests dishonest
       scales,
   but accurate weights find favor
       with him.

2 When pride comes, then comes
       disgrace,
   but with humility comes
       wisdom.

3 The integrity of the upright
       guides them,
   but the unfaithful are
       destroyed by their
       duplicity.

4 Wealth is worthless in the day of
       wrath,
   but righteousness delivers
       from death.

5 The righteousness of the
       blameless makes their
       paths straight,
   but the wicked are brought
       down by their own
       wickedness.

6 The righteousness of the upright
       delivers them,
   but the unfaithful are trapped
       by evil desires.

7 Hopes placed in mortals die
       with them;
   all the promise ofᵃ their power
       comes to nothing.

8 The righteous person is rescued
       from trouble,
   and it falls on the wicked
       instead.

9 With their mouths the godless
       destroy their neighbors,
   but through knowledge the
       righteous escape.

10 When the righteous prosper, the
       city rejoices;
   when the wicked perish, there
       are shouts of joy.

11 Through the blessing of the
       upright a city is exalted,
   but by the mouth of the wicked
       it is destroyed.

12 Whoever derides their neighbor
       has no sense,

ᵃ 7 Two Hebrew manuscripts; most Hebrew manuscripts, Vulgate, Syriac and Targum *When the wicked die, their hope perishes; / all they expected from*

but the one who has understanding holds their tongue.

13 A gossip betrays a confidence,
    but a trustworthy person keeps a secret.

14 For lack of guidance a nation falls,
    but victory is won through many advisers.

15 Whoever puts up security for a stranger will surely suffer,
    but whoever refuses to shake hands in pledge is safe.

16 A kindhearted woman gains honor,
    but ruthless men gain only wealth.

17 Those who are kind benefit themselves,
    but the cruel bring ruin on themselves.

18 A wicked person earns deceptive wages,
    but the one who sows righteousness reaps a sure reward.

19 Truly the righteous attain life,
    but whoever pursues evil finds death.

20 The LORD detests those whose hearts are perverse,
    but he delights in those whose ways are blameless.

21 Be sure of this: The wicked will not go unpunished,
    but those who are righteous will go free.

22 Like a gold ring in a pig's snout
    is a beautiful woman who shows no discretion.

23 The desire of the righteous ends only in good,
    but the hope of the wicked only in wrath.

24 One person gives freely, yet gains even more;
    another withholds unduly, but comes to poverty.

25 A generous person will prosper;
    whoever refreshes others will be refreshed.

26 People curse the one who hoards grain,
    but they pray God's blessing on the one who is willing to sell.

27 Whoever seeks good finds favor,
    but evil comes to one who searches for it.

28 Those who trust in their riches will fall,
    but the righteous will thrive like a green leaf.

29 Whoever brings ruin on their family will inherit only wind,
    and the fool will be servant to the wise.

30 The fruit of the righteous is a tree of life,
    and the one who is wise saves lives.

31 If the righteous receive their due on earth,
    how much more the ungodly and the sinner!

12

Whoever loves discipline loves knowledge,
    but whoever hates correction is stupid.

2 Good people obtain favor from the LORD,
    but he condemns those who devise wicked schemes.

3 No one can be established
　　through wickedness,
　but the righteous cannot be
　　uprooted.

4 A wife of noble character is her
　　husband's crown,
　but a disgraceful wife is like
　　decay in his bones.

5 The plans of the righteous are just,
　but the advice of the wicked is
　　deceitful.

6 The words of the wicked lie in
　　wait for blood,
　but the speech of the upright
　　rescues them.

7 The wicked are overthrown and
　　are no more,
　but the house of the righteous
　　stands firm.

8 A person is praised according to
　　their prudence,
　and one with a warped mind is
　　despised.

9 Better to be a nobody and yet
　　have a servant
　than pretend to be somebody
　　and have no food.

10 The righteous care for the needs
　　of their animals,
　but the kindest acts of the
　　wicked are cruel.

11 Those who work their land will
　　have abundant food,
　but those who chase fantasies
　　have no sense.

12 The wicked desire the
　　stronghold of evildoers,
　but the root of the righteous
　　endures.

13 Evildoers are trapped by their
　　sinful talk,
　and so the innocent escape
　　trouble.

14 From the fruit of their lips
　　people are filled with good
　　things,
　and the work of their hands
　　brings them reward.

15 The way of fools seems right to
　　them,
　but the wise listen to advice.

16 Fools show their annoyance at
　　once,
　but the prudent overlook an
　　insult.

17 An honest witness tells the
　　truth,
　but a false witness tells lies.

18 The words of the reckless pierce
　　like swords,
　but the tongue of the wise
　　brings healing.

19 Truthful lips endure forever,
　but a lying tongue lasts only a
　　moment.

20 Deceit is in the hearts of those
　　who plot evil,
　but those who promote peace
　　have joy.

21 No harm overtakes the
　　righteous,
　but the wicked have their fill of
　　trouble.

22 The LORD detests lying lips,
　but he delights in people who
　　are trustworthy.

23 The prudent keep their
　　knowledge to themselves,
　but a fool's heart blurts out
　　folly.

24 Diligent hands will rule,
　but laziness ends in forced
　　labor.

25 Anxiety weighs down the
　　heart,
　but a kind word cheers it up.

26 The righteous choose their
      friends carefully,
   but the way of the wicked leads
      them astray.

27 The lazy do not roast[a] any game,
   but the diligent feed on the
      riches of the hunt.

28 In the way of righteousness
      there is life;
   along that path is
      immortality.

13 A wise son heeds his father's
      instruction,
   but a mocker does not respond
      to rebukes.

2 From the fruit of their lips
      people enjoy good things,
   but the unfaithful have an
      appetite for violence.

3 Those who guard their lips
      preserve their lives,
   but those who speak rashly
      will come to ruin.

4 A sluggard's appetite is never
      filled,
   but the desires of the diligent
      are fully satisfied.

5 The righteous hate what is
      false,
   but the wicked make
      themselves a stench
   and bring shame on
      themselves.

6 Righteousness guards the
      person of integrity,
   but wickedness overthrows
      the sinner.

7 One person pretends to be rich,
      yet has nothing;
   another pretends to be poor,
      yet has great wealth.

8 A person's riches may ransom
      their life,
   but the poor cannot respond to
      threatening rebukes.

9 The light of the righteous shines
      brightly,
   but the lamp of the wicked is
      snuffed out.

10 Where there is strife, there is
      pride,
   but wisdom is found in those
      who take advice.

11 Dishonest money dwindles away,
   but whoever gathers money
      little by little makes it grow.

12 Hope deferred makes the heart
      sick,
   but a longing fulfilled is a tree
      of life.

13 Whoever scorns instruction will
      pay for it,
   but whoever respects a
      command is rewarded.

14 The teaching of the wise is a
      fountain of life,
   turning a person from the
      snares of death.

15 Good judgment wins favor,
   but the way of the unfaithful
      leads to their destruction.[b]

16 All who are prudent act with[c]
      knowledge,
   but fools expose their folly.

17 A wicked messenger falls into
      trouble,
   but a trustworthy envoy brings
      healing.

18 Whoever disregards discipline
      comes to poverty and
      shame,

---

[a] 27 The meaning of the Hebrew for this word is uncertain;
the meaning of the Hebrew for this phrase is uncertain.   [b] 15 Septuagint and Syriac;   [c] 16 Or prudent protect themselves
through

but whoever heeds correction
is honored.

¹⁹ A longing fulfilled is sweet to the
soul,
but fools detest turning from
evil.

²⁰ Walk with the wise and become
wise,
for a companion of fools
suffers harm.

²¹ Trouble pursues the sinner,
but the righteous are rewarded
with good things.

²² A good person leaves an
inheritance for their
children's children,
but a sinner's wealth is stored
up for the righteous.

²³ An unplowed field produces
food for the poor,
but injustice sweeps it away.

²⁴ Whoever spares the rod hates
their children,
but the one who loves their
children is careful to
discipline them.

²⁵ The righteous eat to their hearts'
content,
but the stomach of the wicked
goes hungry.

14 The wise woman builds her
house,
but with her own hands the
foolish one tears hers
down.

² Whoever fears the LORD walks
uprightly,
but those who despise him are
devious in their ways.

³ A fool's mouth lashes out with
pride,
but the lips of the wise protect
them.

⁴ Where there are no oxen, the
manger is empty,
but from the strength of an ox
come abundant harvests.

⁵ An honest witness does not
deceive,
but a false witness pours out
lies.

⁶ The mocker seeks wisdom and
finds none,
but knowledge comes easily to
the discerning.

⁷ Stay away from a fool,
for you will not find knowledge
on their lips.

⁸ The wisdom of the prudent is to
give thought to their ways,
but the folly of fools is
deception.

⁹ Fools mock at making amends
for sin,
but goodwill is found among
the upright.

¹⁰ Each heart knows its own
bitterness,
and no one else can share its
joy.

¹¹ The house of the wicked will be
destroyed,
but the tent of the upright will
flourish.

¹² There is a way that appears to be
right,
but in the end it leads to
death.

¹³ Even in laughter the heart may
ache,
and rejoicing may end in
grief.

¹⁴ The faithless will be fully repaid
for their ways,
and the good rewarded for
theirs.

15 The simple believe anything,
   but the prudent give thought
      to their steps.

16 The wise fear the LORD and shun
      evil,
   but a fool is hotheaded and yet
      feels secure.

17 A quick-tempered person does
      foolish things,
   and the one who devises evil
      schemes is hated.

18 The simple inherit folly,
   but the prudent are crowned
      with knowledge.

19 Evildoers will bow down in the
      presence of the good,
   and the wicked at the gates of
      the righteous.

20 The poor are shunned even by
      their neighbors,
   but the rich have many
      friends.

21 It is a sin to despise one's
      neighbor,
   but blessed is the one who is
      kind to the needy.

22 Do not those who plot evil go
      astray?
   But those who plan what
      is good find*a* love and
      faithfulness.

23 All hard work brings a profit,
   but mere talk leads only to
      poverty.

24 The wealth of the wise is their
      crown,
   but the folly of fools yields
      folly.

25 A truthful witness saves lives,
   but a false witness is
      deceitful.

26 Whoever fears the LORD has a
      secure fortress,
   and for their children it will be
      a refuge.

27 The fear of the LORD is a
      fountain of life,
   turning a person from the
      snares of death.

28 A large population is a king's
      glory,
   but without subjects a prince
      is ruined.

29 Whoever is patient has great
      understanding,
   but one who is quick-tempered
      displays folly.

30 A heart at peace gives life to the
      body,
   but envy rots the bones.

31 Whoever oppresses the poor
      shows contempt for their
      Maker,
   but whoever is kind to the
      needy honors God.

32 When calamity comes, the
      wicked are brought
      down,
   but even in death the
      righteous seek refuge in
      God.

33 Wisdom reposes in the heart of
      the discerning
   and even among fools she lets
      herself be known.*b*

34 Righteousness exalts a nation,
   but sin condemns any people.

35 A king delights in a wise servant,
   but a shameful servant
      arouses his fury.

15 A gentle answer turns away
      wrath,

---

a 22 Or show   *b* 33 Hebrew; Septuagint and Syriac *discerning / but in the heart of fools she is not known*

but a harsh word stirs up
    anger.

2 The tongue of the wise adorns
    knowledge,
    but the mouth of the fool
        gushes folly.

3 The eyes of the LORD are
    everywhere,
    keeping watch on the wicked
        and the good.

4 The soothing tongue is a tree of
    life,
    but a perverse tongue crushes
        the spirit.

5 A fool spurns a parent's
    discipline,
    but whoever heeds correction
        shows prudence.

6 The house of the righteous
    contains great treasure,
    but the income of the wicked
        brings ruin.

7 The lips of the wise spread
    knowledge,
    but the hearts of fools are not
        upright.

8 The LORD detests the sacrifice of
    the wicked,
    but the prayer of the upright
        pleases him.

9 The LORD detests the way of the
    wicked,
    but he loves those who pursue
        righteousness.

10 Stern discipline awaits anyone
    who leaves the path;
    the one who hates correction
        will die.

11 Death and Destruction[a] lie open
    before the LORD —
    how much more do human
        hearts!

12 Mockers resent correction,
    so they avoid the wise.

13 A happy heart makes the face
    cheerful,
    but heartache crushes the
        spirit.

14 The discerning heart seeks
    knowledge,
    but the mouth of a fool feeds
        on folly.

15 All the days of the oppressed are
    wretched,
    but the cheerful heart has a
        continual feast.

16 Better a little with the fear of the
    LORD
    than great wealth with
        turmoil.

17 Better a small serving of
    vegetables with love
    than a fattened calf with
        hatred.

18 A hot-tempered person stirs up
    conflict,
    but the one who is patient
        calms a quarrel.

19 The way of the sluggard is
    blocked with thorns,
    but the path of the upright is a
        highway.

20 A wise son brings joy to his
    father,
    but a foolish man despises his
        mother.

21 Folly brings joy to one who has
    no sense,
    but whoever has
        understanding keeps a
        straight course.

22 Plans fail for lack of counsel,
    but with many advisers they
        succeed.

---

a 11 Hebrew *Abaddon*

23 A person finds joy in giving an
       apt reply—
    and how good is a timely word!

24 The path of life leads upward for
       the prudent
    to keep them from going down
       to the realm of the dead.

25 The LORD tears down the house
       of the proud,
    but he sets the widow's
       boundary stones in place.

26 The LORD detests the thoughts of
       the wicked,
    but gracious words are pure in
       his sight.

27 The greedy bring ruin to their
       households,
    but the one who hates bribes
       will live.

28 The heart of the righteous
       weighs its answers,
    but the mouth of the wicked
       gushes evil.

29 The LORD is far from the wicked,
    but he hears the prayer of the
       righteous.

30 Light in a messenger's eyes
       brings joy to the heart,
    and good news gives health to
       the bones.

31 Whoever heeds life-giving
       correction
    will be at home among the
       wise.

32 Those who disregard discipline
       despise themselves,
    but the one who heeds
       correction gains
       understanding.

33 Wisdom's instruction is to fear
       the LORD,
    and humility comes before
       honor.

16 To humans belong the plans
       of the heart,
    but from the LORD comes
       the proper answer of the
       tongue.

2 All a person's ways seem pure to
       them,
    but motives are weighed by
       the LORD.

3 Commit to the LORD whatever
       you do,
    and he will establish your
       plans.

4 The LORD works out everything
       to its proper end—
    even the wicked for a day of
       disaster.

5 The LORD detests all the proud
       of heart.
    Be sure of this: They will not
       go unpunished.

6 Through love and faithfulness
       sin is atoned for;
    through the fear of the LORD
       evil is avoided.

7 When the LORD takes pleasure
       in anyone's way,
    he causes their enemies to
       make peace with them.

8 Better a little with righteousness
    than much gain with injustice.

9 In their hearts humans plan
       their course,
    but the LORD establishes their
       steps.

10 The lips of a king speak as an
       oracle,
    and his mouth does not betray
       justice.

11 Honest scales and balances
       belong to the LORD;
    all the weights in the bag are of
       his making.

¹²Kings detest wrongdoing,
  for a throne is established
    through righteousness.

¹³Kings take pleasure in honest
    lips;
  they value the one who speaks
    what is right.

¹⁴A king's wrath is a messenger of
    death,
  but the wise will appease it.

¹⁵When a king's face brightens, it
    means life;
  his favor is like a rain cloud in
    spring.

¹⁶How much better to get wisdom
    than gold,
  to get insight rather than
    silver!

¹⁷The highway of the upright
    avoids evil;
  those who guard their ways
    preserve their lives.

¹⁸Pride goes before destruction,
  a haughty spirit before a fall.

¹⁹Better to be lowly in spirit along
    with the oppressed
  than to share plunder with the
    proud.

²⁰Whoever gives heed to
    instruction prospers,ᵃ
  and blessed is the one who
    trusts in the LORD.

²¹The wise in heart are called
    discerning,
  and gracious words promote
    instruction.ᵇ

²²Prudence is a fountain of life to
    the prudent,
  but folly brings punishment to
    fools.

²³The hearts of the wise make
    their mouths prudent,
  and their lips promote
    instruction.ᶜ

²⁴Gracious words are a
    honeycomb,
  sweet to the soul and healing
    to the bones.

²⁵There is a way that appears to be
    right,
  but in the end it leads to death.

²⁶The appetite of laborers works
    for them;
  their hunger drives them on.

²⁷A scoundrel plots evil,
  and on their lips it is like a
    scorching fire.

²⁸A perverse person stirs up
    conflict,
  and a gossip separates close
    friends.

²⁹A violent person entices their
    neighbor
  and leads them down a path
    that is not good.

³⁰Whoever winks with their eye is
    plotting perversity;
  whoever purses their lips is
    bent on evil.

³¹Gray hair is a crown of
    splendor;
  it is attained in the way of
    righteousness.

³²Better a patient person than a
    warrior,
  one with self-control than one
    who takes a city.

³³The lot is cast into the lap,
  but its every decision is from
    the LORD.

ᵃ 20 Or *whoever speaks prudently finds what is good*   ᵇ 21 Or *words make a person persuasive*
ᶜ 23 Or *prudent / and make their lips persuasive*

17 Better a dry crust with peace
and quiet
than a house full of feasting,
with strife.

2 A prudent servant will rule over
a disgraceful son
and will share the inheritance
as one of the family.

3 The crucible for silver and the
furnace for gold,
but the LORD tests the heart.

4 A wicked person listens to
deceitful lips;
a liar pays attention to a
destructive tongue.

5 Whoever mocks the poor shows
contempt for their
Maker;
whoever gloats over disaster
will not go unpunished.

6 Children's children are a crown
to the aged,
and parents are the pride of
their children.

7 Eloquent lips are unsuited to a
godless fool—
how much worse lying lips to a
ruler!

8 A bribe is seen as a charm by the
one who gives it;
they think success will come
at every turn.

9 Whoever would foster love
covers over an offense,
but whoever repeats the
matter separates close
friends.

10 A rebuke impresses a discerning
person
more than a hundred lashes a
fool.

11 Evildoers foster rebellion
against God;

the messenger of death will be
sent against them.

12 Better to meet a bear robbed of
her cubs
than a fool bent on folly.

13 Evil will never leave the house
of one who pays back evil for
good.

14 Starting a quarrel is like
breaching a dam;
so drop the matter before a
dispute breaks out.

15 Acquitting the guilty and
condemning the
innocent—
the LORD detests them both.

16 Why should fools have money in
hand to buy wisdom,
when they are not able to
understand it?

17 A friend loves at all times,
and a brother is born for a time
of adversity.

18 One who has no sense shakes
hands in pledge
and puts up security for a
neighbor.

19 Whoever loves a quarrel loves
sin;
whoever builds a high gate
invites destruction.

20 One whose heart is corrupt does
not prosper;
one whose tongue is perverse
falls into trouble.

21 To have a fool for a child brings
grief;
there is no joy for the parent of
a godless fool.

22 A cheerful heart is good
medicine,
but a crushed spirit dries up
the bones.

23 The wicked accept bribes in secret
   to pervert the course of justice.

24 A discerning person keeps
   wisdom in view,
   but a fool's eyes wander to the
   ends of the earth.

25 A foolish son brings grief to his
   father
   and bitterness to the mother
   who bore him.

26 If imposing a fine on the
   innocent is not good,
   surely to flog honest officials is
   not right.

27 The one who has knowledge
   uses words with restraint,
   and whoever has
   understanding is even-
   tempered.

28 Even fools are thought wise if
   they keep silent,
   and discerning if they hold
   their tongues.

18 An unfriendly person pursues
   selfish ends
   and against all sound
   judgment starts quarrels.

2 Fools find no pleasure in
   understanding
   but delight in airing their own
   opinions.

3 When wickedness comes, so
   does contempt,
   and with shame comes
   reproach.

4 The words of the mouth are deep
   waters,
   but the fountain of wisdom is a
   rushing stream.

5 It is not good to be partial to the
   wicked
   and so deprive the innocent of
   justice.

6 The lips of fools bring them
   strife,
   and their mouths invite a
   beating.

7 The mouths of fools are their
   undoing,
   and their lips are a snare to
   their very lives.

8 The words of a gossip are like
   choice morsels;
   they go down to the inmost
   parts.

9 One who is slack in his work
   is brother to one who destroys.

10 The name of the LORD is a
   fortified tower;
   the righteous run to it and are
   safe.

11 The wealth of the rich is their
   fortified city;
   they imagine it a wall too high
   to scale.

12 Before a downfall the heart is
   haughty,
   but humility comes before
   honor.

13 To answer before listening—
   that is folly and shame.

14 The human spirit can endure in
   sickness,
   but a crushed spirit who can
   bear?

15 The heart of the discerning
   acquires knowledge,
   for the ears of the wise seek it
   out.

16 A gift opens the way
   and ushers the giver into the
   presence of the great.

17 In a lawsuit the first to speak
   seems right,
   until someone comes forward
   and cross-examines.

18 Casting the lot settles disputes
   and keeps strong opponents
   apart.

19 A brother wronged is more
   unyielding than a fortified
   city;
   disputes are like the barred
   gates of a citadel.

20 From the fruit of their mouth a
   person's stomach is filled;
   with the harvest of their lips
   they are satisfied.

21 The tongue has the power of life
   and death,
   and those who love it will eat
   its fruit.

22 He who finds a wife finds what is
   good
   and receives favor from the
   Lord.

23 The poor plead for mercy,
   but the rich answer harshly.

24 One who has unreliable friends
   soon comes to ruin,
   but there is a friend who sticks
   closer than a brother.

19 Better the poor whose walk is
   blameless
   than a fool whose lips are
   perverse.

2 Desire without knowledge is not
   good—
   how much more will hasty feet
   miss the way!

3 A person's own folly leads to
   their ruin,
   yet their heart rages against
   the Lord.

4 Wealth attracts many friends,
   but even the closest friend of
   the poor person deserts
   them.

5 A false witness will not go
   unpunished,
   and whoever pours out lies
   will not go free.

6 Many curry favor with a ruler,
   and everyone is the friend of
   one who gives gifts.

7 The poor are shunned by all
   their relatives—
   how much more do their
   friends avoid them!
   Though the poor pursue them
   with pleading,
   they are nowhere to be
   found.[a]

8 The one who gets wisdom loves
   life;
   the one who cherishes
   understanding will soon
   prosper.

9 A false witness will not go
   unpunished,
   and whoever pours out lies
   will perish.

10 It is not fitting for a fool to live in
   luxury—
   how much worse for a slave to
   rule over princes!

11 A person's wisdom yields
   patience;
   it is to one's glory to overlook
   an offense.

12 A king's rage is like the roar of a
   lion,
   but his favor is like dew on the
   grass.

13 A foolish child is a father's ruin,
   and a quarrelsome wife is like
   the constant dripping of a
   leaky roof.

14 Houses and wealth are inherited
   from parents,

---

a 7 The meaning of the Hebrew for this sentence is uncertain.

but a prudent wife is from the
LORD.

¹⁵ Laziness brings on deep sleep,
and the shiftless go hungry.

¹⁶ Whoever keeps commandments
keeps their life,
but whoever shows contempt
for their ways will die.

¹⁷ Whoever is kind to the poor
lends to the LORD,
and he will reward them for
what they have done.

¹⁸ Discipline your children, for in
that there is hope;
do not be a willing party to
their death.

¹⁹ A hot-tempered person must pay
the penalty;
rescue them, and you will have
to do it again.

²⁰ Listen to advice and accept
discipline,
and at the end you will be
counted among the wise.

²¹ Many are the plans in a person's
heart,
but it is the LORD's purpose
that prevails.

²² What a person desires is
unfailing love^a;
better to be poor than a liar.

²³ The fear of the LORD leads to
life;
then one rests content,
untouched by trouble.

²⁴ A sluggard buries his hand in the
dish;
he will not even bring it back
to his mouth!

²⁵ Flog a mocker, and the simple
will learn prudence;

rebuke the discerning, and
they will gain knowledge.

²⁶ Whoever robs their father and
drives out their mother
is a child who brings shame
and disgrace.

²⁷ Stop listening to instruction, my
son,
and you will stray from the
words of knowledge.

²⁸ A corrupt witness mocks at
justice,
and the mouth of the wicked
gulps down evil.

²⁹ Penalties are prepared for
mockers,
and beatings for the backs of
fools.

20 Wine is a mocker and beer a
brawler;
whoever is led astray by them
is not wise.

² A king's wrath strikes terror like
the roar of a lion;
those who anger him forfeit
their lives.

³ It is to one's honor to avoid
strife,
but every fool is quick to
quarrel.

⁴ Sluggards do not plow in
season;
so at harvest time they look
but find nothing.

⁵ The purposes of a person's heart
are deep waters,
but one who has insight draws
them out.

⁶ Many claim to have unfailing
love,
but a faithful person who can
find?

---

^a 22 Or *Greed is a person's shame*

7 The righteous lead blameless
     lives;
   blessed are their children after
     them.

8 When a king sits on his throne to
     judge,
   he winnows out all evil with
     his eyes.

9 Who can say, "I have kept my
     heart pure;
   I am clean and without sin"?

10 Differing weights and differing
     measures—
   the LORD detests them both.

11 Even small children are known
     by their actions,
   so is their conduct really pure
     and upright?

12 Ears that hear and eyes that
     see—
   the LORD has made them both.

13 Do not love sleep or you will
     grow poor;
   stay awake and you will have
     food to spare.

14 "It's no good, it's no good!" says
     the buyer—
   then goes off and boasts about
     the purchase.

15 Gold there is, and rubies in
     abundance,
   but lips that speak knowledge
     are a rare jewel.

16 Take the garment of one who
     puts up security for a
     stranger;
   hold it in pledge if it is done for
     an outsider.

17 Food gained by fraud tastes
     sweet,
   but one ends up with a mouth
     full of gravel.

18 Plans are established by seeking
     advice;
   so if you wage war, obtain
     guidance.

19 A gossip betrays a confidence;
   so avoid anyone who talks too
     much.

20 If someone curses their father or
     mother,
   their lamp will be snuffed out
     in pitch darkness.

21 An inheritance claimed too soon
   will not be blessed at the end.

22 Do not say, "I'll pay you back for
     this wrong!"
   Wait for the LORD, and he will
     avenge you.

23 The LORD detests differing
     weights,
   and dishonest scales do not
     please him.

24 A person's steps are directed by
     the LORD.
   How then can anyone
     understand their own
     way?

25 It is a trap to dedicate something
     rashly
   and only later to consider
     one's vows.

26 A wise king winnows out the
     wicked;
   he drives the threshing wheel
     over them.

27 The human spirit is[a] the lamp of
     the LORD
   that sheds light on one's
     inmost being.

28 Love and faithfulness keep a
     king safe;
   through love his throne is
     made secure.

---

a 27 Or *A person's words are*

²⁹The glory of young men is their
strength,
gray hair the splendor of the
old.

³⁰Blows and wounds scrub away
evil,
and beatings purge the inmost
being.

21 In the LORD's hand the king's
heart is a stream of water
that he channels toward all
who please him.

²A person may think their own
ways are right,
but the LORD weighs the heart.

³To do what is right and just
is more acceptable to the LORD
than sacrifice.

⁴Haughty eyes and a proud
heart—
the unplowed field of the
wicked—produce sin.

⁵The plans of the diligent lead to
profit
as surely as haste leads to
poverty.

⁶A fortune made by a lying
tongue
is a fleeting vapor and a deadly
snare.^a

⁷The violence of the wicked will
drag them away,
for they refuse to do what is
right.

⁸The way of the guilty is devious,
but the conduct of the
innocent is upright.

⁹Better to live on a corner of the
roof
than share a house with a
quarrelsome wife.

¹⁰The wicked crave evil;
their neighbors get no mercy
from them.

¹¹When a mocker is punished, the
simple gain wisdom;
by paying attention to the wise
they get knowledge.

¹²The Righteous One^b takes note
of the house of the
wicked
and brings the wicked to ruin.

¹³Whoever shuts their ears to the
cry of the poor
will also cry out and not be
answered.

¹⁴A gift given in secret soothes
anger,
and a bribe concealed in the
cloak pacifies great
wrath.

¹⁵When justice is done, it brings
joy to the righteous
but terror to evildoers.

¹⁶Whoever strays from the path of
prudence
comes to rest in the company
of the dead.

¹⁷Whoever loves pleasure will
become poor;
whoever loves wine and olive
oil will never be rich.

¹⁸The wicked become a ransom for
the righteous,
and the unfaithful for the
upright.

¹⁹Better to live in a desert
than with a quarrelsome and
nagging wife.

²⁰The wise store up choice food
and olive oil,
but fools gulp theirs down.

---

^a 6 Some Hebrew manuscripts, Septuagint and Vulgate; most Hebrew manuscripts *vapor for
those who seek death*   ^b 12 Or *The righteous person*

21 Whoever pursues righteousness
        and love
    finds life, prosperity[a] and
        honor.

22 One who is wise can go up
        against the city of the
        mighty
    and pull down the stronghold
        in which they trust.

23 Those who guard their mouths
        and their tongues
    keep themselves from
        calamity.

24 The proud and arrogant
        person — "Mocker" is his
        name —
    behaves with insolent fury.

25 The craving of a sluggard will be
        the death of him,
    because his hands refuse to
        work.

26 All day long he craves for more,
    but the righteous give without
        sparing.

27 The sacrifice of the wicked is
        detestable —
    how much more so when
        brought with evil intent!

28 A false witness will perish,
    but a careful listener will
        testify successfully.

29 The wicked put up a bold front,
    but the upright give thought to
        their ways.

30 There is no wisdom, no insight,
        no plan
    that can succeed against the
        LORD.

31 The horse is made ready for the
        day of battle,
    but victory rests with the
        LORD.

22 A good name is more
        desirable than great
        riches;
    to be esteemed is better than
        silver or gold.

2 Rich and poor have this in
        common:
    The LORD is the Maker of them
        all.

3 The prudent see danger and take
        refuge,
    but the simple keep going and
        pay the penalty.

4 Humility is the fear of the LORD;
    its wages are riches and honor
        and life.

5 In the paths of the wicked are
        snares and pitfalls,
    but those who would preserve
        their life stay far from
        them.

6 Start children off on the way
        they should go,
    and even when they are old
        they will not turn from it.

7 The rich rule over the poor,
    and the borrower is slave to
        the lender.

8 Whoever sows injustice reaps
        calamity,
    and the rod they wield in fury
        will be broken.

9 The generous will themselves be
        blessed,
    for they share their food with
        the poor.

10 Drive out the mocker, and out
        goes strife;
    quarrels and insults are ended.

11 One who loves a pure heart and
        who speaks with grace
    will have the king for a friend.

_a_ 21 Or _righteousness_

12 The eyes of the LORD keep watch
over knowledge,
but he frustrates the words of
the unfaithful.

13 The sluggard says, "There's a
lion outside!
I'll be killed in the public
square!"

14 The mouth of an adulterous
woman is a deep pit;
a man who is under the LORD's
wrath falls into it.

15 Folly is bound up in the heart of
a child,
but the rod of discipline will
drive it far away.

16 One who oppresses the poor to
increase his wealth
and one who gives gifts to
the rich — both come to
poverty.

17 Pay attention and turn your ear
to the sayings of the wise;
apply your heart to what I
teach,

18 for it is pleasing when you keep
them in your heart
and have all of them ready on
your lips.

19 So that your trust may be in the
LORD,
I teach you today, even you.

20 Have I not written thirty sayings
for you,
sayings of counsel and
knowledge,

21 teaching you to be honest and to
speak the truth,
so that you bring back truthful
reports
to those you serve?

22 Do not exploit the poor because
they are poor

and do not crush the needy in
court,

23 for the LORD will take up their
case
and will exact life for life.

24 Do not make friends with a hot-
tempered person,
do not associate with one
easily angered,

25 or you may learn their ways
and get yourself ensnared.

26 Do not be one who shakes hands
in pledge
or puts up security for debts;

27 if you lack the means to pay,
your very bed will be snatched
from under you.

28 Do not move an ancient
boundary stone
set up by your ancestors.

29 Do you see someone skilled in
their work?
They will serve before kings;
they will not serve before
officials of low rank.

23 When you sit to dine with a
ruler,
note well what[a] is before you,

2 and put a knife to your throat
if you are given to gluttony.

3 Do not crave his delicacies,
for that food is deceptive.

4 Do not wear yourself out to get
rich;
do not trust your own
cleverness.

5 Cast but a glance at riches, and
they are gone,
for they will surely sprout wings
and fly off to the sky like an
eagle.

6 Do not eat the food of a
begrudging host,

---

a 1 Or who

do not crave his delicacies;
7 for he is the kind of person
who is always thinking about
the cost.[a]
"Eat and drink," he says to you,
but his heart is not with you.
8 You will vomit up the little you
have eaten
and will have wasted your
compliments.

9 Do not speak to fools,
for they will scorn your
prudent words.

10 Do not move an ancient
boundary stone
or encroach on the fields of the
fatherless,
11 for their Defender is strong;
he will take up their case
against you.

12 Apply your heart to instruction
and your ears to words of
knowledge.

13 Do not withhold discipline from
a child;
if you punish them with the
rod, they will not die.
14 Punish them with the rod
and save them from death.

15 My son, if your heart is wise,
then my heart will be glad
indeed;
16 my inmost being will rejoice
when your lips speak what is
right.

17 Do not let your heart envy
sinners,
but always be zealous for the
fear of the LORD.
18 There is surely a future hope for
you,
and your hope will not be cut
off.

19 Listen, my son, and be wise,
and set your heart on the right
path:
20 Do not join those who drink too
much wine
or gorge themselves on meat,
21 for drunkards and gluttons
become poor,
and drowsiness clothes them
in rags.

22 Listen to your father, who gave
you life,
and do not despise your
mother when she is old.
23 Buy the truth and do not sell it —
wisdom, instruction and
insight as well.

24 The father of a righteous child
has great joy;
a man who fathers a wise son
rejoices in him.
25 May your father and mother
rejoice;
may she who gave you birth be
joyful!

26 My son, give me your heart
and let your eyes delight in my
ways,
27 for an adulterous woman is a
deep pit,
and a wayward wife is a
narrow well.
28 Like a bandit she lies in wait
and multiplies the unfaithful
among men.

29 Who has woe? Who has sorrow?
Who has strife? Who has
complaints?
Who has needless bruises?
Who has bloodshot eyes?
30 Those who linger over wine,
who go to sample bowls of
mixed wine.
31 Do not gaze at wine when it is
red,

---

[a] 7 Or *for as he thinks within himself, / so he is*; or *for as he puts on a feast, / so he is*

when it sparkles in the cup,
when it goes down smoothly!
32 In the end it bites like a snake
and poisons like a viper.
33 Your eyes will see strange sights,
and your mind will imagine
confusing things.
34 You will be like one sleeping on
the high seas,
lying on top of the rigging.
35 "They hit me," you will say, "but
I'm not hurt!
They beat me, but I don't feel
it!
When will I wake up
so I can find another drink?"

24 Do not envy the wicked,
do not desire their company;
2 for their hearts plot violence,
and their lips talk about
making trouble.

3 By wisdom a house is built,
and through understanding it
is established;
4 through knowledge its rooms
are filled
with rare and beautiful
treasures.

5 The wise prevail through great
power,
and those who have
knowledge muster their
strength.
6 Surely you need guidance to
wage war,
and victory is won through
many advisers.

7 Wisdom is too high for fools;
in the assembly at the gate
they must not open their
mouths.

8 Whoever plots evil
will be known as a schemer.
9 The schemes of folly are sin,
and people detest a mocker.

10 If you falter in a time of
trouble,
how small is your strength!
11 Rescue those being led away to
death;
hold back those staggering
toward slaughter.
12 If you say, "But we knew nothing
about this,"
does not he who weighs the
heart perceive it?
Does not he who guards your life
know it?
Will he not repay everyone
according to what they
have done?

13 Eat honey, my son, for it is good;
honey from the comb is sweet
to your taste.
14 Know also that wisdom is like
honey for you:
If you find it, there is a future
hope for you,
and your hope will not be cut
off.

15 Do not lurk like a thief near the
house of the righteous,
do not plunder their dwelling
place;
16 for though the righteous fall
seven times, they rise
again,
but the wicked stumble when
calamity strikes.

17 Do not gloat when your enemy
falls;
when they stumble, do not let
your heart rejoice,
18 or the LORD will see and
disapprove
and turn his wrath away from
them.

19 Do not fret because of evildoers
or be envious of the wicked,
20 for the evildoer has no future
hope,

and the lamp of the wicked
　　will be snuffed out.

21 Fear the LORD and the king, my
　　son,
　　and do not join with rebellious
　　　officials,
22 for those two will send sudden
　　　destruction on them,
　　and who knows what
　　　calamities they can bring?

23 These also are sayings of the
wise:

To show partiality in judging is
　　not good:
24 Whoever says to the guilty, "You
　　are innocent,"
　　will be cursed by peoples and
　　　denounced by nations.
25 But it will go well with those who
　　convict the guilty,
　　and rich blessing will come on
　　　them.

26 An honest answer
　　is like a kiss on the lips.

27 Put your outdoor work in order
　　and get your fields ready;
　　after that, build your house.

28 Do not testify against your
　　　neighbor without cause —
　　would you use your lips to
　　　mislead?
29 Do not say, "I'll do to them as
　　they have done to me;
　　I'll pay them back for what
　　　they did."

30 I went past the field of a
　　sluggard,
　　past the vineyard of someone
　　　who has no sense;
31 thorns had come up
　　everywhere,
　　the ground was covered with
　　　weeds,

and the stone wall was in
　　ruins.
32 I applied my heart to what I
　　observed
　　and learned a lesson from
　　　what I saw:
33 A little sleep, a little slumber,
　　a little folding of the hands to
　　　rest —
34 and poverty will come on you
　　like a thief
　　and scarcity like an armed
　　　man.

25 These are more proverbs of
Solomon, compiled by the
men of Hezekiah king of Judah:

2 It is the glory of God to conceal a
　　matter;
　　to search out a matter is the
　　　glory of kings.
3 As the heavens are high and the
　　earth is deep,
　　so the hearts of kings are
　　　unsearchable.

4 Remove the dross from the
　　silver,
　　and a silversmith can produce
　　　a vessel;
5 remove wicked officials from the
　　king's presence,
　　and his throne will be
　　　established through
　　　righteousness.

6 Do not exalt yourself in the
　　king's presence,
　　and do not claim a place
　　　among his great men;
7 it is better for him to say to you,
　　"Come up here,"
　　than for him to humiliate you
　　　before his nobles.

What you have seen with your
　　eyes
8　do not bring[a] hastily to court,

---

[a] 7,8 Or nobles / on whom you had set your eyes. / [8]Do not go

for what will you do in the end
   if your neighbor puts you to
     shame?

⁹ If you take your neighbor to
   court,
   do not betray another's
     confidence,
¹⁰ or the one who hears it may
   shame you
   and the charge against you
     will stand.

¹¹ Like apples[a] of gold in settings of
   silver
   is a ruling rightly given.
¹² Like an earring of gold or an
   ornament of fine gold
   is the rebuke of a wise judge to
     a listening ear.

¹³ Like a snow-cooled drink at
   harvest time
   is a trustworthy messenger to
     the one who sends him;
   he refreshes the spirit of his
     master.
¹⁴ Like clouds and wind without
   rain
   is one who boasts of gifts never
     given.

¹⁵ Through patience a ruler can be
   persuaded,
   and a gentle tongue can break
     a bone.

¹⁶ If you find honey, eat just
   enough—
   too much of it, and you will
     vomit.
¹⁷ Seldom set foot in your
   neighbor's house—
   too much of you, and they will
     hate you.

¹⁸ Like a club or a sword or a sharp
   arrow
is one who gives false
   testimony against a
     neighbor.
¹⁹ Like a broken tooth or a lame
   foot
   is reliance on the unfaithful in
     a time of trouble.
²⁰ Like one who takes away a
   garment on a cold day,
   or like vinegar poured on a
     wound,
   is one who sings songs to a
     heavy heart.

²¹ If your enemy is hungry, give
   him food to eat;
   if he is thirsty, give him water
     to drink.
²² In doing this, you will heap
   burning coals on his head,
   and the LORD will reward you.

²³ Like a north wind that brings
   unexpected rain
   is a sly tongue—which
     provokes a horrified look.

²⁴ Better to live on a corner of the
   roof
   than share a house with a
     quarrelsome wife.

²⁵ Like cold water to a weary soul
   is good news from a distant
     land.
²⁶ Like a muddied spring or a
   polluted well
   are the righteous who give way
     to the wicked.

²⁷ It is not good to eat too much
   honey,
   nor is it honorable to search
     out matters that are too
     deep.

²⁸ Like a city whose walls are
   broken through
   is a person who lacks
     self-control.

---

[a] 11 Or possibly *apricots*

26 Like snow in summer or rain in harvest,
> honor is not fitting for a fool.

² Like a fluttering sparrow or a darting swallow,
> an undeserved curse does not come to rest.

³ A whip for the horse, a bridle for the donkey,
> and a rod for the backs of fools!

⁴ Do not answer a fool according to his folly,
> or you yourself will be just like him.

⁵ Answer a fool according to his folly,
> or he will be wise in his own eyes.

⁶ Sending a message by the hands of a fool
> is like cutting off one's feet or drinking poison.

⁷ Like the useless legs of one who is lame
> is a proverb in the mouth of a fool.

⁸ Like tying a stone in a sling
> is the giving of honor to a fool.

⁹ Like a thornbush in a drunkard's hand
> is a proverb in the mouth of a fool.

¹⁰ Like an archer who wounds at random
> is one who hires a fool or any passer-by.

¹¹ As a dog returns to its vomit,
> so fools repeat their folly.

¹² Do you see a person wise in their own eyes?
> There is more hope for a fool than for them.

¹³ A sluggard says, "There's a lion in the road,
> a fierce lion roaming the streets!"

¹⁴ As a door turns on its hinges,
> so a sluggard turns on his bed.

¹⁵ A sluggard buries his hand in the dish;
> he is too lazy to bring it back to his mouth.

¹⁶ A sluggard is wiser in his own eyes
> than seven people who answer discreetly.

¹⁷ Like one who grabs a stray dog by the ears
> is someone who rushes into a quarrel not their own.

¹⁸ Like a maniac shooting flaming arrows of death
¹⁹ is one who deceives their neighbor
> and says, "I was only joking!"

²⁰ Without wood a fire goes out;
> without a gossip a quarrel dies down.

²¹ As charcoal to embers and as wood to fire,
> so is a quarrelsome person for kindling strife.

²² The words of a gossip are like choice morsels;
> they go down to the inmost parts.

²³ Like a coating of silver dross on earthenware
> are fervent[a] lips with an evil heart.

²⁴ Enemies disguise themselves with their lips,
> but in their hearts they harbor deceit.

²⁵ Though their speech is charming, do not believe them,
> for seven abominations fill their hearts.

²⁶ Their malice may be concealed by deception,

---

a 23 Hebrew; Septuagint *smooth*

but their wickedness will be
exposed in the assembly.
²⁷ Whoever digs a pit will fall into
it;
if someone rolls a stone, it will
roll back on them.
²⁸ A lying tongue hates those it
hurts,
and a flattering mouth works
ruin.

27 Do not boast about tomorrow,
for you do not know what a
day may bring.

² Let someone else praise you, and
not your own mouth;
an outsider, and not your own
lips.

³ Stone is heavy and sand a
burden,
but a fool's provocation is
heavier than both.

⁴ Anger is cruel and fury
overwhelming,
but who can stand before
jealousy?

⁵ Better is open rebuke
than hidden love.

⁶ Wounds from a friend can be
trusted,
but an enemy multiplies
kisses.

⁷ One who is full loathes honey
from the comb,
but to the hungry even what is
bitter tastes sweet.

⁸ Like a bird that flees its nest
is anyone who flees from
home.

⁹ Perfume and incense bring joy
to the heart,
and the pleasantness of a
friend

springs from their heartfelt
advice.

¹⁰ Do not forsake your friend or a
friend of your family,
and do not go to your relative's
house when disaster
strikes you —
better a neighbor nearby than
a relative far away.

¹¹ Be wise, my son, and bring joy to
my heart;
then I can answer anyone who
treats me with contempt.

¹² The prudent see danger and take
refuge,
but the simple keep going and
pay the penalty.

¹³ Take the garment of one who
puts up security for a
stranger;
hold it in pledge if it is done for
an outsider.

¹⁴ If anyone loudly blesses their
neighbor early in the
morning,
it will be taken as a curse.

¹⁵ A quarrelsome wife is like the
dripping
of a leaky roof in a rainstorm;
¹⁶ restraining her is like
restraining the wind
or grasping oil with the hand.

¹⁷ As iron sharpens iron,
so one person sharpens
another.

¹⁸ The one who guards a fig tree
will eat its fruit,
and whoever protects their
master will be honored.

¹⁹ As water reflects the face,
so one's life reflects the
heart.ᵃ

ᵃ 19 Or *so others reflect your heart back to you*

²⁰ Death and Destruction^a are
        never satisfied,
    and neither are human eyes.

²¹ The crucible for silver and the
        furnace for gold,
    but people are tested by their
        praise.

²² Though you grind a fool in a
        mortar,
    grinding them like grain with
        a pestle,
    you will not remove their folly
        from them.

²³ Be sure you know the condition
        of your flocks,
    give careful attention to your
        herds;

²⁴ for riches do not endure forever,
    and a crown is not secure for
        all generations.

²⁵ When the hay is removed and
        new growth appears
    and the grass from the hills is
        gathered in,

²⁶ the lambs will provide you with
        clothing,
    and the goats with the price of
        a field.

²⁷ You will have plenty of goats'
        milk to feed your family
    and to nourish your female
        servants.

28
The wicked flee though no
        one pursues,
    but the righteous are as bold
        as a lion.

² When a country is rebellious, it
        has many rulers,
    but a ruler with discernment
        and knowledge maintains
        order.

³ A ruler^b who oppresses the poor
    is like a driving rain that
        leaves no crops.

⁴ Those who forsake instruction
        praise the wicked,
    but those who heed it resist
        them.

⁵ Evildoers do not understand
        what is right,
    but those who seek the Lord
        understand it fully.

⁶ Better the poor whose walk is
        blameless
    than the rich whose ways are
        perverse.

⁷ A discerning son heeds
        instruction,
    but a companion of gluttons
        disgraces his father.

⁸ Whoever increases wealth by
        taking interest or profit
        from the poor
    amasses it for another, who
        will be kind to the poor.

⁹ If anyone turns a deaf ear to my
        instruction,
    even their prayers are
        detestable.

¹⁰ Whoever leads the upright along
        an evil path
    will fall into their own trap,
    but the blameless will receive
        a good inheritance.

¹¹ The rich are wise in their own
        eyes;
    one who is poor and
        discerning sees how
        deluded they are.

¹² When the righteous triumph,
        there is great elation;
    but when the wicked rise to
        power, people go into
        hiding.

¹³ Whoever conceals their sins
        does not prosper,

---

^a 20 Hebrew *Abaddon*   ^b 3 Or *A poor person*

but the one who confesses
and renounces them finds
mercy.

¹⁴ Blessed is the one who always
trembles before God,
but whoever hardens their
heart falls into trouble.

¹⁵ Like a roaring lion or a charging
bear
is a wicked ruler over a
helpless people.

¹⁶ A tyrannical ruler practices
extortion,
but one who hates ill-gotten
gain will enjoy a long
reign.

¹⁷ Anyone tormented by the guilt of
murder
will seek refuge in the grave;
let no one hold them back.

¹⁸ The one whose walk is blameless
is kept safe,
but the one whose ways are
perverse will fall into the
pit.ᵃ

¹⁹ Those who work their land will
have abundant food,
but those who chase fantasies
will have their fill of
poverty.

²⁰ A faithful person will be richly
blessed,
but one eager to get rich will
not go unpunished.

²¹ To show partiality is not good —
yet a person will do wrong for
a piece of bread.

²² The stingy are eager to get rich
and are unaware that poverty
awaits them.

²³ Whoever rebukes a person will
in the end gain favor
rather than one who has a
flattering tongue.

²⁴ Whoever robs their father or
mother
and says, "It's not wrong,"
is partner to one who destroys.

²⁵ The greedy stir up conflict,
but those who trust in the
LORD will prosper.

²⁶ Those who trust in themselves
are fools,
but those who walk in wisdom
are kept safe.

²⁷ Those who give to the poor will
lack nothing,
but those who close their eyes
to them receive many
curses.

²⁸ When the wicked rise to power,
people go into hiding;
but when the wicked perish,
the righteous thrive.

29 Whoever remains stiff-
necked after many
rebukes
will suddenly be destroyed —
without remedy.

² When the righteous thrive, the
people rejoice;
when the wicked rule, the
people groan.

³ A man who loves wisdom brings
joy to his father,
but a companion of prostitutes
squanders his wealth.

⁴ By justice a king gives a country
stability,
but those who are greedy forᵇ
bribes tear it down.

⁵ Those who flatter their
neighbors
are spreading nets for their feet.

ᵃ 18 Syriac (see Septuagint); Hebrew into one   ᵇ 4 Or who give

⁶ Evildoers are snared by their
   own sin,
   but the righteous shout for joy
      and are glad.

⁷ The righteous care about justice
   for the poor,
   but the wicked have no such
      concern.

⁸ Mockers stir up a city,
   but the wise turn away
      anger.

⁹ If a wise person goes to court
   with a fool,
   the fool rages and scoffs, and
      there is no peace.

¹⁰ The bloodthirsty hate a person
    of integrity
    and seek to kill the upright.

¹¹ Fools give full vent to their
    rage,
    but the wise bring calm in the
       end.

¹² If a ruler listens to lies,
    all his officials become
       wicked.

¹³ The poor and the oppressor have
    this in common:
    The LORD gives sight to the
       eyes of both.

¹⁴ If a king judges the poor with
    fairness,
    his throne will be established
       forever.

¹⁵ A rod and a reprimand impart
    wisdom,
    but a child left undisciplined
       disgraces its mother.

¹⁶ When the wicked thrive, so does
    sin,
    but the righteous will see their
       downfall.

¹⁷ Discipline your children, and
    they will give you peace;

they will bring you the
   delights you desire.

¹⁸ Where there is no revelation,
    people cast off restraint;
    but blessed is the one
    who heeds wisdom's
       instruction.

¹⁹ Servants cannot be corrected by
    mere words;
    though they understand, they
       will not respond.

²⁰ Do you see someone who speaks
    in haste?
    There is more hope for a fool
       than for them.

²¹ A servant pampered from
    youth
    will turn out to be insolent.

²² An angry person stirs up
    conflict,
    and a hot-tempered person
       commits many sins.

²³ Pride brings a person low,
    but the lowly in spirit gain
       honor.

²⁴ The accomplices of thieves are
    their own enemies;
    they are put under oath and
       dare not testify.

²⁵ Fear of man will prove to be a
    snare,
    but whoever trusts in the LORD
       is kept safe.

²⁶ Many seek an audience with a
    ruler,
    but it is from the LORD that one
       gets justice.

²⁷ The righteous detest the
    dishonest;
    the wicked detest the
       upright.

30 The sayings of Agur son of Ja-
    keh — an inspired utterance.

This man's utterance to Ithiel:

"I am weary, God,
　but I can prevail.[a]

[2] Surely I am only a brute, not a
　man;
　I do not have human
　　understanding.

[3] I have not learned wisdom,
　nor have I attained to the
　　knowledge of the Holy
　　One.

[4] Who has gone up to heaven and
　come down?
　Whose hands have gathered
　　up the wind?
　Who has wrapped up the waters
　　in a cloak?
　Who has established all the
　　ends of the earth?
　What is his name, and what is
　　the name of his son?
　Surely you know!

[5] "Every word of God is flawless;
　he is a shield to those who take
　　refuge in him.

[6] Do not add to his words,
　or he will rebuke you and
　　prove you a liar.

[7] "Two things I ask of you, LORD;
　do not refuse me before I die:

[8] Keep falsehood and lies far from
　me;
　give me neither poverty nor
　　riches,
　but give me only my daily
　　bread.

[9] Otherwise, I may have too much
　and disown you
　and say, 'Who is the LORD?'
　Or I may become poor and
　　steal,
　and so dishonor the name of
　　my God.

[10] "Do not slander a servant to
　their master,
　or they will curse you, and you
　　will pay for it.

[11] "There are those who curse their
　fathers
　and do not bless their
　　mothers;

[12] those who are pure in their own
　eyes
　and yet are not cleansed of
　　their filth;

[13] those whose eyes are ever so
　haughty,
　whose glances are so
　　disdainful;

[14] those whose teeth are swords
　and whose jaws are set with
　　knives
　to devour the poor from the
　　earth
　and the needy from among
　　mankind.

[15] "The leech has two daughters.
　'Give! Give!' they cry.

"There are three things that are
　never satisfied,
　four that never say, 'Enough!':

[16] the grave, the barren womb,
　land, which is never satisfied
　　with water,
　and fire, which never says,
　　'Enough!'

[17] "The eye that mocks a father,
　that scorns an aged mother,
　will be pecked out by the ravens
　　of the valley,
　will be eaten by the vultures.

[18] "There are three things that are
　too amazing for me,
　four that I do not understand:

[19] the way of an eagle in the sky,
　the way of a snake on a rock,

---

[a] 1 With a different word division of the Hebrew; Masoretic Text *utterance to Ithiel, / to Ithiel and Ukal:*

the way of a ship on the high
    seas,
  and the way of a man with a
    young woman.

20 "This is the way of an adulterous
    woman:
  She eats and wipes her mouth
    and says, 'I've done nothing
    wrong.'

21 "Under three things the earth
    trembles,
  under four it cannot bear up:
22 a servant who becomes king,
  a godless fool who gets plenty
    to eat,
23 a contemptible woman who gets
    married,
  and a servant who displaces
    her mistress.

24 "Four things on earth are small,
  yet they are extremely wise:
25 Ants are creatures of little
    strength,
  yet they store up their food in
    the summer;
26 hyraxes are creatures of little
    power,
  yet they make their home in
    the crags;
27 locusts have no king,
  yet they advance together in
    ranks;
28 a lizard can be caught with the
    hand,
  yet it is found in kings'
    palaces.

29 "There are three things that are
    stately in their stride,
  four that move with stately
    bearing:
30 a lion, mighty among beasts,
  who retreats before nothing;
31 a strutting rooster, a he-goat,
  and a king secure against
    revolt.*a*

32 "If you play the fool and exalt
    yourself,
  or if you plan evil,
    clap your hand over your
    mouth!
33 For as churning cream produces
    butter,
  and as twisting the nose
    produces blood,
  so stirring up anger produces
    strife."

31 The sayings of King Lemuel — an inspired utterance his
mother taught him.

2 Listen, my son! Listen, son of my
    womb!
  Listen, my son, the answer to
    my prayers!
3 Do not spend your strength*b* on
    women,
  your vigor on those who ruin
    kings.

4 It is not for kings, Lemuel —
  it is not for kings to drink
    wine,
  not for rulers to crave beer,
5 lest they drink and forget what
    has been decreed,
  and deprive all the oppressed
    of their rights.
6 Let beer be for those who are
    perishing,
  wine for those who are in
    anguish!
7 Let them drink and forget their
    poverty
  and remember their misery no
    more.

8 Speak up for those who cannot
    speak for themselves,
  for the rights of all who are
    destitute.
9 Speak up and judge fairly;
  defend the rights of the poor
    and needy.

---

a 31 The meaning of the Hebrew for this phrase is uncertain.   *b 3* Or *wealth*

¹⁰ ᵃA wife of noble character who
can find?
She is worth far more than
rubies.
¹¹ Her husband has full confidence
in her
and lacks nothing of value.
¹² She brings him good, not harm,
all the days of her life.
¹³ She selects wool and flax
and works with eager hands.
¹⁴ She is like the merchant ships,
bringing her food from afar.
¹⁵ She gets up while it is still
night;
she provides food for her
family
and portions for her female
servants.
¹⁶ She considers a field and buys it;
out of her earnings she plants
a vineyard.
¹⁷ She sets about her work
vigorously;
her arms are strong for her
tasks.
¹⁸ She sees that her trading is
profitable,
and her lamp does not go out
at night.
¹⁹ In her hand she holds the distaff
and grasps the spindle with
her fingers.
²⁰ She opens her arms to the poor
and extends her hands to the
needy.
²¹ When it snows, she has no fear
for her household;

for all of them are clothed in
scarlet.
²² She makes coverings for her bed;
she is clothed in fine linen and
purple.
²³ Her husband is respected at the
city gate,
where he takes his seat among
the elders of the land.
²⁴ She makes linen garments and
sells them,
and supplies the merchants
with sashes.
²⁵ She is clothed with strength and
dignity;
she can laugh at the days to
come.
²⁶ She speaks with wisdom,
and faithful instruction is on
her tongue.
²⁷ She watches over the affairs of
her household
and does not eat the bread of
idleness.
²⁸ Her children arise and call her
blessed;
her husband also, and he
praises her:
²⁹ "Many women do noble things,
but you surpass them all."
³⁰ Charm is deceptive, and beauty
is fleeting;
but a woman who fears the
LORD is to be praised.
³¹ Honor her for all that her hands
have done,
and let her works bring her
praise at the city gate.

ᵃ 10 Verses 10-31 are an acrostic poem, the verses of which begin with the successive letters of
the Hebrew alphabet.

TABLE OF WEIGHTS AND MEASURES

	BIBLICAL UNIT	APPROXIMATE AMERICAN EQUIVALENT	APPROXIMATE METRIC EQUIVALENT
Weights	talent (60 minas)	75 pounds	34 kilograms
	mina (50 shekels)	1 1/4 pounds	560 grams
	shekel (2 bekas)	2/5 ounce	11.5 grams
	pim (2/3 shekel)	1/4 ounce	7.8 grams
	beka (10 gerahs)	1/5 ounce	5.7 grams
	gerah	1/50 ounce	0.6 gram
	daric	1/3 ounce	8.4 grams
Length	cubit	18 inches	45 centimeters
	span	9 inches	23 centimeters
	handbreadth	3 inches	7.5 centimeters
	stadion (pl. stadia)	600 feet	183 meters
Capacity *Dry Measure*	cor [homer] (10 ephahs)	6 bushels	220 liters
	lethek (5 ephahs)	3 bushels	110 liters
	ephah (10 omers)	3/5 bushel	22 liters
	seah (1/3 ephah)	7 quarts	7.5 liters
	omer (1/10 ephah)	2 quarts	2 liters
	cab (1/18 ephah)	1 quart	1 liter
Liquid Measure	bath (1 ephah)	6 gallons	22 liters
	hin (1/6 bath)	1 gallon	3.8 liters
	log (1/72 bath)	1/3 quart	0.3 liter

The figures of the table are calculated on the basis of a shekel equaling 11.5 grams, a cubit equaling 18 inches and an ephah equaling 22 liters. The quart referred to is either a dry quart (slightly larger than a liter) or a liquid quart (slightly smaller than a liter), whichever is applicable. The ton referred to in the footnotes is the American ton of 2,000 pounds. These weights are calculated relative to the particular commodity involved. Accordingly, the same measure of capacity in the text may be converted into different weights in the footnotes.

This table is based upon the best available information, but it is not intended to be mathematically precise; like the measurement equivalents in the footnotes, it merely gives approximate amounts and distances. Weights and measures differed somewhat at various times and places in the ancient world. There is uncertainty particularly about the ephah and the bath; further discoveries may shed more light on these units of capacity.

	General Unit	APPROXIMATE AMERICAN MEDICINAL EQUIVALENT	APPROXIMATE Metric EQUIVALENT
Weight			
Length			
Capacity			

A WORD ABOUT THE NIV

The goal of the New International Version (NIV) is to enable English-speaking people from around the world to read and hear God's eternal Word in their own language. Our work as translators is motivated by our conviction that the Bible is God's Word in written form. We believe that the Bible contains the divine answer to the deepest needs of humanity, sheds unique light on our path in a dark world and sets forth the way to our eternal well-being. Out of these deep convictions, we have sought to recreate as far as possible the experience of the original audience—blending transparency to the original text with accessibility for the millions of English speakers around the world. We have prioritized accuracy, clarity and literary quality with the goal of creating a translation suitable for public and private reading, evangelism, teaching, preaching, memorizing and liturgical use. We have also sought to preserve a measure of continuity with the long tradition of translating the Scriptures into English.

The complete NIV Bible was first published in 1978. It was a completely new translation made by over a hundred scholars working directly from the best available Hebrew, Aramaic and Greek texts. The translators came from the United States, Great Britain, Canada, Australia and New Zealand, giving the translation an international scope. They were from many denominations and churches—including Anglican, Assemblies of God, Baptist, Brethren, Christian Reformed, Church of Christ, Evangelical Covenant, Evangelical Free, Lutheran, Mennonite, Methodist, Nazarene, Presbyterian, Wesleyan and others. This breadth of denominational and theological perspective helped to safeguard the translation from sectarian bias. For these reasons, and by the grace of God, the NIV has gained a wide readership in all parts of the English-speaking world.

The work of translating the Bible is never finished. As good as they are, English translations must be regularly updated so that they will continue to communicate accurately the meaning of God's Word. Updates are needed in order to reflect the latest developments in our understanding of the biblical world and its languages and to keep pace with changes in English usage. Recognizing, then, that the NIV would retain its ability to communicate God's Word accurately only if it were regularly updated, the original translators established The Committee on Bible Translation (CBT). The committee is a self-perpetuating group of biblical scholars charged with keeping abreast of advances in biblical scholarship and changes in English and issuing periodic updates to the NIV. CBT is an independent, self-governing body and has sole responsibility for the NIV text. The committee mirrors the original group of translators in its diverse international and denominational makeup and in its unifying commitment to the Bible as God's inspired Word.

In obedience to its mandate, the committee has issued periodic updates to the NIV. An initial revision was released in 1984. A more thorough revision process was completed in 2005, resulting in the separately published TNIV. The updated NIV you now have in your hands builds on both the original NIV and the TNIV and represents the latest effort of the committee to articulate God's unchanging Word in the way the original authors might have said it had they been speaking in English to the global English-speaking audience today.

The first concern of the translators has continued to be the accuracy of the translation and its faithfulness to the intended meaning of the biblical writers. This has moved the translators to go beyond a formal word-for-word rendering of the original texts. Because thought patterns and syntax differ from language to language, accurate communication of the meaning of the biblical authors demands constant regard for varied contextual uses of words and idioms and for frequent modifications in sentence structures.

For the Old Testament the standard Hebrew text, the Masoretic Text as published in the latest edition of Biblia Hebraica, has been used throughout. The Masoretic Text tradition contains marginal notations that offer variant readings. These have sometimes been followed instead of the text itself. Because such instances involve variants within the Masoretic tradition, they have not been indicated in the textual notes. In a few cases, words in the basic consonantal text have been divided differently than in the Masoretic Text. Such cases are usually indicated in the textual footnotes. The Dead Sea Scrolls contain biblical texts that represent an earlier stage of the transmission of the Hebrew text. They have been consulted, as have been the Samaritan Pentateuch and the ancient scribal traditions concerning deliberate textual changes. The translators also consulted the more important early versions—the Greek Septuagint, Aquila, Symmachus and Theodotion, the Latin Vulgate, the Syriac Peshitta, the Aramaic Targums, and for the Psalms, the Juxta Hebraica of Jerome. Readings from these versions, the Dead Sea Scrolls and the scribal traditions were occasionally followed where the Masoretic Text seemed doubtful and where accepted principles of textual criticism showed that one or more of these textual witnesses appeared to provide the correct reading. In rare cases, the committee has emended the Hebrew text where it appears to have become corrupted at an even earlier stage of its transmission. These departures from the Masoretic Text are also indicated in the textual footnotes. Sometimes the vowel indicators (which are later additions to the basic consonantal text) found in the Masoretic Text did not, in the judgment of the committee, represent the correct vowels for the original text. Accordingly, some words have been read with a different set of vowels. These instances are usually not indicated in the footnotes.

The Greek text used in translating the New Testament is an eclectic one, based on the latest editions of the Nestle-Aland/ United Bible Societies' Greek New Testament. The committee has made its choices among the variant readings in accordance with widely accepted principles of New Testament textual criticism. Footnotes call attention to places where uncertainty remains.

The New Testament authors, writing in Greek, often quote the Old Testament from its ancient Greek version, the Septuagint. This is one reason why some of the Old Testament quotations in the NIV New Testament are not identical to the corresponding passages in the NIV Old Testament. Such quotations in the New Testament are indicated with the footnote "(see Septuagint)."

Other footnotes in this version are of several kinds, most of which need no explanation. Those giving alternative translations begin with "Or" and generally introduce the alternative with the last word preceding it in the text, except when it is a single-word alternative. When poetry is quoted in a footnote a slash mark indicates a line division.

It should be noted that references to diseases, minerals, flora and fauna, architectural details, clothing, jewelry, musical instruments and other articles cannot always be identi-

fied with precision. Also, linear measurements and measures of capacity can only be approximated (see the Appendix). Although Selah, used mainly in the Psalms, is probably a musical term, its meaning is uncertain. Since it may interrupt reading and distract the reader, this word has not been kept in the English text, but every occurrence has been signaled by a footnote.

One of the main reasons that the task of Bible translation is never finished is the change in our own language, English. Although a basic core of the language remains relatively stable, many diverse and complex cultural forces continue to bring about subtle shifts in the meanings and/or connotations of even old, well-established words and phrases. No part of the language has seen greater change in the last thirty years than the way gender is presented. The original NIV (1978) was published in a time when "a man" was still used to refer to a person regardless of gender. But the generic connotations of "man" in this sense have eroded over the years. In recognition of this change in

English, this edition of the NIV, along with almost all other recent English translations, substitutes other expressions when the original text intends to refer generically to men and women equally. Thus, for instance, the NIV (1984) rendering of 1 Corinthians 8:3, "But the man who loves God is known by God" becomes in this edition "But whoever loves God is known by God." On the other hand, "man" and "mankind," as ways of denoting the human race, are still widely used. This edition of the NIV therefore continues to use these words, along with other expressions, in this way.

A related shift in English creates a larger problem for modern translations: the move away from using the third-person masculine singular pronouns—"he/him/his"—to refer to men and women equally. This usage does persist at a low level in some forms of English, and this revision therefore occasionally uses these pronouns in a generic sense. But the tendency, recognized in day-to-day usage and confirmed by extensive research, is away from the generic use of "he," "him," and "his." In recognition of this shift in language and in an effort to translate into the "common" English that people are actually using, this revision of the NIV generally uses other constructions when the biblical text is plainly addressed to men and women equally. The reader will frequently encounter a "they," "their," or "them" to express a generic singular idea. Thus, for instance, Mark 8:36 reads: "What good is it for someone to gain the whole world, yet forfeit their soul?" This generic use of the "distributive" or "singular" "they/them/their" has a venerable place in English idiom and has quickly become established as standard English, spoken and written, all over the world. Where an individual emphasis is deemed to be present, "anyone" or "everyone" or some other equivalent is generally used as the antecedent of such pronouns.

Sometimes the chapter and/or verse numbering in English translations of the Old Testament differs from that found in published Hebrew texts. This is particularly the case in the Psalms, where the traditional titles are included in the Hebrew verse numbering. Such differences are indicated in the footnotes at the bottom of the page. In the New Testament, verse numbers that marked off portions of the traditional English text not supported by the best Greek manuscripts now appear in brackets, with a footnote indicating the text that has been omitted (see, for example, Matthew 17:[21]).

Mark 16:9-20 and John 7:53-8:11, although long accorded virtually equal status with the rest of the Gospels in which they stand, have a very questionable—and confused—standing in the textual history of the New Testament, as noted in the bracketed annotations with which they are set off. A different typeface has been chosen for these passages to indicate even more clearly their uncertain status.

Basic formatting of the text, such as lining the poetry, paragraphing (both prose and poetry), setting up of (administrative-like) lists, indenting letters and lengthy prayers within narratives and the insertion of sectional headings, has been the work of the committee. However, the choice between single-column and double-column formats has been left to the publishers. Also, the issuing of "red-letter" editions is a publisher's choice—one that the committee does not endorse.

The committee has again been reminded that every human effort is flawed—including this revision of the NIV. We trust, however, that many will find in it an improved representation of the Word of God, through which they hear his call to faith in our Lord Jesus Christ and to service in his kingdom. We offer this version of the Bible to him in whose name and for whose glory it has been made.

The Committee on Bible Translation, September 2010

More information on the Committee on Bible Translation may be found at: www.NIV-CBT.com.

As you've seen, the Bible is a powerful drama telling us God's story of the world. Our prayer for you is that you will continue to explore this drama. As we said at the beginning, we believe the best strategy with the Bible is to go deep, and read big. Take in whole books, not just isolated bits here and there.

But it's also true that we all need help to read and absorb the Bible well. We need help to understand what these books meant when they were first written. We need help to live out the drama of the Bible today, to find the right way to carry the story of Jesus forward into our world.

For this reason we've developed a website so you can continue your journey deep into the Scriptures. We're committed to continually add more features, insights, links and other follow-up resources. You can check it out on-line at:

BIBLICA.COM/LIVINGTHESCRIPT

We hope this resource will help you make deeper and deeper connections with the Bible. The process of being transformed by God's Word never stops. Of course, we can't give you all the help you need at a website. We also hope you'll seek out other people to read and discuss the Bible with, so you can engage the Bible together. The Bible was meant to be experienced in community. This is key for discovering what it means to live the story today. But perhaps the most crucial thing of all is for God himself to guide you into good understanding. We pray that you will stop and ask him to do just that. In the end, it is his drama that we're all invited into.